4th Edition

Managing Organizational Behavior

Henry L. Tosi, *University of Florida, USA and SDA-Bocconi, Milan, Italy*
Neal P. Mero, *Washington State University*
John R. Rizzo, *Western Michigan University*

First edition published 1986 by Pitman Publishing Inc., USA
Second edition published 1990 by HarperCollins Publishers Inc., USA
Third edition published 1994; reprinted 1995, 1996, 1998

This fourth edition published 2000

2 4 6 8 10 9 7 5 3 1

Blackwell Publishers Inc.
350 Main Street
Malden, Massachusetts 02148
USA

Blackwell Publishers Ltd
108 Cowley Road
Oxford OX4 1JF
UK

Library of Congress Cataloging-in-Publication Data

Tosi, Henry L.
Managing organizational behavior / Henry L. Tosi, Neal P. Mero, John R. Rizzo. – 4th ed.
p. cm.
Includes bibliographical references and index.
ISBN 0-631-21257-4 (hardcover : alk. paper). — ISBN 0-631-20883-6 (pbk. : alk. paper)
1. Organizational behavior. I. Mero, Neal P. II. Rizzo, John R. III. Title.
HD58.7.T66 1999
658—dc21 99-033803
CIP

British Library Cataloguing in Publication Data

A CIP catalogue record for this book is available from the British Library.

Typeset in 10 on 12 pt Sabon
by Best-set Typesetter Ltd., Hong Kong
Printed in Great Britain by TJ International, Padstow, Cornwall
This book is printed on acid-free paper.

Contents

Figures

Tables

"Focus on . . ." features

"Global focus" features

"Diversity issues" features

"Question of Ethics" features

Preface

This book is about the problem of managing people in organizations. We take the view that these issues can only be considered in terms of the interaction between human beings and the organizational context within which they work. Further, just as there are individual differences that help us to understand human behavior, there are differences in organizations which must be understood if we are to manage resources effectively, both human and technical. We are pleased that those who reviewed earlier editions of this book thought that this perspective was a strong point of the book.

Organization of the Book

The framework of the book is fairly conventional, consistent with the ideas which are important and relevant today. We emphasize fundamental concepts about organizations, individuals, and groups in sections that treat what we call the "building blocks of organization." Then, we discuss what managers do to improve organizational effectiveness.

The first building block is the "individual." In chapters 2 and 3, we discuss perception, attitudes, personality, and judgment. Chapter 4 moves the person into the organization, focusing on the process of organizational accommodation, career choice, organizational socialization. Chapter 5 covers motivation theories, important to understand if one wishes to increase the willingness of members to work harder and perform better and chapter 6 illustrates how these theories may be applied at work. Stress, at work and as a result of work, is the subject of chapter 7. Here we show how stress develops, its costs to the organization, and how it can be managed.

The second building block is the "group." The pressures and processes that an individual experiences when interacting with others in a group are discussed in this section. In chapters 8 and 9, group formation, development, and processes that occur in groups are considered. These chapters also cover the important subject of teams in organizations. Chapter 10 describes many of the factors that lead to conflict in groups and organizations.

The third building block is the "organization." In Chapter 12 the important contextual factor, culture, is discussed in detail. In this chapter we show the national culture is embedded in the organizational culture and the effects on so much of what happens in organizations. Chapter 13 describes how the environment and decisions made by managers result in the different types of organization design.

Throughout the text, we examine the things that managers do to improve organizational effectiveness. Chapter 6 describes how motivational strategies are applied in organizations. Decision-making processes are discussed in chapter 11. Interpersonal influence processes are the subject of the chapters on influence, power and politics (chapter 14) and leadership (chapter 15). Chapter 16 discusses some ways to systematically change the organization and those who work in it.

Features in this Edition

- *Chapter Headlines*
  On the opening page of each chapter, we have listed the major topics that will be covered in the chapter. This gives students a good idea of what they will be learning in each chapter. For example, the headlines for the chapter 5, *Motivation*, lists the major theories discussed in the chapter (e.g., need theories, reinforcement theory, and so on).
- *Mini-case chapter openings*
  We open each chapter with a reasonably extensive example of some problem or concept treated in the chapter. These are drawn from our own consulting experiences or from the current press.
- *Preparing for class*
  We have introduced the PREPARING FOR CLASS feature in this edition. These are designed to be thought starters, encouraging the students to focus on how their own experiences might be related to the subject matter of the chapter. Instructors using this version can also adapt these items into class assignments to help students relate text material to their own experiences in organizations. As an example, for chapter 4, *Organizational Accommodation: Careers, Socialization and Commitment*, the student is asked to interview someone who has had a career that might be viewed as successful, or someone who is in a career of interest to the student. The student is then asked to consider career paths discussed in the chapter and to identify the career path used by the person interviewed.
- *Key terms in boldface in the text*
  Key terms and concepts which appear in each chapter are marked in bold text so that students can recognize their importance.

- *Key definitions in the margins*
  Key definitions in each chapter will be located in the margin the first time that they appear in the book so that they are easily accessible to the student.
- *Key concepts at the end of each chapter*
  The key concepts in each chapter are listed at the end of each chapter.
- *Glossary*
  At the end of the text, a glossary of all key concepts with definitions is included.
- *Cases*
  At the end of each chapter, we include a short case. The intent of the case is to illustrate important concepts that appear in the chapter.
- *Study questions*
  Each chapter includes study questions to be used for discussion purposes by the instructor.
- *Guides for Managers*
  A unique feature of this book is the GUIDE FOR MANAGERS that appear at the end of each chapter. These are prescriptive ideas about how to apply the theories and concepts discussed in each chapter.
- *Focus inserts*
  We have taken recent material from the popular press or other useful sources that show the relevance of chapter topics to current management problems. Each chapter includes inserts that focus on global issues, diversity issues, and ethical and management issues.
  - FOCUS ON . . . features relate to topics covered in the chapter.
  - GLOBAL FOCUS ON . . . concentrate on international issues that face manager's in an increasingly global work context.
  - DIVERSITY ISSUES provide discussion, reflection and research in managing an increasingly diverse workforce.
  - QUESTIONS OF ETHICS consider the ethical implications of topics covered within the chapter and are intended to allow instructors to remind students frequently of the ethical issues faced by modern managers.
- *Exercises and simulations*
  We include in each chapter a short simulation or exercise that involves the student in a way so that they understand a particular concept in the chapter.

Finally, we worked very hard on the writing style so that it is not heavy or pedantic. We wanted to ensure that the ideas are easy to understand, with absolutely no compromise of the theory and empirical work which underlies the field.

Henry L. Tosi
Neal P. Mero
John R. Rizzo

Acknowledgments

There are a number of people who have helped us in many ways on this edition and earlier ones. Each has been important and has added constructively to what we have done. Three, however, deserve special mention for the preparation of this edition. Megan Silber, Michelle Franklin, and Samantha Mero brought a high energy level, outstanding administrative skills, and a bright attitude to it. They were a great help to all of us. Others who helped with the focus items were Peter Jones and Elizabeth Campanelli-Johnson.

We also relied very heavily on several people in the production of the manuscript. Bob St. Clair was the first publisher who liked the ideas we have in this book and helped get them into print. Bill Roberts, who is out there somewhere in the publishing business, gave us much help in getting the book where it is, and so did Carol Franco and Rolf Janke.

Finally, this edition is different in an important way from previous ones. Both Steve Carroll and John Rizzo decided to expend their energies in other ways than working on the book. For the senior author, this is the first time in a lot of years that he has written without them. He relied very much on their competence and insights, not only in this book, but also throughout his career in other different ways. For Steve Carroll, especially, this will be the first time in a lot of years that he won't be part of the "Tosi–Carroll" duo.

The addition of Neal Mero to the book is especially gratifying. He is an experienced teacher of organizational behavior who is, at the same time, a very promising researcher. He brought some very important pedagogical concepts to this addition which will make the subject matter of organizational behavior much more accessible to students.

chapter 1

Introduction

A HISTORICAL VIEW OF CONTEMPORARY ORGANIZATIONAL BEHAVIOR
ORGANIZATIONAL THEORY
ORGANIZATIONAL BEHAVIOR
CURRENT TRENDS AND CHALLENGES
MANAGING ORGANIZATIONAL PERFORMANCE
PLAN OF THIS BOOK

Preparing for Class

Consider two organizations you have been associated with in your life. They can be organizations where you have worked, went to school or attended church. Now consider the behavior of individuals within those two organizations. Here are some aspects of that behavior to consider.

1. How do people dress when they are participating in those organizations?
2. How do individuals refer to each other? Do they use titles, first names or some other terminology?
3. Are there rules for members of that organization? If so, are they published in written form or are they communicated in some other way?
4. What are the goals of the organization? Does everyone share them?

Now review the behaviors you listed for both of the organizations.

1. In what ways are they similar and in what ways are they different?
2. Can you provide a theory for the differences?

Bell and Howell has a long history as a producer of high quality audiovisual equipment, but it ran into serious trouble in the late 1980s. In 1990, it not only had a debt of $750 million from a management buy out a few years earlier, but it was trying to shift its strategy from the audiovisual equipment business to an information and systems company in the electronic and online publishing industries (Rehak, 1996). That was about the time when William White took over as chairman and CEO. His job was not easy. Technological and financial problems had to be solved, but there were also many issues related to the people who worked there, both management and workers. White set about cutting costs, increasing sales and, more importantly, solving many of the human and organizational problems that he found. Among the key factors in his success was changing the incentive system to reward activities that contributed to Bell and Howell's objectives and changing the corporate culture so that it gave managers at lower levels in the firm the chance to make decisions and to be held accountable for them. By 1996, William White had turned Bell and Howell around.

This book is about the human problems that companies such as Bell and Howell face in managing organizational performance. Obviously, to manage the performance of organizations and the individuals in them, you have to know about the technical, financial, and economic facets of work, i.e. the nuts and bolts about the situation you are managing. However, that is not enough for effective managers; they must also have "people skills," i.e. an understanding of organizations, how they work, and the people in them. Good managers know that these "people problems" are among the most difficult ones that they face and that "people skills" are among the most important requirements for future managers (Nelton, 1997).

Some think that these people skills are just "common sense," or something that we can learn from our own experiences with others. The problem is that common sense is not so common and, at the same time, it is often contradictory. For example, which commonsense proverb is correct: "Out or sight, out of mind," or "Absence makes the heart grow fonder"? The fact is that research findings show, as in the exercise on page 3, that common sense can lead to some false conclusions about human behavior. In the exercise, think about whether you agree with each statement, and then decide why. You can check your ideas against what the research tells us about the statement by referring to the text pages indicated for each statement.

organizational behavior
The systematic and scientific analysis of individuals, groups, and organizations; its purpose is to understand, predict, and improve the performance of individuals and, ultimately, the organizations in which they work

The Field of Organizational Behavior

The field of study that focuses on the "human skills" which managers need to be effective is called **organizational behavior**. Organizational behavior is the systematic and scientific analysis of individuals, groups, and organizations; its purpose is to understand, predict, and improve the performance of individuals and, ultimately, the organizations in which they work. It applies theory and research from psychology and sociology, and managerial theory that help

EXERCISE

What Does Common Sense Tell You about Dealing with Others in Organizations?

Read these eight statements about some of the subjects that are discussed in later chapters of this book. For each one, indicate whether you agree with the statement by putting a plus (+) sign or disagree by placing a minus (–) sign in the box beside it.

		Agree/ disagree	See page
1	Highly motivated employees are always the best performers in their job.	☐	123
2	Female managers are as effective as male managers.	☐	108
3	A manager's leadership style should be consistent in all situations; otherwise his or her group will be less effective and lose confidence in the manager and the firm.	☐	461
4	Those managers who achieve the highest levels of organizations, such as the CEO, are motivated primarily by success and achievement motives.	☐	138
5	Charismatic leaders are born, and these skills cannot be developed because they are innate.	☐	475
6	Forming a committee of highly intelligent, rational, and wise persons in times of crisis usually guarantees a good decision from them.	☐	328
7	Most important decisions in large business organizations are a result of a careful, analytical decision process that is likely to result in maximizing firm performance.	☐	314
8	Having a spouse has the same effects on the salaries of men and women.	☐	111

us to understand how to use this knowledge to improve the effectiveness of organizations.

To some, the idea of applying theory and research in human behavior to solve work problems is too "academic" – something that is for professors and not for managers; managers are pragmatic and have to solve real, not hypothetical, problems. We think that nothing is further from the truth. The reason is that everyone has personal theories about how to manage or affect others, and these theories guide their actions. For example, every professor has a theory about how to teach a class. It may be rather simple, such as, "Give the students challenging material, test them frequently, give them quick and accurate feedback, and they will learn." A manager may have a theory that workers perform better when their pay is tied to their performance. Both the professor and the manager probably developed their theories after many years of experience.

Student learning for the professor and worker performance for the manager are both dependent on other factors. For the student in the professor's theory, it

independent variables
Factors that can be manipulated by managers or researchers in dealing with or studying organizational behavior

dependent variables
Factors in management or research that are treated as outcomes of other factors or events, and are not directly manipulable

theory
A way of organizing knowledge about something; a way of defining a system into variables and their relationships

hypotheses
Conditional predictions about the relationship between concepts or variables that state how the concepts in a theory go together

is the challenging work; for the manager, it is "linking pay to individual performance for the workers." These can be changed or manipulated by the professor or the manager to affect performance. Challenge in the class can be high or low, depending on how difficult or easy the assignments are. Pay can be increased or decreased, or it may be tied to performance. In theory and research, the factors that can be changed or manipulated are called **independent variables**, like class challenge or pay; the factors that are the outcomes (performance or learning) are called **dependent variables**.

A **theory** is a set of interrelated concepts, definitions, and propositions about tentative relationships between the concepts. These tentative relationships are called **hypotheses**, or conditional predictions about the relationship between two concepts or variables. Hypotheses form the basis for research efforts to test and refine the theory.

To test a theory the researcher states – in the form of a hypothesis – what the theory predicts. The researcher then designs a study and research instruments, collects and analyzes data, and comes to certain conclusions about the validity of the hypothesis. The results may confirm or disprove the hypothesis. If the hypothesis is confirmed, it stays in the theory. If it is disproved, then the theory should be revised, provided that the research was executed properly and assuming that other research continues to produce evidence that disproves the hypothesis.

The ultimate test of the value of theory and research in organizational behavior is if it leads to improved levels of productivity and satisfaction, a lower rate of absenteeism, better retention and learning, or member well-being. We describe many instances of useful and important applications of theory-supported research elsewhere in this book, especially in chapters 6 and 16:

- Goal-setting theory and research has led to the effective use of management-by-objectives (MBO) to improve performance (page 167).
- Positive reinforcement programs have produced some startling improvements in productivity (page 170).
- Total quality management (TQM) programs have been successful in improving quality levels in both manufacturing and service firms (page 179).
- Many firms have successfully become high involvement organizations (HIO) (page 176).

The difference between a manager and a researcher/theorist is not (or should not be) that the manager is not interested in theory and research while a researcher is – it should be only that they do these things differently. The fact is that both are interested in the same thing – what they can do to improve performance. In general, it is safe to say that both developed their theories in the same way: they tested their hypotheses about human behavior by trying – or researching – what affected performance and what did not. The only difference may have been in the way that they did their "research." The researcher tries to do it following the scientific method, the manager does it as he or she works in the organization. One thing is certain, to test their theories, both must be systematic, cautious, and thoughtful about their observations and conclusions because both want to find the right answer.

A Historical View of Contemporary Organizational Behavior

The concern about how to organize people and manage them is not new; it has been with us since the dawn of civilization. The difference between then and now is that, in those early times, most thinking and writing was done in the context of political science, military theory, or religion (George, 1972). There was less attention to the management of commercial activities in ancient times, perhaps because they were not large-scale endeavors like their military, political, and reli-

Global Focus on The Universality of Management Theories

Geert Hofstede, a writer of important books on the role of culture on organizations and management, has raised a caution about much of the research, theory and suggestions for managers that we make in this book. Here is his argument:

> Management as presently used is an American invention. In other parts of the world not only the practices but the entire concept of management may differ, and the theories needed to understand it may deviate considerably from what is considered normal and desirable in the USA.

He argues, for example, that US theories of leadership do not work in Japan, because, in Japan, they have developed their own model for the group-controlled situation; that motivation strategies that work in the USA do not work in Holland; that the matrix organization structure so prominently used in the USA has had little success in France; and that overseas Chinese US firms have few characteristics of traditional US firms.

There are, according to Hofstede, three distinct characteristics of US theories that are not shared by management in other parts of the world:

1 An emphasis on market processes
2 A focus on the individual
3 A stress on managers rather than on workers

He wants to internationalize management theories so that they are more universally applicable.

- What do you think?
- Is he right?
- Why?
- How would you do this?

Source: Adapted from Hofstede (1993)

gious organizations. The development of economic sciences and management practices began around the start of the seventeenth century. The Industrial Revolution and Adam Smith's writing on political economy are key marker events, particularly for most Western management thinkers. While there may be some debate about when serious consideration of management problems began, it is very clear that it became more important when the economic sectors of societies throughout the world became larger and more complicated.

Antecedents of Contemporary Organizational Behavior

specialization
A condition in which a person performs only some specific part of a larger set of tasks

scientific management approach
Emphasizes the systematic study of methods, using techniques such as time study, selection, and incentives to achieve work efficiency

Though contemporary organizational behavior began to emerge as a distinct area of research and academic **specialization** in the late 1950s and early 1960s, it can trace its roots to the late nineteenth and early twentieth century, and its conceptual roots to four approaches to management:

1 The scientific management approach
2 Administrative theory
3 Industrial psychology
4 The human relations perspective

We think that the first major impetus to the field of organizational behavior was the **scientific management approach.** Scientific management focused on the lowest level of organization – the worker and the boss. The basic question it addressed was, "How can the job be designed most efficiently?" Many people were associated with the beginnings of scientific management, but the most

Focus on Management History

If you are a fan of old movies on late night television, you have probably seen the film, "Cheaper by the Dozen." It is a wholesome comedy about the family of two important figures in the history of scientific management, Frank and Lillian Gilbreth. While the film downplays their role in the development of scientific management, it does give some insight to this movement. Frank Gilbreth (played in the film by Clifton Webb) and his wife Lillian (played by Mryna Loy) worked together to develop ways of job analysis and design to make work more efficient.

They were responsible for one of the important concepts in industrial engineering and management, the "therblig" (which is their name, spelled in reverse). Therbligs are standard human motions, such as grasping, selecting, positioning, and holding. For each therblig, a standard time was developed so that, by determining which therbligs make up a job, it is possible to develop a standard time for a job.

Using their methods, they were able to obtain dramatic increases in worker productivity. For example, Frank Gilbreth was able to increase the productivity of bricklayers from 130 to 350 bricks in an hour by decreasing the number of motions in laying a brick from 16 to 5. While in London at a British-Japanese exposition, Gilbreth observed a female worker who was acknowledged to be extremely productive in attaching labels to boxes, fixing 24 labels in 40 seconds. Gilbreth made some suggestions and, in her first attempt with the new method, disposed of 24 boxes in 24 seconds. In her second attempt, the time for 24 boxes was reduced to 20 seconds.

prominent was Frederick W. Taylor – he was to become the "father of scientific management."

Born to a well-to-do Philadelphia family, but unable to complete college due to poor eyesight, Taylor took a job in industry as an apprentice at the Midvale Steel Company in 1878. He quickly rose through the ranks to become chief engineer in 1884, at the age of 28. Based on his experiences and studies, Taylor developed many ideas to increase efficiency and became widely sought as a consultant to other firms. His ideas, when applied, resulted in significant productivity increases. In the well-known shoveling experiment, Taylor found that the optimum-size shovel for handling material carried about 21 pounds of material. He was able to increase productivity from 16 to 59 tons of material shoveled per day while the number of shovelers needed per day was decreased from 500 to 140. Such results were typical when scientific management was applied, and they led to a strong advocacy of scientific management methods. The analysis and redesign of work from methods that Taylor initiated were so widely applied in industry that one social historian, Bell (1970), wrote:

> The prophet of modern work was Frederick W. Taylor, and the stopwatch was his rod. If any social upheaval can ever be attributed to one man, the logic of efficiency as a mode of life is due to Taylor. With "scientific management," as formulated by Taylor in 1893, we pass far beyond the old, rough computations of the division of labor and move into the division of time itself.

By the late 1920s, another perspective on management emerged. A number of writers began to analyze the work of managers. Their ideas concerned understanding the basic functions of management and developing guidelines, or principles, about how to manage effectively, and came to be called "**administrative theory.**"

Management functions are those activities that all executives perform in whole or in part. The administrative theorists defined these and did the most extensive early analysis of the managerial functions of planning, organizing and controlling.

- **Planning** is the determining, in advance of activity execution, what factors are required to achieve goals. The planning function defines the objective and determines what resources are necessary.
- **Organizing** is the function of acquiring and assembling resources in the proper relation to each other to achieve objectives.
- **Controlling** is ensuring that activities, when carried out, conform to plans so that objectives are achieved.

Principles of management are general guides which tell a manager what to do when faced with problems of designing an organization, making decisions, or dealing with people. Principles of management were developed for nearly every phase of the managerial task: leadership, objectives, single accountability, unity of command, equity, and authority. Drawn from real-world experiences, they were meant to facilitate high performance. These principles can, of course, be

administrative theory
Primarily concerned with understanding the basic task of management and of developing guidelines, or principles, on how to manage effectively

management functions
Activities executives perform in whole or part that make up the managerial job

planning
Making decisions about the most effective course of action to take in achieving organization goals and formulating general policies or guides to help in implementing plans

organizing
Acquiring and assembling resources in the proper relation to each other to achieve objectives

controlling
Ensures that activities, when carried out, conform to plans so that objectives are achieved

principles of management
General guides to handling the problems that an executive encounters in work situations

useful guides to action. They give the manager somewhere to start when faced with a problem, and can be very helpful in finding a solution.

industrial psychology
Focuses on both human and physical resources in the workplace; traditionally a study of selection, performance appraisal, work methods, and group behavior

Around 1900, at about the same time that the scientific management movement began to gain impetus, the **industrial psychology** movement began its growth. The driving initial force in this discipline was Hugo Munsterberg. Munsterberg's work was directed at finding the most effective and productive relationship between human and physical resources.

> Munsterberg's *Psychology and Industrial Efficiency* was directly related to Taylor's proposals and contained three broad parts: (1) "The best possible man," (2) "The best possible work," and (3) "The best possible effect . . ." Munsterberg outlined definite proposals for the use of tests in worker selection, for the application of research on learning in training industrial personnel, and for the study of psychological techniques which increased workers' motives and reduced fatigue. . . .
>
> Taylor and others . . . had envisioned contributions from psychologists for research in the human factor. Munsterberg fitted into this scheme, and the ethic of scientific management was readily apparent in (1) the focus on the individual, (2) the emphasis on efficiency, and (3) the social benefits to be derived from the application of the scientific method (Wren, 1972).

An early success of industrial psychology was personnel selection for the US Army in World War I. Faced with the problem of drafting, inducting, and placing millions of men, the Army sought the assistance of the American Psychological Association. A group of psychologists under the leadership of Walter Dill Scott responded (Ling, 1965). To cope with the selection problem, the army Alpha Test was developed, and it proved "extremely valuable in placing draftees and is estimated to have saved . . . millions of dollars" (Miner, 1969).

World War II had another major impact on industrial psychology. The same selection and placement problems of World War I existed but, by now, psychologists had developed refined techniques to improve these processes. For instance, screening instruments were used to predict the probability of success at completing different types of military training. Because of the large-scale production effort to produce defense materials during World War II, under conditions where workers had been lost to the armed services, new techniques for training employees had to be developed.

human relations perspective
Emphasized the personal and social aspects of employee satisfaction and productivity

A quite different behavioral perspective emerged after the Hawthorne experiments at Western Electric in the late 1920s: the **human relations perspective** (Roethlisberger and Dickson, 1939). This was the first widely recognized approach to attempt to utilize the broader range of human potential and to suggest ways to do this. The Hawthorne experiments were carried out in the Hawthorne plant of Western Electric, an AT&T subsidiary in Cicero, Illinois. The studies, started in 1927, were prompted by an experiment that was carried out by the company's engineers between 1924 and 1927. The engineers, in the best tradition of scientific management, were seeking the answers to industrial questions through research.

In perhaps the most famous of the studies, two groups of workers were observed to determine the effects of different levels of illumination on worker performance. In one group, the level of illumination was changed; in the other, it was not. They found that when illumination was increased, the level of performance increased. However, productivity also increased when the level of illumination decreased, even down to the level of moonlight. Moreover, productivity also increased in the control group. These results seemed contrary to reason, and, so, the engineers examined other factors that might have affected the results. The workers were responding in a way that they thought the experimenters wanted and because they were the center of attention. The researchers concluded that how people were treated made an important difference in performance. Obviously, the subjects were responding not to the level of light, but to the experiment itself and to their involvement in it. Since that time, this effect in research has been known as the **Hawthorne Effect.**

Other studies followed and continued to demonstrate the importance of leadership practices and workgroup pressures on employee satisfaction and performance. They showed that the importance of economic incentives in worker motivation was overrated, and they stressed the importance of recognizing that employees react to a wide set of complex forces, rather than to one factor alone.

Contemporary Organizational Behavior

Contemporary organizational behavior took roots in the late 1950s and early 1960s. In addition to those writers already discussed, other psychologists, sociologists, anthropologists, and social scientists had studied worker and management problems from a behavioral perspective before 1960, and managers were always concerned with human problems. However, since 1960, a somewhat unified body of knowledge and thinking has developed that falls under the general label of contemporary organizational behavior.

Flowing logically from the prior works, two distinct but related approaches to the study of human behavior in organizations emerged around this time:

1 A focus on organizations as the unit of analysis, called **organizational theory**, in which individuals and groups are not prominent in the analysis
2 Organizational behavior which is more concerned with the individual and the group as the main object of study, and less so with the organization

organizational theory
A theory concerned with how organizations are structured and how they can be designed to operate more effectively to achieve objectives in a rational way

Our view of contemporary organizational behavior contains both these perspectives.

ORGANIZATIONAL THEORY This theory is concerned with how organizations are structured and how they can be designed to operate more effectively to achieve objectives in a "rational" way. The organizational theorists look at organizational problems rather than at individual problems. This broad view was reflected in the work of Max Weber (1947), a German sociologist who was an important influence on writing and theory about the study of organization. Weber developed a theory of **bureaucracy**, and his analysis considered organizations as part of a broader society. Weber felt that bureaucracy emphasized predictability of behavior and results and showed greater stability over time. He suggested that organizations naturally evolved toward this rational form.

bureaucracy
A form of organization that uses rules and procedures to govern the job behavior of organizational members

Chester Barnard (1938) had a significant effect on organization theory. Barnard developed the concept of the "informal organization" more fully and added much to the thinking about organizations with such concepts as "the zone of indifference" and "the acceptance theory of authority."

Using concepts from Barnard, in their book *Organizations*, James March and Herbert Simon (1958) integrated psychology, sociology, and economic theory. They extended the Barnard view of the organization as a social system. Following Barnard, they presented a more elaborate motivational theory than the scientific management writers and the administrative theory writers. This approach emphasized individual decision making.

contingency theory of organization
Based on the concept that the organization structure and the management approach must be tailored to the situation

Another very important development in the study of organizations is **contingency theory**, a concept based upon the idea that the organization structure and the management approach must be tailored to the situation. Critics of the administrative and scientific management theorists claimed that the early management writers advocated that there is one best way to manage. These critics correctly argued that "it all depended," but they never really told anyone how to proceed to develop a proper managerial strategy. It did all depend – but on what? Some of the answers began to emerge from a study of the Tennessee Valley. The book, *TVA and the Grass Roots*, (Selznick, 1949) described how the structure of an organization is affected by outside restraints, so that the organization develops both formal and informal systems that help it to adapt to the outside environment and, thus, to survive.

In 1961, Burns and Stalker published a study of British firms and found that the differences in the organizational structures of these firms could be traced to the nature of the technology used and to the markets served by the firms (Perrow, 1970):

- When the technological and market environments were uncertain and prone to rapid change, there was a loose, organic organization.
- When the environment was more predictable and stable, a traditional bureaucracy seemed to be more effective.

Burns and Stalker specified more precisely than ever before what the internal structure should look like, given a certain kind of environment.

Lawrence and Lorsch (1969) studied how organizational structure was affected by the rate of technological change for the products produced, the production methods used, and environmental uncertainty. In general, they made two conclusions:

1 Organizations in a stable environment are more effective if they have more detailed procedures and a more centralized decision-making process.
2 Organizations in an unstable environment should have decentralization, participation, and less emphasis on rules and standard procedures to be effective.

ORGANIZATIONAL BEHAVIOR Some of the early contributors to contemporary organizational behavior are Douglas McGregor, Chris Argyris, Rensis Likert, and Lyman Porter. Although others helped to forge the discipline of organizational behavior as we know it today, the work of these scholars deserves special mention. Douglas McGregor (1960), in *The Human Side of Enterprise*, said that most managers make incorrect assumptions about those who work for them. He called these assumptions, collectively, Theory X. **Theory X** assumed that people were lazy, with personal goals which ran counter to the organization's, and that because of this, people had to be controlled externally. In a work context, this meant close supervision and guidance so that management could ensure high performance. **Theory Y** assumptions were based on greater trust in others. Human beings were more mature, self-motivated, and self-controlled than Theory X assumed. McGregor suggested that there was little need for rigid organization or interpersonal controls.

theory X
Assumes humans are lazy, with personal goals which run counter to the organization's and hence, they have to be controlled externally

theory Y
Assumes they are more mature, self-motivated, and self-controlled

Diversity Issues: Mary Parker Follett: A Female Management Guru – from the Early 1900s

Lillian Gilbreth – described in our FOCUS ON . . . *Management History* (page 6) – was not the only woman who contributed significantly to the development of the field of management and organizational behavior. Mary Parker Follett was another. Mary was born shortly after the Civil War and died in 1933. She began her career as a social worker in Boston, but in her late fifties, she drew on her experiences in managing vocational guidance centers and, in the 1920s, began lecturing and writing about how her experience and ideas could be applied to business.

Many important management writers – Peter Drucker, Lyndall Urwick and Warren Bennis to name a few – think that her early contributions were important, but that these were overlooked by others who influenced management thought. For instance, she advocated many things that you will find discussed in later chapters – and attributed to other writers, usually men. For example, she made two arguments:

1. It is possible to make conflict productive by seeking an integrative solution by collaboration rather than using power over others to achieve solutions. Differences can be made to work in a positive way.
2. The use of authority can have negative effects. It does not flow downward but derives from the interaction of processes and people with knowledge.

Her work also emphasized the importance of participative problem solving, high performance teams, collective responsibility and the role of business in society, concerns that are paramount today.

How precursive was her work? After reading some of her work, Warren Bennis, an important contributor to the literature on leadership, said, "It makes you wince when you sincerely believe, as I do, that what you have written about leadership was already literally bespoken by another 40 years before your precious and 'prescient' sentences saw the light of day."

There may be several reasons why Mary Parker Follett's work did not have the impact of other early management theorists. It could be that, as a woman, she attempted to make a contribution in a field dominated by men. Perhaps she wasn't taken seriously because of her experience as a social worker and her emphasis on achieving results by working together, rather than the use of power and authority, an orientation that was more consistent with the business culture in the times that she was writing and lecturing.

Sources: Adapted from Walsh (1995) and Nelton (1997)

Chris Argyris (1957, 1964) also made a strong case for reducing the amount of organizational control. He believed that many constraints placed by organizational structure on human beings were self-defeating to organizational goals of effectiveness and efficiency. The thrust of his argument, along with McGregor's, is that the bureaucratic form of organization is incongruent with the basic needs of the healthy individual and that it treats lower organizational members like children. This fosters dependence and leads to the frustration of the highest-order human needs. This frustration expresses itself in lack of work involvement and antiorganizational activities, such as sabotage.

In 1961, Rensis Likert, a psychologist, published *New Patterns of Management*, a book that was to have a powerful impact on thinking about human problems of management. Likert (1961) believed that "managers with the best record of performance in American business and government [were] in the process of pointing the way to an appreciably more effective system of management than now exists." He proposed that leaders (or managers) would be most effective using a supportive approach. This means that they must create a work environment in which the individual sees his "experiences (in terms of his values, goals, expectations and aspirations) as contributing to and maintaining his sense of personal worth and importance." Likert went on to give details of the characteristics of these managers and organizations.

Lyman Porter (1964) reported an important line of research beginning in the early 1960s that examined how managers' needs, attitudes, and satisfactions were related to organization size, organizational structure, and the nature of the position a person held. Porter's work is significant because it drew attention to the work setting, and, also, it demonstrated that such matters could be studied in a systematic, empirical way.

The work of these writers – and others whom we have not mentioned as well as others we do discuss in this book – is important because they broadened the scope of traditional behavioral approaches and introduced some of the critical factors that the scientific management writers and the administrative theorists had not addressed.

Current Trends and Challenges for Organizational Behavior

Since its birth over 40 years ago, the field of organizational behavior has developed during a time in which the environment in which organizations operate has changed, often imperceptibly but, at other times, dramatically. First, US industrial superiority after World War II eroded as countries worldwide developed strong economies and became more competitive. Second, the Vietnam conflict and its aftermath had a tremendous political significance. The war was not financed properly, setting the groundwork for hyperinflation in the 1970s. In the US, that war disenchanted many, and some analysts believe an era of self-indulgence began which permanently eroded traditional work values (Dyer and Dyer, 1984). Third, during the 1970s, the status of women and minority groups changed. They began entering the work force in increasing numbers and demanded an end to the discrimination they had suffered in the past. Then, in the early 1980s, there was a period of sustained economic growth, but the residual effects of the Vietnam conflict were large national trade and budget deficits that plagued the economy well into the 1990s. Since the early 1990s, however, the US economy has enjoyed a period of sustained economic growth and these deficits have been eliminated.

These are some of the social and cultural forces that have been instrumental in shaping the problems and challenges to managing effectively today. In the following pages, we focus on some of the challenges that managers will face in the future from the changing economy, the changing work force, and some of the important changes in the way that organizations are structured and managed.

The Changing Economy

In the USA, one of the most important changes in recent years has been *changes in the manufacturing sector*. After World War II, basic manufacturing, such as steel, basic metals, and the auto industry which were mostly located in the Northeast and Midwest USA, formed the economic backbone of a strong economy. These industries came out of World War II as dominant world economic forces. However, around 1965, there began a serious decline in productivity. Many production facilities were old and inefficient, but even the newer ones proved to be less efficient than those of foreign competitors with relatively new plants, built since World War II. US firms lagged in modernizing their plant and equipment, partly because foreign competition had not been a serious threat for so long.

Related to the decline in the manufacturing sector was a *decrease in the power and the role of unions*. However, something else was going on, beyond the fact that the number of union jobs was decreasing. With pressures for increased productivity resulting in less labor-intensive operating facilities, management had become more aggressive. This shifted the balance of power in the direction of management. More companies began asking for, and winning, concessions from unions with respect to work rules and wages – a trend that continues today.

The decline in manufacturing, however, was offset by the *growth of the service sector*. The Hudson Institute estimates that manufacturing output in the year 2000 will be 17 percent of gross national product (GNP), dropping from around 21 percent of GNP in the late 1980s (Johnston and Packer, 1987). During the same period, the output of service industries should increase from 69 to 75 percent of GNP. This shift means there will be substantial employment growth in small business (Johnston and Packer, 1987). It also implies that the number of part-time employees will grow. While this may reduce direct wage and fringe-benefit costs to employers, it could give rise to more government programs to provide health care and retirement programs for workers who, in the past, had these benefits as part of their compensation packages in larger manufacturing firms.

Finally, we have seen the *globalization of business*. Companies now compete in worldwide markets in different ways, and the nature of the competition itself is changing. In the past, each country was a separate producer and a separate market. Historically, products and product components would be manufactured in the home country and then exported to foreign markets. For many years, for example, Honda automobiles were built only in Japan and then shipped to the USA. Similarly, US products and parts were built in the USA and exported. Firms are now locating manufacturing facilities in foreign countries. Now Daimler–Chrysler produces the Mercedes in the USA, General Electric builds small appliances in the Far East, and Sony has manufacturing facilities in the USA. The challenge for the multi-national firm is to integrate far flung, and often culturally different, units into an effective organization.

Responding to these changes has led to a major restructuring of business. Many of the problems have been solved by market forces or through cooperation between managers, workers, and investors. The downward trend in US productivity has changed and now it leads both of its major competitors – Germany and Japan – in both capital productivity and labor productivity (*The Economist*, 1996).

The Changing Work Force

In the 1960s, the work force was relatively homogenous. White Anglo-Saxon men dominated the managerial work force and the better-paying manufacturing jobs were also the province of men, though there was an ethnic, but white, diversity that emanated from the European immigration during the first thirty years of the twentieth century. This is nothing like the work force of the future; there have already been major changes in its gender, ethnic, and racial composition – and there are more changes to come. For example, there will be major shifts in the age composition of the work force. The *demographics will change* by the year 2005 (Edmonson, 1996; Johnston and Packer, 1987):

- The size of the work force will increase but the rate of growth will be slower than in the past.
- The number of younger workers (under 35) will decrease from 50 percent to 38 percent of the work force.
- The "baby boomers," the age group between 35 and 54, will expand dramatically and constitute over 50 percent of the labor force, up from 38 percent in 1985.
- Because of the increase in life span, there will be a large increase in the number of people over 65.

The decrease in the working-age population may result in a shortage of labor. This poses some interesting challenges. For instance, it is during the age period from the mid-20s to the mid-40s that people have traditionally advanced in a career. However, if organizations become smaller, requiring fewer managers, and if, at the same time, there are a large number of people in this age group, promotion channels in organizations may become clogged.

If a labor shortage occurs, as some predict, then there are economic incentives for companies to retain older employees. However, changes in attitudes as well as organization practices may be necessary. The conventional wisdom is that older workers are less productive than younger workers, but the evidence on this is mixed. Some research shows that productivity actually increases with age, but older workers receive lower performance ratings (Waldman and Avolio, 1986), while other studies find there is no relationship between age and individual performance. This means, conservatively, that there is no reason for the conventional wisdom and that the older workers can be as productive as younger ones (McEvoy and Cascio, 1989). What is necessary, for sure, is we eliminate the age stereotypes which might hinder retention of older workers.

The *gender and ethnic makeup of the work force* will not be anything like it was in the past. The proportion of white males will decline as more women, Black Americans, Asians, Latinos, Native Americans, and other minorities enter the work force. The cultures of organizations, which have been dominated by the values of white males, will slowly change as these others move into positions of power and influence.

Finally, in the last 40 years, there have been substantial *changes in work values*. Prior to 1960, the **work ethic** was a dominant value in US culture. Most people believed that hard work was good, that it was necessary to provide for one's family, that it would lead to success, and that one could be successful by finding a position in a good company and doing the job well. By 1965, there began a shift away from this perspective toward one that the US value system was too materialistic, that the structure of social relationships was too rigid, and that there were more important things in life than work. The move was away from conservatism and more toward liberalism. By 1975, however, a more conservative attitude reemerged. People again valued work and success in much the same way as they had in the past. If there is a difference, it appears to be that

work ethic
The belief that work is good and that it should be valued

> People today are strongly committed to finding a lifestyle and then a job to support it, rather than the reverse, which was characteristic of the depression-raised generation before them. This calls for more participative styles of leadership, more listening, and considerable democracy in the workplace if these people are to be made more productive and creative (Odiorne, 1983)

Changes in Organizations and the Way They are Managed

The ways organizations are managed have been changing from the past. Prior to the 1960s, the prevailing managerial approach was hierarchical and top-down in most firms. Workers were directed what to do, and they did it; if there were problems, there was usually a union to which the workers could turn for help. As the forces we discussed above began to shape the culture, particularly the work place, not only did the workers change, but companies began to realize that there was unused potential to be tapped in the work force. Many organizations began seeking ways to do this and, today, companies – among them Ford, AT&T, Intel, Motorola, and Xerox – are finding better ways to capitalize on their human resources. They redesign the work to empower employees, and they develop leaner organizations. In some firms, employees are called "stakeholders" or "associates" to reflect a more egalitarian orientation.

One important factor is the *technological revolution* driven by advances in computer technology. Today, computers are used to do so many different things. They facilitate communications within and between organizations all over the world on the worldwide web (WWW). These networks have made possible electronic mail (e-mail) and teleconferencing. Fax machines transmit text materials instantly across telephone lines. With word processing, text material can be produced, edited, printed, faxed almost anywhere in the world, and stored for later use rather easily. Computer networks also make telecommuting possible, where you can work at home or in areas removed from the traditional office.

The integrated circuit has changed the face of manufacturing. Machines can now be programmed to perform very complicated and exacting tasks, often with little or no human help. Currently, robots are welding and painting cars in Detroit and making computer chips in the Silicon Valley.

Computers have changed how we receive and how we spend our money. For example, electronic point of sale (EPOS) systems in supermarkets use optical-scanning devices that have not only changed the cashier's job but, more importantly, now permit managers to obtain information instantaneously about demand and inventory levels. Optical scanning also permits us to use a debit card or a credit card at the point of purchase so that you can pay for dinner at Tremani's Wine Bar in Rome, buy a designer outfit at Armani's on Via Montanapoleone in Milan, pay for suit in Hong Kong, or spend an evening at a local campus bistro without ever actually using the currency of the country until, of course, you have to pay the monthly bill with your own local currency.

One other important change that the computer revolution has meant to organizations is the effect on the importance and status of workers who have the relevant skills to design information systems or to manage them. These skills have become so very important to all large organizations, as well as to most smaller ones, that they provide excellent opportunities for career advancement to those with them – and it is well known that the younger generation of workers possess these skills more so than the older workers, giving them a decided advantage.

The *nature of work* is changing. In the future, jobs will require higher skill levels than in the past (Johnston and Packer, 1987). Virtually everyone must know, one way or the other, how to use computers: from accountants who need to be able to use them for record keeping, data retrieval, and the design of information systems to clerks who need to use them for proper entry of orders and for billing. There could also be more monitoring of work using computers and computer networks. For example, in many large offices where clerical work is performed on networked computers, productivity reports are regularly produced from the information system itself and thus provides feedback to the workers. This impersonal and frequent monitoring may well increase the stress and pressure on workers, and could result in greater alienation.

We also expect to see *increased delegation* of responsibility and authority. More people, both managers and workers, at lower organizational levels have increased authority. Many of the newer management approaches – such as high-involvement strategies, self-directed work groups, and empowerment – require extensive delegation of control. To accomplish this, managers must trust the workers and take a hands-off approach. At the same time, workers must believe that managers will not violate the integrity of those areas which have been delegated to them. This kind of relationship only develops when the work force is well informed about the operations of the firm and they feel secure that management is not hiding anything.

We also can expect to see more **lean organizations.** The use of computers and the downsizing of firms driven by competitive forces have resulted in the need for fewer people to produce the same or more output. The estimates of worker displacement from downsizing range between four million and fifteen million blue-collar jobs (Carroll and Schuler, 1983). This leads to a corresponding decrease in the need for managers. Many firms have flattened the organizational structure, eliminating at least one layer of management in the hierarchy, and reducing the number of managers at other levels. Often, these flatter, leaner structures not only result in a lower managerial wage bill, but they are also very convincing evidence to equity holders that company presidents are taking forceful, effective action to deal with increasingly turbulent environments (Salancik and Meindl, 1984). However, designing these lean structures takes more managerial skill than just reducing the number of workers. When firms reduce the size of the work force alone, they perform no better than average in their industry; when reducing the work force is done in conjunction with other approaches to increasing effectiveness, such as asset restructuring, firms generate better returns on assets and better returns to their stockholders than the average firm in their own industries (Cascio et al., 1997).

lean organization
An organization in which fewer people are required to produce the same or more output due to the use of computers and downsizing

Managing Organizational Performance

Understanding the theories and research on which organizational behavior is built will help you to face these challenges and to manage individual and organizational performance more effectively. However, before you begin studying some of the specific topics in each chapter – such as motivation, personality and organizational design – it is important that you have a clear concept of two things:

1 What do we mean by performance?
2 What is the manager's job like?

What is Performance?

There are several ways to judge whether the performance of an individual or an organization is effective and, depending on your perspective, one of these ways may be more or less important to you. Performance levels can be stated in terms of quantity or quality, and require some subjective judgment by a manager. One person may judge a particular level or type of performance as "high," but the same level may be only "satisfactory," or perhaps "unsatisfactory," for another. For example, if you live in a community, you might judge the effectiveness of a firm based on how many jobs it provides, how little it pollutes your environment, or how much it contributes in taxes. If you work in the firm, you might judge its effectiveness by its ability to pay you in salary and benefits.

In this book, we take a managerial view of performance. That means we define performance in terms of the results that managers must obtain to keep the firm viable as an economic entity. This view of performance includes, as shown in figure 1.1, three dimensions, the task performance dimension, the contextual performance dimension, and the ethical performance dimension. It is achieved by managing what we call the building blocks of organizational effectiveness: the individual, the group, and the organization. We have more to say about these building blocks on page 23 when we outline the plan of the book.

task performance dimension
The set of activities and their results that one must do to accomplish the work

The **task performance dimension** is what most of us focus on: the set of activities and their results that you must do to accomplish the work. For example, if you are manager of a manufacturing plant, you must manage production and quality levels, prepare work schedules, order supplies, deal with subordinates, and run staff meetings. If you are a systems analyst, you must be able to analyze the flow of work through an organization, be able to specify the modification of existing computer software so that it can be adapted to the work flow, and then instruct the users about how to use the system in future.

contextual performance dimension
What one is contributing to the effectiveness of the organization or others in it, in ways other than just your designated work tasks

The **contextual performance dimension**. Another aspect of performance is how you might contribute to the effectiveness of the organization or others in it in ways other than "just doing your job." This performance dimension reflects the extent to which you are willing to go beyond the norms of performance and involvement of your work role. These sorts of actions might be seen by some as

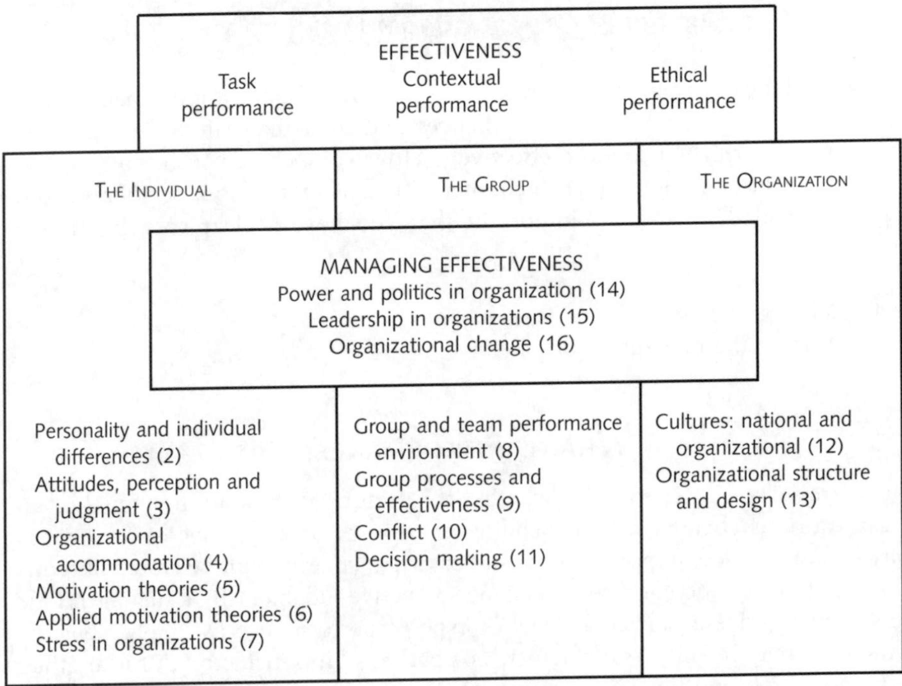

Fig 1.1: Plan of this book

trivial and irrelevant, but they contribute in an important way to the effectiveness of the organization (Organ, 1988). For example, you might assist a co-worker with a task or a personal problem, volunteer extra effort, act in congenial and supportive ways at work, or suggest improvements (Organ, 1988). Such behavior, that goes beyond task performance, is essential if organizations are to excel, because success depends on employees going beyond formal role requirements (Organ, 1988; Borman and Motowidlo, 1993).

The **ethical performance dimension** focuses on doing the right thing. This sounds simple, but the fact is that nearly everyone faces ethical dilemmas at work. One survey of workers (Jones, 1997) reported that almost 50 percent admitted to some kind of unethical or illegal actions at work. The most frequent acts were cutting corners on quality control, covering up some incident, abusing or lying about sick days, deceiving customers, and putting inappropriate pressure on others at work. Here are some of the reasons given for the unethical actions:

ethical performance dimension Focuses on what is the right thing to do

- Pressure to meet budgets and quotas
- Weak leadership
- No management support
- Internal politics
- Poor internal communications
- Work hours and work load
- Lack of recognition by the company
- Insufficient resources
- Balancing work and family
- Personal financial problems

These results suggest that sometimes, by doing what you think is required for your job, you may have a negative impact on stakeholders, including stockholders, who are not customers but are affected by the firm, as well as the members of the firm itself.

How can this happen? Consider first the task dimension of a job. Clearly, the goal of anyone's work is to improve the economic performance of the firm, so, what could you do it faced with these three situations?

1 You are told by your supervisor to ship a product that does not meet quality standards and you feel quite sure that it will fail shortly after the customer starts using it.
2 You are a representative of a US firm doing business in a foreign country where it is traditional, and not illegal, to pay a "fee" for access or consideration to obtain a major contract that could mean substantial profits to the firm and a large commission to you. You know directly from your boss that the firm wants the business, even though such fees may be construed as bribes and they are illegal under US law.
3 You have been asked to charge a fee to a project that you think is excessive and will increase the cost to the client substantially.

Now consider the contextual dimensions of work. These are behaviors that contribute in indirect ways to organizational performance such as being a good colleague and facilitating others in your work group. What would you do if you discovered that your best friend was stealing materials in substantial amounts from the firm?

What creates these dilemmas is fairly simple. It is that, generally, the right thing to do is pretty straightforward: don't cheat, don't tolerate stealing, and don't pay bribes. The problem is that, very often, there are organizational pressures, or pressures from your work group, to do exactly that. Further, there is a good chance that if you do act unethically, no one will be any the wiser and nothing bad will happen to you.

There are some ethical standards and standards of social responsibility that can be applied. You can try to "do the right thing" but the fact is that what is the right, or ethical, thing to do is not easy to define, because different standards and values exist in a society. So, for a firm, there must be some common set of values that are expressed in some way as a guide to deciding about how to act. The most basic guide, but certainly not one that is sufficient, is that our actions must be legal. Usually, however, society demands that we apply a higher standard of what is right.

A Question of Ethics: How Ethics can Collapse in Organizations

Values and attitudes are the underpinnings of ethics. Ethics concerns itself with our conduct and character. It involves the study of principles and methods for determining what is right and wrong, what is good or bad, what ought or ought not be done. Ethical questions arise every day in the world of business, of course, and answers are not always easy to come by. There are many ways for the manager who wants to encourage unethical behavior, including the failure to raise ethical questions before taking action:

- Surround yourself with subordinates who are young, inexperienced, enthralled with power and deep in debt. Youth, ambition and financial dependency create a subordinate unwilling to question an order or challenge a boss.
- Send a clear message that you want results, at any cost. Employees are now likely to act ruthlessly, hide evidence, and falsify facts.
- Be certain the CEO and chairman are tyrannical and prone to anger. Fear is a helpful tool in suppressing free thought and speech.
- When an employee's public statements bring criticism of the company, cut the employee loose. Fire them, or demote, transfer or otherwise render them *persona non grata*.
- When an ethical lapse is discovered, never admit anything. Conceal, spin and gloss. Here, indignation and arrogance are your friends. Trivialize or justify what you've done and brand ethical breaches as "snafus."

Where have you recently seen these behaviors?

Source: Adapted from Jennings (1996)

WHAT MANAGERS DO

Now let us learn about how managers try to manage task, contextual and ethical performance. Managers are a separate and distinct category of employees in an organization. They hold a certain type of job. Approximately 10 percent of the working population in the USA is categorized as a "manager or proprietor." The president of Pepsi-Cola is a manager. So is the afternoon shift supervisor at McDonald's. Though their jobs are very different, there are some characteristics that they have in common with all managerial work (Mintzberg, 1973).

MANAGERS MAKE DECISIONS ABOUT HOW OTHER PEOPLE, PRIMARILY SUBORDINATES, USE RESOURCES Managers usually have formal authority – the right to decide how those who work for them can use resources needed to accomplish the operative tasks, the execution of work. Managers make resource allocation decisions which other people must implement.

A MANAGER IS RESPONSIBLE FOR THE SUPERVISION OF SUBORDINATES What most sharply distinguishes a manager's job from that of others is that the manager must be concerned with the effective use of human resources as well as physical resources. Managers are responsible for the work of other people.

THE WORK PACE IS UNRELENTING Managers work very hard, feel compelled to work hard, and do so at a frantic pace. One reason for this is the wide variety of things that managers are expected to do to complete the work. They are constantly exposed to one problem after another, and most of these need an immediate solution (Mintzberg, 1973).

THE ACTIVITIES ARE VARIED, FRAGMENTED, AND BRIEF Seldom does a manager have the luxury of starting a project and finishing it, without interruption. The work is discontinuous. For instance, a manager may begin a project at 7.30 a.m. and make some progress, but then be interrupted with a question from her boss which needs an answer. She sets aside the project, and finds an answer to her boss's problem. Before she can return to the project, something else interrupts her day. It may be hours before she returns to the work she started in the morning. Also, much of what a manager does takes only a short time. Half of a manager's tasks are finished in less than ten minutes and only 10 percent take more than an hour; telephone calls take an average of six minutes and unscheduled meetings rarely last more than half an hour (Mintzberg, 1973).

MANAGERS PREFER LIVE ACTION Managers tend to do the more active, current, and interesting parts of their work first and set aside the routine parts for later. They are more interested in current information than historical data and more concerned with specific rather than general issues.

THERE IS MUCH VERBAL COMMUNICATION Of the different ways to communicate (mail, memo, phone, face-to-face, meetings, etc.), managers prefer to use verbal communications that can take up to 80 percent of their time (Guest, 1956; Lawler et al., 1968).

THERE IS A VARIETY OF WORK CONTACTS Managers maintain contacts with their superiors, their subordinates, and outsiders. Up to half of this time is spent with subordinates and a large part is also spent with outsiders, both in negotiating the organization's business and in seeking information. This is especially true for CEOs, but it is also true for lower levels and supervisors. Interestingly, contacts with those at higher levels take a relatively short time and they are somewhat formal, usually in the form of requests and written reports.

MUCH MANAGERIAL WORK IS CONTROLLED BY OTHERS An interesting aspect of managerial work is how much of it is controlled by others, meaning that the manager is often reacting. For example, managers are interrupted by their subordinates, called by their bosses, and often must deal with problems that arise unexpectedly.

Focus on A Manager's Job: Why Matt Scott went back to his Work Team

Matt Scott began work at Fore Systems in Pittsburgh in 1994. He was writing computer code in a very unstructured, freewheeling software firm. He liked the work, especially the fact that it was on the cutting edge of developing a system of computer networking that would deliver a great deal of information, including real-time video and voice, at a much faster rate than most existing technologies. He was very good at his job, and this was noted by his supervisors. In 1995, he was asked if he wanted to move into a management position, leading a team of software engineers on special, important projects. He decided to become a manager.

What he discovered was that the job was not what he thought it would be. He was assigned to be the team leader of the group with the responsibility of completing the job, but he encountered problems that he did not like. One was communicating with other team leaders; another was trying to make the members of his own team work effectively and efficiently together, without conflict and controversy.

What he missed was what, for him, had been the most interesting part of the work: the writing of computer code for the design of the system. All of these other managerial things were obstacles to him. In addition, he started to have interpersonal problems with some members of his team. Then his life became even more complicated. His wife gave birth to their first child and he wanted to be more involved at home. All of this became more problematic than he liked. So, he decided to give up the managerial post; instead he returned to the team as one of the members, not as the team leader.

Source: Murray (1997)

Managerial Work and Organizational Level

There are some obvious differences in the work of managers at different levels of an organization.

- Top managers spend most of their time planning and performing general management activities (Mahoney et al. 1965). They are more likely to act as representatives of the firm, to be involved in important negotiations, and to act as a spokesperson for the firm (Pavett and Lau, 1983).
- Middle level managers are more involved in supervision than the top level group, but less than lower-level managerial work. In this supervisory capacity, they perform many leadership activities and monitor the work of others.
- Lower level managers have most of their time (over 50 percent) taken up with supervisory activities (Mahoney et al., 1965; Pavett and Lau, 1983).

The Plan of this Book

In this book, we present the main concepts of field of organizational behavior so that they are easy for you to understand, while at the same time maintaining the integrity of the theory and research on which the field is based. In addition, to help you to understand how these theoretical concepts can be used to improve organizational effectiveness, each chapter concludes with guidelines for using them. Finally, we have integrated some design factors to help you in navigating your way through the book.

The Building Blocks of Organizational Behavior

Figure 1.1 shows the four main content areas that make up the field of organizational behavior. Three of these – the individual, groups, and the organization – can be considered as key building blocks of knowledge. The fourth area focuses on the processes for managing these building blocks.

The individual Some essential aspects of people – such as personality, perception, attitudes, and judgment – are the topics of chapters 2 and 3. In chapter 4, we move the person into the work organization and examine how he or she chooses a career and the way people adjust to work. In chapter 5, we discuss several important motivation theories and, in chapter 6, we describe how these are used by organizations to improve effectiveness. Then, in chapter 7, we show some of the problems that stress can create at work. Many issues are raised in this chapter about the importance of work to individuals and how the work setting can result in serious psychological and physiological reactions.

Groups Individuals work with other people, and are affected by them. The way groups are formed is discussed in chapter 8, and then chapter 9 focuses on group dynamics and how teams can be used in organizations to good effect. Conflict is the subject of chapter 10. In chapter 11, we focus on decision-making processes, both individual and group.

THE ORGANIZATION In this section, we explain some of the broader forces that shape individual and group behavior patterns in organizations. First, in chapter 12, we show how the broader culture and the organizational culture affects individuals, groups, and organizations. Chapter 13 describes the different types of organizational structures within which people work and how these structures are affected by the organization's relevant environment.

MANAGING THE ORGANIZATION Managers do a variety of things to achieve organization effectiveness. Ways that managers exercise power and influence are examined in chapters 14 and 15: power and political process are discussed in chapter 14; leadership is the subject of chapter 15, and this flows logically from the earlier discussion of power and politics. The subject of chapter 16 is organizational change and development. In this chapter, we describe ways that managers may attempt to change organization practices and member behavior when there is a need to do so.

GUIDES FOR MANAGERS The approach that we take to organizational behavior in this book is to present, analyze and discuss the strongest theories and empirical evidence on each subject in each chapter. The ultimate issue, however, is: how do the theories and research help *you* to do a better job as a manager? For this reason, each chapter includes a section called GUIDE FOR MANAGERS, in which we spell out what you can do to use the ideas in the chapter for improving your own performance, or that of others in your work group.

NAVIGATING THIS BOOK

We have designed this book so that it involves you, the reader, with the material seamlessly from the beginning of a chapter to its end. We do this by asking you, before you even start to read a chapter, to draw upon your own experiences of the chapter topic. Then we develop the material so that you become more familiar with the details. We end each chapter with cases and study questions that permit you to test how well you have learned the subject.

PREPARING FOR CLASS It is important that your prepare thoroughly before you cover a new topic in class. We recommend that you read through the relevant chapter to acquaint yourself with the material and tackle the "thought starter" activity given on the opening page of each chapter *before* the first session on that chapter. For example when preparing to learn about leadership, we ask you to think about two personal experiences, one positive and one negative, that you have had with persons in leadership positions . . . What was it they did? Or what they were? What made the good leader good? . . . What made the poor leader poor?

At the beginning of each chapter, there is also a list of the main topics to provide you with a preview of what is to come, and something that might trigger your answers to the "thought starters."

Focus items In each chapter, we have included several "Focus Items" that are examples drawn from the popular press, interesting research studies not discussed in the text, or our own consulting experiences. We have abstracted and rewritten these items to clarify how they are related to the subject matter of the chapter. In each chapter, there are special items:

- Diversity Issues for Managers show how specific aspects of the chapter are related to managing members of different racial, ethnic, or gender groups.
- A Question of Ethics are questions of right and wrong that are relevant for every topic area that we discuss in this book. These focus items illustrate some of the ethical issues for the different chapter topics.
- Global Focus items show how specific topics of each chapter are linked to worldwide matters, because business is so globally oriented today.
- Focus on specific managerial issues are an abstract from the business press that offers an applied example of some concept covered in each chapter.

Key concepts and definitions In each chapter, we have done four things to make it easy for you, the reader, to find information on the important concepts and to understand their meaning.

1 Each Key Concept is highlighted within the text.
2 The Definition of the term is placed in the margin of the book near the highlighted term.
3 There is a list of all of the chapter's key concepts at the end of each chapter.
4 At the end of the book, all of the key concepts and definitions appear in a Glossary (see page 515).

Experiential activities In each chapter, there is a "hands-on" experiential activity. These are high-impact, low-time requirement activities that draw you, the reader, directly into the text material of the chapter. Some are self-diagnostic questionnaires and others are interactive activities between the readers and their instructors. These should give the readers a little assistance in understanding how some of the ideas work and how they might be applied.

Study questions and cases At the end of each chapter, there are Study Questions and a short Case that direct attention to the chapter material and bring to a close the ideas that are stimulated as the reader was Getting Ready for Class. These Study Questions and Cases are written to provide a developmental structure for class discussion that covers the important concepts in the chapter. The cases are, for the most part, short enough that they can be quickly read during an instructional period, and then used for discussion in the same class session.

Summary

Organizational behavior is the study of human action in organizations. It is the systematic analysis of individual and group processes and characteristics. The objective of organizational behavior is to understand, predict, and improve the performance of organizations and individuals. While concern with managing people is as old as human history, it is only recently that organizational behavior (OB) has been considered a separate field of study. Prior to the late 1950s, concern about managing human factors was found in writings on scientific management, administrative theory, industrial psychology, and the human relations approach. Since the late 1950s, many theoretical and empirical aspects of the basic social science disciplines were drawn upon to become integrated into the field which is known today as organizational behavior, a body of knowledge, still incomplete and developing. This book is an introduction to the present state of knowledge in this field, obviously being selective in what is covered, given the limitations of time and space.

Key Concepts

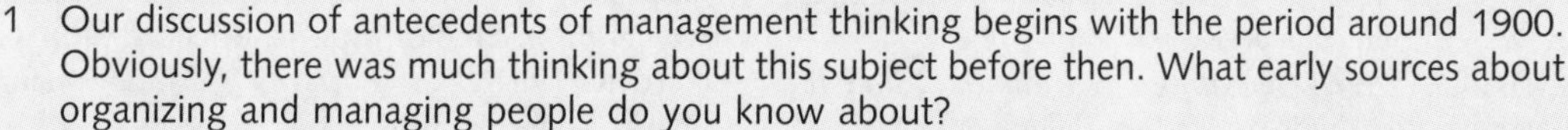

1 Our discussion of antecedents of management thinking begins with the period around 1900. Obviously, there was much thinking about this subject before then. What early sources about organizing and managing people do you know about?
2 What would be the difference in a person's managerial approach if it was guided by scientific management principles, as compared to being guided by concepts from organizational behavior?
3 What are the critical elements in the "administrative theory approach"?
4 What are the main forces that gave impetus to the development of current thinking about organizational behavior and management?
5 What is the difference between organizational theory and organizational behavior? Is this a useful distinction in studying organizations? Is it a useful distinction in managing them?
6 Some people think that managers should know about research and theory so that they can be intelligent consumers of it. Can you think of some other reasons?

Case

Judy Jenkins' First Day in Class

Judy Jenkins was a student at Central State University. She was seeking a degree in business administration and intended to use it later in helping to manage her father's construction business. Primarily, her father built residential homes but he also did small office buildings, sheds and garages. At the beginning of her course in Organizational Behavior, the instructor talked at length about some of the topics they would cover, specifically reinforcement theory, power and politics in organizations, and what happens in small groups and teams.

Judy thought that, while this material might be useful in the large companies that most of her fellow students would be looking for jobs in, it was not very practical for use in her father's construction business. She had never noticed her father using any of these ideas. He just adapted to the requirements of each situation, which were always somewhat unique. She decided to talk to the instructors after class.

She wondered what the instructor would say.

- What do you think was discussed?

References

Argyris, C. 1957: *Personality and Organization: The Conflict Between the System and the Individual.* New York: Harper & Row.

Argyris, C. 1964: *Integrating the Individual and the Organization.* New York: John Wiley.

Barnard, C. 1938: *The Functions of the Executive.* Cambridge, MA: Harvard University Press.

Bell, D. 1970: *Work and its Discontents. The Cult of Efficiency in America.* New York: League for Industrial Democracy.

Borman, W. C. and Motowidlo, S. J. 1993: Expanding the criterion domain to include elements of contextual performance. In N. Schmitt and W. C. Borman (eds) *Personnel Selection in Organizations*, San Francisco: Jossey Bass, 71–98.

Carroll, S. J. and Schuler, R. S. 1983: Professional HRM: Changing functions and problems. In S. J. Carroll and R. S. Schuler (eds) *Human Resource Management in the 1980s*, Washington, DC: Bureau of National Affairs, 8-1–8-28.

Cascio, W. F., Young, C. E. and Morris, J. R. 1997: Financial consequences of employment-change decisions in major U.S. corporations. *Academy of Management Journal*, 40(5), October, 1175–90.

Dyer, W. G., and Dyer, J. H. 1984: The M*A*S*H generation: Implications for future organization values. *Organization Dynamics*, 12, 66–79.

Edmonson, B. 1996: Work slowdown. *American Demographics*, 18(3), March 4–7.

George, C. S. 1972: *The History of Management Thought.* Englewood Cliffs, NJ: Prentice-Hall.

Guest, R. H. 1956: Of time and foreman. *Personnel*, 32, 478–86.

Hofstede, G. 1993: Cultural constraints in management theories. *Academy of Management Executive*, 7(1), 81–94.

Jennings, M. M. 1996: Five warning signs of ethical collapse. *Wall Street Journal*, November 4.

Johnston, W. B. and Packer, A. E. 1987: *Workforce 2000: Work and Workers for the 21st Century.* Indianapolis, IN: Hudson Institute.

Jones, D. 1997: 48 percent of workers admit to unethical or illegal acts. *USA Today*, April 4–6, 1-A.

Lawler, E. E., Porter, L. W. and Tannenbaum, A. 1968: Manager's attitudes toward interaction episodes. *Journal of Applied Psychology*, 52, 432–9.

Lawrence, P. R. and Lorsch, J. W. 1969: *Organization and Environment: Managing Differentiation and Integration.* Homewood, IL: Richard D. Irwin.

Likert, R. 1961: *New Patterns of Management.* New York: McGraw-Hill.

Ling, C. C. 1965: *The Management of Personnel Relations: History and Origins.* Homewood, IL: Richard D. Irwin.

Mahoney, T. A., Jerdee, T. J. and Carroll, S. J. 1965: The job(s) of management. *Industrial Relations*, 4, 97–110.

March, G. and Simon, H. 1958: *Organizations.* New York: John Wiley.

McEvoy, G. M. and Cascio, W. F. 1989: Cumulative evidence of the relationship between employee age and job performance. *Journal of Applied Psychology*, 74(1), February, 11–18.

McGregor, D. 1960: *The Human Side of Enterprise.* New York: McGraw-Hill.

Miner, J. B. 1969: *Personnel Psychology.* New York: Macmillan.

Mintzberg, H. 1973: *The Nature of Managerial Work,* New York: Harper & Row.

Murray, M. 1997: Who's the boss? A software engineer becomes a manager with many regrets. *Wall Street Journal*, May 14, A1–A14.

Nelton, S. 1997: Leadership for a new age. *Nations Business*; 85(5), May, 18–25.

Odiorne, G. S. 1983: HRM policy and program managements: A new look in the 1980s. In S. J. Carroll and R. S. Schuler (eds) *Human Resource Management in the 1980s*, Washington, DC: Bureau of National Affairs, 1, 1–23.

Organ, D. W. 1988: *Organizational Citizenship Behavior: The Good Soldier Syndrome.* Lexington MA: Lexington Books.

Pavett, C. M. and Lau, A. 1983: Managerial work: The influence of hierarchical level and functional speciality. *Academy of Management Journal*, 26(1), 170–7.

Perrow, C. 1970: *Organizational Analysis: A Sociological View.* Belmont, CA: Wadsworth.

Porter, L. W. 1964: *Organizational Patterns of Managerial Job Attitudes.* New York: American Foundation for Management Research.

Rehak, J. 1996: Out of the red and onto the "net". *Chief Executive (U.S.)*, 119, December, 32.

Roethlisberger, F. J. and Dickson, W. J. 1939: *Man-*

agement and the Worker. Cambridge, MA: Harvard University Press.

Salancik, G. R. and Meindl, J. R. 1984: Corporate attributions as strategic illusions of management control. *Administrative Science Quarterly*, 29, 238–54.

Selznick, P. 1949: *TVA and the Grass Roots*. Berkeley: University of California Press.

The Economist 1996: America's power plants; *The Economist*. June 8, 82.

Waldman, D. A. and Avolio, B. M. 1986: A meta-analysis of age differences in job performance. *Journal of Applied Psychology*, 71(1), 33–8.

Walsh, M. 1995: Mary Parker Follet – Review of *Prophet of Management: A celebration of writings from the 1920's*. *Business History*, 37(4), October, 123–5.

Weber, M. 1947: *The Theory of Social and Economic Organization*. Trans. by T. Parsons. New York: Free Press.

Wren, D. 1972: *The Evolution of Management Thought*. New York: Ronald.

chapter 2

Personality and Individual Differences

PERSONALITY

THE BASES OF PERSONALITY

APPROACHES TO LEARNING

PERSONALITY IN ORGANIZATION SETTINGS

Preparing for Class

Since this chapter is about personality, make a list of three or four people that you know. Choose some on your list to be from the same family, but not all of them.

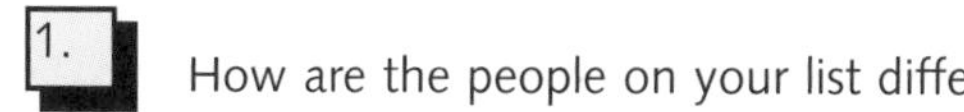

1. How are the people on your list different? How are they the same?
2. To what do you attribute the differences?
3. To what do you attribute their similarities?
4. How are these different people likely to react in their work situation?

Think about these questions (and your answers) as you read this chapter and when you discuss the material in class.

If you believe that people can "make or break" an organization, then it is critical to know something about human behavior. Such knowledge will be useful to you when selecting and training employees, increasing motivation, improving decision making, reducing stress, and enhancing teamwork. Managers cannot be professional psychologists, but they need to know enough to manage from sound principles rather than from myths and guesswork. Had this been the case in the merger of Lotus and IBM, some serious top management problems might have been avoided (Farber, 1995). After Louis Gerstner took over IBM in the crisis years, he set about refocusing the company. One of his important strategic moves was to acquire Lotus. Along with the most of the Lotus staff came Jim Manzi, the former Lotus CEO and President. Manzi was very successful at Lotus and he had a reputation for being a very good, but very tough and often cantankerous manager (Hays, 1995). It was reported that he publicly humiliated employees, made important staff changes on what appeared to be personal whims and, while at Lotus, invested in unwise projects (Hays, 1995). Still, he came along to IBM in the Lotus deal, but only lasted there for a short time, resigning after about three months. His aggressive personal style that worked at Lotus did not fit with the bureaucratic culture of IBM. It appears to have been a case of a bad fit between the person and the organization.

Managing Behavior: A Useful Model

Figure 2.1 is a model of human behavior with four key elements:

1 The environment
2 The person
3 Actual behavior
4 The consequences of behavior

The environment contains the many elements that exist in the world outside the person that may trigger behavior. It interacts with the attributes of the person, which also explain and govern behavior. A few important attributes are shown in figure 2.1, but there are many more. To discover these attributes, we must infer what goes on inside a person or rely on what he or she tells us.

Actual behavior refers to an overt act of the person that can be observed and measured, but tells us little about why it occurred. Observable behavior can never give a complete picture of what goes on inside people, but such behavior does serve as a window to it.

Behavior has consequences; it has intended and unintended effects. For example, behavior at work can produce products for sale, it can lead to conflict, or trigger positive or negative reactions in others. Behavior also has reinforcing consequences that affect the probability of its recurrence. Pleasurable consequences will have a different effect than painful ones.

Finally, the feedback arrows in figure 2.1 show how a person can learn from their behavior and its effects. Also, behavior can change the environment, such

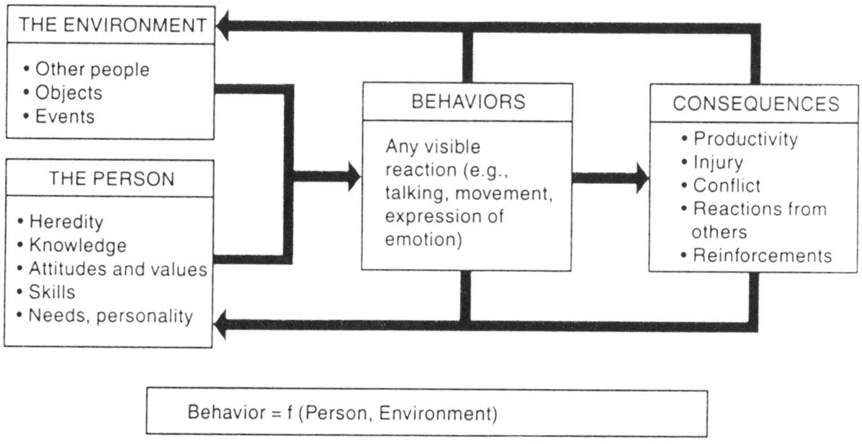

Fig 2.1 : Basic model of individual behavior

as when we turn down the volume on a loud stereo to make it less annoying to others.

Personality

The term personality is used in many different ways. Sometimes we say that a person has a good personality or a bad personality, meaning that he or she is pleasant or unpleasant. Sometimes the word is used to mean an important or famous person, like saying that the President of the USA is an important personality. In this book, we use the term **personality** to mean the relatively stable organization of all a person's characteristics, an enduring pattern of attributes that define the uniqueness of a person. Because attitudes and values are part of the pattern, personality includes predispositions as well as patterns of actual behaviors. Personality plays an important role at work, as the example of Jim Manzi on page 32 illustrated. How else can you explain the reason why he was so successful in Lotus and not so in IBM. It is a wonderful example of the importance of understanding both the person and the environment in which he or she operates. In one environment, his personality was fine; in another, it caused problems.

personality
The relatively stable organization of a person's characteristics; the enduring pattern of attributes which define the uniqueness of the individual

In this chapter, we present several different perspectives on personality because there is no single theory that integrates all we know about personality; each theory and approach has its own way of characterizing it. For example, some approaches emphasize predispositions, and the traits, attitudes and needs that drive behavior (Cattell, 1950; Allport, 1961; Murray, 1962; Maslow, 1970). There are learning theories of personality, such as social learning theory (discussed on page 38). Other approaches stress personality in terms of the perceptions, thoughts, and judgments people engage in as they cope and mature in the world around them (Rogers, 1942). Finally, some theories look at the tensions that exist inside a person, and see personality as the consequence of internal conflicts and how they are resolved. You are probably familiar with the work of Freud who dramatized the struggle between our inner impulses and our moral conscience (Freud, 1933).

HOW AND WHEN PERSONALITY OPERATES

Even though the environment affects behavior, personality-driven behavior can show a good deal of consistency across different situations (Epstein and O'Brien, 1985). This is especially true for a broad disposition such as one's need for social approval. A specific trait such as honesty may vary more with the situation, but even specific traits will affect behavior when conditions are appropriate (Funder, 1991). It is also likely that personality will help to determine the kinds of situations that people enter. Shy persons will avoid social situations. When in these situations, the trait may still emerge, such as when a shy person experiences tension at a party. In some settings, however, personality attributes may be squelched. For example, sociability may be impossible to express in a hostile or threatening environment.

strong situations
Situations where constraints such as clear and precise cues, rules and task demands act to limit behavior

When is personality more or less likely to operate, and to be the main cause of behavior? It seems that personality is less powerful in "**strong situations.**" These are structured situations where constraints such as clear and precise cues, rules and task demands act to limit behavior (Mischel, 1977; Weiss and Adler, 1984). Rewards, tight standards, and expectations can add to the limits, making personality differences between individuals less evident. Think, for example, about watching a military unit in a parade, where the constraints on behavior are very tight: all wear the same uniform, march at the same pace, move on command and salute when ordered. It is impossible to know anything about the personality differences of the soldiers from watching them march – this is the epitome of a strong situation.

weak situations
Situations that are loosely structured and ambiguous and characterized by few cues from the environment

However, the role of personality is much stronger in "**weak situations.**" These are ambiguous situations that are loosely structured, so personality characteristics become a stronger explanation and cause of behavior. You would therefore expect personality characteristics to be more evident in loosely structured organizations with few rules and policies, as compared to bureaucratic settings (Tosi, 1992). This is why you can see prima donna singers or musicians act very individualistically in rehearsals, expecting to be treated special because of their unique skills. However, when it comes time to go on stage, a more controlled situation, usually they play the part and sing on key. Therefore, if you want to understand behavior in personality terms, it is best to observe people when structure is loose or has broken down. Also, if you want personality to operate more fully in a situation so that you might capitalize on personality differences, you may have to loosen controls and expectations, and otherwise permit more situational freedom. This may be helpful when creativity or adaptation to a novel problem is needed.

THE BASES OF PERSONALITY

Some have argued that personality is genetic, i.e. inherited from our parents, while others have argued that personality develops as a result of our upbringing. The **nature–nurture argument** about the bases of personality is an old one. Recent evidence suggests that both sides are right: a significant portion of personality is a result of heredity, but a larger part seems due to the life experiences we have, particularly in our early life. We know, for example, from studies of twins who have been raised in different families, often in very different national cultures, that about 30 percent of the variance in job satisfaction and 40 percent of the variance in work values can be explained by heredity (Arvey et al., 1989; Keller et al., 1992). However, this still leaves a large part of the personality that is likely to develop as a result of how we actually learn in our early experiences to adapt to the world around us.

nature–nurture argument A continuing debate about the role of heredity or the effects of socialization on personality and behavior

THE SOCIALIZATION PROCESS – LEARNING AND PERSONALITY We think that understanding how learning occurs is useful for knowing something about how personality emerges – and that is why we discuss theories of learning here. How do theories of learning help us to understand personality? It works this way. We all start with the genetic makeup that we inherit from our parents. This is the base for personality. Then, as we grow, we are exposed to the socialization process. **Socialization** is the process through which a person learns and acquires the values, attitudes, beliefs, and accepted behaviors of a culture, society, organization, or group. We learn that some behaviors are more rewarding to us while others lead to negative consequences; we learn group norms and values from our parents, as well as observing the behaviors of others. Over a period of time, these experiences shape the way we adapt to the world in which we live. The result is our personality, the unique set of values, attitudes, and behaviors in our adult lives that have been shaped around our genetic character.

socialization The process though which a person learns and acquires the values, attitudes and beliefs, and accepted behaviors of a culture, society, organization or group

APPROACHES TO LEARNING

Learning and socialization are basic to understanding how people acquire knowledge, attitudes, skills and their unique personalities. also, they are central to interpreting how people perceive events and make judgments about them. **Learning** takes place when a relatively permanent change in behavior, or potential for behavior, occurs that is traceable to a person's experience or to practice (Bourne and Ekstrand, 1982).

learning A relatively permanent change in behavior, or potential for behavior, that is traceable to a person's experience or to practice

Learning occurs within the person. We do not see it happen; we can only infer that learning has occurred when we observe a behavior that is different from past behavior given the same stimulus. Learning and behavior are not the same thing:

- Behavior does not always ensure that a person has learned or changed in a significant or permanent way.
- Learning does not ensure that behavior changes will always occur.

Suppose a student is doing poor quality work. He may already have the skill and knowledge to perform better but other factors, such as illness, interruptions, or

Global Focus on An Example of Different Socialization Experiences on Business Practices

One reason for differences in behavior across different nationalities – as you will discover more fully when you read chapter 12 – is that a nation's culture may dictate different societal norms. This can lead to conflict for managers in organizations operating internationally because fundamental differences in behavior offer a difficult situation. Managers must appreciate differences in personality traits and preferences that are unique to a specific national, but different cultures within the same firm. This "culture-clash" gives rise to a variation in personality and behavior patterns within the organization and forces management into a difficult position. One example of such differences has to do with bribery and payoffs. While not nonexistent in the USA, these practices are regarded by most US firms because of government regulation and societal changes, as inappropriate, both professionally and personally.

This creates problems for US firms with divisions in countries where bribery and payoffs are accepted practices. One example is the Maquiladora industry in Mexico. Maquiladoras are assembly, manufacturing, or processing facilities located along the border zone between Mexico and the USA; these exist chiefly due to the lower labor costs available in Mexico for US firms and less government regulation.

Managers from the USA in these plants face the conflict of both imposing norms and beliefs which they developed within the USA or allowing employee behavior which may not productive for the organization as a whole. The point is that the personal decisions and behavior patterns of the Maquiladora employees are directly related to their environment and determining that the "right" standard of behavior is the one determined by American standards seems unrealistic.

Source: Adapted from Butler and Teagarden (1993)

lack of motivation, might account for the poor performance; therefore, learning is not necessary to improve performance. Similarly, the student who learns new ways to improve performance may not apply what he or she has learned.

classical conditioning Model of learning in which a stimulus that causes a reflexive response is paired with another stimulus presented close in time; eventually the second stimulus triggers the reflexive response

One approach to understanding learning is the **classical conditioning** model based on the work of Pavlov (1927). In his most famous study, Pavlov conditioned a dog to salivate at the sound of a bell, just as it would if it were hungry and food were presented to it. Classical conditioning requires the presence of an existing and reflexive stimulus–response pattern such as withdrawing your hand from a hot object or blinking an eye in response to a puff of air. When such a reflexive pattern exists, it is possible to pair the original stimulus (for example, the puff of air) with a new, different stimulus by presenting the two close together in space or time. Eventually the new stimulus will elicit the same response as the original one. The new stimulus is called a conditioned stimulus. For example, suppose a bell is rung just as the air hits your eye. After repeated pairings, the bell alone will cause you to blink; see figure 2.2.

Classical conditioning does not explain how we acquire complex skills such as verbal behavior or skiing, but it does account for much of human learning.

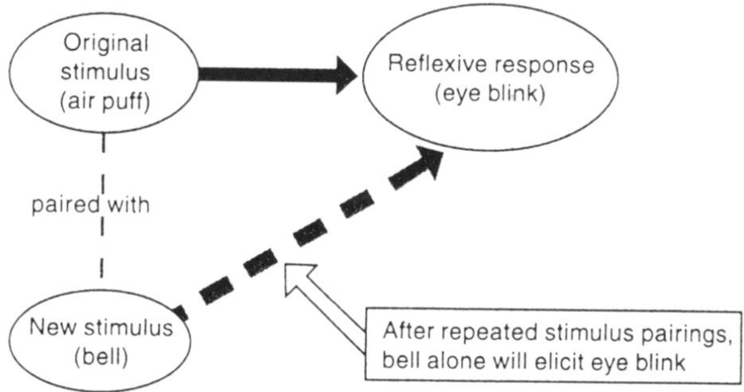

Fig 2.2 : Classical model of learning

Many emotional responses can be understood in terms of the classical conditioning model. The fear and anxiety that you once experienced during an auto accident might well recur when you hear screeching tires that remind you of those heard at the time of the accident.

Reinforcement theories of learning are among the most important concepts in the study of organizational behavior and central to many topics in this book such as culture and socialization, attitude formation and perception, career choices, motivation and training. In this chapter, we introduce reinforcement theory in general terms because it is very useful in understanding how personality develops. In chapter 5, you will come across it again in much more detail; see pages 139–46.

reinforcement theories Learning theories that describe situations where behavior is affected by its consequences

Reinforcement theories are used to describe situations where behavior is affected by its consequences (Skinner, 1938). This approach is shown in figure 2.3. It is also called **instrumental learning.** For example, praise by a coach, teacher or supervisor can be instrumental in sustaining good performance. This is different from classical conditioning because it is not necessary to have a reflexive stimulus–response pattern for learning to occur. The reinforcement approach accounts for a wide range of learning, from the simplest to the most complex behaviors. It explains many aspects of our behavior and attitudes, not only in the workplace but also in everyday life.

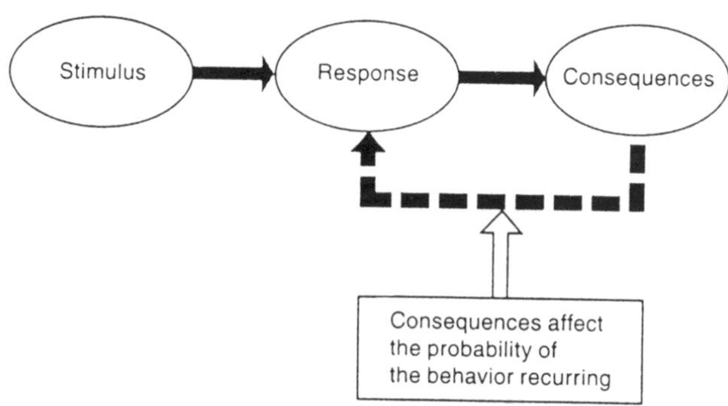

Fig 2.3 : Reinforcement or instrumental model of learning

Though behavior is viewed as having causes, or antecedents, that act as stimuli, reinforcement theory focuses more on the consequences of the response than on the stimuli that begin the behavioral sequence. Stimuli can trigger behavior, such as when we smell food and feel hungry, or when we react to the ring of a telephone. A key point in reinforcement theory, however, is that the particular response to the stimulus is shaped by the nature of the consequence of reacting to it.

Sometimes we control the consequences of our behavior, such as when we take a part-time job to earn money to buy a car. The car is our goal, and earning money is instrumental in affording it. Many consequences, however, are beyond our control. They occur as side-effects of our behavior, or they are controlled by others who react to what we do. For instance, taking the part-time job may require that we work evenings. This could cause a friend to become angry because we are not free to go out together.

We can be very aware of some consequences but not as aware of others. However, consequences that we are less aware of can still affect our behavior, and therefore they affect what we learn. Suppose your parents acted more pleasantly and treated you especially well whenever you do extra schoolwork. You might not be aware that they are rewarding a particular behavior, but it can affect your willingness to take on extra school work in the future.

Consequences always follow from behaviors. Some consequences have very little effect, but others can make a difference. They affect the probability of a behavior recurring. Consequences may be positive (desired) or they may be negative (undesired). Pay and recognition are examples of positive consequences, and physical abuse and firing are examples of negative ones. Basically, we try to repeat those behaviors that result in positive consequences and aim to avoid those that lead to negative ones.

The consequences of behavior can occur in different patterns that affect how quickly a behavior is learned and how resistant it is to change or extinction. These patterns of consequences are called **reinforcement schedules**. Reinforcement schedules are considered further in chapter 5 (page 143); for now, it is enough to say that the strength of a learned behavior, or how resistant it is to change is a function of the reinforcement schedule.

reinforcement schedules Consequences of a behavior occurring in different patterns, which affect how quickly the behavior is learned, and how resistant it is to change

SOCIAL LEARNING THEORY – VICARIOUS LEARNING People can also learn by observing other people and imitating or modeling themselves after what other people do (Bandura, 1977). This is called **vicarious learning** (Wood and Bandura, 1989); it involves more than just reinforcing behavior. It is part of what is called **social learning** theory. This learning involves thinking, including intentions, goal setting, reasoning, and decision making in addition to reinforcements. Learning can take place by reading books, watching television, or interacting with people. Social, or vicarious, learning occurs quite naturally at work. For example, one key to a manager's success is to have a mentor to emulate (Levinson et al., 1978).

social learning Learning that occurs through the observation of others or from modeling (acting) the ways of others

One stage of vicarious learning involves observing and thinking. Another stage occurs when the individual actively engages in new behaviors, or

modeling. Several conditions are involved in vicarious learning (Weiss, 1977; Baron, 1983):

modeling
A type of learning in which people pattern their behavior after others

1 You must have a reason to pay attention to the model or stimulus. Anything that attracts attention, such as expertise or status, will contribute to attention.
2 You need to retain sufficient information to pattern behavior after the model.
3 The person must have enough ability to engage in the model's behavior. Most of us cannot model ourselves after a great athlete or Nobel Prize winner in physics.
4 There must be a motivational or reinforcement element. The person must perceive the probability of rewards and eventually receive reinforcement for imitation. There must be some incentive and encouragement involved.

Personality in the Organizational Setting

Personality is a useful concept for interpreting and managing in many organizational situations. For example, personality measures have long been used as a successful way to select and place applicants for jobs (Tett et al., 1991). Throughout this book, reference is made to personality in explaining a variety of topics.

- Dominant personalities are seen as central to defining an organization's culture.
- Personality is treated as a key factor in understanding adjustment to work and career, coping with stress, and problem solving and decision-making behavior.
- Personality is also viewed as central to the dynamics of motivation, and interpersonal conflict and politics.

attraction-selection-attrition cycle
People are attracted to and select organizational situations they prefer to enter; upon entry, they make the situation what it is; as similar people become attracted, and as dissimilar people leave, the organization becomes more homogeneous

One theory (Schneider, 1987) that has shed some additional light on the relative contribution of personality and organizations on behavior describes the **attraction-selection-attrition cycle** in organizational settings. The cycle says that people are attracted to and select the situations they prefer to enter. Upon entry into an organization, they make the situation what it is. As similar people become attracted, and as dissimilar people leave, the organization becomes more homogeneous. The people who make up the organization define it by establishing norms and maintaining the culture. So, while the situation may affect behavior, it is the people that define the situation. Homogeneity of personalities may become a threat to the organization's survival. If one wants to change such a situation, it is necessary to change the mix of people and to select new people so as to add variability.

There are a few things to keep in mind as you read about these different ways to characterize personality.

1 There are different ways to view people and you will see that some of the approaches are similar in some ways with others, while some are very distinct.
2 Each one represents a motivational force that is likely related to some important organizational behavior, attitude, or perception. As such, some appear elsewhere in the book, especially the chapters on motivation: chapters 5 and 6.
3 Most of the characteristics we are describing represent just one way to describe behavior, and that each of us can be described in terms of any one of the theories, and some more accurately than others.
4 We have selected only some of the more important approaches to highlight in this chapter. As you read other parts of the book, we say again, you will find other ways to characterize personality but these are more strongly associated with a specific subject area in organizational behavior (such as Type A/B personality and stress or Achievement/Power Theory and motivation) that they are better discussed in that section.

Focus on An Extrovert: Bobby Hinds and the Portable Gym

Bobby Hinds is the head of Lifeline USA, a successful company in Madison, Wisconsin that produces a portable gym. It is a device that can be used as a treadmill and a weight machine, yet weighs less than two pounds; it produced more than $12 million in sales in 1998. What makes the Lifeline USA successful is Bobby Hinds' personality. He is "unencumbered by modesty or inhibition . . . outgoing, persistent self-promoter who has been able to convince others of his product's uniqueness." For instance, he brought a CBS camera crew to his plant that prepared a report that would appear on one of the networks major news programs. He has appeared on several late-night television talk shows to promote Lifeline USA and its product.

All of this comes naturally to him. He spent some time in a boy's reformatory as a youth, came out to earn a degree in art and criminology, taught school and was a prizefighter. When asked why he was successful in business, he attributes it to his own drive. "I've been hustling all my life, and this [business] gave me the chance to do it for something I believed in."

Source: Adapted from Wertheim (1998)

THE "BIG FIVE" PERSONALITY DIMENSIONS

A **trait** is some particular relative stable and enduring individual tendency to react emotionally or behaviorally in a specific way. For example, we might characterize a person as being agreeable, responsible, or considerate. Over the years, hundreds of studies have been done which have used specific traits to define personality but they were not very successful. Recently, however, these many trait studies have been analyzed and these traits have been grouped into higher level classifications that have resulted in the identification of the "Big Five" dimensions of personality (Barrick and Mount, 1991).

1 Extroversion
2 Emotional stability
3 Agreeableness
4 Conscientiousness
5 Openness to experience

These are general personality dimensions that reflect similar specific traits and characteristics that fall within each dimension repeatedly in research and theory.

Some of the more specific traits of persons high in **extroversion** are that they tend to be sociable, like to be with others, and are energetic (Barrick and Mount, 1996). Of course, **introverts** are the reverse. They tend to be less sociable, like to be alone and not interact much with others. Extroversion is related to job success for managers and salespeople and success in training.

The **emotional stability** characteristic, viewed from the negative side, is also called **neuroticism**. Among the traits of people low in emotional stability (or highly neurotic), are that they tend to be emotional, tense, insecure, have high anxiety levels, are depressed, easily upset, suspicious and low in self confidence (Barrick and Mount, 1996). There is some evidence that shows that greater emotional stability is related to supervisory ratings of performance (Barrick and Mount, 1991).

Agreeableness is a trait of people who are simply easier to get along with than others. They are likely to be more tolerant, trusting, generous, warm, kind, and good-natured. They are less likely to be aggressive, rude and thoughtless.

Among the traits of highly conscientious persons are being responsible, dependable, persistent, punctual, hard working, and being oriented toward work. **Conscientiousness** is related to success on the job and in training for managers, professionals, salespeople, police, and skilled/semi-skilled workers (Dunn et al., 1995; Barrick and Mount, 1996).

Persons more **open to experience** are imaginative, curious, cultured, broad minded, have broad interests and tend to be self-sufficient. Those who are more open to experiences appear to react very positively to different kinds of training (Barrick and Mount, 1991).

extroversion
Tendency to be sociable, liking to be with others, energetic and forceful

emotional stability
Tendency to be less neurotic, less emotional, less tense, less insecure, have low anxiety levels, are less easily upset, less suspicious and are high in self-confidence

neuroticism
Being highly emotional, tense, insecure, suffering from depression, and easily upset, suspicious and having low self-confidence

agreeableness
Tendency to be more tolerant, trusting, generous, warm, kind, good-natured, and less likely to be aggressive, rude and thoughtless

conscientiousness
Being responsible, dependable, persistent, punctual, hard working, and oriented toward work

openness to experience
Being imaginative, curious, cultured, broad minded, having broad interests and tending to be self-sufficient

POSITIVE AND NEGATIVE AFFECTIVITY – BEING IN A GOOD OR BAD MOOD

positive affectivity Having a strong, positive sense of personal well being, being active and involved and overall, pleasant in most situations

negative affectivity Tendency to be sad, to focus on failure and to view themselves in negative ways

Two general traits that have been related to how people are oriented toward their work are positive affectivity and negative affectivity (George, 1992). **Positive affectivity**, similar to extroversion, means that you have a strong, positive sense of your personal well being, that you think of yourself as active and involved in activities that you like and that you are, overall, a pleasant person in most situations. If you are high in positive affectivity, you are active, elated, enthusiastic, peppy and strong. If you are low in positive affectivity, you are drowsy, dull, sleepy and sluggish (Watson and Clark, 1984). The term that comes to mind for a person high in positive affectivity is "an overall happy, nice human being."

Negative affectivity, similar to neuroticism, means that you are not very happy, you feel under stress and strain, you tend to focus on failure and you tend to view yourself and others in negative ways, even when the conditions in which you are operating do not warrant these perceptions. The high negativity person is distressed, fearful, hostile, jittery, nervous and scornful. The low negativity person is at rest, calm, placid and relaxed. The term that comes to mind for a person high in negative affectivity is "sourpuss."

The research to date suggests that these two traits – positive affectivity and negative affectivity – are independent; they do not exist as separate ends of the same continuum. If they were on the same continuum, it would mean that if you are high on positive affectivity, you must be low on negative affectivity. Instead, being independent means that a person might be high on both positive affectivity and negative affectivity, low on both, high on one and low on the other (Watson and Clark, 1984; George, 1992), as shown in figure 2.4. There you can

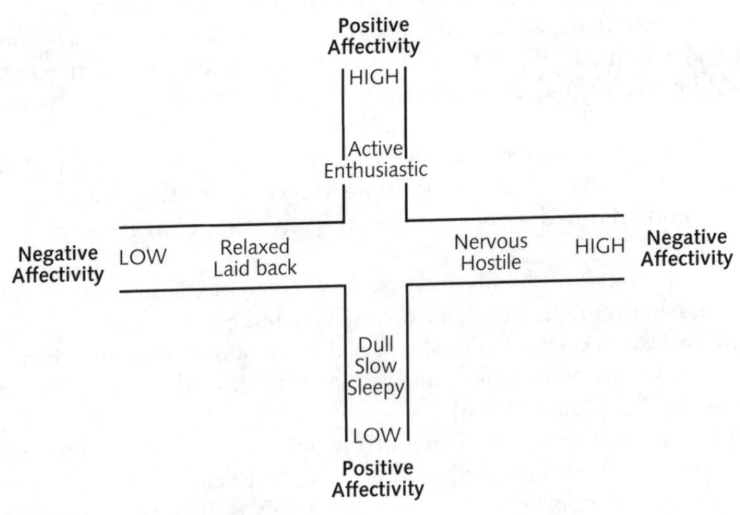

Fig 2.4: Positive and negative affectivity

EXERCISE

Assessing Positive Affectivity and Negativity

This list of words describe different feelings and emotions.

1	Interested	__	6	Guilty	__	11	Irritable	__	16	Determined	__
2	Distressed	__	7	Scared	__	12	Alert	__	17	Attentive	__
3	Excited	__	8	Hostile	__	13	Ashamed	__	18	Jittery	__
4	Upset	__	9	Enthusiastic	__	14	Inspired	__	19	Active	__
5	Strong	__	10	Proud	__	15	Nervous	__	20	Afraid	__

For each one, indicate to what extent you generally feel this way, that is, how you feel on average using this scale:

1 = VERY SLIGHTLY OR NOT AT ALL
2 = A LITTLE
3 = MODERATELY
4 = QUITE A BIT
5 = VERY MUCH

Now, copy the values you have marked for each word in the spaces below, and total the columns A and B.

Column A	
1	
3	
5	
9	
10	
12	
14	
16	
17	
19	
Total A	

Column B	
2	
4	
6	
7	
8	
11	
13	
15	
18	
20	
Total B	

Your score on Positive Affectivity is the Column A total and your score on Negative Affectivity is the Column B total. Which is higher, your positive affectivity score or your negative affectivity score?

- How accurate do you think the discussion of the text was about positive affectivity and negative affectivity?
- Ask some of your classmates what their scores are, and then read again the discussion of positive and negative affectivity. Do their scores reflect their behavior?

Source: Copyright © 1984 by the American Psychological Association. Reprinted with permission.

see what this trait independence means. It shows, for example that the person with high positive affectivity is more active and enthusiastic while the low positive affectivity person is more dull, slow and sleepy. On the other hand, the person high in negative affectivity is more likely to be nervous and hostile, while the low negative affectivity person is more relaxed and laid back.

Having a strong positive or a strong negative disposition can affect your work life. If you are a high on positive affectivity, you are less likely to have accidents at work than if you are high on negative affectivity (Iverson and Erwin, 1997). Or, if you are positive at work, you are more likely to be rewarded by your boss for good performance (George, 1995). Also, effective managers tend to be highly positive (Staw and Barsade, 1993). Highly positive people are seen as better leaders, having higher management potential, and are more satisfied with their work and their life.

ADJUSTING TO WORK AND ORGANIZATIONAL LIFE

Individuals adapt to organizations and organizations adapt to individuals. Anyone who stays in an organization has to resolve conflicts between work and outside interests, establish work relationships, and achieve a minimal level of competence (Feldman and Arnold, 1983). Socialization and personality play a role in the ways a person adjusts to work life, and in the level of satisfaction with the accommodation they eventually make. One approach is to define the characteristics of three patterns of accommodation to organizational life that are called organizational personality orientations (Presthus, 1978):

1 The organizationalist
2 The professional
3 The indifferent

These three orientations will help you to understand better the concept of organizational commitment that we discuss in detail in chapter 4 (page 102).

organizationalist orientation
A strong identification with and commitment to the place of work and the organization

The **organizationalist** is a person with a strong commitment to the place of work. A person with this orientation exhibits these five tendencies:

1 A strong identification with the organization; seeking organization rewards and advancement which are important measures of success and organizational status
2 High morale and job satisfaction
3 A low tolerance for ambiguity about work goals and assignments
4 Identification with superiors, showing deference toward them, conforming and complying out of a desire to advance; maintains the chain of command and compliance, and views respect for authority as the way to succeed
5 Emphasis on organizational goals of efficiency and effectiveness, avoiding controversy and showing concern for threats to organizational success

From their early socialization experiences, organizationalists develop an early respect for authority figures, realizing that they have the power to dispense rewards and/or sanctions. They are success oriented, and seek it in the organizational context. They learn how to avoid failure experiences that stem from being a troublemaker. Often, the organizationalist comes from a family in which rewards are controlled primarily by the father (Presthus, 1978).

Professionals are persons who are job centered – not organization centered – and see organization demands as a nuisance which they seek to avoid. However, that avoidance is impossible since the professional must have an organization in which to work. At work, professionals experience more role conflict and are more alienated (Greene, 1978). A professor who values teaching and research may not be very loyal to the university, but needs the university to teach and research, so this is a very conflicting role for the professional. Professionals exhibit these four tendencies:

professional orientation
A person who is more job centered and tends to view organization demands as pressure or a nuisance

1 An experience of occupational socialization that instills high standards of performance in the chosen field; highly ideological about work values
2 Sees organizational authority as nonrational when there is pressure to act in ways that are not professionally acceptable
3 Tends to feel that their skills are not fully utilized in organizations; self-esteem may be threatened when they do not have the opportunity to do those things for which they have been trained
4 Seeks recognition from other professionals outside the organization, and refuses to play the organizational status game except as it reflects their worth relative to others in the organization. Professionals are very concerned with personal achievement and doing well in their chosen field. Organizational rewards are not without value, however, since they may reflect the professional's importance relative to others in the system. The recognition may be extremely fulfilling, especially when he or she is accorded higher status and pay than others.

In early socialization, the professionals learn that successful performance, not compliance with authority, is more reinforcing. Many professionally oriented people come from the middle class and have become successful through a higher level of education or by other efforts to acquire competence (Presthus, 1978).

Indifferents are people who work for pay. For them, work is not a critical part of their life structure. They may do their work well, but they are not highly committed to their job or the organization.

indifferent orientation
Reflects the belief that work is not a critical part of life

These are some of the characteristics of indifferents:

1 More oriented toward leisure, not the work ethic; separates work from more meaningful aspects of life, and seeks higher-order need satisfaction outside the work organization
2 Tends to be alienated from work and not committed to the organization; more alienated than either organizationalists or professionals (Greene, 1978)

3 Rejects status symbols in organizations
4 Withdraws psychologically from work and organizations when possible

Indifferents often come from the lower middle class (Presthus, 1978). With a limited education, indifferents often work in routine jobs with few advancement opportunities. Research indicates that commitment is lower when jobs have narrow scope and more stress (Fukami and Larson, 1984). Do not assume, however, that only lower-level personnel are indifferents. Some may be organizationalists and others might have a distinctively professional orientation to their work. Also, it could come to be that higher level employees, who once had an organizational orientation and were highly loyal, may no longer follow orders without question. For example, early in a working career, a manager may be extremely committed to the organization. He or she may seek its rewards and want to advance. However, in later career life, after having been passed over several times for promotion, the person seeks reinforcement elsewhere. Thus, it is possible that through their promotion practices, organizations may turn highly committed organizationalists into indifferents.

The Authoritarian Personality

authoritarian personality
A personality type in which the person believes in obedience and respect for authority and that the strong should lead the weak; an excessive concern for power based on prejudices about people

Machiavellianism
A personality type which attempts to take advantage of others, seeks to form alliances with people in power to help serve their own goals, and might lie, deceive, or compromise morality, believing that ends justify the means

Perhaps you have worked for someone who was punitive and rigid and who did not respect you or was trying to demean or control you. You sensed that he or she wanted you to be submissive and seemed intolerant of weakness. These are behaviors characteristic of an **authoritarian personality** (Adorno et al., 1950). Those who have an authoritarian personality believe in obedience and respect for authority, and that the strong should lead the weak. They have an excessive concern for power based on their prejudices about people. They feel that some people are superior and should lead others.

Because of their beliefs in hierarchical order, authoritarians make good followers if they respect and accept a superior. Normally, however, it is not easy to relate to them. True authoritarians will take advantage of others, and the best way to deal with them is to assert your own authority if possible (Maslow, 1965). Extreme authoritarians are not overly common, but some people have such tendencies. This personality type is unlikely to fare well in an organization trying to use more democratic or participative techniques to involve employees in decision making.

The Machiavellians

Machiavellianism is another personality dimension that has interpersonal and leadership implications for the workplace (Christie and Geis, 1970). People who are high Machiavellians (high Machs) have high self-esteem and self-confidence and behave in their own self-interest. They are seen as cool and calculating, attempt to take advantage of others, and seek to form alliances with people in power to serve their own goals. High Machs might lie, deceive, or compromise morality, believing that ends justify means. Truly high-Mach people experience

A Question of Ethics: The Machiavellian Professor

Everyone in the History department at State University was excited to learn that Horace Toth, the Department Chair, had completed negotiations to hire Donald Touchman away from Revere University, a prestigious private university in the northwest. Touchman was a great teacher and an excellent researcher. Everyone thought, certainly, that having Touchman at State University would increase the research productivity of the department, improve its reputation for teaching in the College of Liberal Arts (CLA), and give a boost to its national reputation. The bonus, the History faculty thought, was that during the interview phase of the hiring, they found that he was very clever, witty, charming, bright, and funny. Almost without exception, the History faculty thought that he would be a welcome addition to the very amicable culture of the department.

After he arrived, they were not disappointed. In addition to his writing and teaching, he had a way of making them feel very good about themselves and State University. For example, he talked of how State University was a better place to work than Revere:

> You can't believe how unprofessional they are at Revere, and how arrogant, too. You know Professor Harvey who is there? Well when he came, he negotiated over the color of his file cabinets. How petty can you get? They are all like that. Here, though, the situation is much more congenial.

He also spent a great deal of time with individual faculty members, talking with them about their work and how he saw the future of the History department. Everyone came away from these conversations with very positive feelings about Touchman. For example, he told Jane Fieber, a young Latin-American specialist, "Jane, I just read your last paper in the journal and it was absolutely first rate. It certainly explained the economic problems in Peru much better than I've ever seen. We need more like you." Then he went on, without any motivation from her. "What I'm worried about for the Department is that John's work is not what it used to be. It certainly isn't at the same quality level as yours. Has he turned off? Is he really making any contribution to us at all?" When Touchman left Jane's office, she had a sense of elation and pride. Her work was being highly praised by a good scholar and, more importantly, he seemed to rate it better than the work of John Appley, one of the senior History professors who had a national reputation for his work on Brazil.

By the end of the year, the Department of History contained a group of happy professors, happy because Touchman was apparently such a great addition. However, 18 months later, some strange things began to happen. Adrienne Diest, the Dean of the College of Liberal Arts, called Horace to her office and told him that she wanted the Department of History to do a self-study to find out where the problem areas were, but especially to know which faculty members were not carrying their own load. Horace was puzzled. Nothing like this had happened before in CLA and, besides, he wasn't aware of any difficulties. "Why?" Horace wanted to know.

The Dean responded, "I'm beginning to get some uneasy vibrations from key people in your group that there are problems that need attention. And I also think that it is just a good idea."

When Horace brought the idea up at a departmental meeting, he was surprised to find that the faculty also thought the Dean had a good idea. Many of them, who last year were quite happy with the Department and its position in the CLA, indicated that indeed there were some things that needed examining now. Horace began to have some self-doubt, wondering "Is this a nice way of saying, 'Horace, you're not doing a good job as Chair. Maybe you should think about resigning.'"

Horace pressed on, beginning the self-study by interviewing each faculty member. What dawned on him as these interviews progressed was that each one of them was content with his or her own work, but – and this was the revelation – not very happy about the work of the others. Even more interesting was that the negative evaluations that each had of the others were exactly the sort that Touchman had outlined to him when they had their conversation.

This raised a red flag in the Horace's mind, so he decided to probe more deeply to test an intuition that he was starting to develop by having another talk with two professors, both close friends and whom he trusted implicitly. His intuition was correct: the two separate conversations were almost identical. The first thing that each one told him was that they agreed exactly with Touchman about the strengths and weaknesses of various faculty members. But, and here was the clinching point, John, the Brazil specialist recounted how weak Harold's work on Peru was and Harold told him how deficient John's work on Brazil had become. These were Touchman's evaluations, for sure, but Horace did not agree with them. He thought both John and Harold were still doing good work.

"Could it be," he asked himself, "that the source of all of this negativity is Touchman?" So he met again with Harold and probed more, "How well do you get along with Touchman? Do you agree with his views?" Harold's answer was enlightening. "Yes," he said, "Donald and I have talked at length about the Department. He thinks my work on Peru is very good and holds great promise. He isn't so positive about the others, though, and thinks we need to do something to ratchet up the quality in the department." Horace then arranged to have lunch with John. "How well do you get along with Don Touchman? Do you and he share similar views about the Department?" Horace predicted John's answer. "I've talked a lot with Don," John said, "since he arrived at Revere. He likes my work on Brazil, but has serious doubts about some other senior faculty. For example, he thinks that Harold is on the downslope of his career. His work on Peru is getting sloppy. I haven't looked at it for some time, but I trust Don's judgment on this." Horace talked with other professors and, quickly, his intuition was confirmed. Don Touchman was the person who had created the sense of animosity and uneasiness in the History department.

When he was sure that he was right, Horace went to the Dean to find out if Touchman was behind the self-study. At first, she was reluctant to explain the reasons, but finally admitted that, indeed, Touchman was the instigator of the study. Horace explained to her what he had concluded from the investigation to date. The Dean would, she told the Chair, talk to Touchman about it and form her own opinion.

A week later, the Chair received a phone call from the Dean. She said, "I've spoken with Touchman. He thinks that your accusations are unfair and they are based on the fact that there is a lot of professional jealousy in your group. The others are envious of him because he is such a great teacher and a good researcher. You will have to manage the situation and get things straightened out down there in your group."

"That isn't what is going on." the Chair said. "I think Touchman is very political and I am worried about what his style will do the the Department and to the College."

"Don't be so damned envious," replied the Dean. "He's a good scholar and I'm glad to have him. Don't force me to choose between him and you because you won't like my decision."

"My God," Horace thought to himself, "Touchman's done it with her too. If that's the case, it doesn't make any sense to risk my job over this. I'll just have to be careful. I wonder when Touchman will start on the Dean."

It didn't take long. Within six months there were rumors around the College and the University that the Dean might be leaving, that she was being pushed out by the central administration because there was a lot of grumbling and uneasiness among the faculty that was due to the fact that she was spending much more time with her husband and family, who were located in another university about 200 miles for State University. The Chair knew that Touchman was going after bigger fish now.

no guilt; they somehow detach themselves from the consequences of their actions. They also use false or exaggerated praise to manipulate others. They take care not to be swayed by considerations of loyalty, friendship, and trust. A high Mach might give lip service to such things, but when the chips are down, he or she will not let them stand in the way of personal gain. This gives them a big advantage over those who value friendship and act on trust.

High Machs are able to select situations where their tactics will work: face-to-face, emotional, unstructured, and ambiguous conditions. Not distracted by emotions, they are able to calmly exert control in power vacuums or novel situations. Machiavellianism is not rare in today's society. Studies show that there are many people with moderate to high Mach orientations.

Locus of Control: Who's in Charge?

People can be characterized according to their **locus of control**, i.e. whether they believe what happens to them is externally controlled or whether it is controlled internally by their own efforts (Rotter, 1966). A person who believes that important outcomes are controlled by others has an **external locus of control.** **Internal locus of control**, however, reflects self-control over one's outcomes. A person with an internal locus of control has needs for independence and a desire to participate in decisions that affect them. Internal control is also correlated with better adjustment to work in terms of satisfaction, coping with stress, job involvement, and promotability (Anderson, 1977). People with an internal locus of control also show fewer absences and more involvement at work (Blau, 1987).

Rules, policies, and other management controls can interact with the locus of control to affect motivation. A variety of responses are possible when one's orientation toward control is inconsistent with the environment. Internal locus of control employees might experience frustration and respond with hostility or leave the organization. Those with an external locus of control might react negatively to tasks or jobs that call for independent action. Thus, they might resist efforts such as job enrichment and quality of work life that add autonomy and decision-making responsibility to jobs.

Myers–Briggs Personality Dimensions and Work Style Preferences

The Myers–Briggs approach to personality classifies people according to the kinds of jobs and interactions they prefer, and the ways in which they approach problems (Jung, 1939; Myers and Briggs, 1962). Four **Myers–Briggs dimensions** are used to describe the personality underlying these preferences:

1 Sensing–intuition dimension
2 Thinking–feeling dimension
3 Introversion–extroversion dimension
4 Perceptive–judgment dimension

locus of control
The degree to which individuals feel that they are controlled by themselves or mainly by external forces

external locus of control
A belief by persons that they have little influence over the environment and that what happens to them is a matter of luck, fate or due to the actions of others

internal locus of control
A belief by persons that they can influence their environment, that what they do and how they do it determines what they attain

Myers–Briggs dimensions
A number of personality types, based on Jungian personality theory, which are derived from preferences people have for approaching problems and work

Each dimension forms a continuum that people fall along. **Sensing-oriented people** like structured situations, an established routine, realism, and precise and uncomplicated details. They enjoy using skills already learned. Intuitive people prefer new problems, they dislike repetition, and are impatient with routine. They enjoy learning new skills; they follow their inspirations, and jump to conclusions.

Thinking individuals are unemotional, and often, unknowingly, they hurt people's feelings. They like to analyze and put things in a logical order. They seem impersonal and hard-hearted. Feeling types are more aware of other people, and enjoy pleasing them. They like harmony and are influenced by other people's needs; they relate well to most people.

Introverts prefer quiet concentration and think a lot before acting. They work well alone and can stay with one project for a long time. Much thought precedes action, sometimes without action. Introverts dislike interruptions, they forget names, and can have problems communicating. **Extroverts** show impatience with long, slow jobs and like to work fast, uncomplicated by procedures. They prefer variety and action to contemplation. They are good with people and like them around; usually they communicate quite well.

Perceptive people adapt to change and welcome new ideas. They can leave things unsolved and delay decisions without grave concern. They may start too many new projects, postpone unpleasant ones, and leave things unfinished. Judgment types prefer to plan work and follow the plan. They settle things on just the essentials and are satisfied with conclusions. They decide too quickly and dislike switching off a project in progress.

These four Myers–Briggs concepts can be used in a variety of ways, such as making employees appreciate the different styles of their coworkers or in selecting people for different types of assignments. They can also be used to improve decision making. People can be taught when it is best to exert their sensing, intuition, thinking, or feeling modes. They can also learn when it is best to pair with each other to improve decision making. This is referred to as the **mutual usefulness of opposites** and it works as follows:

1 The sensing type needs an intuitive to generate possibilities, to supply ingenuity, to deal with complexity, and to furnish new ideas. Intuitives add a long-range perspective and spark things that seem impossible.
2 The intuitive needs a sensing type to bring up facts to inspect, to attend to detail, to inject patience, and to notice what needs attention.
3 The thinker needs a feeling type to persuade and conciliate feelings, to arouse enthusiasm and to sell or advertise, and to teach and forecast.
4 The feeling type needs a thinker to analyze and organize, to predict flaws in advance, to introduce fact and logic, to hold to a policy, and to stand firm against opposition.

Frustrating the Mature Personality

Some who write about organizations believe that there is often a fundamental incongruence between the mature personality and the demands that many organizations place on employees. Argyris (1957, 1964) says that as people mature, they go from being passive to active; they develop from a state of dependence to independence, and go from a simple behavioral repertoire to a complex one. Maturity also moves people toward deeper and varied interests, from a short to a longer time perspective, from subordination to equal or superordinate roles, and to higher states of self-awareness and self-control.

Many organizational and managerial practices are inconsistent with the mature personality. Jobs are frequently highly specialized, consisting only of a few simple tasks. Managers, not workers, make most of the decisions and do most of the things that involve judgment and maturity. This makes employees feel dependent, externally controlled, and pressured to be passive rather than active at work. In short, they feel frustrated because they cannot act as mature human beings at work. A sense of failure develops because they cannot pursue meaningful goals. They experience inner conflict, and this will be strongest among those with the most mature personalities. The conflict is also more severe at lower organizational levels, where more directive controls are likely.

If you find yourself in one of these frustrating organizational situations, one way to escape these conditions is by quitting or by being promoted; however, these are not always possible options. If you cannot escape, it is more likely that you might find yourself responding to your work situation by daydreaming, resorting to aggression, or regression, or becoming apathetic and disinterested in work. Employees might also form cliques or unions to protect themselves, and develop norms to withhold productivity, hide errors, and demand increased pay and benefits. At home, frustrated employees might teach their children to become indifferent toward work or their employers.

Frustrating conditions at work often worsen; they rarely improve. As employees react defensively, managers might become more directive, tighten controls even further, or try programs that fail because they are not based on the needs of a mature personality. Thus the situation feeds on itself.

Summary

Managers need to learn all they can about human behavior because people are critical to an organization's success. The knowledge and skills a manager uses in dealing with people should be based on sound behavioral science models and principles. A complete model would include what is known about the person, the environment of behavior, the behavior itself and its effects. Key principles are that much behavior is learned, and the behavior is both stable and changeable.

Learning is a lifelong process. It takes place in a number of ways, such as through classical conditioning, reinforcement, and modeling. Learning theories explain how people acquire knowledge, attitudes, and skills. They are also central to understanding socialization and personality development. Schedules of reinforcement are also important – the timing and frequency of reinforcements makes a difference in how quickly something is learned and how resistant it is to extinction.

Personality is a way to characterize people. Many theories and concepts of personality exist. It is a useful way to understand and predict success at work and accommodations to organizational life. Personality is central to understanding many aspects of work ranging from culture to motivation. For example, the authoritarian, bureaucratic, and Machiavellian personality types are of interest in interpreting interpersonal and hierarchical relationships. Internal or external locus of control may be related to a person's leadership ability and promotability. Clearly, personality can also affect how people approach and solve problems.

Guide for Managers: Understanding Why People Behave as They do

Trying to make judgments about people is one of the most frustrating aspects of managerial work. Too often, as amateur psychologists, we make mistakes about others as we try to judge whether they will work out well. Many times, this is because of attribution errors of the type that we discuss in chapter 3. Having good models about personality to work from is a good place to start, and that is what we have provided you with in this chapter. Here are some things that you can do with these models to help you to make better judgments about the personality of others.

DON'T TRUST EXPLANATIONS

People cannot always fully explain their own behavior (Maslow, 1970). The employee who refuses an assignment might say, "I don't feel very well today," but this does not explain the cause of the resistance. Due to the difficulties in interpreting what people say, we need to seek other information to help us to understand the behavior.

LOOK FOR CAUSES

When interpreting employee behavior, look for causes in both the employee's characteristics and in the environment or situation that might have triggered the behavior. How a person behaves is determined by the person's characteristics interacting with the elements in his or her environment. You must understand this interaction between the person and the environment, and avoid overemphasizing one in favor of the other when interpreting human behavior. You might decide that an unproductive worker is lazy or inattentive (personal attributes) when actually the worker was behaving in response to pressure from peers or faulty equipment (environmental forces).

LOOK FOR SEVERAL CAUSES

Behavior may result from one or more causes. Suppose an employee is very upset over a request to perform an assignment. If you believe that your request is the only cause of the employee's reaction, you might conclude that this is just another case of uncooperativeness. Suppose, however, that you think about other possible causes that might explain the employee's refusal. You might discover that the employee is not only worried about falling behind in his work, but also feels unfairly treated because co-workers are not carrying their share of the load.

ACCOUNT FOR INDIVIDUAL DIFFERENCES

Try to account for individual differences and do not overgeneralize about them when you deal with people. People are alike in many ways, and similarities allow us to generalize about people. Some generalizations are relatively safe (for example, people dislike being embarrassed). Others are more questionable or even dangerous (for example, punishment will eliminate behaviors that cause work accidents). On the other hand, knowing that people are different can complicate things because we might try to treat every person as unique. When dealing with others, it is probably best to err on the side of appreciating individual differences. This, at least, can help to prevent poor generalizations.

USE PAST BEHAVIOR AS A PREDICTOR OF FUTURE BEHAVIOR

Keep in mind that past behavior is a pretty good predictor of future behavior. In many ways people are stable and predictable. There is some truth to the statement that past behavior is the best predictor of a person's future behavior. It is fairly safe for a manager to assume that what a worker has done in the past is quite likely to be repeated unless something significant changes. Stability of behavior, however, does not mean that people do not change. Given the right circumstances, even personality and values may be changed.

RECOGNIZE PERSONALITY DIFFERENCES

Consider important personality differences when selecting and assigning people to jobs. Try to make sure that personality is related to what the job requires for success. For example, do not assume all people are equally dedicated to work or to your organization; know the difference between organizationalists, professionals and indifferents. Try to minimize authoritarian and Machiavellian influences: they create an overemphasis on hierarchy and political behaviors which all too often interfere with task accomplishment. Expect some of your employees to be much more internally motivated, self-controlling and independent. They will expect more freedom and responsibility. At the same time, however, avoid actions that fail to recognize that most employees will exhibit frustration if they are treated as immature rather than as people with adult personalities and needs.

Key Concepts

agreeableness 41
attraction-selection-attrition cycle 39
authoritarian personality 46
classical conditioning 36
conscientiousness 41
emotional stability 41
external locus of control 49
extroversion 41
indifferent orientation 45
internal locus of control 49
learning 35
locus of control 49
Machiavellianism 46
modeling 39
Myers–Briggs dimensions 49
nature–nurture argument 35
negative affectivity 42
neuroticism 41
openness to experience 41
organizationalist orientation 44
personality 33
positive affectivity 42
professional orientation 45
reinforcement schedules 38
reinforcement theories 37
social learning 38
socialization 35
strong situations 34
weak situations 34

STUDY QUESTIONS

1 Think of a recent job you have held.
Explain how the environment made a difference in how well you performed and how satisfied you were with the job.
2 Recall a fellow employee who did things on the job that you either liked or disliked.
What do you think caused his or her behavior? Explain.
3 How does learning take place in classical conditioning?
What use is this theory to a manager?
4 What is the central proposition of reinforcement theory, or instrumental theory, of learning?
Why is this theory so useful to management?
5 Define vicarious learning and the social learning theory elements.
Explain the usefulness of these to managing behavior at work.
6 How do personality and situation interact to affect both behavior and the situation itself?
7 Have you ever met or worked with an authoritarian personality?
How did the experience affect you?
8 Refer to the discussion of the Myers–Briggs types.
How would you classify yourself?
See if another person who knows you agrees with how you perceive your style.
9 Have you ever worked in an organization where managers behaved in the way Argyris's theory would suggest?
What impact did it have on you?

Case

Laurel Bedding Company

The Laurel Bedding Company is in the business of producing a well-known brand of mattresses. Because mattresses are bulky and are costly to ship, the manufacturing is franchised out to various local bedding companies around the nation who produce for local department stores. The Laurel Bedding Company employed some thirty-two assemblers carrying out the various specific operations required in the making of a mattress. The springs inside the mattress were purchased from another company. The mattress core of springs or foam had to be covered with cloth. Different assemblers performed different parts of this operation as the mattress was pushed along the assembly line on rollers. Each assembler had a specific task to perform. For each task there was a performance standard established and a basic incentive was paid for reaching or surpassing the performance standard established by means of time study.

In the spring of 1999, Professor Judy Taylor asked the Laurel Bedding Company if she could conduct a study of the performance of the assemblers. She wanted to administer a number of psychological instruments to the workers and see if variations in their scores were predictive of the actual performance of the workers. One of her instruments measures locus of control – the degree to which individuals feel that their life is controlled by themselves or by events outside of themselves. The former are considered to be "internals" and the latter "externals," depending on the location of the perceived life control. Professor Taylor assumed that most of the workers would probably be "externals," given the fact they were production workers. Much to her surprise, almost all of the assemblers scored quite high as "internals." She wondered why this was so.

- What is your judgment of her findings?

References

Adorno, T., Frenkel-Brunswick, E., Levinson, D. and Sanford, R. N. 1950: *The Authoritarian Personality.* New York: Harper.

Allport, G. W. 1961: *Pattern and Growth in Personality*. New York: Holt, Rinehart and Winson.

Anderson, C. R. 1977: Locus of control, coping behaviors and performance in a stress setting: a longitudinal study. *Journal of Applied Psychology*, 62, 446–51.

Argyris, C. 1957: *Personality and Organization: The Conflict between the System and the Individual.* New York: Harper & Row.

Argyris, C. 1964: *Integrating the Individual and the Organization.* New York: John Wiley.

Arvey, R. D., Bouchard, T. J., Jr, Segal, N. L. and Abraham, L. M. 1989: Job satisfaction: environmental and genetic components. *Journal of Applied Psychology*, 74(2), April, 187–93.

Bandura, A. 1977: *Social Learning Theory*. Englewood Cliffs, NJ: Prentice-Hall.

Baron, R. A. 1983: *Behavior in Organization: Understanding and Managing the Human Side of Work.* Boston: Allyn & Bacon.

Barrick, M. R. and Mount, M. K. 1991: The big five personality dimensions and job performance: A meta-analysis. *Personnel Psychology*, 44, 1–26.

Barrick, M. R. and Mount, M. K. 1996: Effects of impression management and self-deception on the predictive validity of personality constructs. *Journal of Applied Psychology*, 81(3) June, 261–73.

Blau, G. T. 1987: Locus of control as a potential moderator of the turnover process. *Journal of Occupational Psychology* (Fall), 21–9.

Bourne, L. E. and Ekstrand, B. R. 1982: *Psychology: Its Principles and Meanings*. New York: Holt, Rinehart and Winston.

Butler, M. C. and Teagarden, M. B. 1993: Mexico's Maquiladora industry. *Human Resource Management*, Winter, 479–504.

Cattell, R. B. 1950: *Personality: A Systematic, Theoretical and Factual Study.* New York: McGraw-Hill.

Christie, R. and Geis, F. (eds) 1970: *Studies in Machiavellianism*. New York: Academic Press.

Dunn, W. S., Mount, M. K. Barrick, M. R. and Ones, D. S. 1995: Relative importance of personality and general mental ability in managers' judgements of applicant qualifications. *Journal of Applied Psychology*, 80(4), August, 500–10.

Epstein, S. and O'Brien, E. J. 1985: The person-situation debate in historical and current perspective. *Psychological Bulletin*, 98(3), 513–37.

Farber, D. 1995: How will IBM handle Lotus marriage. *PC Week*, 12(41), October 16, 130.

Feldman, D. C. and Arnold, H. J. 1983: *Managing Individual and Group Behavior in Organizations.* New York: McGraw-Hill.

Freud, S. 1933: *New Introductory Lectures on Psychoanalysis*. New York: Norton.

Fukami, C. V. and Larson, E. W. 1984: Commitment to company and union: parallel models. *Journal of Applied Psychology*, 69, 367–71.

Funder, D. C. 1991: Global traits: a neo-Allportean approach to personality. *Psychological Science*, 2(1), 31–9.

George, J. M. 1992: The role of personality in organizational life: issues and evidence. *Journal of Management*, 18(2), 185–213.

George, J. M. 1995: Leader positive mood and group performance: the case of customer service. *Journal of Applied Psychology*, 25(9), May 1, 778–95.

Greene, C. N. 1978: Identification modes of professionals: relationship with formalization, role strain and alienation. *Academy of Management Journal*, 21, 486–92.

Hays, L. 1995: Manzi quits at IBM and his many critics are not at all surprised. *Wall Street Journal*, October 12, A1, A6.

Iverson, R. and Erwin, P. 1997: Predicting occupational injury: the role of affectivity. *Journal of Occupational and Organizational Psychology*, 70(2), 113–29.

Jung, C. G. 1939: *The Integration of the Personality.* New York: Farrow and Rinehart.

Keller, L. M., Bouchard, T. J., Arvey, R. D., Jr, Segal, N. L. and Dawes, R. V. 1992: Work values: genetic and environmental influences. *Journal of Applied Psychology*, Feb 77(1), 79–89.

Levinson, D., Barrow, C. H., Klein, E. B., Levinson, M. H. and McGee, B. 1978: *Seasons of a Man's Life.* New York: Ballantine Books.

Maslow, A. H. 1965: *Eupsychian Management.* Homewood, IL: Richard D. Irwin.

Maslow, A. H. 1970: *Motivation and Personality.* New York: Harper & Row.

Mischel, W. 1977: The interaction of personality and situation. In D. Magnusson and N. S. Endler (eds) *Personality at the Crossroads: Current Issues in Interactional Psychology*, Hillsdale, NJ: Erlbaum.

Murray, H. A. 1962: *Explorations in Personality*. New York: Science Editions.

Myers, I. B. and Briggs, K. C. 1962: *Myers-Briggs Type Indicator*. Princeton, NJ: Educational Testing Service.

Pavlov, I. V. 1927: *Conditioned Reflexes*. New York: Oxford University Press.

Presthus, R. 1978: *The Organizational Society*. New York: St. Martin's Press.

Rogers, C. R. 1942: *Counseling and Psychotherapy*. Boston: Houghton Mifflin.

Rotter, J. B. 1966: Generalized expectancies for internal versus external control of reinforcement. *Psychological Monographs: General & Applied*, 80(1), 1–28.

Schneider, B. 1987: People make the place. *Personnel Psychology*, 40, 437–53.

Skinner, B. F. 1938: *The Behavior of Organisms*. New York: Appleton-Century-Crofts.

Staw, B. M. and Barsade, S. G. 1993: Affect and managerial performance: a test of the sadder-but-wiser vs. the happier-and-smarter hypothesis. *Administrative Science Quarterly*, June, 38(2), 304–28.

Tett, R. P., Jackson, D. N. and Rothstein, M. 1991: Personality measures as predictors of job performance: a meta-analytic review. *Personnel Psychology*, 44, 703–42.

Tosi, H. 1992: *The Environment/Organization/Person Contingency Model: A Meso Approach to the Study of Organizations*. Greenwich, CT: JAI Press, Inc.

Watson, D. and Clark, L. A. 1984: Negative affectivity: The disposition to experience aversive emotional states. *Psychological Bulletin*, 96(3), 465–90.

Weiss, H. M. 1977: Subordinate imitation of supervisory behavior: The role of modeling in organizational socialization. *Organizational Behavior and Human Performance*, 19, 89–105.

Weiss, H. M. and Adler, S. 1984: Personality and organizational behavior. In B. M. Staw and L. L. Cummings (eds) *Research in Organizational Behavior*, 6th edn. Greenwich, CT: JAI Press, 1–50.

Wertheim, L. J. 1998: A marketer who's quick on his feet: Boxer Bobby Hinds started with jump ropes and built a $12 million enterprise. *Sports Illustrated*, October 5, R1.

Wood, R. and Bandura, A. 1989: Social cognitive theory of organizational management. *Academy of Management Review*, 14, 361–84.

chapter 3

Attitudes, Perception and Judgment

THE NATURE OF ATTITUDES

WHY ATTITUDES ARE IMPORTANT

COGNITIVE DISSONANCE

PERCEPTION

JUDGMENT TENDENCIES

Preparing for Class

As you prepare for this chapter, most of you are just beginning to adjust to the course that this text supports. Think about the reaction of your classmates to aspects of the class such as the professor, the content, the classroom or this text. Most students in your class have probably already expressed attitudes about one or more of these aspects of the class. You may have heard these attitudes expressed in class or out of class; you may have inferred them, from student behaviors.

What are your fellow students' attitudes about these aspects of this course?

As you consider those attitudes, try to identify individual beliefs and values that may have contributed to those attitudes.

Do you notice different types of student behaviors from individuals with different attitudes?

Sometimes a "hard-nosed" attitude can backfire, even for the CEO of one of the largest airlines in the USA (Brannigan and White, 1997). Ronald Allen was the CEO of Delta Airlines who took it through a serious financial crisis in the early 1990s. He contributed to these problems by spending over $400 million and assuming a load of debt to acquire Pan American Airlines because he wanted to solidify Delta's overseas market. However, with increased fuel prices and competition, Delta began to suffer severe losses. Allen attacked the problem by cutting costs, curtailing service and reducing the size of the Delta work force. This had pretty severe effects on morale, especially at Delta, because prior to his accession to the presidency, Delta was known to provide very high quality service and was such a worker friendly culture that it had never been unionized. However, he continued his efforts to reduce costs, so much so that morale was at a low point and customer complaints were growing at an alarming rate. In Spring 1995, he was interviewed about the problems and, in the interview, when asked about the dissatisfaction of the work force in Delta, he answered, "So be it!" (Brannigan and White, 1997).

Delta employees, many with long seniority and remembering the time when Delta was both a better airline and a more friendly place to work, were angered. They protested by wearing "So be it" buttons to work. Often managers take strong positions like this, especially when they are in the middle of an economic turnaround in a company.

Soon, Allen's public position was just too much for the board of directors. The board had been concerned about Delta's drop in service quality, the dissatisfaction of employees that had motivated increased union efforts, and the fact that many of their best top executives were leaving. In spite of the fact that Allen had successfully managed to put Delta's financial house in order, the board forced him out. "So be it."

The Nature of Attitudes

This is a good example of how attitudes can have an effect on a person at work. It makes sense to study and know about attitudes because strong attitudes will very likely affect a person's behavior (Perlman and Cozby, 1983). In the world of work, we are concerned with attitudes toward supervision, pay, benefits, promotion, or anything that might trigger positive or negative reactions. Employee satisfaction and attitudes represent one of the key areas for measuring organizational effectiveness.

Sources of Beliefs, Values and Attitudes

The human mind has the capacity to link common events and to generalize across them. These associations may also result from very remote experiences. For example, having long ago had a bad experience with a sales clerk could affect your attitude toward a whole company or toward the sales profession in general. Through socialization, we are exposed to countless personal experiences that have lasting effects. Positive or negative experiences with an object contribute strongly to what you believe and feel about it. We learn firsthand that ice cream tastes good, or that it is risky to be late for work. Parents, relatives, teachers, friends, and many others are critical in shaping your attitudes. They provide reinforcements, they act as models that you emulate, and they serve as sources of information. The mass media can also shape your beliefs. The effects of this exposure can be quite subtle. Simple, repeated exposure can cause us to like something; it does not even require the development of a belief or a value (Zajonc, 1968). Television has been a particular focus of attention because of its supposed impact on children. By the time children reach high school, they spend as much time watching television as doing schoolwork (Oscamp, 1977).

Why Attitudes are Important

Attitudes are important because they serve so many useful purposes for people. For example, suppose someone on your work team that you admire and look up to comes under attack in a staff meeting by a team from another department. Your positive attitudes toward her and the things she stands for will help you to come to her (and your own) defense. In doing so, you protect your self-image, and have a motive to express the values that you and your friend espouse. Your attitude toward the attackers could shift toward the negative, providing you an even stronger justification about how to deal with them in the future. Figure 3.1 shows these and other functions that attitudes serve:

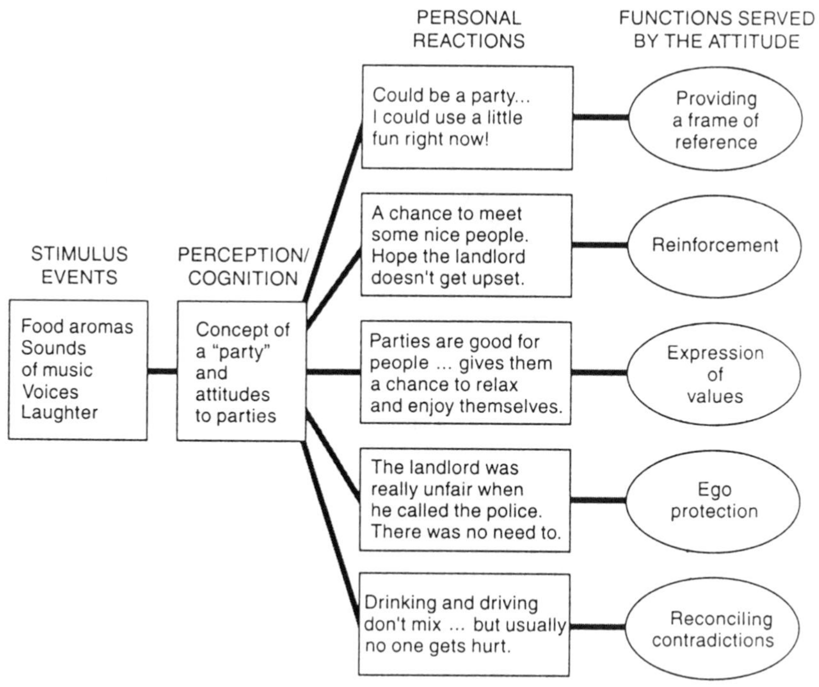

Fig 3.1: What functions attitudes serve

- Providing a frame of reference
- Reinforcement
- Expression of values
- Ego protection
- Reconciling contradictions

PROVIDING A FRAME OF FEFERENCE Attitudes help us to make sense of the world by giving us a frame of reference from which to interpret our world. We selectively perceive only a part of the total world around us. We are likely to select those facts that are consistent with our attitudes and ignore or discount those that are not. For example, recently a large university was severely penalized by their athletic association for violations of rules. Even though there was undisputed proof, many alumni supporters refused to believe that the school should have been punished or even that it was guilty.

REINFORCEMENT Attitudes can serve as means to an end. Suppose a person has threatened us in some way. A negative attitude toward such a person can help us to be on guard and protect ourselves when we are around them.

EXPRESSION OF VALUES Expressing attitudes through words and actions demonstrates our values and allows us to share them with others and to affect the world in which we live (Katz, 1960). Strong democratic values might emerge at work in staff meetings where employees are given a chance to participate in solving a problem or making a decision.

Global Focus on A Clash of Values

The globalization of business puts great pressures on countries on the European continent, at times taking them to breaking point. Countries such as France and Germany are divided internally over the nature and pace of reforms needed. Certain factions are very resistant to a new European currency, to foreign economics, and even to Anglo-Saxon capitalism and free enterprise. They resist budget cutting, corporate downsizing, service sector growth, and changes in legislation that protects against more open competition and markets. Opponents argue that unless reforms continue, Europeans will lose their capacity to compete and survive in a global economy. Some businesses are already selling or relocating noncompetitive businesses and increasing operations outside Europe. They are concerned about economic health, unemployment, and increasing crime rates. At the root of this controversy lies the threat that reforms bring to basic values about what makes for a good society. Those resisting reform defend social security and social solidarity. They favor a humane government as a safety net, and a high standard of living for all workers. They see service sector jobs as lacking in dignity and potential, and as a cause of an economically divided society. Their opponents want economic survival and prosperity in a global environment. Politicians on either side of these issues walk a tightrope.

PROTECTING OUR EGO Attitudes help us to maintain our self-image and self-respect. For example, a supervisor might have feelings of superiority regarding subordinates. An attitude that subordinates are lazy and not trustworthy, or that they are not trained well enough to assume much responsibility, tends to enhance the supervisor's feelings of superiority.

RECONCILING CONTRADICTIONS Most of us have some contradictory attitudes or beliefs, yet, in many instances, these inconsistencies do not cause us to feel uneasy or have a sense of dissonance. This happens when the contradictions between inconsistent beliefs, behaviors, or attitude are reconciled by **compartmentalization**. We are able to place the contradictions in separate compartments and not connect them, thereby reconciling them (Judge et al., 1994). Suppose your new boss treats you in an immature and demeaning way, very different from your previous supervisor. As a result, you become very dissatisfied, and develop a negative work attitude. Yet, at the same time, you are very happy with your family situation, and part of that has to do with the small town in which you live. Do you look for another job in another city? How is such a contradiction reconciled? Compartmentalization occurs when you psychologically separate these two attitudes, compartmentalizing them and taking the position that "work is work and family is family."

compartmentalization
A psychological condition in which one holds contradictory attitudes and beliefs but is able to place them in separate compartments and not connect them

A Model of Attitudes

Attitudes reflect a person's likes and dislikes toward other persons, objects events, and activities in their environment (Bem, 1970). **Attitudes** are tendencies to react in a favorable or unfavorable way toward an object. The object could be almost anything in the world around us.

attitudes
Predispositions or tendencies to react favorably or unfavorably to the world around us

Attitudes can be understood more easily if they are viewed in terms of their components and their dynamics. Figure 3.2 shows that attitudes are tied to values and beliefs, and they precede intentions to behave and actual behavior. Figure 3.3 then shows, for example, the complexity of factors that might affect attitudes toward work.

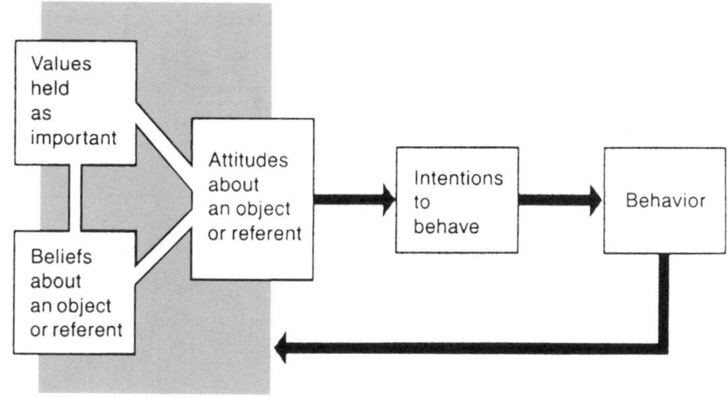

Fig 3.2: A model of attitudes

affective component
The positive or negative emotional tone toward the object of the attitude

THE AFFECTIVE COMPONENT The basic way that we refer to attitudes is to say that they are "positive" or "negative." The **affective component** is the emotional tone generated by or toward the object of the attitude. It simply means that we have some preference – like or dislike – toward the object. Strong and important attitudes are more likely to lead to a behavioral or a psychological response than weak attitudes.

attitude object
The dimension of an attitude that is the identifiable object to which it is directed

THE OBJECT OF ATTITUDES Attitudes always apply to some identifiable **object**. People have attitudes about something or someone, for example, toward the federal government, their supervisor, their job, or the use of seat belts. It is not technically accurate to say someone has a good attitude or a bad attitude without specifying the object of the attitude.

cognitive dimension of attitude
The dimension of an attitude that reflects the positive or negative perceptions that are associated with the object

THE COGNITIVE ASPECT The affective component of the attitude develops as a result of things that we observe in the world around us that we associate, positively or negatively, with the object of the attitude. These are called the **cognitive dimensions of attitude**. If we take the example of attitudes toward the job, or job satisfaction, some of the cognitive components that we might associate with it could be our level of pay, the actual working conditions, the parking facilities, the hours that we work, and so on. Figure 3.3 shows some of

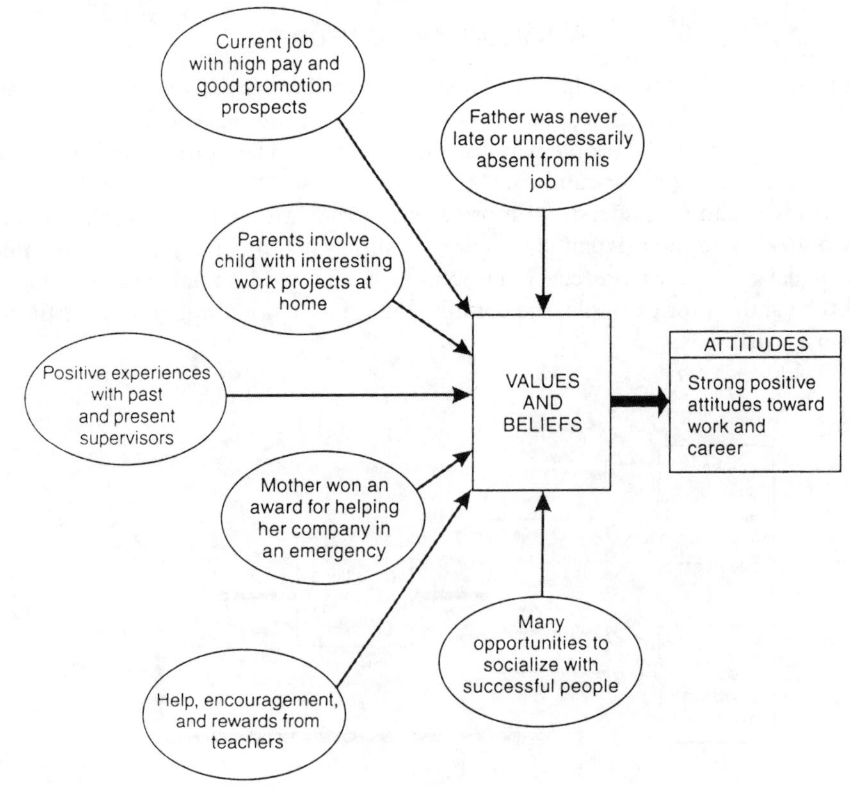

Fig 3.3: Example of the learning and expression of attitudes toward work and career

the cognitions that might be associated with, and will determine, whether our attitude toward work is positive or negative.

What is important is that our specific attitude toward our job will be a function of perceptions and evaluations about these factors. Another person might have a different set of cognitive factors associated with work. For example, someone who is not highly committed to the work might focus on the amount of time available for vacation, the hours worked, the level of strict versus loose supervision. The key point is that these relevant cognitions about work can vary from person to person, in large part depending upon their personality and how they view the world.

Values and beliefs **Values** reflect a sense of right and wrong. Values are more general than attitudes, and they need not have an identifiable object. They define the good life, and identify goals worthy of our aspiration (Myers, 1983). Values are expressed in statements such as "equal rights for all," and "hard work is the road to success."

values
General reflections of people's sense of what they consider to be right

Attitudes formed as cognitions are evaluated in terms of your relevant values. For example, if you value economic well being, then the amount of your pay is assessed to determine if it is consistent with the value that you put on "economic well being." If it is, then a belief is formed that pay is a positive factor and it will contribute to the positiveness of the attitude. If it is seen as a negative factor, then cognitions about pay will contribute to the negativeness of the attitude. We know, for instance, that employees who have high positive affectivity whose basic values are not met at work are more likely to leave, while those who find their values are met will remain (George and Jones, 1996).

Beliefs are the thinking component of attitudes. They do not refer to favorable or unfavorable reactions; they only convey a sense of "what is" to the person (Fishbein and Ajzen, 1975). However, beliefs are not necessarily factual even though they represent the truth for a particular person. Beliefs also can vary in how absolute they are. One might believe that nuclear power plants are all unsafe, or believe that this is only sometimes true.

beliefs
Thoughts and ideas about objects or events, not necessarily favorable or unfavorable

The formation of attitudes Throughout the process of socialization, people develop a whole range of general and specific feelings about objects. This learning process also leads to the development of values. Values underlie attitudes and are usually consistent with them. That is, as cognitions are evaluated against values, and beliefs are formed about whether they are positive, our attitude – positive or negative – takes shape. When there are strong positive beliefs about those cognitions that we associate with work, then we will have high job satisfaction. If they are negative, job satisfaction will be low. If they are mixed, then we might have an indifferent attitude about work.

Attitude and intentions Taking the previous example a bit further, our attitude toward our job might encourage us to take some action. Suppose it is negative and we are frustrated because of what we judge to be low pay and poor working conditions. This could foster intentions, or motivate us, to gain promotion to a job where pay is higher and conditions are better, or maybe even to

Focus on Values and Beliefs: Why Aaron Feuerstein did the Right Thing

Malden Mills, a producer of fabrics for apparel and upholstery in Lawrence, Massachusetts, was founded by Aaron Feuerstein's grandfather over 130 years ago. It has been important to the local economy, employing more than 3,000 employees, providing them with a wage far above the industry average and a very solid package of fringe benefits. In December 1995, a fire destroyed almost all of the manufacturing facilities of Malden Mills.

The decision that Feuerstein faced was to rebuild the mill in Lawrence or to move his new manufacturing facility to a location where the wages and fringe benefits were much lower. Not only did he decide to rebuild in Lawrence, but he began setting up temporary operations almost immediately, and began calling employees back to work. What was most surprising to the employees, however, was that he kept them on the payroll for three months and paid their health insurance for another three, regardless of whether they were working. By March 1996, Malden was again producing at a reasonably substantial level, but at much higher efficiency and quality than before the fire. Two years later, in September 1997, Malden was completely rebuilt and reopened, with nearly all its work force back in place.

It was not a difficult decision for Feuerstein to keep the plant in Lawrence, though other CEOs and owners might have been tempted by the lower labor cost markets in other areas of the USA or overseas. His belief is that most business leaders have lost their commitment to workers and communities and focus primarily on the shareholder. He said, "There's some kind of crazy belief that if you discard the responsibility to your country, to your city, to your community, to your workers, and think only of the economic profit, that somehow not only your company will prosper but the entire economy will prosper as a result. I think that is dead wrong."

> For Feuerstein, a devout Jew, a driving force in his life has been a 2,000 year old saying from the Jewish tradition that his father taught him. It says, in essence: When everything is moral chaos, try your hardest to be a "mensch," or a man of the highest principles (Coolidge, 1996).

Source: Adapted from *Time* (1997) and Coolidge (1996)

seek a job elsewhere. Our choice will depend on which alternative we feel has the greatest likelihood of success.

ATTITUDES AND OVERT BEHAVIOR Attitudes often lead to overt behaviors, but not always. Except for behavior, all other aspects of attitudes are internal to the person; they are not observable. The behavioral component of attitudes is important because people draw inferences about attitudes, beliefs, values, and intentions by observing what you say and what you do. For example, if you have a co-worker who has been spending a great deal of time working late at the office, you might infer that he or she has a very positive attitude toward work and the company. However, it could be something else, such as an overdue credit card bill.

Attitudinal Consistency and Cognitive Dissonance

An attitude does not usually exist in isolation. You do not, for example, have an attitude toward your work that exists independently of other attitudes that might also be linked to work. It is likely, for example, that your attitude toward your place of work is linked with your attitudes toward the work itself that you do, your co-workers, the location of the workplace and so forth. These related attitudes form an **attitude cluster** and more than likely, though not always, they will be consistent with each other as well as the specific values, cognitions and beliefs for each specific attitude in a specific attitude cluster. However, they also will be consistent with other attitude clusters to which they are strongly linked. For example, it can be said that you have a work attitude cluster, a family attitude cluster, and a political attitude cluster. Each of these will include specific attitudes that make up the cluster; see figure 3.4. One attitude cluster might or might not be linked to another. For example, the work attitude cluster might be very tightly linked to the family attitude cluster but not to the political attitude cluster.

attitude cluster
A set, or group, of attitudes consistent with each other, as well as with the specific beliefs, values, and cognitions for each specific attitude in the cluster

The theory of **cognitive dissonance** is based on the idea that people need to have consistency between their behavior and attitudes, beliefs, or thoughts (cognitions) (Festinger, 1957). When there is inconsistency (dissonance), we are motivated to reduce it because we experience discomfort. Another basic idea of this theory is that we are motivated to explain or justify our behavior, thoughts, or feelings. In short, feelings, thoughts and behaviors each must be consistent with each other. Suppose you are quite happy with your work and have been for a long time because the specific attitudes that make up the work attitude cluster (how you feel about the job, the supervisor, and the location) are all positive. Then, along comes a new manager and you find that his actions with the work group are demeaning, demanding and distant, resulting in your attitude toward your boss to become negative. Now you have a dissonant attitude in the work attitude cluster. One way to deal with this is to modify your overall attitude toward work by reducing your level of job satisfaction. You might cite examples of times when you had problems with him, how he deals in negative ways with

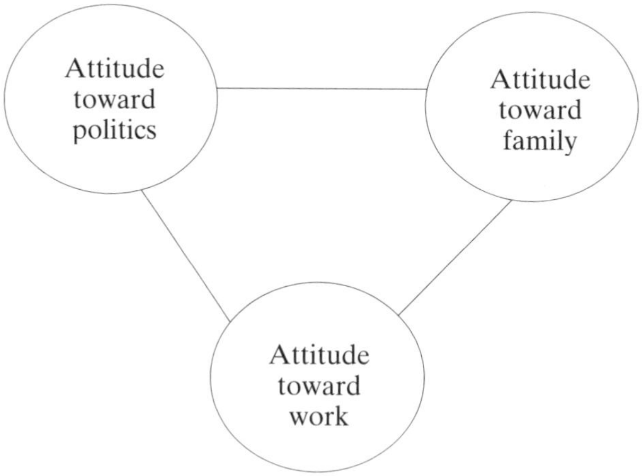

cognitive dissonance
A condition that exists when a person experiences a discrepancy among behavior, attitudes, beliefs, or thoughts

Fig 3.4: Cluster of related attitudes

other workers, or tell others that he is not important to your success. If your work attitude cluster does become negative and, if at the same time, there are cognitive elements that are common with your family attitude cluster, this could produce dissonance. It has been shown, for example, that there is strong positive relationship between work satisfaction and life satisfaction (Judge et al., 1994). This means that some cognitive dimensions will be common in both the work and the life attitude cluster. For example, one cognitive dimension of your work attitude cluster and your family attitude cluster could be "location." You like your job because it is located near other members of your family and, at the same time, you are contented because your spouse and family are happy there. This overlap will lead to some discomfort when things at home are going well, but you are dissatisfied at work. However, suppose that there is no overlap of cognitive elements with your political attitude cluster, as shown in figure 3.4. This poses no adjustment problems.

A Question of Ethics: Values and Cognitive Dissonance

In the business environment, where maximization of shareholder wealth is often the ultimate goal, the prospect of ethical practices may seem unrealistic for most managers. Typically, a given manager may feel torn when their personal ethics clash directly with the ethical standards (or lack thereof) expected by the corporation. A manager must not only make judgments conducive to business practice, but should, for obvious internal peace, make decisions appropriate for personal morality. Is such a compromise possible?

To begin with, it should be noted that most of the decisions of the business will certainly not fall into blatant categories of right and wrong. Many times, the manager is faced with decisions that, while beneficial to the corporation and not illegal, may make for an uncomfortable personal burden. Just the opposite is also true. Managers will often face a possible outcome that makes for a greater ethical satisfaction, yet leaves the company in a more difficult position. Herein lies the problem: where on this "ethical spectrum" should you position yourself to stay true to your personal ethics *and* maintain a professional approach to your employer's needs?

Although the position on this spectrum may fluctuate as corporate positions change, the overall keys to finding that ethical compromise remain the same. One such key lies in the repeated consideration of the ethical implications of even simple day-to-day decisions. This repetition of considering the ethical implications of each decision allows for the manager to become better skilled at determining that satisfactory ethical level. Over time, decisions will become more obviously ethical or unethical. Further, this repetition creates an awareness among the manager's co-workers. The number of unethical prospects put forth by employees will decrease substantially. Finally, it is recommended that the manager starts in small steps. This allows for an easier transition to increasing the emphasis on ethical behavior as opposed to making important, highly public decisions based on a new found ethical ideal.

Obviously, finding this balance between business and personal ethics is not a trivial endeavor. The ability to perceive and accurately judge such a situation must be developed and adjusted over time. Still, the balance is not impossible to maintain. It has been successfully implemented by many managers and will continue to be so in the future.

Source: Adapted from Dumville (1997)

Dissonance can arise when there is **insufficient justification** for what you do. This is called **decisional dissonance**. Dissonance can be reduced before you take action Suppose your new boss tells you to reprimand a subordinate, a behavior that you find unpleasant and harsh. If you were ordered to do so, you may have little or no dissonance because your boss has given you **sufficient justification** (a direct and clear-cut order) to do it. However, in the absence of such an order, the justification may be insufficient. Following the act, the dissonance may remain strong and the motivation to reduce it persists. You would therefore have to rationalize your action. You might justify the reprimand by convincing yourself that your boss wanted you to do what you did but just did not say so. If the employee has a hostile reaction to the reprimand, it can serve to confirm that he deserved it, reducing your dissonance even further.

Dissonance also arises when there are **disconfirmed expectations**. If a customer complains about one of our products, dissonance arises because it is inconsistent with our image of the company's reputation. Here again, developing a belief that rationalizes, or explains, the condition can reduce dissonance. We might think that the complaint was triggered by the customer's failure to follow directions in using the product.

Not surprisingly, dissonance is more severe when we are personally involved, such as when our own decisions lead to an unexpected problem. People often refuse to admit they have made a mistake. Dissonance theory predicts that people will persist in the original decision. They will even repeat it as a way of justifying it, thus compounding the bad decision rather than face the dissonant admission that they were wrong in the first place (Staw and Ross, 1987a,b). In one study (Staw, 1976), students played a business game in which they allocated funds to different projects. Those students who allocated funds to unsuccessful projects made subsequent further investments in the same unsuccessful project, especially when they felt responsible for the bad decision.

insufficient justification
A condition that fosters cognitive dissonance and blocks its reduction when a person lacks a good reason to act against his or her beliefs or attitudes

decisional dissonance
Cognitive dissonance that is experienced before a decision is made and possibly reduced as a way to justify the decision

sufficient justification
A condition helping to reduce cognitive dissonance, when a person is provided with enough reason to act against their beliefs or attitudes

disconfirmed expectations
Cognitive dissonance that arises from perceptions of reality not meeting the person's expectations

Employee Attitudes, Job Satisfaction and Performance

How employees feel about their job situation and their commitment to the organization are among the most critical consequences that managers can strive to improve. For example, employee attitudes about their pay and benefits, their coworkers and supervisor and about work hours and conditions are among the many factors that both managers and researchers have considered important to examine.

Attitudes and satisfactions also affect different measures of effectiveness. For example, there is evidence that employee satisfaction is correlated with contextual performance dimensions – see page 18 in chapter 1 – such as lateness, attendance, and turnover (Bateman and Organ, 1983). Organizations suffer significant direct and indirect costs when workers miss work. When they quit, the costs of recruitment, selection, and training the new employee to full productivity can be considerable.

There is also a long history or evidence that shows there is a positive, but relatively weak, relationship between job attitudes and task performance (Vroom, 1964, Iaffaldano and Muchinsky, 1985). The reason is that many employees, regardless of whether their work performance is high or low, may be quite satisfied with many other aspects of their employment and do not feel any need or motivation to do more. You should not conclude from this, however, that as a manager you have no need to worry about **job satisfaction**. Because of its link to both task performance and contextual performance, one of the key goals in managing behavior in organizations is to create linkages between employee performance and their satisfaction. Many managerial strategies such as redesigning organizational structures and tasks discussed throughout this book are aimed at strengthening this link. Similarly, we will show how motivation theories and strategies focus on creating work environments that link satisfaction with having done a good job.

job satisfaction
The attitude toward work in general, or to specific facets of the work

However, it is not always easy to change attitudes in ways to increase job satisfaction. The reason is that, as you have seen, attitudes toward work may be only one important aspect of the person's structure of attitudes. It might be linked strongly to other important ones, making it deeply embedded, and thereby limiting how much managers can succeed in altering the way employees feel and act. However, particular attitudes and satisfactions at work can and do change, sometimes quickly, as events change (Maier, 1973). An employee who is happy and productive one day can become dissatisfied and resentful overnight as a consequence of some managerial action. Reflect on the employee reactions in Delta that were triggered by the CEO's statement, "So be it!" This is one of the reasons why many organizations pay close attention to attitudes by conducting periodic **attitude surveys** of employees, and by seeking feedback in other ways.

attitude surveys
Data collection techniques conducted to assess attitudes and serve as a source of management feedback

Perception

Perception is the psychological process of creating an internal picture of the external world. It is the way that we organize information about people and things, the attribution of properties to them on the basis of the information and the way we make cause/effect attributions about them. It is a process of interpreting what information our senses provide to us so as to give meaning to the environment we are in. The resulting interpretation is the perceiver's reality, and even though several people may observe the same environment the perception of it can vary widely from person to person. Perception is a dynamic process, a search for the best interpretation of available data (Gregory, 1977), though that does not necessarily mean that the interpretation is an accurate one.

perception
The process of using our five senses to create an internal representation of the external world

In this next section, we focus on the feeling and thinking aspects of perception, with emphasis on just two sensory channels: what we see and what we hear. Then we examine how our perceptions affect behavior. We discuss

EXERCISE

MAKING INFERENCES

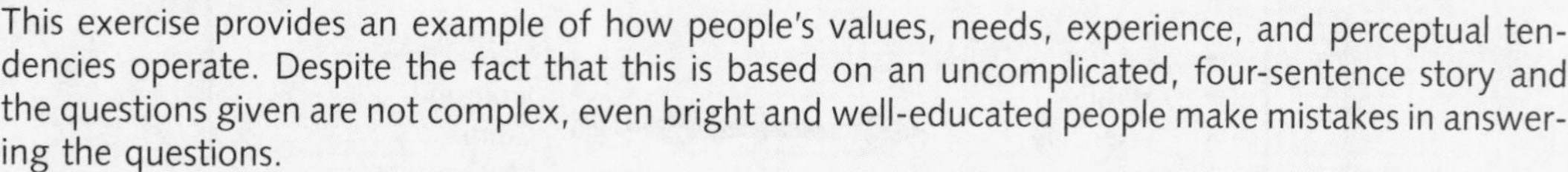

This exercise provides an example of how people's values, needs, experience, and perceptual tendencies operate. Despite the fact that this is based on an uncomplicated, four-sentence story and the questions given are not complex, even bright and well-educated people make mistakes in answering the questions.

Instructions

Read the story below slowly at least three times. When you have completed this, write down your answers to the six questions as you read each question. Do *not* refer back to the story. Score your answers using the answer key provided.

The story

A businessman had just turned off the lights in the store when a man appeared and demanded money. The owner opened the cash register. The contents of the cash register were scooped up, and the man ran away. A member of the police force was notified promptly.

The questions

Answer these questions by indicating T (true), F (false), or ? (can't tell or don't know):

1 A man appeared after the owner had turned off his store lights. ☐
2 The robber was a man. ☐
3 The man did not demand money. ☐
4 The owner opened the cash register. ☐
5 After the man who demanded the money scooped up the contents of the cash register, he ran away. ☐
6 While the cash register contained money, the story does not state how much. ☐

Consider reasons for any answers that you marked incorrectly. The (?) or "can't tell" answer are cases where people's perceptions, judgments, and inferences come into play in mentally interpreting and organizing the story. Question 4 is particularly interesting because it is taken verbatim from the story itself, yet people answer it incorrectly.

- Do you believe the errors are caused by problems with attentiveness? Selective perception?
- What similar behaviors occur in the workplace? For example, how might quick judgments and assumptions affect a superior–subordinate relationship such as during a performance appraisal or discussion over a work-related incident?

Note: The correct answers are as follows: 1. ? 2. ? 3. F 4. T 5. ? 6. ?

the perceiver, the event or object being perceived, and the situational context in which the perception occurs. Figure 3.5 illustrates these elements and shows that they interact to determine both the interpretation and the action that takes place.

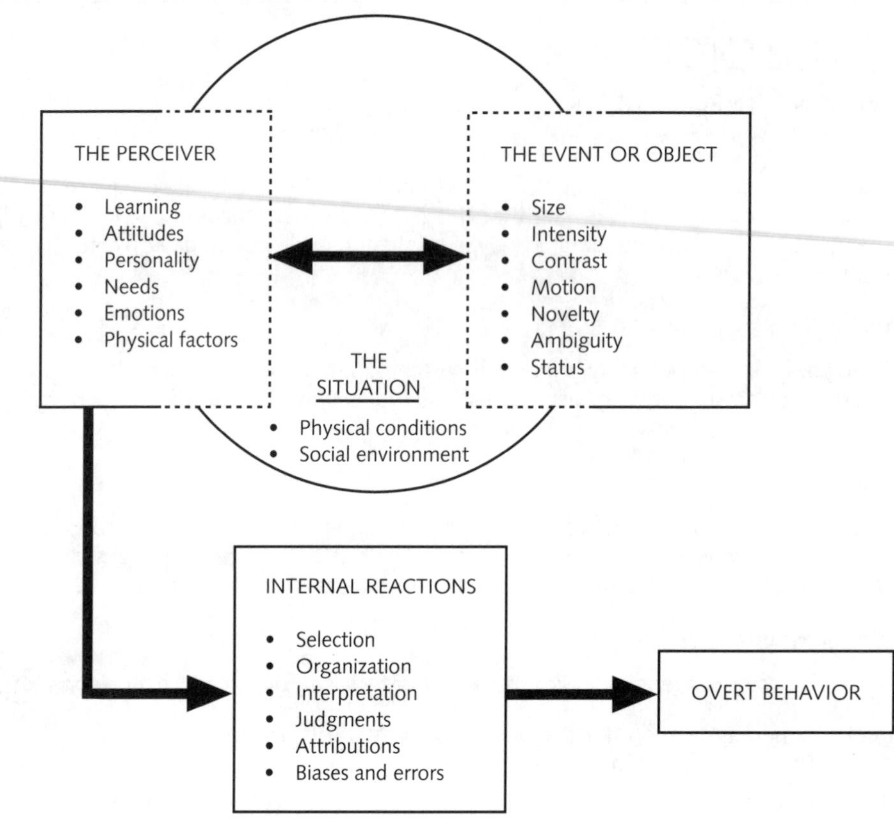

Fig 3.5: A perceptual model

selective perception
The tendency to sense some aspects of our environment while paying less attention to or ignoring other aspects

perceptual organization
The tendency to group stimuli into patterns so that they become "meaningful wholes" rather than fragmented parts

schemas
Patterns of information that we have learned from our past experiences; also called categories

THE PERCEIVER

The way we perceive is learned, and what we learn affects our perception. **Selection** is at the heart of the perceptual process, and it is driven by our personal characteristics, attributes of the object itself, and the situation in which perception takes place. For example, Inuits have no concept that corresponds to what most people call snow. They actually perceive different kinds of snow depending on its particular characteristics and its potential uses, and have several concepts for it. There is good reason for this: Their survival depends upon snow. This means that out of the many stimuli that bombard people, only a few actually penetrate and become part of their experience and are used in making judgments. The remainder are excluded.

Another powerful mechanism is **perceptual organization**. The reason is that information has an expected pattern that we have learned from our past experiences: a pattern that might be very general and abstract or very specific and detailed. These patterns are called categories, or **schemas**. As you are exposed to information in the environment, you tend to group certain stimuli into patterns so that they become meaningful wholes rather than fragmented parts. The way that they are grouped depends upon your schemas. An example is the words that you are now reading. The separate letters are ignored in favor of the whole word. Another example is the inclination to see physical patterns. It takes only three dots for us to see a triangle and four to see a rectangle or square. Suppose one of your subordinates is late for work and is working slowly, producing below par. You are going to organize these facts in a way that makes sense to you, perhaps that slow work and lateness go together. Perhaps your schema about this set of information is that it reflects lack of caring and indifference. You may explain the behavior, then, in terms of laziness and irresponsibility. You would also seek consistency in surrounding events. Irresponsibility explanations would be reinforced if there was union trouble in the plant and you believed the worker was slowing down under union pressure. However, if there were no union problems and you believed the worker was a loyal employee, it would be more consistent to believe his behavior was due to a temporary condition, such as an illness.

Diversity Issues: Perceptions about Women and International Assignments

The role of perception in day-to-day business transactions is an extremely important one. As managers create that internal portrait of the world around them, their past experience and expected information comes into play. The flawed perceptions that can occur based on a personal bias can be extremely damaging to an organization. Since perception forms the basis for our judgments, perceptual errors can lead to errors in judgments that can be extremely costly for the organization.

One such judgment error that can occur could be the result of a manager's flawed perceptions about whom to assign to a particular task. Despite multiple opportunities now available, gender-based errors in perception are still encountered. For example, in determining who to send on various global assignments, it has been documented that some managers may tend to lean more towards men as a general rule. Their reasoning can be attributed to familiar errors in their perceptions of the ability of women. Women, they reason, may have difficulty with the stress associated with travel, may be faced with a lack of respect by other cultures, and may lack the aggressive nature needed to close a deal. These perceptual errors based on stereotypes may lead them to choose a less capable employee for the assignment.

In examining such gender-based misperception, studies show that reality is far different than the perception. It has been shown that women are capable of a resiliency equal to and often times greater than their male counterparts; the idea that they could somehow be more vulnerable to travel stress seems entirely baseless. Further, the notion that other cultures prefer male representatives is also suspect. Studies have shown that female consultants' very nature makes for a more open, personal, and comfortable exchange of ideas. The skill needed to negotiate and close a potentially profitable alliance lies in this same natural ability.

The basis for these misguided perceptions is easily understood; assumptions and dated norms can lead to inaccurate opinions. The lesson here is in the care with which perceptions should be formed. A manger's lack of concrete data and inherent personal bias offer more than just room to make a poor assignment. In the case documented above, a poor perception can yield lost opportunities, and that is not good business.

Source: Adapted from Fisher (1999) by Pete Jones

Physical and emotional states can also shape and determine our reality. When a person is hungry, sights and sounds that point to food tend to become salient. Emotional states can distort perception, as the example of the level of excitability of eyewitnesses to a crime. Eyewitness perceptions may be so inaccurate that one must wonder why they are relied on so often (Loftus, 1984). Some eyewitnesses report things that never happened, and overlook both small details and glaring stimuli. For example, some may fail to see a bright red shirt or hear an important statement made by a person committing a crime.

Effects of the Event or Object

Certain attributes of events and objects affect whether they are perceived and how they are perceived.

- Size effects
- Intensity effects
- Contrast effects
- Motion and novelty
- Ambiguity
- Characteristics of other people

size effect
Larger objects being more likely to be perceived than smaller ones

intensity effect
Particularly strong, or extreme, cues being more likely to be perceived than smaller ones

contrast effect
Cues that stand out against their background being more likely to be perceived

Size has an effect: larger objects are more likely to be seen than smaller ones. **Intensity** of stimuli is another factor: particularly loud noises are likely to be heard, and bright or shining objects will likely be seen. **Contrast effects** also affect perception, so anything that stands out against its background is more likely to be attended to. Motion and novelty also facilitate perception: a moving object or unusual things draw attention. Experts in advertising creatively manipulate such characteristics of objects and apply them to magazine and newspaper ads, to billboards, and to radio and television commercials.

Ambiguity also has an impact on perceptions. Ambiguous or incomplete events are actually more subject to personal interpretation. Ambiguity is discomforting, and can be reduced by adding meaning to the stimuli or attributing motives to a person associated with the stimuli. For example, after interviewers talk to an applicant for a job, they often draw conclusions that are not justified by the applicant's behavior. They often fill in gaps about the applicant's past experience, and do it in a way that confirms their good feelings or negative suspicions about a candidate with no good reason.

Finally, characteristics of other people affect perception. One example of this is how the status of a person affects perception. Higher-status people are more likely to be noticed, and they usually are perceived to be more knowledgeable, accurate, and believable.

Situational Effects

Under different conditions, the same cues can easily result in different perceptions. Imagine seeing a person holding a knife in a kitchen in which food is being prepared for a meal. Now imagine the same person holding a knife the same way in the middle of a public demonstration. The knife is often unnoticed in the kitchen setting but would be prominent in the demonstration. Furthermore, your predictions about what might happen would probably be different for each situation.

Perceptions can also be affected by the presence of another person. Suppose you are criticized by your boss in the presence of a higher-level manager. You might conclude that your boss is seeking favor from the higher manager. If the higher manager is absent, you are less likely to draw such a conclusion. In short, perceptions occur in a context, which predisposes us to expect certain events and lends an additional ingredient to how we interpret, judge, and react.

It is clear, then, that perception plays a huge role in how accurate we are in the conclusions and judgments we make about others. Of particular interest are judgments that distort or misrepresent the facts, or that disagree with the perceptions of others. Distortions and disagreement are at the root of a host of problems in managing people.

Judgment Tendencies

In addition to inaccurate perception, other human tendencies lead to inaccurate or unreliable judgments. Optical illusions are a good example of how the actual characteristics of an object are not the same as what they seem to be; see Figure 3.6.

For managers, the most important **perceptual biases** are those that arise in relationships with other people. There are many such situations at work: performance appraisals, selection interviewing, group meetings, customer relations, and so on (Parsons and Liden, 1984). Perceptual biases create distortions that are particularly crucial to understand. Once understood, it is easier to overcome judgment errors (Cardy and Kehoe, 1984). Figure 3.7 shows various ways we might react to others and the types of errors that can occur.

First Impressions

Strong and lasting impressions of others tend to be formed very early in a relationship. Since early interactions are usually of a short duration, these early impressions may be based on very limited information. This tendency is a critical problem because **first impressions** are often lasting ones. In other words, we use only a few cues when judging others, and then continue to maintain the judgment.

There are two reasons why first impressions are so strong: the principles of closure and consistency. The **principle of closure** is that humans need a relatively complete conception, or idea, about things. The **principle of consistency** is that the conception should be congruent with other attitudes, perceptions and beliefs. Suppose you meet someone for the first time. It is very difficult to know most of the things that you should know to form an accurate impression. What happens

perceptual bias
Any tendency on the part of a person to distort or otherwise misrepresent or organize perceptions in a personalized way

first impressions
Impressions of others, formed early in a relationship; usually lasting impressions

closure, principle of
The need for a relatively complete conception, or idea, about things

consistency, principle of
The principle that a person's attitudes and perceptions will be congruent with other attitudes, perceptions, and beliefs

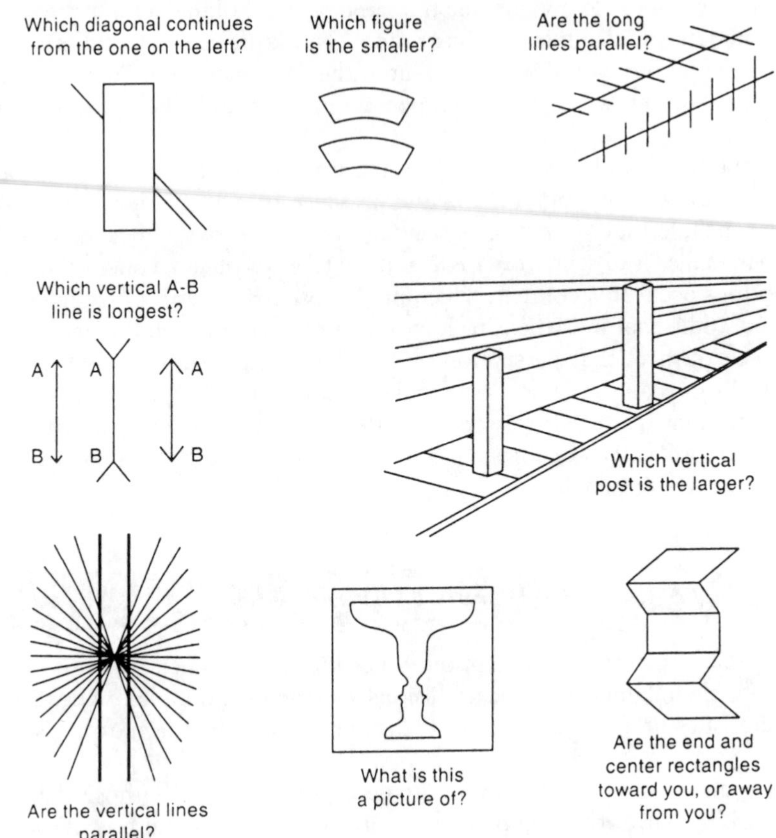

Fig 3.6 : Perceptual teasers

is that you focus on those cues that strike you as important at the time and then use these as a basis for "completing" your picture of the person. When this happens, you no longer have limited information, but a fairly full model of the other person, made up of the relatively few cues gathered in your first impression and those that you added to it, which will be consistent with the first information. Later information obtained about the person should be evaluated against this more complete image that you have created, but because you have created this more complete concept now, it becomes difficult to change it when you receive the new information.

halo effect
A judgment tendency in which one or a few characteristics of an individual affects the evaluation of them on other characteristics

Halo: One Characteristic Tells All

The use of one or a few characteristics of a person to affect the evaluation of other characteristics is called the **halo effect**. Many people find a particular attribute that they like or dislike strongly in others. For example, if how one

Fig 3.7 : Judgment tendencies

dresses is an important concern for a person, it can become a dominant basis to make biased judgments about others – positive or negative – if the halo effect is operating. How another person dresses would determine their overall evaluation. We see this often in the case of employment interviews when the interviewer makes a judgment that a job candidate is dressed in a way that seems consistent with the dress norms of the company. The interviewer assumes because the candidate is dressed well she will fit well in the firm and, during the interview, has his or her other judgments colored by this factor.

Halo is likely to be related to our own self-image. We tend to have very positive evaluations of those who possess characteristics we believe we have. A manager who is always on time for work is more favorably disposed toward subordinates who are punctual; they may be negatively disposed toward those who arrive late.

Projection

Projection is a psychological mechanism by which people attribute their own traits to others. Sometimes the trait is one that we like in ourselves. For example, we might attribute potential success to an interview applicant because we dis-

projection
A form of defense mechanism by which people protect themselves against undesirable characteristics that they themselves possess by projecting their own characteristics or feelings onto others

cover that she, like us, pays particular attention to spelling and neatness on her resume and other application materials. Sometimes, the trait is one we dislike in ourselves. For example, we might blame a co-worker's mistake on sloppiness when sloppiness is one of our own faults. If others do not possess what we project onto them, our behavior is governed by the false impression, and further misperceptions will likely follow.

IMPLICIT PERSONALITY THEORY

implicit personality theory
A tendency to link personality characteristics of others into a pattern

Statements such as "honest people are also hard working," "late sleepers are lazy," or "quiet people are devious" all link together two characteristics of a person. When we make such linkages, we are creating our own **implicit personality theory**. Any of the linkages could be wrong. Hard work and honesty need not go together. The late sleeper might have a medical problem. The quiet person might simply be shy. Engaging in implicit personality theory is amateur psychology at its worst. It is much safer to link two characteristics together only if we witness both characteristics on repeated occasions.

STEREOTYPING

stereotyping
Connecting characteristics of people to characteristics of the group into which we place them

In **stereotyping**, we link characteristics of people to characteristics of a group with which we associate them. Surely not all members of a given group possess the characteristic they are said to have, yet stereotyping is common and widespread. It persists because it is useful, and helps us to organize the world around us. Often, however, stereotyping is nothing more than a perpetuation of old myths and prejudices. It is fed by prejudices and ambiguity, and sometimes by fear or threat, and reinforced in many ways. For example, if we know that someone is Italian, we might conclude he is emotional and likes good wine; if he is Irish, we might conclude he drinks whiskey and is prone to be quick-tempered. Countless other examples exist, often very negative. Ethnic groups, older people, men, women, lawyers, used-car salesmen, or just about any other group can be stereotyped.

Stereotypes also appear in our language, in words such as "chairman" or "cleaning woman." They are often so embedded in society that they are difficult to change. Think of how women are portrayed in many television commercials and movies. Women's rights organizations spend much time and energy fighting to try to change stereotypes.

It is a fact, however, that members of groups do share certain values and beliefs, and will exhibit similar traits or behaviors. In some cases, therefore, it is quite safe to draw conclusions about people based on their group membership. We are usually correct in concluding that professional athletes are healthy, or that the average weight that women can lift is less than the average men can lift. However, even these generalizations require qualification and have to be carefully stated. For example, there are women who can out-perform men in lifting weights.

Attribution Theory: Finding Causes of Behavior

It is fundamental to human nature to want to explain the causes of our own and others' behavior. An unexplainable event can leave us in a state of dissonance which motivates us to explain the situation to reduce the dissonance. If we know why something happened, it helps us decide how to react to an event. Suppose our supervisor gives us an unpleasant assignment. If we see the assignment as caused by unfairness, we are tempted to fight it. If we attribute the cause to a higher manager's wishes, we might have a different reaction to the whole situation.

Attribution theory explains why and how we determine these causes. It focuses on key errors people make in attributing causes. The attributions are judgments that subsequently affect our feelings, our behavior, and the conclusions we draw about our experiences (see figure 3.8). Wrong inferences about causation will create problems similar to those created by perceptual errors.

attribution theory
An approach to understanding how and why people attribute causes to their own and other people's behavior

JUDGING OTHER PEOPLE'S BEHAVIOR Earlier we pointed out that behavior is determined by the person and the environment, but when we judge others, we have a strong tendency to attribute causes of behavior to the internal characteristics of the person. This is called the **fundamental attribution error** (Ross, 1977), overestimating the role of the person relative to the environment as a cause of behavior. Thus if we see people steal, we are more likely to characterize them as dishonest than we are to conclude that their family is starving.

fundamental attribution error
A tendency to attribute causes of behavior to the internal characteristics or motives of another rather than to the situation

We have a tendency to underestimate the situation as a cause of behavior even when we are told the person was forced or instructed to behave as he or she did.

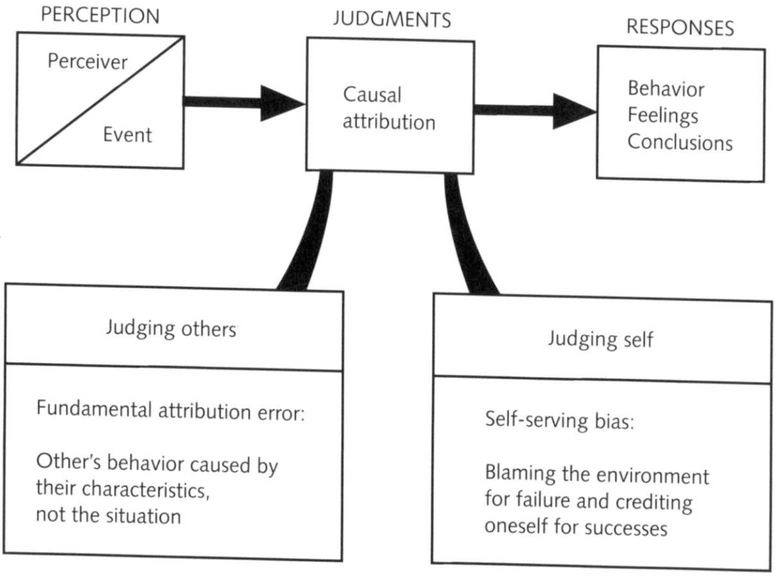

Fig 3.8: A model of attribution theory

For instance, if we observe a debate in which participants are assigned to defend a defined position, we will most likely attribute their arguments to their beliefs rather than to the debating rules they are following. Somehow, what people say or do, even under instructions or other situational pressures, leads us to conclude more about them than about the situation. Perhaps this is because we see the situational influences as operating through people and not independent of them.

There are several reasons for the fundamental attribution error. First, if you believe that the other has free choice in the situation, you are more likely to attribute causality to him or her personally. This makes sense, for you can conclude that the person was free to do otherwise, but chose to act as he or she did.

Second, you are more likely to attribute internal motives to people when they take action you view as important, and especially when those actions affect us personally. Suppose someone dents your car in a parking lot but left the scene before you appeared. You would characterize them unfavorably for failing to leave a note or call a police officer. If, however, you seek a situational cause, you might speculate that he or she had to rush home to take care of a dire emergency.

There are several other factors that affect our attributions about others (Kelly, 1973):

1 *Consistency* If a person behaves the same way in similar situations, we are more likely to see the behavior as internally motivated, such as when a friend is almost always late.
2 *Distinctiveness* Distinctive behaviors are those that are relatively unique to a situation. If a behavior is more distinctive, we are less likely to make internal attributions. If our friend was always on time, we are apt to evaluate a lateness as due to some unforeseen difficulty thrust on them.
3 *Consensus* When the person we are judging acts differently than others act in the situation, we are more likely to think of that person's behavior as internally motivated.
4 *Privacy of the act* Actions that are taken in the absence of other people are more likely to be judged as internally motivated. When others are present, we might attribute the action to social pressure. When people are alone, we attribute the action to them.
5 *Status* In general, higher-status people are seen to be more personally responsible for their actions. They are thought to have more control over their own actions and decisions and do things because they choose to, not because they have to.

automatic information processing The recognition of some key information, or stimuli, that causes recall of schemas or categories into which that particular information fits, leading our judgment to be biased toward general characteristics of that category

One important reason for making the fundamental attribution error – as well as the use of first impressions, halo, projection, stereotyping, and the use of implicit personality theory – has to do with the way that we process information. Recall that we said earlier that perception has to do with how we organize information. We often make these errors because we use **"automatic" information processing.** This means that when we recognize some key information, or stimulus, we recall schemas or categories into which that particular information fits and our judgment is then biased toward the general characteristics of that category. Take the use of stereotypes as an example. Suppose we have a negative stereotype of lawyers and then we learn that a dinner guest is a lawyer. If we automatically use our occupational stereotype, then we are likely to attribute all of the negative aspects of the stereotype to him, without ever having taken the time to learn anything more about him. Automatic processing obviously occurs in performance evaluation but it is more likely to occur when a rater observes positive performance of the performance being rated. Then they are more likely to attribute other positive characteristics to the person that have not been observed and to make relatively quick judgments (Kulik and Ambrose, 1993).

To avoid the fundamental attribution error and the other perceptual problems, it is necessary to use a "controlled" approach to information processing. In the **controlled information processing** approach, we pause and reflect on the situation as well as the person and try to identify both the situational forces and the personal causes of behavior, before making our judgment. This approach requires searching for more data. While this can complicate and delay matters, it may lead to a more accurate and less biased judgment. This is the approach raters used when they had observed negative performance of a person being rated (Kulik and Ambrose, 1993). They took more time and had more accurate recall of the negative aspects of the person's performance.

controlled information processing
Pausing and reflecting on the situation to try to identify both the situational forces and personal causes of behavior before making a judgment about cause/effect relationships

JUDGING OUR OWN BEHAVIOR Self-judgments are affected by a **self-serving bias** – a tendency to perceive oneself favorably. People credit themselves when they succeed but blame external factors when they fail (Zuckerman, 1979). Success is usually attributed to hard work, ability, and good judgment. Failure, on the other hand, is attributed to bad luck, unfair conditions, or impossible odds. If you play golf, for example, think what happens when you are playing a close match. When your opponent makes a long putt, you tell her, "You're lucky." When you make a long putt, it is because of your skill.

self-serving bias
A judgment tendency reflecting a bias to perceive oneself favorably; crediting oneself when one succeeds but blaming external factors when one fails

Self-serving attributions and self-congratulatory comparisons operate in many ways (Jones and Harris, 1967). We tend to overrate ourselves on nearly any factor that is subjective and socially desirable (Felson, 1981), seeing ourselves as better than average in intelligence, leadership ability, health, life expectancy, interpersonal skill, and so on. We believe flattery more readily than we believe criticism. We overestimate how well we would act in a given situation and overestimate the accuracy of our judgments. For example, a psychologist who is well known for his work in the development of selection tests and who advocates their widespread use was asked what he thought about a candidate for a position at his department. He had only spent thirty minutes or so with the candidate, who was not selected through the use of any test. When asked what he thought of the candidate, he replied without hesitation, "We shouldn't hire him. He will never work out here. I could tell it in the first five minutes of our discussion." This is a good example of how he trusted his own selection judgment without the test, but it is likely that he would not trust the judgment of others unless selection tests had been used.

When we deal with others, we often see our own actions as externally justified, but attribute others' actions to their internal disposition. You are angered by your boss because you were provoked by a "stupid" order that he or she gave. However, when your boss is angry with you, it is attributed to his or her "neurotic personality." The objective truth hardly matters, and the self-serving attributions persist even in the face of contrary evidence.

Interestingly, the self-serving bias seems to be strongest among people with high self-esteem. People with low self-esteem are more self-deprecating and engage in self-blame rather than blaming external events for failure. They are less likely to exhibit the self-serving bias. On the other hand, when low-self-esteem people have a strong need for respect, they could be more likely than the average person to exhibit the self-serving bias. This is why some people constantly talk about their own activities, exploits, and successes. The self-serving bias acts as a boastful cover for their feelings of low self-esteem and is an attempt to gain recognition and thus to enhance self-esteem.

SOME ORGANIZATIONAL IMPLICATIONS OF ATTRIBUTION BIASES

We have already given several examples of how perceptual distortions and attribution biases can affect people at work. We now discuss three specific areas that should be specially noted:

1 Problem solving and decision making
2 Performance appraisal
3 Managing workplace diversity

PROBLEM SOLVING AND DECISION MAKING Effective management requires making good decisions when solving problems, and effective problem solving requires identifying the most likely cause of the problem. Biased attributions can occur in identifying problems. For example, a committee will blame other groups or departments when problems occur. Here, the self-serving bias can damage cooperation between groups and fail to uncover the true causes of the problem. Another difficulty in problem identification occurs because we tend, when looking at difficult situations, to interpret them in terms of our own experiences and capacity to solve problems. It has been shown, for instance, that when faced with identifying problems to be solved in a complex business situation, managers are most likely to have a tendency to emphasize more strongly a problem definition that reflects their own functional competence than other functional areas (Dearborn and Simon, 1958; Walsh, 1988). This means, for example, a human resource manager is more likely to perceive a problem to be based on personnel deficiencies while a production manager is likely to see the problem as having more technical issues that must be solved. The importance of correct problem identification is obvious: Trying to solve the wrong problem will not correct the situation.

PERFORMANCE APPRAISAL Performance appraisal is another situation where attribution biases operate. The attribution errors can create serious disagreements between raters and ratees about performance. Some research shows that we look at both effort and ability in evaluating performance but give more weight to effort (Knowlton and Mitchell, 1980). Effort is weighted higher for both good and poor performance: good performance is rated higher and poor performance lower when effort, rather than ability, is seen as the cause. Thus we are evaluated more on how hard someone who is judging us thinks we are trying. If our boss feels we put in a lot of effort, we will be appraised higher when we succeed. If we are seen as not trying very hard, we will be rated more poorly when we fail.

MANAGING WORKPLACE DIVERSITY Perceptual errors are even more critical problems when ethnic or sex differences are added to the situation. The work force in the USA is now far more multi-cultural than ever, but still the number of women and minorities in management jobs is underrepresented. One reason for this situation lies in how these groups are evaluated. One evaluation of the research on selection procedures and performance evaluation shows that minorities are rated lower by supervisors (Martocchio and Whitener, 1992). Hiring biases are also affected by other factors such as gender (Latino women suffer less hiring discrimination than Latino men), the source of recruitment (private employment agencies are more discriminatory), the type of job (there was more discrimination for jobs not requiring college degrees), and location of the job (there was greater bias when selecting for inner city jobs) (Bendick et al., 1991). However, the bias issue does not exist only in the dominant white male group. For example, a survey of males, females, African Americans, Asian Americans, native Americans, and Hispanic Americans reveals that there is bias and stereotyping of other groups by these groups. In addition, there is bias and stereotyping within their own groups as, for example, the view of women by men within each group (Fernandez, 1991).

Other studies uncovered a tendency to attribute female successes to hard work or luck rather than to ability (Feldman-Summers and Kiesler, 1974). Males, on the other hand, are more protected from adverse evaluations. Interestingly, both males and females make these biased attributions. Their successes usually are attributed to competence, and their failures to bad luck. Such gender-biased attributions insult women and place them at a disadvantage because they are given less credit than males for their skills. From a woman's perspective, it is better if her successes are attributed to ability, rather than to effort or situational conditions.

Summary

Attitudes, perceptions, and judgment tendencies have widespread and important implications in the world of work. Employee attitudes can make a huge difference in the effectiveness of an organization. They affect such things as attendance, retention, work commitments, and interpersonal reactions. Perceptions and judgments are critical because they enter into so many work situations: selecting applicants, making assignments, appraising performance, giving feedback, solving problems, and so on.

Attitudes refer to what people like and dislike; they predispose them to act favorably or unfavorably toward an object or event. They function in several ways to help people to adapt to their world. Attitudes are related to beliefs and values. All three are acquired from infancy through our experiences and associations with people, events, and the media. Specific attitudes can be learned at any time and apply to any experience. Employee attitudes about various aspects of their job are often studied by employers, because it is known that attitudes affect satisfaction, performance and constructive voluntary contributions to organizational success.

The study of perception is central to understanding how people react. Each of us has certain perceptual tendencies that define the world from our own personal point of view. Values, emotional states, needs, and personality all come into play. Characteristics of the object and situation also affect what we select, how we organize what we perceive, and how we make interpretations. Most critical are the errors in judgment we make about the world around us. An important tendency is how we make causal inferences about what we perceive. We tend to attribute other people's behavior to their personality rather than to situational forces. When judging ourselves, however, we are more likely to have a self-serving bias. We also attribute our successes not to external forces, but to our own skills and abilities.

Guide for Managers: Making Better Judgments

MAKING BETTER JUDGMENTS ABOUT ATTITUDES

There are a number of things that we can do to make better judgments about attitudes of others in evaluating their suitability for almost everything that goes on in organizations. For example, in interviews, prospective employees are often asked, "How do you feel about working here?" or "How satisfied were you with the type of work that you did in your previous job?" Attitudes are also important when evaluating someone for promotion. We hear comments like, "He doesn't have a good attitude toward affirmative action" or, "He just doesn't believe enough in quality to do the job right." This means that we should be very careful about judging attitudes of others (as well as our own, we might add).

Focus on specific, rather than general attitudes

Rather than generalizing, such as saying that an employee has a good or a bad attitude, it is better to try to focus on employee attitudes in terms of their more specific objects, such as attitudes toward pay, toward supervision, and so on. This helps you to decide what you have to change in the organization, such as modifying the pay system or training supervisors. There is often very little that you can do about these general attitudes, since they may reflect the positive or negative affectivity of the person.

Notice depth of feeling and behavior

Do not dismiss or underestimate the depth of feeling and the behavior associated with attitudes, values and beliefs. Do not trivialize the attitudes of others by thinking or telling them that their feelings are not important. Attitudes are very important to the psychological well being of people and some are strongly held, especially those linked to the person's self image. More importantly, they may be related to attitudes, values and beliefs that are not directly related to work itself.

Understand how attitudes work at work

Negative attitudes toward the job or the organization may lead an employee to want to avoid work or to quit, and they may do so because job satisfaction is negatively related to turnover and to commitment. However, never assume that a satisfied employee is always a productive employee or that a productive employee is always satisfied. There is a weak relationship between attitudes and task performance, though it is statistically significant.

Periodically assess employee attitudes and satisfaction

It is a good idea for organizations to evaluate attitudes and satisfaction with periodic employee surveys. It is also useful to involve the employees in the design, collection, and interpretation of the study. However, never conduct surveys unless you are fully committed to act on the findings and report the actions you have taken.

Accept people's tendency to justify, rationalize and explain their beliefs

This helps them reduce cognitive dissonance, and appear consistent to themselves and others. However, you should strive to ensure that they understand, as clearly as possible, what is expected in terms of work performance and that you can accept their attitudes so long as they do not have negative effects on others or on their own performance.

USING THEORIES OF PERCEPTION AND OF THE ATTRIBUTION OF CAUSES AND EFFECTS

Theories of perception and of the attribution of causes and effects are also useful to managers. Think about problem solving, for example. We can solve only those problems of which we are aware, or that we perceive. However, beyond simply recognizing that a problem exists we are faced with the question, "What is the cause?" The same is true for evaluating the performance of another. We need to know why performance is high or low. Here are some ways to sharpen your perceptions and attributions.

Do not assume your reality is another person's reality

Perceptions of events (selecting, interpreting, organizing) will vary from person to person, and become each person's individual reality. Many things affect the accuracy of a perception. It pays to seek confirmation of events. If you are part of a group trying to solve a problem, attempt to find a consensus definition of the situation. Be careful, however, not to be stampeded into an agreed upon, but wrong, set of perceptions.

Keep the common judgment tendencies in mind

You can reduce the common errors that lead to inaccurate assessments by not rushing to judgments based on stereotyping, halo, and so on. These can be reduced through training and other techniques that seek factual data from several sources. Also, remember that the self-serving bias is widespread and impossible to eliminate, so it must be accepted as a factor in interpreting what other people say and do. Also, remember that it applies to you too.

Fight the fundamental attribution error

Seek environmental or situational causes to explain someone's behavior instead of blaming their personality. This is particularly important wherever judgment tendencies and errors are causing problems, such as when women, minorities or any employee is unfairly treated as a consequence. Examples may be found in how performance appraisals, task assignments or promotion decisions are made.

Key Concepts

affective component 62
attitude cluster 65
attitude object 62
attitude surveys 68
attitudes 61
attribution theory 77
automatic information processing 78
beliefs 63
closure, principle of 73
cognitive dimension of attitude 62
cognitive dissonance 65
compartmentalization 61
consistency, principle of 73
contrast effect 72
controlled information processing 79
decisional dissonance 67
disconfirmed expectations 67
first impressions 73
fundamental attribution error 77
halo effect 74
implicit personality theory 76
insufficient justification 67
intensity effect 72
job satisfaction 68
perception 68
perceptual bias 73
perceptual organization 70
projection 75
schemas 70
selective perception 70
self-serving bias 79
size effect 72
stereotyping 76
sufficient justification 67
values 63

STUDY QUESTIONS

1 Define and differentiate between attitudes, values, and beliefs. How are these three concepts linked together to explain behavior?
2 In what various ways are attitudes, values, and beliefs formed?
3 What functions do attitudes serve for people?
4 List five people, objects, or events about which you have strong attitudes, positive and negative. In what ways might these attitudes affect your behavior as a manager? How will subordinates react to such behavior?
5 What kinds of new attitudes do you think you might learn as you advance upward in management?
6 Define cognitive dissonance. Cite several factors that help to cause dissonance.
7 What characteristics of an event or object are likely to affect how it is perceived?
8 Define the major judgment tendencies or errors that people commonly commit.
9 Describe three work situations that show how a particular judgment error might damage the relationship between a superior and a subordinate.
10 According to attribution theory, what are the two basic judgment errors people commit? Cite several organizational implications of attribution errors.
11 List the ways in which an applicant for a job can behave so as to affect or control the judgment tendencies of the interviewer.

Case

A Bad Day in Boonetown

Tom, the plant manager of the Boonetown facility, sat with his elbows on his desk, holding his head. "What a day! I've never seen it like this," he said aloud, though he was alone in his office. He was relieved that, in a few minutes, he could climb into his car and head for the golf course. He could not remember when it all began, but knew that Carl had burst into his office before he'd finished his first cup of coffee.

"Those guys in Production wouldn't give you the right time of day!" said Carl, sales manager. "All I wanted was to get this big order scheduled, and you'd think I was asking for the moon. Those production people are all the same. They hate to touch a thing once a schedule is set." Tom tried to calm him down, but Carl went on. "I even tried to talk to Cranston. I figured maybe a new guy would help me out. But I should have known better. Last week at the welcoming party for him, I sensed he wasn't any different. I guess I was right. I shouldn't have wasted my time on him."

Tom told Carl he'd look into the matter, though he knew this wasn't anything new. He also knew he needed to get Production and Sales to cooperate more. After answering a few phone calls, Tom strolled out to the Production area to see what he could find out. He didn't even have to let on that Carl had come to see him. They were hot under the collar in Production, too. Peter Kenilworth, production manager, and Bonnie Baines, chief scheduler, were discussing Carl's visit and turned to Tom for counsel. Bonnie began: "I'm not sure how concerned those sales people are for production schedules and costs. They all think we can stop a run and set up for a new order in five minutes. I think they're conditioned to bark three times every time a customer calls. I'll bet half of them let their kids tell them what to do!" Peter had his own ideas as well. He stood up and paced the floor, yet in a controlled voice said, "Sales needs some appreciation for the total company. I can't figure out why they constantly tie us up in knots. They make impossible promises to customers. They should know better. Where did they get their training? Don't they value what our situation is? I'm pretty sure no one in this company is forcing them to make the delivery commitments they make!"

Tom did what he could to soothe bad feelings, and promised Peter and Bonnie he'd have a meeting in a day or two to discuss these issues. He was particularly upset with Bonnie's attitude. On more than one occasion she had gotten very critical toward other people. He wondered whether she had what it took to do the job. Much of her performance was good, he admitted. She certainly put in enough hours trying to improve and enforce the production schedule.

- How many perceptual and judgmental tendencies do Tom, Carl, Peter, and Bonnie exhibit?

References

Brannigan, M. and White, J. P. 1997: So be it: Why Delta Airlines decided it was time for the CEO to take off. *Wall Street Journal*, May 30, 1, 8.

Bateman, T. S. and Organ, D. W. 1983: Job satisfaction and the good soldier: The relationship between affect and employee citizenship. *Academy of Management Journal*, 26, 587–95.

Bem, D. J. 1970: *Beliefs, Attitudes, and Human Affairs*. Belmont, CA: Brooks-Cole.

Bendick, M., Jackson, C. W., Reinoso, V. A. and Hodges, L. E. 1991: Discrimination and Latino job applicants: A controlled experiment. *Human Resource Management*, 30(4), 469–84.

Cardy, R. L. and Kehoe, J. F. 1984: Rater selective attention, ability, and appraisal effectiveness: The effect of a cognitive style on the accuracy of differentiation among ratees. *Journal of Applied Psychology*, 69, 589–94.

Coolidge, S. D. 1996: "Corporate Decency" prevails at Malden Mills. *The Christian Science Monitor*, March 28, 1.

Dearborn, D. C. and Simon, H. A. 1958: Selective perception: A note on the departmental identifications of executives. *Sociometry*, 21, 140–4.

Dumville, J. C. 1997: Business ethics: A model to position a relative business ethics decision and a model to strengthen its application. *Employee Responsibilities and Rights Journal*, 8(3), 231–43.

Feldman-Summers, S. and Kiesler, S. B. 1974: Those who are number two try harder. The effect of sex on the attribution of causality. *Journal of Personality and Social Psychology*, 30, 846–55.

Felson, R. B. 1981: Ambiguity and bias in the self-concept. *Social Psychology Quarterly*, 44, 64–9.

Fernandez, P. 1991: *Managing a Diverse Work Force*. Lexington, Mass: Lexington Books.

Festinger, L. 1957: *A Theory of Cognitive Dissonance*. Evanston, IL: Row, Peterson.

Fishbein, M. and Ajzen, I. 1975: *Belief, Attitude, Intention and Behavior: An Introduction to Theory and Research*. Reading, MA: Addison-Wesley.

Fisher, A. 1999: Overseas, U.S. business women may have the edge, *Fortune*, 138(6), September, 304.

George, J. and Jones, G. R. 1996: The experience of work and turnover intentions: Interactive effects of value attainment, job satisfaction and positive mood. *Journal of Applied Psychology*. June 1996, 81(3), 318–26.

Gregory, R. 1977: *Eye and Brain: The Psychology of Seeing*, 3rd edn. London: Weidenfeld & Nicholson.

Iaffaldano, M. T. and Muchinsky, P. M. 1985: Job satisfaction and job performance: A meta-analysis. *Psychological Bulletin*, 97, 251–73.

Jones, E. E. and Harris, V. A. 1967: The attribution of attitudes. *Journal of Experimental and Social Psychology*, 3, 2–24.

Judge, T. A., Boudreau, J. W. and Bretz, R. D. 1994: Job and life attitudes of executives. *Journal of Applied Psychology*, 79(5), October, 767–82.

Katz, D. 1960: The functional approach to the study of attitude change. *Public Opinion Quarterly*, 24, 107–8.

Kelly, H. H. 1973: The process of causal attribution. *American Psychologist*, 28, 107–28.

Knowlton, W. A., Jr and Mitchell, T. R. 1980: Effects of causal attributions on a supervisor's evaluation of subordinate performance. *Journal of Applied Psychology*, 65, 459–66.

Kulik, C. T. and Ambrose, M. L. 1993: Category based and feature based processes in performance appraisal: Integrating visual and computerized sources of performance data. *Journal of Applied Psychology*, 78(5), October, 821–30.

Loftus, E. F. 1984: Eyewitnesses: Essential but unreliable. *Psychology Today*, February, 22–6.

Maier, N. R. F. 1973: *Psychology in Industrial Organizations*, 4th edn. Boston: Houghton Mifflin.

Martocchio, J. J. and Whitener, E. M. 1992: Fairness in personnel selection: A meta-analysis and policy implications. *Human Relations*, 45(5), 489–97.

Myers, D. G. 1983: *Social Psychology*. New York: McGraw-Hill.

Oskamp, S. 1977: *Attitudes and Opinions*. Englewood Cliffs, NJ: Prentice-Hall.

Parsons, C. K. and Liden, R. C. 1984: Interviewer perceptions of applicant qualifications: A multivariate study of demographic characteristics and nonverbal cues. *Journal of Applied Psychology*, 69, 557–68.

Perlman, D. and Cozby, P. C. 1983: *Social Psychology*. New York: Holt, Rinehart and Winston.

Ross, L. D. 1977: The intuitive psychologist and his shortcomings: Distortions in the attribution process. In L. Berkowitz (ed.) *Advances in Experimental Social Psychology*, 10th edn, New York: Academic Press.

Staw, B. M. 1976: Knee-deep in the big muddy: A study of escalating commitment to a chosen course of action. *Organizational Behavior and Human Performance*, 16, 27–44.

Staw, B. M. and Ross, J. 1987a: Knowing when to pull the plug. *Harvard Business Review*, (March–April), 68–74.

Staw, B. M. and Ross, J. 1987b: Behavior in escalation situations: Antecedents, prototypes, and solutions. In L. L. Cummings and B. M. Staw (eds) *Research in Organizational Behavior*, vol. 9, Greenwich, CT: JAI Press.

Time 1997: Good old factory values. *Time*, September 29, 101.

Vroom, V. H. 1964: *Work and Motivation.* New York: Wiley, 8–28.

Walsh, J. 1988: Selectivity and selective perception: An investigation of managers' belief structures and information processing. *Academy of Management Journal*, 31(4), 876–96.

Zajonc, R. B. 1968: Attitudinal effects of mere exposure. *Journal of Personality and Social Psychology Monograph Supplement*, 9, 1–27.

Zuckerman, M. 1979: Attribution of success and failure revisited, or the motivational bias is alive and well in attribution theory. *Journal of Personality*, 47, 247–87.

chapter 4

Organizational Accommodation: Careers, Socialization and Commitment

CAREERS AND CAREER PATHS
ORGANIZATIONAL SOCIALIZATION
ORGANIZATIONAL COMMITMENT
DIVERSITY AND WORK IN ORGANIZATIONS

Preparing for Class

Choose and interview someone you know that has had a career that you view as successful. Perhaps you could interview someone who is in a profession that you are interested in pursuing. Interview that person about their background and the jobs they have had that led up to their current position. Consider these questions:

Have they always worked in the same profession?

Do they view their career path as traditional for individuals in their profession?

What unusual steps did they take in their career?

Consider the career paths discussed in this chapter. Which path is most descriptive of the career of the person you interviewed? Be prepared to discuss your conclusions.

When Jennifer Thomas was considering her career opportunities in her last semester of program in accounting, she narrowed it down to two alternatives. One was the large, national prestigious CPA firm, Smith, Finch, and Krupinski, located in Capital City in which her uncle has been a senior partner for many years. The other alternative was her father's smaller CPA firm, also located in the state capital.

She considered all the factors that she thought were important in the choice. First, she wanted to live in Capital City because she was born there and her family was in that area. Second, after long conversations with her uncle and her father, she concluded that there would be no substantial long-term financial advantage working for either firm. Her father's income and her uncle's income were almost equal and had been throughout their careers. Third, there were some advantages to working in the large national firm, but there were other, different advantages in the small firm. For example, in large national CPA firms, there were opportunities to develop a high level of competence in a specialized area, but at the same time office politics can be very vicious. In her father's firm, the office politics were minimal, but work was more varied. Her choice came down to what kind of accounting she thought she would like to practice. In Smith, Finch, and Krupinski, Jennifer would specialize in one area of accounting. During her first two years as an associate of the firm, she would have a chance to work in different areas. However, in her third year, they would allow her to specialize in tax, an area that she especially liked in her accounting program. In her father's firm, Thomas and Associates, she would be a member of a firm with a general practice. They did some corporate work, but mostly for small local firms. They worked on virtually every kind of problem that a CPA firm might handle, and they were expected to do it well.

As she evaluated the two alternatives, she was initially inclined to go to Smith, Finch, and Krupinski, primarily because she felt it would not be a good idea for her to go to work in Dad's firm, as she called it. However, her father planned to retire in six years, so Jennifer would be on her own. It would be Thomas and Associates, but the "Thomas" would be Jennifer, not her father. After long discussions around the dinner tables of her uncle and her father, she decided to go with Smith, Finch, and Krupinski. Her reasoning was that she would gain wonderful experience and make good connections. If she later wanted to move to Thomas and Associates, it would not be difficult.

She decided on the Smith group and began working there four years ago. She was happy with her choice and they were happy with her work. During that period, she met C. J. Snow, a part-time student-intern. They eventually married and began a family. Jennifer was happy that they were to have a child, but now she was career-conflicted again. C. J. had finished school and he too was working at a major CPA firm, earning enough income to support a family. However, what about her career? What should she do? What could she do? What was the right thing to do? Was there a right thing to do?

During her pregnancy, Jennifer spoke often with the senior partners about her options. They had given her several. After a period of time to recover from the birth of her child, she could come back full-time, an outcome that they preferred because she was a valued member of the firm. Alternatively, they could arrange a reduced schedule for her that would allow her to stay home with the child. If later she decided she wanted to return full-time, that was possible. Work alternatives became even more complicated when her father made a similar proposal. "Have the baby, stay home for a while, then decide what sort of work schedule you want," he told her. "Come to work with me when you are ready and I'll simply retire a few years later." There was another alternative that no one spoke about very much but which was on Jennifer's mind: the possibility of not returning to work at all, but staying home and caring for her family.

In this chapter, we address some of the problems Jennifer has faced, and will face, in her choices about a career in a work organization. We focus, first, on the concept of a career. Second, we discuss some of the factors that led to her career choice, then organization socialization and commitment are discussed, and how that is affected by the person's orientation toward work. Finally, we suggest some things you can do to manage a career.

Careers

How would you judge whether Jennifer has been successful in her career to date? What about her success in the future? A career is more than just the job or sequence of jobs a person holds over a lifetime. A **career** is the individually perceived sequence of attitudes and behaviors associated with work-related experiences and activities over a person's life (Hall, 1976). The conventional standard for a successful career is to judge how high you go in the organization, how much money you earn, or the standing you attain in a profession. This is too simple a concept, however. Career success should be judged on several dimensions (Hall, 1976):

career
The individually perceived sequence of attitudes and behaviors associated with work-related experiences and activities over a person's life

- Career adaptability
- Career attitudes
- Career identity
- Career performance

Career adaptability refers to the willingness and capacity to change occupations and/or the work setting to maintain a standard of career progress. It is important if you aspire to career advancement. You must be able to handle different jobs and to make frequent moves. It is especially critical today because people change jobs more often than in the past. For example, in 1981, the average job tenure in US firms was twelve years but, by the end of 1992, it was under seven years and is still decreasing slightly (Cascio, 1993).

career adaptability
The individual's willingness and capacity to make changes in the occupation and/or the work setting so as to maintain his or her own standards of career progress

Another need for career adaptability is corporate downsizing, which affects workers at all levels. For example, in the USA between 1993 and 1996, there were more than 500,000 jobs and about 140,000 workers that were affected by layoffs. These cuts – across a range of industries and firms, such as Apple (in computers), ABC (in broadcasting), Signet Banks (in banking), Levi Strauss (the jean manufacturer) and Marzotto (an Italian fashion house) – have made very significant reductions in the numbers of managerial, technical, and the lower-level workers.

career attitudes
Attitudes about the work itself, where one works, the level of achievement, and the relationship between work and other parts of a person's life

Career attitudes are your attitudes about the work itself, where you work, your level of achievement, and the relationship between work and other parts of your life. Career attitudes begin to be formed early in life, before you have a job, and they continue to be shaped by your work experiences.

career identity
That particular facet of a person's identity related to occupational activities

The **career identity** is that particular facet of your identity related to occupational and organizational activities. Individual identity is the unique way that a person believes he or she fits into the world. One way to think of it is that you have several subidentities that constituted your total identity. These subidentities center around family, social relationships, and other parts of a person's life. An example is shown in figure 4.1 (Hall, 1976). A woman like Jennifer Thomas, the CPA at the beginning of this chapter, who is married, with children and a career has subidentities that overlap and, taken together, represent the way she views herself. At any one time, one of these subidentities may be more important than others, but the importance can change over time. For example, in early career stages, the work identity may be very important to Jennifer but, later, her emphasis may shift to the family. Also, the importance of subidentities of different persons in the same career stage may not be the same. One person may identify more strongly with family and children; another may have greater identification with work.

objective career success
The evaluation of career success based on measurable factors such as increases in pay and staus at work

Career performance can be judged by both the level of **objective career success** and the level of **psychological success**. Your pay, a good reputation or reaching a high office in an organization, usually reflects objective career success. For example, if you earn $75,000 each year, it is thought that you are more successful than someone who earns $50,000; if you are the company president you are "objectively" more successful than a vice president. Objective career success may also be measured by the reputation you have with colleagues. To some, to be recognized as a "leader" in a field may be a more important indicator of career success than money.

Attaining objective career success usually depends on how well you perform your job and whether that sort of performance is valued by others in the firm.

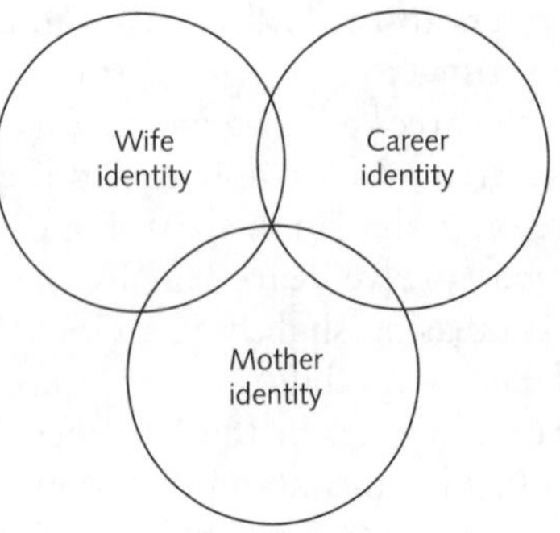

Fig 4.1: Different subidentities

While it is generally true that the best performers are the most successful, this is by no means always the case. Sometimes two people may be equally capable, but their careers might progress at different rates because they work for different firms or in different industries. For example, there are greater advancement opportunities in the computer industry than in, say, the steel industry. Other times, a very good performer may be passed over for another who is not quite so effective. The reason is that a person's attitudes, values, and beliefs enter into advancement decisions, so if yours are consistent with those of the individual or group making the promotion decision, you have a better chance of advancing than if they are not. We call this the **Good Enough Theory of Promotion.**

Good Enough Theory of Promotion
Based on the assumption that a person's attitudes, values, and beliefs enter into advancement decisions, and that if those beliefs are consistent with the individual or group making promotion decisions, that person has a better chance of advancement than if they were not

According to the Good Enough Theory, it is not necessary to be the best candidate of those under consideration for promotion. It is only necessary to be judged to have adequate competence – in other words, to be "good enough" – to do the job. To show this theory, in figure 4.2, we have divided performance, both task and contextual, into two categories, "not good enough to be promoted" and "good enough." To have any chance of being promoted, you must be considered to be at least "good enough." The other axis indicates whether you are judged to have attitudes and values that are "organizationally appropriate" or "not organizationally appropriate." If you fall into the "yes–yes" cell, you are much more likely to be promoted than candidates in other cells. For most promotion decisions, there are usually enough people in the "yes–yes" category so that anyone who falls into the "yes-ability/no-attitude" cell is usually passed over.

Psychological success is the second measure of career performance. It is achieved when your self-esteem, the value you place on yourself, increases (Hall, 1976). Of course, psychological success and objective success may be related. It may increase as you advance in pay and status at work or decrease with job disappointment and failure. However, self-esteem may also increase as you begin to

psychological success
A measure of career performance that is achieved when self-esteem increases

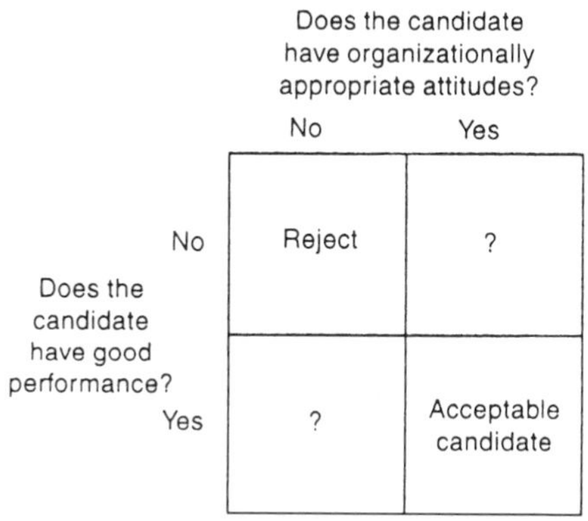

Does the candidate have good performance? \ Does the candidate have organizationally appropriate attitudes?	No	Yes
No	Reject	?
Yes	?	Acceptable candidate

Fig 4.2: The good enough theory of promotion: Performance and attitudinal requirements for advancement

sense personal worth in other ways, say through family involvement or by developing confidence and competence in a particular field. Objective career success may then be secondary in your life. This happens sometimes after a person has achieved some degree of economic security, enough to be certain that personal and family commitments can be met. Becoming psychologically successful explains why some people who had been advancing rapidly but then slowed down can be quite happy with their life.

CAREER PATHS

People move through a career along different paths. For many years, it was thought that the normal career path was to take a position with a firm and work your way through a series of jobs towards the top, leaving it when you retired. Alternatively, you entered an occupation or a profession, such as medicine or law, and did that for the rest of your working life. Today, while these traditional patterns exist, there appear to be other career paths that you might follow during a working life (Brousseau et al., 1996). We look at four such career paths:

1 The linear career path
2 The expert career path
3 The spiral career path
4 The transitory career path

linear career path Associated with long-term work in a large, bureaucratic organization with a tall pyramid structure where advancement involves a series of upward moves in the organization until you reach your career limit

expert career path A career path built on personal competencies or the development of a profession in which the person invests heavily in acquiring a particular skill and then spends most of his or her working time practicing that skill

The **linear career path** is the stereotypical structure associated with long-term work in a large, bureaucratic organization with a tall pyramidal structure. It involves a series of moves *upward* in the organization until you reach your career limit. You might work in several different functional areas of the firm – such as marketing, finance, and production – as you move up the ladder. In organizations with these paths, the persons who follow them tend to be highly oriented toward success defined in organizational terms and they exhibit leadership skills. They are very likely to have the organizationalist personality orientation and motivational pattern described on pages 44–6 in chapter 2 (Brousseau et al., 1996).

On the **expert career path** are those who build a career on the basis of personal competence, or the development of a profession. They invest heavily, often both personally and financially, in acquiring a particular skill and then spend the major portion of their working life practicing that skill. They are likely to have the professional personality orientation that we described in chapter 2; see page 45. Examples of expert career paths are law, medicine, teaching, acting, plumbing, bricklaying, and other craft areas.

Expert career paths are found in organizations that tend to be relatively flat, have departments in which there is a functional emphasis, emphasize quality and reliability, and have reward systems that have a strong recognition component. The amount of work is usually highly variable and there is usually the need for groups of experts to work together on larger projects.

Focus on Careers: The Expert Career Path

Georgia Stokes had become very successful at US West where she attained the position of vice president associate general counsel; she was in line for the top legal job of chief counsel. The fact was, however, that she was not happy with that position and very ambivalent about moving up in the company. In 1990, she decided to try another job in US West, taking the position of general counsel of the company's marketing resource group. She liked the job better but it was a step down in her career. When others let her know that they thought she had made a mistake, she began to have doubts. Then her marriage began to fall apart and, by the end of 1992, she decided to retire.

She moved to the Sonoma County wine country in California after visiting friends there and finding the area to be charming, beautiful and climate-conducive to the kind of life she thought she wanted. She settled there.

It was not long before she became uneasy away from work. She read, gardened, and visited with friends but that was not enough. In her mid fifties, she began to think about returning to work again. A lawyer, she found a part-time position with a social service agency in the area, but that was not enough either. She heard that Coca-Cola was looking for a general counsel, the position that she might have had at US West and was interested in it. With her qualifications, she was a strong candidate. In fact, she was so strong that she was offered the job.

Source: Morris (1998)

Those on the **spiral career path** make periodic moves from one occupation to another. People who follow this career path tend to have high personal growth motives and are relatively creative. Usually these changes come after you have developed competence in the occupation you are working in and you think it is time to change what you do. The ideal spiral career path is to move from one occupation (say human resource management) to an area related to it (for example, counseling psychology) (Brousseau et al., 1996). This permits you to use some of the basic knowledge that you developed in your past work and to transfer it to the new occupation.

spiral career path
A career path in which one makes periodic moves from one occupation to another

This differs in an important way from the linear career path. In linear careers, you might move from one type of work to another, just as in the spiral career. The major difference is that focus and the movement in the linear career path are upward, while the mobility pattern in the spiral path is more lateral.

People who take the **transitory career path** cannot seem to, and perhaps do not want to, settle down. The pattern is one of consistent inconsistency in their work (Brousseau et al., 1996). One type of work characterized by this career path is that of a general consultant who can take on a wide range of tasks in different firms for different periods of time. What marks them particularly is their capacity to do many different things reasonably well. They value independence and variety, and they work best in relatively loose and unstructured organizations that tolerate the type of freedom that they demand in their work.

transitory career path
A career path in which people seem to not be able to settle down

Organizational Socialization: Learning How to Accommodate to Work

In chapter 2, you read about how the socialization process affected the development of personality and how it was related to learning about work and careers long before you ever take a job. For example, what happened to Jennifer is illustrated in figure 4.3. She learned a lot about what it meant to be an accountant during her early socialization experiences, being exposed to her father and uncle, both accountants. Her work orientations and values were further shaped during a stage of preliminary work socialization, while she was studying accounting in the university and developing the skills necessary to perform as an accountant. She took the results of this with her when she began her job with the Smith group. There, she learned how to accommodate and what emerged was the type of commitment that she had toward the firm.

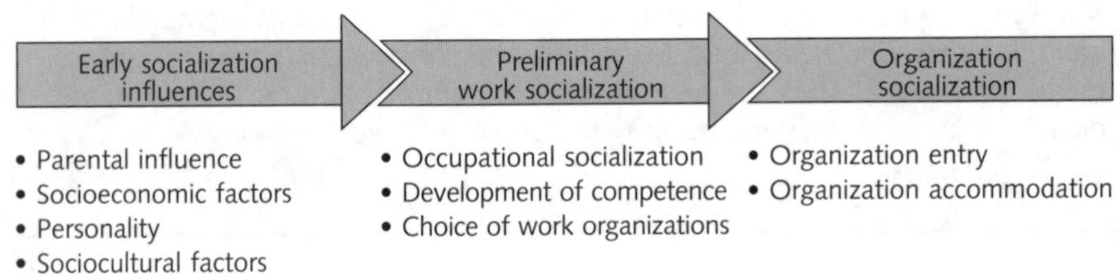

Fig 4.3: Socialization and work

EARLY SOCIALIZATION EXPERIENCES

In your very early years, you begin learning how to respond to authority and authority figures, such as parents and teachers. These authority figures have power, can give rewards or withhold them, and can administer punishment or refrain from its use. Responses to parents learned at home become further developed and reinforced in churches, schools, and other organizations. These experiences set the stage for the development of work values, all affected by parental influence, socioeconomic background, sociocultural factors and personality.

career exploration stage
The period, typically before the twenties in which an individual acquires work values

This period, called the **career exploration stage**, is from birth into the early twenties. During this time, you begin to acquire work values through your socialization experiences that affect later feelings about work (Pulakos and Schmitt, 1983; Staw et al., 1986). Toward the end of this period, you begin to separate from family and early friends, and take steps toward independence and into the adult world. Preliminary organizational and career choices are made, and usually some commitment to training of some kind. Those who attend college pick a major, some join the military, others go into vocational training, or take entry-level work positions (Levinson et al., 1978).

Parental influence One way that parental influence has an effect on career choice is whether the child rearing practices of the parents lead to an orientation "toward people" or "not toward people" (Roe, 1957; Roe and Seigelman, 1964). A person who has developed an orientation toward people is likely to have a career in the service industry, business, or in the arts and entertainment; they are likely to have come from a home that generated a loving, overprotective environment (Osipow, 1973). Those whose early home atmosphere was one in which there was avoidance by the parents and, perhaps, rejection are likely to be oriented "not toward others," and seek careers in science, technology, or in some form of work in the outdoors.

Socioeconomic factors Your social class (upper, middle, or lower), family income, occupational status, and education levels also affect work orientations. First, parents from higher social classes tend to earn more and have better connections that they can use to help their children (Tinto, 1984). Second, children from higher social classes usually aspire to careers in business or in the professions, while children from lower-class families tend to believe that they will work in service trades. Third, children initially aspire to a career similar to that of the father and other family members (mothers and grandparents) and are likely to choose one that resembles it (Osipow, 1973; Beck, 1983). This, of course, is determined to some extent by the educational opportunities available, which are most often dependent on family income.

Higher social classes also pass different work values on to their children than those in lower classes. For example, fathers from the upper classes place a higher value on self-direction and less value on conformity, while the opposite is true for fathers from the lower classes (Kohn and Schooler, 1969). One way that this is reflected is in the ways that young managers from higher socioeconomic status react to career mentoring at work. Those from higher socioeconomic backgrounds who had good career mentoring had higher promotion rates and pay than those from lower socioeconomic backgrounds who had similarly good mentoring (Whitely et al., 1991). More than likely, they are able to capitalize at work on what they learned in early years from their family experience.

Personality Career choices are also an extension of personality because most of us try to implement our broad personal behavior styles in the context of work (Super, 1957; Osipow, 1973). This means that, to some degree, occupational choice is the result of a long developmental process during which you are learning about yourself and developing a self-concept (Super, 1957). In your early years (before the age of 25), you are attempting to find out what kind of human being you are, and to discover your strengths and weaknesses. The self-concept that you form then becomes an important determinant of your occupational choice.

PRELIMINARY WORK SOCIALIZATION

You begin to develop more specific orientations toward a certain career – or orientations relevant to a particular type of organization – during **preliminary work socialization** *before* beginning a career in a work organization. This occurs in three ways:

1 You begin to develop some specific competence.
2 You experience some degree of occupational socialization.
3 You make choices about your first place of work.

The early phase of this aspect of work socialization, from age 17 to about 33, is called the **career novice stage** (Hall, 1976; Levinson et al., 1978). During this period, the center of your life will probably shift from your family to your own world. You become immersed in a career and in an organization, but, as an apprentice, a novice, a beginner, learning the relevant skills, attitudes, and culture of a specific organization and a specific job.

Occupational competence is developed as you make early choices about what knowledge and skills to acquire. Each of us does some things better than others and is encouraged in selected directions. The young person who thinks about a career in business may go to college and major in accounting, finance, or economics. Another who has had early success in mathematics may choose an engineering program or computer science. Specialized training has two important effects.

1 You learn certain things (say, accounting) and not learn others (such as engineering). This limits your initial career opportunities to the chosen field.
2 You begin to discover how someone in your chosen area attacks problems and thinks. If you are studying accounting, you start learning to act like an accountant before ever working as one, and you begin to form relatively specific expectations about the job itself and the accounting firm in your accounting classes, usually long before spending the first day on the job.

Becoming competent in an occupation and learning the ropes takes several years (Levinson et al., 1978). For instance, even great artists and chess players do not achieve prominence until they have worked at their craft for at least ten years (Simon, 1982). You can expect the same thing for your work career. By the end of this stage, however, if you have worked at it, you can achieve a level of competence so that you can be a full contributor to an organization.

For some careers, **occupational socialization** begins in professional school, where the would-be professional is first exposed to the perspectives, values, and ways of thinking characteristic to the chosen field. Students in clinical psychology or architecture, for example, not only learn technical aspects of their field but also learn how to act like psychologists and architects, as they work on projects or as psychology or architectural interns.

preliminary work socialization
A period prior to joining an organization or beginning a career during which a person begins to develop more specific orientations related to a certain career or to a particular type of organization

career novice stage
An early phase of work socialization during which the employee begins to develop some specific competence, experiences some degree of occupational socialization, and makes choices about their first place of work

occupational competence
The job related skills, activites, and attitudes that are necessary to perform work tasks in a particular field or occupation

occupational socialization
The cultural learning process by which an individual learns the norms, values, and behaviors required in a particular work area or occupation

A QUESTION OF ETHICS: SOME CAREERS HAVE TOUGHER PROBLEMS THAN OTHERS

Ethics issues arise in any career. Executives are often faced with dilemmas about pricing, bribery, and other decisions that they must make. In some careers, particularly in medicine, the ethical questions often revolve around life itself. Nurses, for example, may have to confront situations in which their beliefs about the sanctity of life conflict with the desire of patients.

- What does a nurse do when a patient wishes to forego life-sustaining treatments such as CPR, forced nutrition, or hydration when the patient expresses the wish to not receive them?
- What happens when a patient requests an abortion and the nurse's own belief is in the right to life?
- How can the nurse, or the physician for that matter, make an ethical choice when the patient desires to be assisted in suicide?

None of these are easy issues.

Occupational socialization can be a very controlled process, such as what happens in medical schools, seminaries, convents, and military academies. If you were to choose these careers, you would find yourself, in the early years, separated from other parts of society and becoming submerged in the organization culture as well as learning the skills of the profession. Professional values are fostered by participation in student groups, by taking courses, and through interaction with teachers. After successfully completing this training, the person is admitted to the field and is commissioned, ordained, or passes through some other acceptance ritual. By this time, important organizational and occupational values have become deeply embedded.

On the other hand, most preliminary work socialization is less formal, as your experience in secondary schools, universities, and colleges and sometimes what you learn in a part-time job during your early years. These less formal and less controlled forms of occupational socialization do not have as strong effects, but they still shape later work experiences (Chatman, 1991).

When choosing where to work, people tend to pursue an "ideal job" (Soelberg, 1966) that is a function of their self-perception (Korman, 1970), personality (Roe and Seigelman, 1964), beliefs about being successful (Blau et al., 1956), and the information one has about the company (Gatewood et al., 1993). For example, the image that most college students have of a firm comes from the general reputation of the company and the information they read in recruitment brochures (Gatewood et al., 1993). The more information and the more frequent their exposure to it, the more positive the corporate image that they have. In one study of how college students chose which job to take after graduation, it was discovered that they considered job alternatives in parallel, rather than sequentially (Soelberg, 1966). They would follow some leads but not others and job alternatives were not compared on similar criteria; each alternative was considered against different standards. A "favorite" job was usually selected early and was the one that was closest to the person's job goals. The ranking of the job alternatives was done *after* the "favorite" job was chosen. The purpose of the ranking was to confirm the person's "favorite." Job search continued even after a person had a number of acceptable jobs. This was a lengthy process during which the person resolved the uncertainties and problems with the "favorite" job and, at the same time, arrived at a way to justify the "favorite" choice as rational. If they received information that was inconsistent with their perception of the "favorite" job, it was distorted to make the "favorite" appear a much better choice.

People who have skills that are in demand may have several job alternatives and can make choices about where they are going to work. Chance, luck, and economic factors play an important role in taking jobs at all occupational levels, but they may be especially important at lower ones. People with limited skills and few work alternatives may have little choice; they may have to take a job where one is available, just to earn a living.

organizational socialization
A learning process through which you learn to adapt to the organization

norms of performance
Norms that specify the specific task performance components that are to be done and the minimal acceptable levels of performance

norms of involvement
The expectations that an organization has about the contextual performance and the acceptable ways for its members to show commitment and loyalty

psychological contract
The mutual expectations between an individual and an organization

ORGANIZATIONAL SOCIALIZATION

After you have joined a work organization, **organizational socialization** begins: adapting to the unique culture of the organization. There are three important things to learn during this stage.

1 How the competence you have already developed and bring to the organization will be used by it
2 The organization's **norms of performance**
3 The organization's **norms of involvement**

Some norms of involvement are more important than others. The most important are called *pivotal norms*, those that must be accepted by everyone in the organization. Failure to comply with pivotal norms results in pressures to leave from others in the organization (Schein, 1970). For example, an important and large retailing organization has a "customer is right" norm for returning purchases. If a salesperson questions and angers a customer, he or she is very likely to be fired.

Peripheral norms are less important. They are desired, but it is not essential that the person accept them. An example of a peripheral norm is the recent custom of "dress down Friday," a day on which employees in professional offices may, if they wish, wear more casual clothes instead of coats and ties for the men, or skirts and jackets for the women.

These norms and expectations are reflected specifically in the **psychological contract**, the mutual expectations between an organization and its members. "These expectations not only cover how much work is to be performed for how much pay but also involve the whole pattern of rights, privileges, and obligation between the worker and organization" (Schein, 1970). The psychological contract is informally and continuously negotiated throughout the organization socialization process and during your career in the organization. It is an important and useful concept that you will see later in chapter 5 (page 146) as well as in chapter 14 (page 422).

Diversity Issues: The Psychological Contract and Women in Procter and Gamble

The case of how Procter and Gamble (P&G) changed its organizational culture to accommodate women managers is a good example of how learning the organizational norms of performance and norms of involvement do not necessarily lead to better performance. In the early 1990s, women recruited for managerial positions in P&G, like men, were led to believe that P&G rewarded high performers with promotion and advancement, not an uncommon thing to promise in the recruiting process. However, until recently, there were not many women in high-level positions and women were actually leaving the company at a very high rate.

P&G discovered, in an analysis of managerial turnover, that two of every three good managers who quit were women. Analyzing the exit interviews, the most frequent reason that the women gave was that they wanted to spend more time with their families. Yet, nothing was further from the truth. P&G dug further into the matter, finding and interviewing some of the women who had left.

They found that many of these women were in high-level, high-pressure management jobs, often more demanding and more stressful than the work at P&G. What they also discovered was that these women left because they perceived the norms and practices of P&G were not consistent with a "family friendly" work environment. For example, when women said they wanted to spend more time with their family, the P&G response was to suggest that they take a part-time position. Because this would remove them from the promotion stream, many of the women wanted more flexible working schedules that would protect their advancement opportunities. The norm of performance, then, was not just that high performance leads to advancement (what they thought when they took the job), but that also that performance had to be executed during the conventionally accepted working hour. What is strange about this is that long hours are expected but does it really make a difference *when* the work is done, so long as you can be there when you must meet with others?

When these problems were discovered, P&G undertook a serious effort to change things, and created a number of task forces to attack them. One conclusion was that "there was a gender aspect to [P&G's] culture that was not intentional, but very real." This strong force that determined the norms in P&G, needed changing if the turnover of women was to be reduced.

P&G did several things to work on these issues. One was to create a mentoring program in which women worked with male managers to help them to understand the power of the culture and what could be done to change it. Another solution was to create more family-friendly benefits, allowing all employees more choice in how they took the benefits. Because P&G is so good at marketing, it also undertook to sell the changes internally. One of these internal marketing strategies was to produce a video in which senior female executives in P&G talked about their jobs and their families, and how they had tried to integrate these two facets of life.

These efforts were successful in changing the expectations of both P&G and female employees. After five years of effort, the turnover rate of women managers is the same as for male managers, women form more than 30 percent of the general managers, and, recently, a woman was appointed to the Executive Committee, the first in P&G's history.

Source: Parker-Pope (1998)

ORGANIZATIONAL ENTRY The first significant exposure to the organization's expectations in the psychological contract comes during the phase of organizational entry, the time after you join the organization and experience it for the first time as one of its members. It is a period when you aware of what differences exist, if any, between your personal values and the requirements of the organization. This can be a disrupting experience as you face changes, contrasts and a few surprises, and have to make some sense of all this (Louis, 1980).

person–organization fit The degree of congruence between organizational values and your own individual values

Organization entry is affected by a number of factors. One is the **person–organization fit**, the congruence between patterns of organizational values and your own individual values. When this fit is good, you are likely to be more satisfied and have stronger intentions to stay in the firm (Chatman, 1991).

A second factor is the expectations that you bring to the job. Before starting the job, most people have positive but often inaccurate expectations about the company, working conditions, co-workers and opportunities for advancement. When these expectations are not met, the results are lower job satisfaction, lower organization commitment, higher intentions to leave, lower organization tenure, and lower performance (Robinson, 1996; Wanous et al., 1992).

The form of the organization socialization process itself is a third factor. For example, persons may be brought in with a group and experience group socialization, while in other instances they come in singly, one at a time (Van Maanen, 1978). Group socialization is often used when large numbers of recruits are brought into an organization at one time. Indeed, many firms have extensive management training programs to socialize college graduates who all join the firm following spring graduation. One study which examined these different organization socialization practices found that those who entered in the formal group process were more satisfied with their job and had less conflict between their job and family roles as compared to those who were brought in individually (Zahrly and Tosi, 1989).

ORGANIZATIONAL COMMITMENT AND ACCOMMODATION

After being in an organization for while, you eventually reach some level of psychological and behavioral commitment and accommodation to it. This means two things:

1 You have demonstrated at least enough competence so that the organization decides to retain you.
2 You have resolved conflicts between your work and outside interests (Feldman and Arnold, 1983).

career establishment stage A period, typically from the early thirties to the mid-forties, during which a person becomes established in a career

All this is not to say that you will have high job satisfaction and be highly committed to the organization itself. It only means that equilibrium has been achieved between the way that you relate to the firm and the way that it relates with you.

The type and the level of organization commitment and accommodation tends to become relatively stable during the **career establishment stage** (Levinson et al., 1978). This is a period from the early thirties to the mid-forties, during which a person becomes established in a career. In the early part of the establishment stage, you will have "junior" status at work, even though you have developed organizationally relevant skills. A senior person, a mentor, may be very helpful in showing you how to operate effectively in the organization during this period. Managers who have had a career mentor tend to have more rapid promotion and are more satisfied with their pay than those who did not (Dreher and Ash, 1990; Whitely et al., 1991).

People move at different speeds during the establishment stage. Some may begin to slow down in their rate of advancement. Others may continue to advance more rapidly. They will begin to outpace their peers and start to encroach into the areas of more senior personnel. They may be seen by some as being too "aggressive." Toward the end of this stage, the career is fairly well established. The person becomes a senior member of the organization and is able to "speak more strongly with [your] own voice, and to have a greater measure of authority" (Levinson et al., 1978).

Accommodating to an organization is usually expressed in two ways.

1 One is how willing you are to meet the norms of task performance requirements, and the norms that apply to contextual performance requirements. This is a very basic and key aspect because it means that you can perform your job at least well enough that the organization sees your performance contribution as good enough (remember the Good Enough Theory of Promotion!).
2 The second aspect of accommodation is that you achieve some level of organizational commitment. **Organizational commitment** is the degree to which you identify with the organization, relative to other factors that affect you at work, such as the work itself or factors outside the organization that compete with it for your commitment and identification.

organizational commitment
The degree to which a person identifies with or feels connected to the organization

We take a **multi-focal view of organizational commitment.** This means that there are at least three facets that pull on you from the work perspective and that you will have some level of identification, or orientation, toward each. As we have pointed out earlier, this results from your socialization experiences both before and after you enter a work organization. These three facets of commitment can be easily understood if you refer to the three organizational personality orientations that we described on page 44 in chapter 2: the organizationalist, the professional, and the indifferent:

multi-focal view of organizational commitment
The view that there are several facets of work and the different levels of identification, or orientation, toward each

- *Organizationalists* have strong identification with and commitment to the place of work, the organization itself. They are easy to manage and direct because they respect organizational authority and the chain of command.
- *Professionals* are job centered, not organizational centered. Their socialization experiences have taught them that successful performance of the job, not compliance with authority, is more reinforcing to them.
- The *indifferent orientation* is a perspective in which neither the organization nor the work itself is the most critical element in the person's life. The

indifferent works for pay. They tend to be more alienated toward work and the organization, and will withdraw psychologically from work and organizations when possible.

It is useful to think of these three orientations as a commitment profile. It is unlikely that a person would be oriented toward only one of the foci and not toward any of the others (Tosi, 1992). Instead, it is probably safer to make these three points:

1 At any one time, you may have a dominant focus of commitment. For example, figure 4.4 illustrates a person with a strong organizational commitment, but with weak professional and indifferent foci. Figure 4.5, on the other hand, shows a person with a strong indifferent orientation, with moderate levels of organizational and work commitment.

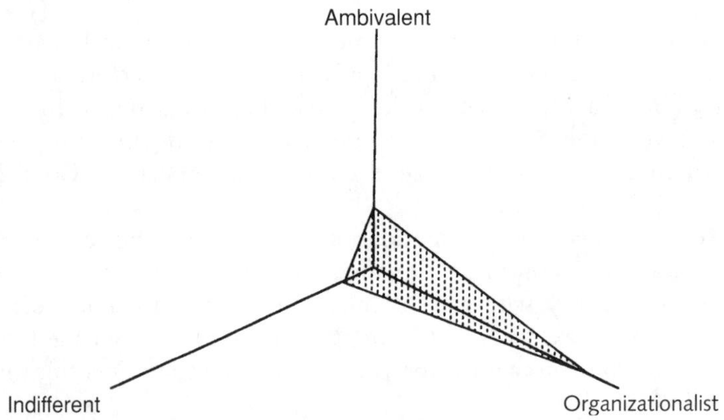

Fig 4.4: A strong organizationalist orientation

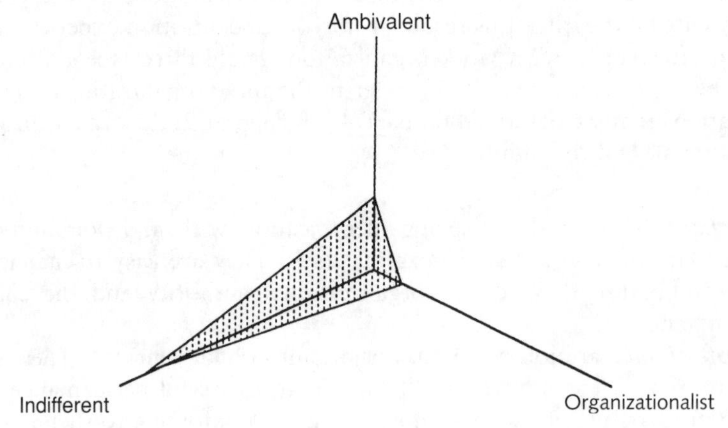

Fig 4.5: A strong indifferent orientation

2 The dominant orientation at the time of job choice will affect the kind of position you seek. If you have a strong organization focus, you are likely to seek a position in an organization that offers you opportunity for career advancement *within* the firm. You will prefer, but not necessarily be able to adhere to, the linear career path discussed on page 94. If you have a strong professional orientation, you will be looking for work that will give you plenty of freedom to work in your chosen work area.

3 The focus of commitment may change over time. There are many circumstances that may lead you to change. For example, if you start with a strong organizational focus but find that you are passed over several times for promotion, that orientation may diminish and an indifferent orientation might become stronger as your positive reinforcement from the organization is reduced. Similarly, a senior executive with the organizational orientation might suffer a serious medical problem, like a heart attack, and become indifferent as he or she begins to question what is important in life.

There are different motivations for sustaining the identification you have with an organization, regardless of your organizational personality. Those who have studied organizational commitment have identified three different reasons for, or bases of commitment (Dunham et al., 1994):

1 Continuance commitment
2 Affective commitment
3 Normative commitment

With **continuance commitment**, you stay with an organization because you feel you cannot afford to leave. You might not be able to find a higher paying job; you might believe that to leave you will be working in a company with lower status or reputation; or you might not want to lose the long-term investment that you have made that will be paid off in terms of a good set of pension benefits.

continuance commitment An organizational commitment to stay with an organization because one cannot afford to leave

With **affective commitment**, you identify strongly with the organization because it stands for what you stand for; you believe strongly in its goals and objectives. For example, many whose work careers are with political parties make that choice because of their own political beliefs and those espoused by the party are the same.

affective commitment A strong identity or connection with the organization because it stands for what the person stands for

Finally, some people may have **normative commitment**, and stay with an organization because of pressures from others in their life who think they should be there. For example, you might work in the same company that your mother or father worked in for many years, simply because they made it clear to you that they believe this is the best place for you to work.

normative commitment A sense to stay with an organization because of pressures from others in their life that think they should be there

Table 4.1 shows how these different bases of commitment and the organizational personality orientations may be related. For example, you can see that a person with a professional orientation may have continuance commitment, affective commitment, or normative commitment. Obviously, when the basis of commitment is not consistent with the organizational personality orientation, you can expect some uneasiness and stress to occur.

EXERCISE

WHAT IS YOUR ORGANIZATION COMMITMENT?

Some people are highly committed to their job, others are loyal to the organization, and others are more oriented to external factors. The purpose of this exercise is twofold:

1 To illustrate the differences in the way people view their work as it relates to other parts of their life
2 To help you to think about different things you expect from your work

Listed below are a series of nine statements, each one having three possible responses.

- Indicate your reaction to a statement by choosing the response that most nearly approximates your view, and enter a 1 to the right of that response.
- Then decide which is second closest to your views on the statement and enter a 2 in the blank to the right of that response.
- Finally, fill in the remaining blank with a 3.

When you are finished, add up the figures in columns A, B, and C.

		A	B	C
1	I am most interested in . . .			
	. . . things about my company.	....		
	. . . things I usually do around the house or in the community.		....	
	. . . things about my job.			....
2	I prefer to have as friends people who . . .			
	. . . share my leisure interests.		....	
	. . . have work like mine.			....
	. . . work in the same company.	....		
3	I believe that, in general, . . .			
	. . . helping my fellow human beings is more important than anything else.		....	
	. . . my career in the company is more important than anything else.	....		
	. . . the work I do is more important than anything else.			....
4	Interruptions bother me most when I am talking to someone . . .			
	. . . about my work.			....
	. . . about the office or plant.	....		
	. . . about my family.		....	
5	In my free time at work, I would rather talk about . . .			
	. . . whatever comes up.		....	
	. . . the things I am working on.			....
	. . . other things going on in the company.	....		
6	I hope my children can . . .			
	. . . work in any occupation, but in a company like the one I am now working in.	....		
	. . . work in the same kind of occupation as mine.			....
	. . . concern themselves with work and company less than I have.		....	

7	I would like to be . . .			
	. . . a more important member of my church, lodge, club, or other nonwork organization.		....	
	. . . a more important member of my company or office.	....		
	. . . specially recognized by those who have work like mine.			....
8	It is harder for me to listen to criticism of . . .			
	. . . my work.			....
	. . . my company.	....		
	. . . my family.		....	
9	When I am worried, it is usually about . . .			
	. . . things that happen at home.		....	
	. . . what people in the company think of me.	....		
	. . . how well I am doing in my career.			....
	Total	....	....	....

Now answer these diagnostic questions.

1 What is your score for column A, B, and C?
2 What type of organization orientation does column A reflect?
3 What type of organization orientation does column B reflect?
4 What type of organization orientation does column C reflect?
5 What do you think are some implications for the kind of work preferred by one who holds a view reflected by a high score in column A? Column B? Column C?

Source: Adapted by Henry Tosi and John Jermier from a questionnaire designed by Robert Dubin, as a Central Life Interest Scale. We thank him for his tolerance about what we did to his instrument and for his permission to use it.

As you might expect, a high level of organizational commitment is something that most firms would like to see in their employees have because it reduces some managerial problems. For example, strong organizational commitment is related to lower turnover and absenteeism (Lee et al., 1996) and to the level of contextual behaviors, or organizational citizenship activities, that a person is willing to engage in at work (Organ, 1997).

Commitment, Careers and Work Force Diversity

Much of what has been written on accommodating to work organizations and careers is based on studies of white males because, during the time that the research was done, they constituted the bulk of the work force and held virtually every important management position. Now that situation has changed. Today, the work force of US companies is far more diverse, creating some serious problems that managers must face.

Table 4.1 Organizational personality orientations and different bases of commitment

	Organizationist	*Professional*	*Indifferent*
Bases of commitment			
Affective	You have been positively reinforced over your work career by pay increases and promotion for your performance and loyalty.	You are a specialist working in an organization whose major product is what you do occupationally, e.g. pharmacologist in a pharmaceutical firm.	You are not likely to have high affective commitment.
Continuance	You are well paid and in a high level position, but it unlikely that you would be able to better yourself by changing firms.	You are a research scientist in a prestigious university who would like to move to a warmer climate, but all of your opportunities are at lesser schools or places with inferior research facilities.	You have a job that permits you to spend more time at your real love (fly fishing), so even though the pay is less than you want, you will not leave.
Normative	You have a promotion opportunity to another firm located elsewhere, but do not accept it because your spouse and family are happy in your present city.	You have an opportunity to move to another position with a better research facility but do not move because it would mean leaving your project team and good colleagues.	You would not think of moving to another company because the pay is good and most of your family has worked in the same place for past 30 years.

WOMEN AND CAREERS

Since 1900, the percentage of women in the work force has increased from less than 20 percent to over 50 percent (Ross et al., 1983; Hall, 1986) and, in the year 2000, 65 percent of the entrants in the work force will be women (Powell, 1983). The important thing about this growth is that it is not only in traditionally female-dominated occupations (e.g. nursing and teaching) but also in the professions. Women are in 45 percent of managerial or administrative positions, 53 percent of the professionals (which includes scientists, engineers, lawyers, nurses, teachers, etc.) and 48 percent of all technicians (Powell, 1983).

WOMEN, PAY AND PROMOTIONS Overall, women are not promoted at the same rate as men, nor do they receive the same wages as men for similar work. These differences in career attainment and pay cannot be attributed to major differences in managerial performance between men and women. An analysis of studies that compared leader effectiveness of men and women show that, on average, women are evaluated as being as effective as men (Eagly et al., 1995), though there are some important differences. For example, men are seen as more effective when the work context and work roles tend to be defined in more "masculine" terms or the group is numerically dominated by men, as for example in military situations. Women, on the other hand, are more effective when the leadership role is more female-congenial, meaning that interpersonal skills are dominant requirements. This suggests that, overall, there are no meaningful differences in ability between men and women and that women can manage as well as men, but that there are some situations that facilitate male or female leaders in different ways (Tyler, 1965; Dobbins and Platz, 1986; Eagly et al., 1995).

While there has been both significant career and wage improvements for women in recent years, and although it is dramatically better than the past, as a group, they are still behind men in pay levels and organizational attainment (Fields and Wolff, 1991). On average for the whole working population, women earn 71 percent of what men earn. This is somewhat misleading in one sense because the large proportion of women in the work force are in much lower paying jobs than men, jobs such as secretaries and retail clerks. However, even when women work in jobs similar in level, authority, and skill requirements as men, there is still a substantial wage gap. For example, female accountants earn about $10,000 a year less than men, and male teachers average about $4,000 per year more than women teachers. In addition, while a few women such as Donna Karan (the fashion designer), Carly Fiorina (Hewlett–Packard), and Ellen Gordon (head of Tootsie Roll) have become the top executives in their companies and earn over one million dollars annually, women make up only 2 percent of the top-five earning managers of the *Fortune 500* companies (Jackson, 1996). However, there is some indication that this is improving; women still lag behind men in salary progression but, overall, they experience similar promotion rates as men (Stroh et al., 1992). Interestingly, women seem to be breaking through the "glass ceiling" more frequently in high-technology firms, advertising, media and entertainment, and publishing (Creswell, 1998).

There are several reasons for this pay discrepancy. First, women are paid less than men for jobs of similar difficulty (Kemp and Beck, 1986). This could be, in part, because of different starting salaries paid to men and women (Gerhart, 1990). In one company, there were significant pay differences between men and women when they were initially hired. Ten years later, the pay discrepancies in the study group had diminished some, but they were still relatively large and, still, attributable to the different starting pay rates. One reason for this difference was the college major of the women and the men, the men coming from more traditional fields. If this is so, then, since the number of women entering these higher paying areas is increasing, the starting pay gap should narrow in the future.

Second, there are more women, proportionately, in low-paying industries, particularly the service sector, where there are low profit margins, low job skill needs, and lower wage rates (Ward and Mueller, 1985). Even in those industries where women tend to be over represented, they are more likely than men to be in lower authority positions, and men are more likely to be higher paid when they perform in the same type of managerial jobs.

Third, in some organizations, women may be in jobs doing less complex work and/or at lower organizational levels rather than in jobs with more autonomy and that require higher skill. These jobs, in most organization, have lower pay rates (Form and McMillen, 1983).

Fourth, a portion of the discrepancy can be attributed to different rates of pay and promotion at lower and higher organizational levels. Women do well at lower levels of the organization, where their promotion rates and salary progression equals or exceeds that of men (Stewart and Gudykunst, 1982; Tsui and Gutek, 1984; Markham et al., 1985; Gerhart and Milkovich, 1987). They do not seem to be moving into higher levels in the same numbers (though they do as well proportionately) as men, where salary progression rates are much higher (Stroh et al., 1992).

One explanation of these changes in pay and promotion rates could be that many women leave the workplace to raise children during the critical establishment stage of a career, from the early thirties to the mid-forties, when persons in a career cohort begin to advance at different rates. Some begin to outpace others. Being out of the organization during this period could cause one to lose valuable experience, which extracts its price later, in the form of lower salaries relative to others in the cohort.

OCCUPATIONAL STATUS Women, even though they may be in traditionally "male" occupations such as engineering or law, do not have the same high status and prestige as men in the same occupations (Powell and Jacobs, 1984). This could be because they have yet to reach, in large numbers, higher level positions (Jacobs, 1992). When they do enter the labor force in positions with the same status as men, working women's occupational prestige does not increase as much over the career cycle as men (Marini, 1980). While these status discrepancies do not affect women's level of performance, they are related to their attitudes and perceptions. For example, men and women who work in relatively similar management jobs have similar levels of job satisfaction, but men rate themselves as better performers than the women, attributing their high performance to their ability more than women do (Deaux, 1979). Male managers also report better relationships with their supervisors than female managers with their supervisors. When there are large occupational status discrepancies between men and women, women tend to have more liberal political attitudes than when the status discrepancies are small (Auster, 1983).

WORK EXPECTATIONS Historically, women have had lower occupational aspirations than men and wanted different things from work (Fottler and Bain, 1980). Women, for example, seem to prefer more interesting work. They are more likely to prefer staff positions and positions in human resource management that tend to be lower-paying jobs than higher-paying positions such as finance and marketing. Their salary expectations are also lower (Fottler and Bain, 1980) and this creates a problem because job candidates with higher pay expectations are offered higher starting salaries than those with low pay expectations (Major and Konar, 1984).

MARRIAGE AND CAREERS Having a wife is related to higher wages for men but it seems that married women are penalized (Hill, 1979; Pfeffer and Ross, 1982; Jacobs 1992). When spouses have **dual careers**, it creates strain on both wives and husbands. Generally, dual-career couples suffer more job stress and poorer mental health than single-career couples (Srivastava and Srivastava, 1985; Sund and Ostwald, 1985), which is worse when interests of females shift from the home to work and the interests of men shift from work to home. There is greater role conflict both at work and within the family for dual-career spouses who have high job involvement and high work expectations (Higgins et al., 1992). They are also likely to experience greater strain between work and family demands. The effects of these role strains are lower quality of work life and lower quality of family life.

dual careers
A situation where both husband and wife pursue work careers

Global Focus on Dual Career Expatriates

The increasing global market gives rise to a number of difficult situations for management. Although profits can be high, the potential problems associated with international business are numerous. One such example of these problems lies in the expatriate managers. Turnover for these international managing positions has been alarmingly high in recent years.

The advantages of using expatriate managers in foreign assignments is fairly obvious; an organization will benefit by having a long-time company employee involved directly in a project located far from corporate headquarters. While the screening process for these international duties consider individual qualifications, it has been documented that a multinational corporation will typically make these assignments without considering a given manager's spouse and family. This has been a key mistake for these corporations.

The relationship between dual-career couples can certainly be strained given the mammoth lifestyle change foreign duties can involve. The spouses of the expatriate managers are left with an unpleasant decision to make: they can either give up their current career standing and follow their partner to the foreign assignment, or they can continue with their American job and attempt to preserve the marriage via a long-distance relationship. Either way, problems are bound to surface. To stay with a current job means financial and emotional stress in living across two nations. The alternative offers an end to the career to which the spouses had dedicated their life.

The costs associated with training and compensating the international manager are extremely high. In fact, in comparison to domestic duties, international managers are three times as expensive. Further, the international manager's duties, when halted suddenly due to resignation, can be very damaging to the company in terms of lost customers and increased HR duties. It is therefore in the best interest of international businesses to incorporate spouse and family into assignment decisions; the benefits of using this criteria will almost certainly pay off in the long run.

Source: Adapted from Harvey (1966)

The problems facing dual-career couples stem in part from the circumstances that all working couples face.

- Finding two desirable jobs in the same geographic region may be difficult. If the couple must work in separate and distant locations, this strains the relationship.
- The separate careers may advance at different rates. If a wife's career advancement is more rapid, this could lead to strains since it is inconsistent with the traditional model in which the male holds the primary occupation in a family (Ross et al., 1983).
- Children add complications to the lives of dual-career couples. While the number of children does not seem to be related to the job performance of either spouse, it does affect the allocation of responsibilities at home. As the number of children increased, the burden for child care fell disproportionately on the wife (Bryson et al., 1978).

RACIAL AND ETHNIC DIVERSITY

The work force in the US is far more multi-cultural than ever. For example, Digital Electronics Corporation has a plant that employs 350 workers who are from 44 different countries and speak 19 different languages (Dreyfus, 1990). US West, has a work force in which 13 percent of the managerial force are African Americans, Hispanics, Asians, or American Indians and their objective is to have a work force in each location which mirrors the racial, gender, and ethnic distribution of the regional work force (Caudron, 1992). As we noted in chapter 3 (page 81), this has been a dramatic change in the last several years. For example, the number of Hispanic Americans in the US increased by 30 percent in just seven years in the 1980s. The numbers of Asian Americans have increased as well (Fernandez, 1991).

In spite of these increasing numbers, there are still few Hispanic Americans, Asian Americans, and African Americans in management. Similar to women, they experience a "glass ceiling" which restricts their advancement (Domingues, 1992). While some very slow progress has been made in promoting women through the glass ceiling, the progress for African Americans, Hispanics, and other minorities of color is almost non-existent (Fernandez, 1991).

There is much to be done to manage diversity better, and a good place to start is to recognize the nature of the biases against women, minorities, and ethnic groups. We pointed some of these out in chapter 3 (page 81).

Summary

A career includes all the jobs that a person will hold in a lifetime, plus the training and preparation necessary to qualify for such jobs. A career is an important part of an individual's life but is by no means the only critical life component. Individuals must make adjustments among their various life roles, such as spouse, parent, and occupation.

A number of different factors contribute to career choices and the organizations in which we have a career. Child-rearing practices that affect the individual's personality and self-concept influence occupational choice. The occupation of parents and the cultural values transmitted to the child also play a part in such decisions.

Work socialization follows occupational choice. Individuals must learn about the characteristics and culture of their work organization and of their chosen occupational field. In learning about the more important, or "pivotal," norms of their organization or occupation, they may be directly taught by others, they may learn through the process of observing others, or they may learn through the process of conditioning by behaving in certain ways and having such behaviors responded to in different ways by others.

If we do not adjust well to our job or the organization in which we work, it can negatively affect an individual's performance, morale, and health as well as those of others associated with us, both at work and as family members and friends. One factor that complicates adjustment to work and organization is the changing nature and role of women in the work force. Women form an increasing part of the work force and are moving into different types of work than in the past, such as professional and managerial. However, there are still pay and opportunity discrepancies between men and women that do not seem to be related to capability. Another issue is the dual career.

All these problems must be resolved in the future. The current interest in career and organizational adjustment can provide important dividends in lessening the dysfunction that may result from poor career and organization choices.

Guide for Managers: Managing Your Career

Because of the corporate restructurings, downsizings, and the growing globalization of business, "our views of organizational life, managing as a career, hard work, rewards, and loyalty will never be the same" as they were in the 1960s and 1970s (Cascio, 1993). This means that you are well-advised to be active in self-career management. Rather than waiting for fortune, good or bad, to strike, you can work to develop the skills required for success and to create opportunities for it. There are several important things you can do to help yourself.

HAVE A CAREER GOAL

A career goal provides an anchor and some direction, yet these career goals should not be static. You should set specific goals but change them as you learn more about yourself and the work situation. For example, you might enter college with the goal of becoming a journalist but find that a marketing career is more desirable after you learn something about it.

DEVELOP COMPETENCE

A person must develop both career competence and occupational competence.

- **Career competence** refers to the skills that contribute to a person's career maturity such as being able to appraise one's strengths and weaknesses, having and using information about job and career opportunities, and planning how one can achieve goals are career competence skills (Hall, 1976).

- **Occupational competence** is the job-related skills, activities, and attitudes that are necessary to perform work tasks.

One occupational competence strategy is to be narrow – to learn some job-specific skills in college, vocational school, or an apprenticeship program. For example, the student who studies engineering or bricklaying is ready to work in an organization immediately after training is completed. A second approach is to develop broad competence, that is, to learn a general set of skills that would be applicable in different jobs. For example, if you take courses in mathematics or liberal arts you will have the skill to work in a bank or in a manufacturing plant. If you take this broad approach, it is likely that you might start at a lower salary than one who has followed a more narrow approach, but studies show that on average, salary and advancement at work generally even out in the long run, whether you take a narrow or a broad approach.

ASSESS THE WORK SETTING

There are two important things about the work setting:

1 The organization in which you work
2 The specific job that you have

Knowledge about the organization is important for several reasons.

- Rates of promotion may be much slower in firms in more traditional industries.
- Some career paths are more promising than others.

We now look at some other things you should know about.

What are the promotion rates?

This will give you some idea of how quickly people are promoted. You will find higher promotion rates in growing firms than in more mature ones.

What is the nature of careers in the organization?

Some firms seem to keep their employees until retirement, whereas in other firms, people "burn out and bail out." One major US firm is noted for hiring young managers and paying them very well, but using them up. An ex-manager from the firm said, "No one ever retires from there. You quit. You can't stand the strain."

Where do managers go?

It is particularly helpful to know the promotion ladders in an organization. This is the chain of jobs held by those who are rapidly promoted within the firm. It is also useful to know where people go when they quit or are hired away. This will tell you something about how others value the experiences offered by the firm.

Find out what your specific job entails

Some jobs are dead-end positions with little or no opportunity to move out of them. For instance, in one manufacturing plant, all plant superintendents and plant managers have been promoted from production management positions. No one has been promoted to plant manager from jobs in personnel, production control, accounting, or quality control. In this organization, these jobs are dead ends. If you want to be a plant manager, you must avoid them. If you take one of these dead-end jobs for experience, work your way out of it later, and back into the promotion track.

Is the job challenging?

Job challenge gives you a chance to stretch your skills. Succeeding in a challenging job will be noticed by those who make promotion decisions.

How successful were others who held this job?

There is more to being successful than just having the right attitude and plenty of ability. Sometimes the job itself can be a critical factor. Any job requires a certain set of behaviors and interaction with others, which do not change drastically when another person takes the job. If the job was a losing proposition for the person you are replacing, it could be the same for you. One way to assess the impact that a job may have on your career is to find out how successful previous incumbents were (Stogdill et al., 1956).

WORK AT EXCELLENCE

Performing well requires ability and motivation, but also an understanding of the criteria used to judge performance. Find out what people are rewarded for doing. Listen to what others tell you about the performance and involvement norms, and observe the behavior of those who have advanced.

DEVELOP CAREER MOBILITY

In this period of downsizing, career mobility is very important. One type of mobility is to move to other jobs within your current organization. You may want to do this if you are dissatisfied with either the content of your present job or its advancement opportunities. Another type of career mobility is to leave your present firm. For this, you must have the occupational competence that is needed by a different employer. Note though that the demand for your skill in the market is related to economic factors; in a recession, it is more difficult to change jobs than in periods of growth.

There are risks to moving to another firm. You may have unrealistically high expectations that, if they are not met, could lead to significant economic and psychological costs. For example, a company recruited a person who was believed to be the "best quality control specialist in the industry." During the recruiting period, the company executives and the candidate were excited about future prospects. However, in the euphoria of evaluating the new job, he failed to consider some important differences between the job he left and the one that he took. Six months later, he was fired. What were the costs? He had moved his family from another part of the country. He still had an unsold home in the city from which he moved, and he was between jobs and with no immediate prospects.

CONSIDER THE EFFECTS OF YOUR CAREER CHOICES ON OTHERS

How a job will affect a spouse and children and how it will change family life are some of the problems that you must think about. The quality control manager's career choices affected his family life. Because work and family are so interrelated, one is going to affect the other, and career choices must be made with these factors in mind.

MONITOR YOUR CAREER

You should regularly assess whether your career is advancing as you think it should. If not, what steps should you take? Should you revise your aspirations? Should you change jobs? Should you leave the organization? You will also want to make a judgment about the relationship of your career progress to the other components of your own life structure.

Key Concepts

affective commitment 105
career 91
career adaptability 91
career attitudes 92
career establishment stage 102
career exploration stage 96
career identity 92
career novice stage 98
continuance commitment 105
dual careers 111
expert career path 94
Good Enough Theory of Promotion 93
linear career path 94
multi-focal view of organizational commitment 103
normative commitment 105
norms of involvement 100
norms of performance 100
objective career success 92
occupational competence 98
occupational socialization 98
organizational commitment 103
organizational socialization 100
person–organization fit 102
preliminary work socialization 98
psychological contract 100
psychological success 93
spiral career path 95
transitory career path 95

STUDY QUESTIONS

1 In what ways can psychological success and objective success be related? Can you have one without the other?
2 What are the phases of organizational socialization?
3 How can the behavior of parents affect job and career choices? How would you say your parents affected your career choice?
4 What is occupational socialization? Differentiate it from organizational socialization. Analyze to what extent you have experienced occupational socialization at this stage in your life.
5 Give some examples where there is strong occupational socialization before one actually assumes an occupational role.
6 Select two personality orientations discussed in chapter 2. What are the implications of these types for management and control? Can you relate these personality types to people you know?

Case

Harrison Electronics and Sarah Cunningham

Harrison Electronics is a large, profitable hi-tech firm located in New Jersey. It designs and produces advanced electronics products mostly for the space program or for specialized industry applications. The president of Harrison, John Dowd, was a professor of electrical engineering at an important state university before he took a job at Harrison and moved quickly to the top. Dowd is a tough, hard-nosed manager who expects results. His philosophy is to make tough demands and to reward high performers. If he has one fault it is that he is quick to call someone on the carpet. When he believes a person did not do the job, he lets him or her know, in clear terms.

The major units in Harrison are the production division and the research group. There is a very small government contracts division. The research division is Dowd's pride and joy. Most of the staff are highly trained physical scientists. Dowd boasts that Harrison will always be a growth company as long as they have such strong technical personnel. In fact, Harrison does have a good growth record and there are always opportunities for advancement for those executives who Dowd thinks are good.

Recently Harrison had a contract to develop some specialized computers in a government contract. As a result, several people in the company, especially Dowd, thought the product had potential as a personal computer, so they decided to enter the personal computer business. Dowd set his research group out to the task of developing the hardware and software necessary for the new product line. He and his staff put together a very ambitious schedule to complete product development and put the personal computer on the market.

Harrison added a vice-president of marketing, Sarah Cunningham, who was hired from one of the leaders in the retailing industry. Sarah was a successful top manager in the appliance division, located in California, before coming to Harrison. Sarah was thirty-five years old, unmarried, and had lived on the West Coast all her life. Sarah hired a marketing staff and began to develop a plan to sell the new product. She brought in several top people from other firms.

However, soon Sarah began to run into problems. She could not win the ear of Dowd for marketing problems; he and the other top people were, it seemed, more concerned with the technical matters. Most of Sarah's programs had to be approved by the executive group, all engineers except her. It became difficult to achieve anything. Soon the project began to run into scheduling difficulties. The best engineer assigned to the personal computer project was pulled off by John Dowd to work on a new government contract. It became known around the company that the project was in serious difficulties and there were rumors that it would soon be dumped.

John Dowd called a meeting of the group responsible for the personal computer project. He was very angry about the progress. He told them: "I don't know why you people can't make this thing work. You've got the resources of the best technical staff in the country. I've spent a lot of money on the project. If it fails, it's your fault. I am holding you all personally responsible."

Sarah became a little concerned. She thought the criticism was unfair. She asked John Dowd, "Don't you think that's a little harsh judgment? After all, we've had serious technical problems and our best engineer has been pulled from the project."

Dowd looked at her and glared. "Sarah," he said, "I don't know what you did in that damned department store where you used to work. Here we deal with hardware, not with fashion. We get results. That's what I want. If you can't get them, maybe you should look for something else to do." Then he turned and walked out of the room.

Sarah didn't know what to do or what to say, John Rice, an old Harrison hand, leaned over to her and said quietly, "Sarah, don't worry. The old man is going through one of his phases. This happens every time something gets behind schedule. He'll be O.K., and so will you."

Sarah wasn't so sure.

- What would you do if you were Sarah? Why?
- What are the important factors about the company and the situation that should have been considered by Sarah before she took the job at Harrison?
- Would a career failure at Harrison hurt Sarah? Why?

References

Auster, C. 1983: The relationship between sex and occupational statuses: A neglected status discrepancy. *Sociology and Sociology Research*, 67, 421–38.

Beck, S. H. 1983: The role of other family members in intergenerational mobility. *The Sociological Quarterly*, Spring, 24, 173–285.

Blau, P. M., Gustad, J. W., Jessor, R., Parnes, H. and Wilcox., R. S. 1956: Occupational choice: A conceptual framework. *Industrial Labor Relations Review*, 9, 531–43.

Brousseau, K. R., Driver, M. J., Eneroth, K. and Larsson, R. 1996: Career Pandemonium: Realigning organizations and individuals. *Academy of Management Executive*, 10(4), 52–66.

Bryson, R. J., Bryson, B. and Johnson, M. F. 1978: Family size, satisfaction and productivity in dual career couples. *Psychology of Women Quarterly*, 3, 67–77.

Cascio, W. 1993: Downsizing: What do we know? What have we learned? *Academy of Management Executive*, 7(1), 95–104.

Caudron, S. 1992: US West finds strength in diversity. *Personnel Journal*, March, 40–4.

Chatman, J. 1991: Matching people and organizations: Selection and socialization in public accounting firms. *Administrative Science Quarterly*, 36, 469–84.

Creswell, J. 1998: *Fortune*'s first annual look at women who most influence corporate America. *Fortune*, October 12, 85–7.

Deaux, K. 1979: Self-evaluations of male and female managers. *Sex Roles*, 5, 571–80.

Dobbins, G. H. and Platz, S. J. 1986: Sex differences in leadership: How real are they? *Academy of Management Review*, 11(1), 118–27.

Domingues, C. M. 1992: Executive forum: The glass ceiling. Paradox and promises. *Human Resource Management*, 31(4), 385–92.

Dreher, G. F. and Ash, R. A. 1990: A comparative study of mentoring among men and women in managerial, professional, and technical positions. *Journal of Applied Psychology*, (75)5, October, 539–46.

Dreyfus, J. 1990: Get ready for the new work force; if demographics are destiny, companies that aggressively hire, train, and promote women and minorities – the growing segments of the US labor market will succeed. *Fortune*, April 23, 21(9), 165–70.

Dunham, R., Grube, J. E. and Castaneda, M. B. 1994: Organizational commitment: The utility of an integrative definition. *Journal of Applied Psychology*, 79(3), 370–81.

Eagly, A. H., Karau, S. J. and Mikhijani, M. G. 1995: Gender and the effectiveness of leaders: A meta-analysis. *Journal of Applied Psychology*, 117(1), 121–45.

Feldman, D. C. and Arnold, H. J. 1983: *Managing Individual and Group Behavior in Organizations*. New York: McGraw-Hill.

Fernandez, J. P. 1991: *Managing a Diverse Work Force*. Lexington, MA: Lexington Books.

Fields, J. and Wolff, E. N. 1991: The decline of sex segregation and the wage gap: 1970–1980. *Journal of Human Resources*, Fall, 26(4), 608–22.

Form, W. and McMillen, D. 1983: Women, men and machines. *Work and Occupations*, 10, 147–77.

Fottler, M. D. and Bain, T. 1980: Sex differences in occupational aspirations. *Academy of Management Journal*, 23(1), 144–9.

Gatewood, R. D., Gowan, M. A. and Lautenschlager, G. J. 1993: Corporate image, recruitment image, and initial job choice decisions. *The Academy of Management Journal*, 36(2), 319–48.

Gerhart, B. A. 1990: Gender differences in current and starting salaries: The role of performance, college major and job title. *Industrial and Labor Relations Review*, 43(4), April, 418–33.

Gerhart, B. A. and Milkovich, G. T. 1987: Salaries, salary growth, and promotions of men and women in large, private firm. Working paper, Center for Advanced Human Resource Studies, New York School of Industrial and Labor Relations. Ithaca, NY: Cornell University.

Hall, D. T. 1976: *Careers in Organizations*. Pacific Palisades, CA: Goodyear Publishing Company.

Hall, R. H. 1986: *Dimensions of Work*. Beverly Hills, CA: Sage Publications.

Harvey, 1966: Addressing the dual-career expatriation dilemma. *Human Resource Planning*, 19(4), 18–39.

Higgins, C., Duxbury, L. and Irving R. 1992: Work–family conflict in the dual career family. *Organizational Behavior and Human Decision Processes*, 51(1), 51–75.

Hill, M. S. 1979: The wage effects of marital status and children. *Journal of Human Resources*, 14, 579–93.

Jackson, M. 1996: The gender gap. *Work Life, Gainesville Sun*, December 23, 10–19.

Jacobs, J. 1992: Women's entry into management: Trends in earnings, authority, and values among salaried managers. *Administrative Science Quarterly*, 37, 282–301.

Kemp, A. and Beck, E. M. 1986: Equal work, unequal pay. *Work and Occupations*, 13, 324–46.

Kohn, M. L. and Schooler, C. 1969: Class, occupation, and orientation. *American Sociological Review*, 34, 659–78.

Korman, A. 1970: Toward a hypothesis of work behavior. *Journal of Applied Psychology*, 54, 31–41.

Lee, T. W., Ashford, S. J., Walsh, J. P. and Mowday, R. T. 1996: Commitment propensity, organizational commitment and voluntary turnover: a longitudinal study of organizational entry processes. *Journal of Management*, 18(1), 15–18.

Levinson, D., Barrow, C. H., Klein, E. B., Levinson, M. H. and McGee, B. 1978: *Seasons of a Man's Life*. New York: Ballantine Books.

Louis, M. R. 1980: Surprise and sense making: What newcomers experience in entering unfamiliar organization settings. *Administrative Science Quarterly*, 25, 226–51.

Marini, M. M. 1980: Sex differences in the process of occupational attainment: A closer look. *Social Science Research*, 9, 307–61.

Major, B. and Konar, E. 1984: An investigation of sex differences and pay expectations and their possible causes. *Academy of Management Journal*, 27, 779–92.

Markham, W., South, S., Bonjean, C. and Corder, J. 1985: Gender and opportunity in the federal bureaucracy. *American Journal of Sociology*, 91, 129–51.

Morris, B. 1998: Executive women confront midlife crisis. *Fortune*, September 18, 60–86.

Organ, D. W. 1997: Organizational citizenship behavior: It's construct clean up time. *Human Performance*, 10(2), 85–97.

Osipow, S. H. 1973: *Theories of Career Development*, 2nd edn. New York: Appleton-Century-Crofts.

Parker-Pope, T. 1998: Inside P&G, a pitch to keep women employees. *The Wall Street Journal*, September 9, B1–B6.

Pfeffer, J. and Ross, J. 1982: The effects of marriage and a working wife on occupational wage attainment. *Administrative Science Quarterly*, 27, 66–80.

Powell, G. 1983: *Women & Men in Management*, 2nd edn. Newbury Park, CA: Sage.

Powell, G. and Jacobs, J. A. 1984: The prestige gap: Differential evaluations of male and female workers. *Work and Occupations*, August, 11, 283–308.

Pulakos, E. D. and Schmitt, N. 1983: A longitudinal study of a valence model for the prediction of job satisfaction of new employees. *Journal of Applied Psychology*, 68, 307–12.

Robinson, S. 1996: Trust and breach of the physical contract. *Administrative Science Quarterly*, 41(4), December, 574–600.

Roe, A. 1957: Early determinants of occupational choice. *Journal of Counseling Psychology*, 4, 212–17.

Roe, A. and Seigelman, M. 1964: *The Origin of Interests*. The SPGS Inquiry Series, No. 1, Washington, DC: American Personnel and Guidance Association.

Ross, C., Mirowsky, J. and Huber, J. 1983: Dividing work, sharing work, and in between: Marriage patterns and depression. *American Sociological Review*, 48(6), 809–23.

Schein, E. A. 1970: *Organizational Psychology*. New York: Prentice-Hall.

Simon, H. A. 1982: *Solving Problems and Expertise*. Symposium. University of Florida.

Soelberg, P. 1966: Unprogrammed decision making. *Proceedings of the Academy of Management*, 3–16.

Srivastava, K. and Srivastava, A. 1985: Job stress, marital adjustment, social relations and mental health of dual-career and traditional couples: A comparative study. *Perspectives in Psychological Researches*, 8(1), 28–33.

Staw, B. M., Bell, N. E. and Clausen, J. A. 1986: The dispositional approach to job attitudes: A lifetime longitudinal test. *Administrative Science Quarterly*, 31(1), March, 56–77.

Stewart, L. P. and Gudykunst, W. B. 1982: Differential factors influencing the hierarchical level and number of promotions of males and females within an organization. *Academy of Management Journal*, 25(3), 586–97.

Stogdill, R., Shartle, C., Scott, E. L., Coons, A. and Jaynes, W. E. 1956: *A Predictive Study of Administrative Work Patterns*. Columbus, OH: Bureau of Business Research, Ohio State University.

Stroh, L. K., Brett, J. M. and Reilly, A. H. 1992: All the right stuff: A comparison of female and male managers' career progression. *Journal of Applied Psychology*, 77(3), 251–60.

Sund, K. and Ostwald, S. 1985: Dual earner families' stress levels and personal life-style related variables. *Nursing Research*, 34(6), 357–61.

Super, D. E. 1957: *The Psychology of Careers*. New York: Harper & Row.

Tinto, V. 1984: Patterns of educational sponsorship to work. *Work and Occupation*, 11(3), August, 309–30.

Tosi, H. 1992: *The Environment/Organization/Person Contingency Model: A Meso Approach to the Study of Organizations*. Greenwich, CT: JAI Press.

Tsui, A. S. and Gutek, B. A. 1984: A role set analysis of gender differences in performance, affective relationships and the career success of industrial middle managers. *Academy of Management Journal*, 27(3), 613–35.

Tyler, L. 1965: *The Psychology of Individual Differences*, revised edn. New York: Appleton-Century-Crofts.

Van Maanen, J. 1978: People processing: Strategies of organizational socialization. *Organizational Dynamics*, Summer, 64–82.

Wanous, J. P., Poland, T. D., Premack, S. L. and Davis, K. S. 1992: The effects of met expectations on newcomer attitudes and behaviors: A review and meta-analysis. *Journal of Applied Psychology*, June, 7(3), 822–9.

Ward, K. B. and Mueller, C. M. 1985: Sex differences in earnings: The influence of industrial sector, authority hierarchy, and human capital variables. *Work and Occupations*, November, 12(4), 437–63.

Whitely, W., Daughterty, T. W. and Dreher, G. F. 1991: Relationship of career mentoring and socioeconomic origin to managers' and professionals' early career progress. *Academy of Management Journal*, 34(2), 331–50.

Zahrly, J. and Tosi, H. 1989: The differential effect of organizational induction process on early work role adjustment. *Journal of Organizational Behavior*, 10, 59–74.

chapter 5

Theories of Motivation

NEED THEORIES OF MOTIVATION

THE JOB CHARACTERISTICS APPROACH

ACHIEVEMENT–POWER THEORY

REINFORCEMENT THEORY

GOAL-SETTING THEORY

JUSTICE THEORIES OF MOTIVATION

Preparing for Class

Consider three behaviors that are relevant to this course:

1. Your choice of academic major

2. Your choice of profession that you are pursuing or hope to pursue.

3. How hard you are working in this class

Note that two of these behaviors involve choices made through some form of decision process and one involves level of effort. After reviewing the motivation theories discussed in this chapter, choose which theories best explain the three behaviors you listed.

1. Were some theories more useful than others in explaining certain types of behaviors?

2. Do the theories complement each other or do they provide very different explanations for behavior?

For most managers, the words motivation and performance go together. That is certainly what government officials of the state of Kentucky thought when they developed a plan to improve the quality of state schools by providing cash incentives to teachers when their school's scores on a test to evaluate student performance increased (Seclow, 1997). The idea was simple and straightforward: reward teachers for improved student performance. A test was created to evaluate students in mathematics, science, and the humanities. There was a heavy emphasis on writing skills to assess the students' capacity for critical thinking and exposition. If it was discovered that student performance dropped, a plan was in place to provide the school with administrative and managerial assistance to move it in the right direction. Between 1995 and 1998, more than $518 million in bonuses to teachers were paid out.

Not all was going well with the new incentive approach. In an evaluation of student writing samples in more than 100 schools, it was found that over 95 percent of the grades were much too generous. This was attributed to the fact that these writing exams were graded by teachers in the school, the very teachers who would receive bonuses if students improved. It was a case of improvement by reducing grading standards. In addition, it was discovered that all was not as expected for the portions of the exam that were graded by an outside consulting firm. It was discovered that, in some schools, teachers did a number of things to help students do better that were outside the realm of normal classroom teaching. For example, some reviewed the questions that were on the test before the test was given. Others permitted the students to ask questions to clarify parts of the exam while they were taking it.

There were some other unanticipated problems. One of the features of the system was that when a school received a "bonus" for high performance, it was the teachers themselves who voted on how to distribute it. This caused not only some dissatisfaction among the teachers themselves, but also with other groups in the school, such as cafeteria workers and bus drivers, who thought that they deserved part of the bonus. As you read this chapter, you will find some of the answers to the question you have in your mind about this program, "Why didn't it work?"

Like the state officials in Kentucky, motivation is a seductive subject for many managers who believe in it for many reasons, some right and some wrong. One reason is that work motivation is an important value in Western society. In Western society in general, and particularly in the USA, there has been a historical stress on the "**work ethic**." The work ethic belief – that work is good and that it should be valued – is so strongly ingrained in some that if they do not have an opportunity to work, they have psychological and social problems. Health statistics from areas experiencing long and extensive layoffs show increases in anxiety, depression, and often suicide.

work ethic
The belief that work is good and that it should be valued

Second, many managers believe the improved performance resulting from motivation is free. Imagine that you hire a worker for $10 per hour who produces five units per hour. The unit labor cost is $2. If the worker has the potential to produce 10 units each hour and does so without buying new equipment, the unit labor costs drops to $1. To make such a gain with improved equipment would cost money; through motivation it seems to be free. However it is not the case that improvements can be made through motivation without cost. A highly motivated work force only comes with good selection, sound compensation practices, training, and the use of good human resource management practices, all of which "cost."

Third, motivation is an explanation of why some organizations are more productive than others. Suppose you take a tour of two breweries and there are no identification signs to inform you whether you are in the Coors brewery or one owned by Anheuser-Busch. The equipment looks very similar. The two buildings look alike. If there are any differences in productivity and the equipment is the same, it is only logical to conclude that these differences arise because of the people involved. The problem with this perspective is that it generally attributes the responsibility for poor performance to the worker and ignores the possibility that the management is poor. This is exactly the conclusion that many reached about the decline in market share of the US automobile industry and the increased share of the Japanese manufacturers over the last 20 years. Many believed that the Japanese workers were more motivated and that the problems in US firms were a result of strident unions and unwilling workers. It took several years for the US firms to believe, first, that there was a market for smaller cars and, second, to change their approach not only to the manufacturing process but also their approach to managing the work force. The recent successes of US automobile manufacturers to compete with foreign car companies, especially exemplified by Ford's Taurus suggest that the industry may have learned how to deal with some of their problems, but it took more years than it should have.

Motivation and Performance

Consider this situation: Lance Roberts has a burning desire to be a good tennis player. He spends hours practicing, reads all the instructional magazines, regularly takes lessons, and plays a match every day. Blaine Davis is one of Lance's regular weekly matches. Every Wednesday afternoon they play and Blaine usually wins. It is especially frustrating to Lance because Blaine hardly practices and plays only twice, at the most three times, each week.

This example illustrates that performance (or results) is a function of two things: motivation and ability. This is the basis of a very fundamental relationship for understanding human performance in organizations.

$$\text{Performance} = f\,(\text{Ability} \times \text{Motivation})$$

Figure 5.1 shows how these three factors are related. On one axis is performance and on the other, motivation. The lines in the figure represent the abilities of both men. They show that Lance has less tennis ability than Blaine. Therefore, if both are equally motivated (say at point X), then Blaine will always win. Lance will only win when he has high motivation (at point Y) and Blaine is not highly motivated to perform (near point Z).

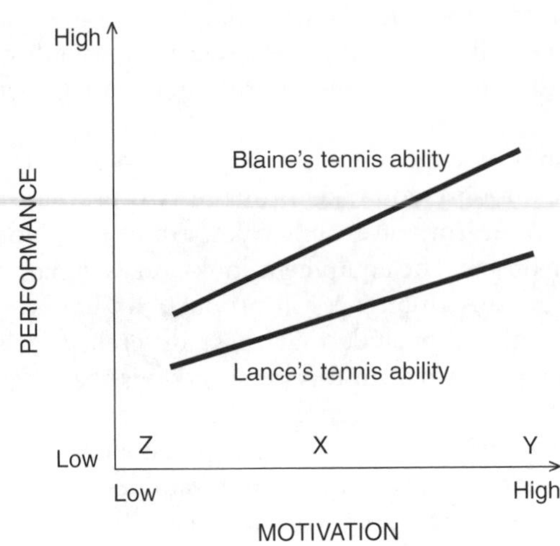

Fig 5.1 : Relationship between performance, motivation, and ability

What Do We Mean by Performance?

Performance results from mental or physical effort. Performance levels can be stated in terms of quantity or quality, and require some subjective judgment by a manager. A particular level of performance may be judged as "high" by one person, but the same level may be only "satisfactory," or perhaps "unsatisfactory," for another. It is a little more complicated when we think about job performance because most jobs have several distinct elements and therefore require several different types of performance.

performance components
A relatively discrete subtask for which the requisite ability to perform is different from other abilities

The different elements are called **performance components**, relatively discrete subtasks or behaviors which require different abilities and which might have different motivational predispositions. You will recall from our discussion about performance in chapter 1 (page 17) that we said that jobs had task performance components and contextual performance components.

task performance component
An element of the person's job that is required to perform the job itself

- **Task performance components** are the activities required to do the work itself. For example, a plant manager must have the ability and the motivation to manage production and quality levels, prepare work schedules, order supplies, deal with subordinates, and run departmental meetings.
- **Contextual performance components** are behaviors that go beyond task performance and are essential if organizations are to excel, because success depends on employees going beyond formal task role requirements (Borman and Motowidlo, 1993).

These performance components are also referred to as prosocial or organizational citizenship behavior (Borman and Motowidlo, 1993; Organ, 1988) and reflect the extent to which a person is willing to go beyond the norms of performance and involvement of his or her work role (Organ, 1988). Several contextual performance behaviors which reflect organization citizenship are discussed in chapter 9:

- Altruistic behavior
- Conscientious behavior
- Sportsmanlike behavior
- Courtesy
- Civic virtue

ABILITY

Ability is the capacity to carry out a set of interrelated behavioral or mental sequences to produce a result. For example, to play the piano requires that one be able to read music, understand chord structures, and have the manual dexterity to finger the keyboard. Generally, it is easy to see ability differences between two individuals; it is often apparent among individuals who perform similar jobs.

ability
The capacity to carry out a set of interrelated behavioral, or mental, sequences to produce a result

It is also important to remember that individuals have different abilities. A person may be a highly skilled architect but have very low communication skills. Since most job performance is multidimensional, it follows that the person who is assigned to do the job must have adequate ability for each different performance component. For example, the plant manager's job involves scheduling work, dealing with subordinates (handling grievances, supervision, etc.), and running departmental meetings. Each of these separate activities requires different skills and a person can be good in some and poor in others.

THE ROLE OF TECHNOLOGY Technology interacts with ability to affect performance, but in different ways. **Technology** refers to the methods, tools, facilities, and equipment a person uses in performing a task. Auto workers "use" a complex production system with highly independent activities to manufacture a car. An artist's technology may be a canvas, paint, and brushes.

technology
The tools, machines, facilities, and equipment a person uses in performing a task

Most task performance components involve the use of some technology, but, for some of them, technology is more important than for others. For example, the technology of the production line is critical for the task performance component "managing production levels" of a plant manager's job. However, for the task performance component "dealing with subordinates" the impact of technology is minimal; human skill is more important.

Since technology plays different roles, we think it is useful to think of any specific task as being either skill-dominated or technology-dominated. In **skill-dominated tasks**, individual skill is the most important factor. A clothing designer's job is an example of skill-dominated work. Giving a designer better equipment is likely to have only a marginal effect on performance, just as giving Blaine and Lance, our tennis players, better rackets and shoes will probably not improve their game very much because tennis, like most sports, is a skill-dominated task.

Contrast this with assembly-line work, an example of a **technology-dominated task**. Only limited human skills are required in the job; technology is the

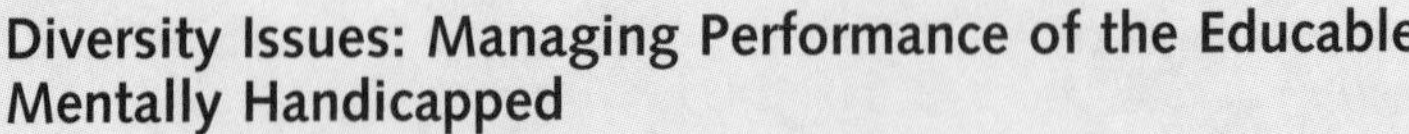

Diversity Issues: Managing Performance of the Educable Mentally Handicapped

Usually, when we think about high work performance, we have in mind a situation in which a specific job has some defined acceptable level of output that is exceeded. When a person does not have the ability to achieve that acceptable level, our tendency is to see him or her as less than competent. However, the example of what the Marriott Hotels of Chicago in conjunction with the International Association of Machinists (IAM) have done to accommodate to problems of the educably mentally handicapped employees can be helpful to understand the performance/motivation/ability relationship.

In general, most of the entrance level jobs at the Chicago Marriott are too complicated for many educably mentally handicapped people. However, through a joint program of the hotel and the IAM, there has been a good deal of success in training and placing these workers in productive jobs. What did they do?

First, jobs were selected that these employees can handle reasonably well – the jobs are selected properly. For one thing, most of the employees work in jobs that require no contact with guests. They work, for example, in the laundry, housekeeping, or in other areas in which they work as members of a team or group. Some have even worked in the HR department doing light office work.

Second, there was a serious attempt to redesign tasks, where possible, so that the employees' limitations did not limit their performance. For instance, a bell-station job was redesigned so that the same person was not assigned the task of handling luggage for guests, but rather had the responsibility for cleaning and polishing the carts.

You can see from this approach how motivation and ability are related to affect performance. Be redefining what was acceptable performance (i.e., maintaining the appearance of luggage carts but *not* handling the luggage), the employees' ability was sufficient, if they were motivated, to do the job.

Incidentally, motivation was no problem for any of these employees. Not only did the hotel find these employees effective at the work, there is also a lower level of turnover among this group.

Source: Adapted from Laabs (1994)

most important factor. Figure 5.2 shows how technology can affect performance. Here you have enough motivation and ability to perform at a minimum level, for instance, to start the machine. From there on, the equipment determines how well the job is done. The lower and upper limits of performance are set by the technology. When technology sets such limits, one cannot expect performance to increase simply because one obtains competent or more motivated people.

There are several important things to learn when viewing performance in this way.

1 Specific and different abilities are required for the various parts of a job. A person may be more talented in one performance component and less in another. A quarterback for a football team may be an excellent passer but a very poor runner.
2 A person may be more motivated (willing to put forth more effort) for one performance component than others; the plant manager, for example,

might rather manage production and quality than spend time in dealing with subordinates.

3 For some performance components, significant levels of technology may be required to achieve results. For example, required production levels in a plant cannot be achieved unless the appropriate equipment is operating effectively. Technology is not critical, however, in running a meeting; for this, human skill is most crucial.

4 Technology and human skill may be interchangeable. When technology is substituted for human skill, it often leads to more predictable and dependable performance. Consider a task so simple as making coffee. Until the introduction of automatic coffee makers, making a good cup of coffee required a great deal of skill. With the automatic technology, it is a task that a child can do.

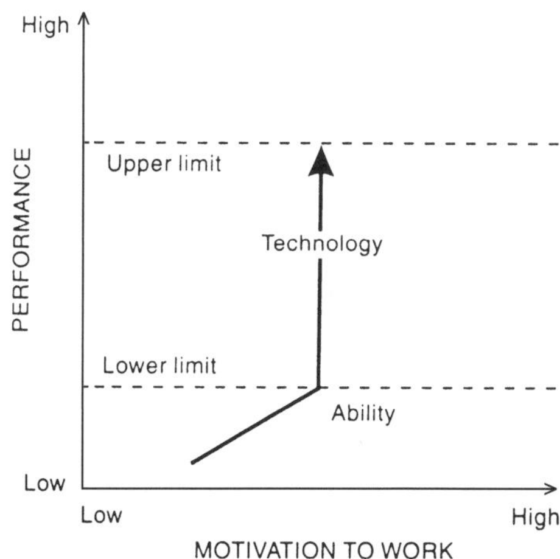

Fig 5.2 : Technology-dominated work

What Do We Mean by Motivation?

motivation
An internal mental state of an individual that causes behavior; also defined as a management activity, or something that a manager does to induce others to act in a way to produce the results required organizationally

The term **motivation** has both a psychological and a managerial connotation in the field of organizational behavior. The psychological meaning of motivation is the internal mental state of a person which relates to the initiation, direction, persistence, intensity, and termination of behavior (Landy and Becker, 1987). The managerial meaning of motivation is the activity of managers to induce others to produce results desired by the organization or, perhaps, by the manager. In this latter context, we might say, "The role of every manager is to motivate employees to work harder or to do better."

The managerial concept of motivation is illustrated in figure 5.3, which shows the relationship between motivation, ability, and performance for two football teams about to play each other. For simplification, we assume that the teams are

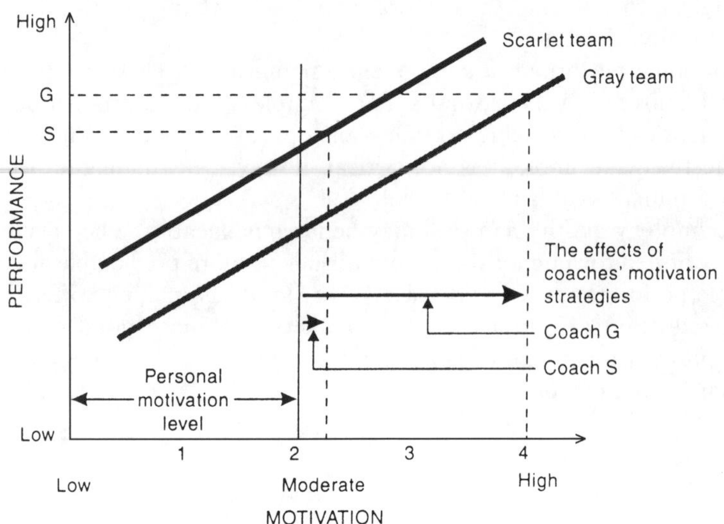

Fig 5.3: Role of managerial motivation strategies

equal in personal motivation (at level 2), but that they differ in overall ability as shown by the diagonal lines in the diagram. Suppose the coach of the Scarlets takes the game between the teams lightly because of the Scarlets' superior ability. He gives the team only a little boost to level 2.25. The coach of the Grays recognizes the Scarlets' superior ability and inspires his team to put forth a great deal more effort. If the coach of the Grays can move the players to a high level of motivation (to level 4.0), they will win the game despite having less ability.

CLASSES OF MOTIVATION THEORIES Any motivation theory attempts to account for the reasons why people behave as they do and the processes that cause the behavior

- Those which focus on "what" motivates behavior are called **content theories of motivation.**
- Those theories that focus on "how" behavior is motivated are called **process theories.**

We use this distinction between content and process theories of motivation because it highlights the main orientation of a particular formulation about motivation. However, content theories have some process orientation and process theories usually have some content dimensions. For example, content theories usually focus on a human need of some type. The strength of that need – and the specific way that a person wishes to satisfy it – are usually learned through socialization, a process that can be understood in reinforcement theory terms. As you study the theories in this chapter, you will see that these two orientations – content and process – are present in each of them.

A Question of Ethics: Motivational Practices and Unethical Behavior

In the early 1990s, Sears had a set of procedures and a compensation program for mechanics that motivated them to cheat customers. Mechanics were charging customers for service never performed or parts not installed. Sears, at the time of the problem, had no controls for either poor or unnecessary work. With high sales quotas, the mechanics found that it was a simple matter to pad customer bills, and they were rewarded for it. After the problem was uncovered, Sears took action to solve it, changing the method of compensation and the quality control system. However, as late as 1999, Sears was again faced with similar suits. Apparently, some in the company never got the message.

Sears is not alone with this type of problem. There are studies that show that nearly 50 percent of workers in US firms acted in unethical or illegal ways such as disregarding quality standards, abusing sick leave, lying to someone at work, deceiving customers, or taking credit for someone else's work. In part, this kind of behavior is because some people are not completely honest. However, some of this behavior is actually motivated by company policies and management practices. It seems that over 50 percent of all workers feel pressure to act in illegal or unethical ways – and the pressure is worse than it was five years ago.

What this means is that the motivational practices in some firms are such that they encourage illegal or unethical action. The reasons are pretty simple. Companies in today's global economy are subject to severe competitive pressures to keep costs down and to increase revenue. Managers often set difficult objectives for subordinates and do not care how these goals are achieved; the employees are worried because if they do not perform as expected, they might be fired or, if the firm does not do well, downsizing is a threat. Situations like this lead to a climate and culture that oftentimes motivates socially and organizationally undesirable actions by employees.

Source: Adapted from Greengard (1997)

Motivation – The Content Theories

Content theories of motivation emphasize the reasons for motivated behavior; that is, "what" causes it. A content theory would explain behavioral aspects in terms of specific human needs or specific factors that "drive" behavior. For example, you might say that "Joan is motivated to work for higher pay" or "John did that because he has a high need for power." In this section, we discuss four different content theories:

content theories of motivation Theories that emphasize the reasons for individual behavior

- Need theory and, in particular, Maslow's need theory and ERG theory
- Herzberg's two-factor theory
- the job characteristics approach
- McClelland's achievement–power theory

NEED THEORIES

needs theories
Motivation or personality theories focusing on needs

needs
When a person senses a discrepancy between a present (or future) condition, and some desired state that leads the person to feel tension and act to reduce it

Need theories of motivation assume that people act to satisfy their needs. A **need** (or a motive) is aroused when the person senses that there is some difference between the present (or, perhaps, a future) condition and some desired state. When a "need" is aroused, the person feels some tension and acts to reduce it. This sequence is shown in figure 5.4.

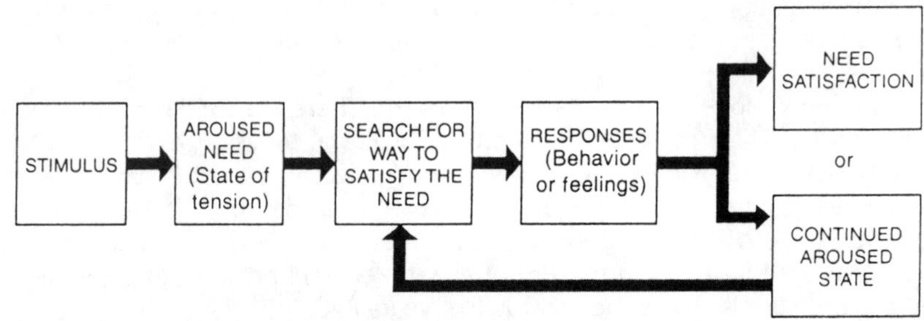

Fig 5.4: A needs approach to motivation

Suppose a manager tells you about a vacancy at a higher organizational level and that the position will be filled by the most productive worker in the group. This may arouse your desire for advancement, achievement, or more pay. If your need is aroused, you will search for ways to satisfy it. You might work harder – which is what the manager wanted. If your harder work leads to a promotion then the need is satisfied. If it does not, the desire for promotion may be suppressed and lead to frustration or you might decide to seek a job elsewhere.

Ways to satisfy needs are learned through socialization, and so people differ with respect to the needs that are important to them. We learn through experience that some situations are more rewarding than others and seek these out; other situations, we try to avoid.

Need theory is elegant in its simplicity and appeal. If, as the theory suggests, people are concerned with satisfying their needs, then all that has to be done is to provide for need satisfaction opportunities in the work place. Yet, for a very simple reason, this is not so easy to translate into practice: a particular need may be satisfied in different ways for different people. For example, one person's need for self-esteem may be satisfied by being recognized as the best worker in a department; another may find this need satisfied by others' recognition of his or her dress style – being acknowledged as the sharpest dresser in the group.

MASLOW'S NEED THEORY In organizational behavior, the most popular need theory of motivation by far is the one developed by Abraham Maslow (1943). He believed that human needs could be categorized into five categories:

1 **Physiological needs** are the basic requirements for survival. Humans must have food to live, and shelter is necessary. Physical well-being must be provided for before anything else can assume importance for a person.
2 **Safety needs** reflect a desire for protection against loss of shelter, food, and other basic requirements for survival. Security needs also involve the desire to live in a stable and predictable environment. It may also involve a preference for order and structure.
3 **Belonging needs** reflect the person's desire for love, affection, and belonging. The need to interact with others and have some social acceptance and approval is generally shared by most people. For some, this need may be satisfied by joining groups. Others may find sufficient affection from their family members or other individuals.
4 **Esteem needs** are those human desires to be respected by others and for a positive self-image. Individuals strive to increase their status in the eyes of others, to attain a good reputation or a high ranking in a group. Self-confidence is increased when self-esteem needs are satisfied. When self-esteem needs are thwarted, feelings of inferiority or weakness often result.
5 **Self-actualization needs** are the individual's desire to do what he or she has the potential of doing. The desire for self-actualization is called the "highest-order need."

These basic needs are arranged in a **hierarchy of needs** as shown in figure 5.5. Maslow hypothesized that unsatisfied needs dominate the individual's thoughts and are reflected in what the person is concerned about. The higher-order needs

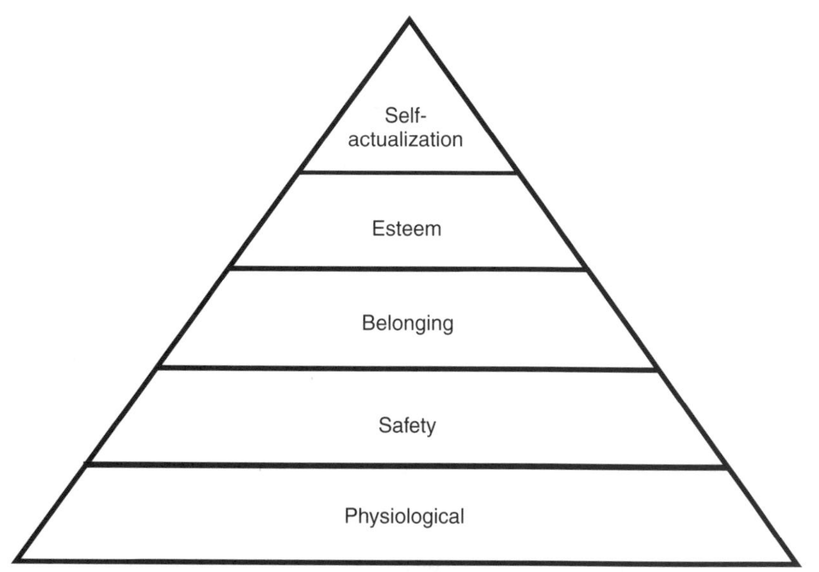

Fig 5.5: Maslow's hierarchy of needs

physiological needs
Basic human requirements for survival such as food and shelter

safety needs
The desire for protection against loss of shelter, food, and other basic requirements for survival

belonging needs
A desire for love, affection, and belonging; the need to interact with others and have some social acceptance and approval

esteem needs
A human need to be respected by others and to have a positive self-image

self-actualization needs
The individual's desire to do what he or she has the potential of doing; called the "highest-order" need

hierarchy of needs
Hypothesis that human needs are arranged in a hierarchy from lower order (safety and physiological needs) to higher order needs (belonging, self esteem, and self actualization)

(belonging, esteem, and self-actualization) are not important until the primary, or lower-order needs (safety and physiological) are at least partially satisfied.

Maslow also feels that a person is not motivated by a need that is satisfied. Once a need is satisfied, the person is concerned with the next level of the need hierarchy. A person seeks to move up the hierarchy of needs, generally striving to satisfy the need deficiency at the next-highest level.

ERG theory
A modification to needs theory; three basic needs: existence needs, relatedness needs, and growth needs

existence needs
Needs that encompass psychological and security needs for material things

relatedness needs
Security needs for interpersonal matters, love, and belonging needs, and the needs of an interpersonal nature

ERG THEORY ERG theory is similar to Maslow's approach, though there are important differences. In **ERG theory** there are three, not five, basic need categories (Alderfer, 1972). They are existence needs, relatedness needs, and growth needs (hence the label ERG).

- **Existence needs** encompass Maslow's physiological and security needs for material things.
- **Relatedness needs** include security needs for interpersonal matters, love and belonging needs, and needs of an interpersonal nature.
- **Growth needs** focus on the need to confirm personal esteem and self-actualization.

Like Maslow's theory, ERG theory states that unsatisfied needs will dominate behavior and that once a need is satisfied, higher-order needs are desired. For example, the less existence needs are satisfied, the more their satisfaction is desired. As they become satisfied, relatedness needs become more desired. Growth needs continue to be desired even as they are satisfied. Unlike Maslow's theory, ERG theory makes two further statements (Miner, 1980):

- The less relatedness needs are fulfilled, the more existence needs will be desired.
- The less growth needs are fulfilled, the more relatedness needs will be desired.

This implies that if a person is deprived of a higher-order need or does not have the potential to satisfy it, he or she will focus on lower-order needs. In other words, he or she will regress on the need hierarchy.

HERZBERG'S TWO-FACTOR THEORY

The application of need theory to motivate people posed problems for manager, because it is difficult to translate needs into management strategies. Research by Herzberg, Mausner, and Snyderman (1959) provided some guidance for managers in solving this problem. Their study challenged a long-held assumption about how a person's work satisfaction affected performance and motivation. Before, it was assumed that if a person was dissatisfied with part of the job (for example, pay), all that had to be done was to improve the factor (increase pay). This would lead to higher satisfaction, greater motivation, and higher performance. However, Herzberg and his co-workers concluded that there are two sets of factors (hence the name "two-factor" theory) that affect people in the workplace, each of which worked in different ways. These were hygiene factors and motivating factors.

hygiene factors Factors that create dissatisfaction if they are not present

Hygiene factors create dissatisfaction if they are not present. If they are present in a job setting, dissatisfaction will be lower, but satisfaction will not be high. Hygiene factors are associated with the context of a job. They include working conditions, status, and company policy. A complete list is given in table 5.1. Therefore, according to the two-factor theory, providing fringe benefits, nice offices, and good vacation plans serve mainly to minimize dissatisfaction and to keep people in the organization; it does not lead to higher motivation or better performance.

Table 5.1 Basic elements of two-factor theory

Hygiene factors	*Motivators*
1 Technical supervision	1 Responsibility
2 Interpersonal relations – Peers	2 Achievement
3 Salary	3 Advancement
4 Working conditions	4 The work itself
5 Status	5 Recognition
6 Company policy	6 Possibility of growth
7 Job security	
8 Interpersonal relations – Supervisor	

motivators Factors that are related to high satisfaction and willingness to work harder

Motivators are related to high satisfaction and willingness to work harder. When they are present, these job factors may induce more effort, but if they are absent, it will not produce dissatisfaction in most people. Motivators are associated with the content of the job. They are factors such as responsibility and achievement; see table 5.1. Therefore, a person in a challenging job is likely to be satisfied and motivated to perform better. However, the lack of challenging work does not cause dissatisfaction, merely the absence of satisfaction. A person who is well paid will not be dissatisfied; however, high pay will not lead to motivation.

This theory became popular with managers because it gave them a direction in managing motivation. For instance, if worker dissatisfaction is seen as the major problem, then the hygiene factors must be improved. To improve performance the manager must work on the motivators, and this means changing the nature of the work to make it more challenging and **intrinsically rewarding**. That means that the person experiences good feelings of growth and status as a result of doing a good job.

Herzberg's work has been the subject of much research and controversy. First, the results may be a consequence of method bias. He used the incident recall method, an approach in which subjects are asked to think of a good work experience, or to think of a bad work experience. With this method, there is a tendency for the person to attribute good experiences to themselves, as when they did a good job, and bad experiences to others or to the context, as when their supervisor prevented them from doing a good job. This could account for why the particular hygiene and motivating factors were discovered. Studies which used other methods, such as questionnaires, reached different conclusions (House and Wigdor, 1967). Second, individual differences are not considered. For example, self-confidence and skill both may affect whether a job is seen as challenging. A highly skilled systems analyst may find it challenging to design the information system for a new plant while an equally intelligent person with less computer competence may find the same assignment frustrating.

Even with these problems, the two-factor theory made an important contribution. It did provide some guidance to those who design jobs, and it was widely used by practicing managers. Of more importance, though, is that Herzberg's research directed attention in a very dramatic way to the role of the work itself as a factor that affects worker motivation and performance. This is a fundamental premise of several managerial motivational strategies discussed in chapter 6.

THE JOB CHARACTERISTICS APPROACH

job characteristics approach
A theory of motivation based on the concept that it is the properties of the work, the core job dimensions, that affect its motivational capacity

One motivational approach that helps to solve the problem of translating "needs" into management strategies is called the **job characteristics approach**, also called the **job design approach**. Like Herzberg's theory, the job characteristics approach is based on the idea that the nature of the work itself is a factor that affects motivation and performance. Facets of work that are associated with the task itself have a positive motivational effect. Facets of work that are part of the context in which the work is done have little positive motivational effects, but, if they are not satisfactory, they could reduce motivation and satisfaction (Herzberg et al., 1959).

Working from Herzberg's idea that the work itself is an important motivating factor, Hackman and Lawler (1971) set out the first structure of the job characteristics model, which is the basis of the job design approach to motivation. Based on this premise, the job design approach says that when specific job characteristics are present "employees will experience a positive, self-generated response when they perform well and that this internal kick will provide an incentive for continued efforts toward good performance" (Hackman and Suttle, 1977). There are four key elements in the job design approach (Hackman and Oldham, 1976):

1 Work outcomes
2 Critical psychological states
3 Core job dimensions
4 Growth need strength.

internal work motivation
The level of motivation from the work itself, or the person's own desire, rather than from external factors such as pay and supervision

As shown in figure 5.6, there are four important **work outcomes** in this model.

1 **Internal work motivation** is how motivated the person is by the work itself, rather than external factors such as pay and supervision.
2 **Quality of work** results from people having meaningful jobs. Individuals will produce fewer errors, lower numbers of rejected parts, and lower scrap rates. The job characteristics approach does not suggest that people will

produce more, although productivity may increase if an output level is maintained and work quality is improved.

3 **Job satisfaction** is a third outcome that is affected by the characteristics of work.
4 **Absenteeism** and **turnover** are the final set of outcomes in the job characteristics model. Both absenteeism and turnover can be quite expensive for firms when they are high and out of control.

job satisfaction
The attitude toward work in general, or to specific facets of the work

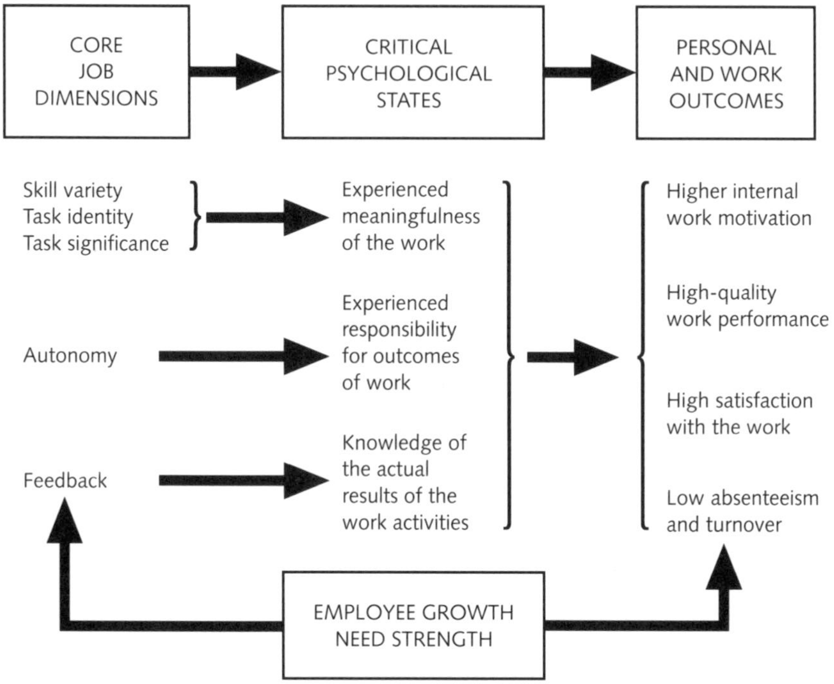

Fig 5.6: The job characteristic's model: the relationships among core job dimensions, critical psychological states, and work outcomes

critical psychological states
Mental states necessary for the work motivation: meaningfulness of work; experience and responsibility for outcomes; and knowledge of results

meaningfulness of work
The belief that work counts for something important either to the person or to someone else

experienced responsibility for outcome
The belief that the person is personally accountable for the results of his or her work

The four work outcomes are affected by three **critical psychological states** that give the person a kick out of doing the work when performing well in a job.

1 **Meaningfulness of work** occurs when the person believes that it counts for something, i.e. that is important either to the person or to someone else. For instance, most Peace Corps volunteers believe that their work is "the toughest job you will ever love." This feeling exists even though a volunteer's work may be a very ordinary task, at a very low pay level, and in very undesirable working conditions. Most volunteers believe that their work makes an important difference, however small, to someone. It certainly makes a difference to the volunteer.
2 **Experienced responsibility for outcomes** of work occurs when a person believes that he or she is personally accountable for the results of work.

This is also the case for Peace Corp volunteers. Usually volunteers are working alone or with only a few others. They know that they are responsible for the success or failure of projects.

knowledge of results
Information that allows a person to make an assessment about the adequacy or inadequacy of work performance

3 **Knowledge of results** is when a person can personally judge the adequacy or inadequacy of work performance. Obtaining knowledge of results is not as simple as it sounds. For instance, the project director for the Mars Pathfinder Mission that successfully landed the Sojourner Walker on Mars in July, 1997 only had feedback about how well he did when the vehicle itself was on Mars and began transmitting pictures. For the prior four years that he and his team worked on the project, they had no idea about the success of the project.

High levels of meaningfulness, responsibility, and knowledge of results exist when certain core job characteristics are present. There are five **core job dimensions:**

1 Skill variety
2 Task identity
3 Task significance
4 Autonomy
5 Feedback

Different core job characteristics contribute to different psychological states:

- Work meaningfulness is affected by skill variety, task identity, and task significance.
- Experienced responsibility is a function of autonomy.
- Knowledge of results is determined by feedback.

skill variety
The number of different abilities and capacities required in performing a job

task identity
The extent to which a person is responsible for the whole job, from beginning to end

task significance
The effect that the work has on others, either in their jobs or their lives

autonomy
The level of freedom an individual or team has to do their job

feedback
The information that a person receives about the results of his or her effort or performance

Skill variety is how many different abilities and capacities are required for the performance components that make up the person's job. A clerk in a secretarial pool who only types outgoing letters has a job that is of a low skill variety. A personal secretary to the CEO, however, may use several different skills such as typing and dealing with different people from both inside and outside the organization.

Task identity is the extent to which a person is responsible for the whole job, from beginning to end.

Task significance is the effect that work has on others, either in their work or in their lives. This occurs when the person can link his or her task to some value created for the customer.

Autonomy is the freedom that you have in the job. High autonomy is the freedom to determine when, how, and where a job is to be done. When autonomy is high, so are perceived feelings of responsibility.

Feedback is the information that a person receives about the results of the job. One source of feedback is from other workers or supervisors. Another form of feedback may be from the job itself; a basketball player has immediate feedback – when a shot goes through the hoop or it misses.

These job characteristics do not affect everyone the same way. The person's growth need strength is very important. **Growth need strength** is the extent to which a person desires to advance, to be in a challenging position, and, generally, to achieve. If you have high growth strength and have a job high on the core dimensions, you are more likely to experience high internal motivation, high satisfaction, high work quality, and low turnover and absenteeism than if you have low growth need strength (Spector, 1985).

growth need strength
The extent to which a person desires to advance, to be in a challenging position, and to achieve generally

McClelland's Achievement–Power Theory

An important motivational model, useful particularly in understanding leadership was developed by McClelland (1965). Two important concepts underlie **achievement–power theory**:

achievement–power theory
A motivational model based upon the relative importance of achievement needs, needs for power, and affiliation needs to the individual

1 Motive
2 The force of motives on behavior

Motives are "affectively toned associated networks arranged in a hierarchy of strength and importance" within a person (McClelland, 1965). Motives are an aspect of the personality, and they develop as the personality emerges. The idea is that, for a particular person, one of these motives is more likely to be dominant, or have the highest position in his or her hierarchy, and that motive will have the strongest effect on behavior.

There are three needs, or motives, that are at the center of this approach:

1 The need for achievement
2 The need for power
3 The need for affiliation

The two most important, discussed in detail below, are the achievement motive and the power motive.

The **achievement motive** is the extent to which success is important and valued by a person. The strength of the achievement motive is related to socialization experiences (Heckhausen, 1967). For example, if your early success experiences were very rewarding, we would expect you to have high achievement motivation. If these success experiences were not rewarding, another motive (say, power) may have a more dominant place in your motive cluster.

achievement motive
An internal drive state of the individual that reflects the extent to which success is important and valued

One person's achievement motive may differ from another's in terms of level and area of focus. Rewarded success in school may lead to high academic achievement motives while rewarded success in a part-time job might lead to work achievement motives. For example, someone high in work achievement may be driven by this motive to be successful in the firm; a person with academic achievement motive may be driven to be successful in an area of science and not seek organization success.

When the achievement motive is generalized, a person wants to succeed in everything. For the high achiever, the achievement motive is toward the top of the motive hierarchy and only minimal achievement cues are necessary to generate the positive feelings of potential success and, therefore, increase the likelihood of trying to succeed (McClelland, 1965). Here are the sorts of cues and conditions that activate achievement motives (McClelland, 1965):

- Success must come from your own efforts, not from those of others or from luck. High achievers wish to take personal responsibility for success.
- The situation must have an "intermediate level of risk." This means that it will be challenging, but not impossible. If the risk is so high that success is impossible, you will avoid it. If it is so low that the task is easy, you would avoid it because it is no real challenge.
- You want concrete feedback about success, because you want to keep track of how well you are doing. You would try to avoid situations where there can be any doubt about their achievement.

Successful entrepreneurs have high achievement motives – those high in achievement motives play a "one man game that need not involve other people" (McClelland, 1975). The entrepreneurial situation in business has most of the characteristics that arouse the achievement motive. Entrepreneurs know that if they win or lose, they are responsible, accountable, and in charge.

Interestingly, it was initially thought that successful managers would have high achievement motivation that would lead to better work performance, faster promotion, and ultimately to high levels of management. It was discovered that many top-level executives did not have high achievement motivation, but instead, they had high **power motives** (McClelland, 1975).

power motive
The need to have an impact on others, or to establish, maintain, or restore personal prestige or power

The power motive is your need to have an impact on others, to establish, maintain, or restore personal prestige or power (McClelland, 1975). It can show up three different ways.

1 You could take strong aggressive actions towards others, give help to others, try to control or persuade others or try to impress them.
2 You might act in a way that results in strong emotions in others, even though the act itself is not strong.
3 This motive can be reflected by a concern for your reputation and, perhaps, doing things that would enhance or preserve it.

Men and women high in the power motive have similar characteristics (McCelland, 1975; Winter, 1988). They hold organization offices, prefer jobs in power-oriented careers (such as business, teaching, and journalism), prefer to be highly visible in their organizations, and tend to acquire prestige possessions. One important difference is that men with high power motives tend to drink heavily while women do not.

personalized power motive
Those with a personalized power orientation prefer person-to-person competition in which they can dominate

The power motive may take one of two different forms: personalized power and socialized power. **Personalized power** is adversarial. Those with a personalized power orientation prefer person-to-person competition in which they can dominate. To them, life is a win–lose game and the law of the jungle rules; the strong survive by destroying the weak. They drink somewhat heavily and gain considerable satisfaction from power fantasies while under the influence of alcohol. These persons are high in the power motive but low in self-control and inhibition (McClelland, 1975).

Those with a **socialized power** orientation want to exercise power for the good of others, to be careful about the use of personal power, plan carefully for conflict with others, and know that someone's win is another person's loss. They have high self-control and prefer a more disciplined expression of their power motivation than those who have a personal power orientation. People with strong socialized power motives, low affiliation needs, and high self-control have a configuration of motives called the "leader motive pattern" (McClelland, 1975).

socialized power motive
A person with a socialized power orientation believes that he or she exercises power for the good of others

Motivation – The Process Theories

We now turn to the second group of motivation theories, the process theories. **Process theories** of motivation focus on how behavior change occurs, or how a person comes to act in a different way. There is less emphasis on the specific factors (or "content") that causes behavior. For example, a content theory would lead you to say that, "Increases in pay can improve satisfaction and performance," while a process theory would explain, one way or another, how that happens. For example, reinforcement theory would lead you to say that "performance will increase if the consequence of high performance is a positive reinforcer." In this case, the reinforcement of the high performance behavior with the desire consequence is the process by which performance improves. As you come to understand the concepts in these theories, you will see the dominant process orientation and the less prominent, but still present, content aspects of each. Four process theories are discussed in this section:

process theories
Motivation theories that focus on how, not why, behavior changes

1 Reinforcement theory
2 Expectancy theory
3 Goal-setting theory
4 Organizational justice theories

Reinforcement Theory

Reinforcement theory is one of the most important and, perhaps, most complicated of the motivation theories. It is very useful to managers because it can help them to understand not only how personality develops (see page 37 in chapter 2), but also how rewarding or punishing behavior affects performance and satisfaction. A good deal of research supports reinforcement theory. The most consistent results are from highly controlled experiments using a wide range of subjects to show the effects of rewards and punishments (Allyon and Azrin, 1965). Research done in the work place, though more complicated because there are just too many factors that prevent the linking of consequences to behavior, also supports reinforcement theory. There are two key concepts in reinforcement theory:

1 The types of reinforcement consequences
2 Reinforcement schedules

We now consider both of these in detail.

TYPES OF REINFORCEMENT CONSEQUENCES In reinforcement theory, several types of consequences can occur:

1 Positive reinforcement
2 Negative reinforcement (avoidance)
3 Punishment
4 Extinction

Figure 5.7 shows the nature of each type of consequence and its effects on the probability of a behavior recurring.

positive reinforcement When a positive reinforcer is linked with a behavior, increasing the probability that the behavior will recur in the same or similar situations

Positive reinforcement occurs when desirable consequences are associated with a behavior. A positive reinforcer increases the likelihood that the behavior will recur in the future. Part (a) of figure 5.8 shows how a manager might use positive reinforcement to improve the quality of your work. When you produce a report, she could point out that it was much better than your previous work and could provide positive reinforcement through praise ("You did great!"). If this continues, the stimulus ("Do good work.") will eventually lead to fewer problems with your reports.

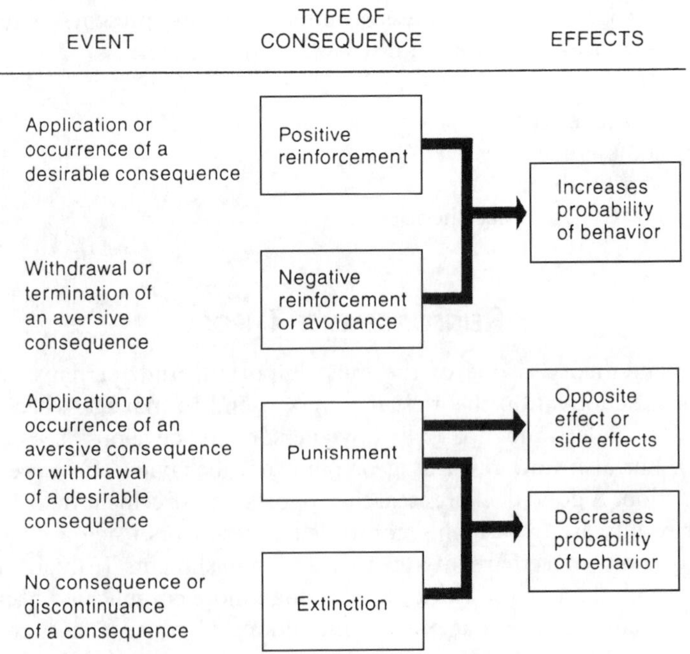

Fig 5.7: Types of consequences and their effects

Negative reinforcement occurs when an undesirable consequence is removed. It also increases the likelihood that the behavior will occur again. Suppose that you work in a very noisy plant and find that wearing earplugs reduces your discomfort from the noise. This should lead you to associate noise (in the plant) and the use of earplugs. The removal of the noise is a negative reinforcer – it strengthens the association between the stimulus (working in high noise) and the response (wearing the earplugs) (Reitz, 1981). This is also called **avoidance learning.** We engage in the response to avoid a negative effect. Just as you stop at a red light to avoid a ticket and fine, so at work you may work hard to meet job standards to avoid negative consequences. Part (b) of figure 5.8 shows what you might do to avoid negative criticism from your boss.

negative reinforcement
Occurs when an undesirable consequence is removed and the behavior is more likely to occur again

avoidance learning
When an aversive event that follows a behavior is terminated, which increases the frequency of that behavior

Some managers think that negative reinforcement is a good way to manage people at work; that is, employees who engage in undesirable behavior should expect something to happen to them. However, there can be some difficulties with this approach. First, it creates a tense environment – it is difficult to work day after day where the main motivation is to prevent unpleasant outcomes. Second, relationships often deteriorate when another person, particularly your supervisor, represents a constant threat to be avoided.

Punishment can take two forms. Negative consequences (undesirable things) can be applied to a response or positive consequences (desirable things) can actively be taken away. Part (c) of figure 5.8 shows how you could be punished

punishment
Occurs when an undesirable or painful consequence follows behavior or when a desirable consequence is removed; may decrease the frequency of the behavior but often has unintended side-effects

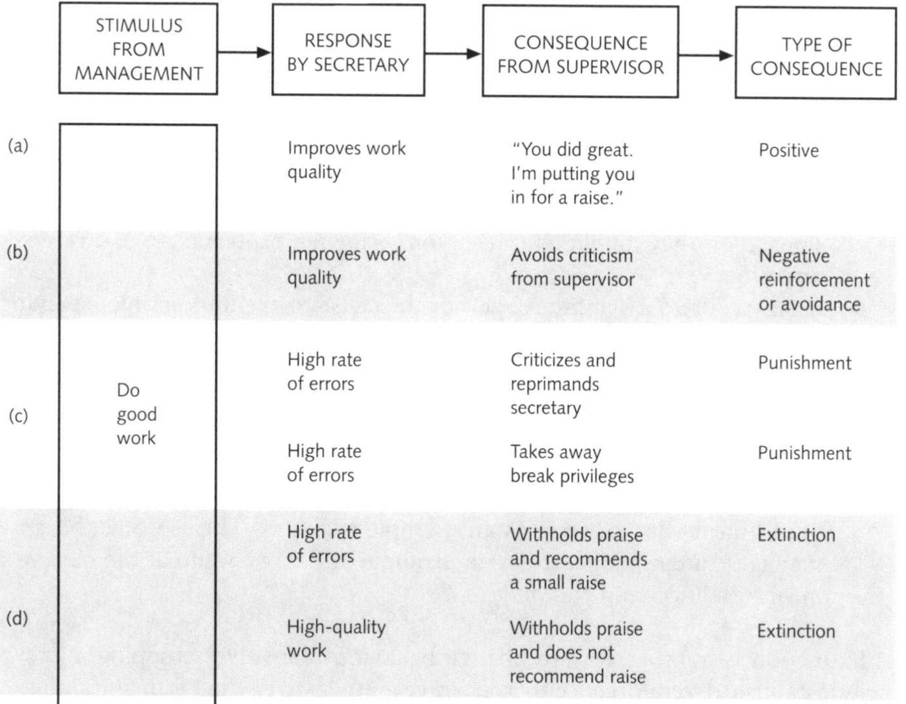

	STIMULUS FROM MANAGEMENT	RESPONSE BY SECRETARY	CONSEQUENCE FROM SUPERVISOR	TYPE OF CONSEQUENCE
(a)	Do good work	Improves work quality	"You did great. I'm putting you in for a raise."	Positive
(b)		Improves work quality	Avoids criticism from supervisor	Negative reinforcement or avoidance
(c)		High rate of errors	Criticizes and reprimands secretary	Punishment
		High rate of errors	Takes away break privileges	Punishment
(d)		High rate of errors	Withholds praise and recommends a small raise	Extinction
		High-quality work	Withholds praise and does not recommend raise	Extinction

Fig 5.8: Examples of consequences in a work setting

when your reports are not well done. Your boss may be very critical and reprimand you. The figure also shows how punishment can be applied by withdrawing positive consequences. Here, the contingent result of a low-quality report is taking away your extra break privileges. In both instances, the response, "poor reports," should decrease.

There is an important distinction between punishment and negative reinforcement. When you are punished, you learn to prevent negative consequences by withholding behaviors. For example, you do not criticize your boss if she treats you unfairly because you are afraid you might be fired. In negative reinforcement, you learn to do things (perform responses) that stop a negative consequence from occurring. You might learn to avoid certain situations at work where you might be made angry by your boss (Stajkovic and Luthans, 1997).

Certainly punishment can affect behavior at work, but it should be a last resort. Reprimands and firing may have to occur, but it is best to try to correct the behavior first. Positive reinforcement is a much better alternative, and many examples exist of its effective use in improving performance and attendance (Locke et al., 1981). There are some serious problems with using punishment:

- It needs to be carefully handled. It cannot be too mild, nor too severe – its magnitude should fit the crime.
- It should be linked to the undesirable behavior and applied as close in time as possible. Punishment is more effective if it encourages an incompatible response or a desirable substitute response.
- It can have an opposite effect and actually become a positive reinforcer. A subordinate who is punished may in fact feel rewarded by having angered his boss or by gaining the attention and support of fellow workers.
- Punishment can have undesirable side-effects. For instance, punishment can reduce the frequency of desirable behaviors. It contributes to a fearful environment in which people may stop taking initiative or trying new things, or they might cut back on bringing problems to their boss's attention.
- It may address a symptom and not the cause of the undesirable behavior. If the cause persists, the behavior will probably persist.
- The manager cannot control how other employees interpret the punishment. It is often the punished employee who controls the information that other employees receive about it. They return to the workplace and give their own interpretation of the situation. If they lack accuracy and completeness in their tale or if they distort their report to save face, the punishment will not serve as an example to others. This is ironic, because managers often punish to set an example but may end up at the mercy of misinformation and rumor.

extinction
The cessation of a previously established reinforcer that is maintaining a behavior

Extinction is another way to change behavior. It involves stopping a previously established reinforcer, either positive or negative, that is maintaining a behavior. Managers may extinguish a response of a worker by not reinforcing it for an extended period of time; the response then becomes less frequent and eventually stops. Part (d) of figure 5.8 shows two examples of extinguishing behavior. In one case, your supervisor withholds both praise and punishment when your reports are not well done. In the other, praise and rewards are withheld when you do a good report. In both cases, the response rates may decrease, but one is desirable behavior and the other one is not.

Managers should be very sensitive to the wide array of possibilities of extinction in the workplace. Employees should not learn that good behaviors have little or no consequences. For instance, when there is no distinction between rewards for average performance and outstanding performance, you soon learn that high levels of performance do not pay off. In short, you have been extinguished from doing more than average or minimal performance. Another interesting case of extinction is when you seek feedback on your performance. You might be told, "I thought you knew you were doing well; I haven't been on your back have I?" A boss who manages by saying little or nothing to the good employee could well be fostering mediocre work performance.

Reinforcement schedules are the timing and frequency that consequences are associated with behavior. They are important because they affect how long it takes to learn a new behavior and how resistant the behavior is to change. Five types of reinforcement schedules are shown in figure 5.9:

reinforcement schedules Consequences of a behavior occurring in different patterns, which affect how quickly the behavior is learned, and how resistant it is to change or to extinction

1 Continuous schedules
2 Fixed interval schedules
3 Variable interval schedules
4 Fixed ratio schedules
5 Variable ratio schedules

In a **continuous reinforcement schedule**, a response is reinforced (or punished) each time it occurs. For example, when learning a new job, an instructor may be constantly present to respond in a reinforcing manner each time a worker does the right thing. It is not easy to apply a continuous schedule in work situations, because it requires the constant presence of someone else; supervisors cannot use continuous reinforcement or punishment schedules unless they monitor subordinates closely. This level of monitoring is probably not advisable, except for short periods where a supervisor is coaching or training an employee on a specific task. Close monitoring creates an unfavorable climate if subordinates feel they are constantly watched and it can have negative effects on the satisfaction and productivity of work groups (Likert, 1961).

continuous reinforcement schedule Reinforcement, every time a behavior occurs

In a **fixed-interval reinforcement schedule**, a response is reinforced after a fixed amount of time has elapsed. These schedules result in irregular performance rates, with behavior at its highest rate closer in time to when the reinforcement occurs. For example, when performance appraisals are scheduled every six months, employees are likely to work harder as the time for appraisal nears. Pay is another example because it is generally given at a regular time of the week or month. It is difficult to say exactly what pay reinforces, but it is unlikely that paychecks reinforce performance because pay is often not a function of performance. The most probable effect of a regular paycheck is to reinforce attendance (if pay is reduced for lateness) or to deter people from quitting.

fixed-interval reinforcement schedule A partial reinforcement schedule in which a response is reinforced after a fixed amount of time has elapsed

CONTINUOUS SCHEDULE

Every response reinforced;
Rapid learning and extinction

	FIXED	VARIABLE
INTERVAL (Time)	FIXED INTERVAL Reinforcement at fixed times Learning fairly slow and connected to time Moderately resistant to extinction	VARIABLE INTERVAL Reinforcement at varied, perhaps unpredictable times Learning is slow and activity high Very resistant to extinction
RATIO (Responses)	FIXED RATIO Reinforcement after a fixed number of responses Learning slow, activity high, and pauses after reinforcement Moderately resistant to extinction	VARIABLE RATIO Reinforcement after a varying number of responses Learning slow, response rate steady and very high Very resistant to extinction

Fig 5.9: Schedules of reinforcement and their effects on learning and extinction

variable-interval reinforcement schedule
A partial reinforcement schedule in which the periods of time between reinforcements to occur is varied

fixed-ratio reinforcement schedule
A partial reinforcement schedule in which a certain number of responses are necessary to produce a consequence

In a **variable-interval reinforcement schedule**, the period of time between reinforcements is not constant. Variable-interval schedules are common in work settings. Supervisors often visit work sites at irregular intervals. Consider the example of a security guard who dare not leave his post because he does not know when the post might be checked by a supervisor.

The problem with variable-interval schedules is that they might also result in the wrong behavior. If subordinates are rewarded by a visit from the boss, the visit might inadvertently reinforce an undesirable act. Suppose the boss makes an unscheduled visit and tells an employee what a good job she is doing, but arrives at the site just after the employee has returned late from a work break. The employee may feel that she is the victim of inconsistent signals or may feel some resentment, e.g., "Why wasn't she here when I did so well the other day?"

In a **fixed-ratio reinforcement schedule**, a certain number of responses must occur before a reinforcement follows. A piece rate payment system is an example of a fixed-ratio schedule at work. The employee is credited with additional pay for increments of productivity. Additional pay is received, say, for each dozen cartons packed or for every three vehicles sold. Fixed-ratio schedules can produce high rates of response that continue so as long as the reinforcement remains powerful.

With a **variable-ratio reinforcement schedule**, the number of behaviors necessary for a reinforcement varies. You might be reinforced after one response or after several, and the number of required behaviors changes. This schedule produces a very high and steady rate of response, typically without predictable pauses or bursts of behavior. Gambling and fishing are good examples of variable-ratio schedules. The payoff occurs at unpredictable times and sustains behavior over long periods. Hundreds of lottery tickets might be bought before a large winning ticket comes along, but there are always small prizes randomly won while you are hoping – and still buying. Likewise, it may take many casts before a fish is hooked.

variable-ratio reinforcement schedule
A partial reinforcement schedule in which the number of behaviors necessary for reinforcements to occur is varied

Variable-ratio schedules occur at work when managers reward irregularly, either by accident or design. Some companies have tried to implement them formally by using lotteries to reduce absenteeism. For example, at Continental Airlines, employees with perfect attendance records for six months are eligible for a drawing in which a new car is the prize. Unless the reinforcement occurs or its perceived likelihood remains, it will not affect behavior. Extinction would take place if the employee attends regularly but *never* wins a prize.

One approach to changing behavior, called **behavior shaping**, involves reinforcing small increments of behavior that are in the direction of desired behavior until a final desired result is achieved. Behavior shaping can be used in all kinds of learning, not just when we are trying to extinguish or overcome old habits. Shaping requires that we break down a desired response into components and think of the desired behavior as a sequence of the components. Then if we can encourage a part of the behavior anywhere in the sequence, it can be reinforced. This continues until the complete behavior is learned. For example, suppose that a manager in your department has been resisting the use of personal computers in his unit. You believe that the reason for his resistance is simply that he is afraid he will not be able to use them easily. Here are some ways that you can begin shaping his behavior so that he will eventually introduce personal computers:

behavior shaping
Involves reinforcing small increments or changes in behavior that are in the direction of desired behavior until a final desired result is achieved

- Take him to the office of another manager who has successfully introduced computers so that he can see the benefits that her department gained.
- Assign him a simple task that requires the use of a computer on which he works with a supportive and helpful computer user.
- Ask him to prepare a brief report on the costs, benefits, and user-friendliness of different computer brands. Throughout this process, you would encourage and positively reinforce any behaviors consistent with your overall goal of introducing computers.

Transfer of learning occurs when behavior learned in one situation occurs in another situation. Sometimes the transfer is appropriate, but sometimes it is not. Suppose you take a job in a company in which there are relaxed standards of dress. So long as you are productive and dress neatly, you can succeed. If you change jobs and join another firm with a more formal dress norm, the way you dress may no longer be acceptable, and you could suffer the consequences despite your good work. What you learned in the first company about appro-

transfer of learning
A condition that occurs when people learn things in one situation and the learned behavior is transferred or applied in another situation

priate dress style transferred negatively to the second. For learning to transfer, it is necessary to have similar conditions to those that existed when the behavior was learned. For example, the use of similar or identical equipment at work as that used in training aids the transfer of learning from the classroom to the workplace. It also helps to maintain the reinforcements and feedback that took place in training.

EXPECTANCY THEORY

expectancy theory Premise that individuals will put forth effort to do those things that will lead to the results (outcomes) they desire; a rational approach to motivation

The basic idea of **expectancy theory** is that you will work (put forth effort) to do those things that will lead to the results (outcomes) that you desire. This is a rational approach to motivation that implies that people make an assessment of the costs or benefits of the different alternatives that they have and then select the one with the best payoffs (Vroom, 1964). Suppose a car salesman has two different ways to approach selling cars (House and Wahba, 1972):

1 He could spend a lot of time telephoning prospective buyers.
2 He could wait until customers come into the store.

What he does depends on his preference for certain outcomes and the expectations about those outcomes. If he estimates that calling customers has a high probability (an expectation) of earning a substantial bonus and a low expectation of earning the bonus if he waits for the customers to come to the showroom, the motivation to call customers is much higher. According to expectancy theory, the salesman would choose the work behavior, telephoning customers.

We must know some other things about the salesman before we can predict his behavior with expectancy theory. For instance, we assumed that the salesman values the bonus and that he feels he can succeed if he tries to sell. However, there are other outcomes associated with both success and failure. For example, failure or success will affect opportunities for advancement, personal satisfaction with work, and, perhaps, relationships with other members of the sales staff. Finally, there is the question of ability. A person with high selling ability will be more successful than one with lesser skills, given similar levels of motivation. These elements of expectancy theory are shown in figure 5.10.

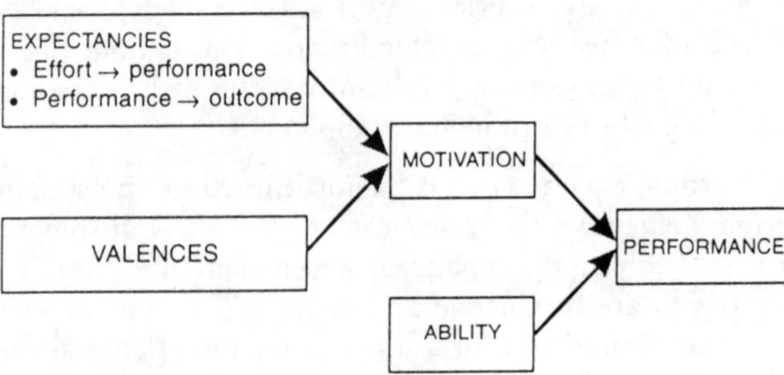

Fig 5.10: Some key concepts in expectancy theory

An **expectancy** is an individual's estimate, or judgment, of the likelihood that some outcome (or event) will occur. It is a probability estimate and can range from 0 (impossible) to 1 (certain). If the salesman believes that to sell one car it is necessary to show cars to five potential buyers, the expectancy is 0.20.

There are two kinds of expectancies; see figure 5. 11.

1 The **effort–performance expectancy** (E → P) is the person's belief about the level of effort made and the resulting performance that it will lead to. For the salesman, the effort–performance expectancy is the relationship between "How hard I work to sell cars," and "How many cars I sell."
2 The **performance–outcome expectancy** (P → O) is the expectation that achieving a given level of work performance will lead to certain outcomes. High P → O expectancies, particularly with respect to attaining rewards, are necessary for high performance. This is called the **performance–reward linkage**, and if it is not made, then we should not expect a person to make an effort.

expectancy
An individual's estimate, or judgment, of the likelihood that some outcome (or event) will occur

effort–performance expectancy
A person's belief about the level of effort put forth and the resulting performance that it will lead to

performance–outcome expectancy
The expectation about the relationship between a particular level of performance and attaining certain outcomes

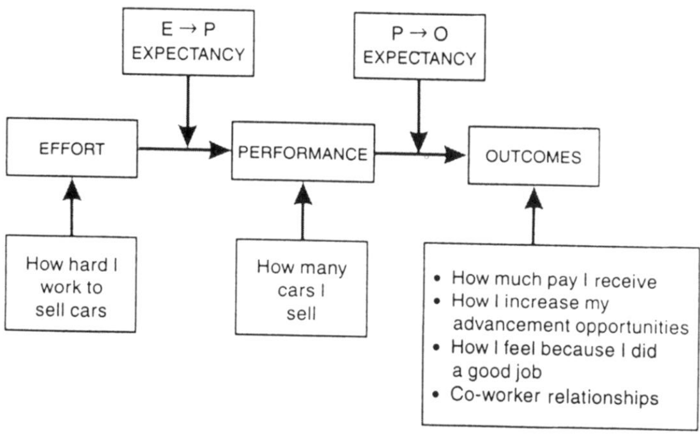

Fig 5.11: Effort–perfomance and performance–outcome expectancies

Figure 5.11 shows four possible outcomes for the salesman's performance, "How many cars I sell:"

1 "How much pay I receive"
2 "How I increase my advancement opportunities"
3 "How I feel because I did a good job"
4 Co-worker relationships

All these outcomes affect the level of motivation. As an illustration, a salesperson may feel that if he works hard, high performance will result (E → P). This may have a high probability of increasing income and self-esteem, but a low probability of improving relations with co-workers. These several outcomes of performance (pay, advancement, self-esteem, and co-worker relations) are all P → O expectations.

EXERCISE

THE BASIC ELEMENTS OF EXPECTANCY THEORY

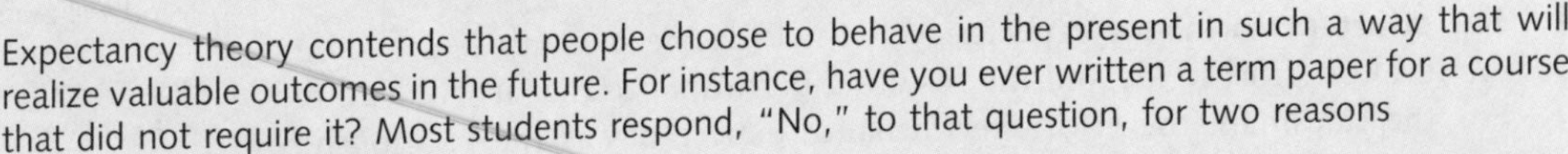

Expectancy theory contends that people choose to behave in the present in such a way that will realize valuable outcomes in the future. For instance, have you ever written a term paper for a course that did not require it? Most students respond, "No," to that question, for two reasons

1 Most undergraduates do not have the information or ability to write it
2 They see nothing "in it for them" for writing one.

These two reasons reflect the basic ideas of expectancy theory. The following short examples are designed to illustrate how the elements of expectancy theory, discussed in this chapter, affect the motivation of a person in an organization.

The Case of "Ike Antt"

Ike Antt works on the production line of a local electronic parts manufacturing firm. Ike has a family and has been struggling to make ends meet during the last few years with most of his small raises being eaten up by inflation. Ike's boss told him yesterday that a foreman's job will open up in about six months and that he could have it if Ike could double his productivity during the six-month period. Ike talked to his wife about it and concluded that the promotion would bring a much-needed pay raise but that he was already working as hard, fast and long as he could without falling sick and that the idea of doubling his current output was totally impossible.

For each of the questions below, circle the correct answer:

• Is the valence or importance of the promotion high or low to Ike?	High	Low
• Is Ike's belief that he will get promoted *if* he doubles his productivity high or low? (This is the P → O belief.)	High	Low
• Is Ike's belief that he *can* double his output *if* he tries high or low? (This is the E → P belief.)	High	Low
• Is Ike, therefore, likely to be motivated to double his output?	Yes	No

The Case of "Noah Get"

Noah Get has worked in the marketing department of Curtis, Inc., for eleven years. Noah is the most likely person to step into the marketing vice president's position when the current executive retires in 18 months. In fact, the current vice president, Mr Edwards, has been grooming Noah to take over. Noah has been putting in 60 hours a week since Mr Edwards told him that if his work output increased significantly, Noah would be given Mr Edwards' strongest recommendation for the promotion. Noah has been working to rise in the Curtis organization since he joined Curtis. His long-range goal is to be the president. Noah has three children about to enter college, so the pay raise that accompanies the promotion would be most helpful. Yesterday, Mr Edwards called Noah into his office and showed him a memo from the president that read: "Due to an immediate need to infuse new blood into our organization to deal with our changing economy and markets, all openings at the senior management level will be filled be experienced candidates from outside Curtis. This moratorium on promotion from within will be in effect for at least the next five years."

For each of the questions below, circle the correct answer:

• Is the valence or importance of a promotion high or low to Noah?	High	Low
• Is Noah's belief that he will get promoted *if* he continues to produce work at his current 60 hour a week level high or low? (P → O)	High	Low
• Is Noah's belief that he *can* continue to produce at the current elevated level for the next few months high or low? (E → P)	High	Low
• Is Noah, therefore, likely to continue to produce at this level?	Yes	No

The Case of Donna Wann

Donna Wann has worked as the local marketing rep for a national paper products firm for nine years. Donna grew up in this area, returned after college, and married her high school sweetheart. She enjoys the company of many childhood friends, in addition to the parents, grandparents, cousins, uncles, aunts, and so on, on both her and her husband's sides of the family. Donna is *very* successful as a marketing rep and could easily increase her productivity if she spent less time with her family and friends. Donna, however, values her close family and friendship ties far more than the rewards of doing more business. Yesterday, Donna's regional manager called and informed her that there would soon be an opening as the assistant to the president and that the top brass at headquarters concluded that Donna was probably the best candidate with the most potential for the position. However, to convince two skeptics on the board of directors, Donna would have to "prove herself" by showing a 15 percent increase in business over the next three months. As Donna considered the offer, she concluded that (a) a 15 percent increase would be easy to do, but (b) since the promotion meant moving to New York City, which was 1,500 miles from "home," she would have to give up her close ties with friends and family which she absolutely did not want to do.

For each of the questions below, circle the correct answer:

• Is the valence or importance of a promotion high or low to Donna?	High	Low
• Is Donna's belief that she will get promoted *if* she increases her business by 15 percent high or low? (P → O)	High	Low
• Is Donna's belief that she *can* increase business by 15 percent *if* she wants to high or low? (E → P)	High	Low
• Is Donna, therefore, very likely to increase business 15 percent?	Yes	No

Now answer these diagnostic questions.

1 What do the experiences of Ike Antt, Noah Get, and Donna Wann tell you about being motivated to put out a great effort to perform well?
2 What could be done to increase the motivation of Ike Antt? Noah Get? Donna Wann?

Not all outcomes are equally valued by a person. The strength of the person's preferences is called valence. **Valences** are anticipated satisfactions (or dissatisfactions) that result from outcomes, or the different degrees of pleasantness (or unpleasantness) of outcomes. So when an outcome has a low positive valence, you will not exert much effort to attain it. The salesman may have a strong desire for some outcomes but not for others. He may, for example, wish to have the pay increase and the advancement but avoid antagonizing co-workers.

valences
Anticipated satisfactions (or dissatisfactions) that result from outcomes; the individual's estimate of the pleasantness – or unpleasantness – of outcomes

Goal-setting Theory

Goal-setting theory is based on a simple premise: performance is caused by a person's intention to perform (Locke et al., 1981). **Goals** are "what a person is trying to accomplish" or intends to do, and according to this theory, people will do what they are trying to do (Locke, 1968). What follows from this is quite clear.

goal-setting theory
A motivation theory in which performance is predicted to be caused by a person's intention to perform (or goals)

- A person with higher goals will do better than someone with lower ones.
- If someone knows precisely what he or she wants to do, or is supposed to do, that person will do better than someone whose goals or intentions are vague.

These are the two basic ideas that underlie the four propositions of goal-setting theory:

1 *There is a general positive relationship between goal difficulty and performance.* This, however, does not hold for extremely difficult goals beyond one's ability. Difficult goals lead to better results than easy goals. This has been shown time after time in very different research settings, using students, workers, and managers (Latham and Locke, 1975; Locke et al., 1981; Tubbs, 1986; Rasch and Tosi, 1992).
2 *Specific goals lead to higher performance than general goals.* This is a particularly important point to remember because managers have a tendency to set goals that are too general for their subordinates (Carroll and Tosi, 1973). The findings from studies with students, keypunch operators, marketing personnel, production workers, and laboratory personnel show that individuals given "specific, challenging goals either outperformed those trying to do their best," or surpassed their own previous performance when they were not trying for specific goals (Locke et al., 1981).
3 *Participation is related to performance through goal acceptance and commitment, and information sharing.* Participation in setting goals does not directly affect performance but it can increase goal commitment and, ultimately, performance, particularly if it leads to some real choices about the way to achieve a goal as well as information about the goal and the task (Erez et al., 1985). This means that participation is a complex process.

It cannot be limited only to narrow areas in which superiors want to have subordinates set goals but must be more broadly based (Carroll and Tosi, 1973). It must also be realistic participation, in the sense that subordinates have some choices about ways to perform the task, the goal levels, and what information they need to perform the task (Scully et al., 1995).

4 *Feedback about performance with respect to goals is necessary.* Clear goals and feedback about performance are both necessary for higher performance (Locke et al., 1981; Tubbs, 1986). A person must know whether the desired level of performance has been achieved. In a study of telephone service personnel that compared the performance of two groups of workers, the group that had goals and received feedback performed better than the group that only had goals. The goals-feedback group had lower costs and a better safety record.

OTHER CONSIDERATIONS IN GOAL-SETTING THEORY A general personality factor that seems related to the effects of goals on performance is the sense of **self-competence**. One measure of self-competence, a general one, is self-esteem. Self-esteem has been found to interact with goals to affect performance. Managers with high self-esteem reported that they worked harder toward performance goals than those managers who had low self-esteem (Carroll and Tosi, 1973). Another is **self-efficacy**, the individual's belief that he or she can perform a task successfully. In a large number of goal-setting studies, self-efficacy has been shown to be an important factor affecting goal success (Locke, 1997).

One problem with this theory is the way it deals with goal complexity. In all the laboratory studies, goals were set for simple tasks. Even many of the field experiments generally studied relatively low-level, simple tasks such as typing or loading trucks. Work goals for managers and professionals are much more complicated. Consider, for example, how one would set goals for the plant manager discussed on page 125, with several performance components. We simply do not know from goal-setting theory, for instance, how the plant manager sets priorities and makes choices between tasks for which goals have been set that are likely to differ in specificity and difficulty. In fact, a review of the research on goal setting showed that goal specificity and goal difficulty had weaker effects for more complex tasks than for simple tasks (Wood et al., 1987).

ORGANIZATIONAL JUSTICE THEORIES

Organizational justice approaches to motivation are based on perceptions of how just or fair you are treated at work.

- **Distributive justice** is the degree to which persons believe that they are treated fairly and equitably with respect to work outcomes, or how much they put into work and how much they gain from it. This is the basis for equity theory.

distributive justice
The degree to which persons believe that they are treated fairly and equitably with respect to work outcomes, or how much they put into work and how much they gain from it

equity theory
A motivation theory based on the idea that people are motivated to maintain fair relationships with others and to rectify unfair relationships by making them fair

outcome justice
Sense of equity that occurs when individuals compare themselves to other important referents

underpayment inequity
A sense of inequity that results from getting less out of the job relative to what others contribute

- **Procedural justice** is the extent to which people believe they are treated fairly in terms of *how* decisions are made about things that affect them in the work place.

OUTCOME JUSTICE THEORY **Equity theory** states that people are motivated to maintain "fair relationships with others and to rectify unfair relationships by making them fair" (Baron, 1983). A fundamental premise is that individuals compare themselves to others and want their efforts and achievements to be judged fairly relative to them. This idea is different from other theories that explain motivation by intrapersonal comparisons (e.g., "what I have now" compared to "what I would like to have"); equity theory explains motivation by interpersonal comparisons ("what I have now" compared to "what others have"). That means that the concern in equity theory is **outcome justice**, or how you perceive your organizational outcomes relative to the contributions that you, and others, make to gain them. In other words, equity theory focuses on how you evaluate your outcome relative to how you evaluate the outcomes of others. There are three key factors used in explaining and understanding motivation in equity theory:

1 Inputs
2 Outcomes
3 Referents (Adams, 1965)

Inputs are what you bring to the job, such as age, experience, skill, and seniority, and contributions to the organization or group. They can be anything that you believe relevant to the job and that should be recognized by others. **Outcomes** are things that you perceive to be received as a result of work. Outcomes may be positively valued factors such as pay, recognition, promotion, status symbols, and fringe benefits. They may also be negative: unsafe working conditions, pressure from management, and monotony. In equity theory, a **referent** is the focus of comparison for the person: either other individuals or other groups. For example, as a department manager, you might compare yourself to one of the other department managers, say Paula Dawkins, or to all the department managers in you firm.

Perceived inequity (or equity) is based on the comparison of two ratios of outcomes to inputs. Equity occurs when your ratio of outcomes to inputs is equal to the ratio of the referent (Paula), as shown in the following equation.

$$\frac{\text{Outcomes (yours)}}{\text{Inputs (yours)}} = \frac{\text{Outcomes (Paula)}}{\text{Inputs (Paula)}}$$

Underpayment inequity occurs when you believe that your inputs are at least equal to Paula's but your outcomes are less than hers. You gain less from the job than does Paula, relative to what you both contribute. This underpayment results in dissatisfaction that stems from anger at being underrewarded and is likely to lead to a reduction in the quality of work (Kanfer, 1990; Cowherd and Levine, 1992), counter-productive behavior such as theft (Greenberg, 1990, 1993), and lower performance (Greenberg, 1988).

There is also **overpayment inequity**. If Paula assesses her outcomes in the same way that you evaluate them, she experiences overpayment inequity. This means that she believes that she gains more from the job relative to her referent (you, in this case). Overpayment inequity leads to dissatisfaction, just as does underpayment inequity, but, in this case, the dissatisfaction results from feelings of guilt that the person (in this case, Paula) develops. The dissatisfaction, whether it arises from guilt or anger, will cause the person who experiences it to do something to bring the situation into a state of equity. For example, when a group of managers were assigned higher status offices than their current position warranted, they increased their performance (Greenberg, 1988). Similar increased levels of performance were found in a study of workers who remain in a firm after downsizing and they have seen their co-workers released (Brockner et al., 1986). If co-workers were terminated because of low performance, those remaining thought that they had performed more favorably on the assignment than those terminated. When co-workers were terminated on a random basis, the remaining workers worked harder, increasing their inputs, as equity theory predicts.

overpayment inequity
A sense of inequity that results from getting more out of the job relevant to your referent

Global Focus on International Pay and Equity

One of the more serious problems that multinational firms face is how to pay their expatriate managers. An expatriate (expat) is a manager from one country (say France) who is working in another country (say Australia) who will return to his or her country of origin for a subsequent assignment. The problem stems from how the pay of the expat is determined.

One common way is to start with the home-based gross income, add or subtract a cost of living allowance (usually firms do not subtract, they just add), add a housing allowance, add any incentives such as mobility or hardship premiums, then adjust for tax differences. The other way is to base their compensation on the host country, that is, where they are working. In this case, you start with the local salary equivalent for the job and add some mobility premiums.

Either way can create equity problems. For example, the first approach makes the expat's pay equitable to his or her colleagues in the home country from which they came. This strategy means that the firm wants its expat managers to have a life style similar to their home colleagues while the second implies that the expat will live like a local manager. If the pay allows the expat to live above the standard of living of his local colleagues, they will experience inequity. However, if the second strategy is used, it implies that the company thinks it is important that the manager live like the others that he or she works with locally. This might result in lower local inequity, but perhaps a sense of inequity on the part of the expat who has a sense of falling behind those in the home office.

Source: Adapted from Frazee (1998)

When inequity is perceived, a person is likely to take some action to restore it, and thus to bring these ratios into balance. This is especially for those who have strong moral values, a strong conscience and high ethical standards (Vecchio, 1981). Here are some of the different ways of achieving an equitable balance:

- *Change the inputs* One way for you to restore equity is to reduce your inputs. You might lower your organizational commitment, put in fewer hours, and not be as concerned with quality as you had been in the past. If Paula experiences overpayment inequity, she could increase her inputs by trying to raise the quality of her work or increasing her effort.
- *Change outcomes* Another way to reduce your feelings of inequity is to try to gain more out of your work. You might seek a pay raise, try to increase your power, or seek more privileges. Paula might alter her outcomes by refusing a pay increase (unlikely!) or by taking on less intrinsically satisfying work.
- *Rationalize the inputs and outputs and psychological distortion* You could increase your outcomes by rationalizing that your job has higher status or is more important than you earlier believed. You could psychologically distort inputs by changing your attributions about how much effort you put into the job, believing that you do less than you believed before. Paula might also "convince" herself that her job is more important than yours. A study found that workers who were forced to take a pay cut but remained on the job elevated the perceived importance of their own work (Greenberg, 1989).

  Psychological distortion of the other person's outcomes and inputs is also possible. You may rationalize that Paula's actual contributions are not as great as yours but that she has done so well because she had the advantage of being a woman during a time when the company was under pressure to treat women more favorably. This would make her inputs seem greater and bring the ratios into balance.
- *Leave the situation* You may decide to move to another job. Then in the new setting, you escape the inequity and may find a fairer situation.
- *Act against the other person* You might try to convince Paula to work harder, thus increasing her inputs. Alternatively, you may be able to decrease her outcomes by a political strategy in which you undermine the confidence others have in her, so that she leaves the company.
- *Change the referent* You may find it easier not to compare yourself to Paula. If you can find another person in the firm who seems to have a similar ratio of outcomes to inputs as you, you will reinstate a sense of equity, your satisfaction will increase, and your anger will decrease.

procedural justice
The extent to which people believe they are treated fairly in terms of "how" decisions are made about things that affect them in the workplace

PROCEDURAL JUSTICE THEORY **Procedural justice** theory focuses on another facet of justice that affects motivation and satisfaction: how you make judgments and your perceptions about whether you believe that the *way* that decisions are made are fair. Perceptions of procedural justice are related to higher levels of organizational commitment, job satisfaction, and higher levels of organizational citizenship behavior, or contextual performance (Folger and Konovsky, 1989; Ball et al., 1994).

Focus on Procedural Justice

Remember the last time that you felt you were treated unfairly at work or in your university and the explanation that you received was, "That is the policy and rule that we follow." The explanation certainly did nothing to make you feel that the decision was fair. For example, Susan, a student, transferred from an MBA program in one state university to another university in the same state system. In negotiating the transfer of credit, Susan was told that she would be required to repeat a statistics course, not because she had a grade that was unacceptable, but because in the first university the course number and designation was for an introductory graduate statistics course (e.g., Sta 5127). The required course number and designation at her new university was for an advanced statistics course (e.g., Sta 6127). Susan discussed the matter with her advisor, even bringing the outline and syllabus from the first course. The fact was that the text, content and level of instruction was more advanced in her first course – and the advisor even conceded that was the case. He refused, however, to allow her the transfer, using the standard bureaucratic argument, "That is our policy here." Obviously Susan was not happy – but she had no choice.

Procedural justice theory is a relatively new motivational approach, but an important one. If you think about it for a minute, you will realize that decisions that affect you, decisions about your pay, your advancement, your work assignment and so on are made in the organization where you work. There are organizational systems of rules, policies, procedures, and operating systems through which these decisions are made and then implemented. Very often, managers believe that simply because they are following these specified procedures, rules, and policies in making decisions that those who are affected by them will accept the decisions and actions as reasonable and fair, and accept them as being equitable.

There could be nothing further from the truth. Though managers might think that the use of standard procedures and policies is fair, there are still feelings of unfairness when managerial action does not result in an outcome favorable to the person or the procedures are seen us unfair. Three factors have to be present to have a sense of procedural justice (Thibault and Walker, 1975). The first is **process control,** or the extent to which you believe that you are allowed to present your position and justify your case before a decision is made. Process control was present in Susan's case above, as we have seen that she was able to bring information about her previous course to her advisor. In unionized organizations, the grievance procedure permits you some level of process control since you are allowed to provide evidence favoring your position at every step in the process.

process control
The extent to which you believe that you are allowed to present your position and justify your case before a decision that will affect you is made

A second factor is **decision control**: the amount of influence you have in the decision-making process. In the example above, the decision was made by the advisor and she was unable to have any influence in the decision outcome itself. One way that she might have been able to exert some influence is if there were some sort of appeal process in which she might ask a committee to review the advisor's decision *and*, at the same time, be able to designate a representative to be on that committee.

decision control
The amount of influence you have in the decision-making process

interactional justice
Your perception about whether the decision that affects you and the decision-making process are fully explained to you and whether you are treated with respect and dignity during the decision process

The third factor that affects perceptions is **interactional justice**: whether the decision and the decision-making process are fully explained to you and whether you are treated with respect and dignity during the decision process (Brockner and Wiesenfeld, 1996). It is a reasonable prediction that if Susan had been given the "It's our policy" explanation that she would not perceive that there was interactional justice.

THE INTERACTION OF OUTCOME JUSTICE AND PROCEDURAL JUSTICE It is quite obvious that the effects of procedural justice on personal reactions depend on whether the result (the outcome) is favorable or unfavorable and, vice versa, that the favorability of any outcome will have an effect on the perceptions of procedural justice (Brockner and Wiesenfeld, 1996). Figure 5.12 shows how these two different justice concepts are related to each other and how they affect the satisfaction of the reactions of those affected. It shows that when the outcome is favorable to a person, then there is high satisfaction, whether or not the procedure was fair. To return to our example of Susan. Suppose that she was given credit for the course she wished to transfer, a decision that is highly favorable to her. She is likely to be similarly satisfied with the procedure that the advisor used to make the decision, whether it was fair and whether it was consistent with the university's policies. Now suppose that the decision was made not to accept the transfer credit, a much less favorable outcome for her. Figure 5.12 shows that if she thought the procedure was unfair ("We won't accept this because it is our policy not to do so!"), then she will have much lower satisfaction than if, say, she was able to appeal to a committee, appoint one member as her representative, and present her case personally to them.

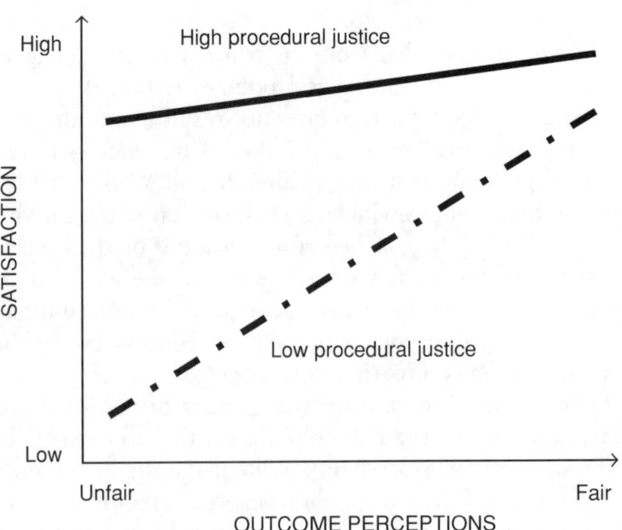

Fig 5.12: The interaction of procedural justice and distributive justice
Source: Adapted from Brockner and Wiesenfeld (1966)

Summary

Several motivation theories were discussed in this chapter. Need theories, a class of content theories, suggest what motivates people. They give clues to managers about what they can change so that increased employee performance and satisfaction as well as organizational effectiveness can result. Maslow's need hierarchy approach, and achievement/power theory are all examples of need theories. The job characteristics approach describes ways that work itself can be modified to build in more motivational power. They suggest a number of strategies designed to activate and satisfy the needs of employees at all levels.

The remaining approaches to motivation emphasize the process of motivation – how it occurs. Reinforcement theory, also discussed in chapter 2, explains behavior and its persistence in terms of consequences associated with the behavior. Expectancy theory is based on the premise that a person will make an effort toward behavior that leads to desirable results. It is a rational approach that suggests people seek to enhance their payoffs. Expectancy theory calls for the management of factors to improve performance and ways to reward it. Equity theory states that people are motivated to maintain fair relationships with others and to rectify unfair ones. A number of conditions can trigger feelings of inequity at work, and these trigger reactions such as withholding performance, seeking better payoffs, or leaving the field. Goal-setting theory predicts how well people perform based on the characteristics of goals they have. Difficult and specific goals and feedback have been consistently associated with high performance.

It is important to note here, though, that there is no one best theory of motivation and some seem better suited to deal with certain topics than others (Landy and Becker, 1987); need theories are most widely used to study satisfaction and work effort; reinforcement theory focuses on effort, performance, and absenteeism and turnover; expectancy theory can be used to predict job and organization choices and withdrawal behavior; goal-setting theory has been related to choice behavior and performance.

Further, since these different theories have psychological bases and concern the same variable, human behavior, it is only logical that they can be related to one another. Expectancies, for example, develop as a result of previous learning experiences. Learning theory may also explain the development of particular motives. Strong achievement needs may result from the positive reinforcement of success experiences in early life. In fact, this is exactly the point we make in chapter 2 in the discussion of learning and personality. In the final analysis, understanding each of these different approaches is useful because it gives the manager several ways to look at problems. As a result, he or she may arrive at better solutions more quickly and effectively.

Guide for Managers: Using Motivation Theories at Work

There are several useful ideas for managers in this chapter. Perhaps the most important is that they must recognize that their primary role is to manage performance, and that low levels of motivation can be one of many factors that contribute to poor performance. There are several indicators that one can check to determine if there are performance problems:

- Increased absenteeism in the work group
- More grumbling or complaining than usual
- Increased tardiness of those in the unit
- Significant changes in performance, up or down
- Major shifts in attitudes or in the level of commitment

These are only indicators that there is a problem to be managed, a problem that may have its source in something other than worker motivation. For example, it is possible that the low performance is a result of deficiencies in ability that may require additional training or, perhaps, shifting a person out of his or her current position and finding a replacement with the skill to perform. It is also possible that some of the indicators above may be attributable to the work context. For example, often performance problems are attributable to equipment beginning to have problems, though these problems may not be immediately obvious to the manager. In this case, surely the solution to poor performance is to fix what is wrong. Once these questions have been addressed and the conclusion is that there are motivational issues that need attention, there are several things that can be done to increase motivation.

CREATE AN INTRINSICALLY REWARDING WORK ENVIRONMENT

This can be accomplished by making the job more challenging and interesting while at the same time increasing the autonomy and responsibility of workers.

DEFINE CLEAR AND CHALLENGING WORK GOALS

The manager should ensure that subordinates know what level of performance is expected in some measurable, quantifiable terms if possible. These goals must be attainable. Unattainable goals have an $E \rightarrow P$ expectancy of zero, and very difficult goals have low $E \rightarrow P$ expectancies.

REMOVE BARRIERS TO PERFORMANCE

By providing adequate resources, training workers, or removing unnecessary bureaucratic constraints, the $E \rightarrow P$ expectancy can be increased.

CLARIFY WHAT IS APPROPRIATE PERFORMANCE

There are often several ways to achieve a goal. For example, cost reduction might be achieved by effective control of all costs or by omitting preventive maintenance programs. A subordinate should know what is considered the preferred way to achieve reduced costs. Clarifying such performance level expectations for subordinates is an important aspect of the coaching role of the manager.

REWARD PERFORMANCE

Extrinsically rewarding good performance can modify the $P \rightarrow O$ expectancy of a person. **Extrinsic rewards** are administered by someone else and are, for example, pay, advancement, and fringe benefits. To the extent that high rewards follow good performance, one can expect an employee to engage in that performance more frequently.

LINK THE REWARD TO THE BEHAVIOR

This can be accomplished by first clarifying what might constitute outstanding performance. The connection can also be made by rewarding very soon after performance or by verbally explaining why the employee is being rewarded.

FIT THE MAGNITUDE OF THE REWARD TO THE MAGNITUDE OF THE BEHAVIOR

A small reward such as a brief word of praise is insufficient for a rather substantial contribution by an employee. It is also possible to over-react to performance, such as putting a story about the employee in the company newspaper and throwing a party when the performance was not sustained or outstanding. This rule requires some judgment.

REWARD BETTER PERFORMERS MORE THAN AVERAGE PERFORMERS

Who complains when every employee receives the same reward treatment? The best performers do, and there is not much that can be said to the best employees when they have not been differentially recognized. Who complains when the best employees are rewarded better? The poorer performers are more likely to make inquiries. Thus, when using such discrimination in rewards, the manager needs to prepare for questions raised by the poorer employees and attempt to improve their performance.

REWARD MORE OFTEN

Many managers are stingy with rewards either because they are embarrassed to give them or because they fear the employee might become "spoiled." Good rewarding does not mean giving employees whatever they want whenever they want it. Good rewarding is based on the existence of performance standards, and if the reward is linked to performance, it need not lead to the spoiling effect.

REWARD AFTER PERFORMANCE

Avoid rewarding before the behavior takes place. For example, suppose a supervisor grants a merit raise to an employee and explains to the employee that the raise is an act of good faith and that the employee will improve on unacceptable performance in the future. This might work on the rare occasion that the employee agrees he or she needs to shape up and really respects the supervisor. Usually, however, the reward will act as a reinforcement for past behavior. The employee might conclude that his or her behavior could not have been that bad, or the boss would never have granted the merit pay.

REWARD PEOPLE WITH WHAT THEY VALUE

It is important to remember that individuals differ in what they value. A group of employees may have a wide range of preferences. Knowing what those preferences are, the manager may be able to tailor some rewards to the specific values of employees and, unless someone values a reward, it is not likely to affect their behavior. There are several ways to discover what people value. One is to use consequences that are widely valued, such as praise, a smile, or recognition. Another is to ask people. A third is to observe how a person uses free time on and off the job to find out what they like or dislike.

ADMINISTER RULES AND POLICIES FAIRLY

Rules and policies should be applied in a consistent, fair and impartial way. Inconsistent application will surely result in feelings of favoritism, unfairness and dissatisfaction by those who are negatively affected by decisions that they think have been made differently for others.

PROVIDE DUE PROCESS FOR YOUR STAFF

When a person has a complaint or criticism, every attempt should be made to provide a fair hearing. If there is a union involved, you should follow the bargained procedure. If there is not, but there are organizational policies that specify a procedure, follow them. If there are neither, then use your good judgment to treat the complaint as you would want yours treated.

Key Concepts

ability 125
achievement motive 137
achievement–power theory 137
autonomy 136
avoidance learning 141
behavior shaping 145
belonging needs 131
content theories of motivation 129
continuous reinforcement schedule 143
core job dimensions 136
critical psychological states 135
decision control 155
distributive justice 151
effort–performance expectancy 147
equity theory 152
ERG theory 132
esteem needs 131
existence needs 132
expectancy 147
expectancy theory 146
experienced responsibility for outcome 135
extinction 142
feedback 136
fixed-interval reinforcement schedule 143
fixed-ratio reinforcement schedule 144
goal-setting theory 150
growth need strength 137
hierarchy of needs 131
hygiene factors 133
interactional justice 156
internal work motivation 134
job characteristics approach 134
job satisfaction 135
knowledge of results 136
meaningfuless of work 135
motivation 127
motivators 133
need 130
need theories 130
negative reinforcement 141
outcome justice 152
overpayment inequity 153
performance components 124
performance–outcome expectancy 147
personalized power motive 138
physiological needs 131
positive reinforcement 140
power motive 138
procedural justice 154
process control 155
process theories 139
punishment 141
reinforcement schedules 143
relatedness needs 132
safety needs 131
self-actualization needs 131
skill variety 136
socialized power motive 139
task identity 136
task performance component 124
task significance 136
technology 125
transfer of learning 145
underpayment inequity 152
valences 150
variable-interval reinforcement schedule 144
variable-ratio reinforcement schedule 145
work ethic 122

STUDY QUESTIONS

1 Why are managers so deeply interested in motivation?
Why are the different definitions of motivation important for managers to know?
2 Differentiate between content theories and process theories of motivation.
3 Compare and contrast the approaches of Maslow, ERG theory, and McClelland.
4 Discuss the key elements of the job characteristics approach to motivation.
Analyze the motivational character of a job you have had in terms of the approach.
5 What are the characteristics of a person high in achievement motivation?
Power motivation?
What is the difference between personalized power motivation and socialized power motivation?
6 Explain the relationship between motivation, ability, and performance.
7 What are the key concepts of expectancy theory?
Describe the relationship between the concepts of expectancy theory.
What is the theory seeking to predict?
8 What are the concepts in goal-setting theory?
What is the relationship between participation in goal setting and goal success?
Do you agree with this? Explain.
9 Distinguish between the different consequences of behavior in reinforcement theory.

Case

Paul Peters' Raise

It was Friday afternoon and Paul Peters, a computer programmer at the Kalamazoo Lock Company, was feeling nervous. So was his boss in the nearby office, Ms. Fenwich. The time had come for Paul's first annual performance appraisal interview.

Paul felt he had performed well in the first year, especially in the past six months. However, it was always hard to tell what Ms. Fenwich thought, because she was usually busy, as well as being the quiet type. He did not know how she felt about some of the mistakes he had made or how many of them she knew about. Paul did try to make some of his recent improvements apparent to Ms. Fenwich, but she had not said much about them either.

Before inviting Paul into her office, Ms. Fenwich had reviewed the year and concluded that Paul needed a lot of improvement. His early mistakes had been costly in time and money to the company. However, he had shown some progress. The question was how much, and whether to give Paul a merit raise. Ms. Fenwich disliked appraising performance, but she took a deep breath and called Paul into her office.

After a friendly greeting, Ms. Fenwich pointed out Paul's good work and attitude. She pointed out how much she appreciated a recent program that Paul had written, which Paul took as a pleasant surprise. He also enjoyed finding out that Ms. Fenwich thought he had a good attitude.

Then the boom fell. Ms. Fenwich began to recount several of Paul's early errors, especially the time he was late with an inventory control program which took a long time to debug. After ten minutes of this, Paul became quite tense, because he was being hit with more surprises and did not have much of a chance to defend himself.

However, much to Paul's surprise and relief, Ms. Fenwich informed him that she was going to give him a merit increase anyway. She said, "Despite the fact that we both know you didn't have a good first year, the merit increase gives you an incentive to improve the coming year. It's our way of saying we have faith you can earn this raise by better and better performances."

With that, the appraisal interview ended. Paul went back to his desk pleased about the merit money, but feeling a bit bewildered. A number of things were still bothering him.

- Did Ms. Fenwich use good learning and reinforcement techniques in Paul's first year? Explain. What effect did this have on Paul?
- Will the merit raise act as an incentive for Paul to improve performance, or will he view it as a reward for past performance?
- Paul is likely to experience cognitive dissonance because he received two conflicting messages: he was told he didn't have a good year; and he was given a merit raise. How can Paul reduce this dissonance?
- How would you use expectancy theory and reinforcement theory to improve Paul's performance?

References

Adams, J. S. 1965: Inequity in social exchange. In L. Berkowitz (ed.) *Advances in Experimental Social Psychology*, vol. 2, New York: Academic Press, 267–99.

Alderfer, C. 1972: *Existence, Relatedness, and Growth: Human Needs in Organizational Settings*. New York: Free Press.

Allyon, T. and Azrin, N. 1965: The measurement and reinforcement of behavior of psychotics. *Journal of the Experimental Analysis of Behavior*, 8, 357–83.

Ball, G., Treviño, L. K. and Sims, H. 1994: Just and unjust punishment: Influences on subordinate performance and citizenship, *Academy of Management Journal* April, 37(2), 229–323.

Baron, R. A. 1983: *Behavior in Organization: Understanding and Managing the Human Side of Work*. Boston: Allyn & Bacon.

Borman, W. C. and Motowidlo, S. J. 1993: Expanding the criterion domain to include elements of contextual performance, in N. Schmitt, W. C. Borman and Associates (eds), *Personnel Selection in Organizations*, San Francisco, CA: Jossey Bass, 71–98.

Brockner, J. and Wiesenfeld, B. 1996: An integrative framework for explaining reactions to decision: Interactive effects of outcomes and procedures. *Psychological Bulletin*, 120(2), 189–208.

Brockner, J., Greenberg, J., Brockner, A., Bortz, J., Davy, J. and Carter, C. 1986: Layoffs, equity theory, and work performance: Further evidence of the impact of survivor guilt. *Academy of Management Journal*, 29(2), 373–84.

Carroll, S. J. and Tosi H. L. 1973: *Management by Objectives: Applications and Research*. New York: Macmillan.

Cowherd, D. M. and Levine, D. I. 1992: Product quality and pay equity between lower-level employees and top management: An investigation of distributive justice theory. *Administrative Science Quarterly*, 37(2), 302–20.

Ellis, J. W. 1997: AT & T links diversity to specific unit goals. *Advertising Age*, 68(7), February, 14–16.

Erez, M., Early, P. C. and Hulin, C. 1985: The impact of participation on goal acceptance and participation. *Academy of Management Journal*, 28(1), 50–66.

Folger, R. and Konovsky, M. 1989: Effects of procedural and distributive justice on reactions to pay raise decisions. *Academy of Management Journal*, 32(1), March, 16–131.

Frazee, V. 1998: Is the balance sheet right for your expats? *Workforce*, 77(9) September, S19.

Greenberg, J. 1988: Equity and workplace status. *Journal of Applied Psychology*, 73(4), 606–14.

Greenberg, J. 1989: Cognitive reevaluation of outcomes in response to underpayment inequity. *Academy of Management Journal*, 32(1), March, 174–85.

Greenberg, J. 1990: Employee theft as a reaction to underpayment inequity: The hidden costs of pay cuts. *Journal of Applied Psychology*, 76(5), October 562–9.

Greenberg, J. 1993: Stealing in the name of justice: Informational and interpersonal moderators of theft reaction to underpayment inequity. *Organizational Behavior and Human Decision Performance*, 54(1), February 81–104.

Greengard, S. 1997: 50 percent of your employees are lying, cheating & stealing. *Workforce*, 76(10), October, 44–5.

Hackman, J. R. and Lawler, E. E. 1971: Employee reactions to job characteristics. *Journal of Applied Psychology Monograph*, 55, 259–86.

Hackman, J. R. and Oldham, G. R. 1976: Motivation through the design of work: Test of a theory. *Organizational Behavior and Human Performance*, 16, 250–79.

Hackman, J. R. and Suttle, J. L. (eds) 1977: *Improving Life at Work: Behavioral Science Approaches to Organizational Change*. Santa Monica, CA: Goodyear Publishing.

Heckhausen, H. 1967: *The Anatomy of Achievement Motivation*. New York: Academic Press.

Herzberg, F. A., Mausner, B. and Snyderman, B. 1959: *The Motivation to Work*. New York: John Wiley.

House, R. J. and Wahba, M. 1972: Expectancy theory in managerial motivation: An integrated model. In H. Tosi, R. J. House and M. D. Dunnette (eds) *Managerial Motivation and Compensation*, East Lansing, MI: Michigan State University, Division of Research, College of Business Administration.

House, R. J. and Wigdor, L. 1967: Herzberg's dual factor theory of job satisfaction and motivation: A review of the evidence and criticism. *Personnel Psychology*, 20, 369–89.

Kanfer, R. 1990: Motivation theory and industrial

and organizational psychology. In M. D. Dunnette and L. Hough (eds) *Handbook of Industrial and Organizational Psychology*, Palo Alto: Consulting Psychologists Press, 75–170.

Laabs, J. J. 1994: Individuals with disabilities augment Marriott's work force. *Personnel Journal*, 73(9), September, 46–53.

Landy, F. J. and Becker, W. S. 1987: Motivation theory reconsidered. In L. L. Cummings and B. M. Staw (eds) *Research in Organizational Behavior*. 9th edn, Greenwich, CT: JAI Press, 1–38.

Latham, G. and Locke, E. A. 1975: Increasing productivity with decreasing time limits: A field test of Parkinson's law. *Journal of Applied Psychology*, 60, 524–6.

Likert, R. L. 1961: *New Patterns in Management*. New York: McGraw Hill.

Locke, E. A. 1968: Toward a theory of task motivation and incentives. *Organization Behavior and Human Performance*, 3, 152–89.

Locke, E. A. 1997: The motivation to work: What we know. *Advances in Motivation and Achievement*, Jai Press, 10, 375–412.

Locke, E. A., Shaw, K., Saari, L. M. and Latham, G. P. 1981: Goal setting and task performance: 1969–1980. *Psychological Bulletin*, 90, 125–52.

Maslow, A. H. 1943: A theory of human motivation. *Psychological Review*, 50, 370–96.

McClelland, D. A. 1965: Toward a theory of motive acquisition. *American Psychologist*, 20, 321–3.

McClelland, D. A. 1975: *Power: The Inner Experience*. New York: Irvington.

Miner, J. B. 1980: *Theories of Organizational Behavior*. New York: Macmillan.

Organ, D. W. 1988: *Organizational Citizenship Behavior: The Good Soldier Syndrome*. Lexington MA: Lexington Books.

Rasch, R. H. and Tosi, H. L. 1992: Factors affecting software developers' performance: An integrated approach. *Management Information Systems Quarterly*, 16(3), 405.

Reitz, H. T. 1981: Behavior in Organizations Homewood IL, Richard D. Irwin.

Scully, J. A., Kirkpatrick, S. and Locke, E. A. 1995: Locus of knowledge as a determinant of the effects of participation on performance, affect and perception. *Organizational Behavior and Human Decision Processes*, 62(3), March, 276–88.

Seclow, S. 1997: Kentucky's teachers get bonuses, but some are caught cheating. *Wall Street Journal*, September 2, 1–A6.

Spector, P. E. 1985: Higher-order need strength as a moderator of the job scope-employee outcome relationship: A meta-analysis. *Journal of Occupational Psychology*, 58, 119–27.

Stajkovic, A. D. and Luthans, F. 1997: A meta-analysis of the effects of organizational behavior modification on task performance, 1975–95. *Academy of Management Journal*, 40(5), October, 1122–50.

Thibault, J. and Walker, L. 1975: *Procedural Justice: A Psychological Analysis*. Hillsdale, NY: Erlbaum.

Tubbs, M. E. 1986: Goal setting: A meta-analytic examination of the empirical evidence. *Journal of Applied Psychology*, 71(3), 474–83.

Vecchio, R. 1981: An individual difference interpretation of the conflicting predictions generated by equity theory and expectancy theory. *Journal of Applied Psychology*, 66, 470–81.

Vroom, V. H. 1964: *Work and Motivation*. New York: John Wiley.

Winter, D. G. 1988: The power motive in men and women. *Journal of Personality and Social Psychology*, 54(3), 510–19.

Wood, R. E., Mento, A. J. and Locke, E. A. 1987: Task complexity as a moderator of goal effects: A meta-analysis. *Journal of Applied Psychology*, 72, 416–25.

chapter 6

Applied Motivation Theories

MANAGEMENT BY OBJECTIVES

POSITIVE REINFORCEMENT PROGRAMS

GAINSHARING

HIGH INVOLVEMENT ORGANIZATIONS (HIOS)

Preparing for Class

One key theme in this chapter is high involvement organizations (HIOs). After reviewing this chapter, consider how this course would be designed if you applied the concepts of an HIO in this classroom.

1. How would you change aspects of the course syllabus to increase student involvement in their education?
2. What components of this class reflect strategies to increase student involvement in their education?
3. Can the concepts of HIOs be applied in the classroom?
4. What are the difficulties in making the classroom an HIO?
5. Are there similarities with the difficulties faced by managers trying to develop a HIO?

Motivation theory was the subject of chapter 5; how the theories may be applied to improve performance in organizations is the focus of this chapter. None of the theories are easy to implement because there is a great gap between theory and practice – the real world is not as neat and well defined as the theoretical models. One reason for this is that people are involved – both managers and workers – and they find ways and reasons to muddle things up. Take, for example, the attempt by Eaton Corporation to implement a high involvement organization (HIO) approach in its small forge plant in South Bend, Indiana (Appall, 1997). The basis of the strategy was to empower the workers in the plant so that they could take action without too much managerial supervision. **Empowerment**, a very hot concept at this time, is based on the idea that workers should be able to make more decisions about the work that they do, extending these decisions from the task itself to other areas such as selection and discipline of co-workers. Fundamentally, management authority is delegated to the lower level employees in the organization.

empowerment
The idea that workers should be able to make more decisions about the work that they do

There is much more involved, though. One key in the Eaton plant was to increase the accountability of the workers and this was done through the creation of self-directed, or autonomous, work teams. These teams were usually given the responsibility for a broad range of tasks that were required to do the job and any specific work activity was not the province of any single worker but the whole team. Basically, jobs were redesigned and enriched by adding more tasks to them. The idea behind this comes from the job characteristics approach described in chapter 5 (page 134). This also increased the responsibility and the accountability of workers, though it did increase the variety of task activities that a worker could do.

Team members were expected to exercise their own judgment about how to allocate work and complete it. This was accomplished in team meetings where team members were expected to participate and contribute to solving whatever problems they faced. There was a serious attempt in the plant to minimize the appearance and the impact of the managerial hierarchy. Everyone, for instance, wore the same uniform so that workers were not differentiated from managers by the fact that managers wore shirts and ties while workers dressed in coveralls or work clothes.

Many of the workers at the Eaton plant liked the system. It gave them flexibility and control over their work that they were not used to from previous jobs. One employee worked at Eaton for a while, then left because she felt the work was too hard. She found a job in a unionized plant, but did not like it. She returned to Eaton because she did not like supervisors watching her in the unionized shop. The team concept was better for her, she thought.

However, for others, there were problems. Some of the workers found it difficult to speak up at team meetings about production problems of other team members. Some could not accommodate because they did not like the team idea, many of these because they had previous experience in unionized plants. Others felt uneasy because, instead of managers now observing their performance in the work place, it was fellow team members.

The managerial motivation strategies discussed in this chapter, like the Eaton approach, are attempts to act on the human factors, technological factors, and organizational structural factors in ways that increase the person's motivation to perform, so that they exert more effort and achieve a higher level of performance. Figure 6.1 shows an example: Peter and Paul differ in their ability and come to work with, we assume, personal motivational levels that are similar, designated by the arrow A. The role of the **managerial motivation strategies** is to elevate that personal motivational level, perhaps by the increment shown by the arrow B. That is what managerial motivation strategies are intended to do. In this chapter, you will learn about approaches such as management-by-objectives (MBO) that incorporates goal setting and reinforcement theory, positive reinforcement programs, a strategy that is based primarily on reinforcement theory, and high involvement organizations (HIO), an approach which usually attempts to integrate a number of different theoretical ideas.

managerial motivation strategies Attempts to act on the human factors, technological factors, and organizational structural factors in ways that increase the person's motivation to perform, so that they exert more effort and achieve a higher level of performance

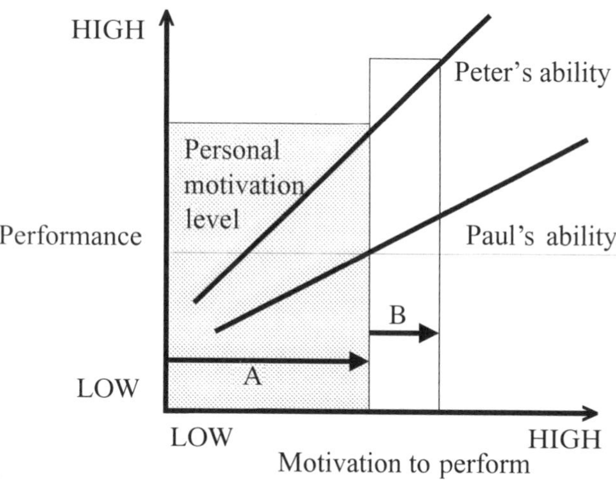

Fig 6.1 : The role of managerial motivation strategies

Management by Objectives (MBO)

Management by objectives (**MBO**) is a process in which a manager and a subordinate work together to set the subordinate's goals, relying on a participative approach to goal setting. It is probably the most popular and most widely implemented approach to managerial motivation used over the past 30 years. Many of the largest firms in the USA and Europe – among them companies such as Service America, Black & Decker, ARA Services, and Tenneco – have made systematic efforts to build MBO into their management philosophy.

management by objectives (MBO) A process in which the superior and subordinate, together, establish objectives for the subordinate

Goal-setting theory is the underlying basis of MBO. From goal-setting theory, we know that there are three specific process components of a sound MBO system:

EXERCISE

How Motivating are Your Work Experiences?

In this exercise, you will focus on your own work experiences (or other experiences in groups or teams if you have no work experiences that fit). The idea is to understand what is different about "motivating" and "non-motivating" work – and how some of the theories and approaches discussed in this chapter and in the previous one can help you understand these differences.

First, think about a job or experience that you had that you feel was one in which you felt like doing a good job. Let's call that the "high motivation experience." Next, think of a situation that you disliked, one that we will call a "low motivation experience."

Now, systematically analyze some of the differences between these two situations. Use this scale to indicate the extent to which the characteristics listed below were present in the two situations.

Scale:
4 = Always present
3 = Present most of the time
2 = Occasionally present
1 = Never present

	The High Motivation Situation	The Low Motivation Situation
• I had the chance to have a major say in what I did.	....	....
• I had the chance to set my own work goals.	....	....
• I was rewarded when I did a good job.	....	....
• When the unit did well, there was something extra for me.	....	....
• The job gave me a chance to do many different things.	....	....
• My work group had a chance to develop our own approaches to doing the job.	....	....
• My supervisor left me alone unless there were really serious problems.	....	....
• There was little emphasis on the differences between managers and workers.	....	....
• I was given the job because someone I knew recommended me.	....	....
Total points:	....	....
Now, indicate with a check in the appropriate column which of the two situations you liked the most	☐	☐

Now let's do some analysis. In the spaces next to each of the job characteristics, indicate which motivational approaches discussed in the chapter make use of the specific motivational strategy

	Motivational approach
• I had the chance to have a major say in what I did.	__________
• I had the chance to set my own work goals.	__________
• I was rewarded when I did a good job.	__________
• When the unit did well, there was something extra for me.	__________
• The job gave me a chance to do many different things.	__________
• My work group had a chance to develop our own approaches to doing the job.	__________
• My supervisor left me alone unless there were really serious problems.	__________
• There was little emphasis on the differences between managers and workers.	__________
• I was given the job because someone I knew recommended me.	__________

What conclusions do you draw, personally, from this analysis about motivational settings? Are they the same as others in your class?

1 Goal setting
2 Feedback
3 Participation

feedback
The information that a person receives about the results of his or her effort or performance

However, trying to use these processes on an organizational wide basis as MBO means that each must be done in such a way that the individual members of an organization work with one another to identify common goals and coordinate their efforts in reaching them. This makes it a much more complicated matter than simply setting goals with specific individuals without regard for the more broad organizational context within which these goals are set.

This leads to the major problem that many organizations have when trying to implement MBO: it is not strongly supported by management throughout an organization (Rodgers and Hunter, 1991). If some managers use it and others do not, then the positive effects are unlikely to occur (Carroll and Tosi, 1973). This is, perhaps, the most important reason why MBO fails in organizations, in spite of the strong evidence of its positive effects on organization performance. When the top management is strongly committed to building an objectives-oriented approach into its organizational culture and philosophy, the payoffs can be very high. Organizations with a culture of high commitment to MBO report an average productivity gain of 56 percent in the first several years; in firms with a low implementation commitment, the gain is only 6 percent, a dramatic difference (Rodgers and Hunter, 1991). In addition, the job satisfaction of those managers who use MBO increases, regardless of the degree of organizational commitment or the increase in productivity.

Diversity Issues: Using MBO to make Diversity Programs Work

In many cases, firms give lip service to intentions to broaden the diversity of their work force with elaborate statements and with general goals that have no serious impact. Using an MBO approach can make diversity programs work. What is necessary is that goals for units be specified and then used in appraising and rewarding the responsible managers. For example, managers in Xerox began to take diversity seriously when they found that 15 percent of their performance appraisal depended on their efforts to increase the representation of women and minorities in their work groups. When AT&T decided to make diversity a serious objective in 1984, the character of their work force began to change. Between 1984 and 1995, the percentage of minority managers increased from 0.5 percent of senior management to 12 percent and the percentage of women increased from 2 percent to 12 percent.

Source: Adapted from Stoner and Russell-Chapin (1997) and Ellis (1997)

The responsibility for developing this commitment to MBO lies with the top management. Typically, it begins with the development of strategic organizational goals by the CEO and the board of directors. Once these strategic organization goals are developed, functional subunit goals (marketing, production, etc.) are then prepared, usually in the form of general plans. These are then communicated to the next lower levels. This process continues down through the organization through a series of cascading meetings between superiors and their subordinates and work groups, until there is an unbroken chain from the top management level to the lowest levels of supervision.

Two things must be done for MBO to be effective: it is necessary to implement it organization-wide; and each manager and subordinate must be willing and able to work with goal setting. A superior and a subordinate attempt to reach a consensus:

- What goals the subordinate will attempt to achieve in a given time period
- The means by which the subordinate will attempt to accomplish the goals
- How and when progress toward goals will be assessed

Later, during the following period, the superior will review performance, possibly quarterly, along with a final performance at the end of the year.

organizational behavior modification (OB Mod) Proposes that to improve performance (change behavior) it is necessary to change the stimulus (antecedents) and the consequences (reinforcers, punishments, etc.)

Positive Reinforcement Programs

Positive reinforcement programs – also called **organizational behavior modification (OB Mod)** programs – seek to improve performance (i.e. to change behavior) by changing the stimulus (antecedents) and the consequences (reinforcers and punishments). These motivational strategies, based on reinforcement theory, have been used in some of the very largest and best-managed US organizations, such as Connecticut General Life Insurance, General Electric, and B.F. Goodrich. They have led to major improvements in productivity, reductions in turnover, and improved safety (Luthans et al., 1981; Orpen, 1982). These firms used praise, recognition, and other nondirect compensation (time off or freedom to choose activities) as reinforcers for production workers which proved quite effective in bringing about improvements in attendance and increased performance (Hamner and Hamner, 1976). Other firms have designed reward systems to encourage managers to pay more attention to long-run, rather than short-run, interests of the organization (Tosi and Gomez-Mejia, 1989).

Figure 6.2 illustrates the steps in a positive-reinforcement program (Hamner and Hamner, 1976). Suppose that you wish to improve the quality of secretarial work. In the first stage of a positive-reinforcement program, you would record the error rates of each secretary in the office. You have to identify the specific behaviors that are to be changed; they must be accurately and reliably observed and then recorded. The behavior should be observable and measurable. Behav-

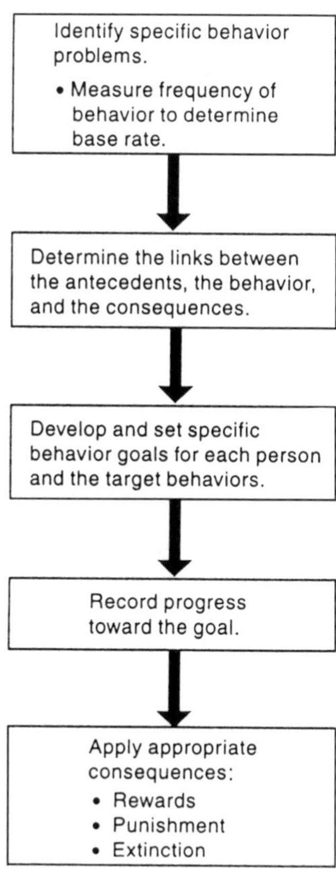

Fig 6.2 : Positive reinforcement program components

iors are observed and usually recorded to establish a base line rate against which behavior change is measured.

The second step is to determine the links between the target behavior, its consequences, and its stimuli. We have diagrammed these links in Figure 6.3 and found that there are no negative consequences for low performance nor are there positive consequences for high performance.

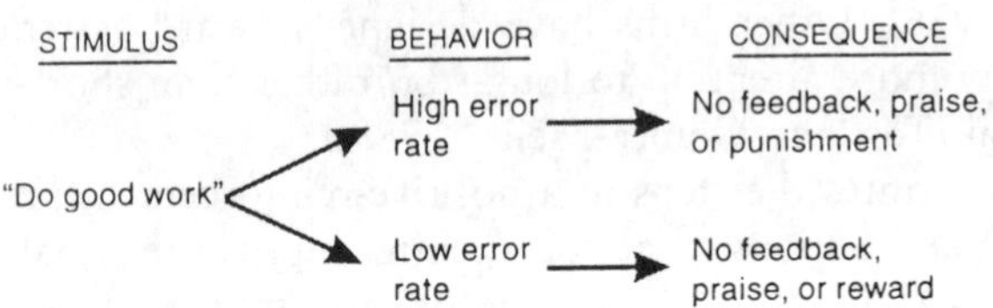

Fig 6.3 : Behavioral diagnosis in positive reinforcement

The next step (in figure 6.2) is to develop a specific goal for secretary's target behavior, that of reducing error rates. A target goal should be stated in the same way as the behavior was defined in the first step. You might, for example, start with a goal of reducing typing errors by 30 percent.

> Recording progress toward the goal is the next step. Generally it is best for the person to maintain his or her own personal record to measure progress. This process of self-feedback maintains a continuous schedule of reinforcement for the worker and helps . . . obtain intrinsic reinforcement from the task. Where employees [know their] own results, they can see whether they are meeting their goals and whether they are improving over their previous performance levels (Hamner and Hamner, 1976).

The final step is to ensure that the consequences of behavior are the ones that are likely to lead to the desired result. Basically, you must make every effort to positively reinforce the desired behavior when it occurs. This can be done by observing the charted record. When the secretary makes performance changes in the desired direction, you must apply positive consequences.

Positive consequences can take many forms. One of the strongest is praise and recognition for good work. Others are money (when it is a consequence of good performance), some autonomy in choosing work assignments, opportunities to improve one's status and self-esteem, and, lastly, power to influence co-workers and management. Table 6.1 lists some rewards that managers believe they can use for reinforcers. Many more could be added to such a list.

Positive reinforcement is good rewards management. It shifts the emphasis and energy of the manager toward a larger number of employees, rather than focus all the attention and time mainly on poorer employees. It can be handled in a way that makes all but the worst employees feel that the organization recognizes and appreciates their effort and contribution.

There is some good evidence about the effects of OB Mod in organizations (Stajkovic and Luthans, 1997). It tells us that it is more effective in manufacturing organizations than in service industries. In these manufacturing cases, the use

Table 6.1 Classifications of on-the-job rewards

Consumables	*Manipulatables*	*Visual and Auditory*	*Tokens*	*Social*
Coffee-break treats	Desk accessories	Office with a window	Money	Friendly greetings
Free lunches	Personal computers	Piped-in music	Stocks	Informal recognition
Food baskets	Wall plaques	Redecoration of work environment	Stock options	Formal acknowledgment of achievement
Easter hams	Company cars	Company literature	Movie passes	Feedback about performance
Christmas turkeys	Watches	Private office	Trading stamps (green stamps)	Solicitations of suggestions
Dinners for the family on the company	Trophies	Popular speakers or lecturers	Paid-up insurance policies	Solicitations of advice
Company picnics	Recommendations	Book club discussions	Dinner/theater/ sports tickets	Compliment on work progress
After-work wine and cheese parties	Rings/tie pins		Vacation trips	Recognition in house organ
	Appliances and furniture for the home		Coupons redeemable at local stores	Pat on the back
	Home shop tools		Profit sharing	Smiles
	Garden tools			Verbal or nonverbal recognition or praise
	Clothing			
	Club privileges			

Source: Reprinted with permission from Luthans and Kreitner (1985, p. 127)

of financial reinforcement and other types of reinforcement produced positive results. Interestingly, however, there was no difference in the effects between complex reinforcement packages and those that were nonfinancial interventions. This would suggest that the most effective managerial approach is to use the nonfinancial reinforcements and not become involved in the extra cost, "time and effort to apply the [financial reinforcements]" (Stajkovic and Luthans, 1997).

Financial reinforcers seemed to work better in service organizations (Stajkovic and Luthans, 1997). However, they are far more effective when they are combined with social reinforcers. Still, the effect of these social reinforcers was very high, justifying a recommendation that they may well be used alone with good results (Stajkovic and Luthans, 1997).

gainsharing Compensation approach in which employees receive bonuses or other forms of additional pay based on cost savings or profitability increases which occur as a result of the employees' contribution of ideas or more productive work effort

Gainsharing Approaches

There are several types of incentive plan that provide bonuses to employees based on profit improvement, cost savings, or productivity increases achieved as a result of the employees' contribution of ideas or more productive work effort (Scarpello and Ledvinka, 1988). These **gainsharing** systems can have very positive effects on firm performance regardless of how big the firm is, whether there is a union, technology differences, or the firm's environment (Bullock and Tubbs, 1990).

Focus on Gainsharing: A Project at Henle

As part of a plan to improve its financial performance, the Henle Commercial Aviation Division in Phoenix developed a gainsharing plan that shared financial improvements with the employees. First they defined and measured the activities and outcomes expected from individual employees that were necessary to achieve better results. Having done this, they discovered that there was a serious mismatch between those behaviors and the way that employees were compensated.

To attack this problem, they created a team of 25 employees and set them the task of designing the pay system. The members of the committee included secretaries, machinists, engineers, and department managers. This committee went out and learned about different facets of compensation, trends in pay, methods of pay, and other important factors that might affect the plan that they were going to develop. Then they worked for several months to create the gainsharing plan. Basically, the plan put a proportion of employee pay "at risk" depending upon the attainment of business goals of the division, but it also gave employees the opportunity to earn a good deal more than their annual pay if the company performed well.

An amount was set aside – some percentage of the available budget – for merit pay to be used for the "risk-sharing" portion, and this risk-sharing portion was distributed based on the division's performance. For example, if the merit increase budget was 3.5 percent of the previous year's pay budget, an amount equal to 1 percent could be allocated to the risk pool. This 1 percent would be given as a lump sum payout if the division reached 80 percent of its annual financial objectives. If the division did not achieve those goals, then no one receives a payout and the money stays in the "risk pool" until it does. However, the "risk pool" was not to exceed 3.5 percent of an employees' salary.

This plan also provides for employees to share in success when the division exceeded its objectives. If the division bettered its objectives by 20 percent, there was a bonus payout of 5 percent. This gave the employee an increase of 8.5 percent of the base salary – 3.5 percent from the risk pool and 5 percent success bonus.

Henle understood that this was a complicated program and that it touched pay, a very important and emotional factor for any employee. To work on this aspect of the problem, Henle developed and implemented a training program that provided information on business goals, financial measures, profit, working capital, economic value added, and the concept of risk and risk-sharing.

In the first year of the gainsharing program, the division exceeded its goals by 10 percent and the work force achieved all of its goals. Since the division goals were not exceeded by 20 percent, there was no "success" payout, but the work force received an increase of 3.5 percent, all the money from the risk pool.

Source: Adapted from Caudron (1996)

THE SCANLON PLAN

The **Scanlon Plan** is one of the more widely known and oldest of the gainsharing approaches but many of the current gain sharing plans use elements from it. The Scanlon Plan was developed as a way to integrate the interests of the work force with the interests of the company so that there would be a strong spirit of cooperation between labor and management. This is achieved by creating an environment in which the employees have a good deal of information about the company's situation, both problems and successes, and an opportunity to contribute to the solution of the problems. A key element of this plan is that the employees benefit, through pay, from the problems that they help to solve (Milkovich and Newman, 1987).

Scanlon Plan
A compensation plan that includes a system of committees for intergroup cooperation between labor and management in which efforts are made to reduce costs and share the cost savings with the workers

The Scanlon Plan is a participatory philosophy of management that involves a pay incentive system and a suggestion system (Milkovich and Newman, 1987). It is not simply a method of incentive payment, such as a sales commission plan or a piece-rate system. It is much broader than that because, in the Scanlon Plan, the work force must be involved in many different ways. It requires not only a commitment to participative decision making and joint problem solving but also an organizational structure and management style that is congruent with participative decision making and joint problem solving (Lawler, 1976). The organizational culture must be based on a high level of trust between the workers and management. Both groups must be willing to take responsibility for their actions and to share the responsibility of decision making. Together, they seek ways to improve the operation so that productivity increases. Productivity increases result in a bonus to the workers when the workers are responsible for them.

HOW THE SCANLON PLAN WORKS The core of the Scanlon Plan is a system of committees for intergroup cooperation between labor and management in which efforts are made to find ways to reduce costs and a formula for determining and sharing the cost savings. These cost savings are shared by the workers and by the company.

There are two types of committees in the Scanlon Plan: production committees and screening committees (Alderfer, 1977). **Production committees** are spread throughout the organization. There are members of management and labor on these committees, but the committee is usually dominated by the workers. They meet regularly to find ways to operate better. When the production committee agrees on a suggestion for improvement, it is implemented. If there is disagreement or if the proposal requires the cooperation of other units, then the proposal goes to the screening committee.

The **screening committee** is a plant-wide group with equal representation from the workers and the management. This committee has three roles (Hackman, 1977):

1. To determine the bonus for the month
2. To hear reports from management about any factors that might influence future operations of the plant

3 To act upon any issues that have come to them from the various production committees.

The formula for calculating cost savings that are the basis for the bonus paid to the workers is an important element in the Scanlon Plan. The savings must be a result of the worker suggestions, since capital improvements arising out of technological improvements are not part of the Scanlon Plan savings for distribution to workers. Obviously, complicated accounting matters enter into this calculation, sometimes making it questionable. These formulae often take several years to work out so that they are "right." A base cost point is selected against which current costs and cost savings can be compared, and the cost savings are split between the company and the workers (Milkovich and Newman, 1987).

High Involvement Organizations (HIOs)

high involvement organizations (HIOs)
A motivational strategy that promotes employee motivation and improves the effectiveness of the organization by changing the adversarial relationship between workers and managers to a cooperative approach

job enrichment approach
A work design approach in which the activities of a person in a job are changed so that the person does more different things as opposed to a few routine activities, with more autonomy and responsibility for quality of performance

Many organizations in today's competitive global environment are trying to create a **high involvement organization** (**HIO**). The HIO organization is one that promotes employee motivation in the work place; it improves the effectiveness of the organization by changing the adversarial relationship between workers and managers that dominates many firms and replacing it with a cooperative approach. HIOs may use a number of different management practices that include, but are not limited to, participative decision making, self-directed work groups, job design programs to enrich work, total quality management (TQM), improved safety and working conditions, innovative compensation plans to emphasize gainsharing and skill development, the elimination of organization levels, and minimization of bureaucratic processes and practices. A survey of 1600 organizational units found that more than 50 percent used some aspect of HIO practices (Hoen, 1987). In this section, we discuss some of the more common and more important aspects of HIOs: job enrichment, self-directed work groups, compensation practices, and lean organization structures.

Job Enrichment

The design of work in HIOs, usually based on the Job Characteristics Model (Hackman et al., 1975), is aimed at increasing skill variety, task identity, task significance, autonomy and feedback so that workers will have more meaningful jobs, a greater sense of responsibility, and more feedback. In the **job enrichment approach**, there are five basic ways to redesign jobs, as shown in figure 6.4, to increase their motivating potential and affect the core job dimensions, critical psychological states, and personal and work outcomes (Hackman et al., 1975).

1 *Combining tasks* Narrow tasks, especially those that are "fractionalized," should be combined into larger, more complex tasks. If the new task is too large for one person, it may be assigned to a team. Combining tasks increases skill variety and task identity.

2 *Forming natural work units* Tasks should be grouped into work units so that as much of the work as possible can be performed in the same organizational group. This leads to a sense of ownership of the job, increasing task identity and task significance.

3 *Establishing client relationships* It is a good idea, when possible, to link the worker with the purchaser of the product or the service. Since the worker cannot often interact directly with a customer, it may be possible to devise ways that the customer can give the worker feedback. If client relationships can be established, skill variety, autonomy, and feedback should improve.

4 *Vertical loading* The job should be enriched by **vertical loading** (adding responsibilities from higher organization levels) as opposed to **horizontal job loading** (adding more tasks from the same level). Vertical loading gives the person more responsibility and control at work which should lead to an increase in the level of perceived job autonomy.

5 *Opening feedback channels* There are two ways to provide feedback: job-provided feedback occurs when the person knows how to judge performance from the job itself; management feedback comes from the supervisor or from reports such as budgets and quality reports. Removing obstacles to increase job-related feedback will improve performance.

vertical loading
Enriching a task by adding responsibilities from higher organization levels

horizontal job loading
Increasing the job requirements of a person by adding tasks or other activities from the same organizational level

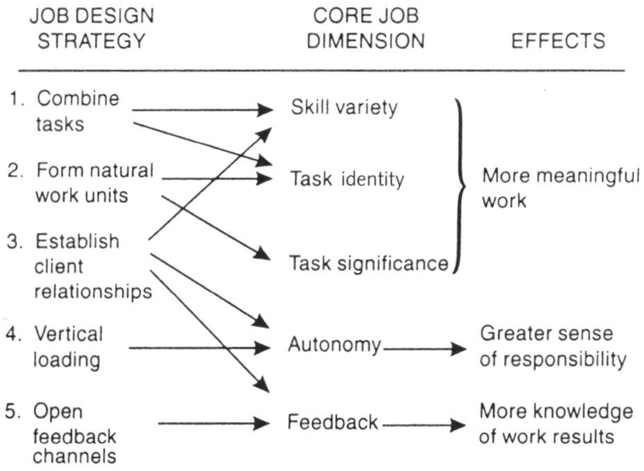

JOB DESIGN STRATEGY
CORE JOB DIMENSION
EFFECTS
1. Combine tasks
2. Form natural work units
3. Establish client relationships
4. Vertical loading
5. Open feedback channels
Skill variety
Task identity
Task significance
Autonomy
Feedback
More meaningful work
Greater sense of responsibility
More knowledge of work results

Fig 6.4: Strategies for implementing job redesign and their relationships to job characteristics

Self-Directed Teams

Self-directed teams place even more responsibility on the individual team members, and usually have responsibility for some decisions once reserved for management. The teams may be headed by a person from the managerial ranks or may have a member of the team designated as "team leader," but is usually one of the more highly skilled members, and leadership may rotate from person to person. The members of teams are encouraged to work together as a unit, to identify problems and look for solutions to them, to help and train each other

self-directed teams
Teams which place more responsibility on team members, usually with some management responsibility

while maintaining high quality production. Often they have responsibility for controlling other team members through self-regulating activities such as recommending disciplinary action if necessary, making individual work assignments, and sometimes deciding on member pay increases (Tosi et al., 1990). As you read in the case of Eaton on page 166, these self-regulating activities are sometimes very difficult for the team members to perform since they threaten interpersonal relationships at work.

Focus on Teams: They don't always Work

In 1992, Levi Strauss and Company, the manufacturer of jeans, decided to discard its old piecework system and move a team-based concept in its US plants. Under the piecework system, each worker performed a specific operation on a pair of jeans, for example setting pockets, putting on the belt loops, and stitching the fly. For each unit completed, the worker received the piece rate. Under the team concept, groups were assigned the responsibility for completing a pair of jeans and each team was staffed so that all the necessary skills were included in the group. The piece rate pay system was changed so that each team had a quota to reach and the average wage would be higher than under the existing piece rate system.

Levi Strauss implemented this new concept slowly so that it was not until 1997 that it was spread throughout all of the US operations. However, there were problems that began to appear early. For example, many of the best workers, who earned the highest wages under the piece rate system, found that their pay dropped. This happened most often in the less skilled teams, because the slower workers held down the productivity of the whole group. For example, one worker's pay dropped from around $9 per hour to $7, because of slow teammates.

Tension also developed in many teams, as the members pressured slow or absent workers to keep up. One team member said, "If one person has a lot of flaws, that costs everyone their bonuses." When someone was absent, workers argued about dividing up their work. There were cases where workers were actually threatened by team members for failing to keep up their end of the work.

Supervisors were not helpful in solving this problem because either they were not there (remember these organizations have leaner management structures) or they had not been trained to handle these problems.

Unfortunately, in addition to these problems, Levi Strauss, at the time of the report, had not experienced any performance improvements. In 1998, it was estimated that costs were 10 percent higher to produce a pair of jeans than in 1992.

Source: Adapted from King (1998)

cross training
Training workers to learn the various skills necessary to perform a wide range of jobs

HIOs invest heavily in training to achieve work force flexibility because permanent work assignments are often discouraged in favor of job rotation by team members. For example, the initial group of employees at the GM Saturn Plant received as much as 700 hours of training in the early stages of the Saturn startup (Woodruff, 1993). To achieve this work force flexibility, HIOs use skills cross training, problem-solving training, and interpersonal training. In **cross training**, workers learn the various skills necessary to perform the required tasks of the group. Training also becomes an instrument of worker socialization, an important element in the screening process to be discussed below (page 181).

NEW COMPENSATION APPROACHES

While the use of profit-sharing or gainsharing plans, like the Scanlon Plan, are common in HIOs, many of them use other compensation strategies to complement cross training and to reinforce job rotation. In one such pay strategy – a **skill-based pay** system – workers are paid for the skills they possess, not for the job on which they are working, as in more traditional pay systems. The idea is that a more versatile worker is more valuable to the organization (Tosi and Tosi, 1986). For example, Anheiser-Busch opened a new plant in which one of the key elements was skill-based pay. At first, many managers were skeptical whether skill-based pay would work and felt that it would be even more difficult in an industry characterized by "hard nosed" union relationships. Instead, they found that the workers accepted the skill-based pay system, and that productivity and profitability were very high. Surprisingly, there was much more management flexibility since workers were willing to move to different jobs as needed since they would not suffer any wage rate change that might occur under a more traditional wage system.

skill-based pay
A pay approach in which workers are paid for the skills they possess, not the actual work that they do

Another innovative pay approach is to use **team-based incentives** instead of individual incentives. Team-based incentives provide similar pay increases to the whole team instead of the more traditional approach of providing differential individual incentives. The purpose of the team-based incentive is to reinforce the team concept.

team-based incentives
Providing similar pay incentives to the whole team instead of the individual members to reinforce the concept of cooperative work

Devising a team-based incentive approach is not simple. In addition to the sorts of problems that were described with the Scanlon Plan, there is the further problem of trying to ensure that each member contributes equitably to team performance and does not become a "free rider," or a person who fails to carry his or her load yet receives the same incentive increases as everyone else.

LEANER MANAGEMENT STRUCTURES

When redesigned compensation systems and jobs increase motivation, then responsibility, self-direction, and less supervision is required. To put it another way, if workers are able to monitor their own job performance because accurate task feedback is available about a challenging job for which there are performance incentives, there is less need to have a supervisor looking over the workers' shoulders. After successful implementation of HIO philosophy and practice, it is often possible to eliminate at least one level of management. In the Anheiser-Busch plant described above, the use of the self-directed work teams, skill-based pay, and higher worker participation resulted in one less layer of management than similar plants in the industry. This meant that there were three to five fewer managers, a saving of between $300,000 and $350,000 each year.

total quality management (TQM)
A system of organizational processes and values that focuses on continuous product or service improvement

TOTAL QUALITY MANAGEMENT (TQM)

A sharply focused effort on improved product or service quality may be a part of the HIO philosophy and process, often with some sort of **total quality management (TQM)** program (Ciampa, 1992). The guiding principle of TQM is to create a system of organizational processes and values that are totally dedicated to the customer. The goals are to create highly loyal customers, to minimize the time required to respond to problems, to develop a culture that supports teamwork, to design work systems that increase motivation and lead to more satisfying and meaningful work, and to maintain a focus on continuous improvement.

There is no single method for organizations to achieve these quality goals, though there seem to be some techniques common to most approaches to TQM. For example, statistical quality control methods are used to identify causes of quality problems and to measure improvements, close relationships are developed with suppliers (such as just-in-time (JIT) inventory systems) to minimize inventory expenses, and benchmarking is used to identify other organizations to be used as a base for comparison to the firm's activities. TQM also uses some approaches from other MBOs (goal setting) and positive reinforcement programs (recording quality levels and recognition for attaining high quality performance).

Global Focus on Total Quality Management (TQM)

TQM, by definition, refers to any program that creates a system of processes within the firm that are totally dedicated to the customer. While somewhat straightforward in definition, there can, however, be many ways to implement such an idea. We have made reference to statistical methods, goal setting, and positive reinforcement within the text. Just as there are many forms of TQM available for management use, so can an application of such a program yield many different results. At times, cultural characteristics can have an effect on the success or failure of a given type of TQM; an example occurred recently in Scotland.

Local Scottish government services attempted to implement TQM. Managers of individual sectors were allowed to choose the most appropriate quality technique. One quality technique in particular, known as the "charter mark," performed poorly when compared to other methods.

The charter mark focuses not on internal service procedures, but on the quality of service delivered to the public. Citizens are provided with a set of principles and ideas for public services to use in raising performance standards and their input is then incorporated into an evaluation of each government agency. If the analysis is favorable enough, the charter mark award is bestowed. The benefits of achieving the charter mark are numerous: an awards ceremony, the mark is embossed on company literature, and an association of quality is made for years to come. Despite these positive aspects, the incentive of the charter mark did not work well in Scotland. The question is: Why?

One explanation for the failure of charter mark is that when it was introduced, it was seen as coming from a government headed by a conservative Prime Minister. This program – called the Citizen's Charter – was associated with a Conservative movement to reduce government involvement. These Scottish workers, however, were strongly politically aligned with the more liberal Labor party. They viewed support for the charter mark program as support for the Conservative government. As a result, the charter mark program failed. The failure of this motivation program was not because of the quality of the ideas. Similar programs have been very successful in other cultures.

Source: Adapted from Douglas and Gopalan (1996) by Pete Jones

Minimizing Worker–Management Status Differentials

The lean management structure, along with the use of self-directed work groups, has another implication for managers. Instead of the traditional managerial role of direction and supervision, managers must take more facilitating roles, place more trust in the workers, and take a hands-off approach. At the same time, workers must believe that managers will not violate the integrity of those areas in which the group has been delegated the responsibility for self-direction. Some companies refer to employees as "stakeholders" or "associates" to reinforce the more cooperative and trusting culture that they are trying to develop. This trust relationship can only develop when the work force is well informed and feels secure that management is not hiding anything, and after some history develops that management does, in fact, trust the work groups. Managers must therefore give up hierarchical control and must necessarily act as team leaders, coaches, and facilitators.

Nontraditional Selection and Socialization Strategies

It should be obvious by now that the HIO requires an organization culture which is different from the more hierarchical, traditional models of management to which many employees are accustomed. This means that the selection process may be of a different type than in traditional firms. Often, bringing people into HIOs is done with an approach that is specifically designed to bring "a 'whole' person who will fit well into the organization's culture" (Bowen et al., 1991).

HIOs tend to use relatively "thick" screening procedures and carefully designed socialization processes, especially when the HIO is a startup organization. This thick screening process, for example, will include the assessment of technical knowledge, skills, and abilities, using written tests or performance tests. Personality tests, which assess the capacity to work in teams, to act independently, to accept responsibility, and to tolerate ambiguity can also be used. Usually applicants face a series of interviews both with managers and members of the team on which they might work. Finally, there are strong socialization processes such as training or other "rites of passage" for successful applicants (Bowen et al., 1991).

The thickness of the screening process may vary, depending upon the desire to ensure that members fit well with the culture. For example, in one startup organization, the selection screen was very thick. First, every applicant for non-managerial jobs was required to attend, without pay, a pre-employment course in which basic manufacturing skills were taught. The course was designed by the company and covered such areas as blueprint reading, mathematics, safety, and mechanical design and repair. There was competence testing during the course, and individual scores on the tests were among the factors used in selection. Second, the applicants were interviewed by at least seven managers, including team leaders. The goal of these interviews was to assess technical skills, interpersonal skills, and potential for working within the HIO culture. Interviewers looked for initiative, good communication skills, the ability to work without supervision, and a high achievement orientation. Third, employment offers were made by the plant manager to the successful applicants in the presence of spouses or significant others so as to impress them about the level of commitment that was desired for their HIO organization.

Focus on Selection: The Thick Selection Screen at a Toyota Plant

One company that takes selection seriously is Toyota. It could take as long as two years from the time that you submit an application until you are finally hired. There are several steps, any one of which could disqualify you. You start with an initial application. Next there is a more extensive formal application and a formal test. If you are successful at this stage, you are then asked to participate in up to eight hours of group discussions and problem solving which is used to evaluate your ability to work with others, your leadership, and the general suitability of your personality. After that is the "Day of Work." In this stage of selection, you work for four hours on a simulated assembly line. You use an air gun to tighten lug nuts on wheels, spend time screwing and unscrewing nuts and bolts, and inspect parts. This phase of selection is grueling and tests your physical stamina. If you are successful, then there is a formal interview. If your performance in these is acceptable, you are then entered into an "applicant pool" and when an opening occurs, you might be called.

Source: Adapted from Maynard (1997)

The Effectiveness of HIOs

There are many well-documented instances of firms, large and small, which have successfully created HIOs, among them General Foods and the General Motors Saturn Plant. One of the most famous and earliest cases is that of Volvo (Schleicher, 1977). In Sweden, Volvo changed the process of auto manufacturing from an assembly-line process to a work team system. Work teams were responsible for different components and for the assembly itself. In one plant, the workers were organized with 30 teams of 15–20 workers. These teams not only worked on the assembly process but also met with management to discuss problems and recommend ways to improve performance. In this plant, turnover was drastically reduced and down time was cut. There were some cost increases, but these were thought to be short-run problems.

There is even stronger support than the anecdotal case study provides. Three analyses of several research studies show that enriched jobs are associated with higher performance and higher job satisfaction and had stronger effects than other types of motivational interventions (Guzzo et al., 1985; Stone, 1986; Fried and Farris, 1987). However, the effects were not large. One reason for the modest effects is what happens to many programs that organizations adopt to raise motivation levels – they lose their impact because managers begin to take them for granted and fail to continue to support and use the concepts (Marks et al., 1986; Griffin, 1988).

Perhaps the strongest evidence supporting the HIO concept is from a study of human resource practices in over 700 firms (Becker and Huselid, 1997). This research identified a cluster of firms that implemented **high performance work systems**. These firms were able to create complementary and supportive relationships among such practices as rigorous recruiting and selection, performance management and incentive systems, and employee development and training activities. Other groups of firms tended to use more narrow approaches, relying primarily on compensation or other human resource strategies to manage their personnel. It was estimated that, on average, the HIO firms that used the elements of the high performance approach produced very substantial increases in shareholder value per employee.

A Question of Ethics: Motivation Strategies and Ethical Problems

When examining motivation as it relates to managerial practice, it may often be thought of merely in terms of urging employees to work with more enthusiasm or a higher emphasis on quality. Motivation can be identified as a means of extinguishing certain types of behavior, as well. For instance, managers may be confronted with a situation wherein employees are abusing company policy. In such a situation, management may be called on to end certain types of unethical behavior within the organization. The New York State Department of Health was confronted with such an instance of unethical behavior.

Leave abuse has traditionally been a problem in many organizations. Sick leave – a benefit intended to help to maintain productivity and offer restitution for situations outside an employee's control – is often abused. The national average for absenteeism on a typical weekday is approximately 2.1 percent; the New York State employees' absentee rate, however, was estimated to be closer to 4.1 percent.

The Department of Health attacked this problem by utilizing analytical tools, the idea being that abuse of sick leave would show up in statistical data. The first step in this program was simply to monitor individual levels of absence within appropriate categories and time intervals. For instance, partial and consecutive days, generally not abuses of leave, could be eliminated. This individual measure, in conjunction with measures of expected and actual leave data for each department, helped to form a picture of specific absentee patterns by organizational unit. Finally, a means of analyzing trends was developed to help managers to determine levels of improvement and to set appropriate goals. The result was that abuses of sick leave were more easily identified. The absentee rate dropped dramatically.

In sick-leave pay, this program saved approximately $180,000 per year for the New York State Department of Health. Over and above monetary gains, there is most likely some intangible increases in employee dedication and output. This form of organizational behavior modification can help to extinguish unethical behavior. While attempts to end these sorts of behavior can be difficult for management, both in terms of execution and personal struggles, the end result may justify the necessity of such actions.

Source: Adapted from Gardiner (1999) by Pete Jones

Summary

Managerial motivation strategies are attempts to act on human factors, within technological constraints, to increase a person's drive to perform. In this chapter, we considered several ways that organizations attempt to develop company-wide approaches to motivation of members.

The HIO is an approach that has been growing in popularity in the USA. The goals are to increase productivity, quality, and satisfaction of the work force. There are many variations in the elements that make up HIO programs; self-directed work groups, worker participation, leaner management structures, total quality management, and job enrichment are some of the more frequently used elements.

MBO is the organizational application of goal-setting theory. In MBO, managers at all organizational levels set goals with subordinates. This goal setting, if done correctly, coordinates activities within the firm as well as providing specific and difficult targets. The goals set also provide a useful basis for performance appraisal.

Reinforcement theory is the underlying basis of organizational behavior modification (OB Mod) programs. They focus on changing the antecedents (stimuli) and consequences of behavior (reinforcers, punishments, and so on) to improve performance. This approach can be quite effective when the conditions are such that desired behaviors can be identified and rewards associated with them.

Productivity gainsharing is an attempt to increase the involvement of workers and management more directly in the performance of the organization, by giving them a greater stake in the firm's profitability. In all gainsharing programs, workers and/or managers make income above regular wages and salaries if profitability can be increased through their contributions. These increases may be a share of increased earnings or a share of increased savings.

All of these managerial motivation strategies are complex and difficult to implement effectively in organizations. They demand a great deal of managerial knowledge and persistence but have potential to bring about improvements in performance.

Guide for Managers: Making Motivation Theories Work

It is much easier to implement an HIO philosophy and structure for a new organizational unit, such as a new manufacturing plant. The reason is that the different elements can be in place when the managers and workers begin operating it. There will be no need to change an existing culture. The greater challenge is to be successful in creating an HIO to replace the management philosophy and approach of an existing organization. In either case, however, the implementation efforts must be widely supported in spirit by the effort of the management. There is often resistance to HIO concepts from both the worker side and the management side which must be overcome. Resistance arises because changes are not well understood by some workers and by some managers, and such problems may have implications for the redistribution of power (Bowen et al., 1991). In some instances, supervisors lose power and feel threatened. Also, unions have not always supported such efforts because they believe that changes in jobs should be a subject of contract negotiation.

Some guidelines for implementing these concepts come from an analysis of the differences between successful and unsuccessful job design programs (Hackman, 1977).

EVALUATE TOP MANAGEMENT COMMITMENT

The results of research on the effectiveness of the managerial motivation approaches discussed in this chapter shows that perhaps the most critical factor is whether there is top management support and commitment. What this means, in essence, is that the top management is willing to spend the time, money and effort to ensure that the program is well designed, that they are willing to use the approaches themselves in the management of their subordinates and that they are willing to have the same approaches applied to them. One way to know that this commitment is lacking is if you hear the top executives say something like, "This is something that will be good for the employees. We don't need it to be applied to us." That is a sure sign of no commitment.

ENSURE THAT ALL KEY PERSONNEL UNDERSTAND HOW TO USE THE CONCEPTS PROPERLY

Many of these approaches are complicated and require a clear understanding of both the concepts underlying them and the techniques necessary to use them. For example, positive reinforcement programs are based on reinforcement theory so it would be wise for managers to understand the basic concepts as well as how to provide positive reinforcement.

MAKE SURE THAT REWARDS ARE REWARDING

This is particularly a problem when firms attempt to introduce incentive compensation programs. In some cases, the incentives may be relatively small, making them meaningless.

DELIVER WHAT YOU PROMISE

There is a case of a firm that implemented a profit sharing program during a period when the firm was having serious financial difficulties. They convinced the union and the workers to forego a cost of living pay increase and participate in the profit sharing plan. Of course, during the period that there were losses, there were no profits to share. Finally, things turned around and the firm began to make money. At that time, the company arbitrarily modified the profit sharing program to reduce the payments to workers who had been promised a share.

Another case is when firms seek to use self-managed work teams. In this case, it is important for managers to relinquish authority and to trust the teams to manage themselves. Some managers are unable to do this and they interfere. It takes no time at all for the teams to understand who is to manage whom.

DIAGNOSE THE ORGANIZATIONAL SYSTEM

When there is a major change in work, other effects must be anticipated. Usually there are policies, procedures, practices and processes that might act as barriers to implementing motivational strategies. One of the most frequently encountered problems is with the compensation system that is in place. Usually these have been part of the operational structure for some years and they were put in place for reasons other than the one you have in mind. Further, these compensation systems sometimes have political implications. For example, pay systems that provide for regular cost of living adjustments are generally favored and supported by unions, so moving to another approach might result in union resistance. A problem that often occurs when you are implementing job redesign is that some jobs cannot be easily changed because the technology limits much modification. To try to change these tasks may end in failure. A diagnosis will point to those jobs that show greatest potential for improvement and will highlight problems that need to be solved before any job design is implemented.

DEAL WITH DIFFICULT PROBLEMS EARLY

Some important matters must be resolved before these complex programs are implemented. These must be discussed openly and consensus reached early. These are some of the more difficult issues:

- How strong is the commitment of the worker, the management, and the union, if there is one?
- What standards will be used to evaluate the success of the HIO effort?
- How will problems that are uncovered be solved?

ENSURE THAT THE ORGANIZATIONAL CULTURE IS CONSISTENT WITH THE HIO CONCEPT

Often managers are attracted to the HIO concept because of its potential for improving organization effectiveness, yet they fail to understand that managerial practice and the organizational culture must be HIO-compatible. For example, an authoritarian culture which fosters status differentials between managers and workers will be a disastrous context for a HIO organization. Therefore, early in the implementation process, the culture should be analyzed to determine this fit, and appropriate organizational development methods should be undertaken, if necessary.

Key Concepts

STUDY QUESTIONS

1. What is management by objectives (MBO)? Relate it to goal-setting theory.
   What are some differences that you can see between goal-setting theory and the practice of MBO?
2. Do an analysis of your own study habits using the positive-reinforcement/OB Mod approach.
3. Why is it difficult to link reinforcements to performance at work?
   For what type of work can this be done most easily?
4. What is the Scanlon Plan?
   How does it work?
   Under what conditions can it work best?
5. Reflecting on other relevant chapters in this book, what does it take to create effective self-directed work groups?
6. What are the strengths and weaknesses of skill-based pay?
   Based on your knowledge of reinforcement theory, which behaviors should increase?
   Which behaviors should decrease?
7. Analyze the TQM concept from the perspective of goal-setting theory and reinforcement theory.
   How does it differ from organizational behavior modification (OB Mod)?
8. The HIO movement is growing in the USA. Why do you think so?
   What are some implications for the work force?
9. What are the key implementing concepts for job design?

Case

National Oil Company

National Oil Company was one of the most profitable oil companies in the USA although it was only medium-size compared to the industry giants. In the early 1970s, income soared as the OPEC nations raised the price of oil to heights only imagined before. Many of the oil companies such as National found themselves awash in cash and expanded their work force and provided their employees with very high salaries and benefits. Investments from the general public rose also to new heights. The morale of the company's employees was very high and the company attracted many top graduates of the better universities in the nation. However, the price of oil began to drop to more normal levels over the next several years and, while it took some adjusting, National and the other firms were able to be profitable.

In the late 1990s, though, the price continued to drop, this time to very low levels. For example, from September 1998 to January 1, 1999 the price dropped from around $15 a barrel to $12. As the price of oil slumped and investments in the industry fell off, National was forced to change some of its strategic plans and had to lay off some of its work force. The layoffs amounted to only about 6 percent of the company's employees, but a shock went through the company and morale plunged. A significant number of the company's best new employees who were not laid off quit the company anyway. The company's personnel office wondered what to do about the problem.

- What would you suggest to them? Explain.

References

Alderfer, C. 1977: Group and intergroup relations. In J. R. Hackman and J. L. Suttle (eds) *Improving Life at Work: Behavioral Science Approaches to Organizational Change*. Santa Monica, CA: Goodyear Publishing.

Appall, T. 1977: Not all workers find the idea of empowerment as neat as it sounds. *Wall Street Journal*. September 8, 1, 1–2.

Becker, B. E. and Huselid, M. A. 1997: The impact of high performance work systems and implementation alignment on shareholder wealth. Paper, Academy of Management Annual Meeting.

Bowen, D. E., Ledford, G. E. and Nathan, B. R. 1991: Hiring for the organization, not the job. *Academy of Management Executive*, 5(4), 35–51.

Bullock, R. J. and Tubbs, M. E. 1990: A case meta-analysis of gainsharing plans as organization development interventions. *Journal of Applied Behavioral Science*, 26(3), 383–404.

Carroll, S. J. and Tosi, H. L. 1973: *Management by Objectives: Applications and Research*. New York: Macmillan.

Caudron, S. 1996: How pay launched performance. *Personnel Journal*, 75(9), September, 70–6.

Ciampa, D. 1992: *Total Quality: A User's Guide for Implementation*. Boston, MA: Addison-Wesley Publishing Company.

Douglas, K. and Gopalan, S. 1996: Application of American management theories and practices to the Indian business environment: Understanding the impact of national culture. *American Business Review*, 16(2), 30–41.

Douglas, K., Brennan, A. R. and Ingram, M. I. 1996: Missing the mark: A preliminary survey of the Scottish Charter Mark experience. *Total Quality Management*, 9(4/5), 71–4.

Ellis, J. W. 1997: AT&T links diversity to specific unit goals. *Advertising Age*, 68(7), February 17, S14–15.

Fried, Y. and Farris, G. 1987: The validity of the job characteristics approach: A review and meta-analysis. *Personnel Psychology*, 40, 287–322.

Gardiner J. C. 1999: Tracking and controlling absenteeism. *Public Productivity & Management Review*, 19 15(3), 289–300.

Griffin, R. 1988: Consequences of quality circles in an industrial setting: A longitudinal assessment. *Academy of Management Journal*, 30(2), 338–58.

Guzzo, R., Jenne, R. D. and Katzell, R. 1985: The effects of psychologically based intervention programs on worker productivity: A meta-analysis. *Personnel Psychology*, 38, 275–91.

Hackman, J. R. 1977: Work design. In J. R. Hackman and J. L. Suttle (eds) *Improving Life at Work: Behavioral Science Approaches to Organizational Change*, Santa Monica, CA: Goodyear Publishing, 96–162.

Hackman, J. R., Oldham, G. R., Janson, R. and Purdy, K. 1975: A new strategy for job enrichment. *California Management Review*, 17, 57–71.

Hamner, W. C. and Hamner, E. P. 1976: Behavior modification on the bottom line. *Organization Dynamics*, 4, 8–21.

Hoen, J. C. 1987: Bigger pay for better work. *Psychology Today* July, 57, 15.

King, R. 1998: Jeans therapy: Levi's factory workers are assigned to teams and morale takes a hit. *Wall Street Journal*, May 20, A1, A6.

Lawler, E. E. 1976: New approaches to pay: Innovations that work. *Personnel*, 53, 11–24.

Luthans, F. and Kreitner, R. 1985: *Organizational Behavior Modification and Beyond*. Glenview, Ill: Scott, Foresman.

Luthans, F., Paul, R. and Baker, D. 1981: An experimental analysis of the impact of contingent reinforcement on salespersons' performance behavior. *Journal of Applied Psychology*, 66(3), 314–23.

Marks, M. L., Hackett, E. J., Mirvis, P. H. and Grady, J. F. 1986: Employee participation in a quality circle program: Impact on quality of work life, productivity and absenteeism. *Journal of Applied Psychology*, 71(1), 61–9.

Maynard, M. Toyota devises grueling workout for job seekers. *USA Today*, August 11, 3b.

Milkovich, G. T. and Newman, J. M. 1987: *Compensation*. Plano, TX: Business Publications, Inc.

Orpen, C. 1982: The effects of contingent and noncontingent rewards on employee satisfaction and performance. *Journal of Psychology*, 110(1), January, 145–50.

Rodgers, R. and Hunter, J. E. 1991: Impact of management by objectives on organizational productivity. *Journal of Applied Psychology*, 76(2), 322–36.

Scarpello, V. and Ledvinka, J. 1988: *Personnel/Human Resource Management*. Boston, MA: PWS-Kent.

Schleicher, W. F. 1977: Volvo: New directions in work technology. *Machine Tool Blue Book*. Wheaton, IL: Hitchcock Publications, 74–85.

Stajkovic, A. and Luthans, F. 1997: A meta-analysis of the effects of organizational behavior modification on task performance. *Academy of Management Journal*, 40(8), 1122–49.

Stone, E. F. 1986: Job scope-job satisfaction and job scope-job performance relationships. In E. A. Locke (ed.) *Generalizing from Laboratory to Field Settings*, Lexington, MA: Lexington Book Company.

Stoner, C. R. and Russell-Chapin, L. 1997: Creating a culture of diversity management: moving from awareness to action. *Business Forum*, 22(2–3), Spring–Fall, 6(7).

Tosi, H. L. and Gomez-Mejia, L. 1989: The decoupling of CEO pay and performance: an agency theory perspective. *Administrative Science Quarterly*, 34, 169–89.

Tosi, H. L. and Tosi, L. A. 1986: What managers need to know about knowledge-based pay. *Organizational Dynamics*. Fall, 52–64.

Tosi, H. L., Zahrly, J. and Vaverek, K. 1990: *The Relationship of Worker Adaptation and Productivity to New Technology and Management Practices: A Study of the Emergence of a Sociotechnical System*. Organization Studies Center, Graduate School of Business Administration, University of Florida, 1990.

Woodruff, D. 1993: Saturn: Labor's love lost? *Business Week*, February 8.

chapter 7

Stress in Organizations

STRESS AND COPING
STRESS MANIFESTATIONS
SOURCES OF STRESS
STRESS AND INDIVIDUAL DIFFERENCES

Preparing for Class

As you prepare for this chapter, team up with another student who is taking this course and with whom you are willing to discuss the issues involved in this activity. Independently, both of you should answer these three questions.

1. Write a general description of the level of stress you are feeling in your life at this time.

2. What are the main aspects of your life that are contributing to the stress you are feeling? (Look at the "Sources of Stress" section on page 200 for a list of the type of events that can lead to stress.)

3. List the activities that you do to manage your own stress. (If you need help here, consider which of the ideas provided in the GUIDE FOR MANAGERS on page 214 that are applicable to your life.)

Now, compare your answers with those of your teammate.

1. Are the stressors in each of your lives similar?

2. Do you have different ways of managing the stress?

3. Can either of these aspects explain the differences or similarities in the stress you said you were feeling?

4. Where there are differences, can they be explained by the individual differences mentioned in the text?

Sam Allen was admitted to the hospital with a bad case of hives. Large red welts had broken out all over his body causing such serious pain that his physician, John Gibbs, put him in the hospital. Sam did not like – and did not believe – John Gibbs' explanation of why he had the hives. John told Sam that it was his new job as Director of Marketing that caused the problem.

Sam had time to think about that explanation. When Arnie Heston had told him that he was going to be the new director of marketing, Sam was pleased. For the past six years, he had put in long, hard hours in his job as a sales engineer, and it had paid off.

After he moved into the director of marketing's office, he was struck by how different the job was from his old one as sales engineer. As a sales engineer, Sam had set his own schedule. He was away from the office most of the time because he was calling on his customers, and he had control over when and where he worked. He worked hard, but he worked on his own schedule. Another part of his old job he liked was that he always knew how well he was doing by simply looking at his current sales figures.

The new job was different. Sam had more status, a nicer office, a better car, and a secretary. However, things began to bother him: the things that were out of his control. For instance, his appointment calendar was always full. Usually these appointments were made by someone other than Sam. Now he reported to Bryan Kraft, the vice president of marketing. Kraft was a high producer, but he was difficult to work for. For example, at least once a week he would, on short notice, call a meeting at 4.30 p.m. that would last until 7.30 or 8.00 p.m. Bryan always apologized for "cutting into family time," but after the meeting he would want everyone to come out for dinner and drinks with him. It was his way of making up for the imposition. Most of the staff went because they thought Bryan wanted them to go along. For Sam that meant he would not reach home till midnight. He missed putting his children to bed and his wife Adrienne, a lawyer, was not particularly pleased with the late hours.

Sam also began to feel uneasy about the fact that now he had no control over his own success. Instead of producing his own sales, now the people who worked on his staff had his future in their hands. This was the first time he had ever been in such a position.

Sam tried to meet all his new commitments. He went out of his way to spend more time, and better time, with Adrienne and the children. He tried to leave a little unscheduled time in his calendar for some projects that he wanted to start. He started to sleep less and he was tired. Sam started to smoke again, after being off cigarettes for ten years. One night, Adrienne told him that she thought he was drinking a little more than he had in the past.

Sam knew he was under pressure, but that was part of the job, he thought. When Sam broke out with hives, he did not think that went along with it.

Sam Allen's reaction to the strain of his new job is not uncommon. People often experience symptoms such as hives, migraine headaches, depression, and back pain when stressed. Other, more serious physiological effects can be caused by stress, such as ulcers, hypertension, and coronary heart disease. Some symptoms of stress, perhaps those that are most conventionally associated with it, are psychological. People who work in stressful work settings are more likely to have a sense of futility and lower self-esteem, which may lead to lower levels of mental health and physical well-being (Cooper and Marshall, 1976). Blue-collar workers have disproportionately high levels of mental health problems (Shostak, 1980). Stress can lead to divorce, broken friendships, and frustration. Also, physical or psychological illness is often thought to be a sign of weakness by the person.

Organizations pay a high cost for employee stress. First, critical levels of stress can lower work performance. There are also very high direct costs due to stress-related lawsuits, workers' compensation, and healthcare premiums. For example, in California in 1992, 99 percent of the claims for psychological and stress-related problems were litigated at a cost of around $11,000 each (Stevens, 1992). The cost to California was so high that it enacted a law that increased the burden of proof by employees that the illness was stress related. Prior to the law it was necessary to show that only 10 percent of the disability was caused by workplace pressures. The law raised the threshold to 51 percent and there was a dramatic reduction in claims, though they are still quite high (Schachner, 1994).

In this chapter, we focus on stress in work organizations. We examine the meaning of stress, its causes, how it is manifested by individuals, some personality factors that are important, and how it can be managed. Generally, the focus is on work-related stress, but we discuss some extra-work considerations because we believe that stress may emanate from many sources and has effects beyond the workplace.

A Model of Stress and Coping

Figure 7.1 shows one way to conceptualize stress. You are constantly interacting with the environment, objective and psychological, in which there are stimuli, called **stressors**, that can induce stress. Stress may be manifested in physiological, psychological or behavioral responses. The nature of the response depends upon the individual. Some people are more sensitive than others to the presence of stressors; some use more effective coping mechanisms.

stressors
Environmental factors and forces that cause stress

Stress is a non-specifically induced psychological state of an individual that develops because the individual is faced with situations that "tax or exceed available resources (internal or external), as appraised by the person involved" (Lazarus, 1980). This means that, usually, there are several factors in the environment, often several of which you might not be aware, that lead to stress. Stress is a dynamic condition in which the person is confronted with one of three things (Schuler, 1980):

stress
A psychological state that develops because a person is faced with situations that tax or exceed available resources as appraised by that person

1 An opportunity
2 A constraint
3 A demand for which resolution is both uncertain and important

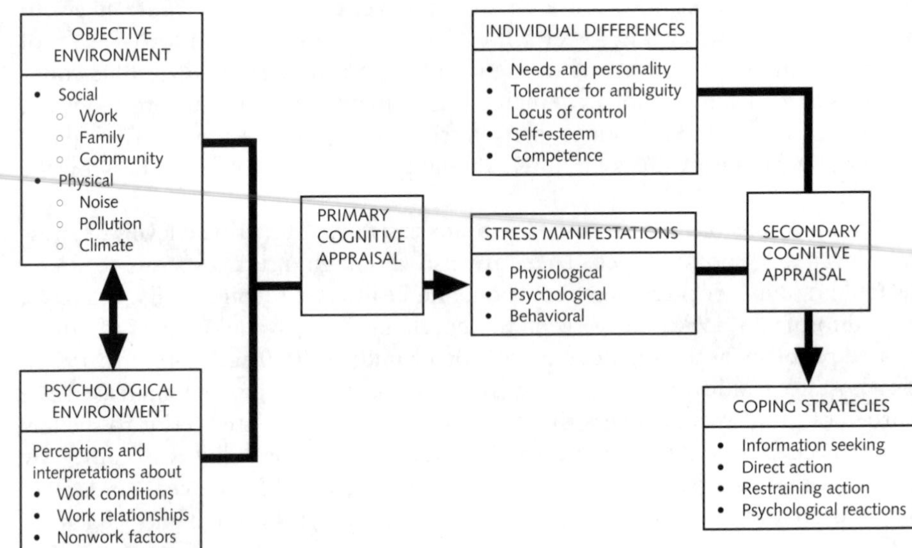

Fig 7.1: A model of stress and coping

Its effects are not always negative, as they were for Sam Allen. Each of us has experienced a stress-inducing situation that was a positive learning experience. For instance, preparing to take your first examinations in college might have been very stressful. As the time came closer you become more tense, worried about the exams, and studied harder. When you walked into the classroom and took your seat, butterflies were in your stomach, and your palms were sweaty. If you were well prepared, these reactions disappeared when you started on the exam and found you could solve the problems or answer the questions. You learned that you were able to perform well on examinations, and as a result, later exams were not as stress inducing as the first.

Even performing poorly could be a positive developmental experience if you learned where you went wrong, what your limits are, and how to do better next time. You became stronger, and the next time you faced the examination situation, you knew what to do. Over time, exams could become less and less stress inducing.

eustress
A positive, healthy, and developmental stress response

distress
Stress responses that weaken a person's physical and psychological capacity to cope with environmental stressors

A positive, healthful, and developmental stress response is called **eustress** (Selye, 1974). Just as tension causes muscles to strengthen, some level of stress may lead to better performance and a more adjusted personality. **Distress** includes those stress responses that weaken a person's physical and psychological capacity to cope with environmental stressors. As you becomes less resistant to stress, you may perceive a larger number of more severe stressors in the environment. This may make it more difficult to cope, leading to more serious physiological and psychological problems.

These different responses to stress are shown in figure 7.2.

- Under low levels of stress, you experience little stimulation. There is no challenge, and boredom sets in because mental and/or physical skills are underutilized.

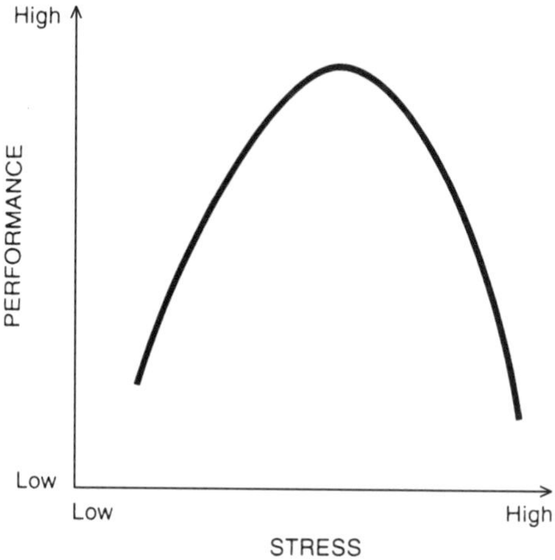

Fig 7.2 : Relationships between levels of stress and performance

- Under moderate stress levels, performance is high because physical and mental capacities are challenged. You are motivated but not anxious, and your mental attention is focused on the task at hand. A moderate level of stress is likely to result in higher performance.
- When you experience high stress, personal resources are strained – you are stretched beyond physical and mental limits.

The Objective Environment

The **objective environment** contains those conditions in which you are embedded and that may affect you. Working conditions, other people, noise, and heat are all examples of possible stressors in the work environment. Nonwork elements such as social pressures, demands from spouses and children, and community problems may also induce stress, and they can certainly affect what happens on the job. These are important pressures because, as we have pointed out in chapter 4 (page 92), the relationship between work and family and other critical aspects of a person's life must be resolved.

objective environment The actual conditions in the world in which you are embedded and that may affect you

The Psychological Environment

The **psychological environment** is the way that you experience the objective environment. For instance, if you are in a job that requires dealing with people outside the organization (a fact of the objective environment), you are likely to feel more incompatible job demands or role conflict (an aspect of the psychological environment) than someone who works completely within the organization (Katz and Kahn, 1978).

psychological environment The way that a person experiences and interprets the objective environment

Individual Differences

Some individual differences are associated with stress and stress responses:

- Tolerance for ambiguity
- Locus of control
- Achievement needs
- Self-esteem
- Individual competence
- Affectivity
- Type A/Type B patterns

alarm reaction
A reaction to stress that causes physiological changes that warn the body that it is under pressure

resistance stage
The second stage of reaction to stress in which the body tries to restore its balance

exhaustion stage
The last stage in a person's reaction to stress, in which the person simply wears out

cognitive appraisal
The way a person assesses the significance of the various aspects of the environment

primary cognitive appraisal
The cognitive appraisal that determines the intensity and quality of the individual's emotional response to stressors

They affect, in some part, how a person adapts to stressors which are perceived to be frequent and intense (Selye, 1974). The first thing that happens when stressors are perceived is an **alarm reaction**: physiological changes that warn the body it is under pressure. Adrenalin flow increases, blood pressure rises, and muscles become tense. Next there is the **resistance stage**, when the body tries to restore its balance, expending physical and psychological energy to seek this equilibrium. People use different physiological, psychological and biological responses to respond to stress. The final stage is the **exhaustion stage**. If the resistance is not successful, the person simply wears out. Over time, the stressors may use up all the person's psychological and physiological energy. When a person reaches the exhaustion stage, both physical and mental illness may occur.

Stressors do not necessarily have the same effects on different individuals, and the outward appearance of individuals under stress is not necessarily related to their physiological response. In stressful situations, some are "hot reactors" and experience dramatic physical changes. Blood pressure shoots up, heart rate may increase or decrease, and blood vessels may become more or less resistant to blood flow. Other people are "cool reactors" – under stress their bodily functions change more or less at rates appropriate to the situation. At the same time, both the hot reactor and the cool reactor may appear to be very calm on the outside. The hot reaction may overstimulate the body's nervous system and lead to arterial spasms and other circulatory problems. It also causes the body to increase its production of adrenalin, potentially a serious problem because adrenalin stimulates both physical and mental activity, and the person may become addicted to it. That is, the person is able to operate best only under conditions of an adrenalin surge.

Individual differences affect how people experience the objective environment. The way you perceive and interpret may be different from the way others would react when exposed to the same situation. This occurs through a process called **cognitive appraisal** – the way you assess the significance of the various aspects of the environment (Lazarus, 1980; Motowidlo et al., 1986). In the case of Sam Allen, he could have judged the demands as stressful, positive, or neutral. How they are actually judged depends on the person, so that one person could feel stressed while another feels neutral. This assessment, called a "**primary cognitive appraisal**," determines the intensity and quality of the individual's emotional response (Lazarus, 1980). When your primary cognitive appraisal is positive, you will have reactions such as pleasure, joy, and relaxation. When your environment is appraised as stressful, your reaction will be anxiety, fear, and so forth. Suppose your boss says to you, "Your annual report is incomplete." You may appraise this event in at least two ways as shown in figure 7.3. You might believe, "My boss called me incompetent. He shouldn't do that. I can't stand to be called incompetent." Such a cognitive appraisal may lead to feelings of job anxiety, low job satisfaction, and frustration because you are not sure how to improve your report-writing skills. Another, but positive, way to appraise the same event is, "I am a human being and I have some faults. I am not perfect. This is good feedback. I am going to strive to do better." This may lead to more constructive actions to deal with exactly the same event (Tosi and Tosi, 1980).

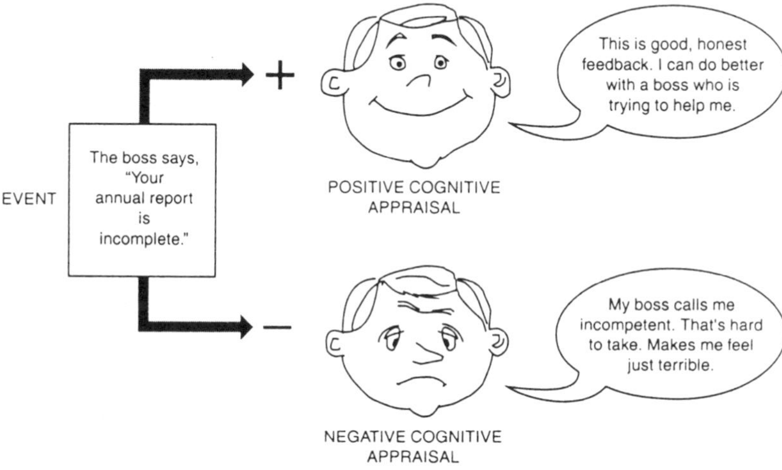

Fig 7.3: The effects of two different cognitive appraisals of the same event

We know that these sorts of processes are important because they do have effects on how you feel about yourself and your work. Research has shown, for instance, that when persons have negative and dysfunctional thoughts and thought processes, they are more likely to be less satisfied with their jobs, as well as feel that they are not in good physical and mental health (Judge and Locke, 1993). However, it is possible to alter the these negative thought processes by **cognitive restructuring** (Tosi et al., 1987). This is done by:

- identification of positive and negative self thoughts and statements
- substitution of positive ones for the negative ones.

cognitive restructuring The identification of positive and negative self thoughts and statements, and substitution of positive ones for the negative ones

This will increase self-efficacy and lead you to believe that you have the ability to perform the task or to cope with the stress. Suppose, for instance, that your first reaction to feedback from your boss might cause you to feel quite stressed. However, if you reappraise the situation and cognitively restructure it, you might conclude, after all, that you are not incompetent. You could, therefore, affect your stress level by what you think and tell yourself about the situation.

STRESS MANIFESTATIONS

stress manifestations Individual responses to stressors; physiological, psychological, or behavioral actions that are triggered by the cognitive appraisal of the situation

Reactions to stressors – called **stress manifestations** – may be physiological, psychological, or behavioral reactions that are triggered by the cognitive appraisal of the situation.

PHYSIOLOGICAL RESPONSES Bodily functions change when you are stressed. These changes may be immediate or long-term reactions. When a stressor is recognized, an immediate biochemical bodily reaction initiated by the brain leads to an increased flow of adrenalin. In response to stressors, blood sugar increases, the heart beats faster, muscles tense, perspiration increases, and all senses become heightened.

The longer-term physical reactions are, perhaps, more of a problem. As you experience stress over long periods, the body begins to show signs of wear and tear. Serious health problems such as coronary heart disease and cardiovascular illness have been associated with occupational and organizational stressors (Cooper and Marshall, 1976; Karasek et al., 1981; Ganster and Schaubroeck, 1991). Other specific illnesses associated with stress are ulcers, hypertension (high blood pressure), headaches, and migraine headaches. Some believe that even illnesses not normally associated with stress, such as cancer, can be due to stress because stress leads to a breakdown in the body's immune system and this will increase susceptibility to other illnesses (Fox et al., 1993).

PSYCHOLOGICAL RESPONSES The psychological manifestations are the ones that we conventionally associate with stress. Psychological responses are thoughts and feelings that may be work-specific or nonwork-oriented. There are several work-specific responses to stress. For example, nurses who experienced more frequent and intense work stressors were more depressed, had greater work anxiety, and were more hostile toward coworkers (Motowidlo et al., 1986). Other work-specific responses are lower job satisfaction, lower confidence in the organization, anxiety about work and career, increased alienation, and lower commitment to work (Kahn et al., 1964).

Nonwork-oriented responses are either short-term or long-term changes in the individual's psychological state. When these effects persist, they may reflect a change in personality, which is in itself a coping response. Some of these nonwork psychological responses are lower self-confidence (or self-esteem), denial of the situation, an increased sense of futility, neuroticism, tension, general anxiety, irritation, hostility, and depression (Beehr and Newman, 1978; Motowidlo et al., 1986).

BEHAVIORAL RESPONSES People may act differently when they are under stress. Increased use of alcohol, smoking, and changes in eating patterns are symptoms shown by people under stress. Stress has also been associated with increased absenteeism, tardiness, lateness at work, poor performance, reduced work concentration, composure, perseverance and adaptability, and lower work quality (Beehr and Newman, 1978; Cohen, 1980; Motowidlo et al., 1986).

Stressed individuals are less interpersonally effective. When exposure to stress resulted in higher depression for a group of nurses, they were less tolerant with doctors and showed less warmth toward other nurses. Highly stressed persons are more aggressive toward others, they are more competitive, and group cohesiveness is lower (Cohen, 1980). Communication with others may also be reduced. All these responses may be part of a more general coping syndrome of withdrawal from others, avoiding contact, and rejecting influence attempts from those who may be exerting pressure.

Coping Strategies

coping strategies The way a person responds to stress

Coping strategies are the way that you handle either the stressors or yourself when you experience stress (Lazarus, 1980). If you are sensing a stressor either consciously or unconsciously, you choose a way to respond to it. This occurs through a **secondary cognitive appraisal** process, which is different from the primary cognitive appraisal in which one becomes aware of the stressor.

There are two functions of coping (Lazarus, 1978). The first is a problem-solving function; you may try to change the environmental stressor or your own behavior so that the stressor is less likely to occur or to be so severe. For instance, suppose you feel stress because you constantly receive negative feedback about your performance. If you are actually doing well, you might be able to change this feedback by making sure that your boss receives the correct information about your performance. You might also change the feedback by improving your performance if you have not been up to par.

The second function of coping is to manage the physiological and emotional reactions to stress "so that they do not get out of hand and do not damage or destroy morale and social functioning" (Lazarus, 1978). Basically, this means managing your emotions.

There are four different strategies to cope with stress (Lazarus, 1980).

1 Seeking information
2 Direct action
3 Restraining action
4 Psychological coping reactions

Information seeking is trying to find out what the stressors are and what causes them. Because uncertainty is a property of stress, information seeking can be productive if the result is reduced uncertainty. However, it is possible that "ignorance is bliss." Sometimes the truth may be quite disruptive. Stress was found to be higher for employees who actively sought and obtained information about a major organizational change which might have had negative effects on them (Ashford, 1988).

Direct action may take several forms. When experiencing job stressors, you may work harder, take pills, drink more, change jobs, or change the environment in some way. You might try to escape it by removing yourself from the immediate danger, or you might choose to respond by taking direct or indirect actions to remove the stressors. Another form of direct action is to seek and develop *social support* Communication of positive feelings and behavior from others who are important people in one's life

social support. Acceptance and help from others may buffer the effects of the stressors as well as help you to find more constructive solutions. If you are experiencing stress because of conflicting demands from your boss, you might seek out an older colleague (perhaps a mentor) with whom you can discuss the problem and find a solution that helps.

Restraining action is dealing with stress by doing nothing, especially when taking action might lead to other, less desirable outcomes. For example, acting on an immediate impulse to a problem at work might lead to a person becoming so angry when another person is promoted that he or she might resign in haste. This could result in serious upheaval to family, a significant change in a person's career, and other undesirable results. Waiting before doing something is probably a more effective way to cope with such stress.

Psychological coping reactions are very common responses to stress. Emotions, and often subsequent behavior, are determined in part by what the person says to himself or herself about the situation. Denial of the existence of a problem, psychological withdrawal from the situation, and other defense mechanisms may change the perceptions of the objective environment so much that the perceived environment is one in which the person can operate more comfortably, at least in the short run. When psychological coping modes distort reality and are used extensively, they may represent a poor adjustment to stress. For example, if a person who consistently has a difficult time performing a job but denies the failure or attributes it to wrong causes may continue to stay in an unsuccessful situation. In the long run, this may diminish self-esteem.

COPING AND PERSONALITY Because people will differ in their cognitive appraisal of the same situation, they will use different coping strategies, the choice of which is affected by personality. Personality effects on coping strategies were demonstrated in a study of a new plant start-up (Tosi et al., 1986). Workers who were impatient, aggressive, and precise about details (characteristics of a Type A orientation, see page 209) chose direct action strategies of simply working harder at the new job. Those with low self-esteem reported that they psychologically withdrew from the jobs. For example, they were more likely to let their minds wander, take breaks, or go to get something to eat or drink. Those who considered work a central element in their life structure tended to complain about the work situation and sought help in learning and doing the job.

Sources of Stress

Stress is a result of the transaction and interaction between the person and the environment. In this section, we discuss environmental stressors. Some are in the objective environment, most are part of the psychological environment. We distinguish between "work factors" and "nonwork factors" which are sources of stress, as well as individual differences that affect our propensities to react to stressors or how we cope with it.

WORK FACTORS

There are good personal and organizational reasons to reduce stressors in the work context. For the person, work can be hazardous to your mental and physical health, an idea which is not consistent with the Western work ethic that work is rewarding and valued in and of itself. For the organization, work-induced stress has serious financial effects. It has been estimated, for example, about 95 percent of workers' compensation claims resulting from mental stressors may be due to cumulative psychic workplace trauma, which is caused by employee abuse by managers (Wilson, 1991). In this section, five work-setting stressors are discussed.

1 Occupational factors
2 Role pressures
3 Participation opportunities
4 Responsibility for people
5 Organization factors

OCCUPATIONAL FACTORS Some jobs are more stressful than others. Blue-collar workers are more likely to be exposed to working conditions that lead to physical health problems because many of their jobs are more physically dangerous or they are exposed to more toxic substances (Shostak, 1980). Studies have shown that those who work in routine jobs have high levels of alienation from work and boredom, and that machine-paced work was more strongly related to tension, anxiety, anger, depression and fatigue than non-paced work (Kornhauser, 1965; Hurrell, 1985).

Studies of occupations and coronary disease give us a clue about why some jobs are generally more stressful than others. Coronary disease is considered to be related, in part, to stress, and those jobs with the highest levels of coronary disease have two common characteristics: they are high in "psychological demands" and low in "decision control;" see figure 7.4. People in these jobs are constantly under pressure from others, say a customer, and they must respond in a way that the other person wishes, not in the way they would like to. Consider a waiter. When the customer is ready to order, the waiter must be there. Food cannot be delivered until it is prepared by the cook. The waiter is in the middle between the cook and the customer, and subjected to demands from both while having little control over the situation. High demand/low control jobs are shown in the lower right quadrant of figure 7.4. Cooks, assembly line workers, fire fighters and nurses have higher coronary disease risks (Karasek et al., 1981; Fox et al., 1993). One study of nurses in the high-risk quadrant found they had lower job satisfaction, higher blood pressure, and higher levels of salivary cortisol. Blood pressure is typically associated with coronary risk and cortisol is associated with reduced immune reactions and depression. These nurses also carried stress reactions to home after work, increasing their chances for longer-term negative health effects.

ROLE PRESSURES Individuals are more effective at work when they are clear about what is expected of them and when they do not have severe role conflict and role

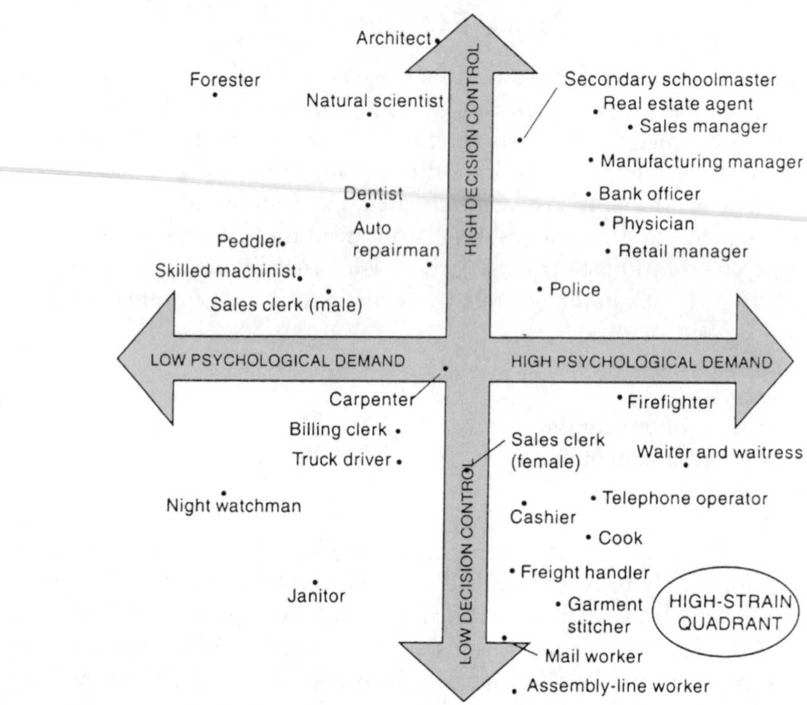

Fig 7.4 : Stress at work

ambiguity at work (Kahn et al., 1964). Role conflict and role ambiguity are both associated with a broad set of negative work reactions, including higher job tension and anxiety, lower job satisfaction, lower organization commitment, and a higher propensity to leave an organization (House and Rizzo, 1972; Jackson and Schuler, 1985). A moderate negative relationship also exists between individual performance, role conflict, and role ambiguity (Jackson and Schuler, 1985).

A Question of Ethics: Ethical Climates in Organizations and Role Strain

One way to minimize certain aspects of role conflict and role ambiguity is to foster an ethical climate in an organization. An ethical climate requires more than a code of ethics and ethical statements by top managers. It is important that a complex set of policies, procedures, and reward systems are in place that reinforce "doing the right thing." Studies show that when there is a strong ethical climate, there are less serious ethical violations, greater capacity to act ethically when situations arise and, for sales personnel, less ethical conflict with their sales managers.

Source: Adapted from Bartels et al. (1998) and Schwepker et al. (1997)

Role conflict occurs when a person is in a situation where there are pressures to comply with different and inconsistent demands. If the person complies with one demand, it is difficult or impossible to comply with other demands. Suppose a student has a Tuesday evening history class in which the instructor schedules an exam, but then finds out that her statistics exam is to be given during the same Tuesday evening class period. She cannot do both exams.

role conflict
Results when a person is unable to meet conflicting demands

The particular type of role conflict depends on the sources of the demands. An **intrasender role conflict** is inconsistent expectations from a single person. A manager, for instance, may expect you to increase production but does not give you the necessary additional resources. Often managers resort to this kind of demand when there are cost-cutting drives or other programs to increase efficiency.

intrasender role conflict
The inconsistent expectations that one faces from a single person

Diversity Issues: Role Conflict and the Working Woman

Stress will certainly be a part of everyone's life in the work environment. The daily pressures of any job will need to be addressed by the workers. It has been documented that the levels of stress are certainly not the same for individual employees. Different work responsibilities, personality types, and home lives can all have a dramatic effect on the stress level faced at one's job. However, there may also be a distinct connection to a given employee's stress level and the *gender* of that employee. Recent data suggests that the pressures women face are far beyond those difficulties addressed by their male counterparts.

Although constantly improving, it is no secret that women in the workplace are still faced with traditional, gender-based discrimination issues. Recent data shows that, despite making up over 40 percent of the workforce, women still hold less than 3 percent of top management positions. This 'glass ceiling', as well as more blatant forms of sex discrimination and stereotyping (i.e. stark differences in pay rates), continue to be a factor in the day-to-day efforts of women.

These difficulties, just on their own, would make for a more stressful work environment. However, there is more to this problem than simply discrimination and stereotypes. Despite the entry into the workforce, the majority of women perform the traditional familial duties of old. Their day simply does not end at 5 p.m. Household chores, child care, and other homemaking duties make for an extremely rigorous and pressure-packed day. It is interesting to note that, despite similar feelings of work–family conflict, men, as a whole, may not have yet embraced such family-oriented responsibilities. A recent US survey showed that women spend four times as much of their day on household labor than do their husbands, despite both parents having full-time employment.

It is certainly not surprising then that many women have much more extreme feelings of pressure and frustration. Managers and their organizations should therefore be conscious of potentially higher levels of stress for their female employees' situations. Flexibility for family life would be an initial step towards assisting women in their struggle for balancing full-time careers with family care expectations.

Source: Adapted from Yang (1996) by Pete Jones

intersender role conflict
When two different individuals place incompatible demands on a person

Intersender role conflict occurs when two or more individuals place incompatible demands on a person. For example, the quality control manager of a plant may expect the production supervisor to reject more units of the product while the production manager wants increased production output and therefore fewer rejections.

person–role conflict
When organizational demands are in conflict with one's values

Person–role conflict occurs when organizational demands are in conflict with one's values. An example of this is the "whistleblower." Whistleblowers call public attention to unethical or illegal actions by an organization, even though there can be great personal costs, often because they are motivated by personal beliefs about ethical responsibilities. In most organizations, person–role conflict is not likely to be a serious problem, since individuals who have serious personal differences with organizational values would probably discover this early in their organization socialization and leave.

role ambiguity
When people feel uncertain about what is expected of them

There are two types of **role ambiguity** – the uncertainty about the expectations of others:

task ambiguity
Uncertainty about the work requirements themselves

social–emotional ambiguity
Ambiguity about how you are evaluated by another person

1 **Task ambiguity,** refers to uncertainty about the work requirements themselves. This is common, for example, when you take a new position and are trying to learn how to do the job. It also occurs when responsibilities are not clear because of vague job descriptions or unclear instructions from a manager.
2 **Social–emotional ambiguity** is uncertainty about how you are evaluated by another person. This happens when work standards are unclear and performance judgments are subjective. It is also a problem when someone does not receive feedback from others.

role overload
Occurs when the work requirements are excessive and exceed the limit of time and/or ability

role underload
A condition in which the work does not make use of a person's abilities

Two more stressors are role overload or role underload.

- **Role overload** occurs when the work requirements are so excessive, they exceed the limits of time and/or ability.
- **Role underload** is when work does not make use of a person's abilities. For security guards and receptionists, where the person is underutilized, their jobs require "few of the worker's skills and abilities (although they make heavy demands on those few)" (Katz and Kahn, 1978). Persons in such jobs characterize them as boring and monotonous. This kind of work is associated with higher levels of absenteeism, lower job satisfaction, and alienation.

PARTICIPATION OPPORTUNITIES Managers who report higher levels of participation in decision making feel much lower stress, job anxiety, and threat than those who report low participation (Tosi, 1971). Participation is important for two reasons.

1 Participation is associated with low-role conflict and low-role ambiguity (Kahn et al., 1964; Tosi, 1971).
2 Participation gives you the feeling of some control of the stressors in the environment, reducing the effect of stressors compared to when you have no real or perceived control (Cohen, 1980).

Responsibility for people Responsibility for others may lead to stress at work (Cooper and Marshall, 1976). As a manager, your effectiveness depends on those who work for you. If for any reason you do not have confidence in them or in your ability to manage them, then you are likely to experience stress because you do not perceive control over the situation. In addition to that, responsibility for others calls for making decisions about pay, promotion opportunities and career paths of others, and exerting a good deal of influence over their lives.

Organizational factors The organization itself affects stress. For instance, many believe that when organizations are restrictively bureaucratic, it does not maximize human performance potential; others believe that when they are too unstructured they are more likely to release human productive capacity (Argyris, 1964; Presthus, 1978). Four characteristics of organizations can be stressors:

1 Organizational level
2 Organizational complexity
3 Organizational change
4 Organizational boundary roles

At top organization levels, executive work has a good deal of role overload, executives have responsibility for others, and a good deal of conflict and ambiguity is present in the job. Managers tend to have more time constraints and efficiency problems. The very characteristics of the managerial role, such as constant interruptions, short times on any one activity, and so on, make effective use of time difficult. Workers at lower levels are more likely to have role overload and role conflict due to conflicting demands from supervisors and lack of resources (Parasuraman and Alutto, 1981).

Regarding organization complexity, excessive rules, requirements, and complicated networks that exist in large organizations can be stressful. Role strain tends to become increasingly a problem as work becomes more specialized, more levels of supervision are introduced, and more complexity is added (Kahn et al., 1964).

When there are any kinds of organizational changes that modify your job and responsibilities so that you have to accommodate to them, stress reactions are possible. Some changes reduce a person's job security, status, and power. Mergers, acquisitions, retrenchment, and downsizing will create uncertainty, job anxiety, and higher stress.

An organizational boundary role is one in which you must interact with, and be accountable to, others in your own organization at the same time that you are interacting with persons from other organizations who place demands on you. These are more stressful because you are subjected to role conflict which emanates from both internal and external sources. For example, sales personnel must meet customer demands at the same time that they must satisfy company requirements.

Global Focus on Stress and International Jobs

International business is becoming an increasingly necessary part of many corporations' day-to-day operation. Just as these overseas efforts are becoming more common, so also are the problems associated with business travelers. One such problem in international business is the stress level of sales executives who are given these international assignments.

There are many factors associated with international travel that contribute to employee stress. An unfamiliar place, being away from home, jet lag, poor nutrition, and dehydration are just a few of the problems encountered. It is not surprising that these travelers are much more in danger of developing psychological problems related to stress than their coworkers who stay in the US. Recent studies have shown that international travelers are *twice* as likely to suffer stress-related conditions such as anxiety attacks, depression, social withdrawal, and coping problems. Another recent survey stated that some 75 percent of frequent business travelers not only recognize the stress of being away from home and family, they also suffer anxiety over work awaiting them when they return.

There have been many remedies proposed for these stress-related problems. One such strategy has been to encourage employees to become familiar with the country as much as possible before their visit. While not intended to be a full immersion in the other nation's culture, this approach was developed to assist travelers in basic social norms of the host country. Helpful tactics include determining the best ways to travel from place to place, how to say a few simple words in the national tongue, and determining what sites close to the destination are worth visiting. Some travelers also face worries associated with being away from home, and are limited in telephone communication due to time zone differences. However, encouraging the use of fax and e-mail technologies have helped to reduce this common stressor. Another approach, designed to assist travelers with families, is to involve family members in discussions of the destination before departing.

While the international traveler will most likely always have an added burden of stress associated with his duties, the above remedies can help reduce the stress level.

Source: Adapted from Ligos (1998) by Pete Jones

NONWORK FACTORS

Suppose that two administrative assistants have been working for you for several years. They may both have very similar work assignments, and both be exposed to the same set of work stressors in their objective work environment. How will this affect them?

- They are likely to experience different levels of stress and will exhibit different stress responses.
- They may make different cognitive appraisals of the same objective environment.
- Personality differences may account for their different reactions.
- One may be experiencing stressors in the nonwork environment, such as divorce, the recent death of a parent, a very ill child, or marital difficulties that are not in the environment of the other.

In this section, we show the relationship of stress responses to some of these nonwork environmental factors such as life structure changes and social support.

LIFE CHANGES Some of the natural flows of life can induce stress as you go through the transition periods of life and career stages. For instance, most of us will experience the death of a spouse or a close family member. Each of us faces the prospect of changing jobs. One approach to assessing the impact of such changes is the "social readjustment rating scale" (Holmes and Rahe, 1967). The scale lists over 40 stress producing events and changes that most people will experience at one time or another in their life. Table 7.1 shows some of these events with weights that indicate the difficulty of coping, or dealing, with the events. The table shows, for example, the death of a spouse is very stressful; changing jobs less so. The nonwork events are more severe stressors than the work events. Basically, the idea is that if you accumulate a large number of stressor points in a relatively short period, you are more likely to show a stress reaction.

High life stress is related to how individuals seek information to cope with stress-inducing events. Studies show that when faced with high life stress, individuals tended to seek help off the job (Weiss et al., 1982). They seek help from friends, take continuing education courses, or seek a new job. When faced with work stress, people tend to seek help from others at work, looking for help from workers and superiors.

Table 7.1 Relative difficulty of adjustment to selected life changes

Nonwork		*Work*	
Event	*Weight*	*Event*	*Weight*
Death of spouse	100	Fired at work	47
Divorce	73	Retirement	45
Jail term	63	Business readjustment	39
Death in close family	63	Change in responsibilities	29
Marriage	50	Trouble with boss	23
Death of close friend	37	Change in hours/working conditions	20
Wife begins/stops work	26		

Source: Holmes and Rahe (1967)

SOCIAL SUPPORT Social support is the communication of positive feelings of liking, trust, respect, acceptance of one's beliefs, and, sometimes, assistance from others who are important people in one's life (Katz and Kahn, 1978). It is important because it affects a person's psychological environment. When you have social support, events may seem less stress inducing because the resources that you draw on are greater – help from others – and therefore the demands of the environment can be met. It is perhaps as simple as the fact that you have some help in dealing with pressure. For example, losing a job is stressful and it has been related to such effects as arthritic symptoms, cholesterol elevation, and escapist drinking (Katz and Kahn, 1978). However, these effects are not as strong when you have a social support system to help you to deal with the situation.

Individual Differences and Stress

We have already told you something about the role of individual differences and how they relate to stress in chapter 2. Now we turn to a specific set of dimensions:

- The self-concept and hardiness
- Locus of control
- Type A/B behavior patterns
- Flexibility/rigidity
- Negative affectivity
- Ability

The self-concept and hardiness Individual self-perceptions affect the way that you handle stressful life events. One of the more important facets of self-perception is self-esteem, i.e. the way that you perceive and evaluate yourself. Those who have a positive and a reasonably accurate concept of "self" have high self-esteem. They tend to have confidence in themselves – not that they charge headlong into unknown situations with adventurous disregard, but that they know their capacities and potential and act accordingly. Self-esteem seems to moderate how you respond to stressors (Howard et al., 1986; Nowack, 1986). In one study, workers with low self-esteem withdrew psychologically from the stress of starting a new job in a new plant (Tosi et al., 1986). People with low self-confidence tend to have more intense reactions to high stress than those with high self-confidence (Kahn et al., 1964).

hardiness
A psychological condition of how much a person feels in control, confident of their own ability and orientated toward challenge and adventure

The concept of **hardiness** is a bit more complex than self-esteem. "Hardy" persons tend to feel more in control, less alienated from themselves, have a clear sense of personal values and goals, are confident of their abilities and are more oriented toward challenge and adventure (Kobasa, 1979; Rhodewalt and Agustsdottir, 1984). Hardy persons cope with stress better than those who are not (Lawler and Schmied, 1992). Over 800 executives in a large public utility were studied to find out if those who experienced a high degree of stress without falling ill were more "hardy" than those who become sick under stress (Kobasa, 1979). Life stress was measured for the managers using the "social readjustment rating scale." Recent illnesses of each executive were also assessed to determine how often and how severely each had been sick. Lastly, "hardiness" was assessed. Executives who experienced high stress but low levels of illness were more hardy than those who experienced high stress and had high illness rates. Here is an example of how a hardy executive might respond to a job change:

> The hardy executive does more than passively acquiesce to the job transfer. Rather, he throws himself actively into a new situation, utilizing his inner resources to make it his own . . . [He has] an unshakable sense of meaningfulness and ability to evaluate the impact of a transfer in terms of a general life plan with its established priorities (Kobasa, 1979).

The sense of self-complexity is also related to how people respond to stressful events. Those with complex self-perceptions deal differently with stressful events than those with simple self-conceptions (Linville, 1987). When they were exposed to stressful events, those with cognitively multi-dimensional lives were less depressed, perceived lower stress, and had fewer incidents of flu and other illnesses than those with simple cognitive representations of themselves. Perhaps the impact of a negative event occurs to a smaller portion of their self-representation (Linville, 1987), reducing its effect.

Locus of control To have real or perceived control over stressors is related to reduced stress levels and active coping responses (Cohen, 1980). Specifically, the locus of control has been shown to moderate stress reactions. Internals, i.e. persons with an internal locus of control (see chapter 2, page 49) believe that they can influence their environment, that what they do and how they do it determines what they attain. Externals, those with an external locus of control believe that they have little influence over the environment and that what happens to them is a matter of luck, fate or due to the actions of others (Rotter, 1966).

Internals manifest stress in different ways from externals. Internals faced with a stressor are more likely to believe that they can have a significant effect on outcomes while externals are more likely to acquiesce, to be passive, and to see events as more stressful (Williams and Stout, 1985). When faced with stressors, internals report lower stress levels and are less likely to become severely and frequently ill (Kobasa, 1979; Williams and Stout, 1985; Ashford, 1988).

Internal's coping strategies are different than external's (Anderson, 1977; Lawler and Schmied, 1992). For example, after a hurricane that devastated several small towns in central Pennsylvania, entrepreneurs whose business was ruined and who were internals perceived the situation as less stressful than the external entrepreneurs (Anderson, 1977). The external entrepreneurs tended to be more defensive. The internals brought their businesses back more quickly from the disaster. When they faced the stressful situation, they took control of events with more task-oriented coping behavior.

Type A behavior pattern Those who are hard-driving, highly competitive, impatient with others, irritated when they are in situations that they believe prevent them from achieving their goals, and strive to accomplish more and more in less and less time manifest a **Type A behavior pattern**. The **Type B behavior pattern** is the opposite. Those who exhibit this pattern tend to be less aggressive, less competitive, and more relaxed (Matteson and Ivancevich, 1980).

Type A behavior pattern
People who are hard-driving, highly competitive, impatient with others, irritated when situations prevent them from achieving their goals

Type B behavior pattern
People who are less aggressive, competitive, and more relaxed than Type A people

EXERCISE

Managerial Health: Are You Dying to Succeed?

This questionnaire is designed to help you to diagnose your own personal style and approach to work, and to give you some initial insight into whether your lifestyle and work might be leading you to ill health. Listed below are statements that describe personal actions or feelings.

		Score
A	Once I start something, I must finish it as soon as possible.	-----
B	It is very important to pay attention to details and be precise.	-----
C	I like to compete and I like to win at whatever I do, work or play.	-----
D	If I am in a conversation and I have something to say, I interrupt the other person.	-----
E	I do everything at a fast pace, playing, working, eating, walking.	-----
F	I have very little patience if I have to wait for something.	-----
G	I am very ambitious. I want to succeed and be the best at what I do.	-----
H	I always set tight, but achievable deadlines.	-----
I	I try to do more than one thing at a time.	-----
J	I evaluate people by hard objective criteria such as how much work they do or how much profit we make. I don't like subjectivity.	-----
	Total	-----

Indicate the degree to which you think the item describes how you behave or how you feel. However, *before* you do this, make a copy of the list and give it to someone who knows you very well, and ask them to indicate the extent to which they think that the item describes you. Both of you should use this scale:

1 A completely inaccurate description
2 Mostly inaccurate
3 Slightly inaccurate
4 Neutral
5 Slightly accurate
6 Mostly accurate
7 A very accurate description

Now transfer your score to the Type AB scale below to see where you fall.

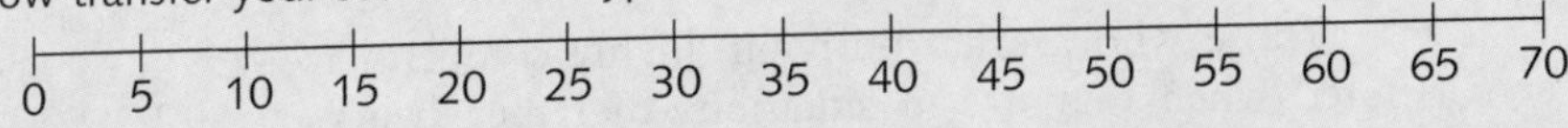

55–70 If you scored this high you are in the strong Type A category. This means that you are prone to all the problems discussed in the chapter about Type A persons.

40–50 Your propensities are strongly in the Type A direction. It makes some sense for you to be careful in the same ways that strong Type A persons should.

30–40 This is a healthier pattern. You are more balanced than either the Type A or Type B person.

15–25 You are a near Type B if you are at this point. You are likely to be pretty relaxed and not likely susceptible to Type A problems.

10–15 You need not worry about the Type A effects, though this does not mean that you may not have stress reactions for other reasons.

Given your score, what do you think about your likelihood of your experiencing high stress at work? Are you pleased with your results? Why or why not? What could you change to minimize the stressors in your environment?

Different responses to stress have been linked to the Type A behavior pattern and the Type B behavior pattern. Physiologically, Type As tend to have more extreme bodily responses to stress and to recover more slowly than Type B individuals (Hart and Jamieson, 1983). Those who are Type A are more likely to have a higher incidence of risk factors associated with cardiovascular disease as well as having a higher incidence of coronary disease itself (Matteson and Ivancevich, 1980). They have higher pulse rates when faced with challenging tasks and also tend to have elevated blood pressure when their self-esteem is threatened (Pittner and Houston, 1980). In a study of a new plant start up, Type A workers reported more sexual problems and a higher frequency of headaches (Zahrly and Tosi, 1987).

Behavioral responses to stress for Type A individuals may contribute to the more extreme physiological responses. For example, when they have perceived control of the situation they perform better, but behaviorally they are less able to handle conflict through accommodation (Baron, 1989). Type A individuals tend to smoke more and are more impatient, act in aggressive ways, and report higher levels of physical problems (Zahrly and Tosi, 1987; Puffer and Brakefield, 1989).

Psychologically, Type A persons experience more subjective stress in their environment that is moderately uncontrollable or uncontrollable. When exposed to stressors they are more angry, time pressured, and impatient (Hart and Jamieson, 1983; Rhodewalt and Agustsdottir, 1984; Motowidlo et al., 1986). They also respond more cognitively to stressful situations: they are more likely to use denial and suppression than a Type B person.

One reason for these different reactions is that the Type A may internalize stress and, perhaps, failure. When they fail, they try again and again to solve the problem. If they are not successful, they feel that they did not try hard enough, leading to greater frustration and annoyance. They feel ineffective and attribute the failure to themselves. The cost of their exposure to stressors and coping with them is very high (Brunson and Matthews, 1981).

FLEXIBILITY/RIGIDITY Flexible people experience different stressors and have different stress reactions than rigid people (Kahn et al., 1964). **Flexible** people are relatively adaptive to change, somewhat free and open and responsive toward others. They may show some indecisiveness because they may struggle more with decisions. The flexible person does not have clear-cut rigid rules for handling situations.

flexibility
The characteristic of being relatively adaptive to change, somewhat open and responsive toward others

Role overload and role conflict (page 201) are the main stressors for flexible people (Kahn et al., 1964). Their flexibility makes them susceptible and willing to respond to many pressures because they can be easily influenced. Perhaps this openness reflects "interest in variety and innovation, and their general expansiveness leads them to undertake many tasks that are not specifically required. . . . [They are] fall guys to work imposed by others; they tend to overload themselves. Their jobs continue to grow until they are overtaxed" (Kahn et al., 1964). Flexible people try to change their behavior as the situation demands so as to reduce pressures. They make performance promises, a commitment to complete the job. When the demands are high and the deadlines are near, a second strategy comes into play. The flexible person turns to peers and subordinates for help and collaboration.

The rigid person is closed-minded, generally somewhat dogmatic toward life. Rigid people have a preference for neatness and orderliness. They are also inconsiderate of others, tend to be critical in judging others, and not very tolerant of others' weakness. Rigid people respond differently to stressors.

- They deny or reject the pressures; in other words, the rigid person simply may not react when experiencing stressors, but will ignore them.
- The rigid person sometimes pushes away those who are pressing too hard.
- Under pressure, a rigid person may become increasingly dependent on his or her boss. This is a useful way to cope with any role strain because a superior can often protect a person from role conflict (by giving the person priorities for compliance), role ambiguity (by clarifying responsibilities), and role overload (by reducing work load requirements).
- A rigid person responds to work stressors by trying harder. He or she may spend more time and effort on the job trying to achieve more and ignore other facets of his or her life. To the extent that results are achieved, the rigid person has accomplished two things: removing the stressor by completing the work and being seen as more valuable to the organization.

NEGATIVE AFFECTIVITY Those persons high in negative affectivity tend to be sad, focus on failure and view themselves in negative ways so you would expect that they are more likely to see their world as more stressful (Burke et al., 1993). For one thing, they report that they experience more role conflict and role ambiguity (Spector and O'Connell, 1994). They also are more likely to manifest stress through behaviors such as higher absence rates, more visits to physicians and report that they have more physical problems (Chen and Spector, 1991).

ABILITY There is not much evidence to show how ability affects responses to stress (Beehr and Newman, 1978), however, it is reasonable to think that it does. In times of crisis, experts are called in to solve problems. A physician trained in trauma medicine knows what to do in a serious automobile accident emergency, whereas a psychiatrist may not. Professional athletes are regularly involved in competition with severe time pressures and extreme performance demands. They know what to do and, perhaps more importantly, are able to focus intensely on relevant factors, not extraneous ones. Some research does indirectly support this – in stressful conditions, supervisors with more experience perform better than those with less experience (Frost, 1983; Murphy et al., 1992).

There are at least three reasons why those with high ability may perform better in stressful situations.

1. It is less likely that they will experience role overload. The greater the ability, the more one can do.
2. They tend to know their upper limits. They are, therefore, better able to assess their likelihood of success in stress-inducing situations. You will recall that stress occurs in situations that are uncertain and important. The

high-ability person will probably face less uncertainty than the low-ability one.

3 High-ability people have more control over a situation than low-ability people, and situational control affects how a person responds to stressors.

Research on social facilitation can tell you something about the effects of ability, performance, and stressors. Social facilitation refers to the effect of the presence of other people on performance. In the presence of others, some people perform very well, whereas others do not. The difference has to do with the person's ability: high-ability people tend to do better in the presence of others, whereas those with low ability seem to do worse (Baron and Liebert, 1971).

Summary

Stress is a major determinant of health problems – both physical and mental; and much stress comes from the work setting. Since stress depends on the relationship of a person to the environment and what is happening in that environment, you must look for the causes of stress in the person as well as environmental forces.

The objective environment is the actual context in which you live, both at work and away from it. The psychological environment is the way that you experience the objective environment. Different people might psychologically experience the same job conditions in quite different ways because they have different needs, concerns, and personalities and therefore appraise the situation differently.

We also know that an individual can experience too much stress or too little stress. Too much stress may cause poor health, absenteeism, emotional breakdowns, and other dysfunctional behaviors. If there is too little, the motivation of the individual will be inadequate. The organization can manage stress in a situation by careful selection of personnel and by the manner in which the work of individuals is arranged or designed. The selection approach – selecting "internals" rather than "externals," those with high self-confidence, those who are flexible rather than rigid people, and high-ability people – can reduce the amount of stress experienced by individuals in the organization. In designing work, it appears that stress may be lower if employee decision control over work is higher, if there is less ambiguity about what is to be done on the job, and if a person does not have to comply with different and inconsistent demands.

Guide for Managers: Dealing with Stress

There are several ways to manage stress. It may be possible to change the objective environment to remove a stressor or to alter the psychological environment that you experience. Perhaps it is possible to alter the stress symptoms in some way so that they will not have debilitating long-run effects. All of these general approaches work, and the most effective way to manage stress may be a broad attack on several dimensions.

PERSONAL APPROACHES TO STRESS MANAGEMENT

Stress can be managed, at least in the sense that you can avoid stressful conditions, change them, or learn to cope more effectively with them. There are so many ways to do this that an extensive discussion of each is beyond the scope of this chapter. However, some that are currently thought to be useful and seem particularly relevant to organizational stress are discussed here.

Manage the environment in which the stressor exists

Change some activity or behavior to modify the environment. Suppose you are experiencing high stress from work. One way to resolve the problem may be by changing jobs within the company or leaving the firm.

Managing your life can diminish stress and its symptoms. Many stress-inducing situations occur because of poor personal planning and time management. For example, students often have test anxiety because they do not believe they have enough time to prepare for tests. Here is a typical scenario. A student has two midterm examinations scheduled in the next week. Because both exams cover a lot of material, the student begins to worry, especially if it is important to gain good grades. She goes to one of her instructors to ask for permission to take a make-up exam. The reason given is, "I don't have time to prepare." In cases like this, the anxiety can easily be avoided or at least reduced by preparing earlier in the term, instead of waiting until the last minute.

Change your cognitive appraisal of the environment

You can restructure the way that you think about and appraise the environment by telling yourself that the situation is not as destructive as when you felt stress from it. You can also change your behavior at work, perhaps by performing your job in a different way.

Relaxation, meditation, and biofeedback are a few of the mind-clearing approaches that you might use. These approaches either detach you from the stressor or help you to focus on other, less-stressful situations. They may also have important and positive effects on physiological stress symptoms. For example, relaxation approaches can reduce hypertension and heart rates.

Get help

Counseling and psychotherapy have long been used to solve stress-induced problems. A second party trained in mental health intervention works regularly with the person to determine the source of stress, to help the person to modify his or her outlook, and to develop alternative ways to cope. Often this is done by helping a person gain enough self-confidence and self-esteem to try a different way of coping with stress.

Therapists and counselors use many different approaches. These methods tend to be based on learning theory and the use of internal or external reinforcements. They are behavioral self-management tools to help you monitor, facilitate, and modify your own behavior. The role of the therapist is to teach you these methods and then withdraw so that you can use them independently (Osipow et al., 1980).

Develop social support

Having a group of close friends is helpful. They may provide a listening ear, a less-biased assessment

Focus on Discharging Stress: Some Conventional and some Unconventional Ways

While many top executives are workaholics and have little time for a life outside work that might help them to cope with stress, that is not the case for everyone. For instance, the CEO of Honeywell, Mike Bonsignore, escapes under the sea where he pursues his hobby of deep sea photography. He equates the weightlessness and quiet underwater to the best form of meditation. It is better than other ways to relax, like golf. "I play two games a month and rarely break 100. That's not renewal to me."

Francis Luzuriaga, an executive vice president at Mattel, is a dancer. She dances as much as she can, especially when traveling. She carries her tights and ballet shoes with her and relaxes that way. She continues a practice that many ballet dancers start when they are very young, dancing *The Nutcracker* every Christmas with a regional ballet company near Los Angeles.

Paolo Fresco climbs mountains. Mr. Fresco, General Electric vice chairman, started climbing when he was a teenager growing up in Milan, Italy during family vacations. He finds the stimulation a way to recharge himself for when he returns to work from the mountain.

Buzzy Krongard, the CEO of Alex, Brown and Sons, a brokerage firm, describes himself as an "adrenaline junkie" and he relaxes doing things that are likely to give him his adrenaline kick. Besides parachute jumping, he regularly trains and practices kung fu.

It is not likely that these are the sorts of things that you might think about as ways of handling stress, but the key point is that they work for the specific individual. That is what makes them effective.

of the situation, some help in working your way out of a stressful situation, and, finally, suggest ways to change your behavior so that you become more adaptive.

Improve your physical condition

Being in good physical condition will help you to deal more effectively with stress. Proper exercise, a wise diet, and not smoking will result in positive physiological effects for anyone. Heart rate decreases, blood pressure is generally reduced, and the body becomes more resistant to pressures.

ORGANIZATIONAL APPROACHES TO STRESS MANAGEMENT

Many organizations realize that if they can reduce the number and intensity of stressors or help employees to cope more effectively with them, there should be increased performance, reduced turnover and absenteeism, and substantial reductions in costs. This problem can be attacked through the implementation of employee wellness programs and by management practices which modify the work environment.

Employee wellness programs

Over the last 15 years, an increasing number of organizations have instituted some type of employee wellness program, including stress management. These programs include health risk assessments, exercise facilities and programs, individual counseling when employees feel job or personal strain, clinics to deal with the use of alcohol and regular seminars and lectures. Dow Corning's approach is to send health and wellness magazines to its employees, offer seminars to help them to quit smoking, programs to reduce stress, and health screenings that include prenatal checkups (Woolsey, 1993).

Wellness programs are effective in reducing work stress (Rose and Veiga, 1984). They are also very cost-effective when they have the support of top management and are accessible to a large number of employees. For example, Adolph Coors Company saved an estimated $1.9 million over the last decade by reducing medical costs and sick leave, and by increasing productivity (Caudron, 1990).

Implement management practices to improve the work environment

There are several ways that some work stressors can be affected by good management practices:

- *Improving communication with employees will reduce uncertainty.* This is a way to lessen role ambiguity and may also have direct effects on role conflict if better communication clarifies lines of responsibility and authority.
- *Effective performance appraisal and reward systems reduce role conflict and role ambiguity.* When rewards are clearly related to performance, the person knows what he or she is accountable for (reduced role conflict) and where he or she stands (reduced role ambiguity). When a good coaching relationship between a superior and a subordinate exists along with the performance appraisal system, the person may perceive more control over the work environment. He or she may also sense some social support for the task of getting the job done well.
- *Increasing participation in decision making will give the person a greater sense of control over the work environment*, a factor associated with less negative reactions to stress. There is a strong relationship between participation and job satisfaction, role conflict and role ambiguity. Increasing participation requires decentralization of decision making to more people and delegation of responsibility to those who are already accountable for work performance.
- *Job enrichment* gives the person more responsibility, more meaningful work, more control, more feedback. Uncertainty will be reduced, greater control over the work environment will be perceived, and there will be more variety. Job enrichment increases motivation and encourages higher work quality, especially among those with high growth needs.
- *An improved match of skills, personality, and work* is also a way to manage stress at work. There is nothing so frustrating as being placed in a job that you cannot handle and do not have the potential to perform well (Motowidlo et al., 1986). Similarly, some jobs have a good deal of natural stress just because the work is set up that way (Karasek et al., 1981). For these tasks, organizations should seek highly skilled and competent persons with personalities that help them cope effectively.

Key Concepts

STUDY QUESTIONS

1 What are the key elements in the stress and coping model?
2 What is meant by the statement that stress is "nonspecifically induced"?
3 How is the psychological environment related to the subjective environment in the stress model?
4 What is a "cognitive appraisal"?
What is the difference between a "primary" and a "secondary" cognitive appraisal?
5 Distinguish between coping responses and stress manifestations.
What are some ways to cope with stress?
Apply these concepts to a stressful situation you personally experienced.
6 How can stress have positive effects?
7 What key characteristics about a job seem to be related to stress?
8 What is role conflict?
What is role ambiguity?
What are some other types of role strain?
Show how you experienced each of these on a job.
9 How can the work setting itself contribute to stress?
Interview a manager or visit a company and document sources of stress.
10 How are "life events" related to the effects of stress?

Case

John Baxter

John Baxter was a new young manager at National Metals Corp. As a recently graduated MBA, John was eager to learn as much as possible about the company and to advance quickly through management levels to a top management position. Being single enabled John to work extra hours on the job and to volunteer for membership on various task forces attempting to achieve better coordination among organizational units and to install newer and more efficient work technologies and procedures. His own field of information systems was, in itself, changing rather rapidly, also requiring him to spend much time reading new technical material.

After a year and a half on the job, John appeared to be especially agitated compared to his fellow managers. He would move around the building at a frantic pace. He always appeared to be in a hurry and also appeared quite upset much of the time. He greatly increased his cigarette smoking and appeared to have an extra drink in the evening. His boss and some friends began to worry about him and told him to take it a little easier. None of these talks seemed to do much good.

At the beginning of his third year on the job, John started dating a new MBA working in another company who had just graduated from his university. They became engaged to be married six months later, and did marry four months after the engagement. After the engagement period, John's boss and his friends noticed a significant change in his behavior and attitudes. He was no longer agitated and nervous. He appeared quite calm and in very good spirits. He stopped working extra-long hours at night and on the weekends. His level of work stress appeared to be far lower than it was formerly.

- How do you explain this change in John's behavior?

References

Anderson, C. R. 1977: Locus of control, coping behaviors and performance in a stress setting: A longitudinal study. *Journal of Applied Psychology*, 62, 446–51.

Argyris, C. 1964: *Integrating the Individual and the Organization*. New York: John Wiley.

Ashford, S. J. 1988: Individual strategies for coping with stress during organizational transitions. *Journal of Applied Behavioral Science*, 24, February, 19–36.

Baron, R. A. 1989: Personality and organizational conflict: Effects of the Type A behavior pattern and self-monitoring. *Organizational Behavior and Human Decision Processes*, 44, October, 281–96.

Baron, R. A. and Liebert, R. M. 1971: *Human Social Behavior: A Contemporary View of Experimental Research*. Homewood, IL: Dorsey Press.

Bartels, L. K., Harrick, E., Martell, K. and Strickland, D. 1988: The relationship between ethical climate and ethical problems with human resource management. *Journal of Business Ethics*, 17(7), May, 799–805.

Beehr, T. A. and Newman, J. E. 1978: Job stress, employee health, and organizational effectiveness: A facet analysis, model, and literature review. *Personnel Psychology*, 30, 665–99.

Brunson, B. I. and Matthews, K. A. 1981: The Type A coronary-prone behavior pattern and reactions to uncontrollable stress: An analysis of performance strategies, affect, and attributions during failures. *Journal of Personality and Social Psychology*, 40, 906–18.

Burke, M. J., Brief, A. P. and George, J. M. 1993: The role of negative affectivity in understanding relations between self-reports of stressors and strains: A comment on the applied psychology literature. *Journal of Applied Psychology*, 78(3), June, 402–14.

Caudron, S. 1990: The wellness payoff. *Personnel Journal*, 69, July, 54–60.

Chen, P. Y. and Spector, P. E. 1991: Negative affectivity as the underlying causes of correlations between stressors and strains. *Journal of Applied Psychology*, 76(3), June, 398–408.

Cohen, S. 1980: After-effects of stress on human performance and social behavior. *Psychological Bulletin*, 88, 82–108.

Cooper, C. L. and Marshall, J. 1976: Occupational stress: A review of the literature relating to coronary heart disease and mental ill health. *Journal of Occupational Psychology*, 49, 11–28.

Fox, M. L., Dwyer, D. J. and Ganster, D. C. 1993: The effects of stressful job demands and control on physiological and attitudinal outcomes in a hospital setting. *Academy of Management Journal*, 36(2), 289–318.

Frost, D. E. 1983: Role perceptions and behavior of the immediate superior: Moderating effects on the prediction of leadership effectiveness. *Organizational Behavior and Human Decision Performance*, 31(1), 123–42.

Ganster, D. C. and Schaubroeck, J. 1991: Work stress and employee health. *Journal of Management*, 17, June, 235–71.

Hart, K. E. and Jamieson, J. L. PhD. 1983: Type A behavior and cardiovascular recovery from a psychosocial stressor. *Journal of Human Stress*, 9(1), March, 121–35.

Holmes, T. H. and Rahe, R. H. 1967: The social readjustment rating scale. *Journal of Psychosomatic Research*, 11, 213–18.

House, R. J. and Rizzo, J. R. 1972: Role conflict and ambiguity as critical variables in a model of organizational behavior. *Organizational Behavior and Human Performance*, 7, 467–505.

Howard, J. H., Cunningham, D. A. and Rechnitzer, P. A. 1986: Personality (hardiness) as a moderator of job stress and coronary risk in Type A individuals: A longitudinal study. *Journal of Behavioral Medicine*, 9(3), 19–23.

Hurrell, J. J. 1985: Machine paced work and the Type A behavior pattern. *Journal of Occupational Psychology*, 58, 15–25.

Jackson, S. E. and Schuler, R. S. 1985: A meta-analysis of research on role ambiguity and role conflict in work settings. *Organizational Behavior and Human Decision Processes*, 36, 16–38.

Judge, T. A. and Locke, E. A. 1993: Effect of dysfunctional thought processes on subjective well-being and job satisfaction. *Journal of Applied Psychology*, 78(3), June, 475–91.

Kahn, R. L., Wolfe, D. M., Quinn, R. P., Snoek, J. D. and Rosenthal, R. A. 1964: *Organizational Stress: Studies in Role Conflict and Ambiguity*. New York: John Wiley.

Karasek, R. A., Baker, D., Marxer, A., Ahlbom, A. and Theorell, T. 1981: Job decision latitude, job demands, and cardiovascular disease: A prospective study of Swedish men. *American Journal of Public Health*, July, 71, 694–704.

Katz, D. and Kahn, R. 1978: *The Social Psychology of Organizations*. New York: John Wiley.

Kobasa, S. 1979: Stressful life events, personality, and health: An inquiry in hardiness. *Journal of Personality and Social Psychology*, 37, 1–11.

Kornhauser, A. 1965: *Mental Health of the Industrial Worker*. New York: John Wiley.

Lawler, K. A. and Schmied, L. A. 1992: A prospective study of women's health: The effects of hardiness, locus of control, Type A Behavior, and psychological reactivity. *Women and Health*, 19(1), 27–41.

Lazarus, R. S. 1978: *The Stress and Coping Paradigm*. Paper presented at the conference: Critical Evaluation of Behavioral Paradigms for Psychiatric Science.

Lazarus, R. S. 1980: The stress and coping paradigm. In C. Eisdorfer, D. Cohen and P. Maxin (eds) *Models for clinical psychopathology*, New York: Spectrum.

Ligos, M. 1998: Traveler's advisory. *Sales and Marketing Management*, 150(4), 58–63.

Linville, P. W. 1987: Self-complexity as a cognitive buffer against stress-related illness and depression. *Journal of Personality and Social Psychology*, 52(4), 663–76.

Matteson, M. T. and Ivancevich, J. M. 1980: The coronary-prone behavior pattern: A review and appraisal. *Social Science and Medicine*, 14, 337–51.

Motowidlo, S. J., Packard, J. S. and Manning, M. R. 1986: Occupational stress: Its causes and consequences for job performance. *Journal of Applied Psychology*, 71(4), 618–29.

Murphy, S. E., Blyth, D. and Fiedler, F. E. 1992: Cognitive resource theory and the utilization of the leader's and group member's technical competence. *The Leadership Quarterly*, 3, Fall, 237–54.

Nowack, K. 1986: Who are the hardy? *Training and Development Journal*, 40(5), 11–118.

Osipow, S. H., Walsh, W. B. and Tosi, D. J. 1980: *A Survey of Counseling Methods*. Homewood, IL: Dorsey Press.

Parasuraman, S. and Alutto, J. A. 1981: An examination of the organizational antecedents of stressors at work. *Academy of Management Journal*, 24, 48–67.

Pittner, M. S. and Houston, B. 1980: Response to stress, cognitive coping strategies and the Type A behavior pattern. *Journal of Personality and Social Psychology*, 39, 147–57.

Presthus, R. 1978: *The Organizational Society*. New York: St Martin's Press.

Puffer, S. M. and Brakefield, J. T. 1989: The role of task complexity as a moderator of the stress and coping process. *Human Relations*, March, 42, 199–217.

Rhodewalt, F. and Agustsdottir, S. 1984: On the relationship of hardiness to the Type A behavior pattern: Perception of life events versus coping with life events. *Journal of Research in Personality*, 18, 212–23.

Rose, R. L. and Veiga, J. F. 1984: Assessing the sustained effects of a stress management intervention on anxiety and locus of control. *Academy of Management Journal*, 27, 190–8.

Rotter, J. B. 1966: Generalized expectancies for internal versus external control of reinforcement. *Psychological Monographs: General & Applied*, 80(1), 1–28.

Schachner, M. 1994: California stress claims fall: stricter injury standards cut employers' comp costs. *Business Insurance*, 28(17), April 25, 17.

Schuler, R. S. 1980: Definition and conceptualization of stress in organizations. *Organizational Behavior and Human Performance*, 2, 184–215.

Schwepker, C. H., Ferrell, O. C. and Ingram, T. L. 1997: The influence of ethical climate and ethical conflict on role stress in the sales force. *Journal of the Academy of Marketing Science*, 25(2), Spring, 99–109.

Selye, H. 1974: *The Stress of Life*. New York: McGraw-Hill.

Shostak, A. B. 1980: *Blue-collar Stress*. Reading, MA: Addison-Wesley.

Spector, P. E. and O'Connell, B. J. 1994: The contribution of personality traits, negative affectivity, locus of control and Type A to subsequent reports of job stressors and strains. *Journal of Occupational and Organizational Psychology*, 67(1), March, 1–13.

Stevens, H. J. 1992: Stress in California. *Risk Management*, 39, July, 38–42.

Tosi, D. J. and Tosi, H. L. 1980: ABCD model of cognitive, affective and behavioral responses. Paper. University of Florida.

Tosi, D. J., LeClair, S. W., Peters, H. J. and Murphy, M. A. 1987: *Theories and Applications of Counseling*. Springfield, Ill: Charles C. Thomas.

Tosi, H. L. 1971: Organizational stress as a moderator of the relationship between influence and role response. *Academy of Management Journal*, 14, 7–22.

Tosi, H. L., Vaverek, K. A. and Zahrly, J. H. 1986: *Personality Correlates of Coping Strategies on New Jobs*. Paper delivered at the annual meeting of the Academy of Management.

Weiss, H. M., Ilgen, D. A. and Sharbaugh, M. E. 1982: Effects of life and job stress on information search behaviors of organizational members. *Journal of Applied Psychology*, 67, 60–6.

Williams, J. M. and Stout, J. K. 1985: The effect of high and low assertiveness on locus of control and health problems. *The Journal of Psychology*, 119(2), 169–73.

Wilson, C. B. 1991: U. S. businesses suffer from workplace trauma. *Personnel Journal*, 70, July, 47–50.

Woolsey, C. 1993: Encouraging workers to care for themselves. *Business Insurance*, 27(19), May 3, 4.

Yang, N. 1996: An international perspective on socioeconomic changes and their effects on life stress and career success of working women. *S.A.M. Advanced Management Journal*, 63(3), 15–19.

Zahrly, J. and Tosi, H. L. 1987: *Antecedents of Stress Manifestations*. Paper delivered at the annual meetings of the Academy of Management.

chapter 8

Group and Team Performance Environment

Preparing for Class

Consider the groups or teams that you have been associated with in your sports, academic or professional experience. Make two columns on a sheet of paper. In one, list those teams that you believe were effective; in the other column, list those teams that were not effective. With these two lists in mind, consider these questions:

What criteria did you use when you determined effective teams from ineffective ones? Were they subjective or objective measures of performance? Was your criterion based on the level of success the team/group achieved or was it the process and experience of working with this particular team?

As you look at your list of effective teams, are there any characteristics of the environment that this team or group operated in that are similar and that may explain its success? Were there similarities within the environments among the teams or groups you determined were ineffective?

Develop your own model of group or team effectiveness. While you can consider the components from figure 8.2, use your own experience to develop a model that you feel helps to explain why some groups or teams are effective, and why others are ineffective.

Monarch Marking Systems had tried numerous programs to increase the involvement of its employees in improving the efficiency of the production processes. Employee empowerment through the use of employee teams had often been tried and this led employees to be extremely skeptical about the typical "program-of-the-month" syndrome. In 1995, Monarch's new CEO, John Paxon, wanted to change this mentality that existed within Monarch's work force. His objective was to harness the collective intelligence of the group without making employees feel like it would be just another failed experiment in leaders pretending they wanted employee input when really they did not. In 1997, the results of Monarch's effort to improve group effectiveness were remarkable. Paxon reports a 100 percent increase in employee productivity, 70 percent decrease in the square-footage required for the product assembly area, reduction in work inventory by $127,000, and a reduction in past-due shipments by 90 percent, a remarkable achievement that led to the team receiving the "work-force-excellence" award from the Nation Association of Manufacturers (Pettinger, 1997).

Among the changing trends in modern organizations, few have generated more interest than the use of teams. In 1996, 73 percent of US companies used some form of team within their organization (Novak, 1997). Teams are so important to organizations that some have adopted a strategy of acquiring other organizations as a means of buying human talent – specifically buying a smaller company to acquire new product teams.

Focus on Teams: Team for Sale?

Cisco Systems Inc. of San Jose, California – like other high-tech firms – has been an active acquirer of other companies. In fact, since 1994 it has bought 19 software companies. While this merger and acquisition behavior is not unusual, one of the motivating factors behind the mergers is unique. Cisco is buying teams! It views the ability to build teams from scratch as a luxury and is willing to pay high prices (as much as $2 million dollars per employee) to bring in an accomplished new product team. Many other high-tech firms are following this strategy because they are willing to buy production teams rather than building their own from scratch (*Wall Street Journal*, 1997).

At lower levels in countless organizations, teams and teamwork seem to be a part of the US corporate strategy to become more productive and competitive. Self-managed teams, cross-functional teams, product-teams, and virtual-teams, teams which rely on information technologies for communication and may never meet face-to-face, are all commonly used in the modern workplace. However, the use of this potentially powerful management tool has met with mixed effectiveness and often with high cynicism. Some have said that half of the decisions reached by teams are never implemented and the other half should not have been implemented.

Why are some teams effective and other teams ineffective? What factors within the organizational environment influence that effectiveness? Are there leadership strategies that can be implemented along with teams that would increase their chance of success? This chapter reviews what we know about group and team effectiveness.

Groups and Teams: Definitions

A **group** is defined as two or more people who interact and are dependent upon each other to achieve some common objective. Patients in a doctor's waiting room or passengers on a bus do not constitute a group because while they may have some interaction, they do not depend on each other. Without interdependence, several people in proximity to one another are referred to as a **collection**. People in collections are usually aware of one another, such as in a movie theater.

The term "team" has gained increased popularity in organizations. Researchers who study groups often use this term when studying the same processes. **Teams** are a special form of a group that have highly defined tasks and roles, and demonstrate high group commitment (Katzenback and Smith, 1993). In this chapter, we use the terms team and group interchangeably.

group
Two or more people who interact and are dependent upon each other to achieve some common objective

collection
Any group or aggregate of people that do not interact or influence one another

teams
A special form of a group that have highly defined tasks and roles and demonstrate high group commitment

Why Groups Form

Before we begin our discussion of group factors that influence the overall effectiveness of groups and teams, we should consider the factors that influence group formation. People join groups for a variety of reasons and are often willing to endure great hardships and financial costs to belong to a group. However, in many common organizational situations, individuals often have little choice about the groups and teams to which they are assigned. Understanding the basic theories of group formation can help us to understand groups we associate with willingly, and more carefully analyze those we associate with because of our job requirements. Figure 8.1 shows the factors critical for group formation:

- Personal characteristics
- Interests and goals
- Potential to influence
- Opportunity for interaction

Personal Characteristics

Our social groups, which we usually join willingly, are often formed with those who share our beliefs, values, and attitudes. It is much easier to interact with those who share our attitudes: it permits us to confirm our beliefs, to deal with others with minimal conflict, and to express ourselves with less fear of contradiction. In our earlier discussion of the development of our beliefs, attitudes and values, we discussed the role association and interaction with others had in reinforcing these structures (page 59). Groups also form around political

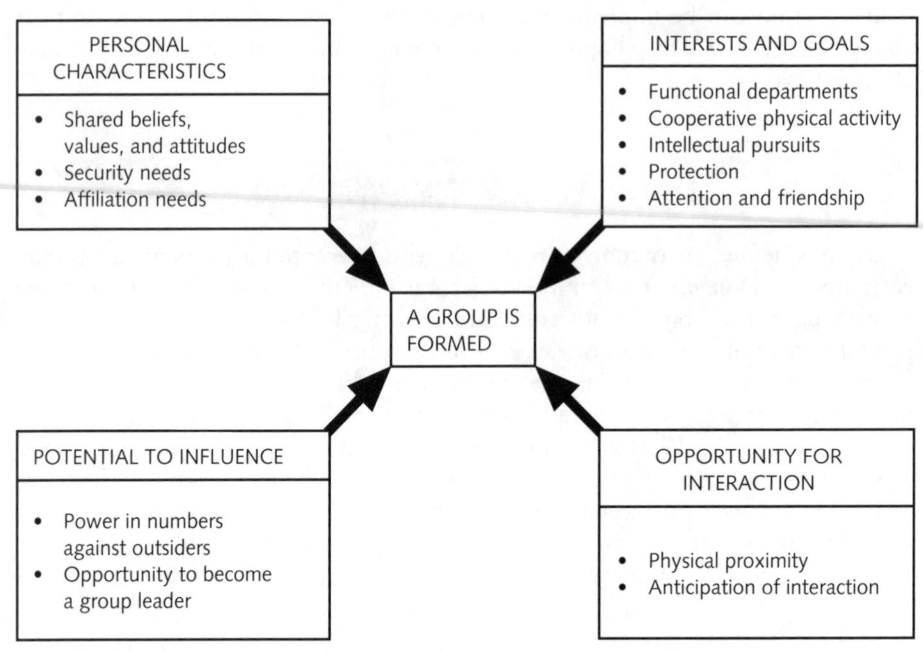

Fig 8.1 : Factors in group formation

philosophies and parties, ethnic and religious affiliations, or factors such as gender, age, or intelligence. While a common notion is that opposites attract, research into group formation does not confirm that conclusion.

Over time, our work groups can also have many of the same characteristics of our social groups. While the beliefs, attitudes and values of group or team members may not be consistent initially, socialization can have a strong influence on their development over time. Organizations who use intensive socialization processes often attempt to develop in members the factors required for group formation. Early socialization processes in the military emphasize the need for new recruits to value the importance of the group for their social and security needs.

INTERESTS AND GOALS

Shared goals that require cooperation are a powerful force behind group formation. Managers organize employees around functions such as sales, production, accounting, or maintenance. If people in these groups also have similar characteristics, the basis for group formation and cohesion may even be strengthened.

Individuals may form their own groups or teams to achieve common goals. Common interests can include physical activities such as golf, softball, or bowling. Groups may also form due to shared interests in personal or professional development such as among individuals who are interested in learning more about a particular subject or in learning a new skill.

One formal group found in organizations is a union. Employees may be more prone to join a union if they perceive that the union has the ability to meet their needs and interests (Youngblood et al., 1984). Recent developments in the workplace have found traditional adversaries may work together if they realize the importance of cooperation to achieve important goals.

Focus on Productivity: Look Who's Pushing Productivity

Common goals and shared needs are influencing organized labor as they have formed new partnerships with companies to improve productivity. In an effort to protect jobs and encourage corporate growth, the International Association of Machinists has begun to increase labor–management cooperation through the creation of teams systems and joint decision-making councils. Productivity gains and job protection are common goals for both groups. Labor organizations are interested in keeping, and potentially increasing, the number of organized jobs in manufacturing and insuring increase in wages by increasing the size of the "pie" eventually shared by management and labor (Business Week, 1997).

POTENTIAL TO INFLUENCE

Many managers have been approached by a group of workers with a complaint or a request. The work group knows that a manager might be more prone to listen when any complaint is prefaced with a "we" instead of an "I." Co-worker support may be necessary to gain attention and action. Groups also provide opportunities for individual members to influence each other. In an informal organization, the role of informal leader can be very important to some employees. If an employee can gain acceptance as an informal leader, he or she can satisfy many personal needs and gain visibility that could even boost his or her career.

OPPORTUNITY FOR INTERACTION

Individuals often form groups with others just because their jobs force them to be in close contact with others. Physical proximity and interaction permit relationships like these to develop and this can lead to friendships and group formation. We often associate with groups that developed from relationships that began in college dorms, apartment complexes, and work organizations (Shaw, 1981).

Interaction and group formation can be influenced in an organization, for example, through the design of office space. Pathways and barriers can affect group membership and identification. People are more likely to form groups with others in their vicinity. Managers often cooperate with architects to design space so as to foster interactions. Employees who work closely together can be located near each other to increase interaction and allow the needed cooperation to take place.

Types of Groups

We are all members of some type of group. Since birth, most of us were members of a common group, our families. As we grew, we participated in groups or teams formed in our schools, neighborhoods, and work organizations. Each group added to our knowledge of how to behave in group settings and we learned that roles and expectations may differ, based on the type of group or team and its objectives. There are several common types of groups.

- Reference groups
- Formal groups, e.g. functional groups and task groups
- Informal groups

REFERENCE GROUPS

reference groups Groups which shape our beliefs, values, and attitudes

Reference groups, or primary groups, are groups which shape our beliefs, values, and attitudes. These groups are formed of members whom we trust enough to rely on for testing ideas and giving feedback, guidance, or support. They serve as standards of comparison against which we evaluate our own behavior. A person facing a decision might draw on a reference group's values, or talk with someone in that group, before making a choice. Our family, our running partners, a local volunteer group, or a work team can also be reference groups.

FORMAL GROUPS

formal groups Groups, such as project teams, that are designed into and make up the formal organization structure

functional groups Groups comprised of individuals who accomplish a similar task within the organizational structure

task groups Groups that are used to accomplish a specific organizational goal

Formal groups are those created as part of the formal organization structure. The formal organization is the hierarchical structure and the various departments that exist within that structure. Formal organization is reflected in the goals, policies, rules, and procedures that are designed to accomplish the organization's tasks. Any group that is purposely designed into this configuration is a formal group.

One form of formal group, a **functional group**, is comprised of individuals who accomplish similar tasks within the organizational structure. Functional groups exist for an unspecified period of time. Many organizations organize around functional groups assigned to related work activities such as accounting, marketing, production, research and development (R&D) or other related task groupings. Universities are usually organized into functional groups called departments.

Task groups are groups that are used to accomplish a specific organizational goal. They are usually established by the organization and exist for a specified period of time. In task groups, social benefits for members are secondary or may even be absent. Committees, project teams, and employee participation teams are all organizational task groups. They usually have a defined purpose, deadlines to meet, specific work assignments, and a reporting relationship in the organization. Some task groups are relatively permanent; others are temporary groups.

Diversity Issues: Diversity Task Groups

One type of task group being used increasingly by organizations is a task group focusing on issues such as diversity. These groups are often called **task forces** or **councils**. These single-purpose groups allow managers to achieve important goals and are especially relevant when those goals are to change beliefs and attitudes of organizational members such as those related to diversity. Groups or teams appointed to achieve these types of changes can only be successful when membership includes representatives from all levels of the organization. These are especially interesting groups to consider because they often have a significant challenge in overcoming resistance throughout the organization. Here are some suggestions for having effective diversity task groups.

- Members should be appointed by the CEO.
- The organization should provide clear and realistic mission statements and adequate support and resources. Members should be trained in diversity issues, definitions and company programs.
- White males should be included and placed on an equal footing with all participants.
- Team-building activities should be used to help members to develop improved group processes.
- Supervisors of team members should be advised in advance of the team appointment and be made aware of the commitment of team participants.

As you will see in this chapter and the next, many of these issues are relevant to the effectiveness of all teams. They are especially critical for teams working on issues such as diversity where strong organizational support and member acceptance are critical to success.

Source: Adapted from Baytos (1995)

INFORMAL GROUPS

Informal groups arise out of individual needs and the attraction of people to one another. While out of the normal structure of the organization, these groups can have a significant effect on organizational performance. Membership is usually voluntary and is based on common values and interests. Sometimes the origin of these groups is social in nature.

Social or interest groups are a type of informal group. **Social groups** exist primarily to provide recreational or relaxation outlets for members. For example, friends may eat together at work or socialize after work. Most softball teams, bowling groups, and gourmet clubs exist so that people can enjoy themselves in good company. Sometimes work goals could be involved, as might be the case for a company softball team or computer club, but the work is secondary to the social benefit.

On other occasions, an informal group develops in response to the organization, such as when workers band together to protest an unpopular management action. Informal groups arise at work because many employees are concerned about their freedom at work, about control over their jobs, and about establishing good relationships with others (Katz, 1965). Informal groups may develop

informal groups
Groups that arise out of individual needs and the attraction of people to one another; membership is usually voluntary and based on common values and interests

social groups
Groups that exist primarily to provide recreational or relaxation outlets for members

to bypass company rules or to enhance the members' power. They might consist of people who also like and trust each other and perhaps interact outside work in a church group or neighborhood.

Informal groups can be both effective and powerful. This may explain why some managers view them with doubt and suspicion. They tend to see informal groups as disruptive and potentially harmful to the formal organization. Some managers seek ways to gain the support of informal groups and informal leaders to reduce their threat or to enhance some company purpose.

Since informal groups are an inevitable component of behavior in organizations, as managers, we should attempt to work with these groups so that they contribute to, rather than subvert, organizational goals. Informal groups serve basic needs for employees and are just as important, enduring, and rewarding as the relationship that employees have with the formal organization. The informal group can become a problem when it conflicts with some formal purpose, but even this is not necessarily bad. It may signal some error on management's part or be a symptom of a poor relationship with employees.

Group and Team Effectiveness

In the remainder of this chapter and the next, we discuss the factors that may influence the effectiveness of groups and teams. Figure 8.2 introduces a model of

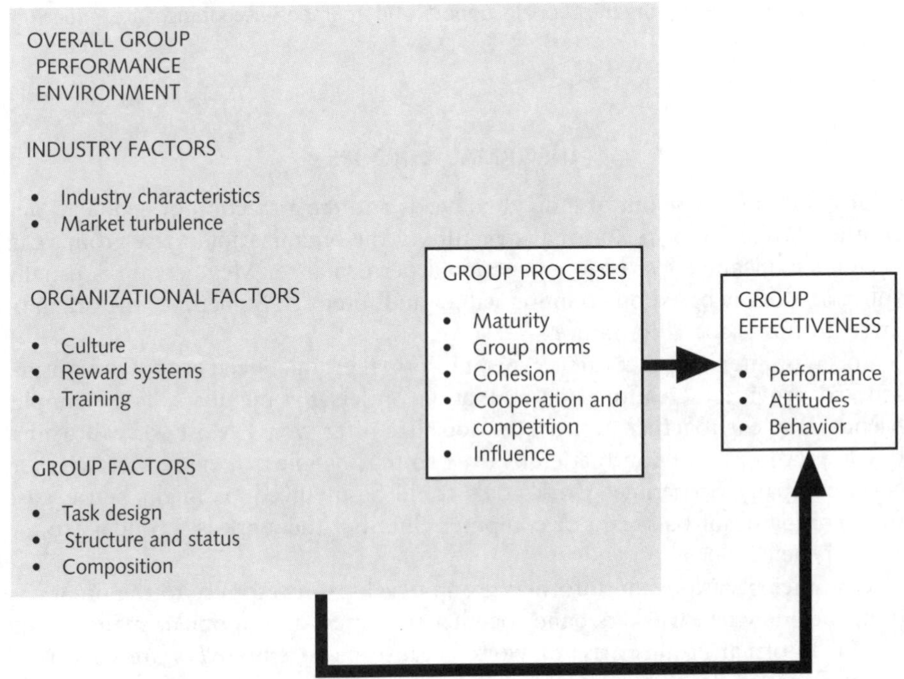

Fig 8.2: A model of group effectiveness

group effectiveness. Groups and teams exist within an environment that can have influences on their performance. This **group performance environment** includes the combined effects of industry, organization, and group factors that form the unique context within which the group operates. These environmental effects on **group effectiveness** are often beyond the control of the group or team. In addition to environment, the **group processes** that exist within the group also affects group effectiveness. The combined effect of internal group processes occurring within the group performance environment determines the overall group effectiveness. Group effectiveness considers measures of group performance and changes in group members' attitudes and behaviors.

group performance environment The combined effects of industry, organization, and group factors that form the unique context within which the group operates

group processes Within-group activities and communications that also affect group effectiveness

Our model suggests that, in addition to influencing effectiveness through influence on group processes, factors that comprise the group performance environment can influence effectiveness directly through factors beyond the control of the group. Notice that, in addition to the influence the environment can have on group processes, there is also an arrow pointing directly towards the measures of group effectiveness. Despite how effective a group's internal processes may be, there may be environmental factors beyond its control that will be a stronger determinant of its overall effectiveness. This is common in team sports such as baseball where effectively performing teams do not win the championship because they did not have enough talent to succeed. Likewise, teams that have best talent are often unsuccessful because of group internal processes such as a lack of team cohesion. We begin our discussion of this model by considering how to measure group/team effectiveness.

Group Performance Environment

As we suggested earlier, group or team effectiveness can be affected by factors outside of the control of the group or team. The environment within which groups or teams function may be critical in determining their ultimate success or failure (Mohrman et al., 1995). We consider three major influences on the group environment:

1 Industry
2 Organization
3 Group

Industry Factors

In this section, we consider two factors, which influence team success from outside of the organization:

1 Characteristics unique to a particular industry
2 Turbulence within an industry

Researchers considering team effectiveness argue that teams may be more successful in certain types of industries. For example, teams may be more effective in knowledge or service industries because of the unique aspects of the work setting. In these industries, where work is less routine, more judgment is required and that judgment may benefit from access to the additional information and feedback mechanisms that can be provided by teams. In manufacturing industries, the routine nature of some tasks may make employee involvement activities such as the use of teams less effective (Cohen, 1994; Smith and Comer, 1994; Mohrman et al., 1995; Cohen et al., 1996).

The amount of turbulence within an industry can also influence a team's success. For example, a highly effective team may develop an excellent new product but because of turbulence in that product's potential market, it may not be successful. Actions by competitors to introduce new technologies or to develop alternative products, or significant changes in consumer tastes, all can adversely effect a team's effectiveness in ways outside of its control. Not surprisingly, studies have found that team effectiveness is higher for teams formed within industries that are in markets categorized as growth markets (Halebilian and Finklestein, 1993).

ORGANIZATIONAL FACTORS

Within the organization, there are also several factors that could influence group or team success:

- Culture
- Reward structure
- Training

Some modern organizations have established a culture where the most common method of organization is through the use of teams. Saturn Corp. is an example of one such company. Teamwork is so important to the culture of Saturn that it is widely discussed in its corporate philosophy and core values. One key statement of philosophy of Saturn's leadership emphasizes the importance of teams:

> To meet our member's needs, we will create a sense of belonging in an environment of mutual trust, respect and dignity. We believe that all people want to be involved in decisions that affect them. We will develop the tools, training, and education that each member needs. Creative, motivated, responsible team members who understand change are critical to success and are Saturn's most important asset (LeFauve and Hax, 1992).

With the above statement, Saturn has established within the culture the importance of teams to organizational success and a commitment to providing team members the tools necessary to carry out their jobs.

A QUESTION OF ETHICS: IS GROUP EFFECTIVENESS AN ISSUE OF TRUST?

One factor critical to team success is trust. Team members must have a basic trust of many issues within a team environment. The existence of an environment where team members can trust each other, and trust organizational leaders, is most likely in organizations with a culture that emphasizes ethical behavior.

Here are some key questions about trust that team members must confront:

- Do I trust the commitment of management to the goals and objectives of the team? (This may be strongly influenced by the history of success of similar teams within the organization.)
- Do I trust that ideas and suggestions developed by the team will actually be implemented and accepted?
- Do I trust that, as a team member, my work on team activities is valued by my supervisor and that he or she will consider work on the team as an important part of my performance evaluation? (This is a key issue for many members of formal groups or teams that are tasked with responsibilities that are not part of their routine work activities.)
- Do I trust that my team members are truly open to a wide variety of ideas and input for all members?
- Do I trust the abilities and skills of other team members?

Trust is a critical component of team effectiveness. In chapter 9, we discuss the process of group maturity and suggest that groups will never reach full-maturity and effectiveness without establishing a high level of trust among members.

Another aspect controlled by the organization is the reward structure. Does the organization have a system of rewards that encourages the cooperation required for successful team performance? There is considerable debate within this research area as to whether individual rewards are more appropriate to encourage team performance or whether team reward systems should be used. Organizations use a wide variety of monetary and non-monetary rewards in team contexts. One study found that, in companies using teams to improve quality, monetary rewards were often restricted to less than $500 to allow organizations to give out more of these type of rewards. Rewards are often linked to improvements in customer satisfaction or other measures of overall product quality (Balkin, 1997).

Saturn uses the concept of team rewards that puts as much as 10 percent of the team's overall compensation at risk based on its effectiveness (Overman, 1995). The purpose of the Saturn compensation system is to use the rewards system in conjunction with other human resource management systems to reward team performance and cooperation.

One of the other HR programs used by Saturn in conjunction with the rewards system is **training**. The importance of training to their team is expressed in the statement on page 230. Many existing and new members of an organization often have little training in team or group participation. While these individuals may have important technical skills to contribute to the team, their placement on the team may have dysfunctional consequences if they lack the appropriate team skills. Training programs provided by the organization can include team-building activities to build member confidence and trust in each other, conflict resolution skills, or a variety of others useful team skills.

Focus on Building Teams: Can a Baseball Team buy its Way to the World Series?

A recent article in the *Wall Street Journal* asks this interesting question and considers the possibility that the success of a major league baseball team can be determined as much by the front office performance off the field as it is by the team performance on the field. Steve Mckee studied the top performing teams during the 1997 Major League Baseball season and found a strong relationship between the amount of money spent on salaries and bonuses and team success (McKee, 1997). Not surprisingly, the four teams in their respective League Championship Series were also among the top teams in salaries. The Baltimore Orioles, Cleveland Indians, Florida Marlins and Atlanta Braves each spent over 55 million dollars on payroll, well over the league average. The 1998 League Championship series included the New York Yankees, Cleveland Indians, Atlanta Braves and San Diego Padres. The Florida Marlins went from being the best team in baseball to the worst. Its team salary also went down to the lowest in the league. This example gives strong support to the idea that despite the best efforts of team members, factors outside of the team's control can often have a greater influence on team effectiveness.

GROUP FACTORS

A final set of factors that contribute to the group performance environment are those factors specific to the group. This section considers those factors that may influence group effectiveness but that are, in some cases, determined by managers who are not part of the group itself.

TASK DESIGN One aspect, task design, considers the nature of the task assigned to the group or team. One component of task design considers clarity of the goals and tasks that are either assigned to the group or that the group or team itself establishes. Groups are often formed with specific goals such as improving the quality of a particular product or resolving a specific problem. Groups can also be formed with less specific goals such as improving the general quality of work life or improving issues within the workplace. Just as in our discussion of individual goal setting from chapter 5 (page 150), group performance is improved when they are handed specific and difficult goals.

On page 222, we introduced Monarch Marking Systems. Monarch is an example of a firm creating a context within which teams could be successful. One factor of its success was Monarch's effort to stop using teams with "open-ended" objectives. Monarch created teams with the specific task of improving a particular aspect of the production process. It also insured that improvements determined by the team could be readily measured. This establishment of teams to achieve a specific purpose, and for a limited duration, was certainly a factor in team success (Petzinger, 1997).

A second component of task design considers the amount of coordination the group must have with others in achievement of its assigned tasks. We consider two potential task characteristics here. **Autonomy** refers to the degree of freedom and independence that the team has to conduct its activities. Teams that operate autonomously are often called self-managed teams. Autonomy appears to have potentially positive and negative effects on measures of team effectiveness. While autonomous workgroups appear to have more positive attitudes towards the organization, this may lead to higher turnover and absenteeism (Cordery et al., 1991). The research is contradictory at this point but one possibility is that autonomous groups work better in organizations operating in environments that have more turbulence (Smith and Comer, 1994).

autonomy
The level of freedom an individual or team has to do their job

Interdependence considers the amount of coordination with, or approval from, others that the team needs to complete its assigned tasks. Monarch's leadership was also concerned with these characteristics of the tasks assigned to the team. Its response was to give the team total control over developing the ideas and implementing the solutions. Jerry Schlagel, Monarch's Vice President for Operations, gave his teams the challenge "go make it happen and then tell us about it" (Petzinger, 1997).

interdependence
A measure of the amount of coordination with or approval from others, the team need to complete their assigned tasks

GROUP STRUCTURE AND STATUS A second factor specific to the group considers the structure of the group and the status of members within the group. As groups develop and pursue their purposes, certain structural characteristics become evident. **Group structure** refers to the roles and relationships among the members and to the forces that maintain the group's organization. Structure is dynamic and changes over time. It can also contribute to the overall effectiveness of the group as many of these structural components are linked to important group issues such as the structure of the rewards and the amount of training the team receives in team processes. A detailed understanding of structure and **status** issues is important to improving our ability to manage and work in teams. In addition, many decisions, such as the determinations of key roles such as leadership, and other factors of team structure, are often determined by the organization and are out of control of team members.

group structure
The roles and relationships among the members and to the forces that maintain the group's organization

status
The relative position or standing of a person in a group that causes respect or deference toward them

People in small task groups engage in certain key functions and assume individual roles. Functions are activities that occur in the group; for example, a project team requires functions such as library research, customer surveys, and data analysis. **Roles**, however, are defined in terms of expectations that members hold for each other's behavior. Groups expect each member to perform his or her role in a certain way. The key aspect of roles lies in the specific expectations that members communicate to each other.

roles
Expectations that members hold for each other's behavior

We now consider the several different types of functions and roles in groups, and the different implications of each (Bales, 1953):

- Task functions and roles
- Socioemotional function and roles
- Leadership roles
- Role complications
- Disruptive actions and roles

Some group member functions and roles are based on the behaviors required to accomplish a particular group task. While we discussed the importance of task clarity as a component of the group performance environment, task and role clarity among group members is also critical. In general, members have to clarify goals, give and seek suggestions and opinions about the task, and help the group to succeed. Specific **task functions and roles** grow out of the purposes of the group and the goals that are established. It follows then that the better the groups' goals are defined, the more adequately specific functions and roles can be made.

Many complications arise in role assignments. In some situations, managers, external to the group, may make role assignments and, at other times, group members may make their own assignments. In either situation, poor planning of assignments causes gaps or duplications of effort, which later slows the group down or detracts from effective performance. When the group assigns tasks, sometimes a member will quickly volunteer for what he or she feels is a "choice" assignment. Other members are then faced with less desirable work. Some members want to do work that is easy for them, while others want to learn a new skill. It is probably impossible to please everyone in assigning tasks. Groups contemplating task assignments may benefit from open and careful consideration of both the desires and the abilities of group members. Figure 8.3 highlights techniques for making task assignments in different conditions of team member desires and abilities. Establishing task functions and roles is the basic activity of organization design, which we examine later in chapter 13.

As the group works on the task and as members grow used to one another, other functions come into play. People give and receive help. They reward or punish each other, and give or receive feedback. Tensions develop that need releasing. Joking

DESIRE TO PERFORM THE TASK	ABILITY TO PERFORM THE TASK: Low	ABILITY TO PERFORM THE TASK: High
High	**Dilemma**: Member wishes to learn a new task. This risks performance; he or she might fail. **Technique**: Train, coach, or pair them with a competent person.	**Dilemma**: No problem here. **Technique**: Assign the person the task. If more than one person fits here, have them share or rotate on the task.
Low	**Dilemma**: No problem here. **Technique**: Avoid assignment to that person. If this leaves a task unassigned, may have to seek outside help or provide training.	**Dilemma**: No desire to perform a needed task. This can leave a gap in group performance. **Technique**: May be necessary to rotate people or equitably distribute undesirable tasks.

Fig 8.3: Dilemmas and techniques in making task role assignments

and laughter are not uncommon, nor are disagreements and arguments. People turn to each other for acceptance and understanding. All of these are examples of the **socioemotional functions and roles** of groups. Socioemotional needs of members are important, yet most groups do not deal adequately with them.

Focus on Socioemotional Roles: Baseball Jokers

Bob Uecker, affectionately known as Mr Baseball, is famous for his antics that often were useful in relieving clubhouse pressure on teams for which he played. His most famous antic was during the pre-game warm-ups for a critical game during the 1962 pennant chase of the St Louis Cardinals. Uecker "borrowed" a tuba from a band that had come on to the field to play the national anthem. He proceeded to use the tuba to catch fly balls in the outfield during batting practice. While its owner did not appreciate the damage to the tuba, Uecker's actions served to introduce laughter to his teammates in a tense situation.

Task and socioemotional roles are not entirely independent, and they both affect all aspects of group effectiveness. Dissatisfied members may perform their assignments poorly, or they might quit the group or psychologically withdraw. These reactions also affect retention and cohesion. If attention is paid to the socioemotional function within a group, that group can be more effective. Actions that show support and acceptance of others contribute a great deal. Listening and showing understanding make people feel positively toward each other.

A critical component of the group factor of the performance environment is the **leadership role**. Leaders control many factors that contribute to group effectiveness. Leaders determine many of the design features of the team or group that we have been discussing. Leadership, within the group and external to the group, can influence reward systems, task assignments, task clarity and other important aspects of the performance environments. Leaders who reward individual accomplishments are likely to find the teams are less effective if those rewards contribute to competition within the team or group. Leaders can influence the group through the clarity with which they understand the organization's goals for the group and how they communicate that vision to group members. Leaders can also determine the structure and autonomy afforded to the group as well as how resources are allocated.

Groups may have leaders who are skilled at task functions and other leaders who are skilled at socioemotional functions. It is rare that one leader has the skills to provide leadership in both areas. As a result, different people may perform leadership within a group at different times.

Groups face many problems that require constant attention, especially in the early stages of group development. Most groups adequately handle task issues, particularly if they make good individual assignments that match member desires and skills. On the other hand, most groups struggle when faced with role difficulties and when group members act disruptively.

role ambiguity
When people feel uncertain about what is expected of them

role conflict
Results when a person is unable to meet conflicting demands

One role complication arises when members experience **role ambiguity**; this occurs when people feel uncertain about what is expected of them or when they are not sure what behaviors will earn them acceptance or rejection. Group members can also experience **role conflict**; this results when a person feels difficulty in meeting conflicting demands, and can take several forms. A person can be a father, a manager, a friend, a husband, a fund-drive chairman, and a Little League coach all at one time. The demands of these roles compete with one another for time and commitment. Within a single role such as manager, conflict can arise from pressure to act in a way that conflicts with the person's values, and from pressure to meet the expectations of others whose request conflicts with one another. Role ambiguity and role conflict were discussed in chapter 7 as an important cause of stress reactions; see pages 201–5.

A final role that surfaces in some group environments is when one member acts in a disruptive way that not only interferes with the task but also can disrupt the social processes of the group. A group member might force his or her ideas on others, and refuse to see different points of view, often generating defensive or aggressive behavior in others.

You have probably had experience working in a group where there was a disruptive member. Perhaps even in your work for this course, you are in a group that has a member who disrupts group effectiveness. Is there a member of your group who comes in late for group meetings, does not complete assignments on time, or interjects comments that causes the group to lose track during a meeting? It is not easy to cope with this type of disruption or to correct it. If the disruptive behavior is rooted in the basic personality of an individual, it is more difficult to handle. Skillful leaders might take disruptive people aside and try to bring about a change. The entire group could also confront a disruptive individual and appeal to his or her sense of fairness and goodwill. If this fails, the group may threaten to ostracize the individual. Sometimes the group might just have to ignore, or work around, the difficult member. Another technique is to seek help from outside the group, perhaps from a higher authority. Few managers who use groups in their workplace or professors who use groups in their classes have not had occasion to help groups to deal with a disruptive member. In chapter 9, we focus more specifically on behavior within group settings.

One aspect of group structure is the hierarchy it often creates within the group. While the hierarchy does help to bring order and control to the group, it is also a way for people to acknowledge and express status differences between each other. These distinctions can be sources of inequity and concern among group members.

Group member status is the relative position or standing of a person in a society or group. It is an index of rank or worth. Like norms, status is a common social force, and often it is habitually accepted. Status is quite apparent and easily identifiable. Here is a partial list of factors that we might use to accord status to a person:

1 Title or position
2 Education, knowledge, or expertise
3 Awards or prizes earned

EXERCISE

Analyzing Role Complications in Groups

Think of a group or team you are now a part of, or one you were a part of recently. Then rate the degree to which the ten conditions described below are true for you in your role in that group. Use this five-point rating scale in responding to each item:

1 Never true of my job
2 Infrequently true
3 Sometimes true
4 Often true
5 Always true of job

		A	B
1	I feel uncertain about how much authority I have.		....
2	I receive incompatible requests from different people.	....	
3	I am unsure about what my responsibilities are.		....
4	I have to buck rules and policies to do my work.	....	
5	Explanations are often lacking about what needs to be done.		....
6	I lack resources and materials to complete assignments.	....	
7	I perform my role without clear plans or objectives.		....
8	I work on unnecessary things.	....	
9	I am unsure whether I divide my time properly.		....
10	I work with other groups who operate differently.	....	....
	Totals	....	....

Now, total column A and column B. Column A scores are for the amount of role conflict and column B for amount of role ambiguity you are experiencing within the group you considered. After determining your score for each area on these scales, consider the conditions in the group that lead to that conflict and ambiguity.

- What are the implications for role problems on yours and other group members' satisfaction, productivity, retention, attendance, etc.?
- How might the implications of these role issues be connected to the experience of stress?

Source: Adapted from Rizzo et al., 1970

4 Income
5 Ownership of resources or property
6 Personal attributes such as appearance, size, dress, age, or sex
7 Behavioral clues such as work or recreational activities
8 Interpersonal clues such as communication patterns or reactions
9 Physical location in relation to others
10 Cultural identification or nationality
11 Physical surroundings, such as home or office

From the list, we can see that status is accorded people on the basis of their accomplishments and characteristics, on the nature of their interactions with others, and on the conditions of the situation, in which they work and play.

Status is rooted in what is culturally valued and results from the evaluation of others. Studies have examined the status of occupations. At the top of the lists are college professors, physicians, Supreme Court justices, scientists, architects, and the clergy. Various managers, some salespeople, nurses, actors, and musicians fall in the middle ranks. Lowest-ranked occupations include trash collectors, newsboys, waiters and waitresses, coal miners, and gas station attendants.

Achieving status is not a simple process. Some factors are within an individual's control, such as how hard he or she works, but some are obviously not controllable, such as family background. In a small group, someone with more education, a respected title, or a fine reputation would probably be accorded high status immediately. However, people can also earn status in a group through their contribution and relationships with others. They could become a respected member or even the group leader.

Global Focus on Group Status Internationally

Americans view status as an individual characteristic. Status in western cultures is traditionally rooted in the individual; it is not that way in all countries. Other cultures, especially eastern cultures view status as more socially dependent. In the list provided above, look at how many of the ways we believe status is communicated that is individually oriented: title or position, education, knowledge, or expertise, awards or prizes earned, income etc. All these are individually attained, as are many others characteristics on the list. How would a similar list look in a Japanese textbook on organizational behavior? It would probably include things like the company they work for, family status, teams or groups they are associated with, etc. These differences in how status is viewed may explain differences in team behavior across cultures. One argument forwarded about the perceived competitive advantage Japanese firms have had over those from the USA, is the ability of Japanese companies to achieve closer member cooperation within teams and groups. This theory is consistent with cultures that hold membership in certain groups as a measure of status.

Can your status change? Factors that determine status depend a great deal on the situation. A short person will have difficulty achieving status on a basketball team or any activity where height counts, but size need not prevent him or her from becoming a national hero or movie star. Status can also have very specific limits. A group of physicians might grant an architect status, but not for his or her knowledge of medicine. In a fair-minded society or group, people can improve their status and earn great respect by providing any valued activity. As long as there are opportunities for an individual to contribute, there is potential for status improvement.

Status distribution in a group is usually uneven: those with high status have disproportionately more than those with low status. This is often a source of conflict within the group. If status were derived from factors such as member competence or contribution, it would be more acceptable. However, status is usually derived from factors that often have little to do with competence or contribution. Furthermore, contributions or competence are quite differently valued. For example, many groups will value a person who actually writes the first draft of a report rather than a person who made skillful contributions to the ideas contained in the report.

It may be reasonable that some contributions are more valuable than others, but if differences are overplayed, group cohesion and individual feelings can suffer considerably. These difficulties worsen when group members disagree on the value of contributions and on the status distribution across members. **Status incongruence** can occur when members are given either more or less status than others feel they deserve.

status incongruence A condition in a group when there is no consensus about a person's position in the status hierarchy

Group composition A final component of the group factor of the performance environment is the composition of the group itself. Groups that form naturally, such as a social group, have much more discretion of different aspects of group composition than do members of a group within a typical organizational setting. Factors such as group size and group member diversity are important components that influence overall group effectiveness.

Groups can vary widely in size, and size, in turn, affects member behavior. On the low side, groups of two or three are sufficiently unique that they deserve special attention. Larger groups show different effects.

Dyads are groups that consist of two people. In this case, no third person is available for an opinion or for help when a disagreement arises. As a result, tensions frequently arise between the two people because they have no outlet, and negative feelings tend to remain unresolved. People in dyads seem to sense this and tend to avoid giving strong opinions or acting in a way that might lead to disagreement. In dyads, opinions are sought more frequently than they are given. Dyads avoid disagreement because it can lead to failure, and this may foster consensus even when it does not exist. Do these characteristics of dyads sound like any marriages or significant relationships of which you know? You should notice that the problems described are similar to those that couples experience. In organizational settings, if two people assigned to a dyad can not deal with disagreement, it may be wise to change group size.

dyads Groups of two people

Triads are groups of three people and pose other problems of their own. Suppose Alan, Betty, and Cathy are on a project team and are assigned to solve a problem. Alan makes a suggestion. Betty agrees wholeheartedly, but Cathy disagrees. The instant Alan and Betty agree, Cathy faces difficulty: the odds are two against one, and Cathy has had no chance to think about it. What choices does Cathy now have? She can go along with Alan and Betty, hoping to have her way another time. If she does not, Cathy must confront the other two or try to sway one or both of them. Now suppose instead that Betty disagrees with Alan; Cathy faces a new bind. Does she side with Alan or Betty? Does she assume the more difficult task of trying to resolve the disagreement, or does she simply withdraw and let the matter sit?

triads Groups of three people

Events like this are a natural consequence of the triad. This is why people often leave triad meetings with considerable tension. Even when people are congenial, repeated imbalances in interactions occur. The triad has very high potential for power struggles, unplanned and planned coalitions, and general instability. Managers should probably avoid the use of triads, especially when the task calls for frequent interaction and influence opportunities.

Small groups are of interest because many of the team structures found in organizations are representative of a small group. For our purposes, a small group has a membership from four to fifteen members. If groups are much larger, it is much more difficult for people to interact. Fewer than ten people can conduct a discussion quite adequately. In larger groups, individuals sense the interaction problems and may become less involved and withhold their ideas. Consider your experience in large classes. Do you notice that class members often avoid speaking up because they intuitively know everyone cannot do so?

There are other considerations in determining the optimum size for group effectiveness. There should be an odd number of members, as even-numbered groups are more likely to have deadlocks. Because of this groups of five, seven, or nine members are more effective. There are four other factors about group size that we should consider:

1 Participation
2 Satisfaction
3 Formality
4 Performance

In larger groups, there is less opportunity to participate. In addition to the natural inhibitions that people experience in groups, the amount of time available to a person to talk is reduced as size increases.

People in smaller groups are generally more satisfied. Positive aspects of group participation like increased interaction and shared goals all positively relate to member satisfaction. In smaller groups, it is easier for members to feel they contributed to the group's success.

To manage a larger group, it must often be broken down into subgroups. This is a natural tendency as group size increases. Control also becomes a problem as groups grow in size, so it is natural for norms and rules to develop. Larger groups even formalize communication by using written memos to supplement face-to-face discussion.

The effect of size on performance depends on the task characteristics. If adding more people to a task helps rather than hinders effectiveness, then size is an asset to performance. If the people work independently, such as in a typing pool, more people usually means more productivity. Size can also be a benefit for some interdependently performed tasks. When the size of groups is increased, errors in problem solving can be reduced. A larger group can be beneficial because people can check work for possible errors.

Researchers are just beginning to explore the effects of group diversity on performance, and the results often offer conflicting results. When diversity is defined as difference in personalities, gender, attitudes, and background, there is a positive effect on creativity and decision making (Jackson et al., 1995). However, when diversity is defined as cultural diversity, initial performance of culturally diverse groups is often poorer. However, that performance may improve over time when compared to less diverse groups (Watson et al., 1993).

Perhaps diversity may initially cause group's difficulty as they deal with values, belief, and attitudinal differences during the initial stages of group development. This may suggest that diverse groups may be less efficient in the short term but may improve performance in the long term (Cohen and Bailey, 1997). The best conclusion from the research on diversity is that more research needs to be done, but increasing the heterogeneity of the group may initially complicate the group formation processes. This puts added pressure on managers and leaders to teach all team members effective team behaviors that would improve the group processes presented in chapter 9.

Summary

People spend enormous amounts of time working within groups, as groups and teams become more common in work settings. In our introduction to groups, we found that groups and teams tend to form around people with similar attitudes and beliefs, and among those who share common interests and goals. Group formation is also facilitated when people need the power of numbers to influence others or to accomplish a task. However, even the opportunity to interact can cause a group to form.

In this chapter, we also proposed a model of team and group effectiveness and have discussed the three factors that form the environment within which groups operate. Group performance is strongly impacted by the context within which the group operates. We considered factors from the industry and organization as well as those specific to the group. Within the industry, characteristics unique to that industry and the market within which it operates can influence effectiveness. Organizational aspects such as culture, systems of reward, and training are also critical factors to group success.

Factors specific to the group consider aspects of the task design, group structure and composition. The basic building blocks of group structure are the functions and roles assumed by its members. A balance of task and socioemotional roles tends to aid success. Disruptive individual roles can threaten the group at any time. One of the key problems is the success of the leadership roles members take. Another central aspect of a group life is the status accorded each of its members. Status can be a force that contributes to group success or it can create difficulties that prevent the group from developing into an effective unit. Groups vary in size, but typically small groups range from four to about a dozen people. The smaller dyads and triads have distinct and different characteristics. Larger groups have a tendency to organize into smaller subgroups to facilitate effectiveness.

Guide for Managers: Creating a Good Team Environment

This chapter has focused on the influences of the environment on a team's effectiveness. Throughout the chapter, we discussed environmental factors that can impact teams. In most cases, those factors are within the control of managers who want to increase the effectiveness of teams within their organizations. Here are some specific suggestions for doing that.

INSTILL WITHIN THE ORGANIZATION THE VALUE OF TEAMS AND GROUPS TO ORGANIZATIONAL SUCCESS

Organizations like Monarch Marking Systems and Saturn have embedded the use of teams within the company's culture. Supporting the use of teams through vision statements, allocation of resources, and developing team-based reward systems all contribute to team success.

DEVELOP SELECTION MECHANISMS FOR ALL EMPLOYEES THAT VALUE TEAM SKILLS WITHIN NEWLY HIRED EMPLOYEES

Employees that come from industries and organizations where teams were not used may have difficulty adjusting to a team-oriented environment. Many organizations focus on technical skills but we suggest you also consider interpersonal and team skills as part of your selection criteria.

IMPLEMENT ORGANIZATIONAL TRAINING PROGRAMS TO INSURE TEAM-SKILLS ARE TAUGHT TO EMPLOYEES WHO MAY PARTICIPATE ON TEAMS OR GROUPS

Behaviors required in team environments are quite different than those needed in other environments. Do not assume that employees are aware of the tools needed to be a successful team member. Training is also important for individuals who will lead teams or groups. As discussed in chapter 9, group leadership requires a complex set of skills and knowledge to be successful.

DEVELOP REWARD STRUCTURES THAT REWARD TEAM PERFORMANCE OR ENCOURAGE TEAM-ORIENTED INDIVIDUAL BEHAVIORS

Compensation programs that provide individual incentives are likely to foster competition rather than cooperation.

PROVIDE CLEAR, SPECIFIC, AND DIFFICULT GOALS FOR THE TEAM OR GROUP

Teams need to understand what they are being asked to do. Where possible, clearly identify effectiveness metrics that will be used to measure team performance.

CONSIDER THE AMOUNT OF INTERDEPENDENCE REQUIRED BY THE GROUP OR TEAM

We recommend erring on the side of allowing the group to operate more autonomously. This prevents groups from being hampered by cumbersome organization structures and processes. It also fosters increased creativity.

ESTABLISH GROUP SIZES CAREFULLY

Unless there are strong reasons to do otherwise, groups of two and three should be avoided. Beyond this, odd-size groups of fewer than 10 members are best, particularly if interaction is required for effectiveness. If groups must be larger, they should be broken into subgroups as a means to facilitate interactive problem solving.

ALLOW GROUP MEMBERS TO SELECT OTHER MEMBERS WHENEVER POSSIBLE

Interpersonal attractiveness can create a strong force toward cohesion and cooperation. Likewise, replacements should be selected carefully so as to minimize disruption. However, diversity of group members should be a factor when creativeness is an important goal.

PROVIDE GROUPS WITH AS MANY OPPORTUNITIES FOR SUCCESS AS POSSIBLE

Participation in goal formation, special assignments, and other methods can give groups a sense of involvement. Successful achievement has a powerful impact on all aspects of group effectiveness. Opportunities for success are especially useful for newly forming groups: success helps to keep them on a track toward maturity as opposed to dissolution.

EMPOWER TEAMS TO BE MORE RESPONSIBLE, MORE SELF-SUFFICIENT AND SELF-MANAGING

Expect teams to identify, select, and solve problems as much on their own as possible, and to evaluate the quality of their own work. Help the group to cross-train members and to share and rotate leadership. Minimize supervisory interventions.

Key Concepts

autonomy 233
collection 223
dyads 239
formal groups 226
functional groups 226
group 223
group effectiveness 229
group performance environment 229
group processes 229
group structure 233
informal groups 227
interdependence 233
reference groups 226
role ambiguity 236
role conflict 236
roles 233
social groups 227
status 233
status incongruence 239
task groups 226
teams 223
triads 239

STUDY QUESTIONS

1 Think of one group you like or want to be in, and another you dislike or would not join. What are the reasons you are attracted to one and repelled by the other?
2 Which of the key values, beliefs, or attitudes that you hold were shaped by a reference group? Describe events that were particularly influential.
3 What holds an informal work group together? What are some key norms that might operate in an informal group? How do relationships with management affect such groups?
4 For a task group you are in, analyze the task, socioemotional, and disrupting roles in the group. Is there one or more than one person in the group who you would call the leader? Explain.
5 Define role conflict and role ambiguity. Should these conditions be eliminated? If so, why?
6 What are the characteristics of dyads and triads that make them unique types of groups? What are some implications for management?
7 Give an example, from your own experience, that shows how a large group you are in suffers the effects of increasing size.

Case

The Same Old Stuff

Just three weeks ago, the Dixon Company had reorganized its thirty factory workers into teams of five. Dixon manufactured various-sized storage units and handcarts for industrial use. The work was often done to customer order because the storage units and carts were designed by engineers to meet special customer needs for size and strength.

Before using work teams, two supervisors kept track of all orders and the blueprints that the engineers and designers developed for special jobs. The supervisors would assign individual workers to different tasks, depending on what was needed. The thirty workers were all capable of just about any task needed to build and assemble the parts that went into storage units and carts. However, from moment to moment, they never knew to which task they would be assigned.

Before teams were formed, morale in the plant was low. Absenteeism and lateness were increasing. The quality of work was not too bad, but a number of errors were found each week that could easily have been prevented. Most of the workers were skilled and experienced, and had been with Dixon for at least three years. The pay was good, and so were benefits, but still Dixon was not perceived as a great place to work.

There were several reasons why morale, attendance, and quality were suffering. These were uncovered by an outside consultant, who eventually recommended that the work teams should be formed. The consultant said that workers did not like not knowing their assignments until the last minute. The workers felt that supervisors gave more pleasant tasks as rewards, and unpleasant ones as punishments. Most often, they never completed a job they had started. They were also upset because some of their fellow workers knew how to hide from the supervisors at the right time. Others were treated with favoritism. Another problem was that every worker knew he could build any storage unit or handcart if he had the blueprint and was left alone to do the work.

The work teams were immediately popular. Teams were formed taking into consideration the workers' own choices of fellow team members. They were given the job orders, blueprints, and deadlines, and set free to work. Team members were allowed to work out their own method of assigning tasks within the group. Management said that teams were not to be used as an excuse to reduce productivity, or else the old method could be reinstituted. Productivity did not diminish, and absenteeism and lateness began to decrease. Fewer quality errors were found.

One day, the consultant returned to see how things were going. Two of six teams were quick to complain, "We're back to the same old stuff!" The consultant soon found out why they were upset. In both cases, the supervisor had entered the team area and reassigned one or more of the team members to a different task. The supervisors had a good reason, they claimed. The customer called and requested that the order be rushed, and they were only trying to meet the new deadline.

However, the workers saw things differently. They wondered if the supervisors really supported the team concept.

- Did the supervisors do the right thing when the customer's deadline was moved up? Explain.
- What happened in the teams when they were set up? What norms were likely to develop, for example?
- How would you explain the improvements in absenteeism, lateness, and productivity?

References

Bales, R. F. 1953: *Interaction Process Analysis: A Method for the Study of Small Groups*. Reading, MA: Addison-Wesley.

Balkin, D. B. 1997: Rewards for team contributions to quality. *Journal of Compensation and Benefits*, 13, 41–6.

Baytos, L. M. 1995: Diversity: Task forces and councils foster diversity success. *HR Magazine*, 40(10), October, 95–8.

Business Week. 1997: Look who's pushing productivity. *Business Week*, April 7.

Cohen, S. G. 1994: Designing effective self-management teams. In M. Beyerlein (ed.) *Advances in Interdisciplinary Studies of Work Teams*, vol. 1, Greenwich, CT: JAI Press.

Cohen, S. G. and Bailey, D. E. 1997: What makes teams work: Group effectiveness research from the shop floor to the executive suite. *Journal of Management*, 23, 239–90.

Cohen, S. G., Ledford, G. E., Spreitzer, G. M. 1996: A predictive model of self-managing work team effectiveness. *Human Relations*, 49, 643.

Cordery, J. L., Mueller, W. S. and Smith, L. M. 1991: Attitudinal and behavioral effects of autonomous group working: A longitudinal field study. *Academy of Management Journal*, 34, 464–76.

Halebilian, J. and Finklestein, S. 1993: Top management size, CEO dominance, and firm performance: The moderating poles of environmental turbulence and discretion. *Academy of Management Journal*, 36, 844–63.

Jackson, S. E., May, K. E. and Whitney, K. 1995: Understanding the dynamics of diversity on decision-making teams. In R. A. Guzzo and E. Salas (eds) *Team Decision-making Effectiveness in Organizations*. San Francisco: Jossey Bass, 204–61.

Katz, D. 1965: Explaining informal work groups in complex organizations: The case for autonomy in structure. *Administrative Science Quarterly*, 10, 204–21.

Katzenback, J. R. and Smith, D. K. 1993: *The Wisdom of Teams: Creating the High Performance Organization*, Boston, MA: Harvard Business School Press.

LeFauve, R. G. and Hax, A. C. 1992: *MIT Management*, Teaching booklet, 8–19.

Mckee, S. 1997: Can a baseball team buy its way to the World Series? *Wall Street Journal*. October 17, New York: Dow Jones & Company.

Mohrman, S. A., Cohen, S. G. and Mohrman, A. M. 1995: *Designing Team-Based Organizations: New Forms for Knowledge Work*. San Francisco: Jossey-Bass.

Novak, J. C. 1997: Proceed with caution when paying teams, *HR Magazine*, 24(4), April, 73–8.

Overman, S. 1995: *HR Magazine*, 40(3), March, 72–4.

Petzinger, T. 1997: The front lines. *Wall Street Journal*, October 17. New York: Dow Jones & Company.

Rizzo, J. R., House, R. J. and Lirtzman, S. I. 1970: Role conflict and ambiguity in complex organizations. *Administrative Science Quarterly*, 15, 150–63.

Shaw, M. E. 1981: *Group Dynamics: The Psychology of Small Group Behavior*. New York: McGraw-Hill.

Smith, C. and Comer, D. 1994: Self-organization in small groups: A study of group effectiveness within non-equilibrium conditions. *Human Relations*, 47, 553–73.

Wall Street Journal. 1997: *Wall Street Journal Interactive Edition*, October 6. New York: Dow Jones & Company. http://www.wsj.com/

Watson, W., Kumar, K. and Michelson, L. K. 1993: Cultural diversity's impact on interaction processes and performance: Comparing homogenous and diverse task groups. *Academy of Management Journal*, 36, 590–602.

Youngblood, S. A., DeNisi, A. S., Molleston, J. L. and Mobley, W. H. 1984: The impact of work environment instrumentality beliefs, perceived labor union image, and subjective norms on union voting intentions. *Academy of Management Journal*, 27, 576–90.

chapter 9

Group Processes and Effectiveness

GROUP DEVELOPMENT

GROUP NORMS

GROUP COHESIVENESS, COOPERATION AND COMPETITION

SOCIAL INFLUENCES

WHAT MAKES GROUPS EFFECTIVE?

Preparing for Class

Conduct a survey of at least five friends, family members or colleagues who are currently members of a group or team in an athletic, professional or academic environment. Ask them these questions:

1. Identify the person who contributes the most to the group or team.
   - What is their formal role within the group?
   - Describe the traits or personality characteristics that they demonstrate.
   - Describe as specifically as you can the behaviors they exhibit that make their contributions so important.

2. Identify the person who contributes the least to the group.
   - What is their formal role within the group?
   - Describe the traits or personality characteristics that they demonstrate.
   - Describe as specifically as you can the behaviors they exhibit that make their contributions so important.

3. Using the information from the survey and your own experiences, develop a profile of the ideal team-member.
   - What traits do they possess?
   - How do they behave?

Developing a diverse group of individuals into an effective group requires both skill and patience – that is what Carl Friedrich discovered when he accepted a position as a manager of a newly formed association of physicians. Working for physicians, Carl had several battles to face. First, he was entering a dynamic industry that, because of the introduction of managed care, was undergoing significant change. These changes put pressure on physicians to reduce costs while maintaining a high quality of health care – objectives that are often in conflict. Second, physicians have typically operated with the utmost autonomy. Managed care was already forcing physicians to work closer with health management organizations to control health care costs and now Carl was asking them to also coordinate their activities within the group. Third, Carl was an outsider who had an MBA but no specific experience in the health care industry. How does an outsider increase the effectiveness of a group of diverse individuals operating in a turbulent industry? Let us focus on the specific actions taken by Carl to turn this association of individual physicians into an effective group (Lancaster, 1998).

After several "shouting matches" with some of the physicians, Carl decided to try different tactics to improve group performance. First, Carl decided to begin with smaller changes to develop the physicians' trust in him and in the benefits of group cooperation. Even though he wanted to eventually consolidate billing operations and increase the sharing of information among physicians, he started out on a small scale by encouraging individual physicians to consolidate their purchasing of supplies. This cooperative effort allowed the group to buy in bulk and, as a result, reduced costs.

Next, Carl considered the personalities and values of the physicians who made up the group. He reasoned, correctly, that they would be reluctant to give up their own decision-making authority. He also understood that the physicians would object to anything that may compromise their ability to make the best decisions for their patients. As a result, he supported the right of the physicians to make important decisions but attempted to limit their options by developing a set of alternative choices from which they could choose one. He found the physicians were much happier following his recommendations when they were allowed to participate in the decision.

A final tactic Carl found to be critical was in how he communicated with the physicians. He found that he needed to spend more time listening to their concerns and responding to issues they felt were important. He found that paying attention to issues that mattered to group members went a long way in building their trust in him and in their understanding of the value of being a part of the group (Lancaster, 1998).

Carl's main challenge was to take a collection of individual physicians and turn them into an effective group. While in chapter 8, we introduced a model of group and team effectiveness and discussed environmental factors that influence a group or team's effectiveness, this chapter focuses on the processes that can lead to increased group effectiveness and the behavior of individuals within a group context.

Figure 9.1 shows a portion of the group effectiveness model introduced in chapter 8. As discussed on page 229, the group performance environment is composed of industry, organization and group factors which can directly influence the processes of the group and affect group effectiveness. We now move our attention to those specific processes.

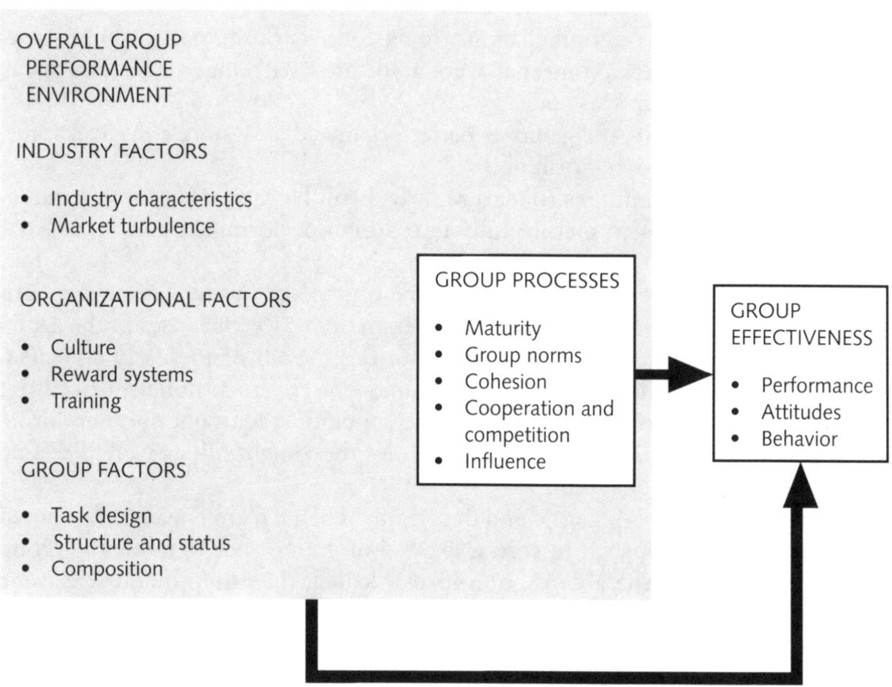

Fig 9.1 : Overall group performance environment and group effectiveness

Group Processes

We know that there are a number of different experiences that a person can have by being a member of a group. For example, when a group initially forms, it takes some time before the members can begin to work together effectively. Also, there are different kinds of pressures that one feels in a group. Some of these group processes are discussed in this section.

Group Maturity

One factor that may strongly influence the effectiveness of a group is the group maturity. Group maturity can be thought of similarly to individual maturity. As individuals, we develop confidence in ourselves and increase our emotional stability over time, partly through our education and interaction with others. Just like individuals, some groups are slower to mature; some never reach full maturity. Research on this issue has considered that groups go through certain stages of development (Bennis and Shepard, 1965; Tuckman, 1965), depicted in figure 9.2.

- Early in the life of a group, members engage in behaviors useful for **forming** the group and orienting members.
- Often a period of conflict or **storming** follows the initial forming stages and the polite behaviors that were associated with that stage. The group often struggles in this stage.
- In the next phase, the group is better organized and more cohesive, sometimes referred to as **norming**.
- As the group continues to mature, it will still have relationship difficulties to resolve if it is to mature fully into a high-**performing** team.

forming
Stage of group development in which the group becomes organized by defining purpose and establishing its activities and priorities

For a group to succeed, it needs to become organized. Initially, there is an orientation period called **forming**. Members seek to define the purposes of the group and begin to establish its activities and priorities. Much of the early conversation revolves around defining group goals and objectives, although it need not be confined to these topics. Members are also acquainted with one another during this stage and are very likely to be seeking roles they might fill, as well as testing the ground rules for behavior.

storming
Stage of group development where group goals, purposes and leadership are debated and tested

This early stage can be chaotic and uncertain. When a formal leader, appointed by the organization, exists, pressure is exerted on him or her to guide the group through this stage. In the absence of a formal leader, the group might select one or simply allow one to emerge. In the early orientation stage, there is little to disagree about, but as goals and purposes surface and as a leader exerts influence, a conflict stage, called **storming**, usually emerges. The leader is usually put to a test, and challenges to leadership could arise. The group may divide over these issues and form two or more subgroups rather than attempt to restructure the group or change the leadership.

ORIENTATION →	CONFLICT →	COHESION →	EFFECTIVE STRUCTURE
• Defining goals • Feeling others out • Sizing up situation • Getting acquainted • Testing ground rules • Defining rules • Uncertainty • Confusion	• Disagreements over priorities and assignments • Hostility, tension • Resistance • Challenging the leadership • Subgroups, cliques	• Consensus • Acceptance of leadership • Sharing, trust • Togetherness • New, stable roles • Cooperation • Standards	• Delusion, disillusion, and acceptance • Intimacy, openness • Flexible, task-relevant roles • Helpfulness • Successful performance
FORMING →	STORMING →	NORMING →	PERFORMING

IMMATURITY ⟷ MATURITY

Fig 9.2: Stages in group development

Focus on Team Building: Kick-Starting Your Group with a Little Team-building?

Many organizations are using **team-building** tactics to try to decrease the time it takes for a team to mature. This is often useful for teams stuck in the conflict stage of group development. One such experience is provided by Outward Bound. Among the courses offered, Outward Bound uses 3–7 day wilderness programs that can be designed to teach participants the value of teamwork and to build specific teamwork skills. Programs also focus on problem solving and goal setting. Many universities have also incorporated similar team-building opportunities into their curricula. At some schools, new MBA students are required to participate in a team-building experience with other new MBA students as part of their initial academic work within the program.

If a group successfully resolves these early conflicts, it is more likely that it will mature, moving into a cohesive stage. If consensus develops around goals and leadership and a sense of liking and trust develops, individuals begin to feel cohesive and express a readiness to move ahead into the **norming** stage. Some groups never make it through the conflict stage. Disagreements and resistance prevail. Energy goes into more conflict, or some people just leave. Others may stay but withdraw psychologically, exhibiting silence and lack of commitment.

If a group survives orientation, conflict, and cohesion, its members move into dealing with problems concerning the structure of the group: the **performing** stage. Here, they face problems that stem from interpersonal/relationships, such as intimacy and openness. These operate on at least two levels.

1 How well does the group deals with emotional tensions that arise out of dissatisfaction of members? For example, do members feel free to say they are being unfairly treated?
2 How is idea generation affected? Unless the participants can freely offer alternative definitions of a problem and differing solutions, problem solving and decisions will suffer.

Other types of conflict can occur and we discuss the topic in chapter 10 (page 275).

If the group is successful in maturing beyond the conflict stage, a stage of acceptance is achieved. Subgroups become less prominent. Communication increases and the needs of individuals are more freely expressed. When the task and the emotional needs of group members are handled well, the group has achieved full maturity. It takes considerable skill from both members and leaders to bring a group to full maturity. Mature groups can be recognized by five characteristics:

team building
A form of planned organization change which focuses on the work team by improving the interpersonal and working relationships of team members

norming
The group development stage where group norms are developed

performing
The final stage of group development in which its members move into dealing with problems concerning the structure of the group

1 The group accepts feelings in a nonevaluative way.
2 The group members disagree over real and important issues.
3 The group members make decisions rationally and encourage dissent, but do not force other members or fake unanimity.
4 All group members have an awareness of the process.
5 Members understand the nature of their involvement.

Mature groups are not that common.

Focus on Teams: The Saturn Experience

"A different kind of company, a different kind of car" is the motto of Saturn Corporation. Saturn has prided itself on its use of innovation both in the technology used in the manufacture of their automobiles and in their team approach to the process. While there were the expected technical glitches in the early stage of the technical development of their automobiles, they were surprised to discover glitches in the development of their team concept. Saturn leadership assumed that the development of teams would take six months. The reality was that it took four to five years.

Saturn's teams went through a series of stages where group members struggled to understand their roles within the teams and adjusted to the new types of behaviors needed to work within the team environment. Saturn found, even though they designed the entire structure of their organization around the team concept, implementation required more than just the right context, it required teaching Saturn employees a whole set of new behaviors required within groups. This process took time and teams went through a series of stages from the initial polite stages to more combative stages. Most of the team failures Saturn encountered were due to teams trying to tackle complex team activities without the team being at the appropriate level of maturity.

COMMONALITY OF GROUP NORMS

norms
Shared group expectations about behavior and how members ought to behave

In our discussion of how group's mature, we discussed the norming stage where maturing groups develop cohesion. Key to this stage is that the group's develop a set of **norms** that are accepted and understood by group members about how members ought to behave. Unlike role expectations, which apply to an individual, norms apply to all group members, but not always equally. For example, we might expect all members to be on time for a meeting but excuse one member under special circumstances. Having a common set of norms is so important to the group process that it is worth discussing in more detail.

FUNCTIONS AND DEVELOPMENT OF NORMS Norms provide groups with control and predictability, and give members a sense of security and comfort. Norms are also the ways we express values, attitudes, and beliefs because they are reflections of the "oughts" and "shoulds" of life. When we believe someone should do something, we are expressing what we feel is right, good, or useful.

Norms put boundaries on member behavior that may be narrow or wide. For example, at a religious service, very little deviance from norms is tolerated. Organizations can also have narrow norms such as a company who has very rigorous dress standards. If an employee were to wear jeans to work at a company with a norm of business dress, the supervisor may quickly rebuke him or her. To improve the organizational climate, many organizations have instituted a "dress-down" day that allows employees to wear more relaxed clothing on a certain day of the week or month. You might expect though that when a program like this is implemented, employees would quickly look to their supervisors and others to understand the new dress standards that would become the new norm for this activity!

Norms benefit both individuals and groups. Even trivial norms, such as how we handle eating utensils, serve a purpose. They make social interaction easy and convey a sense of sharing. They also add to our self-identity and identification with a group or culture. In small groups, people often enter with similar social norms, so that few problems will arise around such matters as eating or dress habits.

Important norms are more likely to emerge around values and behaviors that are central to the group. If attendance at meetings can affect the group's success, being on time and attending all meetings will surely become a norm. The more important the issue and the more it is shared, the more likely and quickly the norm will develop. Important norms are often reflected in bylaws, rules, and procedures that members are expected to follow. However, when values are not shared by all group members or are not considered critical, it does not become a norm.

THE POWER OF NORMS The power of norms lies in two things.

1 They sensitize us to expectations of other.
2 The power of norms is a function of our ability and willingness to act in a way consistent with those norms.

A norm's power to control us depends on how we feel about the consequences of violating it. If we value our membership in a group, we can protect that membership by complying with norms. Some people also have higher needs to be accepted and approved by others, making them more susceptible to group norms.

Groups use rewards and sanctions to enforce norms. They can reward people who comply by giving them acceptance, higher status, and more influence. For those who deviate, the group might use warnings, withdraw privileges, impose a punishment, or actually remove the individual from the group.

WORK GROUP NORMS Many norms in organizations originate from management expectations or from work rules and procedures of the formal organization. They develop and operate in informal groups. A new employee's introduction to an organization requires the learning of its varied norms. The norm may form one basis on which employees are evaluated, and violation of the norms can be personally costly. Sometimes individuals choose to deviate from the norms of the group. They are more likely to be successful in doing this if they are both highly competent, and therefore hard to replace, or they have some political clout to withstand the consequences of ignoring norms.

ratebuster
An individual who performs at a level above what the group will tolerate

Many central work group norms revolve around productivity. Norms can put lower and upper limits on productivity. A **ratebuster** is an individual who performs at a level higher than the group will tolerate. Ratebusters can cause serious problems because workers in a group often have strong norms about what constitutes a fair day's work. Controlling productivity not only spreads the work out to more people for a longer period, but also prevents management from raising its expectations. This group behavior is often seen in college and university classrooms. Have you ever noticed in your classroom how a group of students may try to control the participation of other students? Making sarcastic remarks or laughing after an active student has made a comment are ways members of a classroom control the behavior of ratebusting students. Are there norms that have developed in your classroom?

Some organizations have norms emphasizing social concern for employees (Leventhal, 1976). This norm fosters taking care of people who need it or otherwise contributing to the quality of an employee's life at work. For example, if a death occurs in an employee's family, fellow workers will do all sorts of things to help out. Norms may encourage activities such as giving birthday cards and cakes, sharing rides to work, or bringing lunch to someone who is too busy to take a break. Other norms can exist in organizations including equality and equity norms and social conformity norms.

Management can foster many norms that contribute to organizational success, such as norms effecting work quality, helpfulness, or customer relations. A norm of secrecy may be critical to keep competitors from stealing ideas. In one company, this norm was strengthened by buttons worn by employees which read, "I know a lot but I can keep a secret" (Zachary, 1989).

GROUP COHESIVENESS

cohesion
The degree to which members of a group are attracted to one another and to group membership

Another important element of the group process considers group cohesiveness. **Cohesion** is the degree to which members of a group are attracted to one another and to group membership. Members of cohesive groups have a strong desire to stay in the group. Attractiveness is a key ingredient in cohesion, but it is possible for a person to want to keep membership and yet not be highly attracted to a group. Membership in a country club might be very useful to a person's career success, even though he or she does not particularly like some of the members. However, such motivation will not contribute much to group cohesion. Without attractiveness, cohesion will suffer.

Within the same group, cohesiveness can change over time, depending on the group's experience. Although cohesiveness is important, a group does not have to be highly cohesive to survive; a group can live and work together for a long time without becoming exceedingly cohesive. Figure 9.3 introduces our dis-

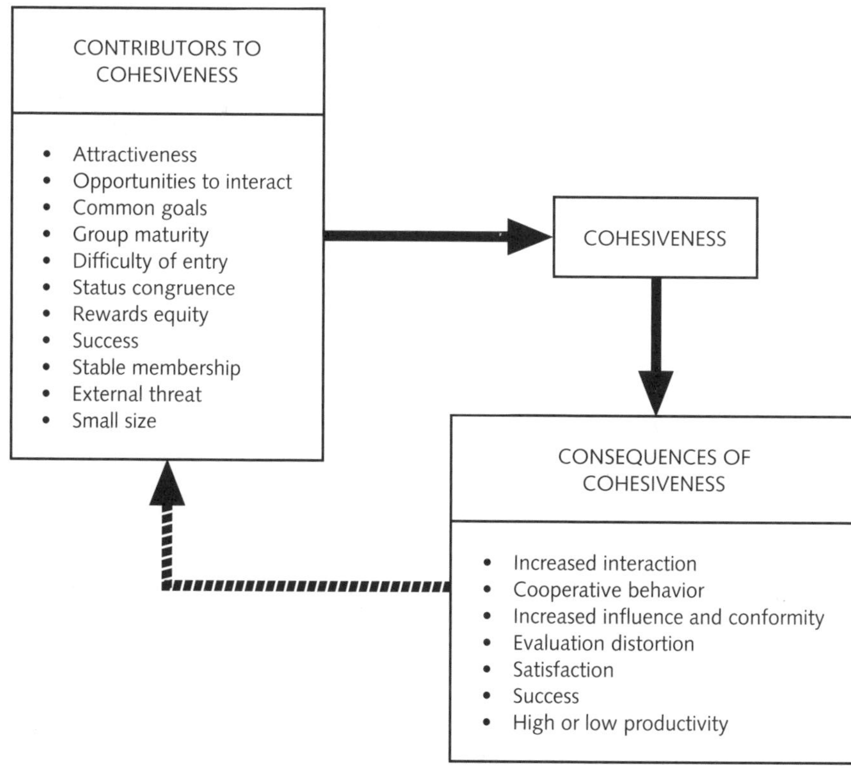

Fig 9.3: Causes and effects of cohesiveness

cussion of some causes and effects of cohesiveness. A number of factors foster group cohesion. Some were suggested in our earlier discussions in chapter 8 (page 223). Other important conditions enhancing cohesion are discussed below.

GROUP FORMATION FACTORS The conditions leading to group formation contribute to cohesion. When people are similar to one another and when they share common goals and interests, the foundation for cohesion is laid. Recall, too, that similarity between people is a powerful basis for mutual attraction and this attraction is central to the definition of cohesiveness. The more important group goals are to each member and the greater they perceive the need to work together to accomplish these goals, the higher the cohesiveness.

DIFFICULTY OF ENTRY Some groups are not easy to join. Members are carefully selected and there may be elaborate rites of entry. The more difficult it is to enter a group, the more status the group is likely to have for someone desiring membership. A personal sense of status and accomplishment will result merely from being accepted into the group. An elitist feeling or attitude can develop that contributes to the spirit and cohesion of the group.

STATUS CONGRUENCE If the criteria for entry into a group are consistently applied, members can start out with similar, though not necessarily identical, status within the group. As members interact, their status can change, and a status hierarchy evolves. Status congruence results if there is consensus among members about this status hierarchy, and each behaves according to his or her status. Status congruence contributes to cohesion. Incongruence, which can lead to both frustration and resentment (Heslin and Dunphy, 1964), can arise when work assignments are made or when status symbols are given. For instance, a group can be disrupted if a low-status member is assigned the best equipment.

FAIR REWARDS ALLOCATION Cohesion is facilitated when rewards are allocated fairly or evenly. To be fair, rewards must be either equivalent to the contribution a person has made or consistent with a person's status level. Equal distribution of rewards can grow out of a group agreement to do so. Cohesion suffers when a member is given rewards inconsistent with what others may feel he or she deserves.

SUCCESS When a group achieves a meaningful and shared goal, cohesion usually increases. Members experience a sense of accomplishment and pride. For example, successful companies, combat units, or sports teams express strong feelings of cohesion.

STABLE MEMBERSHIP Stability of membership helps the group to maintain cohesion. New membership disrupts this. New members may not be accepted easily by the old members, and status struggles can emerge. Patterns of interaction can change, and norms might have to be enforced more actively. This is why it is often difficult for a new member to enter an already cohesive group, particularly if the new member is the leader. A manager who enters a highly cohesive group of subordinates has to tread softly until he or she learns group norms and relationships. The main task is to minimize disruption, particularly if the group is productive and respected.

EXTERNAL THREAT Group cohesion can increase dramatically when group members perceive an outside force as threatening to member goals and interests. Differences between members become less important as they pull together to protect the group and resist the threat. The threatening party will feel less chance of success when faced with a unified response.

SMALL GROUP SIZE Smaller groups tend to be more cohesive than larger ones. Larger groups tend to have interaction and organization problems. With increases in size, subgrouping and formalized procedures are established to prevent disorder. Cohesion is more likely to be stronger within the subgroups that emerge.

Small size contributes to cohesion in several ways. It permits more interactions and increases opportunity to participate. The informality of smaller groups also helps cohesiveness. Member satisfaction is likely to be higher, even for reasons other than cohesiveness.

CONSEQUENCES OF COHESION Consequences of cohesion in groups may be positive or negative. We consider five consequences here:

- Level of interaction
- Power and influence
- Evaluation distortion
- Satisfaction
- Productivity

Cohesive groups have a higher **level of interaction**. Members share needs and problems in cohesive groups more than they do in less cohesive groups. Similarity in interests, common goals, personal attractiveness, and size all contribute to these increased interactions.

A cohesive group can exert a great deal of **power and influence** over its members. They will respond more readily to demands than in low cohesive groups. High susceptibility to influence can be a problem. If members cannot express opinions or feelings for fear of losing acceptance or membership, individualism and self-respect may be reduced. The group may lose the benefit of fresh ideas, and authenticity and honesty can suffer. In chapter 11 (page 328), we show how this can adversely affect group decision making.

However, suppressive influence can be, on occasion, quite functional. A military combat leader in the field needs instant compliance in the midst of a dangerous mission. Democratic and shared influence under these conditions can cost team members their lives. The more appropriate time for individual expression and mutual influence is during planning sessions before the mission takes place, and after the mission is completed.

Another effect of cohesiveness, **evaluation distortion**, occurs when cohesive groups tend to overvalue their own behavior and accomplishments and to undervalue outside groups. A cohesive team in one plant may believe they are the best when, actually, another plant is performing more effectively. High self-evaluations reinforce the group's feelings of worth and togetherness. Outsiders are evaluated lower for several reasons:

evaluation distortion
A condition that occurs when cohesive groups tend to overevaluate their own behavior and accomplishments and to under-evaluate the effectiveness of outside groups

- The group's own status is enhanced by rating another group lower.
- Devaluing the other group is a form of defensiveness, in which the group denies its own weaknesses as a way to maintain togetherness. Stressing the positive may be unrealistic, but it preserves group spirit.
- Devaluing other groups can also give a sense of security.

Members of cohesive groups are more satisfied than members of less cohesive groups. The sources of **satisfaction**, already discussed, are friendliness, support, opportunity to interact, success, and protection against outsiders. Because cohesive groups can pull together against outside threats, satisfaction also grows out of a feeling of security.

Finally, in some contexts cohesiveness can positively influence group member **productivity**. Individuals enjoy the strong bonds that form among members of cohesive groups and members are often focused on a common goal. As a result, highly cohesive groups have a high degree of success in achieving their goals. Unfortunately, those goals are not always consistent with organizational goals. We discuss the factors that influence this complex relationship later (page 264).

GROUP COOPERATION AND COMPETITION

cooperation
Giving support to others, and contributing time and effort in situations where people jointly work together toward some end

Members of a group have choices about whether to cooperate or compete with other members. **Cooperation** means more than just helping; it includes giving support to others, and contributing time and effort in situations where people jointly work together toward some end. Typically, the whole group can benefit from cooperation. As mentioned in chapter 8 (page 228), factors within the group performance environment can have an effect on cooperative behaviors. Sometimes, it occurs as a direct result of how tasks are designed. For example, the layout of a factory or office can be designed for cooperative effort. Cooperation is also a common consequence of team sports such as baseball or basketball. When we use the term "teamwork," we are focusing on cooperative activity.

competition
Team members showing more concern with their own welfare, sometimes at the expense of others

In addition to cooperation, some groups also experience **competition** among members; members are more concerned with their own welfare, sometimes at the expense of others. Competition can impact cohesiveness and encourage group member behavior that may detract from accomplishment of group or organizational goals. Whether it is a basketball player who wants to score the most points and so he or she "hogs the ball," or the sales person who keeps important sales information from colleagues so that he or she can be the top sales person: competition can have negative consequences for group performance.

Competition can also lead to some benefits. Salespeople often compete among each other in rewards programs designed so that they, and the company, gain from improved performance. If awards go to winners, the losers may suffer some, but the gain to the whole group may more than offset it. Therefore, whether competition is damaging or beneficial depends on the balance of benefits and cost that result.

Several factors can tilt individuals and groups toward either competition or cooperation; see figure 9.4. Some factors lie in the characteristics of individuals, some in the group composition and dynamics, and others in the nature of the task or environment of the group (Jewell and Reitz, 1981).

INDIVIDUAL TRAITS Individual differences in traits between people affect their tendencies toward cooperation or competition. For example, men and women differ in competitiveness, and, on average, men are more competitive. In addition to differences between people within a society, anthropologists have found cross-cultural differences in cooperativeness and competitiveness.

GROUP PREFERENCES AND NORMS A group's norms can determine whether cooperative or competitive behavior is acceptable. In some situations, competition is the norm, such as in sports or in the business world. Groups within organizations might compete for the same pool of resources. Balancing cooperation and competition in organizational settings is a delicate and difficult issue.

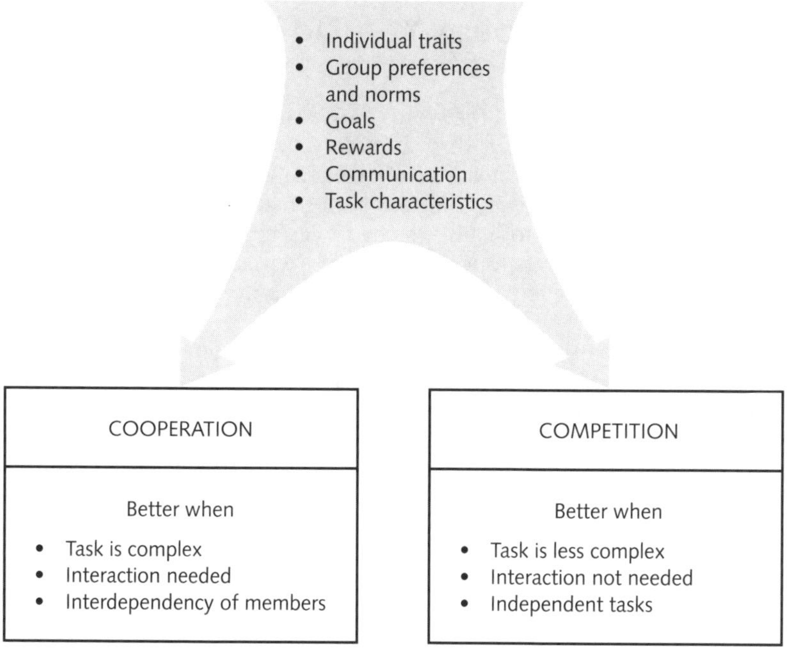

- Individual traits
- Group preferences and norms
- Goals
- Rewards
- Communication
- Task characteristics

COOPERATION	COMPETITION
Better when	Better when
• Task is complex • Interaction needed • Interdependency of members	• Task is less complex • Interaction not needed • Independent tasks

Fig 9.4: Forces and conditions of cooperation and competition

GOALS AND REWARDS Goals and rewards can also influence whether group members cooperate or compete. Cooperation is more likely to occur where there are common goals that are understood, accepted, and believed to be obtainable. It is also fostered by shared rewards. However, when an organization rewards only a few people or a group, competition is a probable result. Competition can reach destructive levels: people hoard resources, withhold information, refuse help, or engage in any behavior that gives them an advantage over others. Rewards can be managed so that they do not cause destructive competition. Competition can be held to acceptable levels if there are few incentives to win at the expense of others. Two divisions of a firm might compete for the introduction of their new products without harm if they both have adequate resources and if they work independently.

Traditional wisdom suggests cooperation is more easily achieved when employees perceive some chance of earning a valued reward. Within work groups, cooperation is maximized when members within the group share rewards equally. Group incentive plans have this attribute. Regardless of individual contributions, the group's product is assessed and rewarded. Group incentives, compared to individual incentives, encourage cooperation and sharing of ideas, and members are more willing to help and give each other feedback. However, not all data supports the contention that rewards for the entire group is the best way to reward team performance. Some argue that individual behavior should be rewarded with one aspect of that behavior being how the person contributes to the team. (*HR Focus*, 1997).

A QUESTION OF ETHICS: WHAT WOULD YOU DO?

Danielle looked at the plaque on her wall and read the words "1998 Sales Person of the Year." She remembered the thrill she had when she found out that, after only five years on the job, she had finally achieved this coveted honor – an award for the pharmaceutical sales person with the combined highest sales and customer satisfaction ratings. The cash bonus that came with the award had also been welcome. It had taken her a while to learn effective sales techniques to deal with the physicians and medical staff that were her clients, but she eventually developed a style that she felt would allow her to compete for this award every year. Her goal was to be the first person to ever win the award two years in a row.

Now Danielle faced a difficult dilemma that she felt might prevent her from achieving her goal. Her regional Vice President had just asked her to prepare a seminar to train others on the sales force to use the techniques that had allowed her to convincingly win this year's awards. Give us your "secrets to success," he had said. She had worked hard to develop those "secrets" – a combination of her style of making sales presentations and her methods of contacting, and making appointments with, the physicians within her region. She reasoned that she had not been given anyone else's secrets, so why should she share hers? Danielle felt she had three options:

1. Give the presentation and share all of the techniques that she had developed over the last five years.
2. Give the presentation but keep her most effective sales strategies a secret.
3. Make an excuse to decline making the presentation.

Right now she just wished she had not been put in this position.

- What would you do if you were in this position?
- Should Danielle share her strategies?
- Should she have been asked to share those strategies?
- What would you do if you were the boss?
- What are the ethical implications of her choices?
- What can we learn about the use of this type of reward system in fostering competition? On the surface, since sales people are assigned separate territories, it appears just a friendly rivalry.
- Is Danielle's reaction understandable?

COMMUNICATION Effective communication results in understanding or acceptance – or both – between the people involved, but understanding and acceptance do not guarantee cooperation or competition. For example, you may understand that other people are angry or hostile but you still may choose to compete with them. Communication is a necessary, though insufficient, condition for cooperation. If people are to cooperate, communication cannot be held back, nor can it be distorted or misdirected. While good communication does not ensure cooperation, poor communication will probably inhibit it.

TASK CHARACTERISTICS The characteristics of the task can effect whether the group members cooperate or compete. With complex tasks, people need to give and receive more information. Complex tasks have more elements than simple tasks. Less is known about how to perform them, and more problems can arise. **Task complexity** can also mean that it is difficult to give someone a clear job description. All this increases the need for interaction and cooperation.

Let us compare a sales team, assigned to contact individual customers to sell a new product, with a product development team, responsible for developing a new product. The sales team can work alone in a separate location, and interactions between members of this team are not necessary to do the work. The product development team, however, has a complex task. Product feasibility, production issues, marketing questions, and technological problems are all woven together, and team members are highly interdependent at all stages of developing a new product. Without interaction, these team members would not know about the work of others, and this may result in duplication and wasted effort. When conditions change, members of the product development team must keep each other informed; they hold frequent meetings and use a variety of communication methods to facilitate cooperation.

Social Influences on Behavior

In this section, we focus on the social influences commonly found in group or team contexts. We consider both functional and dysfunctional behaviors that occur from exposing individuals to the social influences found in group and team environments.

For influence to take place, other people do not have to offer judgments, give orders, or otherwise exert direct pressure. The mere presence of others, without active involvement, can influence behavior. Whether the presence helps or hinders performance depends on the nature of the performance required, or what the group member's response is to the situation (Zajonc, 1965). Generally, when we are in the presence of others, performance on easy or previously learned tasks improves while performance on new or complex tasks worsens. This is an important principle for managers who are attempting to increase the use of groups and teams within their organization to understand. It suggests using groups or teams may improve performance when they do work at which they are proficient. Conversely, when a person is learning new tasks, the principle argues for giving employees a place to learn or practice alone, away from others.

How does this social influence operate? Many of us become apprehensive when we are observed and evaluated (Cottrell et al., 1968). We also become distracted by the presence of others, and this can interfere with our performance. Another explanation lies in individual differences. Some of us are more affected by others, regardless of the task. Some people are simply more aware of others; they are more concerned about others' reactions, and have a greater desire for social acceptance or approval. **Social facilitation** may also mean that the presence of others serves to arouse or sensitize us. Anxiety about evaluation need not be the only factor: performance can be influenced even on tasks where there is no right or wrong answer. In chapter 11, we explore several important social influence phenomena that occur within group decision-making settings.

social facilitation
A social influence condition in which the mere presence of others can influence behavior

HELPING BEHAVIORS There are also positive social influences on individual behavior in team or group settings. Team or group members have many opportunities to exhibit helping behavior. They can assist a teammate with a task or a personal problem, volunteer extra effort, or suggest improvements. These behaviors – referred to as prosocial or **organizational citizenship** behavior (Brief and Motowidlo, 1986; Organ, 1990) – are actions that, in many ways, are not exaggerated, not extreme or heroic, and may seem even trivial and mundane. Still, they contribute in an important way to the effectiveness of the organization.

organizational citizenship
The extent to which a person is willing to go beyond the norms of performance and involvement for his or her work role

People differ in their willingness to help others and there are several factors that influence the presence of helping behaviors in group and team members:

- *Past and present role models*
  Parents, other people, television, radio, and newspapers provide behavioral role models. We can learn helping from our neighbors who organize to clean up the neighborhood or from fellow workers who help each other.
- *Extrinsic outcomes*
  People may be more willing to help when they can obtain valued rewards. Someone might pay you to help him or her with a chore. Doing a good job can be a form of helping an organization to succeed. Many behaviors at work can be truly helpful, especially if others would flounder without such help. Organizations often provide awards to members who demonstrate helpful behavior within the organization or community.
- *Intrinsic outcomes*
  Helping others can simply make people feel good. Intrinsic rewards provide a sense of having done the right thing or a feeling of pride in the action. Self-esteem and self-image are enhanced. Surely if you saved a child from drowning, you would feel quite good even if no extrinsic rewards were forthcoming. There is evidence that volunteers in clinics, libraries, and museums work only to help, since they are unpaid.
- *Group or team norms*
  Norms also affect helping. One widely recognized societal norm is **reciprocity**, based on the idea that helping fosters helping; it is also related to fairness and equity in human social exchange. This norm tells us to return the favor to those who help us. Reciprocity also causes people to expect help from those they have helped. For reciprocity to operate, a person must feel that help really was needed and that the other person gave it voluntarily, with good motives, and in a meaningful way.

reciprocity norm
A norm that tells us to return the favor to those who help us

- *Mood or preoccupation*
  Research shows that intrinsic rewards for helping may be greater when people are in a good mood (Myers, 1983). Many things may effect mood. For example, people who feel fairly treated are more likely to feel better and show helpfulness more frequently (Moorman, 1991).
- *Presence of others*
  The presence of others sometimes reduces the tendency to help. It can also reduce the amount of effort a person contributes to a task. For example, people may feel less pressure to volunteer when surrounded by others. Similarly, they might not exert as much effort when others are added to

the task. An example of this social influence, social loafing, is discussed in the next section.

social loafing
An individual reaction to larger groups that assumes that someone else will do what is needed and thus relieve the individual of the task

SOCIAL LOAFING **Social loafing** occurs in larger groups because, with other people present, we assume that someone else will do what is needed and thus relieve us of the task. People seem willing to pass the buck even though nothing will be achieved if everyone loafs (Baron, 1983). Social loafing helps us to avoid being the one who contributes a lot while others escape with doing less. It also protects us from failing, and it is difficult to fix responsibility or blame when

Diversity Issues: Boomers versus Busters – Does Age make a Difference?

Many of the diversity issues covered in this text highlight gender, racial and ethnic diversity. An additional diversity issue confronting managers is age diversity. As individuals work later in their life, the demographic makeup of a work force can include employees from multiple generations who perhaps have differences in values, motivation, and communication. Two groups that have been the subject of research interest are members of the baby boom generation ("boomers" born during the period 1946–1959) and members of the baby bust generation ("busters" born during 1965–1975). Boomers and busters in the same work force can lead to conflict. Nowhere is that conflict more pronounced than when they are all assigned to the same team.

One researcher discussed boomers versus busters and their attitudes towards teams. She found that boomers liked to work in teams while busters generally preferred to work alone. Boomers also have a preference for group processes and value participation and consensus. Busters have less preference for participation and attending meetings.

- Given these differences in values towards teams, how can managers improve team effectiveness for teams with age diversity?

Like other ways in which we are different, differences in group attitudes can be used positively by managers by capitalizing on individual strengths. One way suggested by career strategist Marilyn Kennedy is to consider individual preferences when assigning work roles.

- If boomers prefer working in groups, they can be assigned tasks that require significant interaction with others.
- Busters, who don't like team work, can be assigned tasks such as research, that requires less interaction.

There are other ways the strengths of these two diverse groups can be used for an advantage.

- Boomers often have significant experience in the field and can share that experience with less-experienced busters.
- By the same token, busters are typically much more comfortable with technology and can mentor their boomer teammates in optimizing the use of technology.

Age diversity, like other types of diversity provides a wide mix of talents and abilities that when managed properly can increase the effectiveness of teams and organizations.

Source: Adapted from Kennedy (1998)

other people are present. When people believe that individual contributions can be evaluated, however, the degree of social loafing is sharply reduced (Williams et al., 1981). Unproductive people do not enjoy being exposed. When contributions to a group are made public, team members are less likely to loaf than when only the group performance is displayed. Individual visibility increases the pressure to perform (Nordstrom et al., 1990).

Social loafing can be a serious problem in work groups and teams. Helping and individual effort might decline because of the presence of others. These effects can be overcome with norms and incentives which help to discourage social loafing, by making individual contributions more visible, and by fostering a culture where individualism and self-interest are replaced by a spirit of commitment to group effort (Albanese and Van Fleet, 1985).

Group and Team Effectiveness Factors

We now turn our attention to the final part of our model of group and team performance to focus on how group effectiveness is measured in organizations. In chapter 1, several of these measures of effectiveness were identified and defined as results or consequences of organizational activities; see page 19. Among them were productivity, satisfaction and other improved employee attitudes, attendance, retention, learning and adaptation, and physical and mental well being. Consistent with recent research in team effectiveness, we have organized the different types of effectiveness into three main outcomes of effective team performance (Cohen and Bailey, 1997):

- Performance
- Attitudinal
- Behavioral outcomes

Performance Outcomes

Group or team performance can be measured in several ways. Performance outcomes have included consideration of productivity improvements. Within our discussion of Monarch Marking Systems in chapter 8 (page 222), we mentioned the 100 percent improvement in Monarch's productivity as a result of implementation of ideas flowing from a team who were studying product assembly processes. Quality can be measured in terms of sophisticated measures of the deviation of final products from performance standards, monitoring product failures or customer returns, as well as through conducting customer surveys on satisfaction with product quality. Subjective measures of team performance such as a manager's assessment of performance or the performance appraisal ratings received by individual team members can also be used to measure performance (Campion, 1996).

Many of the issues discussed in this chapter, and in chapter 8, are important for managers interested in improving group performance outcomes. Both

EXERCISE

WORK TEAM EFFECTIVENESS

This checklist can help you to analyze the effectiveness of a team.

Consider a group or team that you are now a part of or one you were a part of recently. Read the 20 statements and mark your level of agreement that the statement describes conditions found within the group or team you are considering. Use this scale:

1 Strongly disagree
2 Disagree
3 Neither agree nor disagree
4 Agree
5 Strongly agree

		Agreement level
1	The atmosphere is relaxed and comfortable	....
2	Team discussion is frequent and relevant to the task at hand	....
3	Team members have a clear understanding of team goals	....
4	Team members listen to each other's suggestions and ideas	....
5	Disagreements are tolerated and an attempt is made to resolve them	....
6	There is general agreement on most courses of action taken	....
7	The team welcomes frank criticism from inside and outside sources	....
8	When the team takes action, clear assignments are made and accepted	....
9	The relationship among team members is relaxed	....
10	There is a high degree of trust among team members	....
11	The team members strive hard to help the group achieve its goal	....
12	Suggestions and criticisms are offered and received with a helpful spirit	....
13	Team members cooperate rather than compete	....
14	Team goals are set high	....
15	The leaders and members hold a high opinion of the team's capabilities	....
16	Creativity is stimulated within the team	....
17	Team members freely communicate on topics relevant to the task	....
18	Team members feel confident in making decisions	....
19	People are kept busy but not overloaded	....
20	The leader of the team is well suited for the job	....
	Total	....

Now, total the number of points. The greater the total point value, the higher the likelihood that the team you considered is performing effectively and team members are highly satisfied.

Source: Adapted from Dubrin (1982)

cooperation and competition can be useful in improving group effectiveness, depending on the nature of the task performed by the group. Improving cooperation can result in better performance for group tasks that require interdependent action. For example, interaction and communication are critical to the success of a product development team because team members must share information, coordinate their plans and activities, and help each other. Cooperative groups put more pressure on members to achieve group goals (Deutsch, 1949). This is in contrast to a sales team that might be more productive under moderate competition. The productivity of salespeople is possible with minimal interaction with one another. Care must be taken, however, so that lack of cooperation is not damaging to groups such as these. Competition might result in behaviors such as withholding critical information, which could damage the entire sales effort.

Competition within groups may have some positive effects in increasing creativity and innovation but performance may suffer when the parties put more energy into defeating each other, and that suspicion and hostility are undesirable side effects of competition.

Cohesiveness can also contribute to productivity in some contexts (Stogdill, 1972). One study found that, in some contexts, there was no relationship between cohesiveness and productivity. In other contexts, though, cohesiveness was positively related to productivity. In still other contexts, more cohesive groups were among the least productive. These mixed results can be understood if we consider how cohesiveness is related to group goals. A second study of industrial work groups categorized several hundred of these groups into those that had high or low cohesiveness (Seashore, 1954). Surprisingly, the average productivity of both high and low cohesive groups was quite similar, but the productivity of low cohesive groups centered near the average. That is, low cohesive groups were less likely to have high or low productivity. In the high cohesive groups, however, productivity was not near the average but tended to be at the extremes, either highly productive or the least productive.

Figure 9.5 depicts these results. When the cohesive groups had goals and norms that were consistent with organizational expectations, productivity was high. For example, cohesiveness was the strongest predictor of project group performance in a R&D division where goals were clearly understood by the groups (Keller, 1986). When cohesive groups had goals and norms that were not consistent with organizational expectations, productivity was low. This is consistent with the conclusion that cohesive groups influence their members more, regardless of their productivity level.

ATTITUDINAL OUTCOMES

One outcome of group performance can be measured by considering changes in the attitudes of group members. Group or team participation can significantly impact on work-related attitudes of team members. Attitudes of interest include employee satisfaction with the organization, supervision, work relationships and other aspects of organizational life. There is considerable empirical evidence that participation on self-directed work teams is positively related to member

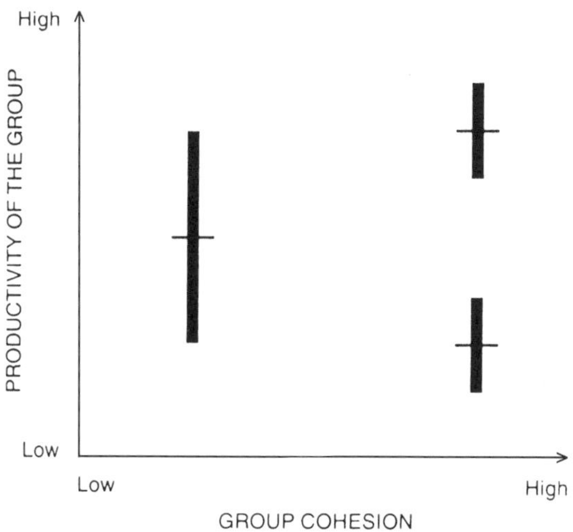

Fig 9.5 : Productivity between and within high and low cohesive groups

satisfaction because of the autonomy provided to the team (Cohen and Bailey, 1997).

Other studies have looked at changes in the commitment of team members both to the team and to the organization. The relationship between team participation and commitment is a complex one. On one hand, team member commitment to the organization can improve team effectiveness (Bishop, 1997); on the other hand, participating on a team can increase an individual's commitment to the organization. This is consistent with our earlier discussion (page 254) of how team cohesiveness increases commitment. When commitment is increased as a result of participation on teams, it can have positive behavioral implications for the organization.

There are also some surprising findings from research on group effectiveness when the aim is to change work-related attitudes of group members. For example, it is not necessarily true that members of cooperative groups are more satisfied than members of competitive groups. The major determinants of satisfaction lie in the members' expectations and the rewards they receive (Cherrington, 1973). It is the rewards that cause satisfaction, and these are different in competing and cooperating groups. Cooperative groups reward members with friendliness, praise, mutual support, and perhaps sharing of bonuses or prizes. Winning can reward competitive group members as well as being given feedback on their skill, or praise from outsiders. Once again, individual differences operate here. Some people prefer competition and the rewards that it provides; others find cooperative activity more rewarding.

In the right context, both cooperation and competition can influence group member attitudes. For example, members of groups with more effective internal group processes – and who are therefore more cohesive – are usually more satisfied than members of less cohesive groups. The sources of satisfaction – already discussed on page 223 – are friendliness, support, opportunity to interact, success, and protection against outsiders. Because cohesive groups can pull together against outside threats, satisfaction also grows out of a feeling of security.

Behavioral Outcomes

The final measure of group effectiveness considers the direct effect of group participation on individual behavior. Group participation can affect member behaviors in terms of their participation in the work place as measured by their rate of absenteeism and the rate at which team members leave the organization (turnover). Several companies have reported a significant reduction in both absenteeism and turnover of members involved in team activities.

In chapter 5 (page 136), our review of job characteristics theory suggested that when a job requires more variety of skills, increases the amount an individual can identify with the task, and increases the significance of the task, he or she should experience greater meaningfulness of work and thus higher motivation. Reliance on a variety of team member skills and strong identification with team goals and activities are often byproducts of team participation. In addition to learning new work skills, team members often develop improved interpersonal skills that contribute to their personal growth and future value to the organization.

There are many factors that contribute to the overall effectiveness of a group. We have attempted to outline several factors in both this chapter and chapter 8.

Global Focus on Measuring Team Effectiveness Internationally

Team effectiveness can be measured in several ways and the many positive organizational benefits of implementing teams can be found in the UK. One example of how job satisfaction can be a direct measure of team effectiveness comes from Nationwide Building Society. In the 1990s, Nationwide began to abandon traditional management hierarchies and opted for flatter structures relying on self-managed teams in their customer service area. Up to that time, employees who worked in customer service had typically showed moderate levels of job satisfaction on the organization's annual survey. In 1997, however, customer service was at the top. In addition, the use of teams is credited with increasing productivity by half and reducing absenteeism by 75 percent. In the same period, overtime was down to zero.

Other UK companies have improved organizational effectiveness through the use of teams. Michelin Tires and Baxi Heating are two examples of UK companies who use teams effectively in the manufacturing setting. In both companies, members are able to use their own knowledge of work processes to improve productivity and product quality.

Source: Scott and Harrison (1997)

Summary

Patterns of group development can either lead to its failure or to group success and maturity, depending on how well the group members handle the stages of its development. Early in its life, a group has to establish goals as well as resolve the question of leadership and personal commitment. Conflicts that surface must be resolved if the group is to become cohesive. Members must also deal with questions of intimacy and openness. Group members can delude themselves into feeling all is well, but when this is not the case, the members become disillusioned and struggle further before the group can mature.

Groups develop norms that define behavioral expectations and contribute to the control necessary for achieving effectiveness. No group can be understood without some knowledge of group norms, and group members cannot adequately operate in a group unless they are aware of norms and help to enforce them.

Effective groups or teams are productive, have satisfied members, and are able to attract and retain members. To remain effective, groups often have to provide learning and growth opportunities for their members. The effectiveness of the team or group can be measured in a variety of ways. Groups can contribute to organizational performance by improving the quality of the product or by recommending ways to improve productivity. There are also attitudinal and behavioral effects of participation on a group or team. Groups have been shown to lead to improved satisfaction with supervisors, coworkers and the increased commitment to the organization. Participation also can affect behaviors such as absenteeism and turnover.

We are certainly not leaving our study of groups and teams. Subsequent chapters – chapter 10 on conflict and chapter 11 on decision making – will consider the role of groups in these important organizational issues. We have all been members of groups or teams in our personal and social lives. If you have not been part of a group or team in your professional life, you probably will be in the future. Understanding the issues involved in group and team effectiveness is an important aspect of insuring that this experience will be a positive one.

Guide for Managers: Encouraging Improved Work Groups

Managers can take a number of steps to foster group productivity, satisfaction, cohesion, and learning. Knowledge of group characteristics and dynamics can be put to good use to increase effectiveness. Some specific ways this can be done follow.

HELP GROUPS TO DEVELOP AND MATURE

Leadership skills, training, or outside assistance can all help a group through its developmental difficulties. Group or team success depends on how well members resolve interpersonal tensions, status issues, and other difficulties. Pay attention to the development of task and socioemotional roles and develop procedures to control disruptive members. Groups should be allowed time and the place to interact so that development is not blocked. In addition to allowing the group time to develop, provide opportunities and resources to support team-building activities such as those mentioned in the chapter.

ENCOURAGE GROUP PRODUCTIVITY NORMS THAT ARE CONSISTENT WITH ORGANIZATIONAL GOALS

The best-producing groups are cohesive ones with norms and goals that contribute to organization success. Some of the steps outlined in the chapter will encourage development of such norms.

DEAL WITH GROUP SITUATIONS WHERE COHESION IS BASED ON NORMS THAT ARE HARMFUL TO THE ORGANIZATION

Unproductive cohesive groups are a sign that something is wrong between employees and management. Employees may feel threatened or have little trust in the organization. This is a difficult situation to deal with, but if the causes can be diagnosed, some sort of conflict resolution strategies can be undertaken; see chapter 10.

VIEW TEAM-MEMBERS AS SOCIAL BEINGS, SUBJECT TO THE INFLUENCE OF OTHERS

Their behavior should be interpreted in light of the surrounding social forces. As a manager, you must understand and accept that the informal organization interacts with the formal organization structure.

USE SYSTEMS OF GOALS AND REWARDS TO COMBAT THE EFFECTS OF SOCIAL LOAFING

This can be done partly by encouraging work teams to develop high productivity goals. It can also be aided by insuring reward systems recognize both individual and team contributions. Group rewards for productivity and for cooperative effort should be used. Individual rewards for team-oriented behavior and for contributions to group goals can augment group rewards.

EXERCISE CAUTION IN USING COMPETITION TO ENCOURAGE GROUP PRODUCTIVITY

If the task requires little interdependence, and opportunities for harmful competition of others are minimized, then competition can enhance productivity. Even under competitive circumstances, such as when sales personnel compete for awards, opportunities for cooperation and mutual helping should be encouraged. In all other situations, managers should encourage and develop norms of helping and cooperation that contribute to productivity, satisfaction, cohesion, and learning.

Key Concepts

cohesion 254
competition 258
cooperation 258
evaluation distortion 257
forming 250
norming 251
norms 252
organizational citizenship 262
performing 251
ratebuster 254
reciprocity norms 262
social facilitation 261
social loafing 263
storming 250
team building 251

STUDY QUESTIONS

1 What are the major stages of development in small groups? What is necessary for a group to achieve maturity?
2 What are the major factors that contribute to cohesion in groups?
3 Suppose as a manager you had a group of workers reporting to you whose cohesiveness was moderate to low. How would you increase cohesion so as to improve productivity and satisfaction?
4 For the same group described in question 3, what might a manager do that would increase the group's cohesion, but *lower* their productivity?
5 What is the best way to manage a cohesive and highly productive group? What can a manager do to change a cohesive but unproductive group?
6 How can a manager encourage and sustain helping behavior in a group?
7 Describe a work situation that would benefit from competition between groups. What kinds of things should be done to keep competition from becoming destructive?
8 What are some key actions a manager can take to increase a group's effectiveness?
9 How is the effectiveness of a group measured?

Case

Design Section E

Stork Aircraft Supplies has an excellent reputation for providing precision parts to the aircraft industry. They design and manufacture a variety of pumps, hydraulic devices, and mechanical controls for jet planes. Their devices are known for their reliability and durability throughout the industry. They have a large R&D Division that designs and tests prototypes before sale and manufacture of them.

R&D usually has 30 or 40 project teams working on new devices and modifications. One support group in R&D is the Design Division. It consists of 20 or so design engineers and draftsmen who serve each of the ongoing projects. On many occasions, demands by project leaders created chaos in the Design Division. To handle special requests and emergency or overflow work, Design Section E was set up. Six employees and a supervisor, Dan Reed, were assigned to the section.

After about a month of operation, Section E was in chaos itself. There were some arguments among his six designers, and dissatisfaction had set in. Three of the designers were upset because Dan kept trying to establish a schedule of assignments. They thought this was foolish, because they perceived the task of the group as not subject to a particular schedule. They felt that Section E was created to respond quickly to special work that was assigned to their unit.

The other three designers were upset and dissatisfied for other reasons. They were angry with Dan because he could not seem to stick to the schedule, or he would change it before it had expired. They also disliked having to set an incomplete project aside whenever a supposedly higher priority design was needed by a project manager. The other three designers exasperated them, too. These other three would often ignore the schedule and suggest various reassignments to meet what they felt were emergency requests.

The tension between Dan and his designers was growing by the day. His group was split down the middle on some key issues. Cooperation between the two subgroups was poor. The teamwork and cohesiveness he wanted was not happening.

- Would Section E benefit more from cooperation or competition given their task? What factors helped or hindered cooperation?
- Is helping important to Section E? Explain.
- What can Dan, the supervisor, do to enhance Section E's cohesiveness? How will cohesiveness help?

References

Albanese, R. and Van Fleet, D. D. 1985: Rational behavior in groups: The free-riding tendency. *Academy of Management Review*, 10, 244–55.

Baron, R. A. 1983: *Behavior in Organization: Understanding and Managing the Human Side of Work*. Boston: Allyn & Bacon.

Bennis, W. G. and Shepard, H. S. 1965: A theory of group development. *Human Relations*, 9, 415–57.

Bishop, J. W. 1997: How commitment affects team performance. *HR Magazine*, 42, 107–111.

Brief, A. P. and Motowidlo, S. J. 1986: Prosocial organizational behaviors. *Academy of Management Review*, 11, 710–25.

Campion, M. A. 1996: Relations between work team characteristics and effectiveness: A replication and extension, *Personnel Psychology*, 49(2), 429–52.

Cherrington, D. J. 1973: Satisfaction in competitive conditions. *Organizational Behavior and Human Performance*, 10, 47–71.

Cohen S. G. and Bailey, D. E. 1997: What makes teams work: Group effectiveness research from the shop floor to the executive suite. *Journal of Management*, 23, 239–90.

Cottrell, N. B., Wack, D. L., Sekerak, G. J. and Rittle, R. M. 1968: Social facilitation of dominant responses by the presence of an audience and the mere presence of others. *Journal of Personality and Social Psychology*, 9, 245–50.

Deutsch, M. 1949: A theory of cooperation and competition. *Human Relations*, 2, 129–52.

Dubrin, A. J. 1982: *Contemporary Applied Management*. Plano, TX: Business Publications, Inc.

Heslin, R. and Dunphy, D. 1964: Three dimensions of member satisfaction in small groups. *Human Relations*, 17, 99–102.

HR Focus, 1997: Across the board. *HR Focus*, 74, 2.

Jewell, I. N. and Reitz, H. J. 1981: *Group Effectiveness in Organizations*. Glenview, IL: Scott, Foresman.

Keller, R. T. 1986: Predictors of the performance of project groups in R&D organizations. *Academy of Management Journal*, 29, 715–26.

Kennedy, M. M. 1998: Boomers vs. busters. *Healthcare Executive*, November, 18–21.

Lancaster, H. 1998: Managing your career. *Wall Street Journal*, November 10. New York: Dow Jones and Company.

Leventhal, G. S. 1976: The distribution of rewards and resources in groups and organizations. In L. Berkowitz and E. Walste (eds) *Advances in Experimental Social Psychology*, vol. 9. New York: Academic Press.

Moorman, R. H. 1991: Relationship between organizational justice and organizational citizenship behaviors: Do fairness perceptions influence employee citizenship? *Journal of Applied Psychology*, 76, 845–55.

Myers, D. G. 1983: *Social Psychology*. New York: McGraw-Hill.

Nordstrom, R., Lorenzi, P. and Hall R. V. 1990: A review of public posting of performance feedback in work settings. *Journal of Organizational Behavior Management*, 11, 101–23.

Organ, D. W. 1990: The motivational basis of organizational citizenship behavior. In B. M. Staw and L. L. Cummings (eds) *Research in Organizational Behavior*, vol. 12, Greenwich, CT: JAI Press, 43–72.

Scott, W. and Harrison, H. 1997: Full team ahead. *People Management*, October 9, 48–50.

Seashore, S. E. 1954: *Group Cohesiveness and the Industrial Work Group*. Ann Arbor, MI: Institute for Social Research.

Stogdill, R. M. 1972: Group productivity, drive, and cohesiveness. *Organizational Behavior and Human Performance*, 8, 26–43.

Tuckman, B. W. 1965: Developmental sequence in small groups. *Psychological Bulletin*, 63, 384–99.

Williams, K., Harkins, S. and Latane, B. 1981: Identifiability as a deterrent to social loafing: Two cheering experiments. *Journal of Personality and Social Psychology*, 40, 303–11.

Zachary, G. P. 1989: At Apple Computer proper office attire includes a muzzle. *Wall Street Journal*, October 6, 1.

Zajonc, R. B. 1965: Social facilitation. *Science*, 149, 269–74.

chapter 10

Conflict

THE NATURE OF CONFLICT

DIAGNOSING CONFLICT

CONFLICT REACTION STYLES

IMPROVING ORGANIZATIONAL RESPONSE TO CONFLICT

Preparing for Class

Review the newspaper from the last few days and count the number of conflicts that are discussed. Classify each situation as either political, organizational and business, or personal conflict. Be prepared to discuss these questions:

1. How many instances of conflict did you find?

2. What factors are involved in each conflict?

3. Using figure 10.5 (page 290), determine if these conflict situations should be easy or difficult to resolve. Prepare to defend your diagnosis.

Consider these three examples:

> The Kosovo and Bosnian peace agreement provide an all too familiar resolution to the years of conflict that have divided the former Yugoslavia. The Bosnian agreement signed in Dayton, Ohio partitions the country into sections where different ethnic factions can live. While some may argue that this is not a peace agreement, because it just partitions the country, it has been a tactic in political relations that has saved many lives. India, Palestine, and Ireland are examples of other countries where conflict became so intense that separating the groups was viewed as the only effective resolution (Kumar, 1997).
>
> A recent agreement between the United Automobile Workers (UAW) and the big three automotive manufacturers (Chrysler, General Motors and Ford) was supposed to have resolved a long-term conflict over the number of jobs available to UAW members. Automotive manufacturers wanted to increase efficiency and the UAW wanted to protect their member's jobs. Despite the agreement, the UAW was still suspicious of the auto manufacturers and continued to stage a series of strikes in an effort to save every job possible. At stake is the long-term health of the US automobile industry and hundreds of thousands of jobs, but even with the critical nature of the conflict, the methods of handling the conflict have even insiders wondering if rational minds are in control of the situation (*Business Week*, 1997).
>
> Nancy felt the energy drain from her body. This had become a common feeling for her in her job as a mediator of disputes that occur within the organization. She saw the look of determination on the faces of Ken, the supervisor, and Bob, his subordinate. Nancy had come to know this as a sign that both parties had taken such a hard line in the negotiations that the resolution would be very difficult. She felt that the initial dispute, which was over Bob's poor performance appraisal rating, was a minor issue now. Both Ken and Bob were in the stage where each person wanted to prove that he was "right." It had become a matter of principle.

These three examples highlight the pervasiveness of conflict in our everyday life. Conflict is a natural part of life and exists in politics, our organizations, and within our personal lives. While some level of conflict is healthy – even necessary – in organizations, it can also increase stress and have dysfunctional consequences as people take sides on issues such as budget allocation, goal priorities, or over how fairly they are being treated. Labor unions and management conflict over compensation and work conditions. Sometimes, the problems are minor and settled easily. Others go unresolved or break out into conflicts of varying intensity from minor arguments to "organizational warfare." However, not all of the effects of conflict are bad. The key lies in how we view conflict and what we do to deal with it.

In this chapter, we discuss the conflict process and how conflicts arise. We explore various styles of reacting to conflict and ways to manage and resolve conflict more effectively.

conflict
A disagreement, the presence of tension, or some other difficulty between two or more parties

The Nature of Conflict

Conflict includes disagreements, the presence of tension, or some other difficulty between two or more parties. It may occur between individuals or between groups. Conflict is caused when individuals or groups of individuals perceive that their goals are blocked. It can be public or private, formal or informal, or be approached rationally or irrationally.

Conflict as a Process

Conflict is not a static condition; it is a dynamic process that involves several stages. Parties can go through the process in many different ways, and do so more than once. Figure 10.1 presents a model integrating different approaches to conflict (Pondy, 1967, 1969; Hickson et al., 1971; Filley, 1975; Thomas, 1976, 1990):

- Antecedent conditions
- Perceived conflict
- Manifest conflict
- Conflict resolution or suppression
- Aftermath

This model is the basis for our discussion throughout this chapter.

Antecedent conditions of conflict are the conditions that cause or precede a conflict episode. Sometimes an aggressive act can start the conflict process. For instance, one of your employees might deliberately hide tools that others need to do a job, or one department may have more resources than another department believes they should. Antecedents of conflict can also be subtle. Pressures on a production department to keep costs down may frustrate your sales manager who wants to fill rush orders on short notice. At this stage, conflict may remain below the surface because neither party presses its position.

antecedent conditions of conflict
The conditions that cause or precede a conflict episode

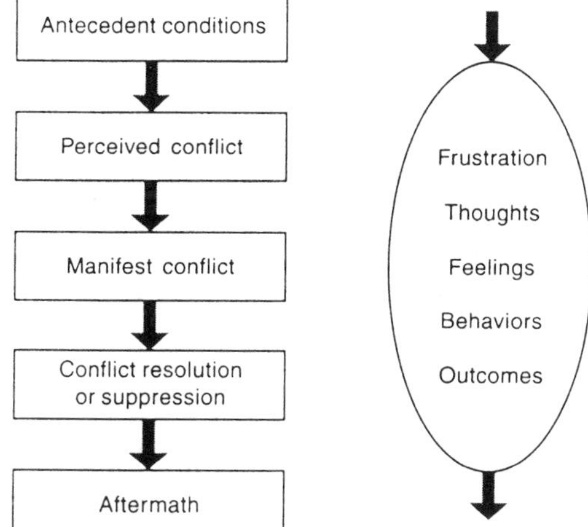

Fig 10.1 : The conflict process

perceived conflict
The requirement that, for conflict to exist, the conflict must be perceived by one or more parties involved

Perceived conflict is necessary for the conflict to progress. The parties must become aware of a threat. Any person might act to the disadvantage of another, but without awareness of the act, little else will happen. Even without an action, people might perceive a threat when none is there. When conflict, real or imaginary is perceived, it may trigger frustration, anger, fear, or anxiety. Those involved start to question how much they can trust each other, and worry about their ability to cope with the difficulty. This stage of conflict is critical because this is when the parties tend to define the issues and start looking for ways to resolve their differences.

manifest conflict
A stage of conflict that occurs when parties that have perceived a conflict behave in a way that makes the conflict observable

Perceived conflict develops into **manifest conflict** when people react to the perception. One of your employees might threaten to file a grievance, prompting you to take defensive steps. Other behaviors that signal manifest conflict include; arguments, aggressive acts, appeal to goodwill, or constructive problem solving.

Conflict resolution can come about in several ways. Parties may agree about how to solve their difficulties and even take steps to prevent it in the future. Conflict can also be resolved when one party defeats another. Sometimes conflict is *suppressed* rather than resolved. This happens when the parties avoid strong reactions or try to ignore each other when they disagree.

Whether conflict is resolved or suppressed, feelings remain. Behaviors during the **conflict aftermath** can be just as varied as the ways conflict is manifested or resolved. Sometimes good feelings and harmony result; a new procedure may be developed that clarifies the relationships between the parties. For example, one of your employees might decide not to file a grievance because you were willing to agree with the union on a new rule that solves the original problem.

Unfortunately, the conflict aftermath can also result in poorer working relationships. If hard feelings and resentment persist, these can trigger the next conflict episode. For example, poor solutions or losses by one party may reduce communication or prepare each party for bigger battles to come. The key question is whether the resolution draws parties into cooperation or drives them further apart.

The Role of History in Conflicts

Linkages between people and units of an organization persist over long periods of time. As a consequence, the parties develop a history of perceptions, attitudes, and behaviors toward each other. If one party has historically been cooperative in its relationships toward others, a single incident of noncooperation is likely to have no significant effect. On the other hand, a history of conflict can cause the parties to mistrust each other continually, making opportunities for cooperation very difficult. In evaluating past behaviors, the parties are likely to put greatest weight on the most recent behaviors of the other.

For example, we already noted the international political conflict in the former Yugoslavia. Conflict in that region, as well as many other regions, has long roots in history, sometimes dating back several hundreds of years. This is complicated when there are unresolved disputes where one or both sides feel they have lost something in the past. These historical traditions of conflict create difficulties for current-day negotiators who attempt to make opposing groups focus on modern issues.

Focus on Conflict: What kind of People do You like to have Around?

There are two managerial responses to organizational conflict manifested in the type of people we like to have around. Managers, who dislike conflict, hire comfortable clones. These are people with similar backgrounds and interests and who "think alike." This "sameness" helps to reduce conflict. An alternative response for managers who value people who think differently than them, is to hire people who can bring diverse viewpoints to the discussion. This too has its drawbacks, as it becomes a significant task to manage the conflict that can occur (Leonard and Straus, 1997). As you can see, as a manager you will often have an important role in making decisions that will help you manage conflict. What kind of people you hire and how you organize their activities are just a couple of the decisions that could eventually avoid or cause conflict.

Viewpoints on Conflict

We look at three viewpoints:

1 Conflict is preventable.
2 Conflict is inevitable.
3 Conflict is healthy.

It is assumed, for example, that conflict can be avoided simply by making employees change their attitudes and behavior so that cooperation can prosper. It is also assumed that conflict is preventable if managers can create positive working relationships through good planning, and with policies and procedures that ensure mutual efforts toward common goals. This perspective has merit, of course, and is part of how managers should view their role. Some conflict in organizations is preventable, and some of it is a sign that something is wrong and can be corrected.

The second point of view – conflict is inevitable and so there is no way to eliminate it entirely – may be true for many reasons; we have cited some throughout this book. For example, not all organizational goals are compatible. The goal of reducing costs is often in conflict with goals that call for innovation. Organizational design also leads to conflict. Employees are grouped into departments of specialists, each with its own point of view. Conflicts may arise between managers and auditors because the required work for each group actually creates problems for the other. Conflict also arises because plans and policies are rarely perfect enough to cover all situations that might arise.

If some conflict is inevitable, then trying to prevent it may be more frustrating (and time consuming) than the conflict itself. The best strategy for you is to accept the inevitability of certain kinds of conflict. Your employees can be trained to anticipate where disagreements are bound to arise, and to resolve them before they become unmanageable. That way, we can keep conflict within tolerable limits and manage it effectively.

The third point of view is that some degree of conflict is healthy for an organization (Cosier and Dalton, 1990). When would this be the case? Suppose that the sales, research, and production departments never experienced tensions or disagreements with each other. The relative peace between the departments might mean that each department is not doing its job effectively. For example, sales may not be responding to new product or market opportunities, so they rarely suggest changes that would create tensions with research and production.

Healthy benefits of conflict include creative approaches to resolving problems and making decisions. In chapter 11, we discuss some dysfunctional aspects of group dynamics such as groupthink. Groupthink occurs when groups attempt to achieve consensus and eliminate conflict. While this is useful so groups can make progress, it has is dysfunctional side-effects.

Figure 10.2 suggests that there is probably some optimal level of conflict.

- *Too little conflict* in an organization can be a threat to effectiveness. Individuals may avoid each other instead of interacting to work on generating new ideas and developing creative approaches to solving problems.
- *Too much conflict* can also hamper effectiveness. With constant disagreement over too many issues, or through failures to appreciate the needs and problems of others, innovations may never come about, customers may be lost, and key issues may go unresolved. The organization will suffer if members are consumed with defending themselves or with winning internal organizational battles.

At the optimum level of conflict, quite different things happen. There are active attempts to improve quality and to introduce changes that might make the organization more competitive and more effective or efficient. Employees are stimulated; they are not bored and withdrawn. Individuals with different perspectives are willing to present their ideas and this may lead to improved performance. Tensions and frustrations are accepted and channeled into productive, rather than destructive, effort (Tjosvold, 1991).

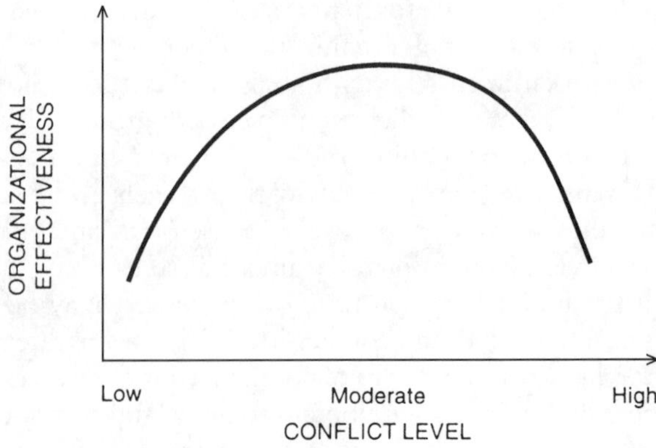

Fig 10.2: Optimum levels of organizational conflict

Intergroup Conflict

When one group is in conflict with another group, certain positive things similar to competition happen. Conflict can stimulate the group members to work harder to accomplish the task, especially if that helps them to protect their group or to look better than the other group. The group becomes more cohesive and coordinates its efforts to present a united front. Internal divisiveness may be avoided because it would weaken the group. In time, with intergroup conflict, members are also more likely to accept directive or autocratic leadership if it helps them in the conflict.

Groups in conflict will tend to view the other party negatively – perhaps even in threatening or hostile terms. Members will increase their alertness to the other group's actions and reduce the communication between groups. A win–lose mentality often develops between the groups. These intergroup behaviors can work against reaching a constructive outcome of the conflict. We discuss several strategies for conflict resolution later; see page 299.

What Triggers Conflict?

To manage conflict, its causes must be understood and, if possible, changed. The causes of conflict are grouped into three major categories:

1 Characteristics of individuals
2 Situational conditions
3 Organizational conditions

Figure 10.3 introduces the causes of conflict.

Individual Characteristics

Individual differences make some people more likely to engage in conflict than others. While you have been introduced to these characteristics in earlier chapters, we want to focus on how they influence conflict.

VALUES, ATTITUDES, AND BELIEFS Our feelings about what is right and wrong, and our predispositions to behave positively or negatively toward an event can easily be a source of conflict. A worker who values autonomy and independence will probably react negatively when supervised too closely. Values also can create tensions between individuals and key groups in organizations. For example, union leaders are likely to have different values than managers. In one study, union leaders valued employee welfare and equality highly, but rated company profit maximization low. Managers' views were quite the opposite (England et al., 1971). In the example on page 276, we describe the conflict between the UAW and the major automotive manufacturers. Their conflict stemmed from an extreme difference in beliefs about what is needed to maintain the strength of the US automotive industry. The union's priority is to save jobs.

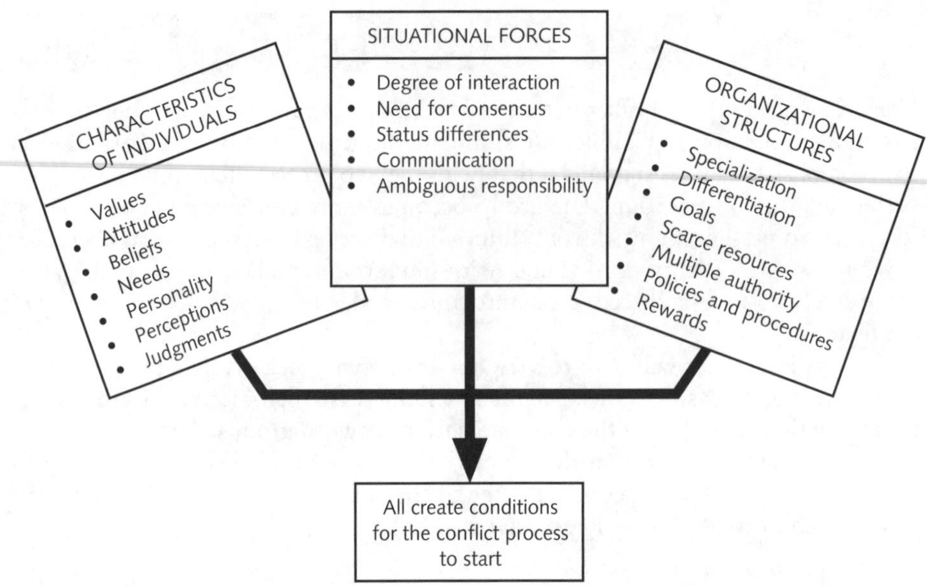

Fig 10.3: Causes of conflict

They view the automotive manufacturer efforts to save costs by outsourcing some production activities to nonunion businesses as a threat. While both sides may value the long-term profitability of the industry, they have different beliefs about how that profitability can be achieved.

NEEDS AND PERSONALITY Another difference that can lead to conflict is when individuals differ in their needs and personality. Consider the case of a chemical company that had several plants making different products (Lawrence et al., 1976). Some of the plants produced products for other divisions in the company. The plant managers cooperated for a time with little difficulty. When some of the older plant managers retired, their replacements from the outside had a different psychological makeup. They were much more concerned about individual achievement and much less prone to cooperate. Disagreements between the old and new managers arose, and performance in some of the plants deteriorated.

PERCEPTION AND JUDGMENT If we perceive another person as a threat, we may act toward them in a way that increases the potential for conflict. Conflict can also arise when people commit judgment errors such as the fundamental attribution error (page 77). One party might blame another for a problem and attribute its cause to the other person's motives. Conflict is more likely when situations are ambiguous because ambiguity contributes to misperceptions and incorrect judgments.

A QUESTION OF ETHICS: CONFLICTS OF INTEREST

Managers of organizations that have significant employee diversity encounter conflicts stemming from differences in individual beliefs and values.

One source of conflict is agreeing what behavior is acceptable to an organization – especially when that behavior has ethical implications.

One issue that is often discussed in today's global business environment concerns conflicts of interest. Consider these work place behaviors and decide which you feel are unethical behaviors.

- A senior vice president for Information Technology takes a free golf vacation as part of a sales pitch by an international supplier who wants him to agree to a multi-million dollar contract.
- A university employee uses her university office computer to set up a web site for a charity where she volunteers much of her personal time.
- A salesperson for a firm that sells electrical supplies takes a potential customer – a senior manager from a major building supply warehouse chain – to dinner and spends over $100 per person on the meal.
- A US computer software firm buys thousands of dollars worth of computer equipment and gives it to an international company so that the company can avoid paying significant import taxes on the equipment. As a result, the international company purchases a great deal of software from the firm. The legal office for the software firm says that the firm has not broken any laws but that the international company is clearly violating laws of their country.

Each of these scenarios could be considered unethical, depending on your individual perspective. Others may argue that they are normal practice of doing business and that organizations have no role in playing moral police in respect to activities of their customers or suppliers.

Differences of opinion on ethical issues like these are a source of conflict in the work place. To cope with conflicts of interest, managers should insure that a written policy that deals with these issues is in place, and that all employees are aware of those standards. Employees should be trained to ask first, when potential ethical conflicts arise.

SITUATIONAL FORCES

A second set of factors that can contribute to conflicts considers the conditions found in different situations. In chapter 2 (page 32), we provide a model which shows that behavior is a function of individual characteristics and the environment. Conflict, as a behavior also has environmental causes. In this section, we focus on common situational causes; in the next section, we consider those found in common organizational environments.

DEGREE OF INTERACTION Conflict is more likely when people are physically close, and when they need to interact. With frequent interactions such as occurs in complex projects, conflict potential increases even more. Interactions are the stuff of life in organizations, but they need not result in conflict. It has been shown that more productive work groups are ones that actively interact with each other by asking questions, working jointly on projects, and by sharing in-

Global Focus on Conflict Across Cultures

Given that individual characteristics are a product of socialization, we would naturally expect many cross-cultural differences on how people deal with conflict. Different styles of reacting to conflict are probably found more frequently in some cultures than others. When organizations have international operations and plants in other countries, they must be aware of such cultural differences since a major aspect of culture is tolerance of and reactions to conflict. In Japan, there is far less toleration of open conflict than in the USA. People also react to others and attempt to gain control over their situation in different ways, a result of differences in child-rearing practices in the two cultures (Kojima, 1984). The Japanese attempt to deal with the issue of control over others with a style of accommodation, whereas the USA culture emphasizes competing or direct confrontational styles (Weisz et al., 1984).

In a recent study, comparisons were made between the USA, Japan, China, Korea, and Taiwan (Ting-Toomey et al., 1991). The researchers examined similarities and differences in how conflict is approached and resolved. Asian cultures are more likely to value group goals and responsibilities than they are to pursue individualistic needs. China, Korea, and Taiwan for example, showed highest concern for the self-esteem and self-image of the other party, and to avoid embarrassing or humiliating them. They gave others the opportunity to "save face" more so than in the USA, and are more likely to avoid conflict. In the USA, there is a stronger tendency to dominate the other party rather than avoid or accommodate. In such individualistic cultures, people show more concern for preserving their own self-esteem, which is the case for both the USA and Japan. Though more competitive, it is interesting that the individualistic emphasis tends also to foster more collaborative behavior. By comparison, Asian cultures are more likely to give in or to accommodate the other party.

formation and achievements (Ancona, 1990). One study demonstrated that in low-conflict organizations, ties between groups were strong and marked by frequent, productive interactions. In high-conflict organizations, ties were strong within the groups, but not between them (Nelson, 1989).

NEED FOR CONSENSUS Conflict may be a function of whether agreements are needed between the parties. For example, many organizational purchases are routine and require little interaction or agreement among departments, but consensus might be needed when purchasing items such as computers or office equipment that may be shared by many users. Conflicts over quality, cost, or location could occur when pressure for consensus exists.

STATUS DIFFERENCES AND INCONGRUENCE A classic analysis of status conflict was done in the restaurant industry (Whyte, 1949). For a variety of reasons, cooks believed they had higher status than waitresses. When waitresses communicated their customer orders to cooks, the cooks often reacted as if people of lower status were personally ordering them around. They often responded to the waitresses by delaying meals. In another study, engineers typically rejected innovative ideas from draftsmen because they felt it was the draftsmen's job to draw what they were asked to draw, not to be equal partners in the design process (Lawrence and Seiler, 1965).

Communication Communication is a two-edged sword. Barriers to communication can cause conflict, but so can the opportunity to communicate. We have seen how the need to interact can stimulate conflict. When we communicate with others, we may discover unfair conditions or begin to see other people as threats. This can start conflict that otherwise would have been avoided with less communication. In one study, conflict between departments was higher when departments were more knowledgeable about each other (Walton et al., 1969). If, for example, communication between departments leads to members of one department finding out that aspects of their work environment, such as pay or equipment, are inferior to that of another department, this can lead to conflict.

Ambiguous responsibilities When there is ambiguity about roles and responsibilities, conflict can arise when individuals or groups posture for position. In one organization, the advertising department took the initiative to locate and order various supplies on their own. The purchasing group accused them of overstepping their authority and violating procedures. This led to continuous conflict and the distractions eventually affected the quality and success of advertising.

Organizational Structure

When large numbers of people come together in an organization, many things can lead to conflict. These are rooted in roles and responsibilities, interdependencies, goals, policies, and reward systems.

Specialization and differentiation Organizations also create expectations that make cooperation difficult. The classic relationships between production, sales, and research units provide a good case in point. Each unit has its own responsibilities and concerns. Sales may concern itself with customers and competition. Production seeks cost reduction and efficiency. Research focuses on technical improvements with emphasis on scientific objectives. These factors sharply differentiate these units and can be the basis for many disagreements. Nevertheless, it is very appropriate for these units to have different priorities. As we said, some conflict is inevitable and healthy, even though it may be difficult to resolve.

The distinction between line and staff departments is also a basis for conflict. Line departments are those that are directly part of the organization mission, such as production departments. Staff units, such as human resources or legal departments, are indirectly involved and exist primarily to support and assist the line units. They often evaluate other units in the organization and develop new programs and procedures for them. Staff units also impose policies and procedures that line units may not understand or cannot accept. The problem is made worse because staff personnel, compared to line personnel, are frequently younger, better educated, and have fewer years of experience. Staff personnel may also use their own jargon, dress differently, and have direct access to organizational leaders.

GOAL SETTING Clear goals can be an excellent source of direction and motivation in organizations, but they do not ensure that conflict is minimized or prevented. Even when goals are clear, the method for achieving those goals may be a source of conflict. Managers all pursuing the same goals can seriously disagree over new products or services or whether to withdraw from certain markets.

Goals can also cause conflict within a single unit of an organization. For example, within a production department, efficiency goals can be incompatible with safety and maintenance goals. A production manager might run equipment at high speeds and reduce maintenance as a way of increasing productivity and reducing costs. This strategy can result in increased accidents and also an increase in long-run costs because poor equipment maintenance may cause them to break down sooner.

SCARCE RESOURCES Resources are almost always scarce in an organization, meaning that not enough exist to satisfy all the desire people might have. When resources are scarce, this may lead to conflict over the few resources that do exist. This engenders sharing of, and competition for, resources, either of which can create disagreements.

MULTIPLE AUTHORITY AND INFLUENCE Many organizations are designed so that each employee has only one superior. In management theory, this is known as the principle of **unity of command**. It is intended to avoid putting employees in a position where they receive conflicting demands from higher-level managers. Unity of command is difficult to maintain, because every employee is subject to many influences besides their immediate superior. A request from any high-level manager in our organizations is difficult for most of us to ignore. In addition, peers can influence a fellow worker. These multiple sources of input can create conflict within the individual.

POLICIES AND PROCEDURES One purpose of an organization's policies and procedures is to reduce conflict by clarifying roles and responsibilities and smoothing the interaction between people. For example, a policy may state that computer maintenance is the sole responsibility of a particular department. If computer problems or failures arise, disagreements about who is to fix it are then less likely to occur.

However, policies and procedures may contribute to conflict when they make people feel frustrated or insulted because they are overly controlled. Controls restrict our freedom and autonomy – something many of us value. We may feel a loss of trust and respect when controls are excessive.

REWARDS Disagreements commonly arise over how we are rewarded. Suppose you work as a medical claims adjuster for an insurance company and are told to provide good service and award claims appropriately without overpaying. When customers call with questions, you take the time to respond to them. When a claim is unclear, you contact the physician or hospital involved. At the end of each month, however, your supervisor tells you that you have not processed enough claims. You realize that to process more claims, you cannot continue to spend so much time talking to customers or clarifying information. You are experiencing tension over whether the quantity or the quality of your work is more important.

Diagnosing Conflict

Figure 10.4 introduces a framework for diagnosing conflict situations (Greenlaugh, 1986). When we attempt to understand the issues involved in a particular conflict situation, there are many dimensions of conflict that we should consider:

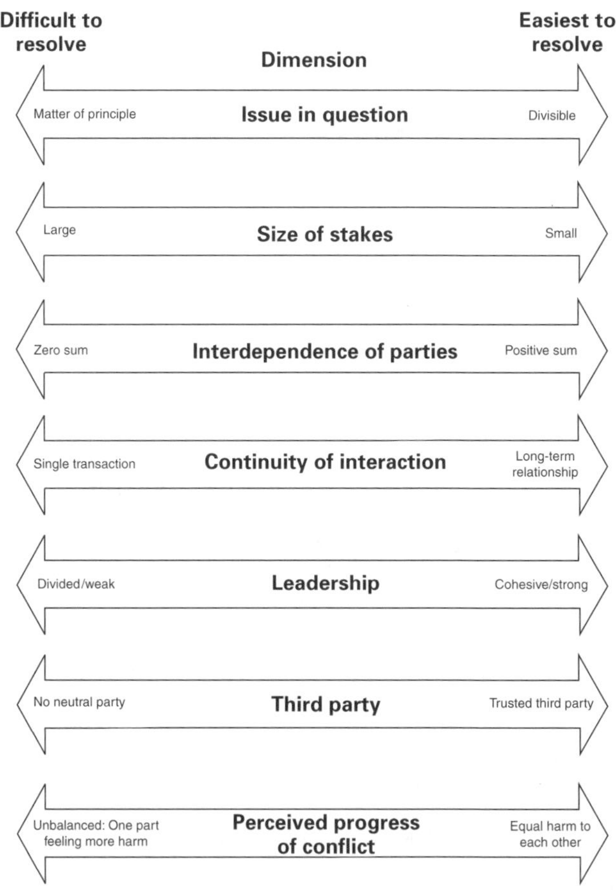

Fig 10.4: Conflict diagnostic model
Source: Adapted from Greenlaugh (1986)

- The issue in question
- The size of the stakes
- The interdependence of parties
- The continuity of the interaction
- The leadership
- The involvement of third parties
- The perceived progress of conflict

THE ISSUE IN QUESTION

Issues that are viewed by participants as matters of principle are the most difficult to resolve. In this case, participants have made the issue one where a possible conflict of values and beliefs systems is involved. Occasionally, participants in conflict make winning the focus and saving face becomes more important than the original issue. This significantly complicates conflict resolution. The easiest conflicts to resolve are those that are easily divided. This allows for compromises in positions so that both parties can view the outcomes as a partial victory at least. For example, if the issue is over a sum of money, compromise is possible because money can be divided.

THE SIZE OF THE STAKES

When the stakes in the outcome are large, conflict is more difficult to resolve than when smaller stakes are involved. As discussed earlier, organizations often experience conflict over budget allocations. The difficulty in resolving this type of conflict is often directly correlated with the proportion of budget that is being debated. If the proportion is considered by participants as large, it is likely that a great deal of debate will occur because the parties are more likely to view the large sums of money involved as important for achievement of their individual unit's goals.

zero-sum interdependence A conflict negotiation condition where a gain by one side means a loss by the other side

positive-sum interdependence A conflict negotiation condition where compromises are possible that would allow gains for both sides

THE INTERDEPENDENCE OF PARTIES

The interdependence of the parties is also an important dimension for diagnosing conflict. In **zero-sum interdependence**, a gain by one side means a loss by the other side. These are more difficult than **positive-sum interdependence**. This is where compromise settlements can lead to gains for both sides of the conflict. Continuing the example of budget negotiations, when finite budget amounts are available and sub-units are conflicting over their unit's share of the budget, it would be a zero-sum negotiation. An increase given to one unit would be at the expense of another.

THE CONTINUITY OF THE INTERACTION

A fourth dimension in diagnosing conflict is the continuity of the interaction among the parties in conflict. This considers the relationship among the parties. If we are talking about a conflict that has arisen between a firm and one of its long-term customers, it is likely that the conflict will be easier to resolve because both parties have an interest in protecting the long-term relationship. As a result, they may be more willing to seek compromise and may be interested in protecting the other side. When negotiations are between parties that have no previous relationship and have no plans for a future relationship, negotiation is likely to be more difficult.

The Leadership

The leadership of conflicting parties is another dimension to consider. When there is a clear leader who has the authority to negotiate and make decisions, conflict should be easier to resolve than when there is a lack of a clear leader. This issue is often evident in labor relation's negotiations. If the chief negotiator for management is not viewed as a party that can make decisions independently and that may be second-guessed by the board of directors or other senior members of the organization, it complicates negotiations. The same can be said for the labor side. When both sides in a conflict have strong leadership who can decisively negotiate an agreement, it increases the confidence of all parties that promises made will be kept and supported, and thus makes the conflict easier to resolve.

The Involvement of Third Parties

Using third parties such as mediators or arbitrators increases the ease of negotiating a resolution to the conflict. The role of third parties is discussed in more detail in the next section but their primary contribution is an objective view of the issues. Third parties may be able to see potential compromises that are not considered by parties who have a strong interest in the outcomes of the conflict negotiations.

The Perceived Progress of the Conflict

Finally, the perception of parties in conflict about the progress of the conflict is important in its resolution. When parties believe that both sides are compromising and giving up something of value, conflict is easier to resolve. When the perceptions of one party are that they have suffered more harm than the other party, they are likely to resist additional compromises until they feel things are more in balance.

Conflict Reaction Styles

Each of us deals with conflict in different ways. Some of us have an initial tendency to escape, and others of us are more prone to become involved. Once involved, people also vary in how they behave. There are five different styles of reacting to conflict, drawn from several important conflict theories (Blake and Mouton, 1969; Hall, 1969; Thomas and Kilmann, 1974; Filley, 1975):

1 Avoiding
2 Accommodating
3 Competing
4 Compromising
5 Collaborating

These five styles are set in a two-dimensional model shown in figure 10.5. The horizontal dimension reflects the degree to which one party has concern for the other party's needs, interests and goals. High concern reflects itself in cooperation and a desire to maintain the relationship. The vertical dimension refers to how concerned a party is for its own needs and goals. If you are high on this dimension, you are assertive, and your main desire is to achieve your own goals, with little or no sacrificing them. The five styles of conflict resolution are combinations of these two dimensions. Each style has different characteristics and different uses (Thomas and Kilmann, 1974; Thomas, 1977).

AVOIDING

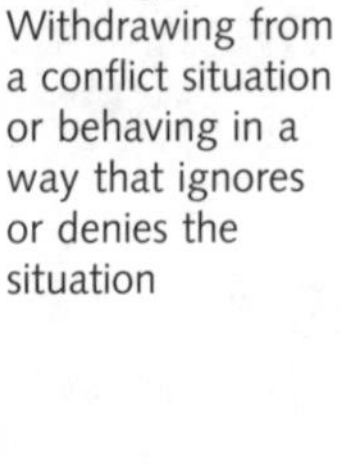
avoiding
Withdrawing from a conflict situation or behaving in a way that ignores or denies the situation

Some of us become emotionally upset by conflict. Painful memories of past conflicts may make us want to withdraw from disagreement. **Avoiding** conflict can be based on a belief that conflict is evil, unnecessary, or undignified. You can withdraw by simply leaving the scene of a conflict. You can refuse to become involved by using silence or changing the topic of conversation. Psychologically, avoiders can also deny the existence of conflict or ignore it when it arises.

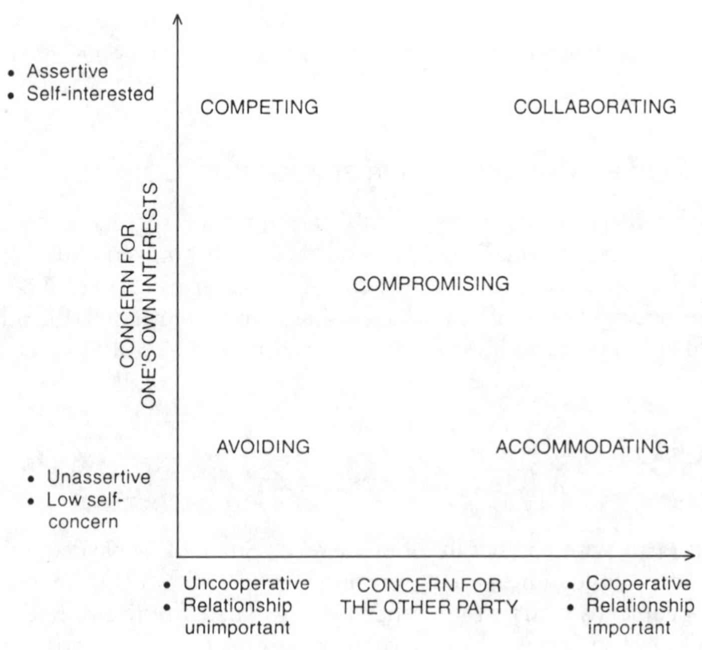

Fig 10.5: A model of personal stylistic reactions to conflict

Avoiding conflict can be wise when issues are insignificant or when the costs of challenging someone outweigh the benefits. It may also be useful when there is little chance of success. Why pursue a lost cause? Avoiding also buys time. It gives others a chance to cool down or to seek more information. Finally, it might be better to avoid conflict when others can resolve it more effectively or when it concerns the wrong issue.

ACCOMMODATING

Accommodating means you give in to the wishes of another person. Accommodators feel it is better to give up their own goals rather than risk alienating or upsetting others. Like avoiders, the value system of accommodators is a perspective that conflict is bad, but rather than avoid, they give in so as to keep or strengthen a relationship. This style can reflect generosity, humility, or obedience. An accommodator may also feel that selfishness, an undesirable trait, is what causes most conflict.

accommodating Giving in to the wishes of another person

Accommodation may be a very good strategy when you are in the wrong; it permits the correct position to win and is a sign of reasonableness. It can be taken as a gesture of goodwill and helps to maintain a relationship. Giving in may be a good thing to do when the issue is much more important to the other party. Fighting is not very productive when the other party has much to lose and you have little to gain.

COMPETING

If your style is to **compete**, you pursue your own wishes at the expense of the other party. The competitor defines conflict as a game to be won; that he or she is not about to become the loser. Competitors are both assertive and uncooperative. Winning means success and accomplishment; losing means failure, weakness, and a loss of status. Competitors will use many different tactics such as threats, arguments, persuasion or direct orders.

competing Pursuing your own wishes at the expense of the other party

A forceful position may be the best style in crises, when there is no time for disagreement and discussion. If the issue is simply not debatable, the manager may have to deal with opposition in a directive manner. As a manager, you may wish to use this style when unpopular but necessary decisions must be made, such as ordering that overtime work is necessary to meet a deadline for an important customer. Competition may also be a style to use when the other party has a tendency to take advantage of you. Competing serves as a way to protect yourself.

COMPROMISING

compromising Give-and-take based on the belief that people cannot always have their way, and trying to find a middle ground they can live with

If you use a **compromising** style, you give-and-take based on the belief that people cannot always have their way; you think you should try to find a middle ground you can live with. As a compromiser, you would look for feasible solutions and will use techniques such as trading, bargaining, smoothing over differences, or voting. You value willingness to set personal wishes and sensitivity to the other person's position. Through compromise, relationships can endure if people hear each other's point of view and if they try to arrive at a fair agreement.

Compromise is a common way of dealing with conflict. It may be a particularly useful technique when two parties have relatively equal power and mutually exclusive goals. Situations like this are zero-sum: what one party gains, the other loses. Compromise can also be useful when there are time constraints. Time may not be available for problems that require a great deal of effort to resolve all the issues. Compromise can allow for a temporary solution until more time can be devoted to unravel and analyze the complexities. Finally, compromise may be useful when collaboration or competition fails to lead to a solution between the parties.

COLLABORATING

collaborating
A willingness to accept the other party's needs, while asserting your own

Collaborating is a willingness to accept the other party's needs, while asserting your own. If you collaborate you believe that there is some reasonable chance a solution can be found to satisfy both parties in the conflict. Such a solution might not be possible, but a collaborator believes that it is worth trying to find one. For example, an organization planning to install a new computer system can use a collaborative approach. Different departments can join together to purchase the equipment or to design the system that meets various needs. Collaboration requires that both the parties express their needs and goals, and work diligently and creatively to generate all kinds of solutions.

Collaboration, therefore, requires openness and trust, as well as hard work. It follows the principles of good problem solving and decision making. Collaboration is useful when each party is strongly committed to different goals and when compromise is potentially very costly. It is also useful when people agree on goals, but disagree on means to achieve them. Collaboration can lead to an appreciation of other people's point of view. Therefore, it can strengthen relationships if mutual respect is maintained. When collaboration is successful, the commitment to the solution is high.

STYLE FLEXIBILITY: OVERUSE AND UNDERUSE

There can be harmful implications if any style is overused or underused (Thomas and Kilmann, 1974). Managers should be flexible enough to use a particular style when it best suits the situation. This would require a diagnosis of the conflict conditions, the selection of an appropriate style, and the ability and willingness to use different styles. Managers should be trained to diagnose and practice each style. Table 10.1 suggests that style flexibility would help to prevent the undesirable consequences of overuse and underuse.

Improving Your Conflict Management Style

conflict management
Strategies in which managers or others take an active role and intervene in the conflict episode

By **conflict management**, we mean that a manager takes an active role in addressing conflict situations and intervenes if needed. A variety of actions are possible,

EXERCISE

Conflict Handling Style

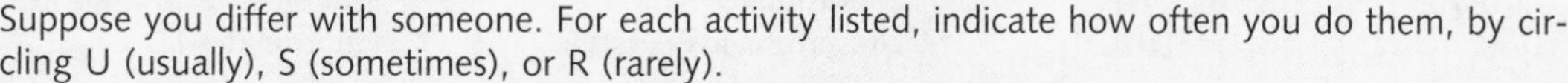

Suppose you differ with someone. For each activity listed, indicate how often you do them, by circling U (usually), S (sometimes), or R (rarely).

1	I explore our differences, not backing down, but not imposing my view either.	U	S	R
2	I disagree openly, then invite more discussion about our differences.	U	S	R
3	I look for a mutually satisfactory solution.	U	S	R
4	Rather than let the other person make a decision without my input, I make sure I am heard and also that I hear the other out.	U	S	R
5	I agree to a middle ground rather than look for a completely satisfying solution.	U	S	R
6	I admit I am half wrong rather than explore our differences.	U	S	R
7	I have a reputation for meeting a person halfway.	U	S	R
8	I expect to express about half of what I really want to say.	U	S	R
9	I give in totally, rather than try to change another's opinion.	U	S	R
10	I put aside any controversial aspects of an issue.	U	S	R
11	I agree early on, rather than argue about a point.	U	S	R
12	I give in as soon as the other party becomes emotional about an issue.	U	S	R
13	I try to win the other person over.	U	S	R
14	I work to come out victorious, no matter what.	U	S	R
15	I never back away from a good argument.	U	S	R
16	I would rather win than end up compromising.	U	S	R

Now, total your choices as follows. Give yourself 5 points for Usually, 3 points for Sometimes, and 1 point for Rarely. Then total your score for each set of statements grouped as follows:

Set A: Items l3–16
Set B: Items 9-12
Set C: Items 5–8
Set D: Items 1-4

You must treat each set of items separately. A score of 17 or above on any set is considered high; scores of 12-16 are moderately high; scores of 8-11 are moderately low; and scores of 7 or less are considered low.

Sets A, B, C, and D represent different conflict-resolution strategies:

A = Forcing: I win, you lose
B = Accommodation: I lose, you win
C = Compromise: Both you and I win some and lose some
D = Collaboration: Both you and I win

Everyone has a basic underlying conflict-handling style. Your highest scores on this exercise indicate the strategies you rely on most.

Source: Adapted from Von Der Embse (1987) and printed with permission from Macmillan Publishing Co.

Table 10.1 Style flexibility, overuse, and underuse of conflict reaction styles

Style	*Overuse: Using the style too much*	*Underuse: Using the style too little*
AVOIDING	Subordinates deprived of help Disagreements persist Coordination suffers Subordinates decide Issues are not raised	Stirs unnecessary hostility Subordinates lose independence Nonavoider is overburdened Failure to set priorities
ACCOMMODATING	Lose self-respect/recognition Deprive others of ideas Seen as indecisive, weak Burdens others excessively Others feel manipulated into reciprocating later	Seen as rigid, unreasonable Prevents goodwill Ignores exceptions to rules False sense of losing face when opposite may be true
COMPETING	Others avoid competitor Makes others repeated losers Cuts off information from others Subordinate reluctance to fight Subordinates give in easily	Lose self-esteem Feel powerless, controlled by others Relinquish decision making Avoid/accommodate too much
COMPROMISING	Others tire of "deals" Gamesmanship atmosphere Game becomes more important than the issues Merits of issues can be lost	Seen as rigid, unreasonable Trapped into dealing and power struggles Lose opportunities to ease tensions
COLLABORATING	Some problems not worth it Unnecessary when stakes are low Can block accommodating Vulnerability to manipulation by others	Lose mutual-gain solutions Unduly pessimistic Lose chances for creativity Lose subordinate commitment Lose team cohesiveness

Source: Adapted from Thomas and Kilmann (1974)

ranging from preventing conflict to resolving it (Tjosvold, 1986; Stulberg, 1987). Although avoiding conflict is a useful alternative, excessive avoidance can be very damaging to an organization (Argyris, 1986).

Figure 10.6 depicts three classes of ways to manage conflict:

1 Selecting and using one of the five styles discussed above
2 Confrontation techniques
3 Improving organization practices

Many people have a dominant style of dealing with conflict and rarely or never use more than one or two other styles. A manager would benefit by appreciating and learning to use all styles. This would broaden the manager's repertoire in coping with disagreements, and help to prevent the costs of overuse and underuse of styles.

CONFRONTATION TECHNIQUES

We are not naturally disposed toward cooperating in the face of disagreement. It takes a special effort on our part to overcome past habits and attempt collaborative approaches. These are often referred to as **confrontation techniques,** and require that parties in conflict decide to face each other on the issues, and

confrontation techniques
Call for the parties in conflict to face each other on the issues, but to do so constructively and peacefully so as to find mutually acceptable and longer lasting solutions

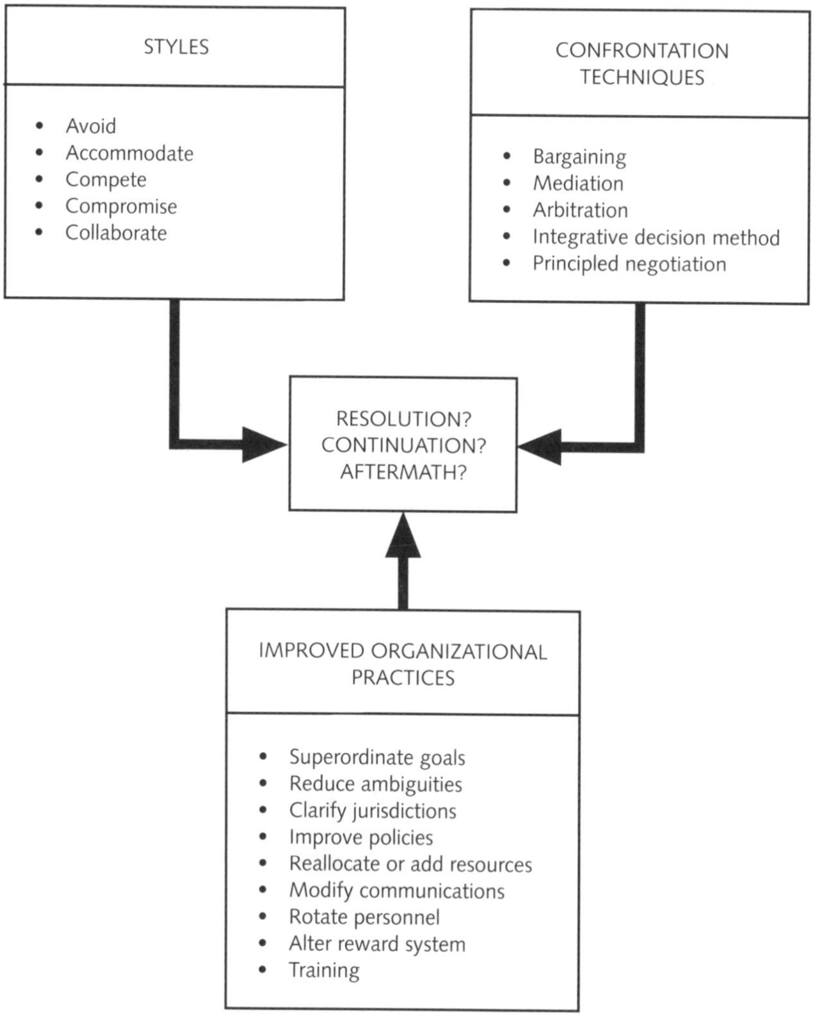

Fig 10.6: Conflict management strategies

do so constructively. The parties must be willing to work together to arrive at a consensus decision, one that both parties can accept. They do not avoid or give in. They may compete or compromise somewhat, but the major emphasis of confrontation techniques is to collaborate to find mutually acceptable and longer-lasting solutions. The aim is for both parties to satisfy their needs and goals to the greatest extent possible. Effective confrontation requires skill and experience and, above all, a positive and constructive attitude in which the parties are open to ideas and information.

In confrontation methods, third parties such as outside consultants or mediators from government agencies that offer such services are frequently used. Sometimes, they come from within an organization, usually from the personnel department. Sometimes, a specially trained manager can act as a third party in conflict resolution. As discussed earlier, the presence of a third party increases the chances of resolution. A third party can see to it that certain steps are followed, be a source of help and advice, make sure all opinions are heard, and assist in many process decisions, such as when to have the parties work separately. In some instances, the third party may even make critical decisions that are binding on the parties.

bargaining
When one person seeks to influence another through the exchange of benefits or favors

Bargaining is primarily a compromising style, but effective bargainers use a variety of techniques. They will occasionally act competitively and use force or threats. They will use accommodation, hoping that a concession on their part will stimulate the other party to concede a point in return. It is also possible for two parties to collaborate on some issues, jointly searching for a solution that is useful to both. One common use of bargaining in work organizations is when labor unions **negotiate** contracts.

negotiation
The process of compromise and bargaining to arrive at a solution to conflict

In many bargaining situations, the goal of each party is to obtain the most it can, often at the expense of the other party. As discussed earlier, one factor that influences this behavior is the continuity of interaction. If the relationship is not a long-term one, people may drive a very hard bargain. You may bargain hard when buying a car, assuming you can buy elsewhere if the bargaining fails. In a labor–management negotiation, though, bargaining is tempered by the fact that the parties must work together when it is over.

mediation
The use of third-party assistance to help arrive at a solution to conflict

Mediation is often used in labor–management negotiations, as well as many other social settings, such as an alternative to going to court (Foldberg and Taylor, 1985; Moore, 1986; McGillicuddy et al., 1987). The parties can use third-party assistance to arrive at a solution. The Federal Mediation and Conciliation Service provides experienced mediators to help with labor–management negotiations. If both parties agree, a mediator is called in. Mediators are not empowered to make decisions or impose a solution, but they use many techniques to resolve differences. They may make suggestions and monitor the interaction of the parties. They can ease tensions with their methods and add objectivity to the process.

arbitration
A third-party approach to conflict resolution, where arbitrators usually make decisions that bind both parties

Arbitration is another third-party approach to conflict resolution. Unlike mediators, arbitrators actually make decisions that bind both parties. Arbitrators are used predominantly in labor–management situations, such as when contract negotiations have reached an impasse. Another use is for grievances. The arbitrator hears both sides and may even follow a courtroom model. The points of view of both parties are presented. When the arbitrator feels he or she has heard enough, the arbitrator takes ample time to study the issues then makes a decision, binding on both parties.

Principled negotiation is based on a collaborative approach to problem solving. Table 10.2 outlines the elements of the technique and its four major requirements are highlighted. Principled negotiation is compared to "soft" and "hard" approaches to conflict resolution.

principled negotiation A collaborative approach to bargaining and conflict resolution; stresses problem solving and other techniques for mutual gain of the parties

- The soft approach is similar to accommodating and emphasizes giving in as a way to maintain a good relationship.

Table 10.2 The principled negotiation technique compared to soft and hard methods of conflict resolution

SOFT (relationship-oriented)	*HARD (goal-oriented)*	*PRINCIPLED NEGOTIATION (problem-oriented)*
Participants are friends	Participants are adversaries	Participants are problem solvers
The goal is agreement	The goal is victory	The goal is a wise agreement
Make concessions to cultivate the relationship	Demand concessions as a condition of the relationship	**SEPARATE THE PEOPLE FROM THE PROBLEM**
Be soft on the people and the problem	Be hard on the people and the problem	Be soft on people, hard on the problem
Trust others	Distrust others	Proceed independently of trust
Change your position easily	Dig in to your position	**FOCUS ON INTERESTS, NOT POSITIONS**
Make offers	Make threats	Explore interests
Disclose your bottom line	Mislead as to your bottom line	Avoid having a bottom line
Accept one-sided losses to reach agreement	Demand one-sided gains as the price of agreement	**INVENT OPTIONS FOR MUTUAL GAINS**
Search for the single answer: the one *they* will accept	Search for the single answer: the one *you* will accept	Develop multiple options to choose from; decide later
Insist on agreement	Insist on your position	**INSIST ON OBJECTIVE CRITERIA**
Try to avoid a contest of will	Try to win a contest of will	Try to reach a result based on standards independent of will
Yield to pressure	Apply pressure	Be reasonable; yield to principle, not pressure

Source: Reprinted from Fisher and Ury (1981) by permission of Houghton Mifflin Company

- The hard approach is similar to competing and emphasizes one party winning over the other.

Principled negotiation emphasizes the problem and tries to make the parties in conflict collaborate toward mutual gain.

There are four steps in principled negotiation:

1 *Separate the people from the problem*
Instead of blaming each other, the parties must share their perceptions and needs, and put themselves in each other's shoes. This reduces the effects of harmful emotions. They must allow each other to let off steam in an accepting way. **Active listening** is essential. The problem must be stated in a way that contains no accusations and does not deny the goals and values of the parties. It is better to say, "The problem is that we cannot agree on how to test the product," than "Your idea of a test is nonsense. We can't afford to do it!"

2 *Focus on interests, not positions*
Each party needs to state its interests and make its position explicit. For example, one party might say, "What I want is a product test that is thorough and realistic." The other party might say, "What I want is a product test that is feasible and done in a month." Focusing on interests legitimizes the expression of needs without demeaning the other party. In a subtle way, the expression of interests also focuses the parties on the problem and on the future, rather than on each other and the troubled past. Together, the parties are hard on the problem, but soft on each other.

3 *Invent options for mutual gain*
The parties jointly generate a number of possible solutions, avoiding premature evaluation that might resolve their disagreement. During this process, they may uncover additional interests. They can examine how much cost and risk they are willing to accept. Common interests can be identified as well. In this manner, options can be generated that are more sensitive to both parties' needs.

4 *Insist on objective criteria*
Eventually, the parties should evaluate the options. Objective criteria consistent with principled negotiation include fairness, workability, and the durability of the solution. The parties should openly ask, "Which solutions do you consider to be fair?" or "Let's identify those solutions that will work and that will be lasting." Solutions should also satisfy each party's interests as much as is possible.

Improving Organizational Response to Conflict

Earlier in this chapter, on page 285, why the organizational context itself might be the cause of conflict in the organization setting was discussed. You should know and understand these causes so you can take steps to try to change them.

Diversity Issues: So You've Increased the Diversity – Now How Do You Decrease the Conflict?

Most successful organizations are increasing the diversity of their work force in an effort to attract and retain the most talented employees available regardless of race, gender, religion or national origin. One impact of this trend is that this diversity of cultures leads to increased diversity of beliefs, attitudes, values and behaviors. These differences, if not properly managed, can increase organizational conflict.

An example of this issue comes from 3Com Corporation's factory in Chicago, Illinois. 3Com employs 1200 people in their factory and those employees represent a wide variety of cultures. 3Com employees speak 20 different languages and many have difficulty with English. The result is that communication is often difficult and this leads to many misunderstandings. The language barriers often provide challenges for individuals who provide training to 3Com's employees. As a result, 3Com relies heavily on pictures and drawings to provide directions to employees on procedures such as operating equipment. According to managers, pointing is also a frequently used method of communication.

Other issues that often lead to conflict at 3Com are customs such as when to say "please" or "thank you." Employees from some cultures seldom say please, and this often leads to hurt feelings. An additional source of conflict stems from the natural cliques that form among people from the same countries or cultures. These cliques are evident in the lunch room as well as on the factory floor where workers have some autonomy in their groupings. Within these sub-groups, members from the same cultures revert to speaking in their natural language – an understandable tendency – but one that leads to concerns by co-workers who do not understand the language. As a general practice, a language etiquette had developed so that if an outsider of the group is present, everyone tries to use English to communicate.

Despite an organization's efforts to increase the diversity of their work force, insuring the success of this effort requires active managerial involvement to make sure this new diverse work force works well together. Overcoming differences in values, attitudes, behaviors, and language are an increasing managerial challenge.

Source: Adapted from Aeppel (1998)

Setting Superordinate Goals

Goals should be set that draw units into collaborative efforts. The dean of a college of business can unite the accounting, finance, management, and marketing departments to work together in a fundraising campaign. If administrators, faculty, alumni and students meet together to plan the campaign, they can decide on how to approach different donors. Goals can also be set concerning how the campaign money will be used. The needs of the college can be integrated with the needs of each department to try to prevent conflict from erupting.

Reducing Ambiguities and Jurisdictional Disputes

There are many ways to decrease ambiguities. The goal-setting process is one of these. Clear and non-conflicting goals clarify responsibilities so that each employee and unit does not interfere or compete with the work of the others. Good job descriptions can also clarify duties and expectations so there is little dispute about whom is responsible for what. Reporting relationships can be clarified by preparing organization charts and discussing who has the authority to make certain decisions.

IMPROVING POLICIES, PROCEDURES, AND RULES

Policies, procedures and rules can often be improved to reduce conflict potential. One such case arose in the research division of a large equipment manufacturer. The scientists and engineers in this division often attended conventions and professional meetings to keep up to date, to present papers, and to work on problems with other scientists. Conflict repeatedly arose over attendance at these meetings. Some employees attended as many as five meetings, others only one. Complaints about fairness put many departments at odds with each other. A committee was established that prepared a fair policy to cover this situation. Costs were contained and conflict over the issues reduced.

REALLOCATING OR ADDING RESOURCES

When there is conflict that stems from resource sharing, personnel assignments, inventory flow and schedules can be reviewed to look for a creative resolution to the problem. In one factory, there was constant conflict between the maintenance department and the production supervisors over maintenance priorities. Favoritism and personalities dominated, and complaints were frequent. The production manager solved the problem by reassigning some maintenance employees to production units. Each production supervisor was given maintenance responsibility and now had the personnel resources to do it. Conflict was virtually eliminated and production delays were drastically reduced.

MODIFYING COMMUNICATIONS

One way to improve communication is to eliminate some of it. Recall the study of the restaurant industry cited earlier (Whyte, 1949). Cooks were resistant to "taking orders" from waitresses, whom they felt were of lower status. The problem was greatly reduced by requiring the waitresses to submit written customer orders and requests. Their orders were clipped to a rotating spindle from which cooks could select. The face-to-face interaction with the cooks was reduced, and so was conflict between them. In many of today's restaurants, orders are transmitted electronically to the kitchen.

ROTATING PERSONNEL

Rotating personnel through different departments helps them to develop a fuller understanding of each unit's responsibilities and problems. Then, when the employee returns to his or her original unit, a basis for cooperation exists. Rotation is often used with new employees.

Changing Reward Systems

The way rewards are administered may decrease the chances of conflict erupting. Managers can be reinforced with positive feedback and good performance appraisals when they promote harmony. Even financial rewards such as bonuses can be consistent with conflict reduction. In one factory, where heavy industrial machines were assembled, employees used to work independently on various tasks such as welding, bolting parts together, and wiring electrical circuits. They argued over assignments, space, and tools. Many saw no benefit in helping each other. Management decided to create work teams and supplied each with enough tools and workspace to eliminate the competition. To prevent further conflict between the teams, productivity and cost-savings bonuses were introduced. In a short time, teams began to help their own team members and offer assistance to other teams.

Providing Training

Many organizations conduct training programs in which employees learn to prevent, anticipate, and cope with conflict. They can assess their own conflict reaction style and learn how to use more than one style. They are given the chance to practice techniques of conflict resolution, especially the demanding confrontation techniques discussed above.

Summary

Since organizations involve so much interdependence between individuals and groups, conflict can easily arise and become a serious threat to organizational effectiveness. However, conflict – when managed properly – can be a healthy aspect of the organization. It can add to creativity, be a sign of health, and bring different points of view to the attention of decision makers.

Conflict, like other organizational behavior often has multiple causes. Certain individual characteristics may lead some of us to become involved in more conflicts than others. Occasionally, characteristics of the situation may make conflict more likely. In our organizations, conflict can arise as a result of many issues that just naturally occur in the workplace. When many diverse individuals work side-by-side in complex organizational structures with numerous goals and agendas, conflict is a natural outcome.

Resolving conflict is an important managerial role. While different managers may choose different styles of dealing with conflict, one thing is certain. Just as there are often multiple causes of individual conflict, managers should consider multiple methods to resolve that conflict. Focusing on organizational goals and structural aspects of the organization are effective means of understanding and eliminating conflict. In our Guide for Managers, we focus on five specific and practical approaches to conflict.

Guide for Managers: Managing Conflict Constructively

In addition to the approaches discussed above, here are a number of practical approaches for managing conflict in ways that will maintain the healthy conflict that allows organizations to maintain creative and innovative energy (Eisenhardt et al., 1997).

FOCUS ON THE FACTS

Many organizations have access to timely data from objective sources. However, it is common to allow discussions about opinions rather than fact to dominate discussions. Attempt to control discussion by challenging ideas and conclusions. Encourage managers to state up front if their comments are based on anecdotal evidence or on factual information.

CONSIDER MULTIPLE ALTERNATIVES

Rather than narrowing the focus to a small set of alternatives, it appears teams with less conflict consider more alternatives. Individuals often suggest an alternative that they may not agree with, in an attempt to increase the options available to the group and induce new ways of looking at existing alternatives (Eisenhardt et al., 1997) Multiple alternatives also may reduce polarization influences given there are more than two positions to consider.

CREATE COMMON GOALS

As discussed on page 286, when parties have conflicting goals, other types of conflict are sure to follow. If common goals can be introduced, it will more likely cause collaboration rather than competition. In chapters 8 (page 224) and 9 (page 270), we discuss the importance of goal clarity on team effectiveness. One reason teams that have no clear and common goals do not perform as well is because of the conflict that occurs.

USE HUMOR

Tension and stress are common byproducts of groups involved in decision making under pressure. It was found that teams that had higher conflict lacked humor in their process. Humor is also an important element in combating the effects of stress.

BALANCE THE POWER STRUCTURE

As with many issues, fairness is a key to acceptance of decisions. When there is a mismatch of power, higher tension is felt by individuals. Creating balance prevents one party from dominating the discussion and the decision process. When members feel that their input has equal value and possibility for acceptance, they are more willing to present their ideas. The openness of the process that ensues leads to higher willingness to the final decision and less conflict in the long run.

Key Concepts

STUDY QUESTIONS

1. Define and describe the various stages in the conflict process.
2. Describe a work situation you are familiar with in which you identify
   (a) preventable conflict conditions
   (b) inevitable conflict conditions, and
   (c) conditions where conflict is a sign of organizational health and effectiveness.
3. Show how individual characteristics and situational conditions operate as antecedents or causes of conflict.
4. Cite five organization structure conditions and show how each one contributes to the likelihood of conflict.
5. Describe the five major styles of reacting to conflict.
   For each one, show how and where it is particularly useful.
6. Which is your preferred style of conflict resolution?
   Which style do you use for backup?
   When do you switch from your preferred style to your backup style?
7. What are the implications of overusing a particular style of conflict resolution?
8. Which style(s) do you rarely use in dealing with conflict?
   What are the risks or costs of not using the style(s) enough?
9. Define and differentiate between the roles of arbitrators and mediators.
10. What are the four major guidelines suggested by the principled negotiation technique?
    Give an example of how to use each guideline.
11. Describe five organizational practices that might help to prevent or reduce the severity of conflict.

Case

Zack Electrical Parts

Bob Byrne's ear was still ringing. Byrne was director of the Audit Staff at Zack Electrical Parts. He had just received a phone call from Jim Whitmore, the plant manager. Whitmore was furious. He had just read a report prepared by the Audit Staff concerning cost problems in his Assembly Department.

Whitmore, in a loud voice, said he disagreed with several key sections of the report. He claimed that had he known more about the Audit Staff's work, he could have shown them facts that denied some of their conclusions. He also asked why the report was prepared before he had a chance to comment on it. However, what made him particularly angry was that the report had been distributed to all the top managers at Zack. He felt top management would have a distorted view of his Assembly Department, if not his whole plant.

Byrne ended the call by saying he'd check into the matter. So he called in Kim Brock, one of his subordinates who had headed the audit team for the study in question. Brock admitted that she had not had a chance to talk to Whitmore before completing and distributing the report. Nor had she really had a chance to spend much time with Dave Wells who headed the Assembly Department. However, Brock claimed it was not her fault. She had tried to meet with both Whitmore and Wells more than once. She had left phone messages for them, but they always seemed too busy to meet, and were out of town on several occasions when she was available. So she decided she had better complete the report and distributed it on time to meet the deadline.

That same day, Whitmore and Wells discussed the problem over lunch. Wells was angry, too. He complained that Brock had bugged him to do the study, but her timing was bad. Wells was working on an important assembly area project of his own that was top priority to Whitmore. He couldn't take the time that Brock needed right now. He tried to tell her this before the study began, but Brock claimed she had no choice but to do the audit. Wells remembered, with some resentment, how Brock was unavailable last year when he needed her help. The staff audit group seemed to have plenty of time for the study when he couldn't give it any attention. Whitmore said he would look into the matter, and agreed that they both had been unnecessarily raked over the coals.

- What were the causes and antecedents of the conflict between the staff audit group and the managers in the plant?
- Describe the conflict that arose in terms of the stages it went through.
- How can staff units work with line managers to minimize such conflict?

References

Aeppel, T. 1998: Babel at work. *Wall Street Journal*, March 30, A1.

Ancona, D. G. 1990: Outward bound strategies for team survival in an organization. *Academy of Management Journal*, 33(2), 334–65.

Argyris, C. 1986: Skilled incompetence. *Harvard Business Review*, September–October, 64, 74–9.

Blake, R. R. and Mouton, J. S. 1969: *Building a Dynamic Corporation through Grid Organization Development*. Reading, MA: Addison-Wesley.

Business Week 1997: Trench warfare in Detroit. *Business Week*, May 5. New York: McGraw Hill.

Cosier, R. A. and Dalton, D. R. 1990: Positive effects of conflict: A field assessment. *International Journal of Conflict Management*, 1, 81–92.

Eisenhardt, K., Kahwajy, J. and Burgeois III, L. J. 1997: How management teams can have a good fight. *Harvard Business Review*, July–August, 111–21.

England, G. W., Agarwal, N. C. and Trerise, R. E. 1971: Union leaders and managers: A comparison of value systems. *Industrial Relations*, 10, 211–26.

Filley, A. C. 1975: *Interpersonal Conflict Resolution*. Glenview, IL: Scott, Foresman.

Fisher, R. and Ury, W. 1981: *Getting to Yes: Negotiating Agreement Without Giving In*. Boston: Houghton Mifflin.

Foldberg, J. and Taylor, A. 1985: *Mediation: A Comprehensive Guide to Resolving Conflict without Litigation*. San Francisco: Jossey-Bass, Inc.

Greenlaugh, L. 1986: SMR Forum: Managing conflict. *Sloan Management Review*, Summer.

Hall, J. 1969: *Conflict Management Survey*. Houston, TX: Teleometrics.

Hickson, D. J., Hinings, C. R., Lee, C. A., Schneck, R. and Pennings, J. M. 1971: A strategic contingency theory of intraorganizational power. *Administrative Science Quarterly*, 16, 216–29.

Kojima, H. A. 1984: Significant stride toward the comparative study of control. *American Psychologist*, 39, 972–3.

Kumar, R. 1997: The troubled history of partition. *Foreign Affairs*, 1, 22–34.

Lawrence, P. R. and Seiler, J. A. 1965: Experiments in structural design. In P. R. Lawrence and J. A. Seiler (eds) *Organizational Behavior and Administration*, Homewood, IL: Richard D. Irwin.

Lawrence, P. R., Barnes, L. B. and Lorsch, J. W. (eds) 1976: *Organizational Behavior and Administration*, 3rd edn, Homewood, IL: Richard D. Irwin.

Leonard, D. and Straus, S. 1997: Putting your company's whole brain to work. *Harvard Business Review*, July–August, 111–21.

McGillicuddy, N. B., Welton, G. L. and Pruitt, D. G. 1987: Third-party intervention: A field experiment comparing three different models. *Journal of Personality and Social Psychology*, 53, 104–12.

Moore, C. 1986: *The Mediation Process*. San Francisco: Jossey-Bass.

Nelson, R. E. 1989: The strength of strong ties: Social networks and intergroup conflict in organizations. *Academy of Management Journal*, 32, 377–401.

Pondy, L. R. 1967: Organizational conflict: Concepts and models. *Administrative Science Quarterly*, 12, 296–320.

Pondy, L. R. 1969: Varieties of organizational conflict. *Administrative Science Quarterly*, 14, 499–506.

Stulberg, J. B. 1987: *Taking Charge/Managing Conflict*. Lexington, MA: Lexington Books.

Thomas, K. W. 1976: Conflict and conflict management. In M. D. Dunnette (ed.) *Handbook of Industrial and Organizational Psychology*, Chicago: Rand McNally, 889–935.

Thomas, K. W. 1977: Toward multidimensional values in teaching: The example of conflict behaviors. *Academy of Management Review*, 2, 484–90.

Thomas, K. W. 1990: Conflict and negotiation processes in organizations. In M. D. Dunnette (ed.) *Handbook of Industrial and Organizational Psychology*, 2nd edn, Palo Alto, CA: Consulting Psychologists Press.

Thomas, K. W. and Kilmann, R. H. 1974: *Conflict Mode Instrument*. Tuxedo, NY: Xicom.

Ting-Toomey, S., Gao, G., Trubisky, P., Yang, Z., Kim, H. S., Lin, S. L. and Nishids, T. 1991: Culture, face maintenance and styles of handling interpersonal conflict: A study in five cultures. *International Journal of Conflict Management*, 2, 275–96.

Tjosvold, D. 1986: *Managing Work Relationships: Cooperation, Conflict and Power*. Lexington, MA: Lexington Books.

Tjosvold, D. 1991: *The Conflict Positive Organization*. Reading, MA: Addison-Wesley.

Von Der Embse, T. J. 1987: *Supervision: Managerial Skills for a New Era*. Indianapolis, In: Macmillan Publishing Co.

Walton, R. E., Dutton, J. M. and Cafferty, T. P. 1969: Organizational context and interdepartmental conflict. *Administrative Science Quarterly*, 14, 522–42.

Weisz, J. R., Rothbaum, F. M. and Blackburn, T. C. 1984: Standing out and standing in: The psychology of control in America and Japan. *American Psychologist*, 39, 955–69.

Whyte, W. F. 1949: The social structure of the restaurant. *American Journal of Sociology*, 54, 302–10.

chapter 11

Decision Making

CHARACTERISTICS OF THE DECISION PROCESS

MODELS OF DECISION MAKING

IMPROVING INDIVIDUAL DECISION MAKING

IMPROVING GROUP DECISION MAKING

Preparing for Class

Using the Internet or your local library, search for discussions of major historical decisions that have affected the USA: Watergate, Bay of Pigs, American involvement in Vietnam, or any of the incidents discussed in this chapter. Consider these questions:

Are there common themes across these different decision contexts?

What went wrong with the decision-making process?

How much was "luck" a factor in the eventual outcome?

Think about problem solving in a group or organization with which you are involved. Consider these questions:

How are problems identified?

Who makes input on possible solutions to the problem?

How are decisions reached about how to resolve those problems?

By what criteria is the effectiveness of those decisions evaluated?

On her way into work one morning, Jean Morgan was reviewing her schedule for the day. As a CEO of a small but growing company that provides memory storage devices for computer systems, she knew her day was full of meetings. She also knew that she would not have additional time to review the material her staff had provided to help her to prepare for the day's activities.

Jean had a breakfast meeting with potential clients at 8.00 a.m. At this meeting, she was hoping to convince them to establish a long-term relationship to purchase memory storage devices from her company. At 9.00 a.m. she had a 30-minute meeting with her sales staff where she was supposed to give them her decision about a possible change from one supplier to a different one. "Well there's a $100,000 dollar decision that I should be more prepared to make," she thought. At 9.30 a.m. she had a meeting with her HR Staff to make the selections for this year's employee of the year, awards that would be presented in a company-wide luncheon meeting at noon. Before lunch she had to make several phone calls to clients who had experienced some shipping delays. Deciding how she should respond to their concerns was a difficult problem for her. They were valued clients and, while the shipping delays were not her company's fault, she wanted to demonstrate that her company was keen to resolve customer concerns.

Jean thought of the stack of reports her staff provided on the day's issues and that she had spent several hours the night before reviewing. She wished she had more time to consider all of the information available. There were the backgrounds of the clients she was having breakfast with, the proposals provided by her sales staff with their recommendations of which supplier they should choose, as well as the records and nominations of employees being considered for employee of the year. As her thoughts drifted to her afternoon schedule, she recalled her strategic planning meeting scheduled with the senior members of her staff. At this point, strategic planning sounded like a foreign concept. "I just don't have time to consider all the information that I should before making a major decision", she thought. "I don't need strategic planning – I need instant decision making!"

Jean Morgan's hectic schedule and desire for the ability to make instant decisions is a common theme heard from professional managers. Her decision-making environment is an important one to consider, especially for those who believe that organizational decision making is usually a rational, reflective process that is a significant aspect of a manager's day. The manager as a reflective, systematic planner and decision maker is folklore and myth (Mintzberg, 1975). The fact is that managers work at an unrelenting pace and that they are strongly oriented to action, not to reflection (Mintzberg, 1975). Many managers feel they cannot afford the luxury of long involved decision-making processes, as their environments became increasingly complex. Managers report spending more time making decisions than planning for those decisions. Modern business environments demand that they are able to process large amounts of information and balance the needs of multiple constituencies within an often very stressful environment. Little time is left for careful information gathering yet decisions made can be costly in terms of lives and money.

Several recent dramatic events provide insight into decision-making environments in complex information contexts. The 1977 Tenerife Air Disaster, the 1986 Challenger Disaster, and the 1994 "friendly fire" shoot down of two US Army helicopters by two US Air Force F-15 fighter aircraft over Iraq are all examples of how simple day-to-day decisions can converge with catastrophic consequences. As we discuss these cases throughout this chapter, what will become strikingly clear is that there are similar causal factors in each case.

What happened in the Challenger disaster? The Rogers Commission determined the direct cause that led to the deaths of seven astronauts was "a failure in the joint between the two lower segments of the right solid rocket motor" (NASA, 1986). However, the report also highlights four other important contributing causes that provide an interesting insight into the nature of decision making in high-pressure environments.

1 Serious flaws in the decision-making process
2 Launch constraints waived at the expense of safety without being reviewed by all levels of management
3 One organization within the space center having a propensity to try to deal with serious problems internally rather than communicating them to other decision-making levels in the organization
4 Reversal of an earlier decision by the management of a major contractor to recommend against the launch after pressure from a major customer

The Challenger example illustrates human decision-making situations with critical consequences. Like other cases discussed in the chapter, managers were confronted with numerous decision-making opportunities where there was information available that would have helped them make a decision that may have avoided the disaster. However, those opportunities were missed and key information overlooked because of some very common problems that occur in decision-making processes.

Of course, many decisions are not as complex or consequential as those highlighted in the Challenger situation. However, most are far from easy to make, and usually not fully effective. Just like Jean Morgan, as a manager, decision making is at the heart of your role. You make small and large decisions in every function you perform. Herbert Simon, Nobel Prize winner for his work on decision making, says that management and decision making are virtually the same thing (Simon, 1976). The consequences of poor decisions may affect many parties, including the decision makers themselves. Managers have even been held personally liable, and criminally charged for failure to meet social and legal responsibilities for worker safety (Garland, 1990).

In this chapter, we discuss problem solving and decision making. We describe characteristics of the process and explore individual and group decision making. Emphasis is given to the difficulties that arise and to methods for improving the process outlined in the model.

Focus on Stress and Decision Making: Disaster at Tenerife

The 1977 Tenerife air disaster demonstrates how very difficult it is to make effective decisions, especially when conditions are stressful (Weick, 1993). A KLM 747 struck a Pan Am 747 on takeoff and 583 lives were lost. Both planes were originally diverted to Tenerife because of a bomb explosion at their intended destination in the Canary Islands. The accident occurred when the KLM plane took off down the runway before the PanAm flight had been cleared out of the way. The decisions that culminated in the accident were negatively affected by the interruption of normal events for both flight crews and for the ground controllers. The difficult conditions of maneuvering jumbo jets at a smaller airport was made even more stressful by time pressures felt by the KLM captain to minimize his delay at Tenerife. Communications were such that information was lost or not processed appropriately. Messages were unclear or misunderstood, and narrowed perceptions diminished the capacity to cope with unfamiliar conditions. There was also a breakdown in coordination within the various teams, in which, for example, subordinates did not challenge or confront openly when the fateful take-off started.

Characteristics of the Decision Process

There are certain common characteristics to decision-making processes that are useful to consider. These are apparent in the catastrophic outcomes of decisions discussed in the introduction as well as in everyday decisions that we make within organizations.

Decisions within Decisions

Often we incorrectly focus on the final decision made as the result of a process. In many cases, the final decision is just one of several decisions that were made and which had a significant impact on the success of the outcome. In the Challenger disaster, there were a series of decisions that were important in both setting the stage for subsequent decisions but that also established a precedent. These are the decisions within the decisions. Decisions not to pass on concerns to higher levels of management. Decisions to stop consideration of alternative solutions at a premature point. Decisions made about key design issues on the space shuttle, many years before, were contributing factors to the eventual outcome.

Focus on Bad Information and Decision Making: Tragedy over Iraq

In April of 1994, two US Air Force jets accidentally shot down two US Army helicopters over northern Iraq. The incident resulted in the loss of 25 lives. In the accident investigation, many mistakes were found.

- Participants not following procedures established by joint agreement between the Army and the Air Force
- Failure of the helicopter pilots to have the correct electronic identification code entered into their on-board equipment
- Failure of the airborne surveillance aircraft to notify the US fighter pilots that there were two US helicopters in the area
- Misidentification of the US helicopters by the Air Force fighter pilots as Russian Hind helicopters commonly used by the Iraqi military.

Deeper investigation into this incident showed that while all of the information needed to identify the US helicopters was available, miscommunication, a reluctance to question information from others, a failure to follow and force others to follow established procedures and other "human errors" contributed to this tragedy.

Small Decisions Accumulate

The fact is that many decisions we make are trivial, or seem to be so, and are made very quickly. Yet the consequences of a series of small decisions can accumulate into a serious problem. In the helicopter situation in Iraq, the air traffic controllers on board the surveillance aircraft decided to allow the army helicopter to stay on a different radio frequency than the one they were required to be on. The helicopter pilots decided not to dial in the correct electronic identification since they were already talking to the controlling aircraft overhead. An equipment failure on the surveillance aircraft led the commander to decide to separate the controllers responsible for monitoring the activities within the area which impaired their communications. None of these decisions alone can be considered the "cause" of the catastrophe, but when it was coupled with misidentification of the US helicopters as Iraqi by the F-15 pilots, the combined effect was disastrous.

This characteristic is evident in even more common organizational situations. Picture an employee who postpones a call to a customer so as to arrive home on time. Another employee overlooks a detail on that customer's order because he has a headache. Later, a shipping clerk leaves the order off a truck rather than make an extra effort to load it. Taken together, these minor decisions can add up to the loss of a major account.

DECISIONS ARE PARTIAL OR TEMPORARY SOLUTIONS

It is almost impossible to prevent errors in decision making. Most decisions, therefore, never completely solve a problem. Even if they come close, the solution often contains seeds of new problems requiring attention. Since decisions are imperfect; they are partial solutions. This means that it is necessary to follow up on important decisions and to be prepared to modify them.

Models of Decision Making

rational or normative models of decision making
Models that attempt to show how people should make a decision and they assume that decision makers apply a carefully applied set of criteria or rationale for their decisions

administrative decision-making model
A model which attempts to provide a more accurate picture of how managers deal with routine and nonroutine problems

There are different ways, or models, for thinking about decision making. Attempts to show how people should make a decision are called **rational or normative models of decision making.** These models are called rational because they assume that decision makers apply a carefully applied set of criteria or rationale for their decisions. They assume the process is rational as well. The term normative is because these models are based on observation of the actual errors that decision makers tend to commit. Certain errors are very common, and, in normative models, an attempt is made to prevent or reduce them.

Perhaps you think the rational model of decision making is inconsistent with the thoughts of Jean Morgan that were introduced at the beginning of the chapter. Her comments suggest that many decisions are not made using the rational process outlined above. The **administrative decision-making model**, a second approach to decision making, was developed by Herbert Simon in an attempt to provide a more accurate picture of how managers deal with routine and nonroutine problems. It also incorporates human tendencies into the process – tendencies that often lead to poorer quality decisions.

THE RATIONAL OR NORMATIVE MODEL OF DECISION MAKING

Normative models are also called rational or economic models (Etzioni, 1967; Miller and Starr, 1967; Simon, 1976, 1977). They have several characteristics (Janis and Mann, 1977). A decision maker should adhere to them even though human abilities and the availability of information put limits on what can be done. Figure 11.1 provides steps that are commonly considered important in the rational decision-making model.

In the rational model, decision making usually begins with a judgment that a problem exists or a change is needed. Sometimes the problem is an uncomfortable or negative condition you want to eliminate, such as a stoppage on a production line. A problem can also exist when you set a goal, because a goal also represents a desire to improve on a current condition. A manager setting a sales goal considers the new sales level preferable to its present level. The problem is how to attain the new sales goal.

Once a problem is recognized and defined, alternatives are sought that could eliminate the negative condition or achieve the goal. Alternatives are activities that you believe will lead to a better state of affairs. When you generate alter-

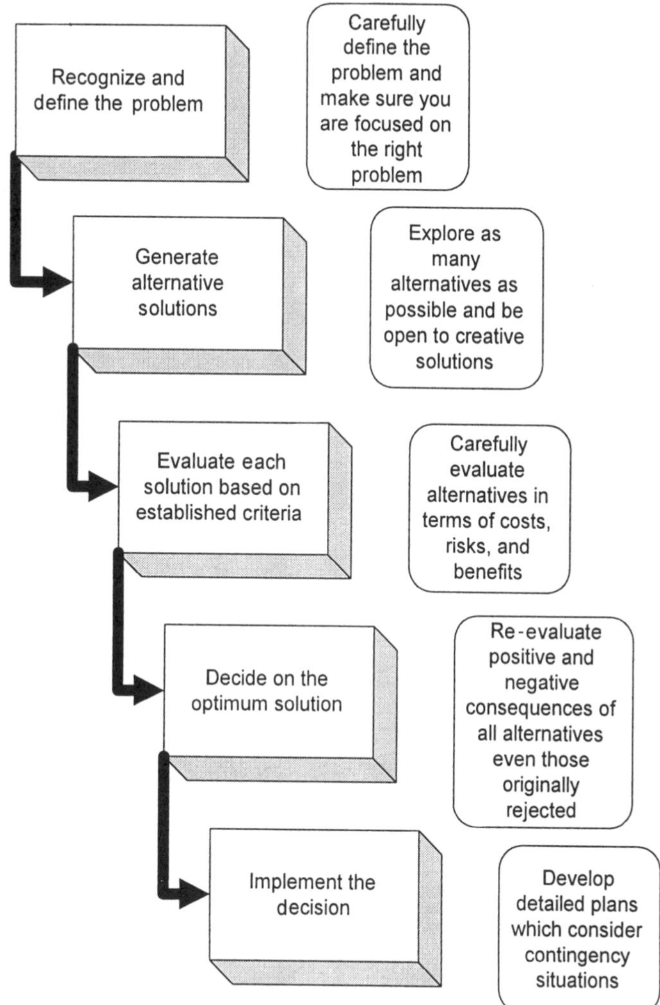

Fig 11.1 : Rational model of decision making

natives, you make assumptions or predictions that certain outcomes will follow. The relationship between alternatives and their outcomes is not a simple one. One alternative can result in a single outcome or several outcomes, or more than one alternative could be required to achieve a single desired outcome. Some outcomes are intended, while others are unintended side-effects of the alternative. For example, a total effort to win a ball game can cause unintended injury to a player who takes some unnecessary risks.

To choose among alternatives, you have to use criteria to evaluate them. Among the most common criteria used are feasibility, time, cost, and personal acceptability. Criteria will usually vary from person to person, and it is not always clear what criteria are being used. Eventually, however, choices are made among alternatives. Once the choice is implemented, it becomes possible to evaluate once again. Here the evaluation can uncover faulty implementation or reveal that errors were made at an earlier stage of the decision process.

The normative approach is prescriptive for managers who wish to improve their approach to decision making. To optimize decision quality, the normative approach requires that you follow these steps.

1 Explore a broad range of alternative courses of action.
2 Survey all possible objectives sought and the values relevant to the choice to be made.
3 Carefully evaluate the positive and negative consequences in terms of costs, risks, and benefits.
4 Search further for new information to evaluate alternatives further.
5 Account for new information and inputs, even when it might not support a preferred course of action.
6 Re-evaluate positive and negative consequences of all known alternatives, even those originally judged unacceptable, before making a final choice.
7 Develop a detailed plan of implementation, including contingency plans to handle risks or new problems should they arise.

Later in this chapter, we discuss ways to improve each one of the steps; see page 316.

The Administrative Model of Decision Making

Researchers who study what managers actually do have questioned the usefulness of normative models. They suggest that the process is much less systematic than the rational process suggests (Simon, 1957; March and Simon, 1958). Two key concepts form the basis for the administrative model of decision making: bounded rationality and satisficing.

bounded rationality
A theory which proposes that decision makers are limited in their ability to be rational because of limits of human abilities, information, money, and time

Decisions are made with **bounded rationality**. This means that decision makers are able to recognize only a limited number of alternatives and are aware of only a few consequences of each alternative. Human abilities are fallible and limited, information is never perfect, and money and time add limits as well. These contextual constraints place pressures on managers to circumvent the rational decision-making process by making decisions more efficiently.

In the PREPARING FOR CLASS section on page 307, we asked you to think about how the group or organization you are familiar with resolves problems. We want to focus specifically on routine problems. Often, in response to problems, organizations will begin a search for "fixes" to that particular problem. This will often result in the introduction of a new "program" which focuses on the most easily identified (or accepted) cause of the problem. When these routines and programs exist, decision makers need not generate a large listing of alternative responses to a problem and perhaps do not even consider alternative definitions of the problem. Pressures due to cost and time may limit the number of options decision makers want to consider. Instead, as alternatives are suggested, they are compared to a set of minimally acceptable criteria. The first alternative that meets those criteria is selected. This process is called **satisficing.**

satisficing
The tendency to accept the first alternative solution that satisfies the established minimally acceptable criteria

Suppose, for example, that, as a manager, you are dissatisfied with the quality of performance appraisals in your department. It would take considerable time and effort to uncover and define elements of this problem. It would also be a major effort to review alternative appraisal systems and thoroughly evaluate each one. Many complications would arise, and many questions would be unanswerable. This is a situation in which some information is unavailable. Alternatives are not easy to identify and are difficult to select. Your ability to be rational is limited by these complexities, and your decisions will be imperfect. In this situation, there are many opportunities to satisfice, such as choosing a rating form that looks quite adequate rather than comparing the form to all possible alternatives.

THE GARBAGE CAN MODEL OF DECISION MAKING

Many forces in organizations complicate decision making. For example, problems are redefined and decisions modified as different people become involved in the process over time. Even with normative approaches, organizational forces will have an effect. One approach to understanding organizational decision making that considers these effects is the **garbage can model**, or organized anarchy (Cohen et al., 1972). The garbage can decision process consists of four elements:

garbage can model
Decision-making model for complex organizations; based on the flow of people, problems, solutions, and opportunities

1 The participants with their various priorities
2 Problems to be solved
3 Solutions to be chosen and applied
4 Decision opportunities

The participants in complex organizations are the many decision makers with different goals and problems. They have limited time and energy, and cannot involve themselves in all decisions. So their involvement depends on their individual needs, goals, and availability. The participation of decision makers can be direct in that they are directly involved or responsible for resolving the problem. Alternatively they can be indirectly related to the decision and can influence outcomes. One example of this would be the role of a supervisor who provides "input" to a subordinate about a decision she or he is about to make. Decision makers may also vary in the priority with which they view the problem. Consider what occurs within cross-functional teams, i.e. teams whose members come from different functions within the organization. While members may bring more ideas and perspectives to the discussion of the problem, they can also bring a different and perhaps competing set of priorities.

Within the decision context, various participants may view the problems differently or may, in fact, be actually working on a different set of problems. They also have ideas they would like to see adopted. Sometimes these ideas are solutions in search of a problem, rather than a problem in search of a solution. For example, a manufacturing manager might want some new equipment he saw at a trade show. He will be sensitive to decision opportunities that will allow him to buy it. Thus, goals are established to justify decisions already made rather than the reverse.

Timing is also an important element in this model. The organization is viewed as a fluid structure in which people, problems, and solutions flow together and apart at different times. Decisions result from a disorderly convergence of these elements, heavily determined by patterns of timing and opportunities (March and Weissinger-Baylon, 1986).

The garbage can model is most likely to operate when goals are ambiguous, methods for achieving goals are not well understood, and organizational units are scattered and loosely linked together. This model is also more likely to operate when an organization has many departments, committees, and task forces, each with vague or overlapping responsibilities. It is also likely to appear in a decision environment with multiple participants representing multiple subunits with varying responsibilities and loyalties.

Focus on Decision Making: Choices in the "Garbage Can"

Let us consider the issues related to the friendly fire shoot down and how the Garbage Can model elements play out. There were numerous participants within the context each with various priorities and problems to be solved. The helicopter pilots had on-board dignitaries and were most certainly worried about protocol issues. The airborne surveillance crew was dealing with the problem of a nonfunctioning console. The F-15 pilots encountered unexpected aircraft within the area and were concerned about the safety of civilians on the ground whom they were supposed to protect. There were numerous potential solutions to be chosen and applied. Using the correct identification codes, recognizing the existence of two friendly helicopters and passing that information on to the F-15 crews and numerous other decisions were available. Finally, there were many decision opportunities within this context. Decisions to allow violation of established procedures, decisions about which codes to dial into the electronic equipment, decisions about recognizing the make of aircraft based on visual observation.

Improving Individual Decision Making

As we look at individual decision making, we can describe how people typically behave, including the errors they make. Once we understand these behaviors, we can turn to ways to improve your individual decision making. Thus, while this discussion follows the steps in the rational process, it provides equally useful ideas for dealing with issues suggested by non-rational models of decision making as well. Many of these decision-making concepts are also used later to discuss the process as it occurs within groups; see page 324.

FACTORS THAT INFLUENCE THE DECISION-MAKING PROCESS

Your values, attitudes, personality, and perception enter the decision process in all of its stages. They affect what you perceive to be or not to be a problem. Beliefs and attitudes enter into the evaluation of alternatives and during implementation. Overall, decision making is an exercise of values. Human biases emerge as you define problems, set goals, and make choices. Group decision making often involves a clash of values and an attempt to resolve differing points of view.

Diversity Issues: How Gender Changes the Decision-Making Process for Promotions

A recent study of corporate decision-making dynamics suggests that, despite an organization's objective to increase the diversity of senior management, aspects of the decision process can undermine those objectives. A study prepared by the Center for Creative Leadership led to some disturbing findings. One study finding was that male decision makers made promotion decisions about male candidates based on perceived comfort level with the person. Promotion decisions about female candidates were made based on their tenure in the lower position. Managers felt more comfortable keeping women in positions longer so that they could ensure they were ready for the higher position. The results of this type of decision process is that women do not move as quickly as men into positions of higher responsibility. This, of course, leads to frustration for women as they see male peers promoted at a faster rate and can subvert an organization's attempt to become more diverse.

These biases are subtle, but critical, components of individual decision making and can have important organizational consequences. The authors of this study suggest that these biases must be made visible and become a topic of discussion among decision makers. One way to assess current organizational practices is to track decision results carefully. Fair decision practices should be reflected in relatively equal promotion rates for men and women. Other factors, such as the retention of women, can provide important clues about the perceived fairness of decision processes. When discrepancies are found, it is important to make decision makers discuss their decision strategies including assumptions, stereotypes, criteria and other factors relevant to the process. Decision makers can often be unaware of how certain assumptions can lead to biases that lead to an unfair decision. Once this discussion occurs, organizational practices should be established that provide training for managers to improve their decision making processes and managers should be held accountable for insuring their decisions are consistent with organizational policies and objectives.

Source: Adapted from *HR Magazine* (1997)

Decision making can be a stressful process and cause considerable anxiety, in part because we are all reluctant decision makers. In one Peanuts cartoon, Linus said to Charlie Brown, "No problem is so big or so complicated that it can't be run away from!" (Janis and Mann, 1977). Not surprisingly, people do not always deal systematically with an important decision. They might overreact and plunge headlong and headstrong into it. They might also show great resourcefulness in avoiding the decision. When facing complex and difficult choices, where the costs and benefits are high, emotion can dominate over reason.

IMPROVING PROBLEM SELECTION AND DEFINITION

As managers, someone else often makes us aware of a problem. This can result in us spending considerable time and resources towards resolving a problem that may, in reality, not exist or that may be a symptom of a larger problem. That is why problem selection and definition are so important to this process.

ISSUES IN PROBLEM SELECTION AND DEFINITION The choice of which problems to work on and the definition of a problem both provide a chance for errors in decision making. Here are some common errors in recognizing, choosing, and defining problems:

1 Biases in our perceptions make us aware of some problems and unaware of others. We block out or ignore problems based on our needs, values, and personalities.
2 Event sequences dictate what we select to work on. Problems are often dealt with in the order in which they arise.
3 Problems we perceive as emergencies and problems we feel are solvable take priority over other problems.
4 We tend to be overly reactive. Given a choice between reflective planning and action taking, we will usually take action.
5 Problems are often poorly defined. Definitions may be inaccurate, incomplete, and not creative.
6 The way we define a problem may lead to a built-in solution that takes the focus away from the problem itself.
7 We often leap to solutions long before the problem is even moderately well defined.
8 Problem definitions are often stated in a way that threatens others.

IMPROVING PROBLEM SELECTION AND DEFINITION A number of steps can be taken to prevent problem selection from being dominated by our perceptions or by the order in which problems happen to arise. The first is to recognize that nothing is a problem until someone calls it that. A problem is nothing more than a personal, subjective conclusion that things are not the way they ought to be. It might be wise, therefore, to check out our perceptions with others before concluding that a problem exists that is worth taking action upon.

Problem selection can also be improved if you make lists of problems and prioritize them. One technique for doing this is to scan and monitor the environment periodically for both problems and opportunities. This may identify conditions that need attention, such as a drop in product quality or new market opportunities.

Value clarification is a process by which we express and clarify the particular values that we hold, especially when they may impact a particular decision. For example, suppose you are considering introducing a new product and you personally value innovation and believe a new product is needed. Others, however, more highly value the reliability and reputation of existing products. Value clarification can lead you in any number of directions. You could seek value consensus, or they might choose to exploit diverse values by working on both new and old products.

Improving problem definition Several things can improve problem definition. The first is to work toward a thorough definition. A second is to avoid the tendency to jump prematurely into solutions before the problem is completely defined. The third comes into play if you fail to do one of the first two. That is, if you have a solution in mind, ask yourself to link that solution back to some aspect of the problem. In other words, when a solution occurs to you, ask yourself how it relates to the problem at hand. This forces you to go back to the problem definition rather than develop the solution. Improving problem definition can help you to obtain and use facts and information that are less ambiguous. When information is ambiguous, managers are more prone to react to threats and to ignore opportunities.

One way that you can provide a better definition of a problem is to determine its causes. Investigate any events that might be related to the problem. Is there a pattern to the occurrence of the events? Does the problem occur at consistent times or within consistent situations?

Many problems can be creatively defined. There is a story that, years ago, the military was looking for ways to improve the efficiency of jet engines on aircraft. The problem was defined by the military as how to burn a higher percentage of fuel in the combustion chamber so that less fuel passed through unburned. Supposedly, a teenager at an air show asked an official why they did not recover the unburned fuel and ignite it rather than try to burn more of it in the first place. The problem was redefined. It became how to catch unburned fuel and how to burn it. Jet engines soon had afterburners that dramatically increased their fuel efficiency.

Improving Generating and Evaluating Solutions

The normative model tells us to generate, explore, and examine all possible solutions in a thorough and exhaustive manner, and to estimate the probabilities and values of all possible outcomes. Methods and criteria are established for evaluating and comparing alternative solutions.

Issues in improving generating and evaluating solutions Even when extensive efforts are made to do this, errors creep in:

1 Alternative solutions are evaluated prematurely. We tend to react positively or negatively to an idea as soon as it arises.
2 Because we evaluate solutions prematurely, idea generation is curtailed. An incomplete set of possible solutions is generated because evaluation works against generation of alternatives. Satisficing is one result.
3 We do not use the definition of the problem as a source of additional solution ideas.
4 A variety of blocks interfere with our search for a solution (Adams, 1974). Perceptual blocks put blinkers on our creative thinking, social and cultural values limit our thoughts, and patterns of thought keep us in mental ruts.

5 We often fail to make our evaluation criteria explicit before using them to judge alternatives. Sometimes we are not even aware of the criteria ourselves.
6 It is difficult to deal with both the value of a solution and the probabilities associated with it. Both are important, but we may ignore one or the other. In other words, if a solution is high risk, we may ignore its value and potential.
7 Emotions can lead to self-deception. We can psychologically rationalize or justify an alternative we strongly prefer.
8 We sometimes rush into making a decision when there may be no need to do so. All we need to do is ask whether postponing a decision could have some benefits.

IMPROVING SOLUTION GENERATION The way in which solutions and ideas are generated makes all the difference in the effectiveness of our decisions. Here are some techniques that you can use to assist in the process.

One important practice is to separate idea generation from idea evaluation. This suggestion is based on the idea that when you evaluate an idea, you cut off the generation of other ones. A positive evaluation is more harmful than a neutral or negative evaluation. If you are neutral toward, or dislike an alternative solution, you have an incentive to generate another one, but if you like an alternative, you might stop your search right there.

brainstorming
A technique of idea generation in decision making that requires we let our minds run free and avoid evaluating what we say or think

Brainstorming requires that you let your mind run free and avoid evaluating what you say or think and do the same for others (Osborn, 1957). All ideas are considered valuable. Using other people to generate additional ideas can often be well worth the effort. First of all, more ideas will result. More importantly, perhaps, these others may not suffer the same perceptual or experience blocks as we. As a matter of fact, lack of experience with the problem may be an advantage. In decision making, experience can work for or against you. It is useful for evaluation, but it puts limits on your ability to see a problem from different perspectives.

bounded discretion
Self imposed moral and ethical limits we put on our decisions

Social and cultural blocks are also difficult to overcome. In fact, we may not wish to ignore values that put moral and ethical limits on our decisions. These limits, referred to as **bounded discretion**, operate in all of our decisions, directly and indirectly (Shull et al., 1970). Robbery to solve a money problem or fraud to save a company might be alternative ways to solve a problem. While bounded discretion is a critical component of behaving ethically, occasionally considering outrageous solutions may spin highly creative ones.

Managers need to be aware of the mental models they use (Senge, 1994). These are assumptions and generalizations about how the world works that affect how we react to that world. These models may also affect our approach to problem resolution. Many of us tend to view problems in terms of linear relationships (Senge, 1994). When looking for causes of problems, we look for the action that occurred immediately preceding the problem surfacing. We then assume causality and go about focusing on a factor that may not be the cause or that may be unrelated to the problem at all. The key is understanding the relationships that exist and our assumptions about those relationships.

IMPROVING SOLUTION EVALUATION Eventually every idea has to be tested. First, it must pass your mental and emotional scrutiny. You can, in some cases, try ideas out before full commitment is made. These tests can take many forms, such as further discussions, computer simulations, or the full-scale construction of a test model, as is done with airplanes.

Another step can be taken to organize alternatives into different clusters before evaluating them. Suppose a manager is deciding how to reduce plant accidents. Alternatives might fall into distinct categories, such as machinery improvements, changing work hours, employee training, and so forth. These clusters may then be evaluated for easier decision making.

Another often overlooked step, is to establish criteria to use for evaluating alternatives. Criteria are not easy to establish, but doing so and making them explicit can help decision making immeasurably. Criteria can then be weighted by importance before the process goes further.

Applying criteria to alternatives can be very complicated. For example, suppose you were looking for a job and salary is one of your criteria. If a job is lacking in that criteria, it is eliminated; for example, jobs that fall below a certain salary level are eliminated regardless of how well they meet other criteria. Another complicating factor can be introduced by considering probabilities: lower-probability events would carry less weight. A number of decision-making techniques apply both probabilities and values.

Solution evaluation is also improved if you know your personal tendencies. Some people take more risk and are more oriented toward seeking success. They are more likely to ignore what can be lost, and rather than protect themselves against losses, they will choose alternatives to maximize gain. Others will avoid the risks of maximum gain and will seek smaller but safer gains. Others may focus on losses rather than gains: their main motivation is to prevent losses, even if it means losing the chance at gaining something. This is a failure avoidance strategy and leads to conservative decision making.

Improving Decision Implementation

Some decisions are implemented easily once we have made a decision. Even a complex decision can have a simple implementation. For example, a company might consider many factors in deciding whether to buy from a particular supplier. Once one is selected, an order can be easily placed. Other decisions may require more complicated implementation. Consider the case of a company that decides to expand into a new product line. The decision is just the beginning of a long process. Hundreds of new problems will have to be solved to prepare the new product. The long and detailed process from design to production, to sales and distribution of the product, will require attention.

The ease of implementation will depend on how often we have implemented a decision in the past. If we have been through it many times, implementation can be a routine matter. However, we are often in new territory when we carry out a decision, and when this is the case, we are always faced with new problems requiring new decisions.

post-decisional dissonance
The anxiety experienced by decision makers that occurs after they have made a decision and that causes them to question the decision and the information upon which it is based

Problems in implementation **Post-decisional dissonance** can impede implementation of a solution. After a decision has been made, people may waver and hesitate. As the decision is executed, anxiety can overcome good judgment. The decision maker can become extremely cautious and overly vigilant. Feelings of regret can set in. Minor setbacks can become signals of concern and evoke new uncertainties about the original decision.

Perceptual errors and cognitive dissonance can also follow a decision. If people are positively disposed toward a decision, they may ignore information that suggests the decision is not working and interpret events to support their original choice. In terms of cognitive dissonance theory, people are motivated to reduce feelings of dissonance. Suppose you strongly favor a particular solution, but information that is unfavorable to your choice creates dissonance in your mind. It is likely to be ignored or distorted to support your original choice. The opposite can happen if you were opposed to a decision. Information favorable to that decision may be distorted.

escalation of commitment Occurs when managers stick with a decision they made even when it appears to be a bad decision

People make decisions and sometimes stick to them over time, even if they are bad decisions. This is called **escalation of commitment** (Staw, 1981; Whyte, 1986). People become trapped or locked into a course of action for several reasons (Staw, 1981; Staw and Ross, 1987a). They resist admitting they made an error so as to appear competent or consistent; they can save face by holding to their original position. They may feel that changing their position will be viewed as a sign of weakness and make them more vulnerable to criticism or exploitation. People may also feel that their original decision was a good one that will contribute to an improved situation. Escalation of commitment can then occur, such as when people pour money into a failing business or when they refuse to admit they are wrong in an argument. Escalation can be a potentially costly behavior if you are wrong (Staw and Ross, 1987b). In some situations, escalation of commitment may decrease or be less likely:

1 The resources to stay with the decision are depleted.
2 The responsibility for the bad decision is shared or when people feel that more than one person was the cause.
3 The evidence is strong that negative things will continue to happen (Garland and Newport, 1991; Whyte, 1991).

Global Focus on Escalating Commitment in Asian Managers

One recent study focused on whether the phenomena of escalating commitment, which has received a lot of empirical support with North American managers, could be found in the behavior of Asian managers (Sharp, 1997). The research hypothesized that Asian managers would be less likely to pursue losing courses of actions when the information about those actions was framed in a negative way. As predicted, the Asian managers chose to not escalate their commitment to the projects when faced with negative information. This suggests that some aspects of decision behavior are culturally dependent and that some US theories of behavior may not apply to other cultures. Perhaps in collectivist cultures, such as those found in Asian societies, individuals are likely to be less motivated by self-interest because the society as a whole provides stronger penalties for such behavior.

IMPROVING IMPLEMENTATION AND EVALUATION You have to accept the fact that post-decisional conflict is natural, and not repress or ignore it. Such conflict is quite common because many decisions are complex and involve a good deal of risk or uncertainty. There are at least three ways to resolve post-decisional conflict (Janis and Mann, 1977).

1 Stick with the original decision, to reaffirm it. After weighing the evidence, you proceed as planned.
2 Modify or curtail implementation. It might be possible to stay with the original decision but slow down a bit in implementing it.
3 Undo the original decision. When the costs and risks of continuing outweigh the benefits of the original decision, it might be wise to drop or change the original choice rather than escalate commitment.

In general, it is wise to consider how common escalation of commitment is and to analyze your own decision-making processes to make sure this phenomena has not overtaken your judgment.

As a decision maker, you can work diligently to seek information of all kinds. This posture of active openness can help to overcome tendencies to pursue feedback selectivity during implementation. Another strategy is to give all information fair and thorough consideration, rather than deny it or rationalize it away. It takes considerable effort to actively seek pros and cons, and to evaluate all sides of an issue.

SUMMARY OF IMPROVING INDIVIDUAL DECISION MAKING: A CALL FOR SYSTEMS THINKING

The practice of systems thinking is useful in resolving problems that occur throughout the decision-making process (Senge, 1994). Systems thinking means that you look for interrelationships among variables within the decision space. For example, a university president was concerned about the declining level of enrollment at her university. Since the traditional student population came either directly from the area high schools or transferred from the local community college, she focused on the enrollments at those "feeder" institutions. As a result, her strategy for increasing enrollments was to focus on attracting more students from the area high school and community college. Extensive funds were spent on marketing the university as the right place for those particular students to study. Unfortunately, this narrow view of the problem ignored a growing market segment that has more nontraditionally aged students returning to universities and colleges across the country. Structural factors such as the lower number of traditionally aged students in the population limited the eventual successfulness of her strategy. However, when she considered the possibility of attracting other types of students and students coming from other areas, she was able to view different possibilities in problem definition and as a result, solution implementation. Systems thinking encourages us to look for alternative or contributing causes of the problem and to alternative solutions.

Improving Group Decision Making

Organizations frequently use teams, committees, task forces, and other types of groups in all stages of the decision process. Usually this involvement or participative management philosophy is an attempt to find better decisions and more commitment by including employees in decisions that affect them, spreading responsibilities for decision making to all employees, not just managers.

Sometimes participation works well, and sometimes it does not. To succeed, the commitment to group decision making must be genuine. In addition, various skills are needed. First, as managers we must learn the steps and techniques of good decision making discussed in the first part of this chapter. Knowledge of group and team dynamics is essential too. We need to know the benefits and disadvantages of group decision making over individual decision making. Finally, leadership is needed to guide the process so that effective decisions have a chance of emerging.

BENEFITS AND DISADVANTAGES OF GROUPS

Using groups for decision making has both assets and liabilities (Maier, 1967). These are shown in figure 11.2. To a large degree, making them an asset depends on the skill of the leader. Compared to individuals, groups have more knowledge and information. Groups also generate a larger number of approaches to a problem, and members can knock each other out of ruts in their thinking. Group participation can increase understanding and acceptance of the decision, and the commitment to execute it. Managerial decisions often fail because of faulty communication of the decision to those who must implement them. Employees often lack knowledge of rejected alternatives, obstacles, goals, and reasons behind the decision. These problems can be overcome when a group is involved in the entire process.

conformity
Tendency to pattern one's beliefs or behavior after others'

A disadvantage of group decision making lies in social pressure for **conformity**. The majority can suppress good minority ideas, or a desire for consensus can silence disagreement. Some solutions, good and bad ones, accumulate a certain amount of support. Once support for a solution reaches a critical level, it has a high probability of being selected and other solutions are very likely to fail. Even a minority can build up support for a solution by actively asserting themselves. Thus, decisions can emerge from this support, rather than from their quality. Members who are hard to control and who persuade, threaten, or persist in their point of view also can dominate groups. A final disadvantage of groups occurs when it becomes more important to avoid disagreement or win an argument than to make a good evaluation of alternatives. Avoidance of disagreement and arguments prevents open and objective discussion. We discuss some of these social pressures later; see page 328.

Some factors can be either benefits or disadvantages depending on the skill of the group leader. If the leader suppresses disagreement or allows it to create hard

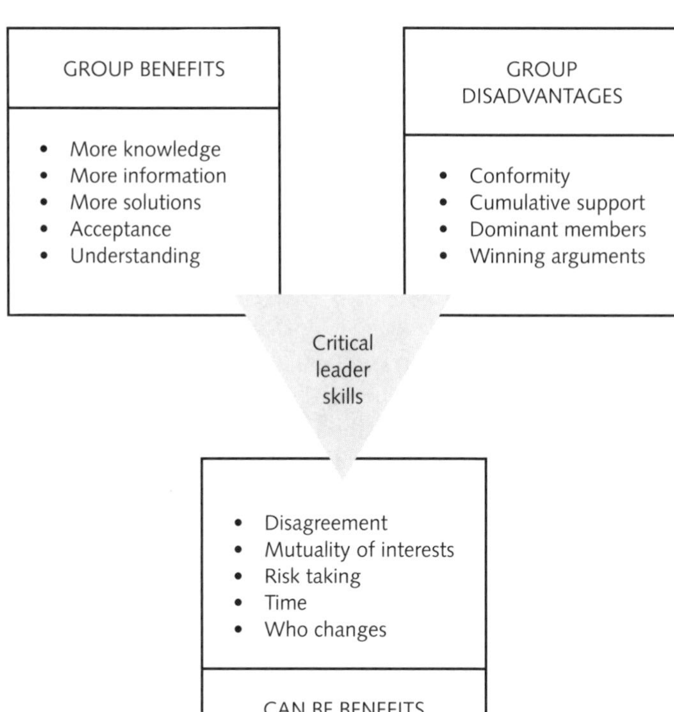

Fig 11.2 : Benefits and disadvantages of group decision making

feelings, it can damage the solution. However, if the leader treats disagreement as acceptable, it can generate innovative solutions. The leader can also make a difference by emphasizing either conflicting or mutual interests. Mutual interests should be explored at all stages of decision making, beginning with the problem definition.

Consensus begins in the process of seeking mutually acceptable solutions, but the leader has to work hard to probe areas of mutual concern. Unless he or she does so, conflict among members might lead to a poor solution. The leader can also affect the level of risk that a group takes: it can be guided toward a very safe and conservative decision, or one that is riskier and more innovative.

Time can also be an asset or a liability. Groups generally take longer than individuals to make decisions. Even if both take an hour to decide, a group of five people has spent five work hours. Leaders who permit rushing to save time can risk losing acceptance and may reduce the quality of the decision. A final factor that can help or hinder a decision is, "Who changes in the group?" If the person with the worst ideas changes, the decision will be better, but if the person with the best ideas is forced to change, the decision will be worse.

DECIDING WHEN TO USE A GROUP

Not every decision that we make can – or should be – made by a group. Managers can make the decision alone or involve others in the decision process. They can assign the responsibility to an individual, a committee, or a task force. The question is, under what conditions is it best to use a group?

QUALITY AND ACCEPTANCE AS CRITERIA Quality and acceptance are useful in deciding whether to engage a group in decision making (Maier, 1963). The quality of a decision refers to the feasibility and technical aspects of a problem and calls for the use of facts, analysis of data, and objectivity. Acceptance of a decision, on the other hand, deals with feelings, needs, and emotions and is subjective in nature.

Decisions can be classified into several types, depending on whether quality, acceptance, or both are important factors. With some decisions, quality is more important than acceptance. These problems are usually technical or scientific in nature, such as how to control pressure in a valve or devising a test to select among vendors' products. When quality is the main concern, you are not likely to become emotionally involved in the outcome or decision, so, as a manager, you need only find experts with the knowledge and experience to find a quality solution. They can research, develop, and test technically feasible solutions. Facts and analysis will dominate decision making.

With other problems, however, acceptance may be the most important criteria. For example, deciding who works overtime is an acceptance issue, assuming that the candidates for overtime are all able to do the work. Other changes that might involve work place procedures or that will significantly impact a particular group and requires their efforts for successful decision implementation increase the importance of the acceptance criterion.

Other problems involve both quality and acceptance: deciding how to increase productivity, introducing new methods or equipment, reducing absenteeism, or developing new safety standards. Here quality solutions are essential, and those affected by them will have strong feelings about them. The decision could fail unless employees accept it and can commit to its implementation.

The decision rule to use is, "Whenever acceptance is critical, the manager must at least consider using a group for the decision process. Unilateral decisions by the manager run the risk of being misunderstood or rejected." Even though shortage of time could argue against participation, group decision is a way to achieve acceptance.

THE VROOM–YETTON MODEL A useful model for deciding whether to use a group has been developed by Vroom and Yetton (1973); see page 330. They propose five different types of decision making, which vary according to the amount of subordinate influence. At one extreme is unilateral decision making by the manager;

this is a quick and efficient way to make a decision. At the other extreme is participative decision making. These five decision styles are listed below. Notice that, as the decision approach moves from AI toward GII (A stands for autocratic, C for consultative, and G for group), the amount of subordinate influence over the final decision increases.

1 *AI*: You make the decision with currently available data.
2 *AII*: Necessary information is obtained from subordinates, but you still decide alone. Your subordinate's role is to provide information data only; they have nothing to do with generating or evaluating alternatives.
3 *CI*: You discuss the problem with relevant subordinates individually. Then, without bringing them together, makes a decision that may or may not reflect their input.
4 *CII*: You share the problem with subordinates in a group meeting, gathering ideas and suggestions, then makes the decision alone, which may or may not take the input of the group meeting into account.
5 *GII*: Problems are shared with the group. In this case, you would be using the participative management style. Your role is to provide information and help, facilitating the group's determination of its own solution rather than the solution preferred by the manager.

This model can help you to decide which of these five decision-making methods to use. The most effective style depends on seven situational characteristics (SC1 to SC7):

- *SC1 – The importance of decision quality*
  How important is it to achieve a high-quality solution? If there is no quality requirement, then any acceptable alternative will be satisfactory to management, and the group can make the decision. For example, groups can decide how to accomplish or assign routine tasks where quality is not critical.
- *SC2 – The extent to which the decision maker has necessary information*
  There are two kinds of information that make an effective decision: preferences of subordinates about alternatives and whether there are rational grounds to judge the quality of alternatives.

  When you do not know your subordinates' preferences, participation can reveal them. If you know subordinate preferences, but the problem is such that an individual decision is more likely to produce a better solution than that of a group, then clearly the situation calls for you to make the decision alone.

  In what kind of situation is a group likely to make a better decision than an individual? Research indicates that an individual can do as well as a group when either the problem has a highly verifiable solution or the solution requires thinking through complicated interrelated stages, keeping in mind conclusions reached at earlier times. A group is superior when the problem is complex, has several parts, and the group members possess diverse but relevant talents and skills. Insight and originality can then be more likely obtained from a group than from an individual (Kelley and Thibault, 1969).

- *SC3 – The extent to which problem is structured*
  In structured problems, the alternatives, or at least the means for generating them, are known. Standard procedures used in most organizations give individuals all or most of the information they need. In an ill-structured problem, the information may be widely dispersed through the organization. Different individuals will probably have to be brought together to solve the problem or to make a joint decision. For example, a computer assembly worker can figure out how to assemble the components given a set of instructions and specifications but may need to consult with others if a new material or component is involved.
- *SC4 – The importance of subordinates' acceptance*
  Acceptance by subordinates is not critical where a decision falls in the boundaries of the psychological contract. In this case, carrying out the decision is a matter of simple compliance. The more commitment required from subordinates in the carrying out of a decision, of course, the more important subordinate acceptance becomes.
- *SC5 – The probability that an autocratic decision will be accepted*
  If a decision is viewed as within the legitimate authority of a manager, it will be accepted by subordinates without participation.
- *SC6 – Subordinate motivation to attain organizational goals*
  Sometimes the objectives of superiors and their subordinates are not compatible. Then participation in decision making may be more risky than in situations where the goals are congruent. Participative decision making works best where there is mutual interest in the problem.
- *SC7 – Subordinates disagreement over solutions*
  Subordinates may disagree among themselves over prospective alternatives. The method used to reach a decision must facilitate resolution of the disagreement, and thus group involvement is necessary.

All of these situational characteristics are presented in the form of questions in the Vroom–Yetton model, shown in figure 11.3. The questions are answered on a yes-no basis. The decision tree format establishes the sequence of the questions to be answered by the manager. At the end of every path in the decision tree is one or more alternative approaches for making the decision.

GROUPTHINK

groupthink
Occurs when a group allows the need for consensus and cohesiveness to be more important than making the best possible decision

Groups can make poor decisions because they fall into a pattern called **groupthink** (Janis, 1972). The need for consensus and cohesiveness assumes greater importance than making the best possible decision. It happens when the group collectively becomes defensive and avoids facing issues squarely and realistically. Groupthink can occur in meetings in any organization, such as when managers meet under pressure to make an important decision. Figure 11.4 provides a model of groupthink.

There are eight key symptoms of groupthink:

1 *Illusion of invulnerability* The group acts as if it is protected from criticism. This gives members too much optimism and encourages extreme risk taking.
2 *Rationalization* The group tends to explain away facts or ideas that press them to reconsider their position.
3 *Illusion of morality* This is a belief that the group is acting in the name of goodness and causes inattention to ethical consequences.
4 *Stereotyping* Rivals or enemies outside the group are treated as evil, too stupid to negotiate with, or too weak to harm the group.
5 *Pressure for conformity* Group members are pressured to go along with the group's illusions and stereotypes. Dissent is suppressed as contrary to group expectations.
6 *Self-censorship* Group members become inclined to minimize their own feelings of doubt or disagreement.
7 *Illusion of unanimity* Silence comes to imply agreement. Perceptions develop that unanimity exists.
8 *Self-appointed mind guards* Some members act to protect the group from adverse information.

Some of the more famous examples of groupthink are found in high-level government decision-making groups (Janis, 1972).

- President Kennedy and his colleagues decided to invade Cuba at the Bay of Pigs, despite good information that the attempt would fail and damage our relations with other countries.
- President Richard Nixon and his staff proceeded with the Watergate burglary of Democratic election headquarters and continued with its subsequent cover-up, despite its serious risks and implications.
- Negative information was ignored by decision makers in deciding to launch the space shuttle Challenger in 1986 (Moorhead et al., 1991).

Causes of groupthink Groupthink is often found in highly cohesive groups. Members' desire to remain in the group contributes to them becoming a victim to one or more of groupthink's symptoms. If the group can insulate itself and has a strong, directive leader, groupthink is more likely. Stress helps too, such as when an important decision is needed but hope is low for finding a solution other than the one desired by the leader or other influential members. Such factors can combine to create disastrous conditions. Consider a situation where a plant manager and his subordinates are under pressure from headquarters to complete a rush order from a customer. They might easily convince themselves that machine breakdowns, employee fatigue, or union resistance will not become an issue. Dissenting members of the team might be pressured to conform, and withhold their opinions.

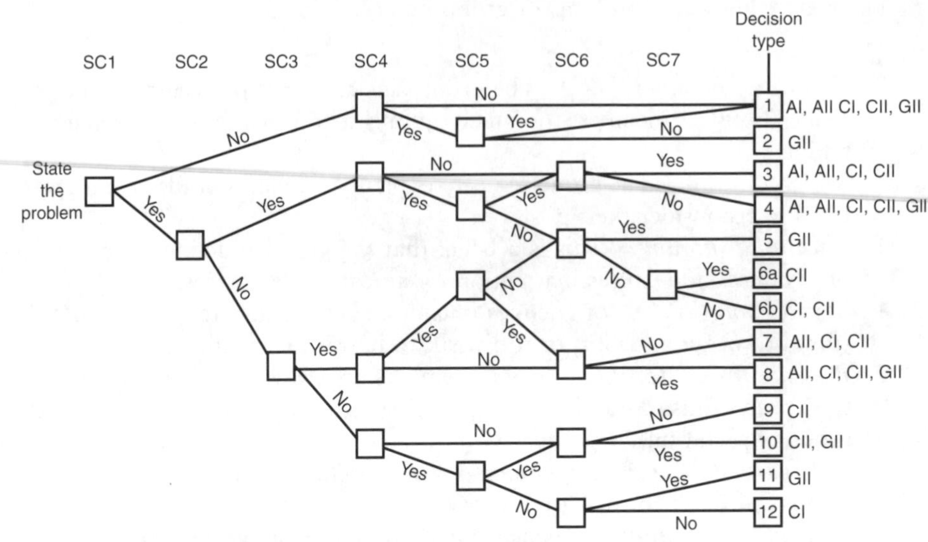

Fig 11.3 : The Vroom–Yetton decision model
Situational characteristics

SC1 Is there a quality requirement such that one solution is likely to be more rational than another?
SC2 Do I have sufficient information to make a high-quality decision?
SC3 Is the problem structured?
SC4 Is acceptance of the decisions by subordinates critical to effective implementation?
SC5 If I were to make the decision by myself, is it reasonably certain that it would be accepted by my subordinates?
SC6 Do subordinates share the organizational goals to be attained in solving the problem?
SC7 Is conflict among subordinates likely in preferred solutions?

EXERCISE

APPLICATION OF THE VROOM–YETTON MODEL

To illustrate how the Vroom–Yetton Model might be applied in actual administrative situations, a case will be presented and analyzed with the use of the model.

Instructions

Read the case description provided below. Note that, while an attempt has been made to describe this case as completely as is necessary for you to make the judgments required by the model, there may be some room for subjectivity.

After reading the case, complete these questions, and circle yes or no based on your response to the questions about the situational characteristics of this case.

SC1	(Quality?)	Yes	No
SC2	(Manager's information?)	Yes	No
SC3	(Structured?)	Yes	No
SC4	(Acceptance?)	Yes	No
SC5	(Prior probability of acceptance?)	Yes	No

		Yes	No
SC6	(Goal congruence?)	Yes	No
SC7	(Conflict?)	Yes	No

Then, work through the decision tree in figure 11.3 to establish the problem type and the feasible set of options.

Problem type (1–12): ....
Feasible set (AI, AII, CI, CII, and/or GII): ....

Case

You are the manufacturing manager in a large electronics plant. The company's management has always been searching for ways of increasing efficiency. They have recently installed new machines and put in a new simplified work systems but, to the surprise of everyone, including yourself, the expected increase in productivity was not realized. In fact, production has begun to drop, quality has fallen off, and the number of employee separations has risen.

You do not believe that there is anything wrong with the machines. You have had reports from other companies who are using them and they confirm this opinion. You have also had representatives from the firm that built the machines go over them and they report that they are operating at peak efficiency.

You suspect that some parts of the new work system may be responsible for the change, but this view is not widely shared among your immediate subordinates, who are four first-line supervisors, each in charge of a section, and your supply manager. The drop in production has been variously attributed to poor training of the operators, lack of an adequate system of financial incentives, and poor morale. Clearly, this is an issue about which there is considerable depth of feeling within individuals and potential disagreement between your subordinates.

This morning you received a phone call from your division manager. He had just received your production figures for the last six months and was calling to express his concern. He indicated that the problem was yours to solve in any way that you think best, but that he would like to know within a week what steps you plan to take.

You share your division manager's concern with the falling productivity and know that your men are also concerned. The problem is to decide what steps to take to rectify the situation.

Authors' Analysis

Based on the case information, the appropriate decision process would be GII. That is, you share the problem with your subordinates and arrive at a decision as a group.

SC1 (Quality?) = Yes
SC2 (Manager's information?) = No
SC3 (Structured?) = No
SC4 (Acceptance?) = Yes
SC5 (Prior probability of acceptance?) = No
SC6 (Goal congruence?) = Yes
SC7 (Conflict?) = Yes
Problem type: 11
Feasible set: GII

- How did your answers compare with ours?

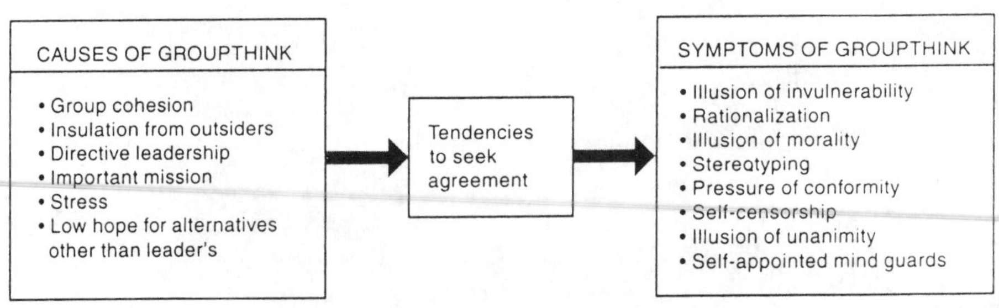

Fig 11.4: A model of groupthink

RISKY SHIFT AND POLARIZATION

Groupthink can be better understood in relationship to other common group phenomena (Whyte, 1989). One issue underlying groupthink is the levels of risk group members are willing to take (Kahneman and Tversky, 1979). As an example, if they view a decision as a choice between two gains, they should have a tendency to choose the option that has the least amount of risk associated with it. If one of those outcomes is a certain loss as compared to a possible gain that has an attached risk of a greater loss, they will tend to choose an alternative that has some possibility of gain even if there is a risk of even greater loss attached (Kahneman and Tversky, 1979).

uniformity
Pressure placed on group members holding a position different than the majority to conform to the majority view

polarization
The tendency that the average group member's position on an issue will become more extreme as the result of group discussion

risky shift
The tendency for groups or teams to make riskier decisions about a course of actions than individuals

A second issue concerns the widely supported concept that there is pressure within groups for **uniformity**. Traditionally, there is pressure on a minority of group members holding a position different than the majority, to conform to the majority view. This conformity occurs as the result of social interaction from discussing the issues. This is coupled with **polarization**, a tendency for enhancement of the initially dominant point of view of members. As discussion and debate occur, the positions become more extreme (Myers, 1982).

One fascinating phenomena found in groups that results from social influences is the tendency for groups or teams to make riskier decisions about a course of actions than individuals. This effect, known as **risky shift**, was the opposite of the widely held belief that groups are conservative or cautious. Later studies showed that the riskier outcome does not always occur in groups, but, together, these studies give some insight into social influences on risk behavior.

What might cause a group to shift to a riskier decision, or a less risky one, compared to individuals? The answer provides a powerful lesson on social influence. In group decision-making contexts, individuals usually have inclinations about a decision before they enter the group discussion. In general, group discussion tends to strengthen these inclinations (Whyte, 1989). The social process of the group discussion causes an individual who favored a particular decision before a group discussion to feel even stronger after the discussion. This process is called polarization and refers to the tendency that the average group member's position on an issue will become more extreme as the result of group discussion. It occurs as a subgroup forms of members of a group who have similar opinions on an issue. Through the decision process, these subgroups become further apart on the issue. For example, suppose the HR Department favors a new appraisal system for first-line supervisors, but these supervisors are predisposed against any change. As members from both sides meet to discuss the issue, polarization predicts that the HR Department will strengthen their inclinations favoring the new system while the supervisors will strengthen their biases against the change. This would create an even larger gap between the two groups. Figure 11.5 shows what will happen if this same process occurs within a group contemplating alternative decisions that have increased risk as the decision options becomes more extreme. Prior to a discussion of the issue, the average pre-discussion positions of subgroup members were closer to the compromise position. However, notice that after the meeting, polarization causes the group members position to move, on average, towards a preference for a riskier decision.

Polarization is one of the key factors in conflict, and there are several managerial solutions to minimize the problem. To reduce polarization, it may be wise to avoid premature meetings of subgroups for and against an issue. It is also helpful to mix membership within groups, or occasionally to invite outsiders or people with different ideas into meetings whenever feasible. Any action that calls for a focus on the total organization mission might reduce the tendency towards polarization. Just making members aware of this tendency may cause members to develop procedures to minimize the impact of polarization in leading their group to make a riskier decision.

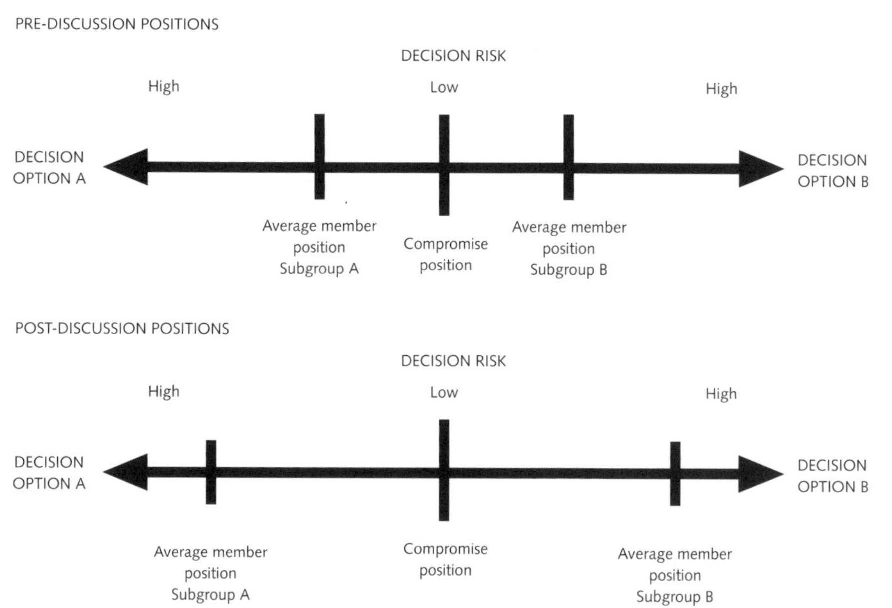

Fig 11.5: Effects of polarization on decision risk

When you understand the ways that groups affect members, it is easier to know how many of the decisions with tragic outcomes occur. NASA leaders may have framed the decision to launch Challenger as a choice between two outcomes (National Aeronautics & Space Administration,1986). One was damage to the public and customer's perception of the reliability of the shuttle program because of the numerous delays that had already been experienced. The other was the potential safety issues occurring from launching in temperatures where performance of the seals was questionable. Additional pressure and negative consequences on NASA was assured if they chose to further delay the launch. There was a possibility, and subsequent discussion reinforced that possibility, that the launch would be successful. The result of the decision to launch Challenger demonstrates the dangers inherent in group decision making.

A QUESTION OF ETHICS: ETHICAL BEHAVIOR IN GROUPS

The discussion of groupthink and the behaviors that support this widely observed phenomena that occurs within a group decision-making context may provide insight into ethical behavior. Within group contexts, members who would normally act ethically individually may be part of a group that makes unethical decisions. Social scientists have studied the invulnerability and illusion of morality of individuals when acting as part of a group. These characteristics when combined with the tendency of groups to accept greater risk should be of concern to managers. One way of protecting against this possibility is openness and disclosure of group processes. Groups who feel they are accountable to others for their decisions and for the process that arrived at those decisions are less likely to feel invulnerable. Groups should continually ask how they could defend their decision to others and should be willing to allow others to observe the decision process. If there is openness, there is less likely to be unethical behavior. If there is hope within the group that some information about their activities does not become public knowledge, there is a good chance that the group is falling into the negative pitfalls of groupthink.

Summary

Decision making is often an imperfect process that requires new decisions to compensate for prior decisions. The basic process includes defining the problem, generating and evaluating alternative solutions, choosing among solutions, and implementing the decision. Both evaluative and creative behaviors are important in all stages. At each step, a number of errors can be made that reduce the effectiveness of a decision. People frequently define problems too narrowly, or fail to generate sufficient alternatives. Premature and incomplete evaluation is also common. Because of such errors, many ideal models and techniques for better decision making have been suggested. These can help decision making significantly but rarely produce perfect, lasting solutions.

Groups that make decisions commit many of the same errors that individuals make. Therefore, it would serve a group well to follow the suggestions offered by ideal models of decision making. One of the first steps consists of deciding when or whether to involve a group in decision making. Group decision making increases the opportunity to gain group acceptance and commitment to a decision, and groups can have a larger reservoir of ideas. However, it takes practice and skill to overcome the disadvantages of groups, such as pressures to conform. A skilled group leader can make a great difference in solution quality and acceptance, not only by overcoming disadvantages but by bringing out the best that the group has to offer.

Guide for Managers: Improving Group Decision Making

The greatest responsibility for group decision making lies with the group leader, who is in a critical position to affect the quality and acceptance of a decision. When you are the leader of a decision-making group, you have to be like an orchestra leader: you do not play an instrument, but rather you conduct and guide group members (Maier, 1963).

The leader has to focus on the process of the group as well as on the actual content of the decision. The leader who focuses on process does things to urge members to define the problem well, helps them to generate alternative solutions, and so on. In focusing on process, the leader ensures that members participate freely and that disagreements are handled appropriately. The leader can affect content by holding to high standards of quality and acceptance, and by preventing the group from making unworkable decisions. Many leaders become too involved in the content of a group decision because they typically know a good deal about the problem at hand and have a natural tendency to offer their ideas and to contribute directly to the decision. Yet it is a mistake to do so, especially if process goes unattended. Shifting your focus to group process takes practice. You must unlearn past thinking habits and practice the acceptance of dissent and experimentation in decision making (Osborn, 1957). Here are some things you can do to manage the group decision-making process (Maier, 1963).

DEFINE THE PROBLEM FULLY AND ACCURATELY

You must overcome the tendency of the group to define problems too quickly or simply. Ask members how they view the problem, and what they feel caused it. Probe the group and work toward a thorough definition. As the group members speak, record their ideas on a chalkboard or on flip charts. The group can be asked to differentiate symptoms from more basic, underlying causes. It is better to put the problem in situational rather than personal terms. For example, it is unwise to state the problem as how to make Charley work evenings. Depersonalizing helps members to respond to various aspects of the problem with more objectivity.

Group members will still move off the problem too quickly and begin to offer solutions too early.

When this happens, you must turn the solution statement back into a problem definition and remind the group, "We are not ready for solutions yet," or say "How does the solution relate to the problem?"

USE THE PROBLEM TO GENERATE SOLUTIONS

A good definition of a problem can be put to productive use. Each element of the definition can be a source of solution possibilities. All you have to do is to keep the group working to generate ideas that respond to all of the problem elements. In this way, you not only encourage various solutions but also help to ensure thoroughness. Solutions are less likely to be incomplete if all the problem elements are attended to.

PREVENT PREMATURE EVALUATION OF SOLUTIONS

The process of idea generation is blocked by idea evaluation. This is especially true when group members quickly agree on a solution and adopt the first acceptable solution that arises. The leader and members should see to it that evaluative statements are withheld until idea generation is at least adequate.

GAIN CONSENSUS

Eventually, group members need to evaluate their ideas and arrive at a decision they can live with. You can help in several ways here. You can summarize the group's progress to make sure the group is ready to make the decision. You can also make members develop criteria to evaluate the alternatives they generated. Questioning where the group agrees or disagrees on any matter before them can directly test consensus. To adequately test and gain a true consensus, you may have to organize and present a review of the group's work.

AVOID LEADER SOLUTIONS

A group leader, especially one with formal authority, should avoid offering solutions to the group. This may be difficult to do. You may want to express your opinions in these situations. The problem is that a superior's idea is evaluated by group members on the basis of the source of the idea and *not* on its worth. Objective evaluation loses out to concern over how the boss will react if the idea is supported or challenged. Rarely is a boss treated as a peer. Better solutions come from groups when they are given no time to prepare or think about a problem (Maier, 1963). When you prepare, you tend to think of solutions that you later find difficult to keep to yourself.

VALUE DISAGREEMENT AND CHAOS

There is more value in disagreement than in quick agreement. When group members agree, solution generation often comes to a close. If a disagreement occurs, however, solution generation is still alive. Train people that if things do not make sense, they must speak up. People in the group should raise their own white flag when they are falling in the trap of reacting without thinking. This is most likely in four situations:

1 When we expect something
2 When we want something
3 When we are preoccupied with something
4 When we finish something

This means that you should embrace chaos (Weick, 1993). Accept that within chaotic contexts, there is pattern. Always look for cues to the pattern and consider numerous methods of problem resolution. Looking across the Challenger disaster, the Tenerife disaster, and the friendly fire shoot down, consistent mistakes were made, mistakes that decision makers should be trained to notice when they might occur so they can avoid them. Leaders squelch disagreement when they say, "If we're going to argue, we'll never get this problem solved." Statements such as this, frustrated sighs, or other nonverbal cues soon tell group members to avoid disagreement. Ideas are accepted because no one wants to incur disfavor.

Disagreements can be made to pay off. This is done when the leader accepts and probes a disagreement. The leader can say, "Phyllis, your idea really contrasts with John's. Tell us what you have in mind, and then we can get John's point of view." This tells the group that it is acceptable to disagree, and no one will be punished for doing so, and opens the door to new ideas. Often the disagreement can be traced to different definitions of the problem, or to goals that the group had not earlier considered. Probing disagreement can prevent the rubber-stamping or the avoiding of ideas. You should program disagreement into discussions with the use of devil's advocate roles or by asking for counter proposals (Cosier and Schwenk, 1990).

Key Concepts

STUDY QUESTIONS

1 Interview a manager or someone you know who recently made an important decision.
2 Evaluative behavior and creative behavior are critical at all stages of decision making. Show why this is true.
3 Define the elements of the normative approach to decision making.
4 What are the different ways to evaluate whether a decision or a solution to a problem was effective?
5 Working alone, or with the help of a friend, identify a problem one of you has that will require a decision.
Was the right problem selected?
Can you improve on how the problem is defined?
6 Briefly describe as many techniques as you can that are useful for generating alternative solutions to a problem.
7 What are the advantages and disadvantages that groups have, compared to individuals, in decision making?
8 What criteria should a manager use to decide whether to use group participation in decision making?
Are there different levels of group involvement? Explain.
9 Name some examples of management decisions where a group should probably *not* be used to make the decision. Then give examples where it might be best to use a group. Explain your choices.
10 Make a list of statements a leader can say that

(a) foster good problem definition
(b) help idea generation
(c) constructively deal with disagreement, and
(d) prevent premature evaluation.

Case

Escapade Travel Agency

Diane Raymond was excited as she left her night class in Personnel Management. Her professor had just lectured on new work schedules that some companies were using. He had discussed compressed work weeks where employees work all their hours on four days of the week, and are given three-day weekends. Sometimes this could be done every other week. He also discussed flextime, where employees worked five days but could come in later or leave earlier, within certain limits. For example, sometimes all employees had to be at work between 10.00 a.m. and 3.00 p.m., but could alter their earlier and later hours. Other variations included putting in more hours on some days so that other days could be shorter. Many possibilities were discussed, including how to cover Saturdays if the organization operated on a six-day week.

Diane felt that a flextime schedule could work at Escapade Travel Agency where she was employed full-time as a travel agent. Personally, it would help her tremendously. Diane was married with two children, and was pursuing a business degree at the local college. With flextime, she could run errands, take care of the children better, and even take a few daytime classes she needed to graduate. She was sure her fellow workers would like flextime, too. They all had problems similar to her own, and even if they did not need flextime, they could probably work their current schedule while others altered their schedules.

Diane had the idea put on the agenda of the next meeting at Escapade. Meetings were usually held early morning before opening time. They were usually led by the owner and manager, Mr Burdick. They were attended by all employees, including the two supervisors of the fifteen agents and two receptionists. Diane hoped for a favorable reaction to her proposal. When her turn came up on the agenda, she described flextime in general terms and paused for a reaction.

She didn't have to wait long. Many of the travel agents were favorably disposed. They saw it as a way to meet many personal obligations without taking time off or asking others to cover for them. They felt they could cover the hours and still complete their work without harming service to customers. Some travel agents resisted the idea, partly because they felt they might lose status by having to cover for receptionists. They also liked the "9 to 5" and felt no need for different hours. The receptionists offered few opinions, and Diane could not tell how they felt.

The greatest resistance came from the supervisors. All they saw was having to spend most of their time making schedules. They just did not think it was workable, especially since they had a hard enough time as it was covering Saturdays and extra evenings during heavy travel seasons.

Throughout all of this, Mr Burdick sat silently and listened to the discussion. No one was sure how he felt. As the clock reached opening time, Mr Burdick said the meeting had to come to a close, and promised to continue the discussion at the next meeting.

- What are the different elements in the flextime problem? Identify them as quality or acceptance issues.
- What are some alternative ways that these problem elements can be solved?
- How should Mr Burdick approach the various decisions that have to be made?

References

Adams, J. L. 1974: *Conceptual Blockbusting: A Guide to Better Ideas*. San Francisco: Freeman.

Cohen, M. D., March, J. G. and Olsen, J. P. 1972: A garbage can model of organizational choice. *Administrative Science Quarterly*, 17, 1–25.

Cosier, R. A. and Schwenk, C. R. 1990: Agreement and thinking alike: Ingredients for poor decisions. *Academy of Management Executive*, 4(1), 69–74.

Etzioni, A. 1967: Mixed scanning. A third approach to decision making. *Public Administration Review*, 27, 385–92.

Garland, H. and Newport, S. 1991: Effects of absolute and relative sunk costs on the decision to persist with a course of action. *Organizational Behavior and Human Decision Processes*, 48, 55–69.

Garland, S. B. 1990: This safety ruling could be hazardous to employees' health. *Business Week*, February 12, 34.

HR Magazine 1997: Managerial promotion: The dynamics for men and women *HR Magazine*, April, 85.

Janis, I. L. 1972: *Victims of Groupthink*. Boston: Houghton Mifflin.

Janis, I. L. and Mann, L. 1977: *Decision Making: A Psychological Analysis of Conflict, Choice and Commitment*. New York: Free Press.

Kahneman, D. and Tversky, A. 1979: Prospect theory: An analysis of decision making under risk. *Econometrica*, 47, 263–91.

Kelley, H. H. and Thibault, J. 1969: Group problem solving. In G. Lindsey and E. Aronson (eds), *Handbook of Social Psychology*, vol. 4. Reading, MA: Addison-Wesley.

Maier, N. R. F. 1963: *Problem-Solving Discussions and Conferences: Leadership Methods and Skills*. New York: McGraw-Hill.

Maier, N. R. F. 1967: Assets and liabilities in group problem solving: The need for an integrative function. *Psychological Review*, 74, 239–48.

March, J. G. and Simon, H. 1958: *Organizations*. New York: John Wiley.

March, J. G. and Weissinger-Baylon, R. 1986: *Ambiguity and Command: Organizational Perspectives on Military Decision Making*. Marshfield, MA: Pitman Publishing.

Miller, D. W. and Starr, M. K. 1967: *The Structure of Human Decisions*. Englewood Cliffs, NJ: Prentice-Hall.

Mintzberg, H. 1975: The manager's job: Folklore and fact. *Harvard Business Review*. July–August.

Moorhead, G., Ference, R. K. and Neck, C. P. 1991: Group decision fiascoes continue: Space shuttle Challenger and a revised groupthink framework. *Human Relations*, 44, 539–50.

Myers, D. 1982: Polarizing effects of social interactions. In H. Brandstetter, J. Davis and G. Stocker-Kreichgauer (eds), *Group Decision Making* London: Academic Press, 125–61.

National Aeronautics & Space Administration. 1986: *Report of the presidential commission on the space shuttle Challenger accident*. June 6, US Government Printing Office.

Osborn, A. F. 1957: *Applied Imagination*. New York: Charles Scribner's Sons.

Senge, P. M. 1994: *The Fifth Discipline*. New York, Currency Double day.

Sharp, D. J. 1997: Project escalation and sunk costs: A test of the international generalizability of agency and prospect theories. *Journal of International Business Studies*, 1, 101–12.

Shull, F. A., Delbecq, A. L. and Cummings, L. L. 1970: *Organizational Decision Making*. New York: McGraw-Hill.

Simon, H. A. 1957: *Models of Man*. New York: John Wiley.

Simon, H. A. 1976: *Administrative Behavior: A Study of Decision Making Processes in Administrative* Organization. 3rd edn. New York: Free Press.

Simon, H. A. 1977: *The New Science of Management Decisions*, 2nd edn. Englewood Cliffs, NJ: Prentice-Hall.

Staw, B. M. 1981: The escalation of commitment to a course of action. *Academy of Management Review*, 6, 582.

Staw, B. M. and Ross, J. 1987a: Knowing when to pull the plug. *Harvard Business Review*, (March–April), 68–74.

Staw, B. M. and Ross, J. 1987b: Behavior in escalation situations: Antecedents, prototypes, and solutions. In L. L. Cummings and B. M. Staw (eds). *Research in Organizational Behavior*, vol. 9, Greenwich, CT: JAI Press.

Vroom, V. H. and Yetton, P. W. 1973: *Leadership and Decision Making*. Pittsburgh: University of Pittsburgh Press.

Weick, K. E. 1993: The vulnerable system: An analysis of the Tenerife air disaster. In K. H. Roberts (ed.) *New Challenges to Understanding Organizations*. New York: MacMillan Publishing Co., 173–98.

Whyte, G. 1986: Escalating commitment to a course of action: A reinterpretation. *Academy of Management Review*, 11, 311–21.

Whyte, G. 1989: Groupthink reconsidered. *Academy of Management Review*, 14, 40–56.

Whyte, G. 1991: Diffusion of responsibility: Effects on the escalation tendency. *Journal of Applied Psychology*, 76, 408–15.

chapter 12

Cultures: National and Organizational

The Hofstede model of national cultures
Organizational consequences of cultural differences
Organizational culture
Types of organizational culture
Organizational culture – special cases

Preparing for Class

Since this chapter discusses two ways that culture is important in organizations, there are two things to do to prepare for class. The first deals with how differences in national cultures affect work organizations. One way to find a sense of this is to talk with a student who you know from another country. Ask them some of these questions to find out how things are done in the places in which they work in their country.

How much control do they have over their jobs?

How do they deal with supervisors and managers?

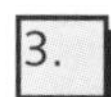
Are there many advancement opportunities for those at lower managerial levels?

Next, you need a sense of how cultures within organizations affect what happens in them by thinking about different jobs you have held or classes you have taken.

List some of the ways that the culture, or the atmosphere, was different between these jobs.

Compare how the students and the instructor in this class differ from some other class that you have taken.

Failure to understand fundamental values in a culture can be disastrous when you are working in it. You might expect, for example, that if you were going to do business in Vietnam that an effective approach would be to use a Vietnamese speaking consultant who was raised in the USA by parents who left during the Vietnamese war for independence. After all, it is very likely, though not always the case, that your consultant speaks the language and is very familiar with Vietnamese customs because, like many first generation US citizens whose parents immigrated from other countries, his or her parents passed on many aspects of their culture.

This is exactly what two of the largest globalized US corporations – one in the oil industry and the other in the food industry – did as they attempted to enter the Vietnam market. Each had, in their upper middle management group, several exceptionally competent Viet-Q (the Vietnamese term for a Vietnamese holding a foreign passport) with MBAs from top programs such as Columbia University, University of Michigan, Wharton and Stanford. It seemed only logical to use their own staff, competent with the language and familiar with the customs, to negotiate the trade deals that would give their firms a footing in the opening Vietnam market in southeast Asia, one of the growth hot spots in the world.

Each sent its best and brightest US trained Viet-Qs to act as interpreters of the language and the customs for a delegation of top managers from the firm for initial meetings with government officials. Unfortunately, the government officials, principally from Hanoi, resented the presence of Viet-Q in this process. The bases for the resentment, in part, were the material wealth and the westernness of the Viet-Q. The Viet-Q were politically and culturally different from Vietnamese nationals. The Viet-Q had been trained in the ways of the USA, Adam Smith and western political thought. The Vietnamese, on the other hand, had been trained in a more socialist society, based on the writings of Lenin and Marx. These values, at least at this time, had become embedded in the culture since the end of the Vietnam War. In addition, Viet-Q were seen by many Vietnamese nationals as having deserted the country in a time of crisis; now they were back to take advantage, once again, of those who stayed and engaged in combat with their "aggressors." All of these factors were among the reasons that both the oil company and the food company had difficulties in establishing themselves as they had anticipated in the Vietnamese economy.

This example gives you an idea of how culture can affect a firm's operation in a foreign country, but what is important to recognize is that problems of this type are much more common than in early parts of the twentieth century. For instance, just in the USA, there are more than 100,000 firms that are involved in global ventures of more than $1 trillion dollars and one in five of all US workers is employed in a firm with international activities (Solomon, 1998). One example is Colgate Palmolive; with 35,000 employees, it has 70 percent of its $8 billion in sales from markets in 194 countries (Anfuso, 1995). One indication of the importance of this global activity is that over 40 percent of firms' revenue is generated outside the country in which its headquarters is located (Solomon, 1997).

Culture, in the broad sense, refers to the social context within which humans live. It affects the very nature of organizations in which people work, and how individuals perceive and respond to the world. Culture is:

culture
Patterned ways of thinking, feeling, and reacting acquired and transmitted mainly through socialization and by symbols that constitute the distinct achievements of human groups

> . . . patterned ways of thinking, feeling, and reacting, acquired and transmitted mainly by symbols, constituting the distinctive achievements of human groups including their embodiments in artifacts. The essential core of culture consists of traditional, . . . ideas, and especially their attached values (Kluckholn and Strodtbeck, 1961).

> . . . a kind of collective software or programming of the mind that distinguishes the members of one human group from another. . . . It is to human collectivity what personality is to an individual (Hofstede, 1980a).

Differences in national cultures emerge from a broad set of forces within a nation to which people must adjust. These forces are a result of a nation's history, geography, resources, climate, and other factors (Hofstede, 1980a). What emerges from these is a set of dominant values and beliefs that govern human behavior and facilitate human relationships in a society. These are so fundamental that their presence and effects make them invisible to its members. It is this invisibility that makes culture so powerful; it drives behavior, perception, and judgment often without the person's awareness. For example, when the USA was settled by Europeans in the seventeenth and eighteenth centuries, they found almost unlimited resources and land. They could spread out, be individualistic, and develop practices which wasted resources. On the other hand, the Japanese, with little arable land and with few natural resources, had to band together in more structured communities. They had to be more frugal in their use of resources for building homes and for obtaining food. Cooperation was especially necessary with the wet agricultural methods for growing rice which required collective effort in building irrigation systems. Farming practices in the US could be quite different. Although some cooperation was needed, much of the work could be done by a single family (Hofstede, 1980a).

For a country, its dominant values are called the **national character**, or the **modal personality** (Hofstede, 1980a). The modal personality represents the degree of homogeneity and strength of the dominant personality orientations in the society. It is a result of **socialization**, the process through which a society instills its members with basic values and beliefs. These values and beliefs begin to take shape early in life. They are the bases for individual control because an overwhelming number of the society's members accept them. Of the many different values acquired through socialization, some of the more important are those related to work, ways of responding to authority, and power orientations.

socialization
The process through which a person learns and acquires the values, attitudes and beliefs, and accepted behaviors of a culture, society, organization or group

Global Focus on Cultural Values in China

Cultural values are an important aspect of doing business internationally. US businesses have often found that a lack of understanding of the culture of the host country can have significant impacts on the success of the international enterprise. Any attempt at understanding cross-cultural management strategies should be based on structured beliefs, existing world views and social relationships. A case in point is the growing international market in China. The Chinese cultural system is influenced by many cultural traits: Confucianism, familyism, group orientation, the Chinese ideal of life and the Chinese character.

Confucianism includes a focus on the relationship between man and man, defined by five virtues:

1 Humanity/benevolence (*ren*)
2 Righteousness (*yi*)
3 Propriety (*li*)
4 Wisdom (*zhi*)
5 Trustworthiness (*xin*)

A second focus includes the hierarchical relationships that are considered natural:

- Ruler and ruled
- Husband and wife
- Elder brother and younger brother
- Friend and friend (considered equal)

These relationships provides the basis for Chinese organizational bureaucracy and the related values of respect for seniority, the role of rituals, ceremonies, as well as business relationships.

Familyism is the basic unit of society where people play out their Confucian roles. The importance of the family unity expands to the employer–employee relationship and is considered familyism. There is a close relationship between work and family activities and employees are provided house, medical care, and education.

In China, group orientation means that the individual exists for the benefit of the group. Identities are formed with reference to others around them. Members accept group goals in exchange for the care of the group. It is suggested that the Chinese social needs are more important than individual needs, perhaps in contrast to US culture.

In the Chinese ideal of life, the emphasis is in enjoyment of the simple life measured by the value of family life and social relationships. The ideals emphasize naturalness and simplicity and lead to attitudes that are carefree, self-satisfied and unhurried.

The character in Chinese society refers to the "maturity" of the state of mind. This is developed through self-awareness and relationships with others.

The Chinese ideal of life and related modes of thinking have heavily influenced the direction of business practices. US firms interested in international operations in China should gain a proper understanding of the Chinese culture based on such mechanisms. These firms must try to maintain an open-mind on the variety of management and negotiation styles.

Source: Adapted from Xing (1995) by Elizabeth Campanelli-Johnson

Ways to Characterize Cultures

There are different ways to characterize national cultures and perhaps the most common is to think of them in terms of cultural stereotypes. Think about your views of Israelis, Turks, the French, and the English. All of these national groups emerge in our mind as pictures and concepts that reflect what we believe about them. One interesting approach to classifying cultures, a variation of the stereotype approach, is the use of **cultural metaphors** (Gannon, 1993): situations, events, or circumstances that occur in a culture and that capture and clarify its essential elements. For example, the symphony orchestra is the metaphor for Germany. Not only is Germany a musical nation with many orchestras, but the country operates like one. In a symphony orchestra, conformity is valued, rules are established, and each person is expected to work for the good of the whole. In business, as the orchestra, strong leadership is preferred, but it should be exercised in such a way that there is considerable delegation of power and decision making to subordinates. The opera is the metaphor for Italy, a country in which drama and emotions are so often intensely felt that they cannot be easily contained within the individual. Among other cultural metaphors are the Japanese Garden, the Turkish coffee house and the Israeli Kibbutz.

cultural metaphors
Situations, events, or circumstances that occur in a culture and that capture and clarify its essential elements

The Hofstede Model

Perhaps the most important model of the way culture affects organizations and work is the **Hofstede model of culture** (Hofstede, 1980a, 1980b, 1992). This model profiles the modal personality of a culture on five different dimensions that are the basis of attitudes and behaviors, organization practices, and social practices such as marriages, funerals, and religious ceremonies:

1 Uncertainty avoidance
2 Power distance
3 Individualism–collectivism
4 Masculinity–femininity
5 Long- versus short-term patterns of thought

In some cultures, people are uncomfortable with high risk and ambiguity; in other cultures, there is a greater tendency to take risks. Societies high in **uncertainty avoidance** tend to prefer rules and to operate in predictable situations as opposed to situations where the appropriate behaviors are not specified in advance. Those with high uncertainty avoidance prefer stable jobs, a secure life, avoidance of conflict, and have lower tolerance for deviant persons and ideas. Japan scores higher than the USA on uncertainty avoidance while both score higher than Sweden. This means that, for instance, in Japan there is far less tolerance for deviations from accepted behavioral practices than in the USA,

uncertainty avoidance
The extent to which individuals and societies wish to have stability and predictability in their lives

while Sweden is generally considered to be a very tolerant society. These differences are reflected in many educational and training programs in Japan devoted to learning the customary behaviors for all types of social situations including how to bow, how to eat certain types of foods, how to behave at a funeral, and other social customs. This desire not to stand out in Japanese society is reflected in a proverb, "The nail that sticks up gets hammered down." (Ferraro, 1998).

In nations low in uncertainty avoidance such as the US, there is less acceptance of rules and less conformity to the wishes of authority figures, unlike high uncertainty avoidance nations such as Germany and Japan (Brislin, 1993). For example, lateness and absenteeism are more serious issues in Japan than in other countries such as Sweden where uncertainty is more acceptable.

power distance
A dimension of culture that is the preferred degree of inequality of power between individuals

Power distance is the degree to which differences in power and status are accepted in a culture. Some nations accept high differences in power and authority between members of different social classes or occupational levels; other nations do not. For example, the French are relatively high in power distance while Israel and Sweden score very low. In Israel and Sweden, worker groups demand and have a great deal of power over work assignments and conditions of work (Cole, 1989; Adler, 1991). French managers tend not to interact socially with subordinates and do not expect to negotiate work assignments with them. The experience of a French MBA student in a US firm illustrates the French sense of power distance. She was surprised to find on the first day of her internship in a US company that some workers called the manager by his first name and talked with him about their weekend activities. She felt that this would rarely happen in a French factory.

There are some other consequences of power distance differences. For example, in low power distance countries such as the USA, powerful individuals can be forced out of their position or can be successfully challenged by less powerful individuals or groups (Brislin, 1993). You saw this happen when Newt Gingrich stepped down as the Speaker of the US House of Representatives in November, 1998 when he came under attack from members of his own political party. This is not likely to happen in a high power distance country. In the low power distance country, individuals feel less discomfort and stress when disagreeing with the boss. For example, in Hong Kong (a high power distance culture), individuals are less upset when they are insulted by high status individuals than in a low power distance culture, such as the USA.

individualism–collectivism
A dimension of culture that is the degree to which those in a society prefer individual action to collective action

Individualism–collectivism refers to whether individual or collective action is the preferred way to deal with issues. In cultures oriented toward individualism – such as the USA, the UK, and Canada – people tend to emphasize their individual needs and concerns and interests over those of their group or organization, while the opposite is true in countries which score high on collectivism, e.g. Asian countries such as Japan and Taiwan. In a collectivist society, you are expected to interact with members of your group. It is almost impossible to perceive a person as an individual rather than one whose identity comes from groups with which that individual is associated (Brislin, 1993). For that reason, when visiting a collectivist society, it is useful to carry business cards that clearly identify your organization and status within that organization.

Often firms in collectivist societies will make decisions without regard for the personal needs of those affected if it is thought that the decision is good for the organization. For instance, employees may be arbitrarily transferred to other locations with little concern for how such a transfer will affect the person or the family. This happened to a Taiwanese manager who was directed to enter an MBA program in the USA. He went against his wishes; his wife was about to have a child, and when the child died in birth, he was not allowed to return to Taiwan. He was told that it was not in the company's interest to allow him to do so and that he should just learn to bear with the situation.

Certain work behaviors may also be affected. For example, in an individualistic society such as the USA, there is a tendency for persons to shirk when tasks are assigned to a group as opposed to when tasks are assigned to individuals. This tendency is not present in the collectivist country of Taiwan (Grabrenya et al., 1985).

The **masculinity–femininity** dimension of a culture refers to the degree to which values associated with stereotypes of masculinity (such as aggressiveness and dominance) and femininity (such as compassion, empathy, and emotional openness) are emphasized. High masculinity cultures such as Japan, Germany, and the USA tend to have more sex-differentiated occupational structures with certain jobs almost entirely assigned to women and others to men. There is also a stronger emphasis on achievement, growth, and challenge in jobs (Hofstede, 1980a, 1980b). In these cultures, people are also more assertive and show less concern for individual needs and feelings, a higher concern for job performance and a lower concern for the quality of the working environment. In countries high on the feminine dimension such as Sweden and Norway, working conditions, job satisfaction, and employee participation are emphasized.

Long- versus short-term patterns of thought reflects a culture's view about the future. The short-term orientation, a western cultural characteristic, reflects values toward the present, perhaps even the past, and a concern for fulfilling social obligations. Long-term thought patterns, characteristic of Asian countries, reflect an orientation toward the future, belief in thrift and savings, and persistence. In countries with a long-term orientation, planning has a longer time horizon. Firms are willing to make substantial investments in employee training and development, there will be longer-term job security and promotions will come slowly (Ouchi, 1981; Jackofsky et al., 1988). Firms will also seek to develop long-term relationships with suppliers and customers (Adler, 1991).

Country clusters There are groups of countries that share somewhat similar modal personalities, language, geography, and religion. These are called **country clusters** and they are shown in Table 12.1. The Anglo cluster values low to medium power distances, low to medium uncertainty avoidance, and

masculinity–femininity
A dimension of culture that reflects the degree to which a culture strongly differentiates between typically "male" roles, which have a strong component of assertiveness, and "female" roles, which are characterized by nurturance

long- versus short-term patterns of thought
The dimension of culture that reflects whether the dominant view about the future is a long-term or a short-term perspective

country clusters
Groups of countries that share somewhat similar modal personalities, language, geography, and religion

Table 12.1 Clusters of nations grouped by culture

ANGLO GROUP
Australia, Canada, Ireland, New Zealand, South Africa, UK, USA
ARAB GROUP
Abu-Dhabi, Bahrain, Oman, United Arab Emirates
FAR EASTERN GROUP
Hong Kong, Indonesia, Malaysia, Philippines, Singapore, South Vietnam, Taiwan, Thailand
GERMANIC GROUP
Austria, Germany, Switzerland
LATIN AMERICAN GROUP
Argentina, Chile, Columbia, Mexico, Peru, Venezuela
LATIN EUROPEAN GROUP
Belgium, France, Italy, Portugal, Spain
NEAR EASTERN GROUP
Greece, Iran, Turkey
NORDIC GROUP
Denmark, Finland, Norway, Sweden
UNIQUE CULTURES
Brazil, India, Israel, Japan

Source: Adapted from Ronen and Shenkar (1985)

high masculinity and individualism. Both Latin clusters showed high power distance preferences, high uncertainty avoidance, and had high masculinity scores, but on individualism, the Latin Americans scored lower than the Latin Europeans.

Still, there are important differences within each cluster. For example, it has been said that the English and Americans are two great peoples separated by the same language (Hall, 1969). Another difference is in how they use space. In the USA, the location of one's home and office is an important cue to status; in Britain, social class is the crucial factor. Another difference is the way privacy is sought. An American who wants to be alone will move into another room and separate from others using a door; the English mostly become quiet, even in the presence of others.

Organizational Consequences of Cultural Differences

There are important ways in which culture affects organizations and those in them. For example, because of power distance differences, you can expect that there are different ways that subordinates interact with higher level managers. For example, in Israel, a high uncertainty avoidance and low power distance culture, effective organizations tend to have clearly defined roles and procedures rather than actively using the hierarchy (Adler, 1991). In countries where uncertainty avoidance and power distance are high, such as Mexico, organizations are modeled after the traditional family. Like the head of the family who has high power, so does the top management. Loyalty is expected in return for protection. Organizations are viewed as pyramids where the lines of communication are vertical, not horizontal, and the hierarchy is more actively used (Adler, 1991).

MANAGERIAL PHILOSOPHY AND CULTURE Cultural differences will be reflected in managerial philosophies. For example, Laurent (1986) conducted an analysis of managers from different countries who work for a large multinational US corporations:

> German managers, more than others, believed that creativity is essential for career success. In their mind, the successful manager is the one who has the right individual characteristics. Their outlook is rational: they view the organization as a coordinated network of individuals who make appropriate decisions based on their professional competence and knowledge.
>
> British managers hold a more interpersonal and subjective view of the organizational world. According to them, the ability to create the right image and to get noticed for what they do is essential for career success. They view the organization primarily as a network of relationships between individuals who get things done through influencing each other through communicating and negotiating.
>
> French managers look at the organization as an authority network where the power to organize and control the actors stems from their positioning in the hierarchy. They focus on the organization as a pyramid of differentiated levels of power to be acquired or dealt with. French managers perceive the ability to manage power relationships effectively and to work the systems particularly critical to their success.

Trying to transplant a managerial philosophy that works in one culture to another can create complications. For example, in the early 1990s, Hayo Nakamura, a Japanese citizen who worked for Nippon Steel in Italy for several years, was appointed the managing director and chief operating officer of Ilva, the state-owned steel group in Italy which was having profitability and production problems. His appointment drew unusual attention because he was the first foreigner named to such a senior post in Italy's very large state-operated economic sector. One thing that he thought would improve performance would be to emulate the Japanese managerial approach by increasing worker involvement, implementing quality circles, and reducing the number of organizational levels. After several months, unsatisfied with the rate of improvement, Nakamura made a strong appeal to the workforce telling them, "L'azienda e' casa tua" (The company is your home) – a very Japanese approach, but not an Italian approach.

A Question of Ethics: Different Cultures, Different Ethics

Ethical issues in business are complicated enough when they arise within a culture. They can become very complicated when they cross cultural boundaries. For example, both legal and cultural constraints govern the employment contract in any particular country. However, there are situations in which the dominant values of the national culture in which the headquarters of a multinational firm is located affect how it operates in other countries where cultural values are very different. This is what happened to, among others, two multinational firms: Nike and Mattel.

Mattel is a toy company and Nike is a sporting goods company, and both have production facilities in foreign countries, particularly Asia. Even though most of these production operations are sub-contractors and operate within legal and ethical standards in their own country, the practices in these firms have come under severe criticism within the USA because they do not meet US standards.

Critics said that Nike not only used child labor but also paid workers in China and Vietnam $1.60 a day and workers in Indonesia less than $1.00 a day when a wage of at least $3 a day is necessary to meet a minimum standard of living. Under this heavy criticism, Nike changed its child labor policies, but critics argue that its pay policies are still a problem.

Mattel, after coming under severe pressure for wage practices and the use of child labor, established a code of ethics for its manufacturing contractors around the world that banned child labor and set a minimum wage standard. The company also terminated relationships with production subcontractors in Indonesia for being unwilling to confirm the age of its employees and, in China, for refusing to meet safety standards.

These problems arise for the simple reason that the concept of what are thought to be proper wages and working conditions often vary from country to country. What is seen as right in one culture can be a problem when viewed from outside. This creates difficulties when there are pressures on the top management to apply these different standards, especially when the economic justification for using these foreign suppliers is the low cost of production. There is a serious conflict between the bottom line and what is right, however that is culturally defined (McCall, 1998).

Organizational design Table 12.2 shows how the cultural dimensions might affect the organizational structure. For example, high power distance means greater acceptance of strong authority systems, high status differentials, and willingness to accept orders from superiors. Therefore, in countries such as Mexico, Venezuela, and Brazil, organizations will have more centralized authority, more organization levels, more supervisors, and a wage structure in which white-collar and professional work is disproportionately more highly valued.

Leadership and managerial style There are cultural differences in the reactions to management and leadership styles (Child, 1981). For example, in Germany and France, leadership and control tends to be more centralized. German managers want to be informed about everything that is going on, and they show less interest in their subordinates. French managers see their job as an intellectual activity that requires intensely analytical work (Beyer, 1981). They value and excel in quantitative analysis and strategic planning. Above all, those who head large firms must be clever. This emphasis on cleverness is manifested

Table 12.2 Organizational characteristics and cultural values in various countries

Low		High
	POWER DISTANCE DIMENSION	
(Austria, Denmark, Israel, Norway, Sweden)		*(Brazil, India, Mexico, Philippines, Venezuela)*
• Less centralization		• Greater centralization
• Flatter organization pyramids		• Tall organization pyramids
• Fewer supervisory personnel		• More supervisory personnel
• Smaller wage differentials		• Larger wage differentials
• Structure in which manual and clerical work are equally valued		• Structure in which white-collar jobs are valued more than blue-collar jobs
Low	UNCERTAINTY AVOIDANCE DIMENSION	High
(Denmark, India, Sweden, UK, USA)		*(France, Greece, Peru, Portugal, Japan)*
• Less structuring of activities		• More structuring of activities
• Fewer written rules		• More written rules
• More generalists		• More specialists
• Variability		• Standardization
• Greater willingness to take risks		• Less willingness to take risks
• Less ritualistic behavior		• More ritualistic behavior
Low	INDIVIDUALISM–COLLECTIVISM DIMENSION	High
(Columbia, Greece, Mexico, Taiwan, Venezuela)		*(Australia, Canada, The Netherlands, UK, USA)*
• Organization as "family"		• Organization is more impersonal
• Organization defends employee interests		• Employees defend their own self-interests
• Practices are based on loyalty, sense of duty, and group participation		• Practices encourage individual initiative
Low	MASCULINITY–FEMININITY DIMENSION	High
(Denmark, Finland, Sweden, Thailand)		*(Austria, Italy, Japan, Mexico, Venezuela)*
• Sex roles are minimized		• Sex roles are clearly differentiated
• Organizations do not interfere with people's private lives		• Organizations may interfere to protect their interests
• More women in more qualified jobs		• Fewer women are in qualified jobs
• Soft, yielding, intuitive skills are rewarded		• Aggression, competition, and justice are rewarded
• Social rewards are valued		• Work is valued as a central life interest
Short	LONG-TERM–SHORT-TERM PATTERNS OF THOUGHT	Long
(France, Russia, USA)		*(Hong Kong, Japan)*
• Shorter term focus		• Strategic long term emphasis
• Organizational socialization left to society		• Formal organizational schemes for thorough organizational socialization
• Focus on results in negotiation		• Focus on the process in negotiation

Source: Adapted from Jackofsky et al. (1988) and Child (1981)

in their recruiting materials, which almost never mention motivation and drive as requisites for a managerial position. The French seem to prefer managers with an analytical mind, independence, and intellectual rigor. They have a strong bias for intellect, rather than action. Unlike the Anglo Saxon view of management, they do not place high emphasis on interpersonal skills and communications that are important managerial attributes in other countries. In the UK, managers delegate and decentralize more, they have a greater interest in their subordinates and, unlike the Germans, they only want to be informed about exceptional events. US managers tend to be hard driving and solution-oriented, while Scandanavian managers are more consensus oriented. Managers take different approaches to problem solving. American managers are more direct, they will give you action plans, Europeans will take a more strategic theoretical look at problems.

THE EFFECTS OF MOTIVATIONAL STRATEGIES Motivational approaches that work in one culture may not work in others because of differences in values and preferences. For example, one large US company operating in 46 different countries with over 20,000 workers found major differences in worker preferences (Sirota and Greenwood, 1971).

- In English-speaking countries, individual achievement was more strongly emphasized than security.
- French-speaking countries tended to place greater importance on security and less to challenging work than the English-speaking countries.
- In northern European countries, leisure time was more important; there was higher concern for the needs of employees and less for the needs of the organization.
- Latin countries, Germany, and southern European countries put more emphasis on job security and fringe benefits.
- Japanese employees put a stronger emphasis on good working conditions and a friendly work environment.

COMMUNICATIONS Effective communication between people from different cultures is universally difficult because people have different values and, therefore, different perceptions. As a result, they do not always agree on the meaning of words and could easily have dissimilar styles of expressing themselves. Ferraro (1998) gives an example:

> Eastern cultures have so many nonverbal ways of saying "no" without directly or unambiguously uttering the word. Needless to say, this practice has caused considerable misunderstanding when North Americans try to communicate with the Japanese. To illustrate, the Japanese in everyday conversation frequently use the word hai ("yes") to convey not agreement necessarily, but rather that they understand what is being said.

You should not expect, either, that communications will not be a problem even within a country cluster that the same language is spoken. For example, English is widely spoken around the world. This makes many Americans feel that they can cope quite well in other countries so long as they deal with individuals who can speak English. This is a mistake for reasons beyond differences in values, perceptions, word meanings, and styles of communicating. For instance, the German mode of communication is slow and ponderous compared to the French, resulting in slower decisions. The Japanese are less willing to make personal disclosures to others while the French have the greatest willingness to express conflict (Ting-Toomey, 1991). Studies have shown that Americans are among the most ethnocentric in their attitudes (Hall and Hall, 1990). They tend to discount what those from other countries say more so than vice versa. For example, in the late 1980s, the American firm AT&T merged with Olivetti, an Italian manufacture of computers, because AT&T wanted to internalize computer manufacturing competence. One of the main reasons for failure of this joint venture was that the AT&T managers working in Italy tended to think that they were right, and the Italians usually wrong.

Organizational Culture

Just as the best way to sense a national culture is when you are out of yours and in another country, you can sense differences in organizational cultures when you move from one to another. The reason is that just like countries, organizations in the same society will have different organizational cultures. The **organizational culture** is the patterned way of thinking, feeling, and reacting that exists in a specific organization or its subsectors. It is the unique "mental programming" of that organization (Hofstede et al., 1990).

organizational culture
The patterned ways of thinking, feeling, and reacting that exist in an organization or its subsectors

The most obvious and general force that shapes the organizational culture is the national character – cultural values such as individual freedom, beliefs about the goodness of humanity, orientations toward action, power distance norms, and so on; see pages 345–8 in this chapter. Then there are other broad external influences such as the natural environment and historical events that have shaped the society over which the organization has little or no control. Finally, and for the organization itself, the most direct source of culture are organization-specific factors. Therefore, while two similar firms in a country would be subject to the same national cultural influences, their separate experiences will lead to differentiated organizational cultures. For example, the Sony corporation has a different organizational culture than the older and more established Mitsui, the oldest Japanese large trading company. This is due, in part, to the fact that Sony was established about three hundred years later than Mitsui when economic and cultural conditions were quite different. Sony could not rely upon employees hired directly from schools and universities for its talent as other companies did because it needed experienced managers and professionals immediately. Therefore, it developed the practice of hiring some employees from other Japanese companies, a rare practice among large Japanese companies.

modal organizational personality
A representation of organizational culture – shows the degree of homogeneity and strength of the dominant personality orientations in an organization

The organizational culture is a direct reflection of its own **modal organizational personality** (Hofstede et al., 1990) the degree of homogeneity and the strength of a particular personality orientation in that organization – and results from four factors:

1 People develop values during socialization so as to accommodate to the types of organizations in the society.
2 Selection processes screen out many who might not "fit," and organization socialization changes those who do join, so that some level of personality homogeneity develops in every organization (Etzioni, 1963).
3 The rewards in organizations selectively reinforce some behaviors and attitudes and not others.
4 Promotion decisions usually take into account both performance and personality of candidates.

There are other organization-specific factors that affect organizational culture, e.g. the industry in which the firm operates. Firms in the same industry share the same competitive environment, the same customer requirements, and the same legal and social expectations (Gordon, 1991). For example, there is a very distinctive culture of direct selling organizations such as Mary Kay Cosmetics, Amway, and Tupperware. These firms do not "have well-defined criteria for recruitment, they discourage competition among distributors, have few rules and managers, spawn charismatic rather than rational leadership ... and encourage employees to involve spouses and children in their selling activities" (Trice and Beyer, 1984).

Significant people in the organization's history are also important. We know from research of the long-term effects on the firm of founders or significant managers such as Bill Gates of Microsoft, Henry Ford of Ford Motor Company, and Mary Kay of Mary Kay Cosmetics. What they do is to build very strong top management groups in their early years that are able to maintain power for many years even after the founder leaves (Boeker, 1990).

Critical events may also become part of the folklore of the organization and are a reference point for members' values and beliefs. For example, when Apple Computer was experiencing serious competitive problems with IBM and having internal organizational and technical difficulties in 1984, Steven Jobs made a powerful speech, animated with a screen descending from the ceiling at the annual sales conference. He challenged IBM in ways which openly excited employees and distributors. There were no changes in financial position, market position, or technology, only changes in "the organization, and how its employees (and competitors and potential customers) felt about it. That was all; that was enough" (Pfeffer, 1992, p. 287). Events like this, as well as the fact that he and Steve Wozniak started Apple, maintain Steven Job's identification with the company over the years.

A Multi-level Model of Organizational Culture

A multidimensional and multilevel model of culture like the one shown in figure 12.1 is one way to understand an organization's culture. Figure 12.1 shows three

Diversity Issues: Corporate Culture and Incorporating Older Workers

Already people over the age of 55 account for 20 percent of the US population, and this figure will increase in the next several years; there will be more older workers in firms, if for no other reason than the percentage of younger workers will be decreasing. Many companies, such as McDonald's, Home Shopping Network, AT&T, and Texas Refinery Corporations have already begun to take advantage of this trend and have successfully incorporated senior employees into their work force. Unlike firms in which there are social and organizational barriers to employ people from these groups, these firms have made a serious attempt to create an organizational culture that values seniors and makes them productive employees. So, what are the characteristics of such a supportive culture?

- It is necessary for others in the organization to understand the economic contribution of senior employees. For example, mature workers – a group ranging in age from 50–60 – stay on the job for an average of 15 years, they have better attendance than other age groups, they have lower accident rates, and the costs of employment (including health care costs) compare favorably with other groups. Mature workers are, generally, highly trainable and can accommodate to many different kinds of work.
- In some instances, it may be necessary to modify the work to accommodate to some physical limitations of the older worker. In one hospital, for example, a nurse's aide is enlisted to move a patient or change bedsheets for a mature individual who has trouble with such strenuous activities.
- Senior-friendly policies that permit, for example, flexible and part-time work, should be developed.
- It is important to maintain pay equity between senior workers and younger workers so that you do not have a second class subgroup of workers.
- It may be necessary to work with younger managers to ensure that they understand that senior workers are likely to have different work values because they were socialized in a different way. For instance, older workers may have different views on authority, on the value of participative decision making, and on the meaning and importance of work in one's life. Another example is that older adults generally place a high importance on work, seeing is as a responsibility, an important part of their life while many younger adults may tend to see work as a means to an end.

While this kind of senior-friendly culture exists in few companies today, it is likely to increase, because it will have to as senior workers become a more important part of the work force and firms will have to employ them if they are to meet customer demand.

Source: Adapted from (Solomon, 1995)

related levels of factors that make up the organization's culture, starting with the basic values of the **dominant coalition.** The goal of that coalition is to ensure that their values are firmly embedded in the firm. Their values form the bases of the next level – the **manifestations of organizational culture.** (These elements – selection and socialization, ideologies, and myths and symbols – are discussed later in this chapter; see page 357.) Finally, for outsiders, the culture is obvious

dominant coalition
The group in an organization that wields the most control and power and whose values are reflected in the organizational culture

manifestations of organizational culture
The specific form of organizational elements that reflect the values and beliefs of the dominant organization coalition

only in the modes of implementation that are apparent when they interact with the firm in different ways. To think of organizational culture in this way should help you to understand why it is so enduring, so powerful and how it is affected by, and affects, selection, socialization, reward practices, and even the firm's products or services (Gagliardi, 1986).

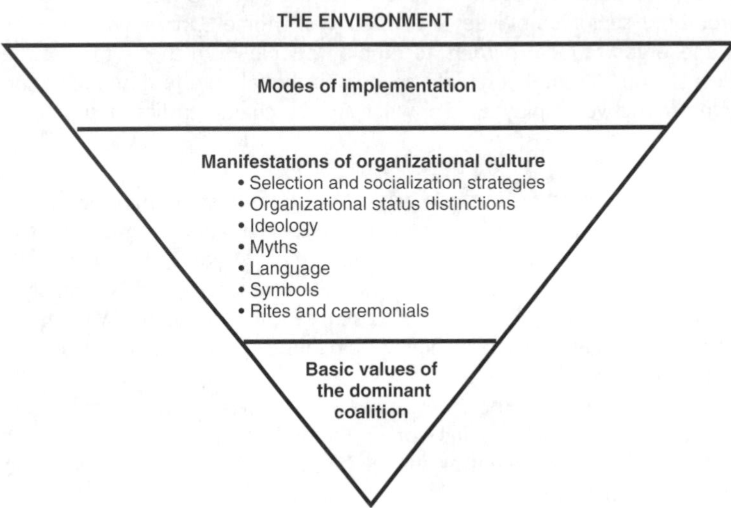

Fig 12.1 : A multilevel model of organizational culture

BASIC VALUES OF THE DOMINANT COALITION

Organization culture has its roots in the basic values of the dominant coalition, the group which wields the most control and power. These values may have originated with the firm's founder and reflect his or her fundamental beliefs about what should be done, how it should be done, who should do it, and the way that members are treated. These values of the dominant are the basis for the **organizational culture profile**, or the general criteria used to judge whether actions, ideas, and attitudes of members are right or wrong. The sorts of values that form the cultural identity of the firm may be the way to which it is oriented (O'Reilly et al., 1991).

organizational culture profile The general criteria in an organization used to judge whether actions, ideas, and attitudes of members are right or wrong

1 *Innovation and risk taking* Seeking new opportunities, taking risks, experimenting, and being unconstrained by formal policies and practices
2 *Stability and security* Valuing predictability, security, and the use of rules to govern behavior
3 *Respect for people* Showing tolerance, fairness, and respect for others
4 *Outcome orientation* Having concern and high expectations about results, achievement, and action

5 *Team orientation and collaboration* Working together in coordinated and collaborative ways
6 *Aggressiveness and competition* Taking strong actions in markets in dealing with competitors

The primary interest of the dominant coalition is to maintain the cultural identity of the firm so that it is consistent with the values of the members in that coalition (Gagliardi, 1986). This permits the members of the coalition to maintain power and control because these values serve to justify crucial organizational policies, practices, and decisions such as key promotions, choices of products or services, and the selection of strategic niches. The recent history of several important firms in the USA is an illustration of what can happen when the top management is able to do this, even in the face of significant environmental changes. The dominant coalitions in both IBM and General Motors were able to remain in power for years by implementing marketing and technology strategies which protected them. As long as IBM was able to remain in the mainframe business, in spite of the technological changes in personal computers, the managerial power structure remained somewhat stable and intact. After some severe losses, John Akers was replaced by Louis Gerstner. He was charged with turning IBM around. The aim literally was to change the way people in IBM think and do business, to change the values which dominated the firm because these values no longer worked. The same thing happened at General Motors. During the 1980s, under the direction of Roger Smith, GM lost a large percentage of its market share to foreign manufacturers. Smith remained in the top position until he was replaced by Robert Stempel. Stempel, however, was part of the same dominant coalition as Smith and while he made some important changes, he was unable to have any substantive effect on GM, though admittedly his tenure was too short for any visible effects to be noticed. He was replaced when the board of directors finally made the decision to intervene and appoint a CEO with a different orientation from that of previous CEOs.

Manifestations of Organizational Culture

The basic values of the dominant coalition are reflected in concepts, meanings, and messages that are embedded in their decisions and in organization practices such as selection and socialization strategies, organizational status distinctions, ideologies, myths, language, symbols, and rites and ceremonials (Trice and Beyer, 1993). These elements have two purposes and, likewise, convey two different types of meaning. One purpose is instrumental and rational; the other is expressive and emotional.

instrumental meanings The ways that the values and beliefs of the dominant coalition are reflected in what the organization can do and how it does it

- The **instrumental meanings** are the ways that values and beliefs are reflected in what the organization can do and how it does it. They broadly and generally define such objectives as the nature of the products or services, the markets that will be served, the philosophy of product quality levels, the orientation toward personnel within the firm, the nature of

expressive meanings
The psychological and sociological meaning to members of the various manifestations of culture

work relationships with the organization, and the general orientation of the organization to its constituencies.

- The **expressive meanings** are the psychological and sociological meanings and effects of those same elements on the members. They create a "symbolic field and seek to protect stability ... They enable the group to maintain its collective identity and offer a recognizable identity to the outside world" (Gagliardi, 1986). They often involve the creation of symbols that have important meanings to the members and are easily identified by others as being associated with that organization.

These instrumental and expressive meanings, and effects, can be seen in what happened when Robert Horton became the chief operating officer of British Petroleum in the early 1990s. The company was in trouble because his predecessor had made some poor major strategic decisions (*The Economist*, 1992). Horton's strategy for turning the company around was to change the corporate strategy, the culture, to reduce costs, and to reduce managerial layers. Under Horton, BP greatly expanded its US refining and marketing operations, spending more than $7.7 billion to take over Standard Oil. Later, BP began making substantial investments in the North Sea, the Gulf of Mexico, and Colombia. To reduce costs, BP eliminated 8,000 employees from the work force. Horton attempted to foster a culture which emphasized teamwork and collaboration, empowering the work force, reducing the bureaucracy, and increasing the focus on globalization. The instrumental effects of these changes were reduced costs and a streamlined organization – exactly the results he intended.

However, the expressive effects were not quite what Horton expected, or wanted. Rather than an empowered culture that Horton wanted, the workers were resentful because they felt that the culture changes had been unilaterally imposed. There was a feeling among many that the cultural change was more of a public relations effort than a serious attempt to change BP's values. Instead of feelings of empowerment because they had more responsibility due to the reduction of layers of management, they felt overburdened with more work and felt that BP was still a top-down managed company.

We now consider each element of the manifestations of organizational culture in turn:

- Selection and socialization strategies
- Organizational status distinctions
- Ideologies
- Myths
- Language
- Symbols
- Rites and ceremonial

Organizations try to select and indoctrinate members with values consistent with the culture. When effective selecting and socializing members results in hiring people with values congruent with the organization culture, the results are increased job satisfaction, higher organizational commitment and lower turnover

(O'Reilly et al., 1991). In one company which was trying to develop a culture emphasizing teamwork, commitment, and cooperation, job candidates were asked in the interview whether they had worked in volunteer fire departments. The reason for such a question was that this type of job required teamwork and a willingness to contribute, both of which were values desired in the firm. In the same firm, the first groups of employees were socialized and trained in groups, with very little individualized training, in an attempt to increase group cohesiveness.

Class distinctions, or **organizational status distinctions** – the accepted power and status relations between individuals and groups in organizations – are one basis for legitimizing influence relationships. The most obvious are hierarchical. These are consistent with the ordering of organizational levels and the delegated responsibility and authority associated with levels.

organizational status distinctions
Accepted power and status relations between individuals and groups

There are also other types of class distinctions. In some organizations, certain positions have higher status than others even though they are presumably at the same organizational level. In universities, there are status distinctions between professors, such as a professor of medicine and a professor of education. Another status distinction could be among occupational groups. These will occur especially when groups of trained professionals work with less trained groups or other groups with different professional training and socialization. The high-status groups will have more power and find it easier to obtain resources.

The culture of any organization is built around a shared **ideology** (Trice and Beyer, 1984) – "the relatively coherent set of beliefs that binds some people together and explain their worlds [to them] in cause–effect relations" (Beyer, 1981). Ideology helps members make sense of decisions. For example, the major US auto firms in the mid-1970s did not respond to the small-car import growth and the oil crisis. They believed deeply that it was unnecessary to move aggressively into small cars because their technical and managerial superiority would, in the long run, win in the marketplace. They felt no need for further justification of this strategy than these beliefs, even in the face of contradictory evidence.

ideology
A relatively coherent set of beliefs that binds a group and explains its world in cause–effect relations

A **myth** is a story of past events that is used to explain the origins or transformations of something. It leads to an unquestioned belief that certain techniques and behavior are right. There is often no demonstrated evidence for the belief, only the acceptance of the myth (Trice and Beyer, 1984). Of course, myths differ in accuracy but they all represent important events or circumstances that are passed on from one organization generation to another and become a basis for action. How much truth and how much fiction are in the myths and stories that arise from the organization's culture is not important. What matters is whether they transmit core organization values to others and that they serve as a basis of control.

myth
A dramatic narrative of imagined events, usually to explain origins or transformations of something

For example, Lee Iacocca, the CEO who navigated Chrysler from near bankruptcy in the early 1980s to a competitive position in the automobile industry in the 1990s, was the topic of many stories and myths. His reputation as an effective, tough-minded manager who can deliver results began in the 1960s during his days at Ford. There were many stories at Ford about him. One of these described his personal role in the development of the first Mustang, which was a very successful Ford product in the late 1960s. Others described his no-nonsense decision-making style. There were stories that he would summarily fire a person, right in a meeting, when he thought the person had done a poor job. During the period of his rise to second-in-command behind Henry Ford II, these stories were told to convey his tough-minded management style in the company. Later, he had a falling out with Mr. Ford and was fired by him. Interestingly, some of these same stories became part of the evidence used to justify his firing.

For a short period, Iacocca was out of work but that was only until the Chrysler bankruptcy crisis. Chrysler needed a tough-minded CEO like Iacocca and he was hired for the job in 1979. Chrysler was a mess organizationally, financially, and from a product-mix perspective. One of his first major moves, a story that lives to this day in Chrysler, is that when he took the position, he publicly announced that he cut his own salary from over $350,000 per year to $1 per year, though he did maintain stock options that later proved to be worth millions. Also, during a strike in which the UAW was trying to negotiate a wage increase to around $19 per hour, Iacocca went into plants to talk directly to the workers. He told them, "Chrysler doesn't have any jobs for $19 an hour, but we have a lot of jobs for $17 an hour." The story is that, even though he was offering no pay increase to the workers, they cheered him because they believed that he was saving their jobs.

A unique **language** exists for every organization. Like the mother tongue of a country, the organization's language is best used and understood by its members. Using it properly is, in fact, a way for individuals to be identified as a member. The organization's language comprises jargon, slang, gestures, signals, signs, jokes, humor and metaphors that allow members to convey very specific and clear meaning to other members (Trice and Beyer, 1993). When the "right" language is used to explain an action, it is accepted because it reflects the culture. For example, when Henry Ford II personally fired Lee Iacocca after a very successful career at Ford Motor Company, Iacocca asked "Why?" Mr Ford is reported to have said, "Because I don't like you." Ford, even though it is among the largest firms in the USA, is still under close family control, and those who work there know it – and have always known it. When this story circulated among employees, everyone there understood – because personal loyalty is very important. The language Henry Ford used was very consistent with the ideology.

symbols
Objects to which organizational meaning has become attached

Symbols – objects to which organizational meaning has become attached – can include titles, parking places, special dining rooms, office size, location, and furnishings and others of position and power (Pfeffer, 1981). In any organization, the specific symbols will be unique and related to the shared perspective of members. One plant manager attempted to convey the concept of egalitarianism in the plant by installing a round table, as a symbol, in the conference room. The idea was that there were no "heads;" everyone should expect to contribute equally. However, another symbol carried a more powerful message: there was only one reserved place in the parking lot – it belonged to the plant manager.

Symbols can also distinguish status and power differences between individuals and groups at the same level. For example, in almost every company, it is simple to know which of the vice presidents (all presumably at the same organizational level) is most important by the location and size of office and pay differentials. In fact, it causes some consternation in an organization when a person wishes to have an office location and size that are different from others with similar status. Likewise, it can also cause problems when a lower-status person acquires symbols that are more appropriate to a higher-level position.

Rites are "relatively elaborate, dramatic, planned sets of activities that consolidate various forms of cultural expressions into one event, which are carried out through social interactions, usually for the benefit of an audience." A **ceremony** is a "system of several rites connected with an occasion or event" (Trice and Beyer, 1984). Like symbols and myths, rites and ceremonies convey important cultural meanings by actions and interactions. Some of the more important organizational rites are discussed below (Trice and Beyer, 1984).

rites
Relatively elaborate, dramatic, planned sets of activities that consolidate various forms of cultural expressions into one event

ceremony
A system of several related rites connected with a specific occasion or event

Rites of passage bring you into an organization or separate you from it. **Induction rites** that bring you into an organization convey some of its important norms and values. They can be very elaborate, like military basic training, or very simple, as when a personnel assistant explains the company rules and policies to you on the first workday. In one firm, to communicate the level of expected commitment, it was standard practice to have the spouses of married prospective employees present when the job offer was made. During this discussion, both the good points and the bad points of the job were accurately described to both.

rites of passage
Rites that are intended to bring a person into an organization and to convey norms and values

Separation rites help you make a clean break with the organization. Retirement parties signal the end of a career, and going-away dinners separate a person from one organization on the way to another. Separation rites often involve elaborate dinners, drinking, and discussions about past life in the organization.

separation rites
Rites that help a person make a clean break from the organization

Degradation rites occur when someone is removed from a position or from the organization. In most organizations, these rites are less formal. At one point in the history of a large entertainment and publishing firm in the USA, releasing a top manager began with a rite of degradation. The CEO would begin to point out that a certain manager was becoming a problem because "he couldn't handle the women." The firm was noted for having many attractive women executives and workers, and it was well known that many men and women had open relationships, regardless of their marital status. However, when the president wished to remove a manager, the degradation rite started this way. Later, some "objective" performance deficiency would be identified and the person would resign or be fired.

degradation rites
Rites that surround the removal of someone from a position or an organization

Enhancement rites elevate the status or position of a person. Awarding recognition through symbols or announcement of promotions are examples. Sometimes these are informal. In one firm, the enhancement rite that precedes promotion to the top levels begins when the CEO asks a junior executive to join him on special public occasions.

enhancement rites
Rites that increase the status or position of a person after they are in an organization

Renewal rites have the goal of strengthening and improving the current social structure (Trice and Beyer, 1984). Training and development programs are one form of these rites. They are usually quite conspicuous in organizations because time must be set aside during which those in the organization must attend classes

renewal rites
Rites that have the goal of strengthening and improving the current social structure

and because these programs usually employ a set of new symbols and language. This was an especially important activity for Service America when the company was restructuring itself after severe economic losses. Under a new CEO, they undertook a series of management development programs which almost all managers were required to attend. While a major part of the development was directed toward improving the managers' knowledge of the latest and best business practices, a substantial effort was devoted toward ensuring that those attending were exposed to the philosophy of the new CEO and understood the type of culture he was seeking to develop.

conflict reduction rites
Rites intended to reduce or avoid conflict in an organization

integration rites
Rites that facilitate and increase the interaction of organization members to make working together easier

Conflict avoidance or reduction is desired in most organizations; yet the nature of organization itself gives rise to conflict. To resolve conflict, organizations use **conflict reduction rites** such as collective bargaining, the grievance process, the "open-door policy" where each manager's door will always be open to hear subordinates' problems, committees in which divergent views can be aired, and ombudsmen who are supposed to represent workers' interests impartially.

Integration rites facilitate and increase the interaction of the organization's members, presumably to make working together easier (Trice and Beyer, 1984). During integration rites, official titles and organizational differences are eliminated for a short time so that people meet others as people. An example of an integration rite is the "dining in" tradition in the US Air Force.

MODES OF IMPLEMENTATION

After you adapt to an organization and live in it for a while (see page 100 in chapter 4), you become unaware of the organizational culture and its effects. On the other hand, if you are an outsider or customer, you have no direct experience of the organizational culture; instead you experience it through the specific modes of implementation – designs for products and services, policies for dealing with customers, approaches to managing human resources, the formal structure and types of controls – all of which can be traced back to the values of the dominant coalition. They are also internally reflected in the sorts of things described above. So, one way to experience the organizational culture is through your perceptions about the company and/or the use of its products and services, how they are designed, their quality level, their price, and the level of service that is delivered. Another way of experiencing the culture is when you seek employment with a firm and are exposed to its hiring practices, promotional material and, perhaps most importantly, the way the hiring decision is transmitted to you if you are a job candidate. You also experience an organizational culture by the symbols, trademarks and logos associated with it. "Joe Camel," the letters "GE," and the Nike "swoosh" convey something to us about these firms. Finally, you sense some of the organizational culture from the way it deals with its social responsibility.

THE MODAL PERSONALITY OF TOP MANAGEMENT AND TYPES OF ORGANIZATIONAL CULTURES

The modal personality of the dominant coalition will determine how these values are translated into actions, policies, and behavior. This group makes the import-

Focus on Rituals – Integration Rites: The Air Force's "Dining In"

The "Dining In" is a formal social event in the US Air Force. It draws on an old tradition of military dinners, which, some think, dates back to ancient military feasts. Its purpose is to bring officers and enlisted personnel together in a setting where they can interact socially, have the opportunity to know each other better and develop closer bonds.

The "Dining In" has a very well-prescribed set of norms that are part of the formal dinner program. These reinforce many of the behaviors expected of military members in other settings. Here are some examples of the formally prescribed "rules of the mess:"

- Thou shalt arrive within ten minutes of the appointed hour.
- Thou should make every effort to meet all guests.
- Thou shalt always use the appropriate toasting procedure.
- Thou shalt enjoy thyself to the fullest.

There are sanctions, far from serious, for violating these norms. On observing a violation, a member of the mess asks to be recognized by the presiding officer. The member then outlines, in a formal manner, the violator and the nature of the violation. If the violation is deemed serious, the violator is penalized, usually by being required "going to the grog bowl" and enduring the punishment of a drink.

The "Dining In" includes much good-natured bantering and roasting within and across ranks, but the effect, it is believed, is a more highly cohesive military unit.

ant decisions about market strategy, organization design, the nature of the reward system, and who is promoted into this group. Their visions, beliefs, and actions are translated through managerial decisions into specific policies, products and practices that will be manifestations of the culture.

One study that tells us a lot about how organizational culture is related to the modal personality is about how neurotic managers create **neurotic organizations** (Kets de Vries and Miller, 1984). The idea of the neurotic organization is similar to the concept of the neurotic person. Neurotic people exhibit extreme psychological tendencies and behaviors, leading to problems that affect them and others. Their problems, however, are not so severe as to justify taking them out of society. Like a neurotic person, a neurotic organization is in trouble, but still able to operate, and headed by executives or groups of executives with neurotic tendencies. The result is a neurotic culture.

neurotic organizations Organizations that are headed by executives or groups of executives with neurotic tendencies

Of course, not all managers are neurotic nor do all organizations have neurotic cultures. Many organizations have healthy cultures that are supportive, innovative, and collaborative, creating a positive social and psychological context for its members. These healthy organizations will have a mixture of personality types, which will be neither dominant nor extreme (Kets de Vries and Miller, 1986). So why study these extreme types of personalities and the resulting organizational cultures? Because it helps understand the culture of "normal" companies. Neurotic cultures are different from normal ones only by a matter of degree. Besides, the processes that lead to neurotic organizations are not qualitatively different from those that lead to healthy cultures – they are simply more extreme and intense. We now look at five cultures:

1 Charismatic culture
2 Paranoid cultures
3 Avoidant cultures
4 Bureaucratic cultures
5 Politicized cultures

charismatic culture
An organizational culture in which the emphasis on individualism is exaggerated, particularly at the top level

dramatic managers
Managers with feelings of grandiosity, a strong need for attention from others, and who try to draw attention to themselves, often seeking stimulation and excitement, but lacking self-discipline

A **charismatic culture** is associated with a dramatic modal managerial personality. **Dramatic managers** have feelings of grandiosity, have a strong need for attention from others, and try to draw attention to themselves. They are exhibitionists, seeking excitement and stimulation. However, they often lack self-discipline, cannot focus their attention for long periods of time, and tend to be charming but superficial. They often attract subordinates with high dependency needs.

In charismatic organization cultures, this emphasis on individualism is exaggerated, particularly at the top level. The executives have a high need for visibility and recognition outside the firm. The goal of the firm is to grow rapidly. Decision making is based on intuition, guesses, and hunches without careful analysis of the environment or the capabilities of the organization. Often the organization structure and human resources are inadequate to handle the desired growth.

The dramatic manager exploits others, and power is concentrated at the top of the organization. This does two things: the top executive keeps close control and at the same time remains the center of attention. The centralized control is facilitated by the kind of people these organizations attract to upper and mid-level positions. They tend to have high needs for dependence, prefer to be directed, and overlook the weaknesses of the leaders. For the subordinates, everything revolves around the top manager or group of top managers. The subordinates have a great deal of trust that those who lead the organization can do no wrong.

paranoid culture
An organizational culture characterized by a strong sense of distrust and a deep sense of suspicion

The **paranoid culture** results from a suspicious modal personality orientation. Suspicious managers feel persecuted by others and do not trust them and behave in guarded and secret ways toward others. They believe that subordinates are lazy, incompetent, and secretly wish to "get" them. He or she feels hostile toward others, particularly peers and subordinates, and acts aggressively toward them. If you work in a paranoid culture, you will feel a strong sense of distrust and suspicion (Kets de Vries and Miller, 1986).

The top managers in paranoid firms are not proactive. Fear and suspicion dominate the organization and this reduces its ability to respond quickly and spontaneously to strategic opportunities. Managements are constantly searching for information about what is going on in their environments. It is acquired through elaborate control systems that provide information the top management believes is required to cope with the external crises that they fear are coming. The information, however, tends to be highly distorted to confirm the suspicions of threat that are the basis for the paranoid organizations. The decision makers look for deeper, hidden reasons for the events that occur around them.

In the paranoid culture, people do not easily share important information with others because they fear that it could cost them some advantage. In paranoid cultures, people tend to act passively and do not actively participate in important organization matters. This results in either organization paralysis or directive action by the top management to initiate events.

The **depressive modal personality** orientation leads to an **avoidant culture**. A depressive person has strong needs for affection and support from others and feels unable to act on, and change the course of, events. These feelings of inadequacy are related to very passive behavior and inaction. Depressives often seek justification of their actions from other significant actors; in the case of managers, these might be experts and consultants.

depressive personality
A person with strong needs for affection and support from others who feels unable to act on and change the course of events

Top management seeks to avoid change in the avoidant culture. They are passive and purposeless. Change is resisted because it may threaten the current organization values and power structure; appropriate action is avoided. The relative low level of external changes and the desire of the management to retain control results in little activity, low self-confidence, high anxiety, and an extremely conservative culture.

avoidant culture
A culture in which top management seeks to avoid change

Managers are more concerned with maintaining the position of the firm in the present environment than with creativity and innovation. Eventually, procedures, rules, and policies are overemphasized, and they often become ends in themselves. In other words, managerial energy goes into ensuring rule compliance, not into seeing that the organization performs effectively.

The **bureaucratic culture** is a result of a compulsive modal organization personality. **Compulsive managers** have high needs for control. They view things in terms of domination and submission. They focus on very specific but often trivial details. Compulsive managers are devoted to their work and to show deference toward those at levels above them and act autocratically toward subordinates. They have strong preferences for well-ordered systems and processes.

bureaucratic culture
An organizational culture in which there is more concern with the rules of working together than with effective performance

In the bureaucratic culture, there is more concern with how things look rather than with how things work. Managers focus more on the rules than on the purpose of those rules. There are usually specific, detailed, formalized control systems, to monitor the behavior of the members. These controls are derived from very specific objectives that have been broken down into very detailed, often trivial, plans of action (Kets de Vries and Miller, 1986). These plans and the performance indicators derived from them then become the criteria against which performance is measured.

compulsive managers
Managers who have high needs for control, view things in terms of domination and submission, and focus on specific, often trivial details

These tight constraints arise because of the obsessive control needs of top management. Careful planning and control processes provide them with a sense of security that is enhanced when they find that careful planning also makes it easy to control the actions of those at lower levels. The high control needs of managers are reflected in the ways that the authority structure is implemented and

politicized culture An organizational culture in which there is no clear direction and there are often power struggles among individuals and groups

detached personality Managers who have a strong sense of disengagement from others and of not being connected to the environment

executed. Rank and position are important, and hierarchical deference is the norm. Ritualistic, deferential behavior toward superiors is expected from subordinates.

Politicized cultures occur in organizations when the top management has a **detached modal organizational personality**. They have a strong sense of disengagement from others and of not being connected to the environment. They believe that interaction with others will lead to harm and tend to avoid emotional relationships because they fear they will be demeaned by others. Aloofness and coldness characterizes their relationships. They are socially and psychologically isolated and do not care about it.

In politicized organization cultures, there is no clear direction. The CEO is not strong, but also not psychologically connected to the organization. Lacking leadership, managers at lower levels try to influence the direction of the firm. There are often several individuals or coalitions competing for power because of the lack of leadership. Managers are involved in these divisive power struggles to enhance their own position and status, and there is only minimal concern with the success of the organization.

ORGANIZATIONAL SUBCULTURES

organizational subcultures Different ideologies, cultural forms, and other practices that are exhibited by identifiable groups of people in an organization

The fact is that most large organizations do not have a homogeneous culture. Instead they are usually a cluster of **organizational subcultures,** or (Trice and Beyer, 1993, p 174):

> different ideologies, cultural forms, and other practices that identifiable groups of people in an organization exhibit. They differ noticeably from the overall culture . . . and from each other.

There can be different types of organizational subcultures that members identify with (Sackmann, 1992):

- Hierarchical subcultures
- Occupational/task subcultures
- Culturally diverse subcultures

EXERCISE

THE ANALYSIS OF NEUROTIC ORGANIZATIONAL CULTURES

This exercise is designed to give you some insight into the dominant orientation of an organization's culture and whether it may be extreme, in the sense we discuss in this chapter.

First, decide on a focal organization – a specific organization that you know well. It could be one where you work presently, one where you have worked in the past, or an organization with which a close friend or relative is associated.

Then, using the seven-point scale, indicate the degree to which you think each characteristic describes the organization as you know it. If the characteristic describes the organization exactly, circle 7. If the characteristic is not very descriptive of the organization circle the 1.

	Not at all descriptive of my organization						Exactly descriptive of my organization
Charismatic cultures							
• The top management is the center of attention.	1	2	3	4	5	6	7
• When the top manager is happy, everyone is happy.	1	2	3	4	5	6	7
• Top management operates on instinctive reactions.	1	2	3	4	5	6	7
Paranoid cultures							
• It is hard to obtain information about what is going on.	1	2	3	4	5	6	7
• We are very concerned that competitors will gain an advantage over us.	1	2	3	4	5	6	7
• You cannot trust many people in this firm.	1	2	3	4	5	6	7
Avoidant cultures							
• Rules are very important.	1	2	3	4	5	6	7
• Managers usually delay decisions.	1	2	3	4	5	6	7
• We are in a good market position and should not risk it much.	1	2	3	4	5	6	7
Politicized cultures							
• Machiavelli would do well here.	1	2	3	4	5	6	7
• Managers are very selfish.	1	2	3	4	5	6	7
• Power struggles are normal events in firm.	1	2	3	4	5	6	7
Bureaucratic cultures							
• The basic rule is to follow the rules.	1	2	3	4	5	6	7
• The position is more important than the person in it.	1	2	3	4	5	6	7
• There are detailed procedures and plans for amost everything to be done in the firm.	1	2	3	4	5	6	7

Now, total the score for each type of cultural category and enter these scores on the appropriate line of the Culture Profile Analysis form below. Connect the points, and then examine the set of scores.

Cultural Profile Analysis

	Low						High
Charismatic	3	6	9	12	15	18	21
Paranoid	3	6	9	12	15	18	21
Avoidant	3	6	9	12	15	18	21
Politicized	3	6	9	12	15	18	21
Bureaucratic	3	6	9	12	15	18	21

- Are any of the culture scores extremely different from others?
- What are some other characteristics of the firm you can describe that have not been discussed in the text or on this scale?
- What kind of employees are in the firm? What kind of managers?

This identification arises for several reasons:

- People share similar attitudes, values and beliefs.
- They have common goals.
- They are able to be more influential with others instead of alone.
- They interact frequently.
- They find their needs satisfied from others who share the same subcultural values. (March and Simon, 1958; Rentsch, 1990).

The stronger these factors, the greater the identification with the particular subculture.

hierarchical subcultures Subcultures that exist at different organizational levels and are visible in the differences in symbols, status, authority, and power between levels

occupational/task subcultures Subculture with members who are likely to have a strong identification with others that have similar skills

pluralism A cultural value that promotes mutual respect, acceptance, teamwork, and productivity among diverse people

Hierarchical subcultures exist at different organizational levels and are visible in the differences in symbols, status, authority, and power between managers and workers. Hierarchical subcultures are most clearly visible and strongest in organizations where there is clear, strong stratification between levels. This occurs when the work at lower levels has been highly task-specialized so that minimal skills are required to do it. This weakens the power of lower levels and results in centralization of control and decision making. It also is facilitated when promotion to the managerial levels requires both competence and values congruent with those of the dominant coalition. The result is a management group with strong homogeneous values that are different from those of the work force in general.

In **occupational/task subcultures**, members have strong identification with the others who have similar skills. These skills are very important to organizational success and have been developed through intensive training during which there is strong occupational socialization. Then, others who share the same occupation or task, inside and outside the organization, will be an important reference group.

Many organizations are experiencing the same phenomena of multi-culturalism as Digital Equipment. In one Digital plant with 350 workers, there are 44 different countries represented and 19 different languages spoken. Multi-culturalism in US organizations in recent years has increased as African-Americans, Hispanics, Asians, and Native Americans have entered the work force in more significant numbers and as companies have made serious efforts to reduce discrimination in selection and promotion practices. The result has been that there are culturally diverse subcultures based on values and beliefs of these groups that may differ in many ways from the dominant organization culture.

Diversity can provide the potential for higher productivity because a wider range of human talents contribute to creativity and there is less chance of "group-think" (Adler, 1991). On the other hand, it can lead to conflict and may make it difficult to develop cohesion. Which outcome occurs depends on how diversity is managed. Some firms have adopted "**pluralism**" as part of their corporate philosophy: a "culture that promotes mutual respect, acceptance, teamwork, and productivity among people who are diverse in work background, experience, education, age, gender, race, ethnic origin, physical abilities, religious belief, sexual orientation, and other perceived differences" (Caudron, 1992). To implement such a philosophy, firms inevitably turn to training and education. For these to be effective, they must, above all, have the strong support of the top management and be reflected in the policies, practices, and strategies. Only then will training and education for multi-cultural, multi-ethnic integration work. When properly conducted, such programs can reduce the use of stereotypes, increase the ability of individuals to see things from the point of view of different cultures or groups, reduce the anxiety of being in the presence of others who are different, and reduce the frequency of non-culturally relative judgments (Brislin, 1993).

Organizational Culture – Some Special Cases

Managers are increasingly recognizing the power and effects of culture on the behavior of people in organizations. They are becoming interested in trying to manage it as a way to contribute to the effectiveness of the firm. However, while there is agreement that cultures exist in every organization and that they do change, there is disagreement over the degree to which they can be managed. We think there are some special situations in which the effects of organizational culture cause serious problems for the management of a firm.

- Implementing culture in a new organization
- Mergers and acquisitions
- Changes in the environment
- Changing the existing culture
- Changing the CEO

Implementing a Culture in a New Organization

In new organizations, it is possible to try to shape the culture through carefully designed selection programs, socialization strategies, and the consistent use of symbols and language. Very quickly, though, the members of the organization modify the values intended by management, and the culture emerges. When starting a new organization, many managers make a conscious decision to implement a healthy culture that supports the type of high involvement organizations (HIOs) discussed in chapter 6 (page 176). This has some important advantages: costs may be lower because less direct supervision is needed, worker morale and satisfaction are higher, and absenteeism and turnover may be reduced.

Creating such a healthy culture to support the HIO is difficult, especially when the basic values and assumptions of the managerial group conflict with the practices required to support it. There is often a serious gap between what managers say they want and the kinds of member behavior that are supported by the organizational culture. This happened in the start-up of a new plant in which the management team wanted to create a culture of participation, self-managed work groups, teamwork, active participation of the work force in decision making, high product quality, commitment, and a sense of trust; see figure 12.2. They sought to do this in several ways. They were very careful in screening and selecting employees. They sought a work force willing to participate in decision making, without previous union experience, with high skill levels, and with a willingness to perform several different tasks. The pay system was based on the skills of the employees, not the tasks that they performed. This was to facilitate the workers' flexibility and willingness to work on different machines.

During the initial phases of the start-up, there was a great deal of worker enthusiasm, involvement, and trust. However, it soon became clear that many of the things that management wanted to instill in the culture were only verbalized values, not implemented practices. For instance, while the plant manager articulated the importance of high product quality, the floor superintendents continued to ship marginally acceptable products to customers.

There were also problems with the espoused value of participation. Initially, workers were told that they could bring any production problem to the attention of any manager in the plant. It soon became apparent that there were certain issues about the new equipment that the plant manager did not wish to discuss. Soon the level of participation decreased to almost nothing.

One reason for the failure to implement the desired culture was that it was inconsistent with the personality of the plant manager. As figure 12.2 shows, he had a dramatic personality that overpowered the attempt to create the articulated values and beliefs of empowerment and participation (Gagliardi, 1986). In fact, the only reason that the empowerment culture was wanted in the first place was that the president of the firm strongly advocated it. The plant manager went along. However, when the president left the company, the plant manager was given more latitude in managing the plant and implementing his own philosophy. In the end, his dramatic personality prevailed.

MERGERS AND ACQUISITIONS

Problems arise when the cultures of two firms involved in a merger are different and, more importantly, incongruent; see figure 12.3. This is what happened in

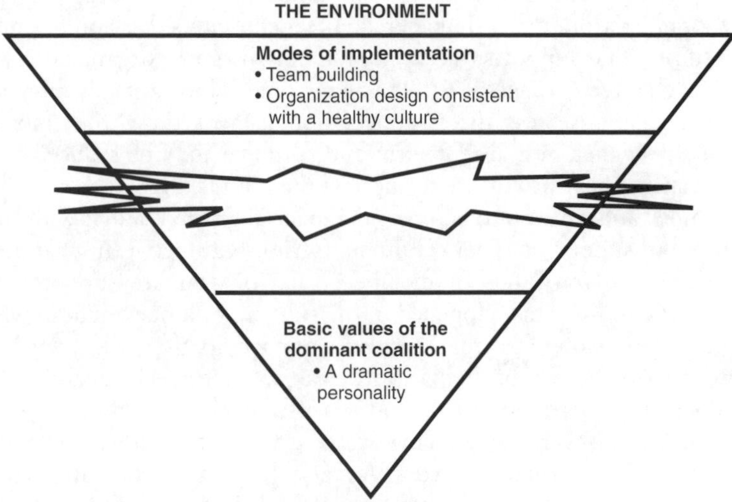

Fig 12.2: Implementing a culture in a new organization

the Kidder, Peabody acquisition by General Electric (GE) (Schwartz, 1989). GE acquired Kidder Peabody in 1986 for $602 million, thinking it to be strategically complementary to its own financial unit, GE Capital. However, while there might have been a strategic fit, there was surely not a cultural fit.

GE had a more traditional structure with managers imbued with the GE philosophy as a result of its extensive management development efforts. The culture is one that seeks to minimize bureaucracy and rely on "just-do-it teamwork" (Stewart, 1996). The idea is that the success of managers is tied to the success of their subordinates. Processes and procedures in the company are designed to support this culture – as does GE CEO Jack Welch's idea that the profitability is a result of teamwork and collaboration.

Kidder, Peabody was a very profitable financial securities firm. Kidder's culture was a very entrepreneurial culture, one in which individuals had a lot of free rein in operating. There was little emphasis on teamwork and collaboration, a fundamental aspect of the GE culture.

After the acquisition, as the GE philosophy and strategy were implemented in the Kidder, Peabody group, the top performers there became dissatisfied. Many left, hurting the profitability of the Kidder unit. As performance dropped, GE began to take more control, which is exactly the opposite of what the free spirited Kidder managers wanted. At Kidder, there was a sense that personal success and the firm's success were not linked – a view that could not be accepted by the GE top management. The result of these differences was GE selling Kidder in 1994 to Paine Webber, another securities firm, for $670 million. The net cost to GE was estimated to be $170 million.

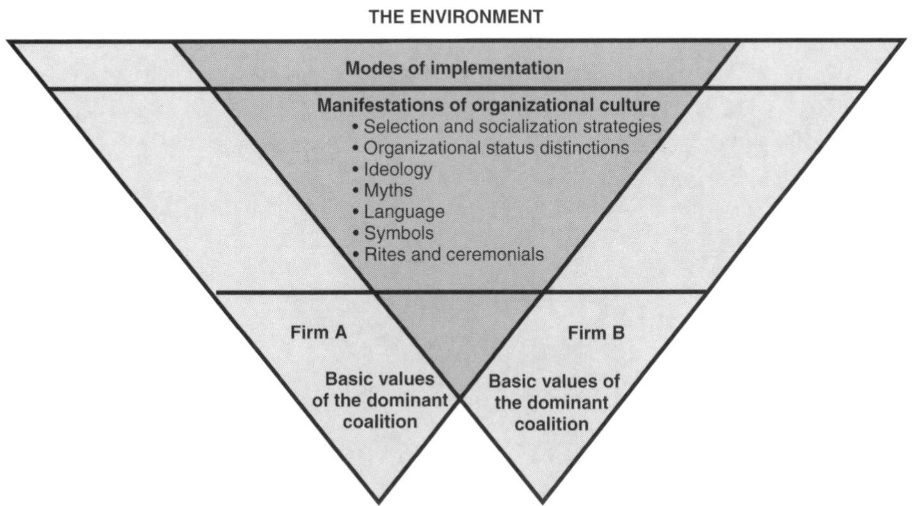

Fig 12.3: Incongruent cultures of two firms in a merger

CHANGES IN THE ENVIRONMENT

Cultures change when there is a significant change in the firm's environment to which it must adapt if it is to survive. Figure 12.4 illustrates the case in which an environmental shift could require a modification of the organization's culture. Suppose that at one time (t_1) a company is operating effectively in the environment as shown bracketed by A. This means that products and services of the firm and the values (basic values A) from which they are derived are congruent. Suppose, however, that over time, the external environment changes and, at t_2, the environment now is shown bracketed by B. This would require different products and services, along with value set B, to operate effectively in it. In many ways, the new outputs for the new environment may be similar to those required by the old one, shown by the area of overlap in figure 12.4. However, the problem of adjustment occurs in those areas where there is no overlap with the previous selection strategies and the other dimensions that reflect the culture.

A good example of the problem of adapting the culture to a changing environment is in the automotive sector in the USA. The environment for Ford, Chrysler and General Motors began changing with the advent of foreign competition beginning in the late 1960s. At that time, GM had a 50 percent share of the US market, with Ford a distant second and Chrysler barely in the picture. However, the environment did not shift sharply and severely in a short time period. Foreign manufacturers kept increasing market share gradually through a strategy of introducing high quality and very competitively priced cars into the US market. All of the American manufacturers made some design changes, but did little to alter their processes to increase product quality. Further, many in this industry were convinced that eventually US consumers would prefer

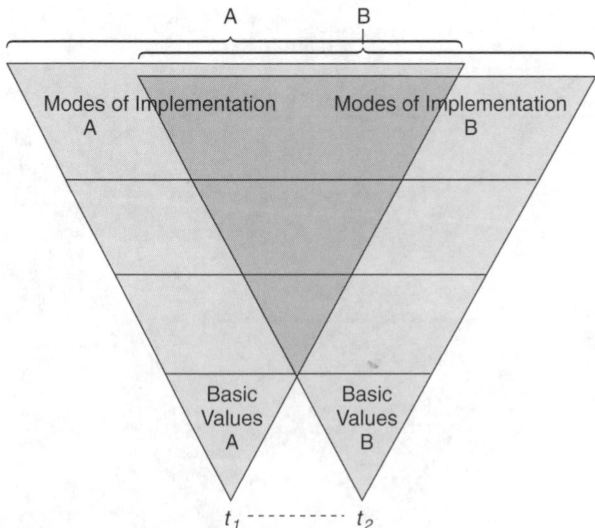

Fig 12.4: Changes in organizational culture as the environment changes

larger, traditional automobiles. Ford adapted nicely, but over some time, to the changing environment. After a long period of resistance, Ford began a serious and successful effort in the mid 1980s to improve its product quality, going through an extreme culture change. The success of this effort was finally realized ten years later in 1992, when the Ford Taurus replaced the Honda as the leader in US auto sales. GM, on the other hand, has not done so well. Its market share is hovering in the late 1990s around 30 percent, down from the 50 percent in the early 1970s. The reason is that, in our judgment, GM has not made the changes necessary in the dominant coalition; one of the major requirements for succession to top management positions has been to be from within GM.

Changing the Existing Culture

It is very difficult to modify the culture of an existing organization, especially when an embedded management attempts to change it by using consultants and formal change programs; see figure 12.5. Usually, attempts to modify culture center around revision of activities and practices. Suppose, for example, a firm is headed by a compulsive chief executive who thinks that productivity might be increased through the creation of an HIO with processes discussed in chapter 6 (page 176). He might decide to change the bureaucratic culture. Trainers and consultants, who use team-building development approaches that give managers experience in working together, might be retained. There might be some organization redesign to facilitate activities among groups by creating new interdependencies. However, because the basic values of the top management managerial groups are not consistent with these practices, the change effort will

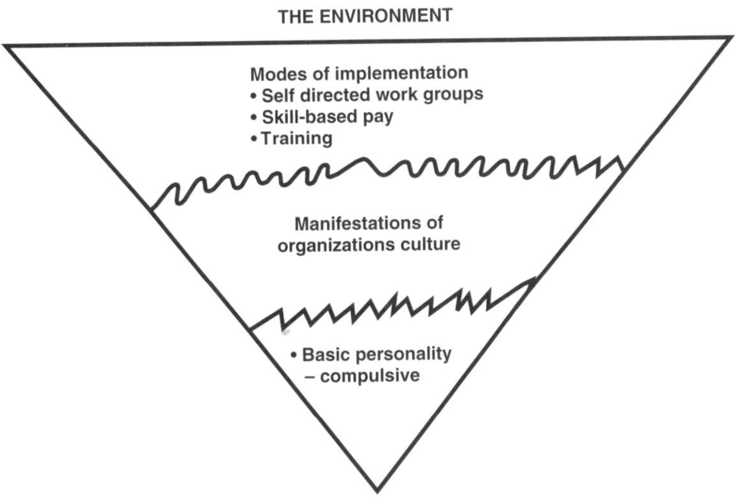

Fig 12.5: Attempting to change an existing organizational culture

fail. The more constructive culture is not consistent with the compulsive modal personality.

CHANGING THE CEO

When a new CEO comes into a firm, a number of things usually happen that affect the culture: Some members of the board of directors are usually replaced; and there is usually a change in the top management group, especially the vice-presidents. The result is a dominant coalition with values more similar to the new CEO that will begin to be reflected in the various procedures and processes that manifest the culture that we have described earlier in this chapter.

Whether the effect on the culture will be strong or weak depends upon the extent to which the values of the new dominant coalition are similar to those of the previous group in power. If the new dominant coalition has values similar to the previous group, there will be little change and things will continue not much different from in the past. This most often occurs when the new CEO comes from within the firm. Then you would expect that he or she has been socialized and then been selected based on the existing culture. Internal succession is a reasonable strategy when the firm has been attaining profitability and performance objectives that are acceptable to its stakeholders, especially the stockholders and the board of directors, and if there is no evidence of a significant change in the environment that would warrant a move to a different culture. The reason for this is that an insider will be already accustomed to the existing culture that is supporting the current acceptable firm performance.

A CEO from the inside is not generally a wise strategy when the firm is performing poorly – unless you can be sure that he or she has a very different set of values from the previous incumbent. When a firm is performing poorly, it usually means that the culture and the operating processes are not aligned with the demands of the external environment, so that the firm is not adopting innovations or is out of touch with the market. An inside replacement could happen under these conditions when the dominant coalition is relatively satisfied and wish to remain in power. This is what happened at GM when Roger Smith was replaced by Robert Stempel in 1990. Under Smith's management, GM lost 11 percent of the market share. Stempel's job as the new CEO was to stop the bleeding and develop a strategy to regain market share. However, Stempel was an old GM hand, having moved through the firm during a career of over 25 years. During that time, he was strongly acculturated with GM values, precisely the ones that were dominant during its years of decline. Stempel made some attempts to turn GM around but was unsuccessful. The board lost confidence in him and, in late 1992, replaced him with Jack Smith. Though Jack Smith was also from inside GM, he was thought to be more innovative and creative than other top managers at his level. When he gained control, he made some key decisions about the product mix of the firm and some significant and effective reductions in the work force. Whether these changes will be effective remains to be seen, at least at this writing.

Focus on A New Actor in the Dominant Coalition: Ted Turner and Time Warner

When Time Warner and Turner Broadcasting System merged in 1995, Time Warner acquired much more than a broadcasting network that specialized in news, Atlanta Braves baseball and old movies. They also acquired Ted Turner as vice-chairman. Turner is an entrepreneurial, outspoken and creative businessman whose reputation for making things work has become legend in the USA and when he began to become more active in the management of Time Warner, he created some waves by insisting that some of the past practices that marked the Times Warner power and status system be changed.

For one thing, the culture of Time Warner was one that permitted, in Turner's mind, it to become an "inefficient collection of free-willed divisions squandering opportunities for synergy and – far worse – often directly wounding each other's businesses." For example, Turner Broadcasting has its own library of films from an earlier acquisition so when Turner discovered that Time Warner had sold a package of movies to CBS for more than $50 million, he was infuriated. He called executive Edward Bleier and let him know in no uncertain terms that he thought the action was inappropriate because he should have offered it to someone in the "family" first. This outburst did little to enhance Turner's standing among the dominant power group in Time Warner, given a number of other invasions into the autonomy of executives who had operated very freely in the media industries.

Next he took on some of Time Warner's status symbols. One thing that he insisted be sold was its art collection of US masterpieces, paintings of museum quality. These paintings decorated Time Warner's board room and executive offices. The pressure from Turner led to the sale of this art. He also attacked the corporate jets that Time Warner top management used for their travels. He thought that if these top people liked this sort of jet travel so much, they could buy their own private jets (Shapiro, 1997).

When the values of an incoming CEO differ from the existing culture, you can expect some serious difficulties. Sooner or later, there will be changes in selection, promotion, policies, procedures and other ways that culture is manifested. During and after the transition in culture, many in the organization may find the new culture uncomfortable and feel a sense of uneasiness and frustration that would lead to high dissatisfaction and turnover. This may be exactly what is needed when the firm is performing poorly and a shakeup is the only way to turn it around. This is the kind of change that Louis Gerstner brought about at IBM when he replaced John Akers, and Lee Iacocca introduced at Chrysler when he took over in the late 1970s. Chrysler had become overstaffed and, even though the top management had a sense of personal security, the firm was in serious financial difficulty. Iacocca focused Chrysler on a more precise market, changed the top management, and above all changed the beliefs of the work force that the firm could survive.

There are times, however, when a new CEO comes into an already effective organization with a strong personality and set of values that are not consistent with the current culture. This is an interesting situation because if the organization is functioning effectively, it is likely that the operating processes and the existing culture are well aligned with its environment. There should be no need for major changes in the culture or the way that things are done. From the multilevel model of culture that we have been discussing, you can predict what might happen in this case. The first thing that will happen, certainly, is that there will be internal resistance to any change from those presently in the organization. If the new manager is successful at changing the culture, there is a real risk that it will lose its culture/process/environment alignment and becomes less effective. It is also possible that the internal resistance might be effective, making it very difficult for the new manager to have a significant effect on the culture. This will lead to significant internal organizational conflict because some will support the proposed changes, particularly if the change will result in more power flowing to them or to their units. Others will oppose it because it threatens their current power and, basing their resistance of the present level of success, might prevail and drive the new manager to leave.

Summary

The fundamental values in a society are strong forces that affect the behavior of those in organizations. Culture is the patterned way of thinking, feeling, and reacting that is characteristic of human groups and that accounts for important differences between them. Values are ideas about what is right or wrong, and good or bad, that are the basis of much human action. Culture is transmitted through socialization.

The organization culture is, of course, significantly affected by the broader society in which the organization exists. However, decisions by key managers, particularly the CEO, give it a more specific form: it will reflect their dominant values. Each organizational culture is unique; there seems to be a distinctive pattern of top management activity and a particular set of policies that emerge in the organization. The culture of an organization contributes to what it is and what it will be. There will be an effort to maintain the culture since it supports the current power structure in the organization. Therefore, it should be expected that the socialization strategies, ideologies and so on will strengthen the current organization value orientations and systems. Likewise, those in organizations may do many things to ensure that the sources of culture do not change in such a way as to require changes in the organizational value systems. Many US firms that have strong capitalistic and individualistic cultures support outside groups and foundations that attempt to strengthen the free-enterprise system. A good example is the extensive business support of the US Chamber of Commerce. These firms also present their own economic and political philosophies directly to the public at large. Even when there are strong external pressures that necessitate internal cultural modifications, the organization will resist. For example, even though there are social pressures and laws that protect women and minorities from discrimination, they still may have problems in work organizations because the culture usually reflects white, male, middle-class, Anglo-Saxon values in its ideologies, socialization strategies, and other manifestations of culture. Those in organizations are sometimes slow to change and, in fact, some resisted when the laws were enacted requiring equal opportunity and access because they know that the organizational culture and, consequently, the power structure will change.

Guide for Managers: Coping with Cultures

DEALING WITH NATIONAL CULTURE

Even if you have not traveled to another country, you know about cultural differences from what you have studied in school and read in newspapers and magazines. It is one thing to travel for vacations to visit foreign lands like China, England, France, Egypt and Israel to see the important places of interest to most of us. It is something else to think about going to foreign countries and to work with their citizens and accomplish something. Here are some things that you can do to make it easier to adapt to a foreign culture.

Preparation is important

Being prepared for working in another culture is more a state of mind than anything else. One thing that most of us do not think about in preparing to travel is to take a good look at our own culture. Since we live in it and have adapted to it, we take it for granted. However, you can be sure that some of your most difficult problems will occur when you expect to act as you would at home and something different is expected of you in the country where you are working. Of course you should learn something about the culture of the country. This information is readily available and helpful. Often these sources provide very good general information about how to travel around, what some of the more important local customs are and, importantly, some information about the local currency.

You will also find it helpful to think again about the question, "Just what is culture?" Read a bit about the concept of culture so that you can refresh yourself about precisely how deeply embedded it is and how it is reflected in a society. This will make you more aware when you arrive. Then you will not be as surprised to see that so many more things are different than you thought would be. You will also be surprised at how many things are the same.

Develop long-term relationships with the locals

If you are going to be in another country for some period of time and you are like most expatriate managers, you will seek other foreign managers in the country, especially those from your own. These are necessary and good sources of local information and psychological support. However, it is useful to be able to operate not only "on the economy" but in it, and having locals as friends to help with this makes life much easier. They can tell you where there are many interesting and useful out of the way places to acquire things that you might like to visit off the tourist track.

Above all, be flexible

If you can develop some local friendship contacts, you will learn about the culture very quickly. Most locals want to expose outsiders to the positive aspects of their own culture. To take advantage of this, though, you must be flexible and willing to take some risks. You should trust your local friends. They will take you to places and offer you things to eat that, at first glance, might seem undesirable. We have all heard some of our foreign friends talk about some of the delicacies in their own cuisine that we thought would not be very good. Your rule here should be, "If they do it, I might like it."

Do not try to force your work style onto others in your work relationships

Perhaps the biggest mistake that you can make when you are working with managers from another culture is to think that your approach is best and that it should be adopted by those managers. If you were to carefully examine the history of "foreign managerial styles," you would discover that, in the late 1960s, there was a great deal of interest in the management approach of the Germans as the Volkswagen and Mercedes began to dominate automobile markets all over the world. In the early 1970s, there was a fear worldwide that US-trained MBAs were so well trained that they would be the dominant force in global business. Then, in the late 1980s, the Japanese approach became the "model."

All of these had their day of popularity, then fell into the background. What is certain is that each culture has its own way to be effective and when you are in it, trust what they do and do not try to force your approach on them.

DEALING WITH ORGANIZATIONAL CULTURE

The most important time that you will have to deal with the organizational culture will be in your early experiences with it. You will be exposed to it in a number of ways, many of which we discussed in chapter 6, Organizational Accommodation. You should read that material on choosing a place to work and organizational socialization. Here are some ways to get an idea of what the culture is like early. (Deal and Allen, 1982).

Do not make quick judgments

Do not make judgments. Don't make the mistake, when joining a new organization, of believing too quickly what you hear and see in your first days. Remember the importance of, and the errors possible from, first impressions; see page 73 in chapter 3.

Listen more than you talk

You will want to become integrated into the firm and to do that you will have to meet your coworkers. When you do, listen particularly to what they say about the firm and its management. If you hear many positive things, that is a good start, but you still should withhold an assessment until you have been able to verify what you have heard.

If you hear negative comments about the firm and its management, that should alert you. It is possible that what you are hearing is an accurate representation of problems; it is also possible that you have found a disgruntled employee and one that you want to be careful with.

Study the Physical setting

Look around to see how consistent the environment is from one place to another. Careful observations can give you some important clues about status differentials in the firm. It will also give you some idea about whether people like to work there by observing things like their mood, how they treat people, especially strangers and visitors. One thing to look at carefully is the company literature. For example, you can tell a lot by how the firm presents itself in words and pictures to the public when you are able to compare that with what you see to be the actual case.

Look for signs of cultures in trouble

Read carefully our discussion of neurotic cultures and look for those signals around you. Try to sense, also, whether there are morale problems, inconsistencies in practices and policies and, perhaps, strong emotions, that are exposed. These will give you some clue that something is wrong.

Look for a way out when you have a bad feeling

First, make sure that you verify negative reactions to the culture when you begin to have them. Make sure, as best you can, that you are not reading more into what is there than is actually the case. Once you feel certain that you cannot exist well in the culture, try to work your way out of it. Do not think you can change it, unless you are entering the firm as its CEO. You cannot – the culture always wins.

Key Concepts

avoidant culture 365
bureaucratic culture 365
ceremony 361
charismatic culture 364
compulsive managers 365
conflict reduction rites 362
country clusters 347
cultural metaphors 345
culture 343
degradation rites 361
depressive personality 365
detached personality 366
dominant coalition 355
dramatic managers 364
enhancement rites 361
expressive meanings 358
hierarchical subcultures 368
Hofstede model of culture 345
ideology 359
individualism–collectivism 346
instrumental meanings 357
integration rites 362
long- versus short-term patterns of thought 347
manifestations of organizational culture 356
masculinity–femininity 347
modal organizational personality 353
myth 359
neurotic organizations 363
occupational/task subcultures 368
organizational culture 353
organizational culture profile 356
organizational status distinctions 359
organizational subcultures 366
paranoid culture 364
pluralism 369
politicized culture 366
power distance 346
renewal rites 361
rites 361
rites of passage 361
separation rites 361
socialization 343
symbols 360
uncertainty avoidance 345

STUDY QUESTIONS

1 Some say that a culture is invisible to those who are in it.
Do you believe that statement is true?
Take a position on this issue and provide arguments for it.
2 How has globalization impacted the education experience that you have had recently?
What changes do you see occurring in the curriculum, student body, and other factors related to the educational process?
3 Think about some foreign students you have met or observed recently.
What differences in their behaviors or thought patterns did you notice that vary from most individuals in your own nationality group?
What underlying cultural differences may be reflected in these behaviors or thought patterns?
4 Consider the possibility of being sent to an overseas post for three years.
What types and amount of training would you like to receive before moving overseas?
5 Of the several countries mentioned in this chapter along with some of their characteristics, which sounds like it would be the easiest for you to live in while conducting business for a US company?
Give reasons for your choice.
6 Discuss the relationship between the culture of a society and an organization's culture.
7 How does the history of an organization affect its culture?
Does it make a difference whether the organization is large or small?
8 What is the advantage of thinking of organization culture as a multi-level concept?
9 What is meant by the organization culture profile?
What are some dimensions that have been found to be useful representations of such a profile?
10 What are the concepts "modal personality" and "dominant coalition"?
How do they relate to organization culture?
11 What is the reason for studying neurotic organizational cultures?
Do you think most organizations have these extreme types of culture?
Select one of the particular types of neurotic organizational cultures that you have experienced in your own work or read about in the popular press.
Describe how this culture is manifested in organization policies, practices, and rituals.
12 What are the consequences of organizational culture?
How do these serve to make the culture resistant to change?
Select a large well-known organization that you are familiar with and that has a culture you think restricts its ability to become more effective.
What would you do to change the culture?

Case

The Graduate School of Business Administration

Garden City University is located in a large Southeastern city. For many years, it has been an important educational institution for the metropolitan area because it provides an excellent undergraduate education for good students who are not able to go to the main state university at College City, about 200 miles away. Garden City has a wide range of programs located in the various colleges.

The College of Business Administration at Garden City has been, predominantly, an undergraduate program. Students who graduated with a bachelor's degree were well trained and most of them found jobs in business firms in Garden City. The College of Business had five departments: economics, finance, marketing, management, and accounting. Each department had 20 faculty members, except economics, which had 30. There was a chairperson for each department who reported to the dean, Delbert Andrews.

The College of Business had only a small MBA program, mainly because the faculty were kept very busy teaching the undergraduate program. As in most MBA programs, the students took courses in marketing, finance, management, and so on. Most of the teaching in the MBA program was done by only eight professors. They had been teaching the graduate courses for two reasons. First, they had more interest in doing so than other faculty members, and, second, they were very good and very experienced at teaching.

Two years ago, a group from the most influential local business firms in town visited the president of Garden City University and proposed that the MBA program be made larger to service their needs for qualified graduate students. These business leaders felt that because Garden City was doing so well in teaching undergraduates, the school would do equally well in training MBAs. They also agreed to support the program through financial contributions and by using the MBA as an element in their management development activities.

After meeting with the group, the president of the university told Andrews about the proposal. Andrews knew that to increase the MBA program would require 20, not 8, faculty members. He told this to the president and asked if he would be able to have the additional faculty positions. Because funds were tight, the president refused, but he did make one important concession. He allowed the College of Business to restrict undergraduate enrollment and thus to free the professors to teach in the graduate program. The president thought that this was justified because, he believed, the support of the business community was especially crucial to raising funds for the whole university.

Now that the new MBA program is two years old, there are some problems. There have been many student complaints that the courses are not well integrated and that the professors who teach are not very effective in the classroom. The uproar has been so critical that a group of the original business executives who supported the program came to Dean Andrews to let him know that they could not continue to support the new program unless some changes were made. One of these executives asked Andrews, "Why do you assign such poor teachers to this program? Don't you know how important it is for the both of us – and for the university?" Andrews replied to the question: "Actually I don't make classroom assignments. That is the role of each department chairperson. The dean's office sends each department a list of courses that must be taught each term, and then the chairperson schedules the time and the instructor for each class. I have told each chairperson about the importance of this program. They know what it means to us, but sometimes it is tough to get the right teachers at the right time."

The executives were surprised. They didn't believe that the dean would delegate such crucial decisions to subordinates without some very clear policy and guidance.

- Why do you think the MBA program has problems?
- What approach should it take for solving this problem?
- What are the problems with the organizational structure of the College of Business that relate to this problem with the MBA program?
- Do you think the organization culture of the university differs from that of most business firms? How would that explain the problems in this case?

References

Adler, N. J. 1991: *International Dimensions of Organizational Behavior*. Boston: PWS-KENT Publishing Company.

Anfuso, D. 1995: Colgate's global HR unites under one strategy. *Personnel Journal*, 74(10), October, 44–51.

Beyer, J. M. 1981: Ideologies, values and decision making in organizations. In P. Nystrom and W. Starbuck (eds) *Handbook of Organizational Design*, vol. 2, London: Oxford University Press, 166–97.

Boeker, W. 1990: The development and institutionalization of subunit power in organizations. *Administrative Science Quarterly*, 34, 388–410.

Brislin, R. 1993: *Understanding Culture's Influence on Behavior*. Fort Worth: Harcourt Brace Jovanovich.

Caudron, S. 1992: US West finds strength in diversity. *Personnel Journal*, March, 40–4.

Child, J. C. 1981: Culture contingency and capitalism in the cross-national study of organizations, in L. L. Cummings and B. M. Staw (eds) *Research in Organizational Behavior*, vol. 3, Greenwich, Conn.: JAI Press, 303–56.

Cole, R. E. 1989: *Strategies for Learning: Small Group Activities in American, Japanese, and Swedish Industry*. Berkeley: University of California Press.

Deal, T. and Kennedy, A. A. 1982. *Corporate Cultures: The Rites and Rituals of Corporate Life*. Reading MA: Addison Wesley.

The Economist, 1992: BP after Horton. *The Economist*, July 4, 324, 59.

Etzioni, A. 1963: *Modern Organizations*, New York: Prentice-Hall.

Ferraro, G. 1998: *The Cultural Dimension of International Business*. Englewood Cliffs, NJ: Prentice Hall.

Gagliardi, P. 1986: The creation and change of organizations: A conceptual framework. *Organization Studies*, 118–33.

Gannon, M. J. 1993: *Cultural Metaphors: Capturing Essential Characteristics of 17 Diverse Societies*. Chicago: Sage Publishing.

Gordon, G. G. 1991: Industry determinants of organizational culture. *Academy of Management Review*, April, 16, 396–415.

Grabrenya, W., Wang, Y. J. and Latane, B. 1985: Social loafing in an optimizing task: Cross cultural differences among Chinese and Americans. *Journal of Cross Cultural Psychology*, 16, 223–42.

Hall, E. T. 1969: *The Hidden Dimension*. New York: Doubleday.

Hall, E. T. and Hall, M. R. 1990: *Understanding Cultural Differences: Germans, French, and Americans*. Yarmouth Maine: Intercultural Press.

Hofstede, G. 1980a: *Culture's Consequences: International Differences in Work-related Values*. Beverly Hills, CA: Sage Publications.

Hofstede, G. 1980b: Motivation, leadership and organization: Do American theories apply abroad? *Organizational Dynamics*, 2, Summer, 42–63.

Hofstede, G. 1992: Cultural constraints in management theories. *Academy of Management Executive*, 7(1), 81–94.

Hofstede, G., Neuijen, B., Ohayv, D. and Sanders, G. 1990: Measuring organizational cultures: A qualitative and quantitative study across twenty cases. *Administrative Science Quarterly*, 35, 286–316.

Jackofsky, E. F., Slocum, J. W. and McQuaid, S. J. 1988: Cultural values and the CEO: Alluring companions. *Academy of Management Executives*, 2(1), 39–49.

Kets de Vries, M. F. R. and Miller, D. 1984: *The Neurotic Organization*. San Francisco: Jossey-Bass.

Kets de Vries, M. F. R. and Miller, D. 1986: Personality, culture, and organization. *Academy of Management Review*, 11(2), 266–79.

Kluckholn, F. and Strodtbeck, F. 1961: *Variations in Value Orientations*. Evanston, Ill.: Row, Peterson.

Laurent, A. 1986: The cross-cultural puzzle of international human resource management. *Human Resource Management*, 25(1), 91–102.

McCall, W. 1998: Critics have Nike stumbling; shoe company blasted for tolerating sweatshops. *Chicago Tribune*, October 11, Sunday, Sports, 6.

March, G. and Simon, H. 1958: *Organizations*. New York: John Wiley.

O'Reilly, C. A., Chatman, J. and Caldwell, D. F. 1991: People and organizational culture: A profile comparison approach to assessing person–organization fit. *The Academy of Management Journal*, 34, September, 487–516.

Ouchi, W. 1981: *Theory Z: How American Business can Meet the Japanese Challenge*. Reading, MA: Addison-Wesley.

Pfeffer, J. 1981: *Power in Organizations*. Boston: Pitman Publishing.

Pfeffer, J. 1992: *Managing With Power*. Boston: Harvard Business School Press.

Rentsch, J. R. 1990: Climate and culture: Interaction and qualitative differences in organizational meanings. *Journal of Applied Psychology*, December, 75, 668–81.

Ronen, S. and Shenkar, O. 1985: Clustering countries on attitudinal dimensions: A review and synthesis. *Academy of Management Review*, 10(3), 435–54.

Sackmann, S. A. 1992: Culture and subcultures: An analysis of organizational knowledge. *Administrative Science Quarterly*, March, 37, 140–61.

Schwartz, F. N. 1989: Management women and the new facts of life. *Harvard Business Review*, January–February, 67, 65–76.

Shapiro, E. 1997: Brash as ever, Turner is giving Time Warner a dose of culture shock. *Wall Street Journal*, March 24, 1.

Sirota, D. and Greenwood, M. J. 1971: Understanding your overseas workforce. *Harvard Business Review*, (January–February), 53–60.

Solomon, C. M. 1995: Unlock the potential of older workers. *Personnel Journal*, 17(10), October, 56–66.

Solomon, C. M. 1997: Return on investment. *Global Workforce*, 2(4), October, 12–18.

Solomon C. M. 1998. Global operations demand that HR rethinks diversity. *Global Workforce*, 3(4), July, 24–7.

Stewart, T. 1996: Why value statements don't work. *Fortune*, June 10, 138.

Ting-Toomey, S. 1991: Intimacy expressions in three cultures: France, Japan, and the United States. *International Journal of Intercultural Relations*, 15, 29–46.

Trice, H. M. and Beyer, J. M. 1984: Studying organization culture through rites and ceremonials. *Academy of Management Review*, 9, 653–69.

Trice, H. M. and Beyer, J. M. 1993: *The Cultures of Work Organizations*. Englewood Cliffs, NJ: Prentice Hall.

Xing, F. 1995: The Chinese cultural system: Implications for cross-cultural management. S. A. M. *Advanced Management Journal*, Winter, 14–23.

chapter 13

Organizational Structure and Design

THE NATURE OF ORGANIZATIONAL STRUCTURE

ORGANIZATIONAL ENVIRONMENTS

ORGANIZATIONAL DESIGN

FORMAL ORGANIZATIONAL STRUCTURES

Preparing for Class

Consider two types of organizations discussed in this chapter: organic and mechanistic.

With these organizational types in mind, think about organizations that you are familiar with. Select one that you feel best represents an organic organization and one that best represents a mechanistic organization.

On a sheet of paper, list the organizational characteristics that you used to classify the two organizations.

Now consider the environments for those organizations.

What environmental factors do you feel most contributed to the organizational form you noticed?

Given your review of the organization's environment, do you feel that the organization has developed the best to compete within their chosen market?

Why?

You can learn something very important and interesting about the design of organizations from observing companies in the personal computer business like IBM, Dell, Gateway and Compaq. What you can learn is this: even though the basic technological and market conditions of these firms are very similar and even though these firms do exactly the same things – they design, manufacture, and sell personal computers – these firms have designed their organizational structure in different ways to accomplish these activities. Further, you can see how often the formal organizational structure is changed as they attempt to become more efficient, as well as increase their market shares in this competitive world. For example, with few exceptions, probably unimportant, the same basic engineering technology is available to all of them. Further, within a similar price class, the basic technical configurations of personal computers have very similar characteristics. Yet each of these companies have gone through, and are continuing to go through, significant changes in the way that they manufacture and distribute their products. For example, at one time, a standard PC line was manufactured and then it was distributed through dealers. Now, companies like Compaq, IBM, and Dell build PCs to order. You can call them and order exactly what you want, and they build it for you. On the distribution side, some of these firms still use distributors; others only sell by direct distribution to the buyer. Procurement is another example of how firms have changed, particularly at IBM. At one time, IBM required that the PC division buy disk drives from internal sources. As part of a reorganizing strategy, IBM changed their policies and permitted the groups in the PC division to buy from outside sources, the same way that other manufacturers buy their drives.

The PC industry is a good example of an important point about the design of organizations: Organizations that do the same things – whether it is to sell personal computers, automobiles, women's clothes, or food – can be organized in different ways. The choices that are made about how the activities, resources, and individuals are organized to achieve objectives can have a significant impact on how the work is done and on the effectiveness of the firm.

Global Focus on Organizational Design at Procter and Gamble

For many years, Procter and Gamble (P&G) used a regional form of organizational structure. There were four regional area divisions for the complete global operations. P&G will now have, instead, seven global product divisions for its product lines; babycare, beauty care, fabric and homecare, feminine products, food and beverage, healthcare and corporate new ventures, and tissues and towels. There will be eight market development organizations in North America, Central and South America, the Middle East and Africa, Central and Eastern Europe, Western Europe, Japan/Korea/India/Australia, China, and Latin America. The role of the market development organization is to develop P&G product portfolios in each of these geographical sectors.

One of the main reasons for the change in the organization structure is that it will shift the orientation of P&G from a regional focus to a product focus. It will also result in more efficient operations at P&G's headquarters (*Manufacturing Chemist*, 1998).

The Nature of Organizational Structure

In this chapter, we explain why organizations are different. Some differences are obvious, as when we observe organizations that are not in the same or similar fields. Hospitals, for sure, are not organized like department stores, and, for more reasons beyond the fact that there are doctors and nurses in hospitals while there are salesclerks and managers in department stores. However, there are also important differences in behavior patterns between companies in the same industry – one day's observation of the women's departments at Sears and a high-fashion boutique will reveal many dissimilarities.

The reason for these differences lies in the fact that organizations are dependent upon the environments of which they are a part. They interact with various environments and, to survive, they must develop some sort of accommodation to them. The idea is straightforward.

1 Organizations must accommodate to the environments within which they exist.
2 For survival, differences in the environments require different activities and different relationships among those activities.
3 Managements have some discretion about how to design and coordinate these activities. These design decisions will have an impact on the effectiveness of the organization.

Some Properties of Organizations

An organization is a group of people, working toward objectives, which develops and maintains relatively stable and predictable behavior patterns, even though the individuals in the organization may change. There are three dimensions that contribute to the patterns of behavior that we observe in organizations:

1 Complexity
2 Formalization
3 Centralization (Hall, 1991).

The patterns of complexity, formalization, and centralization are reflected in the organizational structure and the organizational culture. **Organizational structure** refers to the relationship between the tasks performed by the members of the organization and can be seen in the forms of division of labor, departments, hierarchy, policies and rules, and coordination and control mechanisms. The organizational culture is the set of dominant values, beliefs, attitudes, and norms that is the basis for justifying decisions and behavior as discussed in chapter 12.

organizational structure
The relationship between the tasks performed by the members of the organization

The **complexity** of an organization is the number of different activities, functions, jobs, and number of levels in it. There are more coordination and control problems in more complex organizations because there are more task activities

organizational complexity
The number of different activities, functions, jobs, and levels in the organization

formalization
The existence of written and institutionalized rules, policies, and procedures in organizations

centralization
The degree to which authority and power are concentrated at the higher organizational levels

decentralization
The degree to which power and authority are distributed vertically in an organization

to perform, and there are more numerous interpersonal relationships. Complexity is usually greater in larger organizations.

The degree of **formalization** refers to the number of formal, written policies, procedures, and rules that constrain the choices of members. In a highly formalized organization, members' discretion and freedom of action are limited by the boundaries defined by these organizational devices. In less formalized organizations, there is more freedom of action and choice.

The term **centralization** refers to the distribution of power and authority (Hall, 1991). **Decentralization** refers to the degree to which authority and power are distributed vertically in an organization (Hall, 1991). Organizations are decentralized when most decisions are made by those at lower levels of the organization, guided by policies and procedures. They are highly centralized when decisions are made near the top of the organization hierarchy and the discretion of those at lower levels is constrained by formal rules and procedures.

Authority is the right of decision and control a person has to perform tasks and to meet assigned responsibilities. To have authority means that you can make decisions without having them approved by others. For workers, it means the control over the work itself. For managers, authority is the right of decision and

A Question of Ethics: Formalization and Electronic Mail Snooping

Does an organization have the right to "open" the private email of an employee that is in its own electronic communication system? Should employees use the company's email system for their own personal business or communication?

Email is now a major communication medium that can cause different sorts of problems for a firm. For example, employees might use the firm's email for personal communications or business. Firms might believe that it is acceptable practice to read the email messages that employees receive through the company's system. In fact, in some cases in which employees have had their personal mail at work read by someone in the firm, they have brought a legal suit for invasion of privacy. Usually the firm wins, but it can be an expensive victory.

One approach to alleviate this problem is a formal policy that outlines what is acceptable and what is not. However, a survey found that only 36 percent had any formal policy covering what is acceptable practice. One company that does is DHL Systems, a division of DHL Worldwide. "We felt it was important that everyone knows exactly what the rules are. The idea was to be up front and honest about what behavior is acceptable and what isn't." DHL Systems researched the law on the matter, asked staff members for feedback, and then developed a formal policy that articulates its approach to governing email and online access for its employees. The policy prohibits discriminatory or harassing communication and obscene messages. The email system can be used judiciously by employees for non-business purposes, but employees are not to abuse the privilege. The policy also states that, in general, information created on the firm's computers is private, but DHL Systems reserves the right to review electronic messages and files to ensure that employees are complying with the policy.

Source: Adapted from Greengard (1996)

command about the use of organizational resources by themselves and by others for whom they have responsibility. It is necessary because tasks and the responsibility for their performance are dispersed throughout the organization by the process of division of labor. It is one mechanism for coordination and **integration** of the work of those in the organization.

Authority is distributed both horizontally and vertically in organizations. The **horizontal distribution of authority** is a function of the span of control and occurs through decisions that are made in the departmentalization process, a process that we discuss later (page 401). The **span of control** is the number of subordinates that report to a manager. It is determined by factors such as the subordinates' competence, the decision maker's philosophy about control, the nature of the work to be supervised and organizational size and complexity. For given size organizations, the span of control will determine some critical things about the structure and the number of organizational levels. When the span of control is large, there is more horizontal dispersion of authority, resulting in **flat organizations**. In other words, it will have fewer organization levels. When the span of control is smaller, there will be less horizontal distribution of authority, leading to "tall" organizations with more organization levels.

authority
The right of decision and control a person has to perform tasks and to meet assigned responsibilities

integration
The process of regrouping and relinking system activities into departments in an organization

horizontal distribution of authority
The span of control that occurs through decisions that are made in the departmentalization process

span of control
The number of subordinates who report to a manager

flat organizations
An organization with a large span of control with more horizontal dispersion of authority

relevant environment
The groups or institutions beyond an organization's boundaries that provide immediate inputs, exert significant pressure on decisions, or make use of the organization's output

Organizations and Environment

In this book, we take a **systems view of organizations**, i.e. we think of organizations as systems of related activities that import resources from their external environment which are then transformed, or changed, by these activities into products or services. These product or services may be exchanged with other organizations or groups in the organization's environment, usually for revenues that are then used to maintain the organization itself.

Those groups, institutions or other organizations outside the focal organization that provide immediate inputs, exert significant pressures on the way organizational decisions are made, or make use of the organization's output are called the **relevant environment**. At any one time, some of these are closer and have a more significant effect on what goes on in a firm than do others. For instance, customers and suppliers are always interacting with a business organization. They constitute its most relevant environment. A sudden shift in the level of consumer demand may force internal organization changes, as when a slump in sales causes a firm to lay off workers.

Circumstances might change the composition of external groups that are in the relevant environment. When this causes sufficient pressure, the organization must adapt to it. For example, when federal and state equal opportunity laws were initially passed, many firms had to change their hiring procedures as well as the criteria used for promotion. Now that some states have changed these laws, firms are changing these internal processes again. The relevant environment of an organization may include at least eight external groups:

1 Markets
2 Suppliers
3 Unions
4 Competitors

5 Public pressure groups
6 Government agencies
7 Investors
8 Technology and science

simple environment A relevant environment that contains just a few homogeneous sectors

complex environment A relevant environment that contains many different sectors

market environment The consumers of the output of organizations

technological environment The techniques and the processes that the organization uses to produce the product or service, and the ideas or knowledge underlying the processing or the distribution of the product or service

technology The tools, machines, facilities, and equipment a person uses in performing a task

The relevant environment may be relatively simple or very complex (Thompson, J. D. 1967). A **simple environment** contains just a few relatively homogeneous sectors. For example, the technological environment for companies that sell long-distance service is relatively simple. A **complex environment** contains many different sectors, such as would be the case for an engineering firm which specializes in the installation of manufacturing plants of different types and in different countries.

ENVIRONMENTAL SECTORS While the relevant environment for most large organizations may be relatively complex, it is possible to understand how organizations are affected by taking a more straightforward approach and focus on just two environmental sectors: the market environment and the technological environment. These two sectors are very important to understanding the problems of managing most business organizations and are of traditional importance in the management of economic organizations.

The **market environment** is composed of individuals, groups, or institutions that use what the organization produces, giving value to that output. It could be commodities, products, or services. For business organizations, this means products such as autos, computers, steel, television sets, bread, or the ideas and services that might be provided by advertising agencies, consulting firms, or travel agencies. The market provides the organization with some sort of exchange in return for its output.

The **technological environment** has two components. One is the set of processes that the organization uses to create the product or service. Used in this way, **technology** refers to available methods and hardware from which the organization selects some subset for its own use. What technology is selected and used and how it is organized defines the form of the production activities in an organization. The production activities in an organization cannot be any more advanced than the technology available, but it is possible that a firm does not use all available technology. For example, computers might handle customer credit accounts in a large department store, while the same function in a small specialty store might be performed manually, using a card file.

A second facet of the technological environment is the ideas or knowledge underlying the production or the distribution of the product or service; that is, the way science is translated into useful applications.

CHARACTERISTICS OF THE ENVIRONMENT What complicates the problem of the organization adapting to the environment is the degree of uncertainty, or environmental change. This has major implications for the internal structure of the organization (Burns and Stalker, 1961; Lawrence and Lorsch, 1969), the types of individual who are likely to join it, and the perceptions, attitudes, and values of those in the organization. The most important effect of the environment is whether the activities and processes within the organization structure take on highly routine or nonroutine characteristics.

The degree of change is a continuum: at the opposite ends are stability and volatility. In the **stable environment**, changes are relatively small, occurring in small increments, with a small impact on the structure, processes, and output of the organization. In stable environments, it is possible to make fairly accurate market predictions based on some relatively common indexes. For instance, the level of automobile sales may be predicted reasonably well if you have generally accurate data available about changes in population, income, and the average age of cars on the road.

stable environment
An environment in which the degree of changes are relatively small, occurring in small increments, with a small impact on the structure, processes, and output of the organization

Environmental changes are more likely to affect size dimensions, especially when there is extensive investment in plant, equipment, and distribution methods. Then a firm will use a short-term form of adaptation. This usually consists of reducing or increasing the work force rather than making changes in the product or the method of production. For example, beer is produced by a fairly high-cost system of production, but the final product is still beer. Changes in technology may come rather slowly, but steadily, so the firms can plan relatively easily about how to introduce these changes efficiently and profitably. However, should there be a sharp drop in demand, then the organization will probably not seek new products; instead they would lay off workers until the slump is over.

In the **volatile environment** changes are more rapid, customers may change, and the level of demand may vary widely. The women's high-fashion market is a good example. Product decisions of designers and manufacturers are based on predictions of customer tastes and preferences, and these are highly changeable. Who knows for instance, if the designs of Norma Kamali, Giorgio Armani, Gianfranco Ferre, or Elizabeta Yanigasawa will be the most successful in any one year?

volatile environment
An environment that is more turbulent, with more intense changes than in the stable one

When the technology is volatile, new concepts and ideas are being rapidly generated, and these new ideas affect either the way the production process is carried out or the nature of the processes themselves. The electronics industry, with breakthroughs in integrated circuits, transistors, and miniaturization is a good illustration of how technology changes could affect the nature of a product as well as marketing strategies. These types of technological changes were instrumental in the recent problems of IBM. For many years, the mainstay of IBM's business was large, mainframe computers. Over the years, the computing capacity of microchips increased while costs of computing dropped as the price of a unit of processing power dropped. This led to more powerful personal computers and to price wars among personal computer manufacturers. With the development of networking, it was possible to link together these more powerful personal computers which sharply reduced the demand for mainframes. These developments increased the importance of software, a market that IBM had chosen not to develop and passed on to Microsoft and Bill Gates.

BASIC TYPES OF ORGANIZATIONS Figure 13.1 shows how the dynamics of the environment and the organization that accommodates to it are related to the basic types of organization. On one axis is the technological environment and on the other axis is the market environment. Both of these environments may range from stability to volatility. For simplicity, we have described four basic organization

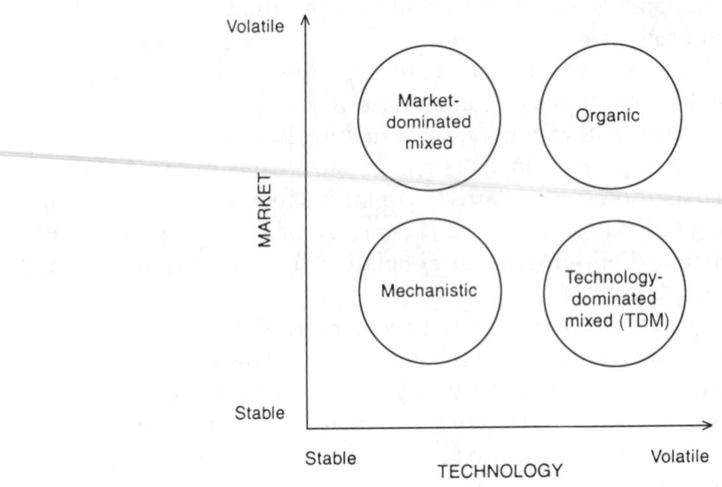

Fig 13.1: The basic relationship between environment and types of organizations

types that fall near the ends of both continua, but if you think about it, you will correctly conclude that organizations can fall at any point in the figure (Tosi, 1992). These are the four basic organizational types:

1 The mechanistic organization
2 The organic organization
3 The technology-dominated mixed (TDM) organization
4 The market-dominated organization.

These **basic organizational types** reflect something different and important about the nature of power and control, how authority is distributed, and the degree of flexibility required to accommodate to the environment. The reason is that in each of the different types, parts of the organization will have different type of interactions with the environment and with each other. For example, functions such as marketing and R&D are always in direct contact with the environment, while the production activities tend to be more deeply embedded and buffered from it. Further, these activities will be affected by the nature of the environment. When it is stable, the activities will take on routine characteristics. When it is volatile, the activities will have to be more flexible.

mechanistic organization
An organization with a very clear definition of responsibility and authority; its management structure is rigid and hierarchical

Figure 13.1 shows that when the market environment and the technological environments are both stable and predictable, there will be a **mechanistic organization.** Examples of mechanistic organization types are automobile manufacturers, steel producers, and fast food restaurants such as McDonalds, Wendy's and Burger King. The reason that they are mechanistic is because when the market and the technology are stable, the mechanistic form is efficient, and efficiency is required for survival (Blauner, 1964). In its production activities, tasks are likely to be highly repetitive. The division of labor will be extreme; the work activities will be standard, relatively small, and simple. You can see this when you observe workers on a manufacturing assembly line or the work in fast food restaurants. When the work is so narrowly specialized, those who perform these jobs will not see clear links between what they specifically do and the rest of the work done in the organization because of the separated, specialized nature of tasks.

In the mechanistic organization, you will find a very clear definition of responsibility and authority. The management structure will be rigid and hierarchical. Much of the communication is vertical, flowing from the top to the bottom. This occurs, in part, because it is possible to use historically developed information that has achieved organizational acceptance and legitimacy for control purposes. The focus of these control activities will be on measuring performance outcomes.

Because of the availability of much cost and other performance information, the tendency is to rely on "hard criteria." This "hard" and objective information is usually centralized and controlled in those units that perform the control functions. Since information is centralized in these units, they are likely to have a great deal of organizational influence.

Decision making in mechanistic organizations tends to be highly centralized toward the top of the organization. Information can be quickly and easily collected and transmitted to the higher levels so that decisions can be made about operations at lower levels without requiring a great deal of involvement of managers at lower levels. This, of course, will put limits on lower level discretion.

Figure 13.1 shows the **organic organization** in volatile market and volatile technological sectors (Burns and Stalker, 1961). Examples of organic organizations are specialized consulting firms, advertising firms, and some research firms that specialize in technology development such as Lucent. Lucent has a wide variety of clients who come to them in search of new solutions to problems. Their professional staff also has a very wide range of technical competence that can be applied to these problems.

organic organization
An organization in which relationships and jobs are more loosely defined to permit an easier process of adapting to the changing environment

Focus on Organizational Types: An Organic Organization

International Creative Management is a talent agency firm that represents very famous and important artists of the likes of Richard Gere, Goldie Hawn, Faye Dunaway, and William Baldwin, just to name a few. The job of Ed Limato, ICM's vice chairman, is to facilitate, to manage, the careers of these stars. His market is the entertainment business, films, the theater and television producers.

You can imagine how unpredictable that market is. So, how does Ed Limato develop a strategy and plan for the careers of his clients? He doesn't "There's no plan in this business," he says.

> Anybody who tells you he has a strategy – it's all [a lie]. That's what they tell a client to sign him up: 'We have a plan.' . . . There is no plan . . . we go to work. We get our hands on every script, we try to get offers on everything, Then we discard what isn't good enough. We say no nicely. Any agent who says he has a plan is snowballing you. There no plan. It's hard work.

ICM is an organic organization. It has to respond to the different needs of its customers, the producers of films, plays and music. You can, from just what you know about these businesses, imagine the uncertainty and volatility of the demands in that market. To deal with it, ICM and Ed Limato have to be very flexible.

Source: Adapted from Reginato (1998)

In an organic organization, relationships and jobs are more loosely defined to permit an easier process of adapting to the changing environment. The result is a continuing shifting and re-definition of tasks as the environment changes, making it difficult, if not impossible to have a well-defined hierarchical structure as found in the mechanistic organization.

This has a number of effects. One is that those who work in these organizations must have a broader range of skills so that they can perform the more varied range of functions. Another is that information is not as easily centralized at the top, making communication more horizontal and less vertical. A person's status and importance are more based on competence than being in a high organizational position.

The management structure in an organic organization has to be more flexible. Few policy guidelines will be used in the decision-making process because the variability of the environment will make well-defined set policies less useful over time. Performance control and evaluation will be more "subjective" and not so much based on "objective" performance measures. Performance indicators will focus on the manner in which individuals perform their work, and how effectively they interact with each other.

In organic organizations, individuals may move from project to project as the need for their skills arises, with a different authority structure for each one, depending on what needs to be done. They may work for more than one manager. Teams will be created to work on particular projects; when the project is completed, team members may move to different teams. This can cause problems unless the individual has a high tolerance for ambiguity and change.

Organic organizations are likely to be relatively small compared with mechanistic organizations. This small size facilitates adaptability to the environment. As an organic organization grows, however, it will begin to develop some degree of rigidity and hierarchy, which may make adapting to environmental changes difficult.

technology-dominated mixed (TDM) organizations
Organizations with uncertainty in the technology environment and stability in the market environment; has a looser structure for internal technical systems

The **technology-dominated mixed (TDM) organization** is a mixed organization type that has both mechanistic and organic elements. Examples of TDM organizations are firms that produce and sell personal computers such as Compaq, Dell, and Gateway. The underlying technology used in computers changes dramatically in short periods of time, following Moore's Law, which states that the amount of data that can be stored on a silicon chip doubles every year. This allows them to build-to-order and configure-to-process. Yet the marketing of personal computers especially is a relatively routine process, with firms like Gateway using mail order distribution.

In TDM organizations, the organic part of the organization interacts with the technological environment because its major threat to survival and effectiveness stems from the uncertainty and volatility there, as we have discussed in the computer industry and also occurred in photography over the last 30 years. Instant cameras by Polaroid started a technological revolution in the 1960s. Later, Nikon and Canon are examples of companies that developed camera systems with automatic focus and shutter speed mechanisms. Now there are even disposable cameras that produce photos of very respectable quality and at a reasonable price, not to mention the developing revolution in digital photography.

Control activities in these TDM organizations are difficult because they must consist of controls for major organizational units that have very different structural characteristics. While the technological and scientific units are organic and flexible, the marketing segments of organization will have a more constrained "bureaucratic" structure because of the stable market. This leads to tensions and conflict between the units.

The management structure of a TDM organization will be different in the major organization units. For instance, in the marketing sector, you can expect to find fairly well-defined job responsibilities, accountability to specific superiors for work, and limited discretion for decisions. On the other hand, those in the technological functions will have more freedom of action. The production units are likely to be caught in the middle, between pressures from research and engineering to adopt newer production methods and the marketing unit's desire to maintain the product relatively as it is.

Another mixed organization type is the **market-dominated mixed (MDM) organization**. These organizations exist in environments that have a stable technological sector, but a volatile market sector. In MDM organizations, the major strategic and policy influence will be from the marketing unit because of the need to stay in close touch with a constantly changing consumer or client group. Examples of MDM organizations are firms in the music industry, the film industry and high fashion. Understanding the volatile market is accomplished more through experience, intuition, and the judgment of those responsible for marketing and product development than through the analysis of standard market information such as population data, income estimates, or traditional buying patterns. For instance, in the fashion or recording industry, the clinical judgment of a designer or a record promoter is more crucial than a judgment made from more systematic market information. What is not a particularly difficult problem to manage in TDM organizations is the way the product is produced. The production of music and films, for example, requires recording equipment or cameras and setups that are readily available to anyone. What makes a difference in the success of the firm is not how the CD, cassette, or film is produced, but whether the producer has been able to find a good song or a good story that the market will accept.

market-dominated mixed (MDM) organization
An organization that exists in an environment that has a stable technological sector, but a volatile market sector

Control activities will be affected by the difference in types of environments. The flexible and dynamic nature of the marketing and distribution system will make collection of historical and relevant cost data difficult, since distribution patterns and systems may be changing. This will lead to performance measurement problems.

The management structure will be relatively hierarchical and rigid in the technical parts of the market-dominated firm. A looser authority structure will exist in the marketing and distribution sectors, which will have more individual discretion and freedom in decision making. Systems to monitor changes in and adapt to the environment will be developed in such a way as to be triggered by decisions made in the marketing sector. The head of a MDM organization will be someone with a marketing or sales background and the organizational culture and tone will be set by those in marketing, since they are the ones with the knowledge and skill to deal with the volatile environment.

As in a TDM, there will be problems in coordinating the organic and mechanistic segments of the organization. The well-defined structure of the technical sector may not only pose adjustment problems for the professionals who work in it but also present difficulties when it interacts with the more organic organization structure in the marketing sector.

formal organization
A configuration of major subunits usually called divisions or departments

department
A distinct area over which a manager has authority for the performance of specific activities

structural differentiation
The process of unbundling all of the work activities in an organization, separating specific sets of activities from others

structural integration
The process of creating a management structure by linking the differentiated subunits back together through authority, responsibility, and accountability relationships

organizational design
The process of creating the internal conditions that facilitate strategic accommodation to the environment and the implementation of the organization's strategy

Formal Organizations: Design and Structure

When we observe an organization chart, we do not see these basic organizational types. We cannot really tell whether a firm is an MDM type or an organic type. Instead, what we see is the **formal organization**, a configuration of major subunits usually called divisions or departments, terms which we use interchangeably in this book. **Departments** engage in a distinct, defined set of activities over which a manager has authority and responsibility for specific outcomes. For example, the activities in a university are embedded in colleges such as Law, Business, and Fine Arts and the responsibility for the college is assigned to a dean. Companies that have multiple product lines, such as Proctor and Gamble, organize their activities into product units such as detergents or dental hygiene products, and assign responsibility to product managers.

These divisions and departments are created through two processes: structural differentiation and structural integration. **Structural differentiation** is the process of unbundling all of the work activities in an organization, separating specific sets of activities from others. For example, the total set of teaching activities of a university may be differentiated, unbundled, in various ways to create colleges and departments. It is common that most courses an accounting major takes are assigned to the School of Accounting and the courses for a music major are assigned to the Music Department.

Structural differentiation may be accomplished in different ways. Subunits may be organized on the basis of products (or services), the work performed (functions), projects, geographical location, and by type of customer. Not all of these are good options for every organization. Some are more logical and more effective than others, depending upon the environmental conditions and managerial preferences. These are discussed in more detail later; see page 401.

Structural integration is necessary when differentiation has occurred because now it is necessary to coordinate the activities of different subunits. It is the process of creating a management structure by linking the differentiated subunits back together through authority, responsibility, and accountability relationships. Like the differentiation process, there are choices about the type and degree of integration. It is possible to create very tight and well-defined linkages or leave them more loosely connected.

The set of decisions about how differentiation and integration is achieved is called **organizational design**. It is the process of creating the internal conditions that facilitate strategic accommodation to the environment and the implementation of the organization's strategy by arranging the complete range of work activities into organizational subunits and hierarchies. First, there are strategic decisions about where to locate the organization in the environment and the tactics for operating in that environment. For example, the market for women's clothes ranges from high fashion to conventional styles, and a firm may select a niche within that range. A firm such as The Limited sells somewhat expensive but more conventional women's clothing, whereas firms such as Armani and Gianni Versace focus most of their efforts in the high-fashion sector. The selection of a niche minimizes adaptation problems in the sense that management can focus on that particular environment but not on the more broad context. It allows the firm to develop a narrow rather than a broad set of competencies.

Second, decisions are then made which result in the organization structure:

1 How the work will be differentiated – the *division of labor*
2 How the work is then grouped into organizational subunits – the selection of the *form of departmentalization*
3 The relationships between the subunits are defined by the *distribution of authority*.

These three decisions create the hierarchical aspects of structures.

Division of Labor and Task Interdependence

The **division of labor** is the way that work in organizations is subdivided and assigned to individuals. Consider this case: suppose that you are a talented woodworker and you decide to start your own business, Cabinets Unlimited. In the beginning, you would perform all the work tasks shown in figure 13.2. You would make the cabinets, sell them, purchase materials, and deliver and install them. You also perform all of the management work of planning, organizing and controlling everything.

division of labor
The way that work in organizations is subdivided and assigned to individuals as a job

If you are successful, and if Cabinets Unlimited is to grow and prosper, you will eventually have to employ someone else do some of the work. In deciding what work you want this employee to do, you will want to arrange to have it done in such a way as to still make high-quality cabinets and maximize profits.

There are two different approaches to deciding how others will work, and they have different implications for what a person does in a task and how it is managed. One philosophy – the **scientific management approach** – is to make jobs simple, have few tasks assigned to a person, have the job supervised by someone other than the person doing it, give the worker little autonomy, and limit the amount of responsibility for the tasks. The other philosophy – the **job enrichment approach** – is to create more complex jobs. They consist of several tasks. The person controls the work more than in scientific management and has higher autonomy and more responsibility. Some important difference between these two approaches are shown in table 13.1.

task specialization
Occurs when a job is broken down into smaller components or task elements; these are then grouped into jobs and generally assigned to different people

In either case, you are engaged in the process of the division of labor. The division of labor leads to specialization. This means that a person performs only some specific part of the whole job. For example, in Cabinets Unlimited, you may decide to hire a person whose only job is to sand and finish the cabinets prior to painting. That is a form of specialization called **task specialization**

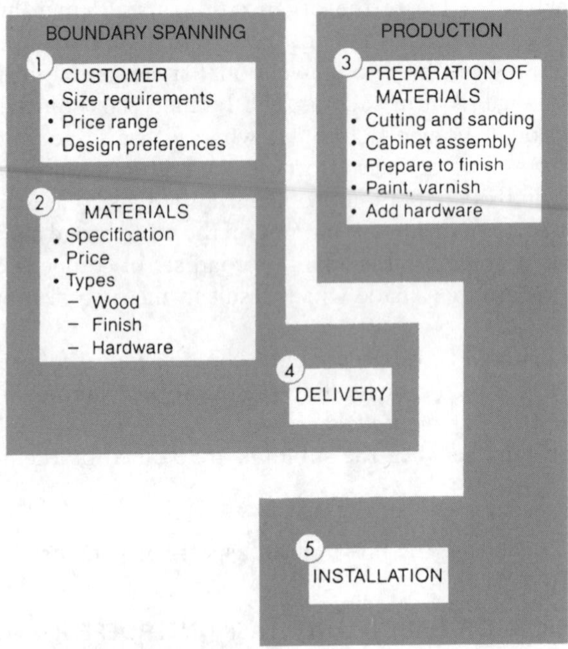

Fig 13.2: Activities required to make and sell cabinets

Table 13.1 Some differences between the scientific management and the job enrichment approach

Scientific management	←	*Work characteristic*	→	*Job enrichment*
Simplify	←	Basic philosophy toward work design	→	Increase complexity
Few	←	Number of tasks in a job	→	Many
By others	←	Supervision and control	→	By self
Low	←	Worker automony	→	High
Limited	←	Level of task responsibility	→	Increased
Low	←	Motivating potential of task	→	High

personal specialization
Occurs when the individual, not the work, is specialized; specialists such as lawyers and doctors often perform such work

(Thompson, V., 1967). Or you may decide to hire another cabinetmaker, who will make the complete cabinets, as you do. This type of specialization is called **personal specialization** (Thompson, V., 1967). The main difference between task specialization and personal specialization is that task specialization usually requires less knowledge and ability; see figure 13.3.

In task specialization, a job is broken down into smaller components, or task elements, which are then grouped into jobs and generally assigned to different people. When work is highly task specialized, it is more repetitive, the person is doing only a small part of the complete task, and the work cycle, the time that

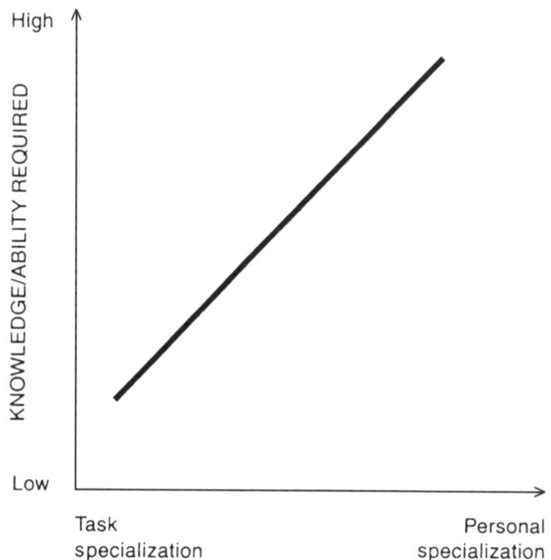

Fig 13.3: The relationship between knowledge–ability and the different types of specialization

elapses between the start of a task and when it begins again, is usually short. Because tasks are more simple and repetitive, they are easier to learn and to do. Therefore face-to-face supervision is not necessary to ensure that the job is done right. Generally, it is possible to tell if the work is done correctly by inspecting the output rather than through the time-consuming task of direct personal supervision. The workers are less involved with their job. High morale and motivation are especially difficult to maintain when the work is routine, repetitive, or highly programmed (Wyatt and Marriott, 1956; Blauner, 1964; Kornhauser, 1965).

Task specialization may have some positive economic effects, such as increased efficiency, but it does have some problems that, according to Presthus (1978) are

> more subtle and pervasive, raising problems of individual autonomy, integrity, and self-realization. [A continuing issue] is a displacement from the intrinsic value of work to its byproducts of income, security, prestige, and leisure. This displacement stems from the impersonality, the specialization and the group character of work in the typical big organization.

Instead of deciding on narrow task specialization, you might decide to hire another first-rate cabinetmaker who would build complete cabinets. This form of specialization is called personal specialization, where the individual, not the work, is specialized. This means that the person can, and does, perform a wide range of the different activities to do the work, instead of the few narrowly specified activities when task specialization is chosen. If you choose personal specialization as the way to design the work in Cabinets Unlimited, then you and your new employee would each make complete cabinets. If business volume increased, it would be necessary to find more skilled cabinetmakers each time you wish to increase production. This might be difficult if skilled cabinetmakers are in short supply, as well as being more expensive than task specialization.

Typically, personal specialization is associated with occupations such as law and medicine. Those with skills in these fields tend to work in small organizations, quite often owned by the physician or attorney. Other personal specialists work in complex organizations. Scientific personnel, engineers, computer scientists, accountants, and human resource personnel are typical specialists found in larger organizations. Personal specialists are extremely important because they bring high levels of skills that are critical to the success of the organization. Personal specialists usually invest a good deal of time, effort, training, and money in acquiring their skill. It takes money, years, and much effort to complete professional training such as at medical school.

task interdependence Exists when several different tasks required to complete a project, product, or a subassembly are performed by different people

sequential task interdependence Where work activities must be performed in a particular sequence and the activities are assigned to different units

reciprocal task interdependence Mutual dependence between two or more units in which interactions vary in complex ways in response to the task

pooled task interdependence When several units of an organization can operate in an autonomous manner, meaning that what one unit does is not entirely dependent on the other groups

When tasks are divided and several different tasks, performed by different people, are required to complete a project, product, or subassembly, there is **task interdependence**. When tasks are highly interdependent, a person cannot complete a job until the work of someone else is finished. For example, there is a high level of task interdependence among workers in a can lid manufacturing plant. The manufacturing process starts with a large press that stamps out the round shell from a large roll of aluminum. The lid travels on a conveyer to a machine that curls the edge and attaches a sealing material to the lid, and then it moves to a machine that attaches an opening tab. From there, it goes to a bagging machine where the lids are bagged and then sent to inventory. The high interdependence is illustrated in a comment of one worker who said, "When one of these machines stops, you get behind, and once you are behind, you never catch up. And most of the time it isn't even your fault."

There are three types of task interdependence (Thompson, J. D., 1967):

1 Sequential
2 Reciprocal
3 Pooled

The work in the can lid plant is an example of **sequential task interdependence**. This is when there are several tasks to be performed and they must be done in sequence. The work flows in a linear fashion through the production unit. An example of sequential interdependence is the organization of the jobs at Cabinets Unlimited shown in figure 13.4.

Reciprocal task interdependence is when the tasks of two or more people are mutually dependent. Reciprocal task interdependence would exist at Cabinets Unlimited if a task specialist is hired and performs the tasks as shown in figure 13.5. The cabinet must go back and forth between the two workers, and each depends on the other to complete the job successfully.

Figure 13.6 shows **pooled task interdependence** in Cabinets Unlimited. If you hired four expert carpenters and assigned each the complete cabinetmaking task, there would be pooled task interdependence. Pooled task interdependence occurs when you work in a more autonomous fashion; what you do is not entirely dependent on the others, but organization success or failure depends on the

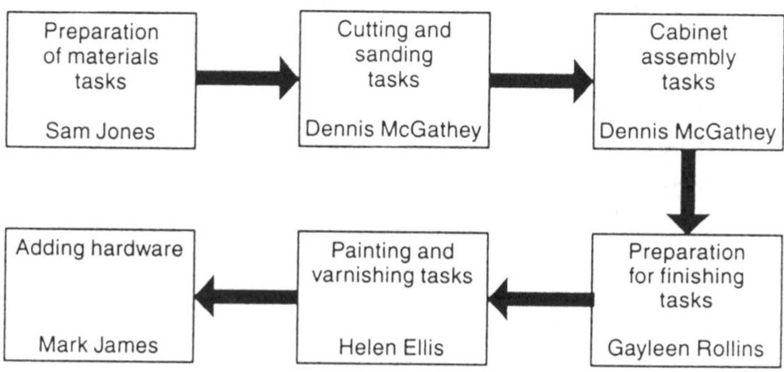

Fig 13.4: Assignment and arrangement of tasks in making cabinets

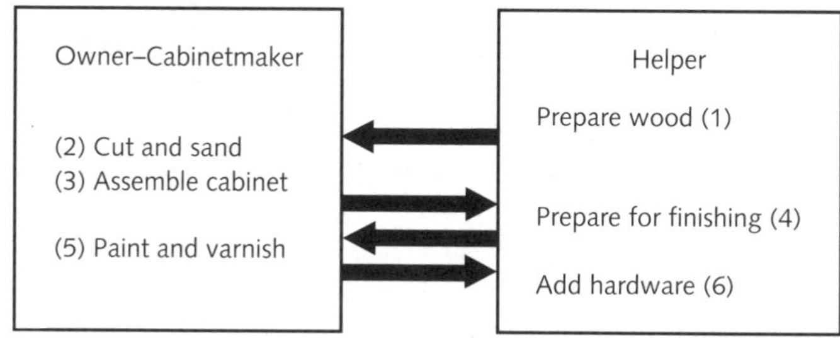

Fig 13.5: Reciprocal task interdependence

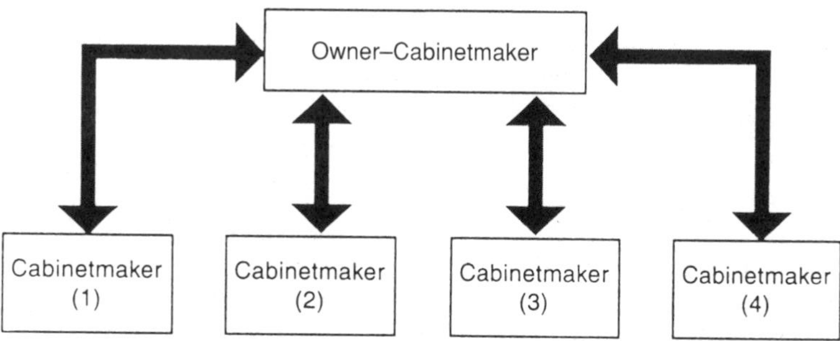

Fig 13.6: Pooled task interdependence

unique contribution of each. Some professionals often have this form of interdependent relationship. Law firms and medical clinics, for example, are set up so that each lawyer or physician works with a high degree of autonomy.

Organizational Design Alternatives

Understanding the ideas we have presented so far is useful to a manager for deciding the critical question of how to design the organizational structure, or the grouping the differentiated tasks into departments and departments into units. For example, there are several bases for grouping activies:

1 Whether they are related to the same product
2 Whether they have similar skill requirements
3 Whether they serve particular customers or clients
4 Whether they are performed in a particular geographic area.

We believe that some organizational designs are better suited to certain basic organizational types. For example, the mechanistic organization is likely to be more effective if the product or functional organizational design is used, mixed-type organizations seem better suited to the matrix structure, while the organic type is likely to use the project organizational structure.

functional organization Activities assigned to major departments are similar

PRODUCT ORGANIZATIONS AND FUNCTIONAL ORGANIZATIONS For mechanistic organizations, the organization will probably take either the product form or the functional form. In the **functional organization**, the major departments are grouped around similar work functions and responsibilities such as accounting, purchasing, production, and personnel. Managers and workers are assigned to units that are responsible for similar tasks. Figure 13.7 shows a functional organization for the hypothetical Eagle Brewing Company, a producer of beer with two brands, American Eagle beer and Ben Jefferson Brew. In a functional organization, the brewing division produces both brands of beer that the company sells. A single brewery might produce American Eagle Beer for a period and then shift its production to Ben Jefferson Brew. The marketing unit is responsible for

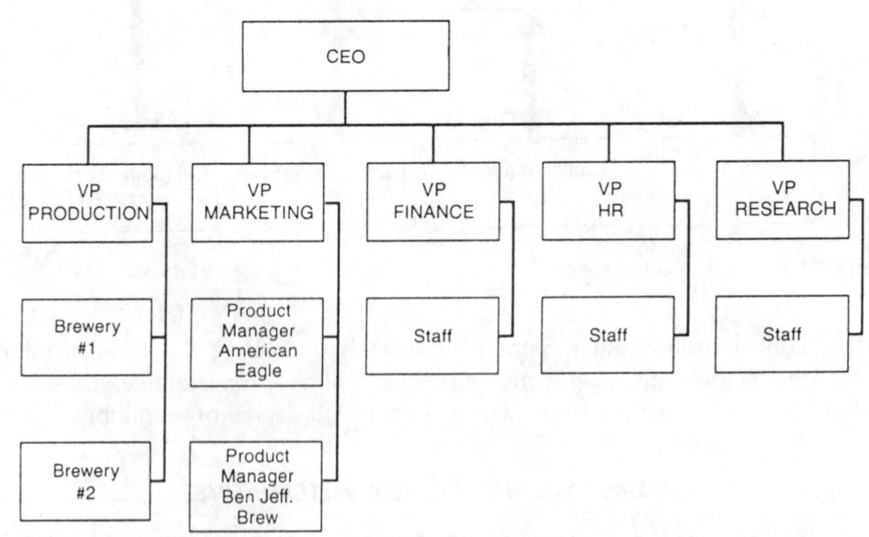

Fig 13.7: The Eagle Brewing Company as a functional organization

selling both products. All the brewing work is the responsibility of one unit and all the marketing work is the function of another one.

Most of the personnel in the units of a functional organization will have similar training and work experience. In Eagle Brewing, this means that all of those in the brewing division are specialists at making beer, while those in the marketing division are specialists in marketing.

Because the work of each major organizational unit is so specialized, the functional form offers great opportunity for increasing operating efficiency, particularly of the production unit. Economies of scale can be more easily achieved because all the production activities are in one department. This similarity of background should also lead to easier communication within the functional departments because the individuals will have a common frame of reference. For instance, the department members will more easily understand the "jargon." On the other hand, there may be communication problems between groups because of the differences in their orientations.

One of the main problems of the functional organization is coordinating the work of these units. For instance, the marketing division would like to have a ready supply of both brands on hand at all times to meet customer demand. However, the manufacturing unit may wish to produce only one brand at a time and have very long production runs to minimize production costs. Each department's interest is best served by different goals (either long production runs or high inventories of both beers).

Diversity Issues: Work Teams with Women and Minorities

Using cross-functional work teams brings a broader range of skills to the solution of complex problems in organizations. Cross-functional teams bring together individuals from different functional areas of the organization with different competencies to work on serious problems, making cooperation an important ingredient to team success.

One factor which works against this is found in teams which are highly diverse, not only in terms of member loyalty to different organizational units, but also when there is gender and racial diversity on the team. This is an increasingly important question since women and minorities are becoming a larger portion of the work force.

A study was conducted in a state government agency that examined this question, focusing on the specific issue of racial and gender composition on how team members themselves and external evaluators judged the effectiveness of teams (Baugh, 1997). One important result is that members of cross-functional work teams with women and minorities perceived their teams as less effective than those on homogeneous teams. However, those on diverse teams did not view their team as having less effective interpersonal working relationships than the homogeneous teams. Another interesting result is that white members of diverse teams believed that the work was less evenly divided than do minority members. However, and this is a key point in this study, the external evaluators do not appear to share the perception of unequal effort within teams with racial variation relative to homogeneous teams. This suggests that while diverse teams may be able to achieve good organizational results, attention must be given to managing the internal group processes.

product organization Departments are created around different products and services

In the **product organization** form, major units are formed around different products or services. Figure 13.8 shows the Eagle Brewing Company as a product organization. Each major unit has its own manufacturing operation, marketing, and so on. Each division is responsible for manufacturing and selling its own product, and each may be very autonomous. Note that within each product division there is considerable functional departmentation. The head of the American Eagle Division will have a production executive, a marketing executive, and other executives in charge of functional units within the product division. It is unlikely that any of them will interact frequently with his or her counterpart departments in the Ben Jefferson Brewing Division.

The product organization simplifies some managerial problems, but it creates others. For example, it is easier to develop accountability systems, reducing internal transaction costs, because production and selling costs can be allocated to the different products, which are almost completely the responsibility of a single unit. However, it is generally believed that some costs are higher for a product organization because it does not offer the same economies of scale associated with grouping similar activities into functional units (Filley, 1978).

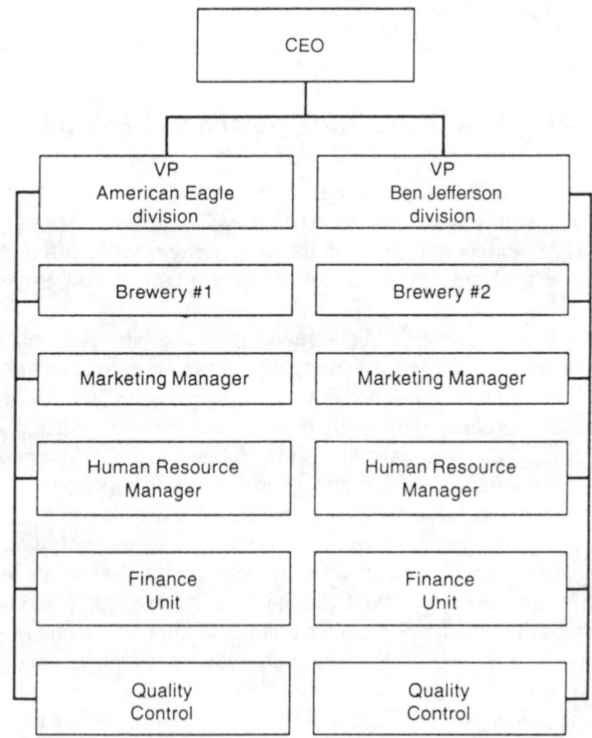

Fig 13.8: Eagle Brewing as a product organization

THE MATRIX ORGANIZATION The **matrix organization** works well for mixed organizations (TDM and MDM). The matrix organization integrates the activities of different specialists while at the same time maintaining specialized organizational units. In the matrix organization, technicians from specialized organizational units are assigned to one or more project teams to work together with other personnel.

matrix organization An organization in which product or project groups are served by and interact with specialist groups

Figure 13.9 illustrates a matrix organization that is used in the Military Aircraft Division of a major aerospace firm in a technologically volatile environment (a TDM organization) and a fairly stable government market. There are six functional units: Product Quality, Business Management, Material, Operations, Engineering and Technology, and Human Resources. The functional departments have a "project manager" from each project who work with them. There are six

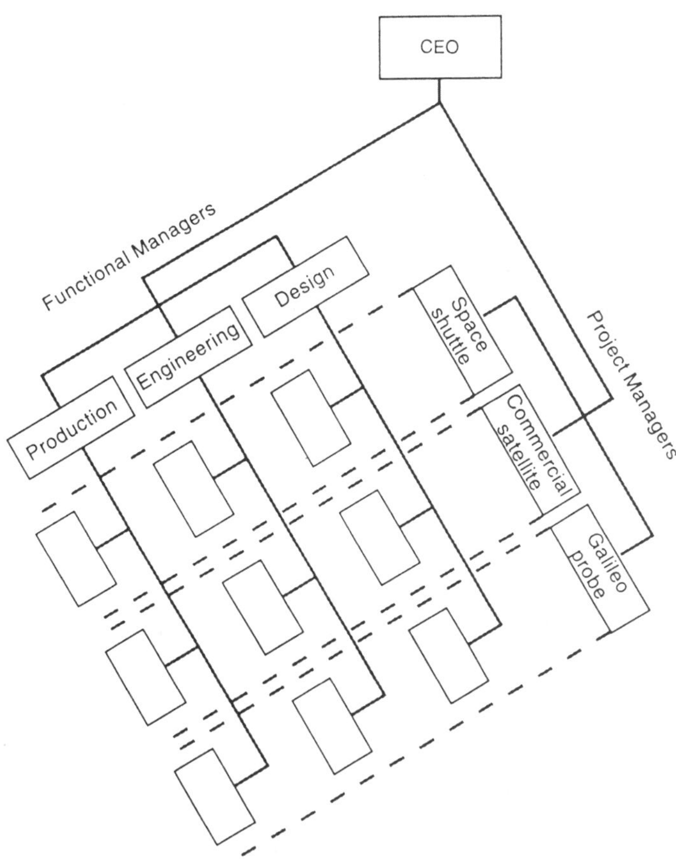

Fig 13.9: A "classic" matrix organization

EXERCISE

THE ORGANIZING PROBLEM

The Apple-Orange Company grows and markets apples and oranges in southeastern USA. Apple-Orange has been in the produce business for the past 50 years and has some of the finest land for growing these fruits. They have also been quite successful in marketing their product. Up until now, Apple-Orange has been a family business operated by old John Graves, whose father and uncle started the business. He has had his son Carl working as his assistant since Carl returned from Vietnam.

Basically, there are three major sets of activities that must be accomplished to grow and market Apple-Orange's products.

- One group of workers and managers work in the fields, handling the growth and harvesting of the apples and oranges.
- Another group of workers and managers work in development research. This group is comprised largely of agricultural scientists who attempt to improve the varieties grown and to increase crop yield.
- Marketing is handled by several sales personnel who call on wholesalers and fruit distributors in the region. The sales staff is very large and has been, like all other employees, very effective.

John and Carl have been managing Apple-Orange without many formal policies and procedures. The company has few set rules, procedures, and job descriptions. John believes that once people know their job, they should and would do it well.

However, Apple-Orange has grown fairly large and John and Carl both believe that it is now necessary to develop a more formal organization structure. They have invited D.J. Blair, a noted management consultant, to help them. D.J. has told them that they have, basically, two choices: a functional organization structure or a product-based organization structure. These two different forms are shown in figure 13.10.

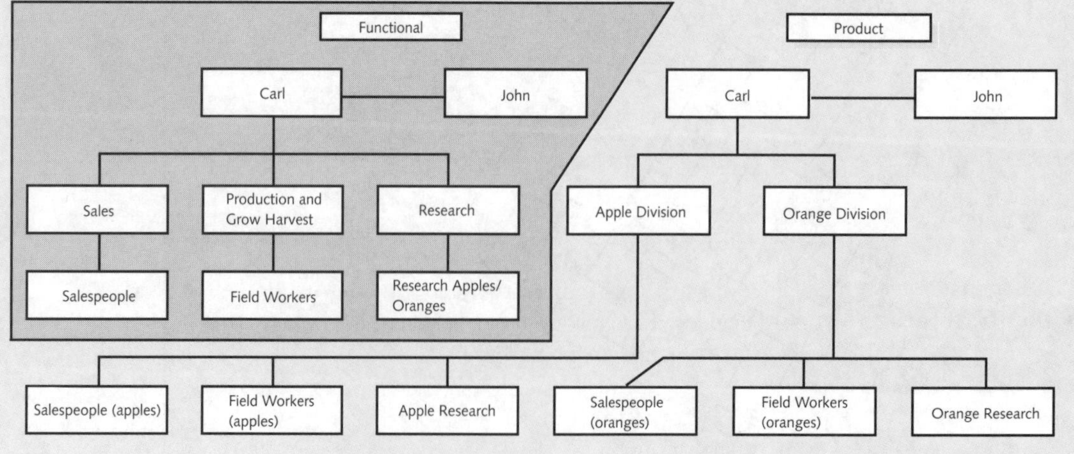

Fig 13.10: Organizational structure options at Apple-Orange

Which would be your choice of structure? Functional or product? Why do you prefer it?

Now, read these ten descriptions of organizational characteristics, conditions, or problems. Tick one box to show which type of organization fits the description of the statement on the left.

		Functional	Product
1	Job specialization will be most extensively developed; in a typing pool one person might specialize in correspondence and another in reprints.	☐	☐
2	Individuals will perform a fairly broad range of activities in their job area. They will be less likely to become specialists.	☐	☐
3	People will very likely be promoted in their field of specialization and will probably supervise several subordinates who do similar work.	☐	☐
4	Managers of major departments are more likely to have subordinates who do a wide variety of jobs.	☐	☐
5	Individuals can learn a lot about their field of specialization because they will be working with people who do similar work.	☐	☐
6	Coordinating and scheduling the activities between production, research, and marketing will be difficult.	☐	☐
7	Coordinating and scheduling production, marketing and research will be easier.	☐	☐
8	Departmental conflict between functional units (production, marketing, and sales) will be less.	☐	☐
9	There is less tendency for those in the organization to be over-specialized in their work area.	☐	☐
10	Individuals will tend to learn a good deal about all the things that must be done to produce the product.	☐	☐

Finally, answer these diagnostic questions.

1. What do you think happens to the product-type organization when it becomes larger?
2. What do you think happens when a functional organization grows larger?
3. Which one of the two forms do you think would be more efficient? Why?
4. Which one would provide the best product, or be more customer oriented? Why?

project managers, each assigned to a different aircraft or aircraft service that the division performs (Overhaul Services, E2C production, E2C modification, F14, EA6B, and S3). You can see that the specialists in the TDM organization come from the engineering side, the units interacting with the more volatile technological sector. However, in an MDM organization, such as a record company, the specialists would come from the marketing sectors. These specialists would be responsible for different areas of music such as classical, rock and roll, and country and western.

People in the matrix organization are accountable at the same time to both the project manager and the manager of the department to which they are assigned. The goals of these different managers may be incongruent. In the aerospace industry, for example, project managers tend to be concerned about meeting their own schedules and producing output within previously planned specifications. Specialized unit managers, on the other hand, are more concerned with high technical performance. Working under such circumstances is certainly stressful.

The matrix organization can result in both high technical performance and integration of diverse specialties at the same time. It demands a great deal of coordination and cooperation rather than competition. Matrix organization has the potential for conflict since often diverse and contradictory objectives and values come together in it, creating a good deal of ambiguity and stress for the individuals involved.

project organization
An organization in which employees work in temporary work teams, each with a specific project responsibility and duration for the life of the project

PROJECT ORGANIZATION When the nature of the work changes rapidly due to changes in the environment, an organization must have a structural form that changes with it. A **project organization** form may be appropriate. A project is a series of related activities required to achieve an outcome, such as a new product or a plan for constructing a new building. Projects are generally unique; no two are the same. In a project organization, individuals are assigned to one or more temporary teams that exist for the life of the project. The specific composition of the team is determined by the project needs. When different skills are needed for different projects, the composition of the team will change.

The Construction Real Estate Development Company, shown in figure 13.11, is an example of project organization. Each house and each commercial building is a unique project, taking a different time to complete. Workers may be assigned to more than one project or moved among the different projects as needed. Each project will have a supervisor who is responsible for the execution of the project plan and must coordinate the construction and manage its capital and human resources. When a building project is completed,

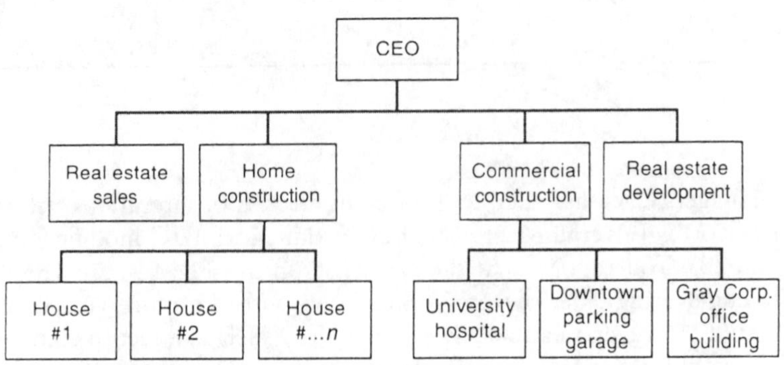

Fig 13.11: Project organization of a construction and real estate development company

a new one will begin and it will have a different configuration of people and resources.

THE NETWORK (OR VIRTUAL) ORGANIZATION Some organizations have recently adopted a relatively new approach called the network or **virtual organization** to adapt to today's fast paced economies, global competitiveness, and meet management's desires for more effectiveness. **Network organizations** are not quite the type of organization that we have been discussing in this chapter so far. We have described, more or less, an organization that includes all of the relevant subsystems within its boundaries. The network organization, instead, should be thought of as a group of firms in the relevant environment with which a focal organization does business. These organizations may be suppliers, customers, or even banks or other sources of capital. What distinguishes the traditional organization in its relevant environment from the network concept is the way that relationships between it and other organizations are governed, or managed. Traditionally we think of these relationships, such as how the firm deals with its customers or suppliers, to be based on economic relationships so that markets are the mechanisms that are important regulating devices for interorganizational relationships.

network organization Groups of firms in the relevant organizational environment in which the relationships are based on complementary strengths, reciprocity, mutual strengths, and trust between the organization

What makes the concept of networks different is that, in addition to economic factors, these relationships are based on complementary strengths, reciprocity, mutual strengths, and trust between the organizations (Powell, 1990; Lorenzoni and Lipparini, 1996). When, for instance, different firms are engaged in the typical long-term buyer–seller relationships, there is usually a contractual agreement between them. There is a different kind of relationship among network organizations. One of the prototype examples of these network organizations is found in the Prato region around Florence, the center of Italian textile production (Voss, 1996). The organization of this textile industry is unique because there are no large, vertically integrated plants that perform the production function from beginning to end. Instead nearly 20,000 firms, most of them very small, perform very specific, specialized functions. Some process new wool, others reclaim old wool. Some spin, others dye; some clean and others cut. All in all, the industry is highly fragmented, but these firms have developed close working relationships. This results in such effective coordination that the wool production process is quite efficient. In large part, this effective coordination stems from basic cultural values. It is based as much on social linkages as on the conventional types of interorganizational linkages common in the USA. Many of the small firms in the Prato region are owned and managed by relatives from an extended family.

You can imagine that this type of network organization might work in Italy because of the values of close family relationships that permit trust to develop more easily. However, there are similar network structures that exist elsewhere. For example, carpet manufacturing around Dalton, Georgia has many of the same characteristics as the wool industry near Florence. So does the consortium of firms called Sematech that was organized to cooperate in the design and manufacturing of semiconductors to enhance the competitiveness of this industry in the USA.

Focus on Organizational Designs: Network Organizations

In the Prato example above, the obvious connecting glue for the firms in the network is strong social relationships. But what about larger, more dispersed network organizations, for which there are not these strong social ties and that are geographically dispersed over a larger area?

Three things that make it work for these large networks.

1 The different, but important complementary competencies of the different firms.
2 A trust relationship that is based on both economic and interpersonal factors.
3 The sophistication and the ease of use of information technology.

Here are some examples:

- A network organization was created to manage the security, press relations, administration and public information systems for the World Cup. The companies that made up this network were Sprint, EDS, and Sun Microsystems.
- Some of the current alliances in the airline industry in which different airlines code share, permitting a traveler to make reservations that might take them on different airlines as they travel, but as though the reservation was with a single carrier. British Airways has such a relationship with US Air and KLM Royal Dutch Airlines works with Northwest Airline.
- West Bend, a manufacturer of household appliances, has its production operations directly connected to WalMart's point of sale information system so that it can easily supply WalMart as its inventory is sold (Christie and Levary, 1998).

The organizational model that we discussed earlier in this chapter can help you to understand the network organization. As the work is differentiated into subunits, it is useful to ask whether or not it might be more cost effective to perform those tasks internally or have them done by some outside group. This is the old "buy or make" decision that firms have always faced. In the case of the network organization, the decision is made to externalize the work and be dependent upon the supplier to provide what the firm needs. Whether some activity is externalized depends on several factors:

1 The costs of performing internally compared to the external costs
2 Whether the activity is critical to the core competence of the firm
3 The criticality of the activity to the organization itself
4 Difficulties of coordinating that externalized activity with internal processes

strategic center
The focal firm in the network that makes critical choices to facilitate the collaboration and cooperation of the network

The focal firm in the network is called the "**strategic center**" (Lorenzoni and Lipparini, 1996). That firm is the one that must scan and monitor the environment, make critical strategic choices about product design, distribution, and internal coordination, and facilitate the collaboration and cooperation of other firms in the network.

Summary

Organizations interact and transact with the environments within which they exist. They take inputs from it, they transform them into products or services, then export these as a form of output. This is accomplished by the activities of the organization that will take on different forms, depending upon the character of the environment. We call these different basic organizational types. If market and technological environments are stable, organizations take on mechanistic characteristics; they are more routine and bureaucratic. Organic organizations are found in volatile market and technological environments; they are more flexible, adaptable, and less bureaucratic. An organization in an environment with both stable and volatile sectors has an internal structure with both mechanistic and organic dimensions. When the technological environment is volatile and markets are stable it is called a technology-dominated mixed (TDM) organization. Market-dominated mixed (MDM) organizations are in stable technological and volatile market environments.

To create the structures that we see when we observe organizations, the activities of these basic organizational types are differentiated and integrated in the process of organizational design. First the activities are divided into organizational tasks. This is called the division of labor. These tasks are then grouped together into organizational subunits. This process is called organizational design and may lead to product-based structures, function-based structures, and matrix structures or project structures. Then an authority structure is created to coordinate and control the activities.

Guide for Managers: Designing Organizations

One of the most important tasks for a manager is to make choices about the design of the organization. There are three critical aspects to this:

1 Understanding what work has to be done
2 How to differentiate these functions, and then group the more specific task into subunits or assign it to individuals
3 To set up mechanisms, both structural and interpersonal, that coordinate and integrate those activities that you have just separated.

For each of these, there are important choices to be made. Here are some of the things that you have to consider in making these choices.

UNDERSTANDING WHAT HAS TO BE DONE

Recognize that your organization is dependent upon its external environment

You have to be aware of what permits the organization to exist. There are customers for your product or service. Your fundamental concern is to ensure that you provide them with the values that they want in your product or service, at the right time, at the right place and at the right cost. If you fail at that, you will also fail to obtain the revenues that are necessary to support the organization activities and make the profit that you want as a manager and/or owner.

This requires an obvious sensitivity to the environment and being willing to adapt to it. In some cases, that adaptation will mean that you need to develop new products. In other cases, if you wish to keep doing what you are now doing, you will have to decide to operate at a reduced level.

Know what work activities the customer is willing to pay for

Customers are willing to pay for production activities that actually create the product, distribution and marketing for delivering it to them, and costs of acquiring materials. They are not so interested in supporting staff activities, like human resources or even quality control. These make your job easier and they often make the product itself better. However, they are not the core work of the firm. Focus first on those core activities, and worry about organizing them most effectively. Let the support activities flow to the part of the organization where they most naturally fall.

FUNCTIONAL DIFFERENTIATION

The organizing function requires disaggregating the activities necessary to do the work and assigning it to different units and/or people. The two primary choices of differentiation are the product form or the functional form:

- In the product design, you group most of the major activities for differentiated products into units that are separated organizationally from other product units.
- In the functional design, you group similar work functions into the same unit, say the production unit, the marketing unit or the human resource department.

All other designs are variations of these two.

Making a design choice solves some problems, but leaves others to be managed

For example, if you choose the product organizational design, you are more likely to maximize customer service (Filley, 1978) but leave problems of efficiency and effectiveness that you must manage. If your firm is a mixed-type, then your most difficult problem will be to manage the interdependence of the various product and functional elements of the matrix organization.

If you have a set of highly differentiated products, the product organization is the better choice

This should be pretty obvious, because these differentiated products will likely require different production, marketing, and staff support. This makes each product unit the relative equivalent of a free standing firm. Here are some of the problems of which you have to be aware:

1 It will be difficult to communicate between product units because each unit will become somewhat insular.
2 There will be duplication of some staff activities. You will probably have, for example, a human resource function in each product unit or different quality control units. This is only a problem if there is duplication of similar activities, not of similar types of subunits.
3 There will be less concern with overall firm effectiveness in the product units and greater focus on the success of their separate activities.

Table 13.2 lists a number of other considerations that differentiate the product form and the functional form.

Understand the political implications of rational organizational design

In general, the choices that are made about the differentiation of activities can be rationalized and justified in terms of some logical organizational objective such as profitability or efficiency. There are, in addition, political implications that will become more clear in chapter 14. At this point, it is enough to say that, in some cases, you will put some units in positions where their activities will control others. This gives the heads of those units the opportunity to engage in political behaviors that may be in their own, and not the organization's, interest.

THE DESIGN OF COORDINATING AND INTEGRATING MECHANISMS

The primary coordinating and integrating device used to pull together the differentiated functions is the organizational hierarchy, especially the distribution of authority. Here are some things to keep in mind when you are making decisions about where and who should have organizational authority:

Delegate authority to the lowest level in the organization possible, consistent with the capacity of the Person in the position to have the information necessary to make decisions

Too often managers are reluctant to relinquish control and are unwilling to delegate authority to lower levels. This is especially a problem as organizations become more lean, with fewer organizational levels. You should keep this thought in mind,

"The person who is doing the work and knows the problems is most likely to be the one who can make the best decision about it."

The person who has the responsibility for a unit should have the authority to make decisions about it

This is an old principle of management, the principle of the parity of authority and responsibility. It simply means that you should not hold anyone accountable for those things that they cannot control.

There are, of course, many other issues that are critical in the design of organization. Many of these will be revealed to you when you begin thinking seriously about the problem and view organizational design in terms of the concepts that we have discussed in this book.

Table 13.2 Some differences between functional and product organization

	Functional	*Product*
Unit communication and coordination issues		
Conflict between major subunits	Higher	Lower
Communication within subunits	Easier	Harder
Communication between subunits	Harder	Easier
Complexity of coordinating mechanisms	Higher	Lower
Human resource issues		
Technical knowledge applied to problems	Higher	Lower
Group and professional identification	Higher	Lower
Training ground for top management	Lower	Higher
Organization effectiveness issues		
Duplication of staff activities	Lower	Higher
Product Quality	Higher	Lower
Efficiency	Higher	Lower
Customer orientation	Lower	Higher
Concern with long-term issues	Lower	Higher

Source: Adapted from Filley (1978)

Key Concepts

authority 389
basic organizational types 392
centralization 388
complex environment 390
decentralization 388
department 396
division of labor 397
flat organizations 389
formal organization 396
formalization 388
functional organization 402
horizontal distribution of authority 389
integration 389
market environment 390
market-dominated mixed (MDM) organization 395
matrix organization 405
mechanistic organization 392
network organization 409
organic organization 393
organizational complexity 387
organizational design 396
organizational structure 387
personal specialization 398
pooled task interdependence 400
product organization 404
project organization 408
reciprocal task interdependence 400
relevant environment 389
sequential task interdependence 400
simple environment 390
span of control 389
stable environment 391
strategic center 410
structural differentiation 396
structural integration 396
systems view of organizations 389
task interdependence 400
task specialization 397
technological environment 390
technology 390
technology-dominated mixed (TDM) organizations 394
volatile environment 391

STUDY QUESTIONS

1 In stable technological and market environments, why is it possible to design the departmental structure of an organization in either the functional or the product form?
2 What would happen if an organization is in a stable market and stable technological environment and the form of departmentation chosen was "matrix"?
3 How do accounting control systems and performance measurement systems differ in the different types of organizations?
4 How do the concepts of differentiation and integration explain organizational design choices?
5 Is the R&D function more important to the effectiveness of a mechanistic or an organic organization? Explain.
6 What are the particular problems of managing "mixed organizations"?
What are the important differences between the technology-dominated mixed (TDM) and the market-dominated mixed (MDM) organization?
7 Compare the strengths and weaknesses of product and functional organizations.
8 What is the relationship between the division of labor and the concept of organizational subsystem?
9 What is the difference between task specialization and personal specialization?
Give some examples of highly professionalized jobs which illustrate that task specialization can exist in jobs other than "blue collar" jobs.
10 What is meant by the term "task interdependence"?
What are the different types of task interdependence?
Give some examples of each from your work experience.
Are there different types of task interdependencies in different types of sports?
Give some examples.

Case

Cole and Wiley

Cole and Wiley is one of the largest drug manufacturers in the world. It has developed some of the most popular drug preparations for a wide variety of diseases and illnesses. Ben Watkins, the New England regional sales manager for the company, was interviewed by Mary Paine, a reporter for a nationally distributed marketing and sales magazine, about the company's system for managing the sales force.

Paine: Let's talk about the situation that your medical representatives typically face in carrying out their job. What, basically, are they supposed to do?

Watkins: Their job is to make sure that physicians know our products and are aware of our products' advantages. They should call on all of the physicians in their area at least once a month. During a visit to a physician, the medical salesperson must talk about whatever preparation we are emphasizing at that particular time. We usually require our sales personnel to discuss two or three products on a single visit, with one product receiving the greatest emphasis.

Paine: What do you do to help them to convince the physician to prescribe your products?

Watkins: We provide them with many different selling aids. Here's one, for example. This little booklet provides a lot of information about epilepsy and an anticonvulsant drug we have developed to deal with it. We also furnish the physician with free samples of our drugs, with articles that report on the use of our products in various research studies, and with other promotional material such as these notepads, or these little flashlights designed to keep the name of a new drug in the physician's mind.

Paine: What else do you do to help to sell your products?

Watkins: Well, of course we carefully select our personnel. We prefer to hire an individual with a master's degree in business and a science undergraduate degree. We need people who are able to converse effectively with physicians. We also spend an enormous amount of time and money on training. Here is a book we had produced to teach our medical representatives about glaucoma. We recently produced a preparation for the treatment of glaucoma that does not have the side-effects of another company's preparation, which was a drug long used for this disease. As you can see, it uses a programmed learning format so that the medical representative can progress at his or her own rate for self-instruction. In addition, we also bring our sales personnel back to Boston for various conferences we run on our new preparations and our current sales programs. We also teach our sales personnel how to make a presentation to a physician.

Paine: So they are supposed to follow a specific procedure in calling on a physician?

Watkins: Definitely. We tell them exactly what to say, when to say it, and how to say it. We work out the best way to get a good result and try to get them to do it that way.

Paine: Do they only call on physicians? Is that the only thing they do?

Watkins: No, they sometimes run meetings in a community where they provide dinner and drinks to physicians and their spouses, and show some film or videotape that our marketing department has commissioned. We send these films to various locations around the country. The films generally deal with some medical problem for which we have developed products. Also, our sales personnel staff booths that we set up at state medical association meetings. In addition, they call on pharmacists as well as physicians.

Paine: What do they do at pharmacies?

Watkins: They tell the pharmacist what drugs the company is promoting in that area at the time so the pharmacist knows that local physicians may be prescribing them. They also check the pharmacists' supply of our products to make sure they have an adequate amount on hand and carry out other promotional programs directed at the pharmacist. We tell our sales staff each month what we want them to do when visiting the various pharmacies in their area.

Paine: Do you assign them a certain number of physician calls to make in a particular period?

Watkins: Yes. Our salespeople have a schedule for each day, which they must follow or explain to us why they deviated from it. Of course, the schedule depends on the amount of travel time necessary for a salesperson to reach a certain community. We do expect the salesperson to stay overnight at those locations that are far from his or her home.

Paine: How do you evaluate their performances?

Watkins: Well, we have a management by objectives system in use in this company. Every medical representative is supposed to produce a given amount of sales for each of our drugs in his district. These are the sales person's goals. We then send these computer sheets that tell the sales for each of our products in his or her district for each three-month period. As you can see, this report tells the medical representative how much the sales are above or below those expected in this area.

Paine: Do the salespeople set these goals themselves?

Watkins: No. This office sends them to them, but if they think the goals are not possible to attain and can convince us that they are unrealistic, we might change them.

Paine: Does the salesperson have any other goals except sales goals for different products?

Watkins: Yes, I set self-improvement goals for each of my subordinates when we have our yearly performance review interviews. For example, here is one for Bob Wills in Vermont: Increased product knowledge in the nonsteroid anti-inflammatory area.

Paine: Do you pay a bonus for reaching or exceeding sales goals?

Watkins: No, we don't want our salespeople to become too pushy in dealing with physicians. You must be careful not to offend them. This company believes that sales will be the result of developing high-quality products and then providing physicians with accurate information about these products.

Paine: How well has your research and development division done in providing your sales personnel with high-quality products?

Watkins: They have done an excellent job. We have far more products coming out than any competitor. Our products are also new and significant, not just "me too" products that are copies of somebody else's.

Paine: What's your research and development unit like? You must have visited your research labs.

Watkins: Yes, I have once or twice. They are located in Pennsylvania and are pretty impressive facilities. They seem to be a very pleasant place to work.

Paine: What types of management procedures do they use? Do they have a management by objectives system too?

Watkins: Oh no. They are pretty informal. It's sort of like a university atmosphere down there. They are not held accountable for reaching specific goals or told how to carry out their responsibilities.

- What type of organization is Cole and Wiley?
- How would its various units be structured?

References

Baugh, S. G. 1997: Effects of team gender and racial composition on perceptions of team performance in cross-functional teams. *Group and Organization Management*, 22(3), September, 366–84.

Blauner, R. 1964: *Alienation and Freedom*. Chicago: University of Chicago Press.

Burns, T. G. and Stalker, G. M. 1961: *The Management of Innovation*. London: Tavistock Institute.

Christie, P. M. and Levary, R. 1998: Virtual corporations: recipe for success. *Industrial Management*, (40), 7–11.

Filley, A. C. 1978: *The Compleat Manager; What Works When*. Champaign, IL: Research Press.

Greengard, S. 1996: Privacy: Entitlement or illusion? *Personnel Journal*, 75(5), May, 74–88.

Hall, R. H. 1991: *Organizations: Structures, Processes and Outcomes*. Englewood Cliffs, NJ: Prentice Hall.

Kornhauser, A. 1965: *Mental Health of the Industrial Worker*. New York: John Wiley.

Lawrence, P. R. and Lorsch, J. W. 1969: *Organization and Environment: Managing Differentiation and Integration*. Homewood, IL: Richard D. Irwin.

Lorenzoni, G. and Lipparini, A. 1996: *Leveraging Internal and External Competencies in Boundary Shifting Strategies*. Working Paper, Faculty of Economics, University of Bologna, Italy.

Manufacturing Chemist 1998: P&G to overhaul its corporate structure. *Manufacturing Chemist*, October, 5.

Powell, W. 1990: Neither market or hierarchy: Network forms of organization. In L. L. Cummings and B. Staw (eds.) *Research in Organizational Behavior* Greenwich, CT: JAI Press, 295–335.

Presthus, R. 1978: *The Organizational Society*. New York: St Martin's Press.

Reginato, J. 1998: Special agent. *WWD*, September, 266–70

Thompson, J. D. 1967: *Organizations in Action*. New York: McGraw-Hill.

Thompson, V. 1967: *Modern Organization*. New York: Knopf.

Tosi, H. 1992: *The Environment/Organization/Person Contingency Model: A Meso Approach to the Study of Organizations*. Greenwich, CT: JAI Press, Inc.

Voss, H. 1996: Virtual organizations: The future is now. *Strategy and Leadership*, 24(4) July–August, 12.

Wyatt, S. and Marriott, R. 1956: *A Study of Attitudes to Factory Work*. London: Medical Research Council.

chapter 14

Power and Politics in Organizations

THE BASES OF INFLUENCE

ACQUIRING AND MAINTAINING ORGANIZATIONALLY BASED INFLUENCE

ACQUIRING AND MAINTAINING PERSONAL-BASED INFLUENCE

USING MANAGERIAL POWER IN ORGANIZATIONS

Preparing for Class

Power in organizations is often evident in aspects of the organizational environment. Individuals who are powerful within an organization often use that power to make their environment more pleasant. Often, we have just learned to expect that more senior supervisors and managers will have bigger offices and better furnishing. In many organizations, to draw many conclusions about organizational power, all one has to do is walk through the building.

To prepare for this class, choose an organization that you can walk through fairly freely. It could be a business or even your university or college. As you walk through the facilities, take note of aspects such as the office size, furnishings and equipment, location of parking spaces, availability and proximity of administrative support, etc.

1. What do you notice about the relationship between power and environment?

2. Besides comfort, are there any trappings of power that you notice that are useful in an individual maintaining his or her organizational power?

A very transparent example of what this chapter is about – power and politics in organizations – is the selection of the CEO to replace Robert Allen at AT&T in 1997. It shows that power and politics can be used in a major way by a person in a top position in a firm – and how you can lose in a big way if your strategy does not work. Allen had been CEO for several years after the splitting off of the "Baby Bells" and the deregulation of the telephone industry. The company had some hard times because it had to compete in the long-distance business with new long-distance suppliers such as Sprint and MCI. The reputation of AT&T changed for investors during this period from a safe, dependable stock that was a sound buy for retirement to a more risky, volatile equity.

As Allen's tenure neared a retirement date, he and the AT&T board of directors began a search for a successor. Normally this search would be done by an independent consultant in conjunction with the board and with some inputs, perhaps significant, from the incumbent CEO. It was very different in this case. The process, in its first go around, was almost completely controlled by Allen. From reports, it appears that Allen had very tight control of the selection process (Dobrzynski, 1997). One thing, unusual in the way CEOs were selected, was to use two executive search consulting firms to find candidates. It was very clear to outsiders that the board's influence in the process would be minimal. In addition, Allen appeared to have a very specific personal agenda: that the new CEO would come in, at first, as a sort of "CEO understudy" to Allen. Then, after Allen stepped down, Allen would remain on the board of directors. In fact, this last point was, more or less, the implied if not explicit price for Allen's support for the candidate.

The control that he had over the process had the effect of eliminating what executive recruiters call the "A List" of candidates (Dobrzynski, 1997). Why would top-notch CEO candidates want to come in as an understudy to an incumbent CEO and be tied to a commitment that he be appointed to the board when they will, for sure, be on other important CEO candidate slates and be able to negotiate more latitude for themselves?

The two consulting firms, Allen, and the board of directors finally found a candidate and appointed John Walter to the position of President and "future CEO." Walter had no experience in the telephone industry or in any area of electronics. He had been the top executive of Rueben Donnelly, the company that produced the Yellow Pages.

Nine months after he had been appointed, Walter resigned from AT&T. It was reported that the board of directors did not think he had the capacity to be CEO (Landers, 1997). Many thought, however, that the real reason is that he could not work with Allen (Keller, 1997). Of course, Walter thought otherwise, but had no choice. The board of AT&T made it easier to swallow the recognition, giving Walter a golden parachute worth over $25 million (Landers, 1997).

Now the search process began again, but this time the board took control of the process from Allen. There were much stronger candidates this time, both from inside and outside the firm. In the end, the board appointed C. Michael Armstrong, chairman of Hughes Electronics. Armstrong had been a candidate in the first selection process but was eliminated early. One rumor is that he would not agree with Allen's demand that he come in as "understudy CEO" and appoint

Allen to the board. After Armstrong took over the job, it was announced that Allen would not be on the board, that he would retire.

In this chapter and in chapter 15, we examine why and how these things happen, why people comply and particularly why important and sophisticated people like those on the board of directors of AT&T might agree with the sort of scheme that Robert Allen had to protect himself in AT&T when he stepped down as CEO. In particular, in this chapter, we discuss the issues of influence, power, and politics, which arise in every organization. We also discuss different types of power, how it is acquired, how it is used, how it is maintained, and how it is related to different types of organizations.

A Model of Influence Processes in Organizations

In the example, Robert Allen had successfully engaged in an influence attempt and the board of directors engaged in an act of compliance. Influence attempts occur when legitimate authority or power is used. These relationships are shown in figure 14.1. It shows that the bases for influence in organizations are the psychological contract, legitimate authority, and power. It also shows that influence attempts lead to results intended by the influence agent or to a modification of the relationship between the influence agent and the target.

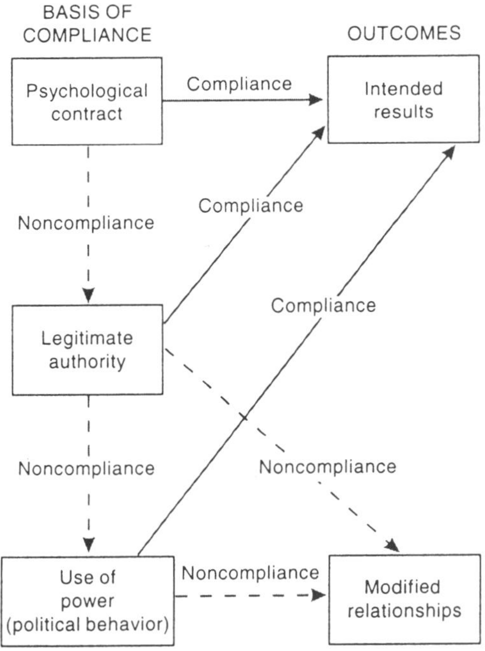

Fig 14.1: The bases of influence in organizations

influence
A process by which the behavior or characteristics of people affect the behavior or characteristics of others

Influence is a process through which you attempt to extract compliance with your intentions from others. For influence to exist, two parties (A and B) must be in an interactive and dependent relationship. This means that the actions of A can affect the actions of B, and vice versa. Influence occurs when one of the parties (A) induces the other (B) to respond in an intended way. Consider the case of Robert Allen and the AT&T Board. Why did the members take a less active role in the selection of a new CEO? Perhaps they believed that their role should not be so active. Or, they might not have wanted to spend the necessary time. Perhaps Allen had demonstrated a great deal of competence in the past, and, for this, the board trusted him. What is clear is that there was a strong dependence relationship between Allen and the members of the board.

dependence
Occurs when one party or both have a need that can be satisfied by the other

commitment
A strong, positive involvement in a dependence relationship

In an organization, there may be different motivational bases for **dependence** (Etzioni, 1961). In some cases, you might want to join an organization or interact with other persons because they share important values. This is usually the case for those who join political parties or religious organizations or become involved with ideological causes. The basis of these relationships is **commitment,** a strong, positive involvement in the dependence relationship. There is something very important that managers must remember about commitment: do not mistake compliance for commitment (Zaleznick, 1971). Compliance can occur for other reasons, as you will see.

In other cases, a dependence relationship may be forced, as when a person is put in a jail or a mental institution. Then the person experiences **alienation** and wants to escape from the relationship. These dependence relationships must usually be maintained by force.

calculative involvement
A dependence relationship where both parties make an assessment of the costs and benefits of maintaining the relationship

The third type of dependence relationship is **calculative involvement**, in which both parties assess the economic costs and benefits of maintaining the relationship. This is the type of dependence relationship that most often occurs in most work organizations (Etzioni, 1961). However, it is obvious that some levels of both commitment and alienation also occur frequently in work organizations.

The strength of influence one party has over another is a function of two factors. One is the need to maintain the relationship. When a person has a choice about whether to remain in a relationship, less influence can be exerted than when the relationship is necessary. A person with strong political beliefs who is a member of a party which espouses similar strong beliefs will be influenced much more by party leaders than others with weaker beliefs. The second factor, power asymmetry, is related to the first, but is not necessarily the same thing. Power asymmetry means that one party (B) is more dependent upon the other, giving the other (A) more capacity to influence.

BASES OF INFLUENCE

The psychological contract is the basis for the distinction between legitimate authority and power which we use in this chapter; see also page 101 in chapter 4. The **psychological contract** is the mutual set of expectations that exist between you and an organization. These expectations cover what pay you will receive as well as "the whole pattern of rights and privileges" (Schein, 1970). In return, you are expected to contribute both work and some commitment. As long as requests, commands, and directives fall within the boundaries of the psychological contract, you will comply. Take the case of Robert Allen, whose hypothetical psychological contract with the board is shown in figure 14.2. In general, he will do anything that falls within the boundary of the psychological contract. As you can see in figure 14.2, Allen would not fix prices or make illegal political contributions. They are not only illegal; they also fall outside his psychological contract.

However, there are two types of boundaries: public and real. The **public boundary** includes those activities that you want others, especially your superior, to believe are the elements of the psychological contract. In this example, the board wants Allen to make regular reports about the return on investment of recent projects, to perform conventional CEO functions, and to represent AT&T in the media.

public boundary Includes those activities that a person wants others, especially his or her superior, to believe are the elements of the psychological contract

In some instances, he may be asked to do something that falls outside the public boundary, but inside the real boundary. The **real boundary** represents the "true" limits of the psychological contract. In our example, we show two activities that fall in this zone, being involved with political parties and taking an active role in the leadership of some religious organizations. For obvious reasons, he will want the board to believe the psychological contract is constrained by the public boundaries because compliance with requests that fall between the real and public boundaries will make it appear that he is "doing a favor" for which there might be some quid pro quo – a favor in return for exceeding the requirements of the job. For example, in the first CEO search, the board of AT&T could have decided that Allen should not be so extensively involved with the process and could have managed it without his help. To do so would have required that they make it clear to him that this was what was going to happen. The fact that the corporate charter permitted this was probably enough that Allen would have been less active, had the point been pushed. They could have taken the position

real boundary The "true" limits of the psychological contract

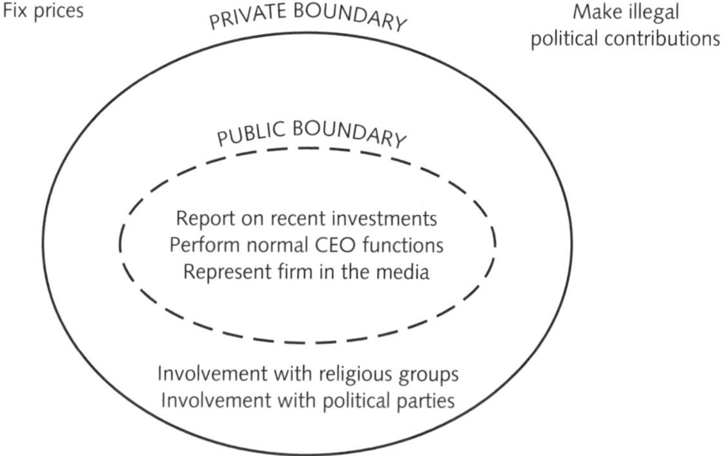

Fig 14.2: The hypothetical psychological contract of a CEO

that his psychological contract really included the expectation that he yield to the board in such matters.

These boundaries are not static; they change. Sometimes they change by mutual consent, as when a person's job changes by promotion. Sometimes they change through the use of power exercised by another person.

We define all those requests from a superior that fall within the real boundary of the psychological contract and are accepted by the subordinate as legitimate authority. Power is used to extract compliance to requests which fall outside the real boundary, and sometimes it is used for directives which fall between the real and public boundaries.

legitimate authority
Refers to whether the person who is the subject of influence believes that it is right and proper for another to exert influence or attempt to exert it

LEGITIMATE AUTHORITY **Legitimate authority** is the right of decision and command that a person has over others. It is sanctioned, or approved, by those in the organization. Legitimate authority is embedded in the psychological contract and, through it, a superior can expect a subordinate to comply with organizationally sanctioned requests.

Authority is seen as legitimate when the person who is the subject of influence believes that it is right and proper for another to exert influence or attempt to exert it. The board would be exercising legitimate authority by requesting Allen to report regularly on company activities. It might fire him if he refuses and could do so because the legitimate authority structure may contain those decision rights for the board use in the case of noncompliance.

Legitimate authority is reflected in the organization's structure, which defines the general distribution of legitimate authority by position location. Higher-level positions have more legitimate authority than those at lower levels. Further, because legitimate authority accrues to a person as a function of his or her organization position, it is transferable from one person to another. This means that when you leave a position, you no longer have the authority associated with it. These are now the rights of your replacement.

There are different patterns of the distribution of legitimate authority depending upon whether it is in a mechanistic or organic organization (Tosi, 1992).

- In mechanistic organizations there will be relatively highly centralized authority, policy, and decision-making mechanisms. In addition, the distribution of legitimate authority will be somewhat stable over long periods of time because there are fewer external pressures to change it.
- In organic organizations, the legitimate authority structure is less stable and will change as the environment of the organization changes and the firm adapts to it. Authority will be less centralized and exist closer to the projects that are being done in the firm. There may also be instances of dual authority as personnel are assigned to different projects or have both technical and functional supervisors, as would be the case in the matrix organization.

The **organizational culture** will also reflect the legitimate authority structure. When large differences in authority exist between levels of managers, there will most likely be very significant differences in status symbols. Managers at the top

A Question of Ethics: CEO Compensation and the Use of Legitimate Authority

Before the problems, Henry Silverman, the CEO of Cendant was regarded as a genius by Wall Street. He had put together Cendant, a conglomerate that included Avis, the car rental company and Ramada, the hotel chain. Unfortunately, it also included CUC, a group marketing discount club. What made the CUC acquisition so attractive was the rapid profit growth that it was experiencing. The acquisition was viewed favorably by investors and the price of Cendant stock rose, as it had done before when such moves were made by Silverman.

The problems that Silverman faced came about because CUC had engaged in some serious accounting fraud prior to being acquired by Cendant, but fraud that was not uncovered until after the acquisition. When the fraud was discovered the value of the stock dropped, between April and December 1998, from over $41 per share to under $12.

This was not only a problem for stockholders outside the firm, it was a problem for Cendant's management, particularly Silverman who held options for 25.8 million shares. However, Silverman, through the board of directors, did not have to worry about taking the loss in the stock market. The "strike price," the price that he would have to pay for his stock options, was lowered when the market price of the stock dropped below the original strike market price. While some think that the board handled it in an appropriate way, it does give one something to think about, how a powerful CEO can turn a loss into a gain (Byrne, 1998; *The Economist*, 1998).

level may have spacious, well-decorated offices set in very desirable locations in the headquarters building, while those at the next lower level may have smaller, less attractive offices.

The acceptance of legitimate authority stems from several sources. First, every culture has a concept of legitimate authority in which it is generally accepted that some forms of authority as well as relationships between superiors and subordinates are appropriate while other forms and relationships are not. For example, highly centralized authority is culturally acceptable in some Latin countries (for example, Italy and Spain) but a more even distribution of authority across different organizational levels is preferred in Anglo-Saxon countries (the UK, Canada, and the USA) (Hofstede, 1980).

Second, when you join an organization, its culture is transmitted through organizational socialization. An important theme in socialization is to rationalize the authority structure of the organization so that you accept it as legitimate. Third, your organizational orientation, initially developed by general socialization, affects legitimacy.

- An organizationalist usually has little trouble with most directives from higher levels.
- If you have professional orientation you may see many directives as less legitimate and respond more readily to influence attempts from colleagues.
- The indifferent responds primarily to reasonable job demands made during working hours and probably views everything else as nonlegitimate.

power
A force that is the basis of influence to extract compliance

organizational politics
The use of power in an organization

reward power
Power based on rewards that a second person desires

POWER **Power** is a force that can be used to extract compliance, but it differs from legitimate authority. Power is not sanctioned by the psychological contract, whereas legitimate authority is (Pfeffer, 1981). The use of power, in fact, distorts the boundaries of the psychological contract. This is possible because the boundaries of the psychological contract are flexible and can be modified, even though it may take considerable pressure. The use of power in an organization is called **organizational politics** (Pfeffer, 1981).

Power can be used to achieve organizationally sanctioned ends or the ends desired by the political actor. A person pressured to act by someone with power in an organizationally unacceptable way may comply to avoid undesirable consequences. Suppose that an organization's culture supports ethical behavior in its practice and the CEO is approached by a competitor to fix prices illegally and, at the same time, some important board members suggest this is a good idea. The CEO might act unethically, at great personal and psychological costs, if the pressure were extreme. If the result is that the firm engaged in price fixing, the board members would have exercised power, not legitimate authority.

People often respond to power even when they are not threatened with physical harm or with economic loss. People often comply when it is exercised by someone with legitimate authority who exerts influence beyond legitimate bounds. People often respond to power even when they are not threatened with physical harm or with economic loss, even though their actions could harm others. This was dramatically shown in research in which subjects were asked to assist the experimenter in a study of the effects of punishment on learning (Milgram, 1974). The subject was asked to be the "teacher." The experimenter's confederate acted as the "learner." The confederate was taken to a separate room where he could be heard but not seen. The experimenter then showed the subject how to operate an alleged shock generator. Shock switches ranged from 15 to 450 volts and were labeled from "slight shock" through "danger: severe shock" to the highest two levels, which were simply marked "XXX." The subject was instructed to apply shock whenever the "learner" gave a wrong answer, and to increase it when more wrong answers were given. Although no shock was actually administered, the subject was led to believe that it was. When mildly shocked, the confederate groaned. As the shock levels increased, the confederate's reaction accelerated to shouts, screams, and cries to quit the experiment. After 330 volts, the confederate became silent. The experimenter prodded the subject to administer stronger shocks when the subject resisted. In one experiment, 63 percent of 40 male subjects, 20–50 years old, applied the maximum 450 volts.

A person may possess different types of power (French and Raven, 1959). The ability to reward or to coerce can extract compliance. So can being an expert or being charismatic.

Reward power exists when you have control over rewards desired by another. The more highly valued the rewards, the greater the power. Individuals in positions with high levels of legitimate authority have the right to make decisions about the allocation of rewards and promotions based on organizationally rationalized criteria. When they use organizationally sanctioned criteria, it is the use of legitimate authority – not reward power. However, reward power can be enacted through politics as a result of a person having legitimate authority. It could happen this way. Based on the Good Enough Theory of Promotion – see page 93 in chapter 4 – a candidate for promotion need not be the most qualified person for a job but must be good enough to enter the selection pool. Usually the criteria to be in the pool are clearly specified and organizationally sanctioned. From that pool, a person is selected who, usually, has the "right" perspective as assessed by the judges. This is especially true when criteria and the judgments may reflect the use of power, not legitimate authority. In this sense, we can say that promotions in organizations are "political" decisions.

Coercive power in an organization exists for the same reason as reward power. The difference is that, instead of rewarding another person, punishment is threatened or applied. Returning to the example of promotions, those who make decisions can exercise their judgment against individuals in punitive ways. For example, in one organization, a manager was removed from a position because her supervisor maintained that she was not performing well and was not a "team player." In several instances, she was late with reports and had experienced some problems working with other managers at her level. When the complete set of facts was analyzed, however, it was found that her unit was among the most productive, her subordinates among the best in the firm, and her customers the most satisfied. However, she had openly disagreed with her boss in meetings, and frequently she was right. She was replaced by another manager who was equally effective. The decision to remove her was justified on the basis that the managerial team would be able to work better together without her. The short-run effect on the organization was not significantly bad, but it was very clear to the other managers that more than competence was necessary to succeed in the firm. They had to be able to work with the boss.

coercive power
Power based on the use, or potential use, of punishment to extract compliance

We rely on and accept recommendations from accountants, lawyers, and physicians because we believe they have the knowledge to make correct decisions in their specific area of competence. The same thing happens in organizations: having **expert power** means that you are able to influence others because you possess some particular skill or knowledge that they do not, and that skill or knowledge is necessary for the performance of their work. For instance, in designing a management information system, systems experts will design the system, specify equipment, and dictate how it should be used. Expert power usually takes time to develop; a person normally spends much time in formal training or developing skills on the job before this type of influence is acquired. Expert power is very task- and person-specific. For example, the systems expert may have a lot of influence in implementing computer information systems but no influence in the design of compensation plans for managers.

expert power
Power based on a person having valued skill or knowledge in a particular area

Because of its specificity, expert power cannot easily be transferred from one person to another in the way that legitimate authority can. For instance, if you become a plant manager, you will have the same legitimate authority as the previous manager. You may even be able to extend it so as to develop reward and coercive power, as discussed above, but expert power develops from your demonstrating competence or having it "given" by others because you have the appropriate education, certification, experience, and appearance. If you only have expert power and leave the organization, your replacement may not have the same amount of influence as you had until it is earned.

Diversity Issues: Expert Power and the Sight-impaired

Michael, a leading expert in the legal and economic aspects of employment issues, teaches the subject in a major university and has written several important books and articles on the subject. His expertise has served him well because he acts as a consultant on these issues and as an expert witness in court cases. He began his teaching and consulting career in his early thirties when he received a PhD and a law degree. Over the years, his research portfolio grew, as did his client list.

A few years ago, Michael began having a vision problem. He began to notice, when he was playing tennis, that it was difficult to see the ball. It appeared to disappear as his opponent was returning it. Gradually, the problem began to spread in other areas of his life. He started having trouble driving, he experienced difficulties reading, and had to be near a person and hear a voice before he would recognize who it was. After about ten years, it was determined the Michael was legally blind, though he still had some sight and could read, though with some difficulty.

That meant that he had to change many things about the way he lived. For example, he needed assistance in his teaching, using some technology for class preparation that the university provided. He also quit driving, finding other means of transportation. He also quit playing tennis. However, his vision problem had no effect on his expertise. He still writes scholarly articles on the subject, though he now uses an assistant to read to him when necessary. He is also still in demand as an expert witness in employment cases. Most of his clients continue to call on him. That is the point about expert power: It is the knowledge that gives Michael the capacity to influence others.

charismatic power
Power that occurs when individuals are susceptible to influence because they identify with another person

Charismatic power occurs when individuals are susceptible to influence because they identify with another person (French and Raven, 1959). It is based on the feeling of oneness that a person has with another, the desire for that feeling, or the personal attraction to be like the other. The stronger the attraction, the stronger the power.

The charismatic leader, a person with charismatic power, is set apart from "ordinary [persons] and treated as endowed with supernatural or superhuman or, at least, specifically exceptional powers or qualities not accessible to the normal person. ... What is important is how the individual is actually regarded by followers" (Weber, 1947). Some political leaders who have been called charismatic are Ronald Reagan, John F. Kennedy, Fidel Castro, and Saddam Hussein. Mary Kay of Mary Kay Cosmetics, Ted Turner of Turner Broadcasting and Herb Kelleher of Southwest Airlines are business leaders who have been called charismatic.

What differentiates someone with charismatic power from those with other types of power is the reaction of the followers. "Followers of charismatic leaders do not feel pressed or oppressed. Charismatic leaders have the ability to engender unusually high trust in the correctness of their beliefs, affection for the leader, willing obedience to the leader, identification with the leader, emotional involvement of the follower in the mission, heightened goals of the follower, and the feeling on the part of the follower that he or she will be able to accomplish the mission or contribute to its accomplishment" (House, 1984).

Focus on A Charismatic CEO: Herb Kelleher of Southwest Airlines

Herb Kelleher has been described as a "chain-smoking, bourbon-loving maverick [who] inspires his employees to break rules and have fun. His enthusiasm has helped make Southwest Airlines profitable for 17 years straight." (Sellers, 1997). He has developed a climate at Southwest that "flying should be fun," and he makes sure that this is carried through in the air to its passengers by the flight staff. He has always been outgoing with Southwest's staff, who know him on a first-name basis. He has such a good relationship with them that, though he is well past the normal age for retirement, they want him to stay. Why? Because he makes them feel very good about working for Southwest Airlines and, especially, him. He does it by joking with them, engaging in self-deprecating humor and, of course, by keeping Southwest at the forefront of the airline industry.

Like expert power, charismatic power cannot be transferred from one person to another. However, it can become institutionalized power when charismatic power is transformed into legitimate authority (Weber, 1947). It happens this way. In the beginning, a charismatic leader will attract followers and, as the number of followers increases, the beginnings of a hierarchy emerge. The charismatic leader appoints others to assist and delegates power to them to make some decisions. Others in the organization comply because they know that the leader chose these persons. Eventually rules, policies, and procedures develop in which the philosophy and practices of the leader are embedded. When the leader dies or leaves, the system of authority stays and becomes the structure of legitimate authority in the organization (Etzioni, 1963). As time goes on, the members comply with influence attempts that, by now, have become reasonable and proper. When new members join the organization, they are socialized to accept this system of legitimate authority (Pfeffer, 1992).

Outcomes of Influence

The use of legitimate authority or power lead to either intended results or to some modification of the relationship between the influence agent and the target; see figure 14.1 on page 421.

INTENDED RESULTS **Intended results** are the outcomes of influence attempts that are desired by the party that exerted the influence. From an organization's perspective, compliance should lead to organizationally valued results, such as high productivity and profitability. However, intended results may also occur because they are the wishes of a particular person, but are not necessarily part of the organizational requirements. For example, Robert Allen wanted the new president to appoint him to the board of directors when he, Allen, stepped out as CEO. This was not the organizationally desired outcome; it was Allen's intended result, and you can see that he achieved it with Walter, but not with Armstrong.

intended results The outcomes of influence attempts that are desired by the party that exerted the influence

Usually when legitimate authority, charismatic power, or expert power is used, the target person will react in a way intended by the power agent. The psychological response of the target is called acceptance, or **compliance**. He or she will engage in the desired behavior, as well as rationalizing and justifying the compliance as being the right way to behave. In fact, that is exactly the response to legitimate authority by the personality type we have called the organizationalist; see page 103 in chapter 4.

Charismatic power and expert power also lead to acceptance. When charismatic power is used, the target's justification is ideological and normative. For expert power, the acceptance is rationalized by the belief that the competence of the expert is necessary to satisfy the target's needs.

There can also be acceptance when reward or coercive power is used. This is particularly true when these types of power are the extension of legitimate authority. An example of this is when Allen, the CEO with legitimate authority exercised power in a political way to try to obtain a later board appointment. For acceptance under these conditions, the power agent must seek organizationally approved outcomes. When Allen used his positions to force Walter to accept his board appointment, the attempt was accepted and ultimately rationalized by the board.

MODIFICATION OF RELATIONSHIPS When a target of influence resists or fails to comply with the influence attempt, there is usually some modification in the relationship between the actors. The idea is usually that the influence agent, particularly when it is a manager, can take some action such as firing or disciplining the target, usually a subordinate. For instance, when Walter eventually had problems working with Allen, Allen and the board forced a resignation. There are other ways a superior could modify relationships with those subordinates who do not comply, such as assigning them to less desirable projects, not supporting them for promotion and pay increases, or changing their personal relationship at work.

There are also ways that the target of the influence can modify the relationship, which is most likely to occur when reward or coercive power are used. One way is by **resistance**, which could take several forms.

resistance Outright sabotage, development of a counter force, or leaving the organization as a way of modifying a relationship

- Appeal to reason is one form of resistance.
- Minimal compliance is another effective resistance strategy. This can be done by following the letter of the law but not the spirit. When air traffic controllers in the USA want to protest, they often do it by slowing down landings at large airports such as Chicago and Atlanta by following the exact formal requirements to maintain the necessary distance between landing planes, which creates delays.
- Outright sabotage is another way to resist. This may be done by tactics from delaying the implementation of decisions to actually destroying information or damaging equipment.
- Development of a counter force is another way to resist power. The person may try to develop their own power base, using approaches to acquiring power discussed in this chapter. They may develop coalitions, increase expertise, influence the environment, or acquire a sponsor. Success at any of these strategies will modify the balance of power.

- Leaving the organization is perhaps the ultimate act of resistance. If you cannot accommodate to the power structure or modify it, you may simply quit and find another, better, situation in which to live and work.

ORGANIZATIONAL AND PERSONAL BASES OF INFLUENCE

You can have influence for different reasons. One is because you are in an organizational position with legitimate authority, while, in other instances, influence is strictly due to some attribute of the influence agent.

ORGANIZATIONALLY BASED INFLUENCE Obviously a person in a higher-level position has more legitimate authority than another lower in the hierarchy, making legitimate authority a type of **organizationally based influence**. Further, studies have shown that a person may have organizationally based power, which is the capacity to influence others beyond the range of legitimate authority, as discussed on page 424 (Milgram, 1974). There are other types of position effects. Often a job description will give a person control over information desired by others. This is a source of power. Similarly, if you can control access to key people, power accrues. Executive secretaries and high level staff assistants are likely to have influence because of this. Also, some people are in jobs where they seem to have some perceived influence over the futures of others, such as the personnel executive who handles transfers, assignments, and personnel reductions.

organizationally based influence
Power beyond the range of legitimate authority based on the position that a person has in an organization

PERSONAL-BASED INFLUENCE You acquire **personal-based influence** when you possess attributes or skills desired by others. These attributes are usually independent of the organization's control. There are two types of personal-based influence:

personal-based influence
Accrues to an individual because he or she possesses attributes valued by others

- Expert power exists when a person has competence required by others.
- Charismatic power exists when one person becomes psychologically dependent upon another.

Acquiring and Maintaining Organizationally Based Influence

The pattern of power and influence relationships among units in an organization is called the **power structure**. For example, the marketing department may be more powerful than the HR department, and the finance group more powerful than both of them. However, the distribution of organizational power and influence is never what it appears to be on organization charts and in job descriptions. It is affected by a combination of situational factors and individual characteristics. For example, deans in a university do not have equal influence and power in the budgeting process. If they did, then budgets would be allocated to colleges on the basis of the number of students served and the cost of instruction. While these factors do count, a department's or college's power and importance also affect how much money it receives (Pfeffer and Salancik, 1974). Some colleges are more important than others, and some deans have stronger predispositions to use influence and power than others.

power structure
The set of influence relationships between different people or subunits in an organization

In this section, we first consider situational factors that affect the power structure of an organization, accounting for some key differences in legitimate authority between subunits. Then we examine individual characteristics related to the acquisition of legitimate authority and the propensity to extend it to become reward and punishment power. Finally, we suggest how organizationly based influence may be maintained.

Situational Determinants of Organizationally Based Influence

strategic contingency theory of organizational power
Theory based on the concept that a subunit's power depends on whether and how much it controls strategic contingencies for the organization

Just saying that more important organization units have more power than those that are less important is not enough. The question is: "What is it about a subunit that makes it more important?" The **strategic contingency theory of organizational power** explains some of these power differences; see figure 14.3 (Hickson et al., 1971). A subunit's power depends on whether, and by how much, it controls strategic contingencies for the organization. "A contingency is a requirement of one subunit that is affected by the activities of another subunit" (Hickson et al., 1971).

There are three conditions that make a subunit strategic.

1 Coping with volatility
2 Substitutability of activities
3 Work flow centrality

Organization subunits that interact with more volatile, threatening, and uncertain environments have more power than those that interact with stable ones. If the subunit can successfully interpret an unclear environment and help the organization to cope effectively, it will be able to influence policy and strategy. This is one of the factors that give physicians so much power in hospitals. They

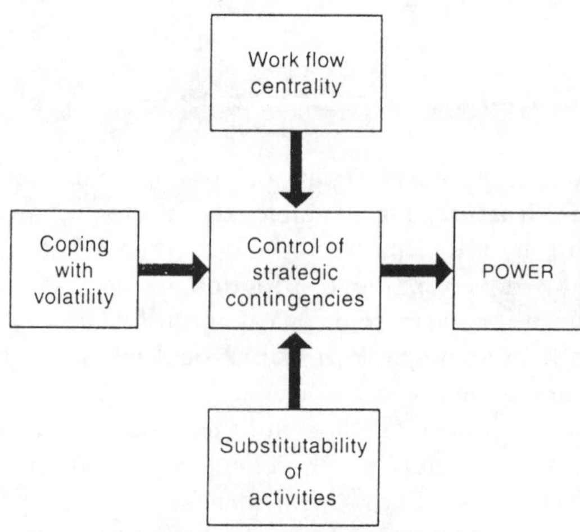

Fig 14.3: Factors affecting power from strategic contingency theory

control three of the critical variables that affect what happens in the hospital: the admissions, the length of stay and the demand for auxiliary services.

When there is no **substitutability for activities** of a subunit, that subunit will be very powerful. For example, physicians in hospitals also are, for the most part, not substitutable, particularly when they are specialists. Because the physician has the technical competence to solve patients' problems and other groups either do not have it or are restricted from using it, they have substantial power.

substitutability of activities When the activities performed by a particular individual or group can be performed by others

Work flow centrality has two aspects. Units with high work flow centrality are interconnected with many others. Most accounting departments have high work flow centrality because they obtain information from many units and provide it to other organization units. A unit with low work flow centrality would be a legal department, which may provide services to only a few other subunits.

work flow centrality The inter-connectedness with many others and the work flow immediacy

The second aspect of centrality is **work flow immediacy**. This is the "speed and severity with which work flows of a subunit affect the final outputs of the organization" (Hickson et al., 1971). The higher the work flow immediacy, the greater the power. Suppose a firm has a policy of maintaining very small finished goods inventories. The production unit has a high work flow immediacy because if production stops, then goods do not flow on to the customer.

work flow immediacy The speed and severity with which work flows of a subunit affect the final outputs

Strategic contingency theory explains subunit power relationships very well. One study showed that the power of the maintenance department in a tobacco factory existed because it controlled the primary uncertainty that affected production machine breakdown (Crozier, 1964). In channels of distribution the power of a supplier was related to three things:

1 Whether there were alternate suppliers
2 Whether the resources controlled by the supplier were critical
3 The level of transactions between the supplier and the customer (Bagozzi and Phillips, 1982).

A subunit's influence in semiconductor firms was related to the characteristics of the market at the time that a firm was founded (Boeker, 1990). In the early stage of the industry, when the primary market was the US military and the defense industry, the R&D units were most dominant in semiconductor firms which began in that stage. Later, the industry faced price competition and, in firms founded during this stage, manufacturing units were the most influential. When the industry moved into a "custom application" stage, the newly founded firms were dominated by the marketing departments.

Environmental Changes and Power

The power structure of organizations tends to be relatively stable because those who hold power are reluctant to let it change. For example, in semiconductor firms, we know that the longer the founding entrepreneur stayed in the firm, the less likely it was that there was a shift in departmental power (Boeker, 1990). The initially dominant departments were able to institutionalize their initial, strong power position.

Power structures are more likely to change in response to significant changes in the environment that destroy the competence of the dominant managerial coalition (Tushman and Romanelli, 1985). This occurs when markets or technologies change in ways that require different skills and competence. For example, the replacement of James Robinson in the early 1990s as chairman of American Express was due to the dramatic loss in profitability and market share. For years, the American Express Card and other financial services provided by the company were unique and resulted in an enviable market niche. Then Visa and MasterCard entered the same market, providing more services in a slightly different, but very competitive package. American Express lost ground to them, in part because the market for financial services, especially the credit card had changed. The top management of American Express under Robinson was not able to cope with the market changes (Tushman and Romanelli, 1985). After some serious attempt to reorganize American Express failed, Robinson was replaced as chairman. After some false starts, under the new management team, American Express has regained some of its market and has become a leader in some specific niches in the credit card business.

Personal Attributes of those who acquire Organizationally Based Influence

Some people have very strong predispositions to seek, acquire, and use power and authority, and they compete with others who have similar predispositions (House, 1988). In this section, we discuss the personal characteristics of those who seek and acquire organizationally based power, specifically legitimate authority and reward and punishment power.

Because legitimate authority depends on the position a person holds in the organization, it follows that to increase it, a person must advance in the hierarchy, increase the amount of discretion in the current position, or move into subunits that are more powerful. Those who seek to do this are likely to have these four characteristics

- Competence
- Self-confidence
- An organizational orientation
- Power needs

Competence is necessary; a person must be good enough at his or her job to be judged capable of performing at higher-level positions. Competence is usually demonstrated by past performance and achievement. Self-confidence is your belief that you will be successful. People with high generalized self-confidence have stronger beliefs that their influence attempts will be successful (Mowday, 1980). An organizational orientation is also likely to be characteristic of one seeking legitimate authority; see page 44 in chapter 2. The organizationalist finds organizational achievement and advancement reinforcing, making high position a sought-after value for them. This orientation will also facilitate advancement because an organizationalist with an adequate level of competence usually has the right combination of factors to be successful, according to the Good Enough Theory of Promotion; see page 93 in chapter 4. **Power**

needs must be very strong. Power needs are a person's desire to have an impact on others, to establish, maintain, or restore the prestige of power; see page 137 in chapter 5. Power needs are one dimension of the leader motive pattern discussed in chapter 15, shown to be related to managerial success (McClelland and Boyatzis, 1982).

In organizations, reward and punishment power stems from the extension of legitimate authority because the person has some discretion in how it can be used. Therefore, the personal attributes already listed above are necessary because you have to be in a position with legitimate authority but they are sufficient to acquire reward and punishment power. In addition, the person must have a political orientation. A political orientation is the willingness or attempt to exert influence beyond the boundaries of legitimate authority (House, 1988). The stronger the political orientation, the more reward and punishment power will be sought and acquired. People with a political orientation have these tendencies: (House, 1984).

- Machiavellianism
- Strong personalised power motives
- Cognitive complexity
- Articulation

Machiavellians have high self-confidence, high self-esteem, and behave in their own self-interest. High Machs are cool, are not distracted by emotion, and can exert control in power vacuums. They use false or exaggerated praise to manipulate others and are able to detach themselves from a situation. **Personalized power motives** will be very strong for those who acquire reward and punishment power. People with a higher personalized power orientation have strong self-interest and exercise power in an interpersonal way with an adversary. A person with **cognitive complexity** is able to find what patterns and relations exist in a situation, even though they are embedded in noise and confusion. This is a necessary skill because if you seek power you must be sensitive to subtle but complex situations in an organization so as to know when to exert influence (House, 1988). Accurate perceptions of the organization power structure are related to a person's power reputation (Krackhardt, 1990). Those who are attributed higher power by others tend to have more accurate perceptions of the power network. Being **articulate** is another important skill. The articulate person will be able to present arguments logically, which should facilitate persuasion. He or she may be able to form coalitions easier and may be chosen by a group to represent them.

Machiavellianism
A personality type which attempts to take advantage of others, seeks to form alliances with people in power to help serve their own goals, and might lie, deceive, or compromise morality, believing that ends justify the means

personalized power motive
Manifested in an interpersonal way between a person and an adversary

cognitive complexity
The ability to make sense out of complicated and ambiguous situations

Maintaining Organizationally Based Influence

Legitimate authority and organizationally based power can be perpetuated and strengthened by maintaining the current structure of organizational relationships and the organizational culture that support stable behavior patterns. This way, the powerful subunit will maintain control over strategic contingencies, retain its centrality, and protect its level of nonsubstitutability. By perpetuating the or-

EXERCISE

THE MACH SCALE

This shortened version of the scale to measure Machiavellianism can be used to give you some indication of your own tendencies. For each statement given below, indicate the degree to which you agree or disagree with the statements using this key:

SD = Strongly disagree
D = Disagree
MD = Mildly disagree
N = Neutral
MA = Mildly agree
A = Agree
SA = Strongly agree

• It is safest to assume that all people have a vicious streak and that it will come out when they are given a chance.	SD	D	MD	N	MA	A	SA
• It is hard to make any progress without cutting corners here and there.	SD	D	MD	N	MA	A	SA
• Most people forget more easily the death of their father than the loss of their property.	SD	D	MD	N	MA	A	SA
• Generally speaking, people will not work hard unless they are forced to do so.	SD	D	MD	N	MA	A	SA
• The biggest difference between most criminals and other people is that criminals get caught.	SD	D	MD	N	MA	A	SA
• The best way to handle people is to tell them what they want to hear.	SD	D	MD	N	MA	A	SA
• Anyone who completely trusts anyone else is asking for trouble.	SD	D	MD	N	MA	A	SA
• Never tell anyone the real reason you did something unless it is useful to do so.	SD	D	MD	N	MA	A	SA
• It is wise to flatter important people.	SD	D	MD	N	MA	A	SA

To find your score, enter the number of times you marked each level of agreement in the spaces here.

□ □ □ □ □ □ □

× 1 2 3 4 5 6 7

Then multiply it by the values shown.

□ + □ + □ + □ + □ + □ + □

Total □

An average score would be between 34 and 38. A high score would be in the range between 58 and 63. A low score would be below 20.

Source: Adapted from Christie and Geis (1970)

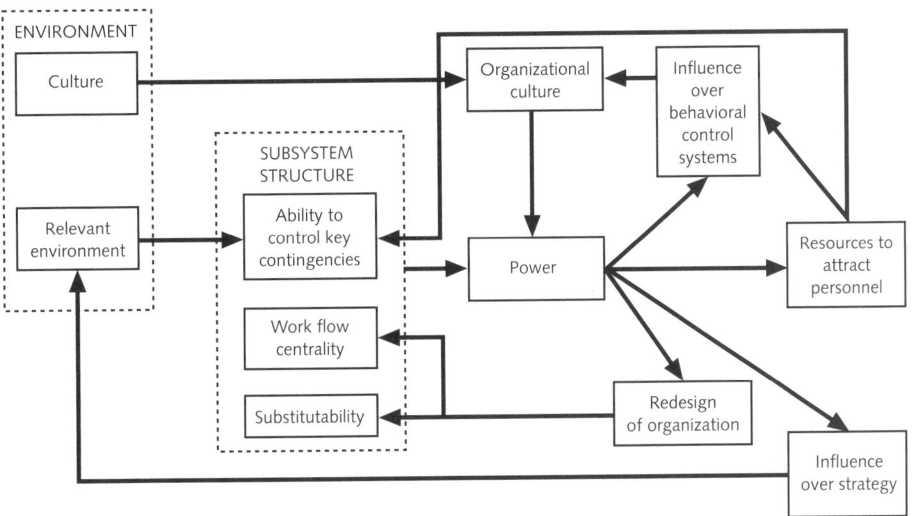

Fig 14.4: Maintenance of organizational-based power

ganizational culture, the norms and values that support the power structure will not change. Figure 14.4 shows some things a subunit with institutionalized power can do to enhance it:

- Influence strategy
- Affect behavioral control systems
- Affect the redesign of the organization structure

INFLUENCE OVER STRATEGY Managers in powerful subunits can affect organization strategy by influencing whether an organization takes an aggressive or a passive approach toward its environment. Stronger subunits can also influence strategic decisions about where the firm is located in the task environment. For example, several years ago a small electronics firm in California designed and manufactured advanced technological components for the defense department and NASA. It used a technology that had several consumer applications. A group from the small marketing department prepared an excellent proposal to develop a consumer products line. It was a well-conceived program that predicted substantial increases in revenue from the new product. The proposal was rejected by the top management group, which was composed mostly of engineers. They argued that the new product line would "change the nature of the firm and cause too much disruption." By remaining in the same market, the technically oriented top management retained its strong power position. It was not until recently, when there were substantial reductions in US defense budgets, that the proposal was resurrected. This has, of course, implications for the power of the engineers in the firm.

ATTRACTING BETTER PERSONNEL An interesting analysis shows how a finance department in a firm perpetuated its power by attracting highly talented people

(Pfeffer, 1981). The firm was experiencing financial control problems, and a large number of very highly talented people were hired in the finance department. Because this was a critical contingency for the firm and because good personnel were attracted, it gave the subunit a greater capacity to deal with the environment. As the competence of the staff grew, so did the unit's power.

INFLUENCE OVER BEHAVIORAL CONTROLS Selection, promotion, compensation, training, and socialization are types of behavior controls. If subunits can control and influence these activities, they will be able to perpetuate the power structure and their place within it. This occurs because the level of commitment and involvement of those who are selected and promoted to key positions will be affected by these processes. They will most likely accept the institutionalized power structure as legitimate.

- *Defining selection criteria* Powerful subunits can affect both the skills mix and general value orientations of those who enter the organizations by influencing selection criteria. For example, on page 2 in chapter 1, we note that one of the important changes in management education since the 1960s was the development of quantitative skills. Since that time, in many colleges of business, quantitatively oriented departments have a great deal of power. They are often successful in influencing other areas to select faculty who have similar skills, even though they may not be particularly necessary to the teaching and research objectives.
- *Affecting advancement criteria* If an error is made in selection, it can be corrected by not promoting those who fail to meet expectations. We have already pointed out the necessity to have both competence and the "right perspective" for advancement. By defining both the required competence and the right perspective, those who are in powerful positions can strengthen the existing culture, which reinforces the present power structure. This is exactly what happened when Lee Iacocca was fired by Henry Ford II (Iacocca and Novak, 1984). During his career at Ford, Iacocca was regarded by almost everyone to be Henry Ford II's successor as CEO and Chair of the Board. For reasons other than his competence, Iacocca was not promoted; for details, see pages 359–60.
- *Influencing compensation* Because pay is important to status, the ability to influence pay criteria and decisions can perpetuate power. In one plant, the plant manager had a very strong interest in safety. When he took charge of the plant, he gave a great deal of legitimate authority to the safety engineering department. This group's power grew, and soon they became influential in most matters of plant engineering and design. They also had a significant effect on a very important compensation decision. The plant manager intended to implement an employee bonus based on achievement of production, quality, and safety goals. Because he wanted to emphasize the interdependence of all activities, it was to be a plant-wide bonus system. The safety group, however, believed that the bonus would have a greater impact on safety if the safety component of the bonus was based on departmental performance. This meant that safety

goals would be set for each department, not the whole plant. In the end, the bonus system had a plant-wide component and the departmental safety component.

- *Influencing training* Because of their strategic position in organizations, powerful units are better able to define the subject of training. This is an important type of influence because in training much information is transmitted about the culture of the organization. For example, when key executives in one firm decided that it should have a management-by-objectives (MBO) approach of managing, they introduced it with a company-wide training program. Before the program was introduced, they were very careful to define what they meant by MBO. They developed very specific definitions of "goal," "tactic," "objective," and "action plan," which were made a basic part of the instructional program.
- *Influencing organizational socialization* The norms and values transmitted through organizational socialization reflect those of the dominant coalition. The effects of controlling socialization on an organization's culture are shown in a study of a new plant startup (Zahrly, 1985). The socialization of the work force was carried out by training that stressed teamwork, group projects that required teamwork, and discussions showing how teamwork was to be a foundation of the plant's management philosophy. Teams were formed and given a great deal of autonomy when they began working. Within 18 months, the teamwork norm was firmly embedded in the plant and transmitted to new employees.

Influencing organizational redesign Through organization design decisions, it is possible to retain control over key contingencies, to maintain work flow centrality, or to protect the nonsubstitutability of activities. The example of economics in colleges of business administration illustrates how this can occur. Because economics groups are often relatively large as well as very powerful, they are able to influence requirements so students in most areas must take economics courses. This makes the work of the economics groups very central to the instructional program. It results in very large enrollments for these courses, justifying the addition of new faculty members in that area and, of course, with increased numbers there is usually increased power.

Acquiring and Maintaining Personal-based Influence

In some instances, influence is entirely a function of personal attributes. The expert attracts a following because of the skills possessed. Entrepreneurs attract loyal subordinates because they believe in the entrepreneur's message. These are examples of expert and charismatic power, both personal based and requiring a fit between the attributes of the power actor and the follower (Pfeffer, 1992). Personal-based power is also important to managers. If they can develop it, it can supplement legitimate power and be helpful in "motivating commitment to the tasks that require high effort, initiative, and persistence" (Yukl, 1989).

However, it is more difficult to perpetuate personally-based power than organizationally based influence.

ACQUIRING AND MAINTAINING CHARISMATIC POWER

Charismatic power results from the identification of one person with another. It is based on personal attraction which develops in certain contextual settings which interact with the personal attributes of those involved.

Charismatic power develops in a crisis situation, when there are high levels of uncertainty and a group needs inspiration and direction. For example, the existence of crises are related to charismatic behaviors of US Presidents (House et al., 1991). As long as the crisis continues, the charismatic leader will continue to have power. Martin Luther King became very influential during the turbulent period of the civil rights movement in the USA. Organization start-ups are another situation in which charismatic influence can develop. In start-ups, members are usually seeking direction and support for their involvement in the new organization.

One explanation for the emergence of charisma in both crisis and start-ups is that the situational context is "weak." There are few cues from the environment, and the situation does not generate uniform expectancies for those in it (Mischel, 1977). When the situation is unstructured, those in it may not know how to respond. In this weak context, the charismatic person can provide psychological boundaries and direction by creating new meanings and beliefs for the followers.

Some of the characteristics we have already discussed as personal attributes of people with the capacity to acquire legitimate authority are attributes of charismatic leaders (McClelland and Boyatzis, 1982):

- Need for power
- Self-confidence
- Articulation skills

In addition, two other attributes are present when charismatic power exists (Hickson et al., 1971).

- *Nonverbal communication skill* The charismatic person has the capacity to convey meaning to followers easily with body language, gestures, and symbols. The manipulation of symbols is very important (Kirkpatrick and Locke, 1996). Revolutions all have slogans, symbols of unity, or other signs that identify the struggle and convey meaning to those involved in them.
- *Strong convictions about beliefs* This belief is transmitted to the followers both verbally and nonverbally.

As long as the crisis or uncertainty exists, the charismatic person will also retain power. When the crisis ends or the problems are solved, charismatic power can be perpetuated only if it has become institutionalized. Then the charismatic leader can remain, at least as a figurehead, because of the symbolic meaning that he or she conveys to the group. In the late 1950s, Fidel Castro led a revolution in Cuba as a young, charismatic rebel. He remained head of the government and had charismatic power for many years. Perpetuating charisma can be done in several ways:

- *Perpetuating the charismatic image* By maintaining images of the leader during the period when charismatic power was the dominant model of influence and control, the perception of charisma can be retained. The way that the group sees the charismatic leader, after institutionalization, is usually very controlled so that the charismatic image is not destroyed. Though much older, Castro still maintains a similar appearance to that which he had during the Cuban revolution. He keeps his beard and generally appears in public in a fatigue-like uniform. Pictures of him appear everywhere in Cuba.
- *Controlling interaction with groups* When the charismatic leader interacts with large groups, it is usually in controlled settings such as speeches, rites, or ceremonies. These can reinforce the organization culture as well as present the charismatic leader in a very positive light. When there is a small group with more interpersonal interaction between the leader and the members, these situations are very controlled. Usually the meetings are of a short duration. Normally, those who are in the meeting are carefully selected because they are loyal to the leader or to the organization. In most cases, they also appear to be representative of the larger group of followers.
- *Evoking specific negative images of the past* A charismatic leader can call to mind specific crises or times of uncertainty for group members. This reminds the group of "how bad it was" (Conger and Kanungo, 1987). Revolutionary political leaders usually refer to very specific cases of tyranny and poverty under previous regimes. The charismatic business leader can evoke the difficult times when he or she was leading the firm through the crisis. The charismatic union leader can bring to union members' minds the low wages, poor safety practices, and unfair working conditions of the past that gave rise to the need for a union.
- *Speaking in general, but positive, terms about the future* (Conger and Kanungo, 1987). This is the counterpart of the previous point. The charismatic leader can evoke images of "how good it will be" in the future. This is most effectively accomplished when the leader speaks in general terms. Avoiding specifics allows followers to project their own meaning into the leader's words. Because of the psychological connection between the group and the leader, this will result in a strengthened bond between them.

ACQUIRING AND MAINTAINING EXPERT POWER

Expert power results from the possession of the ability to do things valued and needed by others.

Expert power exists in situations in which specific skills are necessary in an organization and when the individuals who possess these skills are in short supply. This often happens when the organization's environment is volatile. Then firms must import the newly required skills, and often there is little incentive to try to institutionalize them. Thus, the power remains with the individual.

To acquire expert power, a person must possess the necessary physical, mental, or interpersonal skills that can help others. There is no way, however, to specify what personality factors might cluster around people with expert power because there are so many potential types of expert power. Expert power, however, can be facilitated by the organization or by other external institutions. Both of these can provide legitimacy by giving the expert the appropriate titles, licenses, or certification.

Three conditions are necessary to perpetuate expert power.

1 If you have expert power, you must be able to maintain your skill level. In one large law firm, only one partner is the environmental law "expert." He is important to the firm because he accounts for a large share of the firm's revenue. To maintain his competence, he regularly reads, studies, and attends seminars on the topic. Frequently, he teaches a class in environmental law at a nearby university.
2 It is important to ensure that the dependence relationship between the individual and the organization does not change in such a way as to weaken the expert's position. The law firm needs "environmental expertise" because it is a growing area of practice and an important share of the firm's revenue.
3 The expert must maintain personal control of the expertise. This ensures that others cannot be substituted for him. If environmental law becomes a larger part of the firm's business, it may wish to add other experts in this area, threatening the expert's power. He does this by a careful selection of clients so that new attorneys are not needed or by managing new experts who join the firm.

Managerial Use of Power in Organizations

Studies have shown how managers use some of the influence strategies discussed above (Kipnis, 1984, 1987; House, 1988). Managers from the USA, UK, and Australia were asked to indicate their preferred ways to influence both subordinates and superiors. In dealing with subordinates, this is how managers ranked the use of influence strategies:

1 Reason
2 Assertive behavior
3 Coalition formation
4 Bargaining
5 Appeals to higher authority
6 Use of sanctions

Note that reason was most preferred, but assertive behavior also ranked very high.

Reason is most frequently used as an influence tactic with superiors, as well as subordinates (Porter et al., 1981; Kipnis, 1984). It is an attempt to persuade someone else by providing him or her with information. The information is usually straightforward and presented in such a way that it results in the evaluation desired.

reason
An attempt to persuade someone else by providing them with information

Assertive behavior, direct and forceful approaches toward another, especially subordinates, are often successful. The "**iron law of power**" that states that the greater the discrepancy in power between the influencer and target, the higher the probability of assertive behavior (Kipnis et al., 1984). This usually entails a strong, aggressive effort to obtain compliance from others. For managers with subordinates, this normally takes the form of giving them direct orders. Initially, however, managers prefer not to use assertive behavior. They prefer to start with simple requests and appeals to legitimate authority. If they meet with resistance, then they are likely to become assertive.

assertive behavior
Direct and forceful approaches toward another

iron law of power
The greater the discrepancies in power between the influencer and the target, the higher probability of assertive behavior

Coalition formation is when two or more parties merge interests. Power can be increased because the alliance has greater control over strategic contingencies or more resources. A manager might form a coalition with a group of subordinates to support a particular project. Then when it comes time to bring others on board, they might be more susceptible to the group pressures; see chapters 9 (page 247) and 11 (page 307).

coalition formation
When two or more parties merge their interests

One approach to coalition formation is **cooptation** (Selznick, 1949). You coopt individuals from groups with which you might have problems into the power structure. When this happens, they are likely to adopt attitudes and values similar to those already in power. A striking example of this was illustrated in a classic study that showed how the attitudes of employees changed after they became managers (Lieberman, 1956). The study was done in a large public utility in which there was a very strong union. An attitude survey of the work force was conducted with a follow-up study to be done one year later. Between surveys, several workers had been promoted to supervisory positions and some were elected union stewards. The follow-up study showed that the attitudes of both groups had changed from the previous year. Those who became supervisors now had attitudes like those of the management group. The union stewards shifted their attitudes to become more strongly oriented toward union values. Becoming a member of the different groups changed their values. One year later, several of those who had been promoted or elected had gone back to the work force. Their attitudes reverted back to those held by the rest of the work force of which they became a part again.

cooptation
The process of bringing representatives of other groups into the power structure

In **bargaining**, one person seeks to influence another through the exchange of benefits or favors (Kipnis et al., 1984). Whether bargaining is possible depends on three things:

bargaining
When one person seeks to influence another through the exchange of benefits or favors

1. Whether each has something, a "good" desired by the other
2. Whether either is able and willing to withhold their goods at a cost to the other
3. Whether either is willing to negotiate

When a subordinate is unwilling to act in the way that a manager wishes, one possibility always available for that manager is to appeal to the boss. This has the effect of demonstrating to the subordinate that the directive has more organizational legitimacy, as demonstrated by support from higher management levels.

Managers may also threaten subordinates with sanctions or allocating rewards in punitive ways (Kipnis, 1987). They can do this through the legitimate authority of their position. For example, a common practice in some government agencies is to solicit contributions for political campaigns from employees, even though such demands are illegal in most states. The incumbent politician makes it clear to workers that a "voluntary" campaign contribution is expected. The politician usually receives these contributions because the workers know that negative performance evaluations or undesirable work assignments might result if they are not on the list of contributors.

Managers try to influence their superiors using, more or less, these same strategies. The main difference in the way that they approach their superiors is that assertive behavior was a much less frequently used strategy and, as you might expect, there was no indication of the use of sanctions. This is their order of preference when trying to influence superiors:

1 Reason
2 Coalition formation
3 Bargaining
4 Assertive behavior
5 Appeals to higher authority

shotgun managers Managers who use the following tactics with above average frequency: reason, coalition formation, bargaining, assertive behavior, and appeals to higher authority

tactician managers Managers that attempt to influence others through the use of reason and logic, and about average use of other tactics

Managers use different patterns of these strategies (Kipnis, 1984; Kipnis et al., 1984). **Shotgun managers** tended to use all the tactics with above-average frequency, apparently because they had many different problems to solve. They were also the least-experienced managers in the study. **Tactician managers** attempted to influence others through the use of reason and logic and were about average in their use of other tactics. This group tended to manage technically complex work groups, with skilled employees and work that required much planning. Bystander managers reported below average use of all the influence tactics studied and seemed to exert relatively little influence on others. In general, they were in charge of relatively routine work and supervised a large number of employees. They were also the managerial group in the study that was least satisfied with the effectiveness of their work.

Summary

This chapter explained some of the most important and fascinating topics in organizational behavior: influence, power, politics, and compliance. They are at the heart of what managers do to achieve things with and through others. A model of compliance processes showed that compliance – the degree to which a person acts in accordance with the wishes of another – can occur for several reasons. In some cases, individuals comply because of the psychological contract; in others it is because of legitimate authority, and in other instances the use of power may lead to compliance.

There is a distinction between legitimate authority and power. Legitimate authority is the right of decision and command over others that is accepted as appropriate. Power is the use of force outside legitimate authority. Four types of power were discussed: reward power, coercive (punishment) power, expert power, and charismatic power.

The characteristics of the situation and the individuals are related to the different types of influence that are acquired and exerted. The organizational context for power is related to the extent to which subunits interact with volatile environments, perform nonsubstitutable activities, or are central to organizational functioning.

We also showed how power can be maintained in organizations. Often maintaining power depends on a person's ability to perpetuate the settings in which power was originally developed. This can be done in different ways. In many instances, legitimate authority, reward power, and punishment power can be maintained because the power holders have control of organization processes, such as the choice of strategies, selection of personnel, and promotions.

Guide for Managers: Using Power in Organizations

You must know that if you are going to manage anything, you cannot escape using legitimate authority and power. As we pointed out earlier, power is not based on the psychological contract, legitimate authority is. That means you should have little trouble using legitimate authority. The most important thing that you need to know about it is the boundaries of the psychological contract.

Power is different because you are going outside those boundaries. For that reason, it is best, in organizations, not to use brute force and coercion, but rather use power in much more subtle ways. If force and coercion is used, those in opposition will probably try to use counter force. This will result in force against force, open conflict that organizations try to avoid because harmony is so highly valued. The subtle use of power allows the appearance of logic and rationality to be maintained.

You can have your way without overt pressure and force by using some of the approaches discussed here. However, you must remember two old proverbs when you become involved in the use of power, the game of organizational politics. One is: "What goes around, comes around." The second, maybe a little more precise, is: "Those who live by the sword, die by the sword." This means that even if you are successful in making others do what you want them to do, if they have lost something there may come a time when you will have to pay for your success. Before you start, however, you should ask yourself if you have the stomach for the game. The way to know this is to review the sections of this chapter that discuss the personal attributes of those who acquire organizational and personal power. Without these, you might not fare well in this contest. Here are some things that you can do.

CONTROL THE CONTEXT

If you have the legitimate authority to do so, you can structure the context so that the intended behaviors are likely to occur (Kipnis, 1987). Your legitimate authority can be extended in political ways because a position in an organization gives you some degree of control over the allocation of resources, the distribution of rewards, and the implementation of sanctions. As a manager, you can exert influence in many ways by careful contextual control of others' behavior and decisions. Suppose that you are a vice president of marketing and asked by the CEO to make a recommendation about which one of five new products a firm should develop. A nonpolitical evaluation process would subject each product to a rigorous assessment of costs and benefits. Suppose, however, that you prefer one of the products over the others. You could influence the choice process by appointing a committee composed of people who are likely to favor the product.

DEFINE THE PROBLEM YOUR WAY

As a manager, especially with subordinates, you can often select or define the problem that is to be solved. This limits the range of solutions that can be considered. If the academic vice president of the university asks a committee to develop a program to "enhance the reputation of the university," the committee will attack the issue differently than they would if the problem is "How can the university enhance its reputation as a graduate institution?" People will have an opportunity to exercise some influence over the different ways that the problem is solved but not over the selection of the problem, which by definition was confined to graduate emphasis.

MAKE SUBJECTIVE USE OF OBJECTIVE CRITERIA

An effective way to use political power is to influence the criteria used in decision making (Pfeffer, 1981). For example, as the marketing vice president involved in the product choice decision above, you could define the criteria that will be used in the product evaluation process. In other words, you can "structure" them in a way that will lead to a favorable evaluation of the preferred alternative.

A second related political strategy is to discount objective criteria so that although one of the alternatives appears better than others, the rating of the alternative is lowered for political reasons. Suppose the board of directors has two candidates for the CEO position: one is from inside the firm and the second from outside. Further suppose that the outside candidate is now the president of a small but very profitable firm. Those who favor the inside candidate might argue that the success of the smaller firm is not due to the president but to other factors such as luck, lack of competition, or a special competitive advantage such as a patent. If they are successful in discounting the outside candidate's performance, then the insider will be selected. Though a little different in specifics, this is what Robert Allen did in the example that opened the chapter, on page 420.

USE OUTSIDE EXPERTS

To gain support for your position, you can use outside experts to justify and rationalize decisions (Pfeffer, 1992). This combines legitimate power and expert power. At one extreme, expert opinion can be brought in through research reports and published articles to support a position. At the other extreme, consultants or members at the board of directors can be used to make recommendations, to introduce changes, and to reinforce decisions (Tosi and Gomez-Mejia, 1989). You can see how this worked in the AT&T succession case. Allen was able to use the two consulting firms in ways that furthered his agenda. By letting candidates know that the position would be "CEO in training," neither consulting firm could come up with the "A List" of candidates, leaving those on the list who were more likely to agree to his agenda.

CONTROL THE FLOW AND QUANTITY OF INFORMATION

A person can control when information is released, how much is released, and what others receive. Suppose the board of directors, in the example above, favors an inside candidate for president. The number of outside candidates can be limited in several ways. One is by delaying the announcement of the position and setting an early date for the appointment. The board could also affect the selection by limited release of information. When prospective candidates inquire about the job, the board may provide general, not specific, information about salaries and benefits.

Controlling the agenda of meetings is another way to manage the flow and type of information (Pfeffer, 1981). Both the content of the agenda and the order in which items are considered can influence decisions. This is a common occurrence at stockholder meetings. The board of directors usually determines the agenda, with little time for shareholders interested in other matters to raise them. If such issues are raised, then the board can usually influence the decision because it controls the proxies.

ACQUIRE A SPONSOR

A sponsor is a person at a higher organizational level or in a powerful position who represents and advances the interests of another. Sponsorship provides influence in two ways.

1 The sponsor may be an advocate for a person in a promotion decision. This could result in advancement for the person while at the same time creating a loyal subordinate for the sponsor.
2 The sponsor may advance ideas and projects that are developed by the person. If the projects and ideas are good, the sponsor may even be given some credit for bringing them to the attention of decision makers.

The two things that you have to do to acquire a sponsor is to demonstrate competence and engage in ingratiation. If you do well on important tasks, you will usually come to the attention of someone at a higher-level position, who may be a willing sponsor. Then, by ingratiation, you can increase your attractiveness to others (Liden and Mitchell, 1988). It is usually accomplished through flattery and a display of commitment or potential commitment. Flattery positively reinforces the target. In one organization, a young engineer with high power needs successfully used ingratiation to acquire the sponsorship of a senior project engineer. The senior engineer had been assigned the task of improving the productivity of a plant that was having serious performance difficulties. He had very little support from the plant's staff because they feared that his changes would reduce their status. The young engineer, in a quiet and discreet way, began to let the senior engineer know that he believed the project could work. He gave the senior engineer a good deal of positive feedback about the plans that were being developed. He also made certain that the senior engineer believed that he too thought the resistance from the old staff was unwarranted. While he supported the change project, there was only one problem: because he was new to the organization, he told the senior engineer, it did not seem wise to support the proposals publicly. Because there were no other supporters, the senior engineer began to confide in the younger person. He also started to sponsor him, recommending him for special assignments and early promotion.

USE IMPRESSION MANAGEMENT

One way to develop power is by **impression management** to create the illusion that one has it. This is done by the control of information, or cues, imparted to others to manage their impressions (Thompson, 1967). Specialists practice impression management when they use jargon unique to their profession. The doctor's white coat and use of medical terms does nothing to increase technical competence, but it conveys important meanings to patients. A top executive may try to create the impression of power by high activity levels and demonstrations of organizational loyalty. This may be done by using symbols such as large offices, deep carpets, and special furniture. The executive may also remain aloof and apart from lower-level members to maintain status distinctions.

Those at lower levels can also try to manage impressions of them by superiors. They may seek to give the impression that they are loyal and to create the belief that they are competent in their job and always busy. Being a "good" subordinate may be a way to gain power because superiors may place trust in him or her. Then the subordinate may be able to expand the power from the current legitimate authority base.

Key Concepts

alienation 422
assertive behavior 443
bargaining 443
calculative involvement 422
charismatic power 428
coalition formation 443
coercive power 427
cognitive complexity 435
commitment 422
cooptation 443
dependence 422
expert power 427
influence 422
intended results 429
iron law of power 443
legitimate authority 424
Machiavellianism 435
organizational politics 426
organizationally based influence 431
personalized power motives 435
personal-based influence 431
power 426
power structure 431
public boundary 423
real boundary 423
reason 443
resistance 430
reward power 426
shotgun managers 444
strategic contingency theory of organizational power 432
substitutability of activities 433
tactician managers 444
work flow centrality 433
work flow immediacy 433

STUDY QUESTIONS

1 What is the importance of the concept of dependence in understanding power? How is dependence related to the level of the power that one person has over another?
2 There are three bases of compliance. What are they? Can you link them in any way to the types of organization that were discussed in chapter 2 or the organizational orientations discussed in chapter 4?
3 How is the psychological contract related to the use of power in organizations? Does the psychological contract mean that individuals will comply willingly with orders and directives?
4 In this chapter, we differentiated between power and legitimate authority. What is the difference?
5 What is meant by organizational politics?
6 What is the difficulty with relying on charismatic power as a basis for influence in organizations?
7 What is the basis of the strategic contingency theory of power?
8 List and define the organizationally based power strategies. Can you think of any situations in which you have been personally affected by one of these approaches? Can you think of any situation where you have used one of them?
9 Why is impression management a way to develop and hold power? Give some examples of ways that you have seen it used.
10 Use the ideas in the section "Maintaining Organizationally Based Influence" to explain why it is difficult to bring about a significant change in organizations.

Case

The Brewton School

When Boyd Denton was appointed superintendent of the Washington County School System in 1995 he was given the charge, by the school board, to improve the quality of student performance. His strategy for achieving this was to implement his philosophy of "competence and delegation." First, he would find very strong and very competent principals for each of the schools. Second, he would give each of them a great deal of autonomy. He allowed principals to make hiring decisions, to evaluate teachers, to make salary decisions and to decide how to spend the budget allocated to each school.

From 1995 to 1998, the school system made significant gains in student achievement. However, there was one school, Brewton, which was a problem for Denton. The principal at Brewton was David Starr. Starr was one of the first principals that Denton hired, but now Denton believed that he had made a mistake.

At Brewton, the teachers did not seem to care about the students. They were, by any measure, mediocre. However they were very loyal to Starr. He was well liked by them and they supported him. The reason is that Starr never put any pressure on them for performance and did not really hold them accountable.

When Denton became aware of this, he discussed it with Starr. Starr became angry and threatened to quit. He told Denton that the reason Brewton was not a good school was because Denton did not give them enough resources to do the job right. Denton pointed out the opposite. In fact, by every budget measure, Starr and the Brewton School was well treated.

By 1999, Starr and Denton were on very bad terms. They argued often and all the other principals saw Starr as a prima donna and uncooperative. In one of their arguments, Starr threatened to resign. Denton told him, "Bring me the letter, now." Starr left the office and returned twenty minutes later with a letter of resignation. Denton did not hesitate, "I'll take it," he said.

Denton searched for a replacement and found Joe Melcan, a bright young assistant superintendent in a nearby district. When he hired Melcan, Denton told him:

> I want you to get Brewton straightened out and I'll help you. The teachers are well paid, and you've got good resources there, but the job does not get done.
>
> One of the main problems you will have is that most of the teachers are very loyal to Starr. They won't help you much, but I'll give you whatever help and support you need.

Melcan's approach was a straightforward one. He would let everyone know what was expected of them, make pay as contingent on performance as possible and hire good new teachers. He thought that in three or four years, there would be enough turnover that with subsequent replacement, he could make Brewton into a high performing school.

Denton watched Melcan's progress and he was pleased. Three new young teachers were hired. Melcan instituted a different evaluation approach than Starr, He started to give substantial recognition to the good teachers and less to those who were not so good. This was a major departure from the way Starr had managed and many of the Starr loyalists were angry. Some complained to Denton and some filed grievances. When Denton and the union investigated they found that the charges were without foundation. It is true that things had changed, but now the school was not managed in the style of Starr, but in a performance-oriented style by Melcan.

This was exactly what Denton thought had to be done. Between 1995 and 1998, the student performance improved considerably. However, many of the teachers who were old Starr supporters were dissatisfied. They continued to complain and grumble. Each time, however, they came to Denton, he supported Melcan.

In late 1999, Denton left Washington County to become an assistant to the State Superintendent of Schools. He was replaced by Mitchell Kraut. Kraut had been an assistant superintendent for Denton for several years. There were two things about Kraut that were of concern to Melcan. First, Kraut had been a teacher at Brewton during the first years of Starr's time as principal. They had, in fact, become close friends. Second, Kraut announced that he was going to centralize many activities which had been performed previously by the principals. No longer would the principals make budgeting decisions, evaluate personnel or hire faculty. Joe Melcan was very worried.

- What was the basis of Joe Melcan's power during his tenure?
- What are the potential effects of the change to centralization on Melcan?
- How do you think the supporters of Starr will react to the change? How might they react to Melcan?

References

Bagozzi, R. and Phillips, L. 1982: Representing and testing organizational theories: A holistic view. *Administrative Science Quarterly*, 77, 459–88.

Boeker, W. 1990: The development and institutionalization of subunit power in organizations. *Administrative Science Quarterly*, 34, 388–410.

Byrne, J. 1998: How to reward failure: Reprice stock options. *Business Week*, New York: McGraw Hill, October 12, 50.

Christie, R. and Geis, F. (eds) 1971: *Studies in Machiavellianism*. New York: Academic Press.

Conger, J. A. and Kanungo, R. 1987: Toward a behavioral theory of charismatic leadership in organizational settings. *Academy of Management Review*, 12(4), 637–47.

Crozier, M. 1964: *The Bureaucratic Phenomenon*. Chicago: University of Chicago Press.

Dobrzynski, J. 1997: An ethical role for recruiters. *The New York Times*, July 29, C5.

The Economist 1998: Cendant: Fallen star. *The Economist*, July 18, 56.

Etzioni, A. 1961: *A Comparative Analysis of Complex Organizations*. New York: Free Press.

Etzioni, A. 1963: *Modern Organizations*. New York: Prentice-Hall.

French, J. R. P., Jr. and Raven, B. 1959: The bases of social power. In D. Cartwright (ed.) *Studies in Social Power*, Ann Arbor: University of Michigan Institute for Social Research, 150–67.

Hickson, D. J., Hinings, C. R., Lee, C. A., Schneck, R. and Pennings, J. M. 1971: A strategic contingency theory of intraorganizational power. *Administrative Science Quarterly*, 16, 216–29.

Hofstede, G. 1980: *Culture's Consequences: International Differences in Work-related Values*. Beverly Hills, CA: Sage Publications.

House, R. J. 1984: *Power in Organizations: A Social Psychological Perspective*. Unpublished manuscript. Toronto: University of Toronto.

House, R. J. 1988: Power and personality in complex organizations. In B. J. Staw and L. L. Cummings (eds) *Research in Organizational Behavior*, vol. 10. Greenwich, CT: JAI Press, 305–57.

House, R. J., Spangler, W. D. and Woycke, J. 1991: Personality and charisma in the US presidency: A psychological theory of leader effectiveness. *Ad-*

ministrative Science Quarterly, September, 36(3), 364–96.

Iacocca, L. and Novak, W. 1984: *Iacocca An Autobiography*. New York: Bantam Books.

Keller, J. J. 1997: AT&T's Walter failed to court the man who counted. *The Wall Street Journal*, July 18, A1.

Kipnis, D. 1984: The use of power in organizations and in interpersonal settings. In S. Oscamp (ed.) *Applied Social Psychology Annual*, vol. 5, 179–210.

Kipnis, D. 1987: Psychology and behavioral technology. *American Psychologist*, 42(1), January 30–6.

Kipnis, D., Schmidt, S. M., Swaffin-Smith, C. and Wilkinson, I. 1984: Patterns of managerial influence: Shotgun managers, tacticians, and bystanders. *Organizational Dynamics*, Winter 12, 58–67.

Kirkpatrick, S. and Locke, E. A. 1996: Direct and indirect effects of three core charismatic leadership components on performance and attitudes. *Journal of Applied Psychology*. 3(1), February, 36–42.

Krackhardt, D. 1990: Assessing the political landscape: Structure, cognition, and power in organizations. *Administrative Science Quarterly*, 35, 342–69.

Landers, M. 1997: After nine months, AT&T president quits under pressure. *New York Times*, 146, July 17, C1.

Liden, R. C. and Mitchell, T. R. 1988: Ingratiatory behaviors in organizational settings. *The Academy of Management Review*, 13(4), 572–614.

Lieberman, S. 1956: The effects of changes in roles on the attitudes of role occupants. *Human Relations*, 9, 385–402.

McClelland, D. A. and Boyatzis, R. E. 1982: Leadership motive pattern and long-term success in management. *Journal of Applied Psychology*, 67, 737–43.

Milgram, S. 1974: *Obedience to Authority*. New York: Harper & Row.

Mischel, W. 1977: The interactions of person and situation. In D. Magnusson and N. S. Enders (eds) *Personality at the Crossroads: Current Issues in Interactional Psychology*. Hillsdale, NJ: Erlbaum.

Mowday, R. 1980: Leader characteristics, self-confidence and methods of upward influence in organization decision situations. *Academy of Management Journal*, 44, 709–24.

Pfeffer, J. 1981: *Power in Organizations*. Boston: Pitman Publishing.

Pfeffer, J. 1992: *Managing with Power*. Boston. MA: Harvard Business School Press.

Pfeffer, J. and Salancik, G. 1974: Organizational decision making as a political process: The case of the university budget. *Administrative Science Quarterly*, 19, 135–51.

Porter, L. W., Allen, R. W. and Angle, H. L. 1981: The politics of upward influence in organizations. In L. L. Cummings and B. S. Staw (eds) *Research in Organizational Behavior*, Greenwich, CT: JAI Press.

Schein, E. A. 1970: *Organizational Psychology*. New York: Prentice-Hall.

Sellers, P. 1997: What exactly is charisma? *Fortune*, 133(1), January 15, 68–75.

Selznick, P. 1949: *TVA and the Grass Roots*. Berkeley: University of California Press.

Thompson, V. 1967: *Modern Organization*. New York: Knopf.

Tosi, H. 1992: *The Environment/Organization/Person Contingency Model: A Meso Approach to the Study of Organizations*. Greenwich, CT: JAI Press, Inc.

Tosi, H. L. and Gomez-Mejia, L. 1989: The decoupling of CEO pay and performance: an agency theory perspective. *Administrative Science Quarterly*, 34, 169–89.

Tushman, M. L. and Romanelli, E. 1985: Organizational evolution: A metamorphosis model of convergence and reorientation. In L. L. Cummings and B. M. Staw (eds) *Research In Organizational Behavior*, Connecticut: JAI Press Inc., vol. 7, 171–222.

Weber, M. 1947: *The Theory of Social and Economic Organization*. Translated by T. Parsons. New York: Free Press.

Yukl, G. 1989: *Leadership in Organizations*. Englewood Cliffs, NJ: Prentice-Hall.

Zahrly, J. 1985: *An Analysis of the Source of an Organization's Culture*. Paper delivered at the Midwest Business Administration Association Meetings, Chicago, IL.

Zaleznick, A. 1971: Power and politics in organizational life. In E. C. Bursk and T. B. Blodgett (eds) *Developing Executive Leaders*, Cambridge, MA: Harvard University Press, 38–57.

chapter 15

Leadership in Organizations

Preparing for Class

When you think of a leader, who comes to your mind? Think of someone whom you consider to be an effective leader and someone whom you view as an ineffective one. When you have two individuals firmly in mind, answer these questions:

Did you base your judgment of their leader effectiveness on the behaviors they exhibit? Did you base it on who they were as a person (their traits)? Or did you based it on their success in leading others?

Did you use the same criteria for the ineffective leader as you did for the effective one?

Can you evaluate the reason for the differing effectiveness of the two leaders you considered? Would you attribute their differing effectiveness to behaviors, traits, or measures of success?

What conclusions can you draw about leadership from this comparison?

We are fascinated with leadership – whether it is business, government, or sports – and one of the interesting questions is why someone is thought to be a good leader. An example of this is a study of how Donald Burr, the founder of People Express Airline, was presented in the popular press (Chen and Meindl, 1991). When it started up in the early 1980s, the innovative airline was one of the first low-cost short-haul airlines. People Express was a deviant in the industry. Fares were very low, passengers checked their own bags and employees worked on the flights as well as at ticket counters. During the startup phase, Burr, like most entrepreneurs, was described as evangelistic, entrepreneurial, and charismatic as People Express broke the industry mold with its innovative strategy, even though they were losing money. After that exciting early period, when People Express began to make money, Burr was described in the press as a maverick, a visionary, a whiz, and a competitor, an image consistent with the idea of an innovative and successful manager. Finally, when People Express began to lose money, he was represented still as preacher and visionary, but now a fighter. The failure of People Express was not seen as his fault. The point about this study is that, even though a firm went through a cycle of growth, success, and failure with the same CEO, there was little change in the way he was characterized in the media.

We know from the research, as we know from common sense, that leaders do have strong effects on organizations. For instance, changing CEOs can affect the evaluation of the firm by stock holders. One of the many studies on this issue demonstrated that an announcement of a change in CEOs increased the short-term value of stocks of small firms when the new CEO is an outsider (Reinganum, 1985). CEOs can also affect the strategy of a firm (Smith and White, 1987). More importantly, other studies have shown that CEOs can have a marked effect on a firm's performance (Weiner and Mahoney, 1981; Thomas, 1988). However, there is an important caveat. Simply replacing a poor manager with another is not the answer. A competent replacement is required (Pfeffer and Davis-Blake, 1987). One study of the effects of coach replacements on team performance in the National Basketball Association showed that replacing a coach, alone, had little effect on team success. What made the difference was the competence of the new coach, as measured by experience in the NBA and success in turning around other teams.

Those who select managers and coaches are faced with the difficult problem of predicting success, a problem so difficult that millions of dollars and much time has been spent thinking, talking, and writing about leadership. This theorizing, speculation, and research about leadership has persisted for a long time, always with the same objective: to understand leadership in ways that make it possible to select persons who are likely to be effective leaders and to better training and development of leadership skills. Who makes use of it? Companies like Hewlett–Packard, Fuji, Xerox, GE, PepsiCo, and McKinsey and Company spend large sum of money for the selection and training of their managers (Hadjian, 1995).

leadership
Interpersonal influence – directed toward achieving organization objectives that occurs when one person is able to obtain compliance from someone else because of the relationship between the two

Leadership, as we define it here, is a form of organizationally based problem solving that attempts to achieve organizational goals by influencing the action of others (Fleishman et al., 1991). While this definition places leadership in the broad domain of influence, power, authority, and politics discussed in chapter 14, there is an important difference. In this chapter, the focus is on leadership theory which, almost without exception, focuses on individuals in organizational positions with legitimate authority to make decisions about others. In this chapter, we focus on understanding what makes a leader effective.

The early research on leadership studied it as a collection of personal traits or characteristics of those identified as leaders. Later research emphasized leadership as a series of acts, or a behavioral repertoire, designed to help a group to achieve its objectives. Beginning in the mid-1960s, attention has been directed toward contingency theories of leadership. These theories state effective leadership is a function of the situation in which leader and followers interact. A more recent approach is to focus on the leadership process, an approach that examines not just the traits or behavior of the leader but also the critical dimensions of the relationship between the leader and the followers that lead to leader influence. These themes are the main thrusts of leadership theory and research discussed in this chapter.

Trait Approaches

We often hear that leaders are forceful, tend to be very outgoing, and are persuasive. These common-sense observations form the basis of the belief that personalities of effective leaders are different from non-leaders. **Trait theories of leadership** are based on this idea. Studies have examined factors such as age, height, intelligence, academic achievement, judgmental ability, and insight, all of which were thought to predict successful leadership. These studies were done in a wide variety of settings such as military units, business firms, student organizations, elementary schools, and universities. They led to a rather disappointing conclusion. No specific traits seem to be correlated with leadership in all situations.

trait theories of leadership
Leadership theories based on the idea that personality differences can explain why some people are effective leaders and other people are not

There are several explanations for such a result. First, just because a person has a particular single trait is not a sufficient condition to be in a leadership position or a management job and be successful at it. The person must want the job, seek it, and want to be effective. Also, traits do not operate alone, but in consonance with other factors. Those who have such a grouping of factors, that include leadership traits, have an advantage over those who do not, and over those who have a similar constellation but do not want to be in a leadership or management position (Bass and Stogdill, 1990).

The second reason these research studies produce very divergent results is that the studies have been done in too many different situations. Traits may be related to effectiveness in certain situations but not in others.

Third, there is also the possibility that the trait research tended to focus on very specific traits instead of more general factors. After a careful review of several hundred trait studies, it appears that if specific traits were grouped into general classes of factors, there were differences between effective and ineffective leaders (Bass and Stogdill, 1990). There are five general characteristics:

capacity
An individual's ability to solve problems, make judgments, and generally work harder

1 **Capacity** refers to an individual's ability to solve problems, make judgments, and generally work harder. Specific traits are intelligence, alertness, verbal facility, originality, and judgment.

2 **Achievement:** Effective leaders tend to do better in academic work, have more knowledge, and accomplish more in athletics than ineffective leaders.
3 The specific traits that reflect **responsibility** – another general characteristic of effective leaders – are dependability, initiative, persistence, aggressiveness, self-confidence, and a desire to excel.
4 **Participation** and **involvement** are higher for effective leaders than for ineffective ones. Effective leaders tend to be more active and more sociable, have greater capacity to adapt to different situations, and show higher levels of cooperation than less effective leaders.
5 **Status** is also an attribute of leaders. Effective leaders have higher socioeconomic status and are more popular than less effective ones.

status
The relative position or standing of a person in a group that causes respect or deference toward them

Global Focus on Differences between British and German Middle Managers

There are obvious cultural effects on how managers manage, some of which are demonstrated in a study of the perceptions of 30 British and 30 German middle managers about their jobs and how they actually worked. The study focused on middle managers in the brewing, insurance, and construction industry.

One difference is the way that the British and German managers view how to prepare for a managerial position. The German managers believe that technical training is crucial for managerial effectiveness. Technical competence is an important prerequisite for advancement, but advancement tends to be slow and within their work function. To reach the top, additional formal education is seen as important. In addition, these managers are very task oriented, and are more concerned with the work to be done than the personalities involved.

The British managers place more emphasis on skills in managing people, and, for senior posts, on experience in different aspects of the business. They also prefer a great deal of autonomy in their jobs. In addition, they also do not differentiate as much between their home life and their work life as the Germans. The Germans work hard but tend to leave the job at the end of the day. The British work less intensively during the day but often take work home and work weekends. They also socialize more with their colleagues after work than the German managers.

In managing others, the British prefer persuasion, which means that they must know something about how others will react to their persuasive attempts. Their motivational approaches tend to focus on the individual. The German managers, on the other hand, tend to be more direct, relying on presenting facts and expecting that the facts will make the case. The German managers also place a greater emphasis on teamwork and team spirit, and cooperation that is easy because of their technical credibility.

Source: Adapted from Stewart (1996)

Leader Motive Pattern

An important trait-like leadership approach is the **leader motive pattern** (McClelland and Boyatzis, 1982). This configuration of personality dimensions has been found to be related to managerial effectiveness (McClelland, 1975; 1985):

1 Power needs that are higher than affiliation needs
2 High power inhibition

leader motive pattern A configuration of personality dimensions that consists of higher power needs, moderate affiliation needs and high power inhibition

Low affiliation means that the person does not require interaction with, or positive acceptance by, others. Power inhibition means that the person has discipline and self-control in the use of power. A study of senior managers in jobs at AT&T found that a pattern among those who succeeded (McClelland and Boyatzis, 1982):

1 Managers who are concerned about influencing others
2 Managers who are less concerned about being liked
3 Managers who have a moderate degree of self-control

These managers are more likely to succeed than senior managers without this pattern. These results are impressive because the personality evaluation of the managers in the study was done eight and sixteen years before the measure of success was assessed. Other studies show that the leader motive pattern of branch managers was related to the importance and status of branch offices (Cornelius and Lane, 1984).

Behavioral Approaches

Behavioral approaches to leadership examine how what a leader does is related to leader effectiveness, while the trait approach focuses on what a leader is. How many times does the leader discipline an employee? How often did the leader communicate with employees? There are two classes of behavior that have received much attention in the leadership literature:

behavioral approaches to leadership Theories and models of leadership that are based on the idea that leader behaviors are related to effectiveness

1 Decision influence behaviors
2 Task and social behaviors

Distribution of Decision Influence

Many studies have been conducted on how the distribution of decision-making influence between superiors and subordinates is related to the performance and satisfaction of individuals and work groups. One of the important works in this area was done over 50 years ago (Lewin et al., 1939). A classification of leader behavior emerged that was based on the sharing of decision making between a leader and a follower. Leaders were described in three ways:

1 Autocratic
2 Participative
3 *Laissez-faire*

autocratic leadership
The leader makes all decisions and allows the subordinates no influence in the decision-making process

In **autocratic leadership**, the leader makes all decisions and allows the subordinates no influence in the decision-making process. These supervisors are often indifferent to the personal needs of subordinates. For example, an autocratic manager would assign a worker a task or a goal without any discussion with the subordinate. The manager simply meets with subordinates and gives them a set of goals that the superior prepared.

participative leadership
Leaders consult with subordinates on appropriate matters and allow them some influence in the decision-making process

Participative supervisors consult with subordinates on appropriate matters and allow them some influence in the decision-making process. **Participative leadership** is not punitive and treats subordinates with dignity. The participative leader might set goals with subordinates after talking with them to determine preferences. For instance, a manager might communicate departmental goals to subordinates in a meeting. Using this information, subordinates would then develop their goals, or the superior might develop goals for the subordinate and later meet to arrive at some mutual agreement about the subordinate's goals.

laissez-faire leadership
Leaders who allow their group to have complete freedom in making decisions

In ***laissez-faire* leadership**, supervisors allow their group to have complete autonomy. They rarely supervise directly, so that group members make many on-the-job decisions themselves, such as what jobs they want to do. With such an approach, subordinates set their own goals with no managerial inputs and work toward them with no direction.

These leadership styles can be represented on a continuum that shows different levels of subordinate influence in the decision process, as shown in figure 15.1.

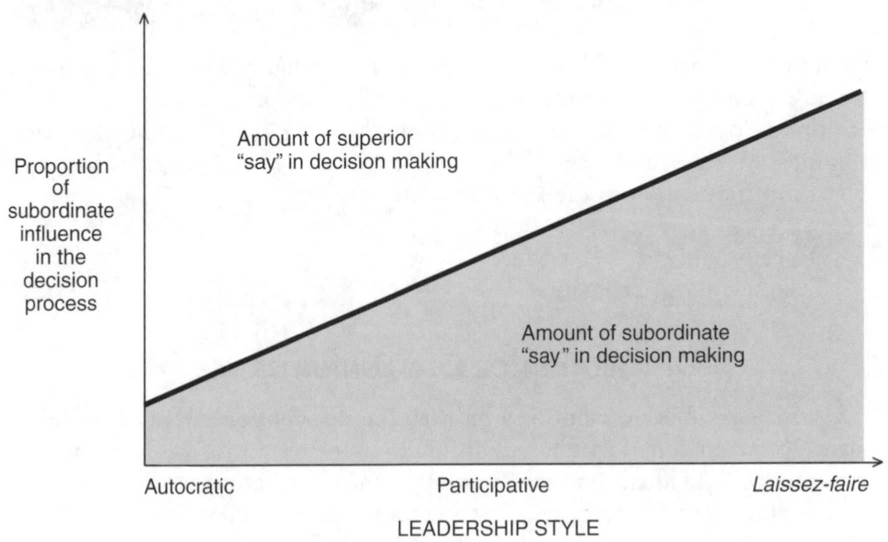

Fig 15.1: Subordinate influence in decision making

Effective groups have had autocratic leaders and participative leaders (Bass and Stogdill, 1990). Participative leadership is associated with higher levels of subordinate satisfaction. Those who work for participative leaders are less resistant to change and show more organization identification than those who work for autocratic leaders. The *laissez-faire* style has not been studied as much as the autocratic and participative styles, but the results are consistent, showing that subordinate satisfaction and performance under *laissez-faire* are lower than under the participative approach but higher than under the autocratic approach (Bass and Stogdill, 1990).

Diversity Issues: US Managers from Middle Eastern Cultures

Like managers of other ethnic origins, many managers with a Middle Eastern background have been successful in the USA. While they tend to adopt a managerial style different than they used in their native countries, they still are affected strongly by their native cultures that are very different from the culture in the USA. For example, Americans are informal, direct, competitive, and achievement oriented. They are uncomfortable with silence, prefer stability, and tend to punctual. The Middle Eastern culture is more diverse and strongly affected by Islam. Middle Easterners tend to be more traditional and family oriented; they value friendship, are more conservative, more intuitive and instinctive, and work in organizations that are male dominated.

A study evaluated how these Middle Eastern immigrant managers differed from US born managers; a study of the managerial styles was done. The Middle Eastern managers were primarily Arabic, but the sample also include several Iranians and some with a Turkish background.

The main finding was that, for the most part, the managerial styles of the two groups were relatively similar. The main difference is that the managers with Middle Eastern backgrounds operate with a style that can be characterized as a "do it the way I tell you" coercive style, providing clear direction by telling subordinates what to do, without listening to or permitting much subordinate input. They expect immediate subordinate compliance or obedience. They like to maintain tight control, often by requiring many detailed reports. They give more negative and "personalized" feedback and motivate by threats of discipline or punishment.

The preference for this management style among Middle Eastern immigrant managers relative to US-born managers was interpreted as resulting from the authoritarian element in the political and social environments of the Middle East societies.

What these results show, overall, however, is that these Middle Eastern immigrant managers have adapted their managerial style reasonably well to their new home (US) culture (Bakhtari, 1995).

Task and Social Behaviors

Two very important programs of research on leader behavior were conducted at Ohio State University and the University of Michigan. They centered on whether effective leaders emphasize task activities and assignments or tend to concentrate on trying to keep good relationships and cohesion among group members, or do both of these things. You will recall that in groups, task functions and socio-emotional functions are the two key sets of activities; see page 233 in chapter 8.

THE OHIO STATE STUDIES From the late 1940s through the 1950s, a group of researchers at Ohio State conducted extensive studies of leadership and effectiveness in industrial, military, and educational institutions (Stogdill, 1974). They developed instruments to measure leadership and evaluated factors that might determine group effectiveness. Two leadership behavior dimensions consistently emerged from these studies:

consideration
The extent to which a leader is likely to have job relationships characterized by mutual trust, respect for subordinates' ideas, and concern for their feelings

initiating structure
The extent to which a leader is likely to define and structure his or her role and those of subordinates toward goal achievement

1 **Consideration** is the extent to which the leader is likely to have job relationships characterized by mutual trust, respect for subordinates' ideas, and consideration of their feelings. Considerate leaders tend to have good rapport and two-way communication with subordinates.
2 **Initiating structure** is the extent to which the leader is likely to define and structure his or her role and those of subordinates toward goal achievement. High initiating structure leaders play an active role in directing group activities, communicating task information, scheduling, and trying out new ideas.

Most studies show that consideration is generally related to high employee satisfaction; it is related much less often to high performance, although it is occasionally. In some studies, initiating structure has been found to be related to job satisfaction but less often to high productivity, low absenteeism, and low turnover (Bass and Stogdill, 1990).

The Ohio State studies had a profound impact on leadership thinking and research. Perhaps its major effect is that wide use has been made of the Leader Behavior Description Questionnaire (LBDQ), for measuring consideration and initiating structure. These concepts have become part of the conventional wisdom about leadership and are the basis of many programs to train leaders (Blake and Mouton, 1969; Hersey and Blanchard, 1988).

production-centered leadership
A style in which the leader is primarily concerned with high levels of production and generally uses high pressure to achieve it

employee-centered leadership
A style in which the leader is concerned about subordinates' feelings and attempts to create an atmosphere of mutual trust and respect

THE MICHIGAN STUDIES At about the same time, the Institute of Social Research at the University of Michigan conducted a number of studies in offices, railroad settings, and service industries. From early studies, the researchers concluded that leadership behavior could be described in terms of two styles: a supervisor may be production centered or employee centered.

1 In **production-centered leadership**, the supervisor was primarily concerned with high levels of production and generally used high pressure to achieve it. He or she viewed subordinates merely as instruments for achieving the desired level of production.
2 In **employee-centered leadership**, the supervisor was concerned about subordinates' feelings and attempted to create an atmosphere of mutual trust and respect.

The group at Michigan, at first, concluded that employee-centered supervisors are more likely to have highly productive work groups than production-centered supervisors. This is an important difference between the Ohio State and Michigan studies. In the early stages of the Michigan studies, leaders were described as engaging in behavior that was either production centered or employee centered while the Ohio State studies characterized an individual on both dimensions (Stogdill, 1974). The Ohio State and Michigan researchers used somewhat different measures, however, which makes their studies less directly comparable.

A later Michigan study by Bowers and Seashore (1966) refined the concept of leader behavior. Four supervisory behaviors, reflecting task and social dimensions, associated with satisfaction and performance were found in a study of 40 agencies of an insurance company:

1 **Support** Behavior that enhances someone else's feelings of personal worth and importance
2 **Interaction facilitation** Behavior that encourages members of the group to develop close, mutually satisfying relationships
3 **Goal emphasis** Behavior that stimulates an enthusiasm for meeting the group's goals or achieving excellent performance.
4 **Work facilitation** Activities that help toward achieving goal attainment by doing things such as scheduling, coordinating, planning, and providing resources such as tools, materials, and technical knowledge.

interaction facilitation
Behavior that encourages members of the group to develop close, mutually satisfying relationships

goal emphasis
Leader behavior that stimulates enthusiasm for meeting the group's goals or achieving excellent performance

Contingency Theories of Leadership

The interest in contingency theories of leadership grew out of the fact that there were some inconsistencies in the research results. For example, initiating structure might be related to performance and satisfaction in some studies, but not in others. Similar inconsistencies were found in studies for the effects of consideration. The idea developed among contingency theorists that there might be different situations in which different leadership styles would be effective. They developed **contingency theories of leadership** that systematically account for how situational factors might result in different relationships between what leaders do and their effectiveness. Contingency theories tell you how a leader's or manager's behavior is related to effectiveness in different circumstances. This kind of work on leadership provides us with more specific prescriptions about how a manager should function in different types of situations. There are three most prominent contingency theories (Fiedler, 1967; Evans, 1968; House, 1971; Vroom and Yetton, 1973):

1 Fiedler's contingency theory of leadership
2 The path–goal theory
3 The **Vroom–Yetton model** discussed in chapter 11.

contingency theories of leadership
Theories of leadership that systematically account for how situational factors might result in different relationships between what leaders do and their effectiveness

Vroom–Yetton model
A contingency model of leadership that attempts to show how the degree of subordinate influence in decision making should vary according to the situation

FIEDLER'S CONTINGENCY MODEL

In 1967, Fiedler proposed a theoretical explanation, called Fiedler's contingency model, of how leadership orientation, the group setting, and task characteristics interact to affect group performance. Much research has been done on this theory since it was introduced and the evidence shows fairly strong support for it (Strube and Garcia, 1981; Peters et al., 1985).

There are three important things about this theory. First, it was the first theory to systematically account for situational factors. Fiedler integrated situational factors such as relationships between the leader and the group, task structure, and leader power into a theory of leadership.

Second, Fielder's concept of leadership considers the leader's orientation, not leader behavior. This orientation is a function of leader needs and personality. Although this may affect a leader's behavior, it is the leader's orientation toward those with whom he or she works that determines how effective the group is.

Third, because leadership orientation is relatively stable, it is not likely that a leader will change orientations when confronted with different situations, though the leader can change his or her behavior when it is necessary and when the leader wants to. There is some evidence, for example, that a person can change behavior from directive to supportive, and vice versa, in different situations (Fiedler and Chemers, 1974; Fodor, 1976). For example, when a critical, stressful situation exists at work, the supervisor is likely to act in a directive way with subordinates. In a low-stress situation, the same supervisor may be much more considerate. This was demonstrated in a study of supervisors' behavior under both stressful and nonstressful conditions (Fodor, 1976). When stress was low, the supervisors were less directive and tended to reward subordinates more. When situations became threatening, the supervisors became more directive and were less likely to reward subordinates.

SITUATIONAL VARIABLES There are three important situational factors that determine leader effectiveness in this theory:

EXERCISE

LEADER DESCRIPTION QUESTIONNAIRE

This exercise illustrates some of the more common concepts that are used in the study of leadership.

Look at the list of 15 items. Each item describes a specific kind of behavior, that may be used to describe the behavior of a superior but does not ask you to judge whether the behavior is desirable or undesirable. The items are grouped but each item should be considered as a separate description. The purpose of these items it to describe, as accurately as you can, the behavior of a supervisor or some manager for whom you have worked. If you have not worked for a manager, then describe the leader behavior of your instructor.

- Read each item carefully.
- Think about how frequently the leader engages in the behavior described in the item.
- Decide whether the leader always (5), often (4), occasionally (3), seldom (2), or never (1) acts as described by the item.
- Draw a circle around one of the five numbers (5, 4, 3, 2, 1) following the item to show which answer you select.

Group I: The leader . . .

		Always	Often	Occasionally	Seldom	Never
1	. . . lets group members know what is expected of them.	5	4	3	2	1
2	. . . encourages the use of uniform procedures.	5	4	3	2	1
3	. . . decides what shall be done and how it shall be done.	5	4	3	2	1
4	. . . assigns group members to particular tasks.	5	4	3	2	1
5	. . . schedules the work to be done.	5	4	3	2	1

Group I total (sum of items 1–5): ☐

Group II: The leader . . .

		Always	Often	Occasionally	Seldom	Never
6	. . . is friendly and approachable.	5	4	3	2	1
7	. . . puts suggestions made by group into operation.	5	4	3	2	1
8	. . . treats all group members as equals.	5	4	3	2	1
9	. . . gives advance notice of changes.	5	4	3	2	1
10	. . . looks out for the personal welfare of group members.	5	4	3	2	1

Group II total (sum of items 6–10): ☐

Group III: The leader . . .

		Always	Often	Occasionally	Seldom	Never
11	. . . stresses being ahead of competing groups.	5	4	3	2	1
12	. . . keeps the work moving at a rapid pace.	5	4	3	2	1
13	. . . pushes for increased production.	5	4	3	2	1
14	. . . asks the members to work harder.	5	4	3	2	1
15	. . . keeps the group working up to capacity.	5	4	3	2	1

Group III total (sum of items 11–15): ☐

Now, look at your three totals and answers these diagnostic questions.

1 What type of leader behavior does the Group I total describe?
2 What type of leader behavior does Group II total describe?
3 What type of leader behavior does Group III total describe?

1 Leader–member relations
2 Task structure
3 Position power

These determine the amount of **situational control** that a leader has (Fiedler, 1978). The more these are present, the more control the leader has over the situation. The level of situational control determines whether a particular leader orientation will be effective.

leader–member relations
The trust a group has in the leader and how well the leader is liked

Leader–member relations refer to the trust a group has in the leader and how well the leader is liked. When leader–member relations are good, there is usually high satisfaction with work, individual values are consistent with organizational values, and there is mutual trust between the leader and the group. When relations are bad, mutual trust is lacking. Group cohesiveness is low, making it difficult to make members work together. If group cohesiveness is high but leader relations are bad, the group works together to sabotage the organization and the leader.

task structure
The extent to which jobs are defined and specified

A job with high **task structure** is spelled out in detail – you know what the goals are and how to achieve them. You have little leeway in doing the job and must follow the instructions. For example, the telephone salesperson who works at a computer terminal has very high task structure. For the whole workday, the person sits at a terminal, answers the phone, enters the order, enters the customer's name and other relevant information, then completes the sale.

Low task structure is present when the objectives of the task or the way it is to be done is somewhat ambiguous. With low task structure, you must decide how to perform a task each time it is to be done. For example, a machinist may work in the tool room of a factory and be responsible for making a wide range of different parts needed to keep equipment operating. The work of managers and many professionals is unstructured.

position power
Power that exists when a leader has much legitimate authority

Position power is a critical factor. High position power exists when you have much legitimate authority, which means that you can make important decisions without having them cleared by someone at higher organization levels. Low position power means that you have only limited authority.

leader orientation
An orientation that is a function of leader's needs and personality, determined by how you view the person you least like to work with

LEADER ORIENTATION – THE LPC SCALE Leader orientation is one aspect of your motivational hierarchy. It is not a leader behavior, but does reflect a behavioral preference (Fiedler and Chemers, 1974). Your **leader orientation** is determined by how you view the person that you least like to work with, whether you see him or her in a positive or a negative way. If you have positive views of least preferred co-workers, you are more likely to act in more considerate ways. If you have negative views, you are more likely to focus on tasks, not people.

Your leader orientation is measured by the **least preferred co-worker (LPC) scale**. You are asked to think about someone that you worked least well with, then indicate if you have positive or negative feelings about the least preferred co-worker. You "may produce a very negative description . . . or a relatively more positive description of the least preferred co-worker" (Fiedler and Chemers, 1974).

Suppose, for example, that there are three persons in your group and John is the one that has been the biggest problem for you and you dislike more than anyone else with whom you have worked. If you are a **high LPC leader**, you have relatively favorable views of your least preferred co-worker, John. High LPC leaders are people-centered and more positively oriented toward the feelings and the relationships of people in the work group. These leaders are able to see some positive things in the people they least like to work with. The high LPC leader wants to be accepted by others, has strong emotional ties to people in the workplace, and has higher status and self-esteem and is more likely to act in a considerate way (Fiedler, 1992). If you are a **low LPC leader**, you have more negative views of your least preferred co-worker, John. Low LPC leaders are more oriented toward the task, and personal relationships tend to have secondary importance for them. They tend to be directive and controlling and to make subjective, rather than reasoned, judgments about those who work with them.

high LPC leader
A leader who has favorable views of the person they least like to work with

low LPC leader
A leader who is more oriented toward the task; personal relationships tend to have secondary importance

LEADER EFFECTIVENESS Either high or low LPC leadership orientations can be effective, depending on the **situational control** that the leader has (Fiedler, 1978). This leader has high situational control

1 Leader–member relations are good.
2 There is high task structure.
3 The leader has high position power.

This leader has low situational control

1 Leader–member relations are poor.
2 There is a low task structure.
3 The leader has little position power.

In this case, obviously, the leadership situation is not a favorable one. Moderate situation control means the situational characteristics are mixed. Some work to the advantage of the leader (for instance, high position power) whereas others do not (poor leader–member relations).

These levels of situational control require leaders with different LPC orientations, as shown in figure 15.2. The low LPC leader, with a strong task orientation, is most effective when situational control is either very low or very high. Weak situational control is good for the low LPC leader. The group may fall apart or it may not attend to the task requirements unless the leader exerts a good deal of direction. When situational control is strong and the conditions are favorable, the low LPC leader is also more effective. The group may be willing to accept the task-oriented leader since success is assured because of their own performance and the vigilance of the leader.

The high LPC leader is most effective when there is moderate situational control. In this case, the high LPC may be more effective in motivating group members to perform better and to be cooperative toward goal achievement. The lower LPC leader does not have tendencies to do those sorts of things. The low

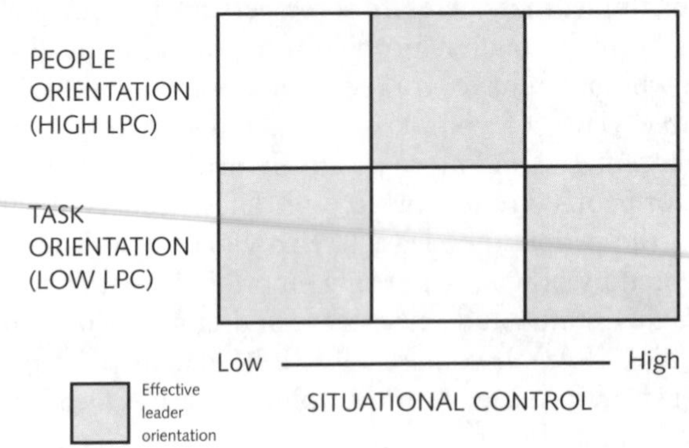

Fig 15.2: Relationships between leader orientation, leader effectiveness, and situational control in Fiedler's Theory

LPC would probably exert pressures to work harder to produce more, which may counteract good performance.

COGNITIVE RESOURCE THEORY A serious weakness of leadership theory, in general, is that leader ability is not considered. With the exception of intelligence, a proxy for problem-solving ability, leadership theory has focused on traits, behaviors, and situational properties. **Cognitive resource theory** is a modification of Fiedler's Contingency Theory that integrates a set of trait-like dimensions, called cognitive resources, into the original model (Fiedler and Garcia, 1987). Cognitive resources are the person's intelligence, job competence, and technical knowledge and skill that can be used in the task of managing.

cognitive resource theory
A leadership theory that integrates a set of trait-like dimensions, called cognitive resources, into Fiedler's contingency model

Cognitive resource theory is based on two assumptions:

1 Managers communicate their plans and strategies to subordinates through directive behavior.
2 Smarter and more experienced leaders can make better decisions than those less intelligent and less experienced.

However, intelligent and experienced leaders will not be effective across all situations. For example, leader experience contributes to performance only in stressful conditions, while leader intelligence contributes only under stress-free conditions (Fiedler, 1992). In the stress-free condition, the leader can resort to normal problem-solving behavior, based on intelligence. However, under stress, the experienced leader can, according to Fiedler (1992):

> fall back on a wide range of previously learned automatic behaviors and . . . will perform better than a less experienced leader who lacks a large repertoire . . . When someone starts shooting at you, it is safer to obey the primitive impulse to run rather than to stop and consider alternative options.

The research support for cognitive resource theory is yet to come, beyond the original research from which it was derived (Fiedler and Garcia, 1987). One study did show leader intelligence was more strongly related to group performance for directive leaders than for non-directive leaders (Vecchio, 1990). Another found that group performance was higher when leaders who had technical training were more directive, but that technically trained groups performed better when the leaders were non-directive (Murphy et al., 1992).

Path–Goal Theory

Path–goal theory links leader behavior to performance using the expectancy theory of motivation (House, 1971; House and Mitchell, 1974). The basic idea of path–goal theory is shown in figure 15.3. To achieve desired organizational results, certain tasks must be performed. The results are the goal; the tasks are the path. When appropriate tasks are performed, the goals are achieved. When the goals are achieved, rewards for the individual should follow. The role of the leader is to ensure that the path to the goal is clearly understood by the subordinate and that there are no barriers to the achievement of the goals (Filley et al., 1976).

path–goal theory
A contingency approach to leadership that focuses on leader behavior and how the situational factors affect what leader behavior is most effective

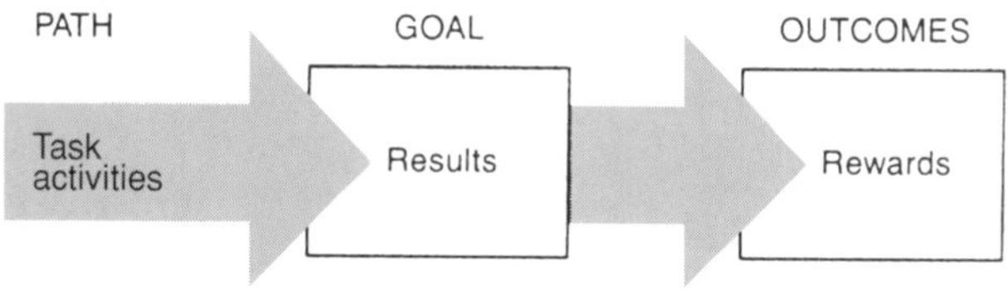

Fig 15.3: Basic premise of path–goal theory

Leader behaviors In path–goal theory, there are four different types of leader behavior which affect outcomes and reward (House and Mitchell, 1974).

1 **Directive leadership** is the style in which the leader gives guidance and direction to subordinates about job requirements. The leader defines the work roles of group members, determines and communicates performance standards to them, and manages using specific policies, procedures, and rules.
2 **Supportive leadership** is a style in which the leader is concerned with the needs of those who report to him or her. The supportive leader is friendly and approachable. Members are treated as equals. This set of behaviors is similar to the style called consideration.
3 **Participative leaders** act in a consultative style. They seek advice from subordinates about problems and consider these recommendations seriously before decisions are made.
4 In **achievement-oriented leadership**, leaders set challenging goals for their work groups. These leaders expect their groups to perform well and they communicate this to subordinates.

directive leadership
The style in which the leader gives guidance and direction to subordinates about job requirements

supportive leadership
A style in which the leader is concerned with the needs of those who report to him or her

achievement-oriented leadership
A style in which leaders set challenging work goals for their work groups

CONTINGENCY FACTORS The appropriate leader behavior depends on two contingency factors to affect subordinate performance and satisfaction, as shown interacting with leader behavior in figure 15.4:

1 Subordinate characteristics
2 Environmental factors

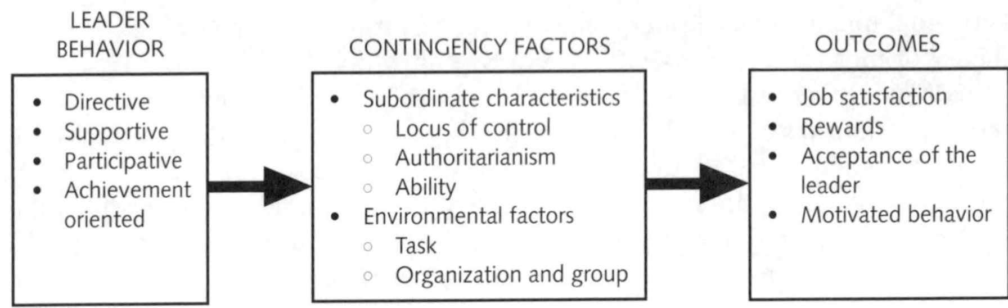

Fig 15.4: Basic factors in path–goal theory

Three subordinate characteristics affect how subordinates perceive the leader's behaviors:

1 Locus of control
2 Authoritarianism
3 Ability

Those subordinates with an internal locus of control react more favorably toward participative leadership. Directive leadership is more satisfying to subordinates with an external locus of control. Participative leadership styles are more acceptable to subordinates who are low in authoritarianism, whereas those high in authoritarianism react more positively to directive leadership. Those subordinates with high ability will see directive leadership as unnecessary and undesirable, and will react unfavorably to it.

There are two environmental factors:

1 The task
2 The organization and group

These may affect performance and satisfaction in several ways. First, the level of task certainly (or task structure) determines the clarity of the path to the goal. When tasks are uncertain, a more directive style of leadership may be more effective. Second, extrinsic rewards are located in the organization and the task environment. Third, significant environmental barriers to performance may exist. Figure 15.5 shows how these environmental factors are related to the task (for example, the path and the goal). It also shows that the role of leader in path–goal theory is to increase task valences and reward valences, remove barriers, and ensure that the right level of task certainty exists.

WHAT LEADERSHIP STYLE? The leader's role in path–goal theory varies, depending on the situation. First, the leader must reduce uncertainty by clarifying expectations about the desired results or the way to achieve them (task uncertainty). Second, the leader should remove barriers to performance. If something is blocking the way, the leader must try to eliminate it. Lastly, the leader must attempt to increase the subordinates valence for the task itself, the achievement of the goal or both.

From figure 15.5, you can make the following predictions about which leadership styles would be most effective. If there is a high level of task certainty because the subordinate knows how to do the job or because the task is very routine, then the path to the goal is clear. The best leadership style here is supportive, not directive. Directive leadership may increase performance because there is added pressure to produce, but it may lead to decreased job satisfaction because of close supervision.

When there is high uncertainty about the task or the goal to be achieved, the leader must clarify them. When the subordinate is uncertain about the best way to do a job, the manager should give instructions. If the goals are not clear to the subordinate, then they should be spelled out. When there is high task uncertainty, the most effective leadership style is to be directive.

RESEARCH ON PATH–GOAL THEORY Path–goal theory is a complex view of leadership. With four different types of leader behavior, three subordinate characteristics, and two environmental factors, it is very difficult to evaluate the whole theory. Most research tests some specific proposition from path–goal theory, and the results are mixed, partly because of the difficulty in testing the theory. However, when path–goal hypotheses are tested in carefully designed studies that reflect the conditions of the theory, the results are more encouraging. In a study done in a bank and in a manufacturing company, directive leader behavior was related to subordinate satisfaction with supervision exactly as predicted by the theory (Schreisheim and DeNisi, 1981). Subordinates who worked in relatively

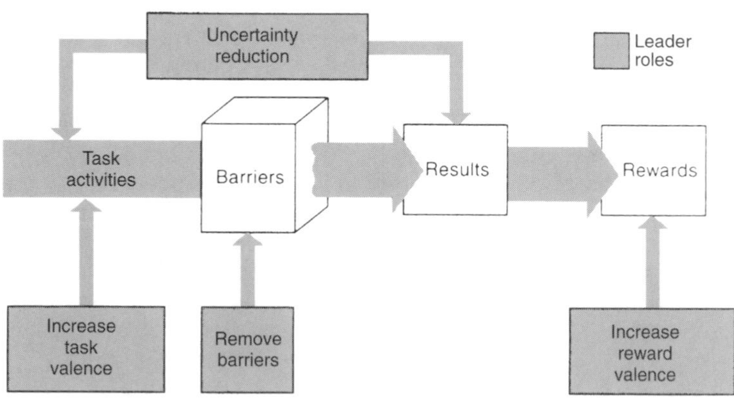

Fig 15.5: Leader role in path–goal theory

Focus on Path–Goal Theory: When being Directive Works for Everyone

Two years ago, Joe Bond was hired as a production superintendent in the new Nelson Appliance manufacturing plant. This plant was designed with the most advanced equipment available and according to some of the ideas of participative management and self-directed work teams. The combination of new technology and more human-resource-oriented management team would, the management of Nelson believed, make the plant efficient and highly competitive.

Joe was hired because he had the reputation of being the best start-up supervisor in the industry. He had been through five other starts, and, in every case, his groups always seemed to develop fastest, and they achieved production quotas, both in quality and quantity, more quickly than other groups.

Joe is a trained machinist. He developed some basic skills in electronics by attending evening courses at a community college and self-study. He has no formal engineering training, but with his experience and knowledge, he has excellent production instincts.

There was never any doubt about Joe's technical competence, but there were some reservations in the mind of Paul Gerrity, the plant manager, about whether Joe could work with the high-involvement management style that Nelson Manufacturing intended for the plant. Gerrity had a long talk with Joe to discuss these concerns and to impress on him that the plant was not going to be one of the "iron-fisted" plants that were common in the industry. Joe told Gerrity, "I'll manage this team the right way. Don't worry." But still Gerrity wasn't sure.

Gerrity watched Joe as the new plant started. Joe worked very differently from the other production supervisors. He systematically rotated all the new employees around to all the jobs in his unit. Each one had to be given the feel of every job. The other supervisors allowed much less rotation.

Another thing that Joe did was to attend all training sessions on the equipment with his team. The machine manufacturers usually taught these training sessions, and they were very important in raising the workers' skill levels. After each training session, Joe would meet with the team to discuss problems that had not been thoroughly solved.

Joe's team also spent the most time of any on maintenance. When there was a breakdown, Joe would shut down the machine and fix it right. Many of the other supervisors would not do that. They would figure out some way to keep the machine running during their shift and let the next shift worry about fixing it. As a matter of fact, Terry Golden, who was the, supervisor of the work team that was on the floor before Joe's team, told the personnel manager it was great to have Joe's team follow his. "That way," Terry said, "I can get the production, and I know that the equipment will be in good shape when we arrive the next day."

This went on for six months, and during that time Paul Gerrity was surprised to see that Joe's production was the lowest of the teams, and it was also hard for Gerrity to understand why Joe's team did not complain about him. After all, Joe was reputed to be a "tough supervisor." The team's quality was always high because Joe never allowed the equipment to run out of "spec" like the other supervisors. He would fix it, so he had few quality problems. Still, his group had the poorest production record. One time when Gerrity complained to Joe about production, Joe said, "We don't run as much as everyone else because we keep fixing their mistakes." Gerrity became angry and pushed Joe a little hard. Joe told him, "I'll manage my group my way. If it's not what you want, I can leave."

About eight months after the plant opened, the productivity of Joe's group began to increase. The team maintained its quality level, but output went up six months in a row. Within 15 months from the plant opening, Joe's team was usually number one, and never below number two, in production and quality.

Joe Bond's approach to managing can be understood in terms of path–goal theory. His training and coaching clarified how the work was to be done properly, and his firm stand on quality left no uncertainty about what results were expected.

routine jobs were dissatisfied with more directive leadership while those who worked on less structured jobs liked it more.

A Summary Comment on Trait, Behavior, and Contingency Approaches to Leadership

One strong conclusion can be drawn from these studies: Making a distinction between leader task-orientation and leader person-orientation seems to be a useful way to describe important ways leaders act. This distinction shows up in many different studies and suggests that the concepts may be a valid way to describe leaders. Figure 15.6 shows the similarities in the way that some of the important leadership approaches use these concepts.

Another important question that arises in this research is the **direction of causality**. That is, is it the behavior of the leader which causes higher performance, or is it possible that follower performance causes the leader to act in certain ways? Much of the leader behavior research consists of field studies that use correctional methodology, which does not prove causality. Some research, on the other hand, supports the idea that leader behavior may be a result of the group's performance as well as affecting it. One very convincing study is an experiment in which managers were hired for part-time student work groups (Lowin and Craig, 1968). Prior to employment, the applicants were introduced to one of the workers and asked to supervise him for a period of time. In some cases, the worker was said to be very competent, but in other instances, the applicants were told that the worker was less competent. Those who managed the competent worker did not supervise him closely and engaged in more consideration and less initiating structure behaviors. Those who managed the less competent worker were more directive. Studies like this show that leader consideration both increases the satisfaction of subordinates and is increased by it (Bass and Stogdill, 1990). The initiation of structure by the leader (if structure is low) improves the subordinates' performance, which, in turn, increases the leader's subsequent consideration and reduces the leader's initiation of structure (Bass and Stogdill, 1990).

Ohio State studies	Consideration		Initiating structure
Early Michigan studies	Employee-centered		Production-centered
Bowers and Seashore	• Support • Interaction facilitation		Goal emphasis Work facilitation
Fiedler's contingency theory	People-centered (high LPC)	Situational factors Position power Task structure Leader–member relations	Production-centered (low LPC)
Path–goal theory	Consideration	Clarity of path–goal relationships	Initiating structure
Vroom and Yetton decision styles (chapter 11)	Consultative (CI, CII) Group (GII)	• Acceptance • Quality • Information • Conflict • Goal congruence	Autocratic style (AI, AII)

Fig 15.6 : Similarity between selected concepts of leadership

Process Theories of Leadership

process theories of leadership Leadership theories that focus on the processes by which a relationship develops between leaders and subordinates

Trait approaches, behavioral approaches and contingency approaches focus mainly on the leader, what the leader is or what the leader does. Some recent theories, called **process theories of leadership**, explain the processes by which a relationship develops between leaders and subordinates. One theory is called transformational leadership theory. Another is called vertical dyad linkage (VDL) theory.

Transformational Leadership Theory

transformational leadership theory Explains how leaders develop and enhance the commitment of followers

transactional leadership The leader and subordinate are bargaining agents, negotiating to maximize their own position

Transformational leadership theory explains how leaders develop and enhance the commitment of followers. In this approach, transformational leaders are contrasted with transactional leaders. In **transactional leadership**, the leader and subordinate are bargaining agents, negotiating to maximize their own position (Downton, 1973). The subordinate's motivation to comply with the leader is self-interest, because the leader can provide payoffs, perhaps both economic and psychological, that are valued by the follower. The transactional view of leadership makes three assumptions (Downton, 1973).

1 Human behavior is goal directed and individuals will act rationally to achieve those goals.
2 Behaviors that pay off will persist over time, while those that do not pay off will not persist.
3 Norms of reciprocity govern the exchange relationship.

This is the style of the transactional leader (Bass and Stogdill, 1990):

1 To use contingent rewards – rewards are associated with good performance and accomplishment.
2 To manage by exception – the leader acts when he or she anticipates that performance is likely to deviate from standards or takes action when standards are not met.
3 To take a hands-off approach – the leader acts in a *laissez-faire* manner, abdicating and avoiding responsibility.

Transformational leadership is based on the leader's effects on the followers' values, self-esteem, trust, and their confidence in the leader and motivation to perform above and beyond the call of duty (House and Singh, 1987). The transactional leader's influence is derived from the exchange process, but it is different in an important way from transformational leadership. Transactional leadership works within the context of the followers' self-interests while transformational leadership seeks to change that context (Bass and Stogdill, 1990).

The transformational leader's influence is based on the leader's ability to inspire and raise the consciousness of the followers by appealing to their higher ideals and values. This occurs because the transformational leader has charisma, and engages in particular behaviors as well. Specifically, this is the style of a transformational leader (Bass and Stogdill, 1990):

1 To use his or her charisma – the charismatic leader creates a special bond with the followers and is able to articulate a vision with which the followers identify and for which they are willing to work; see chapter 14.
2 To be inspirational – the leader creates high expectations and effectively communicates crucial ideas with symbols and simple language.
3 To practice individual consideration – the leader coaches, advises, and delegates to the followers, treating them individually.
4 To stimulate followers intellectually – the leader arouses them to develop new ways to think about problems.

Table 15.1 shows some task behaviors, social behaviors, influence techniques of transformational leaders, and corresponding subordinate behaviors and feelings.

- The task behaviors of the leader are the heightening of task goals, articulating paths to achievement, and proposing innovative strategies. Subordinates become aware of new possibilities, have increased feelings of self-efficacy, are willing to work longer and harder, have higher task identification and stronger achievement motives, and more emotional involvement with the work.
- The socioemotional behaviors of the leader involve showing enthusiasm and trustworthiness, acting in ways to increase group cohesiveness and being approachable and available. The subordinate response is to identify

with the leader and the mission, to try to emulate the leader, to feel increased desire to stay in the group, and to admire and trust the leader.
- The leader's power tends toward the charismatic type, socialized power, unconventional behaviors, and different emotional appeals to subordinates. The subordinates respond with more involvement, trust, compliance, and commitment.

Transformational leaders may have strong effects. We have already mentioned several important executives who fit the description of the transformational leader (for example, Herb Kelleher of Southwest Airlines and Mary Kay of Mary Kay Cosmetics). They were able to build or change organizations in dramatic ways and, at the same time, obtain very high levels of commitment from others

Table 15.1 Transformational leader and subordinate behavior and attitudes

Leader	*Subordinate*
THE TASK OR MISSION	
Discrepant vision and heightened goals	Heightened awareness of new possibilities
Attention focusing, alertness to a need for change	Consciousness aroused for new levels of achievement
High expectations and some risk	Feelings of self-efficacy
Confidence within realism	Identification with a cause
Advocacy but not self-serving	Arousal of task-relevant motives
Paths articulated, innovative strategies	Long hours, hard work
SOCIOEMOTIONAL	
Enthusiastic	Feel on the right side
Available, accessible	Identify with leader and mission
Approachable, likeable	Give leader affection, admiration, trust
Taps deep-rooted values, hopes	Emulate the leader
No betrayal of trust	Feel personally accepted, supported, understood
Considerate individualized attention	Desire to please group, stay in the group
Actions to enhance cohesion	
POWER COMPLIANCE	
Expert, task-connected power	Broad basis for compliance, obedience (leader, task, values, needs, peers, future)
Referent, identification power	Impressed with and committed to leader and mission
Some contingent reward power	Trust
Willingness to influence: uses socialized power	Self-efficacy motivation
Varied emotional appeals, inspirational encouragement	Involvement, participation at various levels (intellectual, emotional, social, physical)
Needs, values, motives arousal	
Personal presence, varied techniques	

in the firm. Transformational leadership effects have also been demonstrated to result in higher performance, member satisfaction, and higher commitment in several studies (Bass, 1985; Bass et al., 1987; Avolio et al., 1988; Deluga, 1988; Hater and Bass, 1988; Seltzer and Bass, 1990). For example, transformational patterns of managers and naval officers are very strongly related to desirable organizational outcomes (Howell and Higgins, 1990; Seltzer and Bass, 1990; Bycio et al., 1995; Kirkpatrick and Locke, 1996). Successful champions, or advocates, of new technologies exhibit transformational leader behavior patterns (Howell and Higgins, 1990).

The concept of transformational leadership raises some interesting questions. First, because of the focus on follower commitment to the leader rather than organization performance, what happens if there is a divergence of interests between the transformational leader and other important stakeholders, such as stockholders? Some evidence shows that, in the absence of stockholder influence, executives manage the firm in their interest, not the owners'. Rather than maximizing owner return, they may increase the size of the firm in ways that increase the owners' risk (Tosi and Gomez-Mejia, 1989). Thus, a transformational leader may manage a firm ineffectively from the stockholders' perspective.

Another question is whether it is possible to develop a transformational style. There is some research, though it is currently rather limited, which suggests that it is possible to develop a charismatic style through training (Howell and Frost, 1989; Kirkpatrick and Locke, 1996). In one study, actresses learned scripts that portrayed charismatic leaders, structuring leaders, and considerate leaders (Howell and Frost, 1989). The emotional state, body language, facial expressions, and other symbolic cues were described and learned for the charismatic role. The charismatic leader was able to gain high productivity from the experimental group. Subjects generated more alternatives and were more satisfied with both the task and the leader.

Vertical Dyad Linkage Theory

The **vertical dyad linkage (VDL) theory** focuses on the relationship between the leader and the subordinate in a different way from other models (Dansereau et al., 1975). In trait approaches, the leader is measured by his or her responses to some form of psychological measurement instrument. For example, achievement motivation and power motivation are assessed by the responses to the Thematic Apperception Test (McClelland, 1975). In behavioral approaches, leader style is measured by descriptions of the leader by subordinates. For example, initiating structure and consideration behaviors are measured in this manner.

vertical dyad linkage (VDL) theory
Focuses on the relationship between the leader and subordinate in different leader–member relationships that are classified into in-group and out-group categories

VDL theory is different. In VDL theory, responses from both the leader and the subordinate about their relationship are considered. The assumption that leadership can be understood best in terms of role relationships between managers and subordinates – members of a vertical dyadic relationship – in an organization. Managers must ensure that the role superior–subordinate relationships are well defined since managerial success depends on subordinate performance. Therefore, managers and subordinates negotiate these role relationships through a range of formal and informal processes that occur primarily in the early stages of their relationship (Dienesch and Liden, 1986).

This negotiation results in different relationships with different subordinates. In VDL theory, the agreement between leaders and subordinates about the degree of trust in the relationship, subordinate competence, loyalty, and similar factors is measured. Leader–member relationships are classified into in-group and out-group categories depending on the level of agreement.

- **In-group relationships** between leaders and subordinates are close, the leader spends more time and energy in them, role participants have more positive attitudes toward the job, and there are fewer problems than in out-group relationships (Dienesch and Liden, 1986). The quality of the linkage affects some subordinate behaviors and perceptions, but has not been related to subordinate performance.
- **Out-group subordinates** spent less time on decision making, did not volunteer for extra assignments, and were rated lower by subordinates (Liden and Graen, 1980).

The quality of supervisor–subordinate relations also affects perception of the organizations climate (Kozlowski and Doherty, 1989). Subordinates who had high quality relationships with supervisors had more positive perception about the climate. Also, their climate perceptions were similar to the supervisors, and there was greater consensus about the climate than was the case for out-group subordinates. There is little evidence, however, that the nature of the supervisor–subordinate relationship is related to subordinate performance (Dienesch and Liden, 1986).

VDL theory is a very useful way to study the relational aspect of leadership. While in-group or out-group status may not be related to the subordinates' actual performance, it seems is linked to several other important aspects of life in organizations. It could be, for example, that the nature of the relationship is an important predictor of subordinate advancement. Further, it may better define the critical dimensions of the leader–subordinate relationship. It also emphasizes the evolution of that relationship, which has received little attention in the other leader literature.

Substitutes for Leadership

leadership substitutes
The subordinate, the task, and the organization; they, not the action of the leader, contribute to success or failure

The very image of the leader in leadership theory is of a person who is able to influence others to act toward organization objectives. This image is reinforced by the popular press, television, and films (Meindl et al., 1985). However, we know that other factors such as ability, intrinsic motivation, the nature of technology, and the structure of the organization also affect performance and satisfaction of members. In fact, in some instances, these factors may be even more crucial to performance than leadership (Kerr and Jermier, 1978; Tosi, 1982). They can serve as **leadership substitutes** because they, not the action of the leader, con-

A Question of Ethics: When there is a Special "In-Group" Relationship

There are some difficult issues, both ethical and organizational, that arise for a manager who takes a romantic interest toward subordinates. On one hand, it is possible that it will be seen as sexual harassment or, perhaps, the creation of a hostile work environment. On the other hand, there is the question of the person's right to consensual relationships with another.

In the past, it was easy. If you were a powerful male manager and you had a romantic relationship with a female subordinate, you were the beneficiary of a double standard. Usually the manager, particularly a powerful one, would have a great deal of license to pursue whom he pleased. If a relationship developed and became even the slightest of an issue, it was condoned for the manager, but the woman was asked to leave, even though the relationship was mutually agreeable.

Today, many companies realize that romantic relationships, sometimes just the perceptions about them, between bosses and subordinates might cause performance and morale problems. A survey of American managers reported that they had at least one office romance during their careers. One-third of the men and 15 percent of the women said that the relationship was with a subordinate and over 20 percent thought that such relationships were acceptable.

The current view in many larger companies is that they recognize that these relationships will occur and think that a better approach is to try to manage these situations. Should these relationships result in marriages, many companies, like AT&T try to make some internal transfers so that the direct supervisory relationship is eliminated.

However, other companies have taken a different approach. They are so concerned with sexual-harassment issues that they are unable to develop policies that are consistent with permitting consensual relationships while there is a clear prohibition of the sort of harassment that often occurs in the workplace (Hymowitz and Pollock, 1998).

tribute to success or failure (Kerr and Jermier, 1978). Suppose that effectiveness of a group depends on two things: performing the task; and good working relationships among members. From a leadership behavior perspective, by initiating structure behavior you could provide the members with knowledge about how to perform the task. Good working relationships can also develop because you as a leader, use a considerate style of behavior.

However, there are other ways that task knowledge and good relations can be present, and they are substitutes for the behavior of the leader. Task knowledge may be present because those who work for you know how to do the job or because there are specific procedures that are well known by them. These work in place of initiating structure. There may be good working relationships because of work group norms, because all the workers are friends, or for many other reasons. These are substitutes for consideration.

There are three types of leadership substitutes: the subordinate characteristics, the task factors, and the organizational dimensions. Specific substitutes are shown in table 15.2. This table shows that, for example, if you receive feedback because the task itself allows you to make a judgment about how well things are going, there is no need to have a manager give you feedback.

Table 15.2 Some substitutes for leadership

Subordinate characteristics	*Task factors*	*Organizational dimensions*
Ability	Repetitiveness	Formalization
Experience	Clarity	Availability of special staff
Background and training	Task-provided feedback	Work group cohesiveness
Professional orientation		Spatial distance between the leader and the group
Indifference toward organization rewards		

Source: Adapted from Kerr and Jermier (1978)

The concept of substitutes for leadership is important for two reasons. First, it suggests that contextual control (discussed in chapter 14) is an alternative to active leadership to obtain good results. The many studies that have been done show that these substitutes can have effects in the predicted direction on employee attitudes, role perceptions and both task and contextual performance. In fact, some have argued that these effects are greater than leadership effects (Podsakoff et al., 1996). This means that for managers, selecting competent and motivated people is one way, and job enrichment is another. In fact, the HIO (see chapter 6) is meant to be a substitute for leadership, trying to improve performance with intrinsically motivating work, supportive working conditions, and a pay structure which provides incentives to learn new skills. Of course, it takes leadership and the use of power to create leadership substitutes and the conditions for them to operate effectively in organizations. The development of HIOs, as one particular example, calls for extraordinary leadership in all phases of formulation and implementation.

Second, there are implications about the interaction of leadership, leadership substitutes, and the nature of the organization. The various factors that may act as substitutes will differ, depending upon the type of organization (Tosi, 1992). For example, in mechanistic organizations, the task itself will provide clarity, formalization will provide direction, and lower-level workers will be indifferent toward organization rewards. In organic organizations, however, task competence, high intrinsic task motivation, and cohesive work groups will be more powerful substitutes.

The effects of leadership substitutes will also vary by organization level (Tosi, 1992). At higher levels in mechanistic organizations, socialization and experience are likely to be more powerful factors that affect performance than at lower levels. At lower levels, formalization and technology may be stronger substitutes.

Summary

Organizations are concerned with leadership because of the need to select and promote individuals into management positions. The manager's role is to make sure the work of the organization is done through the effective use of physical and human resources. Therefore, we believe that an effective manager should be a good leader.

There is a close relationship between leadership and management, but there is more to it than simply understanding the role of the leader/manager. There are many reasons why people are willing to cooperate to achieve organization goals, and many of these are only incidentally related to the superior–subordinate relationship. For instance, the broad shape of the psychological contract is probably constructed in early socialization, before one joins an organization.

However, it is important to know how situational factors, the work setting, and the characteristics of the subordinate interact with the personality and the behavior of a manager/leader to affect the level of individual and organization performance. This chapter has discussed several theories of leadership that illustrate this. Path–goal theory and Fiedler's work explain leadership phenomena with a greater number of situational factors than had been used in earlier approaches. VDL theory contributes to understanding leadership because of its focus on the relationship between the leader and the subordinate. However, we also show how contextual control of members can be achieved through substitutes for leadership, showing that leadership is an aspect of power, as discussed in chapter 14.

Guide for Managers: Choosing a Leadership Style

These theories can help you to do a better job as a leader if you follow their implications in your work as a manager. Perhaps the main idea that you can come away with is to recognize the importance of having a clear understanding about the situation itself – and then do your best to adapt your style to it. First we outline some specific actions that are part of the different behavioral repertoires. Then we suggest some ways to think about the context in which they will occur.

HOW TO ACT LIKE A LEADER

The research on which leadership theories in this chapter is based provides some useful guides for specific actions that are elements of the more broad behavioral repertoires. In addition, you should read again chapter 5; much of what was said there applies here also.

One thing that you must know is your own behavioral tendencies and your own personality. These behavioral tendencies will be your most likely, and probably most comfortable, response when faced with any situation. To be an effective manager, you will sometimes have to cognitively modify your actions to be more appropriate for the situation. Can you do this? The research, and common sense, says that you can, but within reason. You obviously should avoid engaging in any ways that appear to be feigned and forced. Then you will be seen as untrustworthy, something that is a problem for any manager.

Here are some actions that fall within each leader's behavior repertoire.

Directive behaviors

There are times when it is critical to provide direction and guidance to subordinates. A subordinate will generally perceive your actions to be directive if you engage in work-oriented interactions – and you take the initiative in these interactions. However, providing guidance is not the same thing as dominating and demeaning someone. Instead, it is giving direction and clarification as to how to do something or what is expected. This means you have to be careful not to create the perception that you are overly rigid or dominating. Here are some ways to be directive:

- Clearly define responsibilities.
- Provide the necessary information to do the job.
- Emphasize the policies and procedures that should be followed.
- Make regular checks of the subordinate's progress.
- Behave in ways that reinforce status differences between you and your subordinate.
- Provide constructive feedback on a regular basis.

Considerate and supportive behaviors

Like the dangers of appearing too directive and dominating, the dangerous side of acting in a considerate or supportive ways towards subordinates is that some might view it as a sign of weakness and lack of concern for performance. However, if you know when to act in this way and can, you will be rewarded with better performance. Here are some ways that you can be considerate or supportive:

- Show concern for the personal well-being of subordinates.
- Be an active listener. Let the subordinate do most of the talking.
- Personalize the way you deal with subordinates, minimizing organizational status differences.
- Encourage individualism, creativity and initiative.

Transformational leader behaviors

We have discussed the fact that managers have been successfully trained to behave in transformational ways. Here are some of the behaviors that they learn.

- Articulate a vision that subordinates can understand and accept. Do this by providing an optimistic and attainable view of the future.
- Show self-confidence.
- Challenge subordinates, but be sure that they are capable of stretching to achieve the goals.
- Find ways to use non-verbal cues and symbols that are consistent with your message.
- Be dramatic and outgoing, but in ways that are consistent with your personality. This means that you have to sometimes take personal risks that others know about and believe are important to the success of your organization.
- Empower subordinates. This means two things. First, you must be willing to delegate important responsibilities to them to demonstrate your confidence in their ability. Second, you have to use language that lets them know that you believe they can succeed and that you will help them to succeed.

KNOWING WHEN TO USE A PARTICULAR BEHAVIORAL REPERTOIRE

The one thing that is clear from the research on leadership is that one style does not fit all cases. Below are some things that you should consider:

Look first at results, then the person

Before acting in any situation, you want to ensure that you avoid the fundamental attribution error; see page 77 in chapter 3. Otherwise your biases, assumptions and likes for that person will color your evaluation. That means if you have a performance problem with a person with whom you have a good relationship, you will tend to be considerate and/or supportive even though a directive approach might be more effective. Likewise, a performance problem with a person that you do not like as well might lead to more directive actions when a considerate or supportive approach is called for.

When performance of a lower level manager is not up to par, then replace the leader or change the situation

This is one way to attain some congruence between leader behavior and the situation. For example, if it is called for, task structure can be increased or decreased. Jobs can be made more routine and simple or be enlarged and the task structure reduced. The position power of a manager can be increased by delegating more authority and responsibility, or it can be reduced by taking them away. Leader–member relationships may be improved through any number of different training and group development methods.

Identify and remove barriers to performance

Remember that it is not your job as a manager to make someone's job more difficult. You want to make it easier because your success depends upon their success. One of the more important things that you can do, and often one of the easiest, is to make the job of subordinates easier by eliminating difficulties that are in their performance path. Another way to make a subordinate's job easier is to make sure that they have the necessary competence to do the work and that might entail that they have some training.

Know what those in your group are capable of doing

There are two facets to this; their ability and their motivation. If those who work for you are very capable, then you should avoid, when possible, directive leader styles and emphasize the considerate/supportive style. When subordinates do not have the requisite competence, information, or resources, a directive style is probably more effective.

From the motivational side of the issue, it is helpful to know how intrinsically motivated are your subordinates. For those that are highly motivated with high ability, you will want to be considerate/supportive and keep out of their way. For those who have high ability but lower motivation, a more directive style will be effective.

The level of stress that a subordinate is experiencing should also affect your choice of style (Yukl, 1998). The stress could be from organizational sources or external sources. For your subordinates it probably makes no difference; for you, a manager, it does, but not in the way that you might like. Consider stress from external sources first. You might prefer that employees do not bring it to the workplace, but they will; and if they do, the effects of the stressors on their work will be the same as if they are job stressors. So you will have to deal with them. Your leader behavior style in this situation should be, at least at first, considerate/supportive so that you do not make the situation even worse. At some point, if there are still performance problems, you might have to take a more directive approach. You want to be careful, though, and not switch to that style prematurely.

Finally, as a manager you should experiment some and try to find behavior that works for you with your group. What could be the biggest enemy to your effectiveness is your own rigidity and unwillingness to be flexible.

Key Concepts

achievement-oriented leadership 467
autocratic leadership 458
behavioral approaches to leadership 457
capacity 455
cognitive resource theory 466
consideration 460
contingency theories of leadership 461
directive leadership 467
employee-centered leadership 460
goal emphasis 461
high LPC leader 465
initiating structure 460
interaction facilitation 461
laissez-faire leadership 458
leader motive pattern 457
leader–member relations 464
leader orientation 464
leadership 454
leadership substitutes 476
low LPC leader 465
LPC scale 464
participative leadership 458
path–goal theory 467
position power 464
process theories of leadership 472
production-centered leadership 460
situational control 465
status 456
supportive leadership 467
task structure 464
trait theories of leadership 455
transactional leadership 472
transformational leadership theory 472
vertical dyad linkage (VDL) theory 475
Vroom–Yetton model 461
work facilitation 461

STUDY QUESTIONS

1 Define leadership. How is it different from the concept of political activity discussed in chapter 14?
2 What are trait theories of leadership? Why are they deficient as explanations of leadership?
3 How do behavioral approaches differ from trait theories of leadership?
4 How do contingency theories of leadership differ from trait theories and behavioral theories?
5 What are the contingency factors in the path–goal theory?
What are the contingency factors in Fiedler's theory of leadership?
Compare and contrast Fiedler's theory with path–goal theory.
6 What are process theories of leadership?
How do they differ from trait theories and behavioral theories?
7 What are the main characteristics of a transformational leader?
How do they differ from charismatic leaders discussed in chapter 14?
8 Do you believe there is much difference between a transformational leader and a transactional leader? Why?
9 Can you apply the concepts from the substitutes for leadership to a situation in which you have had to work?
10 Analyze the leadership style of the US President using at least two different theories of leadership.
11 How can you integrate some idea about charismatic power (chapter 14) with the concepts of leadership?
12 How would the substitutes for leadership vary by type of organization (see chapter 13)?
By level of organization?
For professionals compared to indifferents compared to organization-oriented personality types (see chapter 2)?
13 What is the important difference between VDL theory and other approaches?
Relate this approach to topics considered elsewhere in the text, for example, the Good Enough Theory of Promotion or attribution theory.

Case

Cliff City Bank

Some years ago, Charles Boyd was appointed president of the Cliff City Bank. At the time, Cliff City Bank was a small, marginally profitable bank controlled by an old Cliff City family, the Oliver family. The bank was having some managerial and financial problems and Bill Oliver, the chairman of the board, thought that Charlie was the person to bring the bank back to profitability. Charles Boyd had the qualifications for the job; he had graduated from State University in 1960 with an MBA. For ten years, he worked with an accounting firm, eventually becoming a partner and he was well-known in financial circles in the state and in the region.

When Charles took charge of the bank, he made some significant changes. First, he was successful in attracting several of Cliff City's largest business firms to use the bank's services. He also made some very sound loans and, more importantly, was able to work out a solution to some of the problem investments that Cliff City had made. Second, he was able to improve the internal operating efficiency of the bank by a careful study of the bank's operating systems.

Over the years, Charles Boyd has become the dominating force at Cliff City. This is because he is an excellent businessman, he keeps almost complete control of all the bank's operations, and he has personally picked all the current managers.

Now Boyd is near retirement. The board of directors, still heavily influenced by the Oliver family, has asked a consultant to help them select a new CEO. The consultant proposed, first, that an analysis of the management structure of the bank would be useful because this would help him understand what kind of person would best meet the bank's needs.

Here is what the consultant found:

- Boyd selected executives who were loyal and committed to him. They were expected to know all the different phases of the bank's operations.
- There were ambiguous job descriptions and policies governing the work of those bank executives who reported to Boyd. Boyd was unwilling to formalize policies and procedures for them.
- Boyd was often vague in making assignments to these managers. Often the goals and the activities assigned to them were not clear. Sometimes he would assign the same project to more than one person. Very rarely did he give anyone enough authority to complete the job. Usually, the manager would have to come to Boyd for approval for some aspects of a project.
- Often Boyd went directly to lower-level managers to find out about problems. It was not unusual for him to short-circuit his direct subordinates.

Now, answer these questions:

- How would you analyze the leadership style of Boyd?
- What is the basis of his power in this organization?
- What kind of replacement would you recommend if you were the consultant?
- What changes would you suggest for the Cliff City Bank? What would have to be done to make them work?

References

Avolio, B. J., Waldman, D. A. and Einstein, W. O. 1988: Transformational leadership in a management game simulation. *Group and Organization Studies*, 13(1), 59–80.

Bakhtari, H. 1995: Cultural effects on management style: A comparative study of American and Middle Eastern Management Styles. (Management and its Environment in the Arab World). *International Studies of Management in Organization*, 25(3), Fall, 97–119.

Bass, B. M. 1985: *Leadership Beyond Expectations*. New York: Free Press.

Bass, B. M. and Stogdill R. M. 1990: *Handbook of Leadership: Theory, Research, and Managerial Applications*. New York: The Free Press.

Bass, B. M., Avolio, B. J. and Goodheim, L. 1987: Biography and assessment of transformational leadership at the world class level. *Journal of Management*, 13(1), 7–19.

Blake, R. R. and Mouton, J. S. 1969: *Building a Dynamic Corporation through Grid Organization Development*. Reading, MA: Addison-Wesley.

Bowers, D. G. and Seashore, S. E. 1966: Predicting organizational effectiveness with a four-factor theory of leadership. *Administrative Science Quarterly*, 11, April, 238–63.

Bycio, P., Hackett, R. D. and Allen, J. S. 1995: Further assessments of Bass's conceptualization of transactional and transformational leadership. *Journal of Applied Psychology*. 80(4), August, 468–99.

Chen, C. C. and Meindl, J. R. 1991: The construction of leadership images in the popular press: The case of Donald Burr and People Express. *Administrative Science Quarterly*, 36, 521–51.

Cornelius, E. T. and Lane, F. B. 1984: The power motive and managerial success in a professionally oriented service industry organization. *Journal of Applied Psychology*, 69(1), 32–9.

Dansereau, F., Graen, G. and Haga, W. J. 1975: A vertical dyad linkage approach to leadership within formal organizations – A longitudinal investigation of the role making process. *Organizational Behavior and Human Performance*, 13, 46–78.

Deluga, R. J. 1988: Relationship of transformational and transactional leadership with employee influencing strategies. *Group and Organization Studies*, 13, 456–67.

Dienesch, R. M. and Liden, R. C. 1986: Leader–member exchange model of leadership: A critique and further development. *Academy of Management Review*, 11(3), 618–34.

Downton, J. V. 1973: *Rebel Leadership: Commitment and Charisma in the Revolutionary Process*. New York: Free Press.

Evans, M. G. 1968: *The Effects of Supervisory Behavior on Worker Perceptions of their Path–Goal Relationships*, PhD dissertation. New Haven: Yale University.

Fiedler, F. E. 1967: *A Theory of Leadership Effectiveness*. New York: McGraw-Hill.

Fiedler, F. E. 1978: The contingency model and the dynamics of the leadership process. In L. Berkowitz (ed.) *Advances in Experimental Social Psychology*, 2nd edn, New York: Academic Press, 59–111.

Fiedler, F. E. 1992: Time based measures of leadership experience and organizational performance: A review of research and a preliminary model. *The Leadership Quarterly*, 3, 5–21.

Fiedler, F. E. and Chemers, M. 1974: *Leadership and Effective Management*. Glenview, IL: Scott, Foresman.

Fiedler, F. E. and Garcia, J. E. 1987: *New Approaches to Effective Leadership: Cognitive Resources and Organization Performance*. New York: John Wiley.

Filley, A. C., House, R. J. and Kerr, S. 1976: *Managerial Process and Organizational Behavior*. Glenview, IL: Scott, Foresman.

Fleishman, E. A., Mumford, M. D., Zaccaro, S. J., Levin, D. Y., Krothin, A. L. and Hein, M. B. 1991: Taxonomic efforts in the description of leadership behavior: A synthesis and functional interpretation. *The Leadership Quarterly*, 2, 245–80.

Fodor, E. M. 1976: Group stress, authoritarian style of control, and the use of power. *Journal of Applied Psychology*, 61, 313–18.

Hadjian, A. 1995: How tomorrow's best leaders are learning their stuff. *Fortune*, 132(11), November 27, 90–7.

Hater, J. J. and Bass, B. M. 1988: Superiors' evaluations and subordinates' perceptions of transformational and transactional leadership. *Journal of Applied Psychology*, 73, 695–702.

Hersey, P. and Blanchard, K. 1988: *Management of Organizational Behavior*. New York: Prentice-Hall.

House, R. J. 1971: A path–goal theory of leader effectiveness. *Administrative Science Quarterly*, 16, 334–8.

House, R. J. and Mitchell, T. R. 1974: Path–goal theory of leadership. *Journal of Contemporary Business*, 4, 81–97.

House, R. J. and Singh, J. V. 1987: Organization behavior: Some new directions for I/O psychology. *Annual Review of Psychology*, 38, 669–718.

Howell, J. M. and Frost, P. J. 1989: A laboratory study of charismatic leadership. *Organizational Behavior and Human Decision Processes*, 43, 243–69.

Howell, J. M. and Higgins, C. A. 1990: Champions of technological innovation. *Administrative Science Quarterly*, 35, 317–41.

Hymowitz, C. and Pollock, E. J. 1998: Office romance isn't the corporate turnoff it once was. *The Wall Street Journal*, February 4, A1(W), A1(E), col 1.

Kerr, S. and Jermier, J. 1978: Substitutes for leadership: Their meaning and measurement. *Organizational Behavior and Human Performance*, 22, 375–403.

Kirkpatrick, S. and Locke, E. A. 1996: Direct and indirect effects of three core leadership components on performance and attitudes. *Journal of Applied Psychology*, 81(1), February, 36–52.

Kozlowski, S. W. J. and Doherty, M. L. 1989: Integration of climate and leadership: Examination of a neglected issue. *Journal of Applied Psychology*, 74, 546–54.

Lewin, K., Lippitt, R. and White, R. K. 1939: Patterns of aggressive behavior in experimentally created social climates. *Journal of Social Psychology*, 10, 271–99.

Liden, R. and Graen, G. 1980: Generalizability of the vertical dyad linkage model. *Academy of Management Journal*, 23, 451–65.

Lowin, A. and Craig, J. 1968: The influence of level of performance on managerial style: An experimental object lesson on the ambiguity of correlational data. *Organizational Behavior and Human Performance*, 3, 440–58.

McClelland, D. A. 1975: *Power: The Inner Experience*. New York: Irvington.

McClelland, D. A. 1985: *Human Motivation*. Glenview, IL: Scott, Foresman.

McClelland, D. A. and Boyatzis, R. E. 1982: Leadership motive pattern and long-term success in management. *Journal of Applied Psychology*, 67, 737–43.

Meindl, J. R., Ehrlich, S. B. and Dukerich, J. M. 1985: The romance of leadership. *Administrative Science Quarterly*, 30, 78–102.

Murphy, S. E., Blyth, D. and Fiedler, F. E. 1992: Cognitive resources theory and the utilization of the leader's and group member's technical competence. *The Leadership Quarterly*, 3, 237–54.

Peters, L. H., Harke, D. D. and Pohlman, J. T. 1985: Fiedler's contingency theory of leadership: An application of the meta-analysis procedures of Schmidt and Hunter. *Psychological Bulletin*, 97(2), 274–85.

Pfeffer, J. and Davis-Blake, A. 1987: Administrative succession and organizational performance: How administrator experience mediates the succession effect. *Academy of Management Journal*, 29, 72–83.

Podsakoff, P., McKenzie, S. and Bommer, W. 1996: Meta-analysis of the relationship between Kerr and Jermier's substitutes for leadership and employee job attitudes, role perceptions, and performance. *Journal of Applied Psychology*, 81(4), August, 380–400.

Reinganum, M. R. 1985: The effect of executive succession on stockholder wealth. *Administrative Science Quarterly*, 30, 46–60.

Schreisheim, C. and DeNisi, A. S. 1981: Task dimensions as moderators of the effects of instrumental leadership: A two-sample replicated test of path–goal leadership theory. *Journal of Applied Psychology*, 66, 589–97.

Seltzer, J. and Bass, B. M. 1990: Transformational leadership: Beyond initiation and consideration. *Journal of Management*, 16, 693–703.

Smith, M. and White, M. C. 1987: Strategy, CEO specialization, and succession. *Administrative Science Quarterly*, 32, 263–80.

Stewart, R. 1996: German management: a challenge to Anglo-American managerial assumptions. *Business Horizons*, 39(3), May, 52–60.

Stogdill, R. M. 1974: *Handbook of Leadership: A Survey of Theory and Research*. New York: Free Press.

Strube, M. J. and Garcia, J. E. 1981: A meta-analytic investigation of Fiedler's contingency model of leadership effectiveness. *Psychological Bulletin*, 90, 307–21.

Thomas, A. B. 1988: Does leadership make a difference to organizational performance? *Administrative Science Quarterly*, 33, 388–400.

Tosi, H. L. 1982: When leadership isn't enough. In H. L. Tosi and W. C. Hamner (eds) *Organizational*

Behavior and Management: A Contingency Approach, New York: John Wiley, 403–11.

Tosi, H. L. 1992: *The Environment/Organization/Person Contingency Model: A Meso Approach to the Study of Organizations*. Greenwich, CT: JAI Press, Inc.

Tosi, H. L. and Gomez-Mejia, L. 1989: The decoupling of CEO pay and performance: An agency theory perspective. *Administrative Science Quarterly*, 34, 169–89.

Vecchio, R. P. 1990: Theoretical and empirical examination of cognitive resource theory. *Journal of Applied Psychology*, 75, 141–7.

Vroom, V. H. and Yetton, P. W. 1973: *Leadership and Decision Making*. Pittsburgh: University of Pittsburgh Press.

Weiner, N. and Mahoney, T. A. 1981: A model of corporate performance as a function of environmental, organizational, and leadership influences. *Academy of Management Journal*, 24, 453–70.

Yukl, G. 1988: *Leadership in Organizations*. Upper Saddle River, NJ: Prentice Hall, ch. 15.

chapter 16

Organizational Change

HOW OUR WORK LIFE IS CHANGING

RESISTANCE TO CHANGE

STAGES OF SUCCESSFUL CHANGE

HELPING INDIVIDUALS TO COPE WITH CHANGE

IMPLEMENTING CHANGE

Preparing for Class

To help you think about change on a small scale, try this experiment with your family, friends, work colleagues or other social group. Make a change to one of the more routine aspects of your interaction within the group. It may be the route you take in going to work or school (if you travel with others), where you sit in the conference room or classroom, or at the dinner table, what time you take lunch or where you go for lunch, or any change in your behavior that will be noticed. Observe how others around you respond and take note of how the changes make you feel.

After your experience, reflect on and record your observations based on the following questions:

1. Describe in behavioral terms how people reacted to your change. What did they do and say? Were they reluctant to go along with the change?

2. Did the change appear to make others uncomfortable? If so, how did they behave?

3. Describe how you felt internally? Were you anxious or uncomfortable? If so, why do think that was?

4. Can you think of the implications of the behavior you witnessed?

5. For our class discussion, were there any of the models introduced in this chapter that were useful for describing your experience?

Amy shifted in her chair and gazed out the window in response to the interviewer's question. "Did I feel threatened when the announcement was made that we were downsizing? I'd have to say yes. In fact, I can't think of a more stressful time in my professional life than the change we have seen in the last 12 months. I went from thinking I would be with this organization until retirement, to wondering how I would make my house payments if I were among those who lost a job. I had trouble eating and sleeping and I spent a great deal of my time trying to figure out what was going to happen. Even now that the organization is telling me that there are no more changes to come, I am skeptical. I am not sure I trust them. I am certainly a different person now and I have a different view of the organization".

Amy is describing her reaction to a significant change in the organization she worked for – a change that fundamentally impacted her mental models of organizational life and subsequently impacted her attitude about the organization. Impacting how she viewed herself, her future, and the organization to which she belonged. Her reaction to the change is normal. In chapter 7, we discussed the "stressed out" employees in the workplace. The uncertainty that restructuring has created is among the top causes of that stress in the workplace. According to an annual survey by International Survey Research Corp., the percentage of workers who frequently worry about being laid off has surged to 46 percent from 22 percent in 1988 (Schellhardt, 1996).

Change affects us all in different ways but the reality is that dealing with change is a complex and stressful process. This chapter focuses on the changing nature of our work. We look at some models of change and build on those models to consider ways of achieving effective change in organizations. We begin by introducing some of the dynamics of modern organizational life that are leading to significant changes in our work lives.

How Our Work Life is Changing

Significant change has become a common occurrence in the modern workplace. Even the largest companies are experiencing significant change in many areas. We are experiencing change in how we work including where we work, change in the structure of our organizations, change in the nature of business to an increasingly global marketplace and change in the increased diversification of our work colleagues. Here are some specific factors that are driving change in the workplace.

Changes to Internal Work Processes used to Complete Work

Perhaps the most common internal change pressure is dissatisfaction with performance. Increased competition, rapid change in consumer tastes, or increased emphasis on service or quality can all trigger pressure to change. Dissatisfaction with employee turnover or performance failures may also instigate change efforts. These changes affect how we work and the skills required for that work. Increases in information technology and a shift from physical activities to intellectual activities have changed the work tasks of workers.

One significant change in workplace activities is the increasing shift toward the virtual office in the Information Age. This has changed the face of the workplace so that, rather than having a specified office in a specific building, many workers nowadays work in their homes, cars, or motel rooms. It is anticipated that the number of employees who work in virtual offices will increase by 10 percent each year for the foreseeable future. Companies such as Hewlett-Packard, Anderson Consulting, Lotus Development, and IBM are all increasingly using virtual office arrangements for their employees (O'Connell, 1998). Not only does this change the nature of how we work; it forces us to learn a new set of skills to cope with the increased use of technology in our work lives.

Organizations are Changing Structurally

Downsizing, rightsizing, mergers and acquisitions are commonplace. In 1998, a focus on just a few of the mergers that occurred gives us a sense of the significant change in structure that is occurring. Compaq computer acquired Digital Equipment Corporation to become the largest computer manufacturer in the world. Washington Mutual and H. F. Ahmanson & Company was the merger of the two largest savings and loan companies in the USA. The American Stock Exchange and the Nasdaq market announced a merger to help them to compete with the New York Stock Exchange. AOL purchased Netscape to become one of the largest organizations designed to support customer access to the Internet. The implications of these mergers are significant for not only the industries within which they operate, But also for the employees associated with those organizations. When Chase and the Chemical Banking Corporation agreed to merge in 1995, the two banks employed about 75,000 people. After their merger, 12,000 jobs were eliminated. As the larger organization continued to acquire smaller companies, it continued changing the size of its work force. A recent New York Times' article describes the effects of these changes. "Chase employees have been aware for some time that layoffs were on the way and a climate of uncertainty has pervaded the bank – an uncertainty that will now be prolonged as Chase carries out the layoffs." That reality came true as, in 1998, Chase announced another 2,250 layoffs (O'Brien, 1998).

Change in ownership also induces organizational change. Typically, in such takeovers, the acquired organization must adopt the management styles, philosophies, and systems of the acquiring organization, often in a very short period of time. Changes in ownership where the new owner is a foreign company creates special change problems for organizations since here there is often a culture clash. The compromises and adjustments that have to be made are often especially severe.

Shifts to a Global Economy

The increased globalization of the marketplace causes several changes that we must accommodate. These changes affect organizations and individuals in many ways. First, many companies have increased need for US employees to work in foreign countries as expatriates. This requires employees to cope with extremely different cultures. Second, global competitiveness has caused organizations to constantly find ways to increase their competitiveness; changes which lead to subsequent changes in the work processes and procedures.

Global Focus on The Myths of the Lives of Expatriates

One significant change in managing organizational behavior is dealing with US employees who are assigned to work units in overseas locations. Here are some common myths of expatriate life as discovered by one expatriate (Fitzgerald-Turner, 1997).

- *Myth 1 – Western Europe is not a third world country*
  While most countries in Europe have many modern aspects similar to life in the USA, there are other aspects that cause frustration for expatriates. Being paid in US dollars, lack of customer service and the expense of living in some areas all cause concern.
- *Myth 2 – Financial incentives resolve most problems*
  Financial incentives often do not improve with changes in the individual's circumstances and often lag well behind change in the valuation of the dollar.
- *Myth 3 – We are sending the best folks who can handle any situation*
  While employees selected for such duties often have special skills such as language and knowledge of foreign travel, many difficulties can arise that are well beyond the ability or experience of the individual. They must cope with unanticipated cultural differences that were often not evident in previous shorter visits to the country.
- *Myth 4 – Support from the home office is always available*
  While senior managers and supervisors may be sensitive to the employee issues involved in living in a different country, support staff at other levels of the organization may be less sensitive. Problems in payroll and personnel are common experiences for expatriates.
- *Myth 5 – Language skills are only critical for the employee*
  Many times these skills are even more important for the family who may have an even more direct interface with the local culture through schools, local employment, or just shopping and living.

An example of this influence in competitiveness was the competition in the automotive market that opened up opportunities for foreign automobile manufacturers that were experienced in making fuel-efficient cars. As foreign automobiles entered the market, US firms were motivated to change their existing product lines and form joint ventures with foreign manufacturers and to sell foreign made automobiles under their own names. This required enormous modifications in company operations. Entire plants, including personnel, technical processes, and administrative procedures, had to change so as to compete more successfully against global competitors. Another result was the significant reductions in the US work force and political pressures to impose quotas against foreign automobile companies. This, in turn, encouraged foreign manufacturers to locate in the USA to avoid the quotas. New problems arose in managing plants in a new culture.

Increased Diversity in the Work Force

The increased diversity within the work force has been a change that has provided challenges for many individuals and organizations. Women increasingly compromise a larger percentage of the work force and bring with them a diverse set of skills and needs. In 1997, African-Americans and Hispanics joined the work force at a much larger rate than their white counterparts (*Wall Street Journal*, 1998). While the increased diversity is seen as good for the competitiveness of US businesses, it brings a different set of issues that result in organizational change.

A Model of Change

As discussed above, modern organizations face many changes in their environment. As a result, for an organization to be successful, it must adapt to those changes to insure survival. To begin our discussion of how organizations change, we introduce a basic model of change that draws from what we know about the adaptation of organisms in a biological sense. This basic model of adaptation to a changing environment is useful in our understanding the basic process which organizations must go through to achieve effective change.

Organism Adaptation

Many of the theories of planned change are based on a basic model of how change occurs and can be attributed to the work of Lewin (1951). If we consider how organisms adapt to change, we have a useful model in understanding the nature of change. From a biological perspective, organisms adapt to pressures in their environment. As the environment changes, the organism must change or it will cease to exist. In many cases, there are opposing forces that affect the organism and so it simultaneously adapts to numerous powerful opposing forces. In a biological sense, this leads to an equilibrium that allows the organism to continue to exist. This is called the resultant and represents the status quo. Given the organism has adapted to these pressures over a significant period of time, it is resistant to any change that would upset that careful balance. To effect future change would require powerful changes in the environment.

Organizational Adaptation

Organizational change can be viewed from this perspective as well. Let us focus on a desired change in an organizational process or procedure – their way of doing things. These processes are often the result of competing organizational pressures caused by conflict, internal political pressures, and diverse needs. A process that evolves from these pressures usually works because it is an equilibrium of pressures. Perhaps any one constituent does not prefer the process but it is a compromise caused by the pressure in the context. Subsequent attempts to change that process may face even greater resistance.

To effect change in the organization, three things must occur.

1 Unfreezing
2 Transformation
3 Refreezing

unfreezing
The process of placing significant pressure on the organism to recognize the need to change

transformation
The process of movement that must occur for the organism to change

refreezing
The process of making change permanent and achieving a new equilibrium point

Unfreezing requires that there be a change in the status quo before there can be a change to a new condition. Just because a change is attempted does not mean it will be effective. The model introduced above suggests the organism will resist the change unless significant pressure can be brought to bear to require the organism to recognize the need to change (unfreeze). For example, one organization introduced a new technology to their assembly line in an attempt to make a procedure more efficient. However, these changes required employees to learn new skills that were unfamiliar to them. They resisted the change because the older procedures were more comfortable to them. Only after significant incentives were introduced were the workers willing to at least try to learn the skills required to operate the new technology. This is the second step in the process and is called **transformation**. It is the movement that must occur for the organism to change. Finally, the change is made permanent through the process of **refreezing** (Lewin, 1951). This becomes the new equilibrium point. Returning to our example, once the assembly line workers accept the need for change and movement occurs, the final step would be to make the change in work processes permanent. This would include training until the procedures were learned and then making sure the new work procedures became permanent.

Resistance to Change

Just like in Lewin's model, there is resistance to change within organizations. Resistance to change may be traced to individual, group, or organizational characteristics. To take a specific example: a consultant had revised an organization's performance appraisal system several times. There was deep resistance to changing the existing system in spite of the fact that it was well known that it was not working well. A general fear of the unknown and a preference for the known appeared to be operating. Supervisors may have felt that a new system would prove even more difficult to use than the present one. They may have thought that their subordinates' performances will look worse under a new system, which might reflect back on them. They may also have feared that they would have to face new problems and decisions for which they lacked experience. Finally, changing may simply not be worth the trouble. The gain is not worth the pain. In this section, we discuss reasons for that resistance.

Global Focus on The Focus of Change Programs are Often a Moving Target

A discouraging feature of change programs that involve an attempt to catch up with competitors in the marketplace lies in the fact that such competitors are often moving ahead in a variety of fronts. If companies catch up with such competitors in some respects, there is a problem of the target moving ahead in other areas requiring constant and never-ending change process.

A good example is the attempts of the US manufacturers to catch up with Japanese competitors. US manufacturers have now improved so much in recent years that the Japanese no longer have a clear lead in many areas and have even fallen behind in areas like reliable delivery. While the gap between the US and Japanese has closed in some areas, a recent survey discovered the Japanese have developed other competitive advantages.

The survey indicated that the Japanese now have been focusing more recently on such competitive factors as more and better product features, flexible factories, expanded customer service, and rapid outpourings of new products. Here the gap between the US and the Japanese firms tends to be fairly substantial reflecting the fact that Japan has pushed for changes in these areas over the past ten-year period. The use of sophisticated computer technologies has helped the Japanese manufacturers to make important positive changes in these areas (Stewart, 1992).

ORGANIZATIONAL CULTURE AND POWER STRUCTURE

The organizational culture and power structure help to maintain stable behavior patterns in organizations. They are self-reinforcing and potentially significant barriers to change. After all, the very nature of change may put them in jeopardy. It is therefore likely that the change efforts will not work unless they are compatible with the organizational culture and the power structure. This is a very well-documented reason why many change efforts fail. Quite often, for example, a top management group decides to decentralize decision making, giving more responsibility to lower-level managers. This requires a climate of trust and willingness to delegate. In an organization that has a political organizational culture, a lack of trust, and strong centralized decision making, decentralizing will be very difficult.

CHANGING SYSTEMS: THE EFFECTS OF INTERDEPENDENCIES

When an organization is viewed as a complex system of interdependent parts, it is clear that resistance to a change attempted in one area may be resisted by other parts of the system. It also suggests that, for change to be effective, it must consider the interdependencies that exist because these interdependencies may interfere with effective change.

Change programs often focus on changes in tasks, people, technology, or structure. In task changes, the duties assigned to individuals are changed. In people changes, an attempt is made to alter individual knowledge, attitudes, or skills. Technological change focuses on the machinery, procedures, work flows, or materials. Structural rearrangements focus on changing how members are grouped together or on the systems and procedures that the organization employs to guide and direct interactions. However, to change any one of these means that the others are very often affected as well. These change interdependencies may cause an effort to fail eventually, even though a desired change in one of the factors had initially taken place. Change efforts directed towards one area may be resisted in another.

The McKinsey 7-S model shows that key interdependencies exist among seven factors that are major determinants of organizational success (see Figure 16.1) (Pascale and Athos, 1981; Peters and Waterman, 1982). The structure of an organization, whether it is organic or mechanistic, must fit the style of management (directive versus democratic), the shared values of organization members (toward collaboration and innovation), and the staff (abilities of people). The strategy of the organization (market focus) must be congruent with the organization's skills (unique organizational abilities) if the organization is to be successful. The systems employed by the organization (reward, control) must be congruent with the type of people employed and their characteristics as well as being compatible with the way people are grouped together by the organization's structure. When one of these elements is changed, others will be affected. We discuss some of these factors more extensively when we discuss leverage points for change.

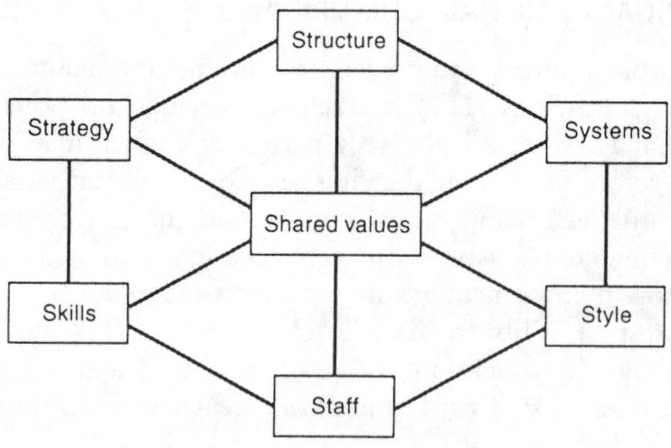

Fig 16.1 : The McKinsey 7-S Framework

The Five Leverage Points of Change

Now that we have introduced some basic models and ideas about change and resistance to change, we can focus on ways of implementing organizational change. The first step is to unfreeze the organization and cause movement. Given the significant resistance to change that can exist, a solid understanding of key organizational components is needed before a manager can effect the required movement that will lead to successful change. These components can be thought of as leverage points for effecting organizational change. There are also potential barriers to successful change if they are not appropriately considered. Archimedes is said to have commented that "give me a lever long enough and single handed I can move the world." This section explores five leverages points thought to be critical to effecting organizational change (Kilmann, 1984, 1989; Kilmann et al., 1988).

1 The setting
2 The organization
3 Management and management skills
4 Culture
5 The team and team building

THE SETTING

The setting includes the potential external barriers of success and also levers that could be catalysts for organizational change. This includes aspects of the organization's history as well as its relationship with the marketplace. Another aspects of the setting are the external stakeholders (Kilmann et al., 1988). This may be government agencies, competitors, or members of the community that have a stake in the organization.

An example of how the setting can be a barrier to change is seen in countless examples across the USA each year. Many communities have limitations on growth and through their planning commissions and zoning boards they can control building or development. This could potentially stop a company who was interested in expanding their business if the construction required them to develop a new process or facilities that required external approval. The setting can also drive change in that governmental regulations often are the source of significant change in organizations. Governmental regulations in the form of environmental laws, employment laws, and taxes are all critical portions of the system within which the organization operates (Kilmann, 1989).

THE ORGANIZATION

The organization's strategy and structure are important levers and potential barriers to change. Strategy encompasses the mission, goals and objectives of the organization. Goals of growth are often a source of organizational change. However, the structure of the organization, its allocation of resources, rules, and policies can be formidable levers of change as well. An example includes the organization's reward system. Are the correct employee behaviors being rewarded? For example, if an organization change requires a team effort, incentives in the reward system that are tied to individual performance may be dysfunctional. On the other hand, organizations that carefully understand the employee behaviors required to effect the change may be able to facilitate those changes more quickly by directly rewarding those behaviors (Kilmann, 1989).

MANAGEMENT AND MANAGEMENT SKILLS

Implementing change in organizations requires managerial skills. It also requires a keen knowledge of critical aspects of the organization. Managers typically control many of the other levers discussed in this section. While top managers control the strategy and structure process, just controlling this does not necessarily mean they hold the skills required to implement effective change.

A key managerial ability is to have a systems perspective of the organization. The McKinsey 7-S model introduced above is an example of a system perspective. A systems perspective allows managers to at least consider the role of each of the levers and barriers discussed in this section in implementing change. We discuss additional managerial skills related to organization change at the end of the chapter (page 511).

CULTURE

There are many aspects of culture that influence organizational members' willingness to change. As we discussed in chapter 12, culture is the characteristic of the organization that pervades every aspect of the organization: the shared values and beliefs of organizational members. Often, those values and beliefs deal with topics like change and organizational identity. Key aspects of culture include members' trust and the quality of communications. Trust is critical in organizations undergoing change. In the opening to this chapter we introduced Amy. One of Amy's reactions to change in her organization was she felt distrustful of future intentions of the organization's leaders. One study of the downsizing that occurred in the federal government in the 1980s and 1990s found that organizational members had to adjust to significant change in their beliefs about the organization. Up until the mid-1980s most employees felt that they had employment for life as part of their "psychological contract" with the government. When significant staff reductions were announced, it came as a shock to many employees because a pervasive aspect of the organization's culture was threatened. The result is that many people now view working for the federal government differently than they did before (Readdy and Mero, 1998).

THE TEAM AND TEAM BUILDING

Effective change often requires members to view themselves as a part of a team. As discussed in chapters 8 and 9, team skills are not common to individuals and often need to be the focus of training. Important in the process of change is developing cooperation among team members. There is significant evidence that participative management and change implementation using groups or teams is a critical lever to achieving successful organizational change – specifically because it affects member commitment to the change (Kilmann, 1989).

In chapter 8 (page 222), we introduced you to Monarch Marking Systems. Monarch provides an example of how teams can be a critical barrier and lever to organizational change depending on how they are used. Monarch's employees initially viewed team participation as "another failed experiment in

EXERCISE

BARRIERS TO EFFECTIVE CHANGE

Here are two situations that introduce an organizational change initiative. On a piece of paper, list six barriers that are likely to exist to making these changes. How could you use the "leverage points" mentioned in this chapter to overcome those barriers?

Situation 1

This year, on your campus, the President has decided that the entire academic curriculum should be available as part of the university's distance learning program. The President has set a goal of having all courses available "on-line" within five years and wants the university to prepare for a decrease of "in-residence" students and an increase in "distance-learning" students. Consider resistance that may come from sources internal to the university (faculty, staff, students, etc.) and those external to the university (the local community, legislatures, alumni, other key constituents etc.).

Situation 2

As the CEO of a large manufacturing firm, you have decided to eliminate the production of one of your product lines (product A) that has been losing money for years. You would like to use the excess capability generated by the reduction to increase the production of two current products (products B and C) that have been more successful. Since your firm is organized by product, this would require all employees from product A to be moved into product B and C organizations. You are confident that you will be able to make the change with only minimal loss of jobs since most employees from product A can be transferred into the other two product divisions. Other reductions in the number of employees can come through early retirement or normal attrition.

leaders pretending they wanted employee input when they really didn't." However, when teams were implemented more effectively, Monarch saw significant improvements in productivity (Petzinger, 1997).

Stages of Successful Change

Successful change depends on moving through the key stages of the change process in a systematic manner. The first stage is the development of motivation to change among those who are initiating it and those who are implementing it (see figure 16.2). This is the unfreezing stage of change. Motivation to change depends on two basic questions:

1 Is it worthwhile to change?
2 Can the change be successfully carried out?

In determining whether it is worthwhile to change, a calculation, at least in a rough sort of way, must be made of the positive and negative outcomes associated with not changing relative to the outcomes associated with changing.

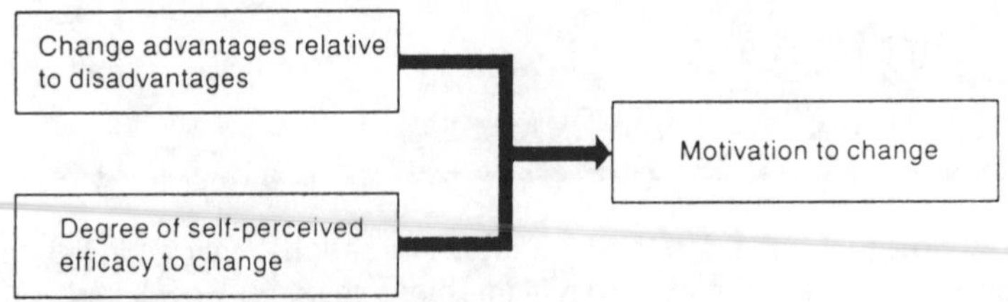

Fig 16.2: Determinants of motivation to change

Motivation to change also requires that those involved believe that it is possible to change and that a change effort will be followed by success. Increasing the motivation to change involves building self-efficacy, the degree to which an individual believes it is possible to achieve a particular performance level or behavioral standard (Bandura, 1982). Self-efficacy can stem from a variety of personal experiences. One source is someone's actual achievements. When a task is performed successfully, the person gains a sense of enactive mastery and will feel capable of performing that way again.

modeling
A type of learning in which people pattern their behavior after others

One way to facilitate self-efficacy is to structure the work setting to ensure that the individual has an opportunity to gain enactive mastery by performing successfully. Self-efficacy can also develop from vicarious learning, or **modeling** (see chapter 2). In organizational change programs, appropriate models should demonstrate the desired behaviors to the targets of change. Verbal persuasion and other types of social influence may contribute to a heightened sense of self-efficacy for change by convincing the change targets that they are capable of engaging in desired behaviors.

The second key stage, when sufficient motivation to change exists, is use of an appropriate change method; (see figure 16.3). This is the stage where transformation occurs. Not all change methods are equally effective. Techniques for knowledge change are different from those for changing skills. Methods for changing individual behavior may be completely ineffective for achieving change at the group level.

The third key stage in successful change is reinforcement of change. This is the refreezing process. New behaviors, working relationships, procedures, and so forth must result in rewarding positive, not negative, outcomes. Otherwise, the

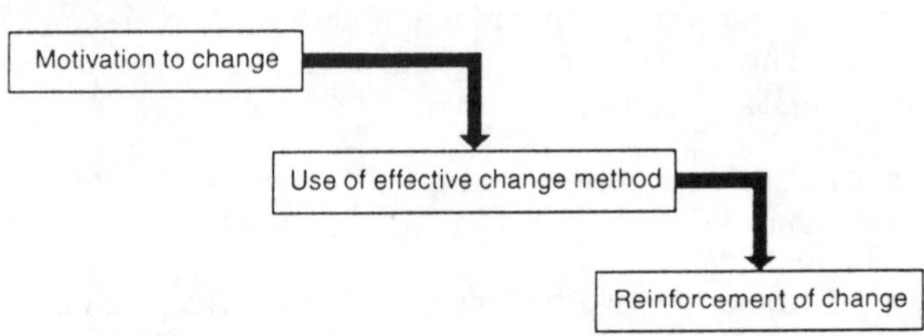

Fig 16.3: Key stages in effective change

individuals, groups, or organizations will revert to previous conditions or look for new ones.

Helping Individuals to Cope with Change

We would like to introduce a model of individual change that is useful to understanding individual reactions to change events. The concepts of trigger events and amended mindsets (Isabella, 1990, 1993) provide a more proactive model for managers to deal with the specific organizational changes. **Trigger events** are those unanticipated events in an organization's history that lead employees to take stock of their situation and interpret the short- and long-term implications of the changing context. As managers attempt to grapple with the significant but not well understood implications of employees' interpretation of events, it may be helpful to view any trigger event as unfolding over a period of time or stages. The resulting interpretation of the change event is called the **amended mindset**. This is a well-developed perceptual interpretation of the event.

trigger events Unanticipated events in an organization's history that lead employees to take stock of their situation and interpret the short- and long-term implications of the changing context

amended mindset The changing interpretation of change events that unfold over a period of time or stages

Within each stage of a change process which involves significant disruption of the work force, such as in an era of downsizing, managers can take several actions which could positively affect the organizational members' psychological response to a change environment. In the next section, we discuss each stage and propose proactive managerial actions to assist members in dealing with the change in a personal and organizational healthy manner.

Before the Change Event

From the perspective of a significant organizational change, trigger events compose four important time frames or stages. First is the pre-event stage that describes the time period when rumors about an impending change abound and complete information is not yet available. Within the pre-event stage is the appearance of rumors or pieces of information from various sources that can create anxiety within the work force. An individual mentally assembles each piece of information along with other bits of information in an attempt to draw meaning and increase their ability to predict the future. It is important to remember that this process of interpretation is a social one, where meanings are discussed among those affected and then jointly constructed. Pieces of information are shared and the input of everyone is considered as each employee copes with the uncertainty created by the event (Isabella, 1990).

Organizational leaders actively help employees to manage the assembly of these complex puzzles (Isabella, 1990). This can be accomplished by quickly, freely, and truthfully sharing information in a public forum and actively helping employees to interpret the surrounding events – maintaining open lines of communication throughout the organization. Managers need to be sure they are in the "communication loop" so they will hear and be able to respond to any rumor that surfaces. Carefully managing the sources of information is also critical. It seems unreasonable to ignore the fact that a rumor presented in the local media would not be the topic of discussion in the break room. Senior leaders typically

A QUESTION OF ETHICS: WHAT WOULD YOU DO?

Manuel Hernandez looked out the window and watched the people in the park across from his office enjoying the beautiful fall day. He wished he was outside enjoying the day as well. In fact, he wished he was anywhere except going into the meeting with his employees scheduled for 15 minutes from now. The meeting had been requested by the employee relations committee and was designed to address rumors that had been running rampant throughout the organization that the company was going to downsize employees to improve their competitiveness.

Manuel was aware of the rumors and had kept in close contact with his supervisor in the corporate office. Based on those discussions, he had been confident that the organization would only try to reduce the work force by freezing hiring, and allowing for normal voluntary attrition. Manuel had agreed to the meeting and had told the leader of the employee relations committee that he would answer their questions as best he could and that they would know "everything he knew." After the last phone call, however, Manuel wished he had not agreed to the meeting.

Manuel reflected on the call he had received from the corporate office telling him that a decision had been made to lay off 20 percent of the staff. While that news was bad enough, he had also been told that he could not announce the layoff until Friday, three days from now. The corporate office was worried about the implications of the announcement for shareholders, customers, and employees and wanted to delay the announcement until a formal plan for managing the announcement could be made. There were also many details about how the layoffs would be made that had not been worked out.

Now Manuel considered his options. He could cancel the meeting, but employee anxiety was very high and doing that would probably only make things worse. He could have the meeting and say that he was unaware of the company's plans. He reasoned that this was a partially true statement because many details of the plan still needed to be worked out. Finally, he could make the layoff announcement and ask employees not to discuss the information.

Manuel had worked to instill ethical behavior as an important value for the organization and now he faced an ethical dilemma. If he kept his commitment of telling employees "everything he knew," he would violate the trust of his boss. If he met with the employees and did not tell them about the layoffs, he would violate his commitment to openness. Manuel recognized the importance of trust in both his relationship with the corporate office and with his employees. He wished there was an easy answer to his dilemma, but he knew there was not one. If there is not an easy answer he wondered, is there an ethical one?

Managers often face dilemmas such as this. In managerial positions, you often know of information that you must keep in confidence. In this case, Manuel must consider that to violate the trust of either his superiors or subordinates could have long-term negative implications on those relationships. He needs to walk a careful line – a line walked by managers every day in organizations across the world.

- How would you have handled that situation?

Your authors recommend that Manuel has the employee meeting and tell employees that he has new information from the corporate office but that he is not in a position to discuss the information – that he is working to obtain complete information to share with them. He should assure them that as soon as he has the full information, he will meet with them and try to answer their questions. While the implications of this are sure to increase employee anxiety, it is critical that Manuel be open about the situation and be open with employees since the ground rules of their relationship have changed.

have better, but often slower, access to accurate information. As a result, a more efficient use of employee time would be for them to go to organizational leadership to receive information. However, this requires managers to be viewed as knowledgeable, reliable and approachable sources. Even if the information gathered has negative implications for the work force, it is critical for the long-term effectiveness of the organization for management to be viewed as a reliable and open source of information.

After the Change Event is Confirmed

The second stage is the **event confirmation stage**, the time period immediately surrounding an official organizational announcement that a change will occur (Isabella, 1990). This critical stage is when employees search for explanations for the change and attempt to understand the personal implications of the action. This stage begins when an official announcement or action confirms that the change will take place. While rumors continue to occur in this stage, employees will immediately begin to consider the personal implications of the change. If the change involves organizational restructuring for example, employees will consider their personal job security and implications of the event on their work environment (i.e. potential changes in colleagues, leadership, work rules or conditions). This is where employees draw from personal experience and the experiences of others to try to improve the predictability of the future. Making comparisons is a standard technique for dealing with the complexity of these events (Isabella, 1990). Individuals may contact their friends or family who have gone through similar experiences to try to understand the implications of the change. Again, the emphasis is to resolve the uncertainty caused by the change.

Managerial actions in this stage vary with the type of change and the setting or context of the change. One critical aspect is to manage the announcement of change. Again, communication is critical. Larger international organizations often include multiple work locations across the world. Management should expressly insure that all organizational members are informed as quickly as possible about everything that is known about the change. If managers are aware that employees are looking for comparisons to reduce uncertainty, they can provide examples of positive past experiences and rationale for why negative past experiences will be avoided. In one organization that had international offices around the world, the CEO had pre-positioned a video with leaders in the field offices of him personally announcing that the organization was going to be acquired by a larger organization. Managers in the field office had been thoroughly briefed on the action and were in a good position to answer employee questions and address concerns. The announcement was well orchestrated and presented to all employees at one time.

The third stage incorporates the time frame in which the actual event occurs and employees are forced to cope with changes in the pattern of events surrounding their work lives (Isabella, 1990). Depending on the significance of the change, employee responses to these events can vary significantly and include anger, cynicism and anxiety to resentment, resignation, retribution, and hope (O'Neill and Lenn, 1995).

In addition to the open communication needed, managers must manage employee perceptions of how critical decisions that relate to the change are made. Cynicism and feelings of helplessness occur and it appears that decision making about the change is a random process or one that employees are not involved in. High employee involvement in change processes is important, not just to enhance the quality of the decision but to influence employee commitment to the change that may occur from implementation of that decision.

Another important role of managers is to focus attention on the opportunities created by any organizational change. Putting change in a positive light, such as emphasizing the opportunity to eliminate redundant tasks and redesigning jobs and work flows to increase efficiency and create more enriching jobs is a critical orientation.

AFTER THE CHANGE

A final stage is the aftermath, the time period when organizational members assess the event and try to understand what they have learned based on their interpretation of the experience (Isabella, 1990). This is certainly the most critical time for the long-term health of the organization as people attempt to evaluate the events of the recent past. Important here is how individuals are thought to make sense of a series of events. Again, openness and honesty are critical in helping individuals to interpret these events. If employees have come to be confident that management will be open and honest with information, it is more likely that management can play a role in how these events will be interpreted.

One suggestion is to create events to help all organizational members evaluate the past. The establishment of groups chartered to study and draw conclusions is an important symbol of this process (Isabella, 1990). After the downsizing and restructuring within the federal government, many task forces and work groups were used to force all organizational elements to look forward to the future – after the change. As Vice President, Al Gore realized the symbolic as well as actual value of this action developed the "reinventing government" theme and "went from agency to agency celebrating reinvention success stories, giving what he admits is 'overdue positive reinforcement to the good folks who are doing a terrific job'" (Shoop, 1994).

Implementing Change

With a basic understanding of the process of organizational change, we now conclude this chapter with a discussion of the methods used to implement change at different levels of the organization. We focus on three levels of change by considering change at the individual level, group, and organizational level.

METHODS OF INDIVIDUAL CHANGE

Many different approaches for individual change have been developed over the years. Indeed, programs for changing a person's health (mental and physical), habits (eating, alcohol consumption, and so on), and competencies for careers are a major industry in the USA. In organizations, common individual change programs include coaching and mentoring, individual counseling, and training. Training is also a method for group change and, for that reason, it is discussed in more detail later in this chapter; see page 504.

One informal type of training is **coaching**; another is **mentoring**. A mentor is an older and more experienced organization member who helps a younger, less experienced person in the organization learn to navigate in the world of work (Kram, 1985). This older person does not have to be the direct supervisor of the younger person. Some organizations have a more formal mentoring program in which mentors are assigned to protégés, but most mentoring arrangements are informal and carried out so as to meet the needs of the two parties (Beer, 1976, 1980; Carroll et al., 1988). Mentoring can be of special value to those who are often excluded from organizational networks, such as women and minorities. Through mentoring, they can obtain valuable information that they would not normally receive in addition to having a champion who can make their talents visible to upper ranks in the organizational hierarchy.

coaching
A superior provides advice and guidance on issues related to subordinates

mentoring
A change method where an older and more experienced organization member helps a younger and less experienced person in the organization to learn to navigate in the world of work

Coaches and mentors can help to cause change in the behavior of younger members of the organization by modeling desired behaviors. This is a method that also helps to perpetuate important aspects of the organization's culture. For example, if a desired organizational change was to introduce a more participative style of leadership, senior managers could effectively influence the behavior of mid-level managers by demonstrating those behaviors within their supervisory relationships.

Counseling is the core of employee assistance programs. These programs help employees to cope with many different types of problems including employee stress. Counseling is a problem-focused interaction process with the object of stimulating learning, growth, and changed behavior (Hunt, 1974). Outside the work setting, counseling is typically utilized for helping individuals to cope with emotional problems. In the work setting, it is usually directed at helping employees to cope with work-related issues, such as relationships with superiors, salary issues, and absenteeism. It has become more important recently in preparing people for career transitions such as retirement, in managing staff cutbacks or organizational restructuring.

counseling
A problem-focused interaction process; its object is learning, growth, and changed behavior

Counseling can have a shallow or a deep focus. That is, it can aim at obtaining some reasonably simple behavior changes, or it can be an approach to produce fundamental changes in the personality or to alleviate significant emotional difficulties. In this latter case, counseling is better called **psychotherapy**. Most organizational counseling programs are of the shallow type; though some firms have professionals available when necessary (Wagner and Hollenbeck, 1992). When a firm does wish to use managers as counselors, they should be restricted to dealing with work problems and trained so that they understand the counseling role, the scope of the problems they can handle, and their limitations in dealing with more serious mental health matters.

Counseling will work when it results in the individual wanting to change, if it builds the individual's confidence in his or her ability to change, when the counseling method is appropriate for the type of problem, and if the counselor provides reinforcement in the desired directions of change.

The research on the effectiveness of employee counseling shows that it can lead to changes and improvements. In one study, 80 percent of the employees who had undergone counseling reported that their situation had improved and 74 percent were content with the treatment received (Weissmann, 1975). In another, a group of frequently absent employees reduced its level of absenteeism after counseling (Skidmore et al., 1974).

METHODS OF GROUP CHANGE

Sometimes the focus is on changing groups. These groups may be intact organization units such as departments and project teams, or organizational level groups, such as first-line supervisors. Many of the specific approaches to developing groups and improving their performance have been discussed in chapters 8 and 9, such as managerial motivation strategies. Identification with others, cohesion, pressures toward conformity, social facilitation, and the strength of group norms combine with the subject matter of the training to produce change. Here we discuss the more generic types of group change processes.

TRAINING There are a number of different training methods that may be used individually or in combination to change knowledge, attitudes, or skills.

Diversity Issues: Action Plan for Change

Effective communication is a critical tool in effectively managing change. This communication is even more critical when that change affects a person of diversity. Here are some suggestions for improving difficult communications within a context of individual change (Mendleson and Mendelson, 1996).

1 *Build rapport and participate in "rituals"*
Key here is demonstrating respect for the practices of others and participating in routine rituals such as meals, celebratory events or other activities that will break down any barriers that may exist.
2 *Carefully discuss the change opportunity*
If the issue involves a change to resolve a problem, a discussion is needed to make sure everyone has the same definition of the problem and the methods of change are agreed to.
3 *Ask for a specific change in behavior*
Based on the success of the earlier steps, the manager should consider alternative tactics and consider alternatives and compromises offered by the employee.
4 *Outline the benefits of the change*
It is important to provide incentives for individual change. Key here is knowledge of the individual and his or her values. In a diverse work force, it would be a mistake to assume everyone is motivated by the same incentives.
5 *Develop an action plan*
This specifies who will take specific actions and determines timelines for implementation of the change. As differences are discovered, sensitivity to those differences is important.

- The lecture method involves one-way communication.
- The case study approach uses complex situations, usually written in the form of the cases at the end of each chapter in this book, which the students must analyze.
- The discussion method, in which everyone participates in the training effort, is widely used.
- Business games and simulations, which attempt to create actual business situations in which the participants make decisions and can see the effects of these decisions, are often used as well.
- In programmed instruction, trainees teach themselves at their own pace by following a prescribed sequence of exposure to concepts and information.
- Role playing, in which the participants act out an interpersonal simulation, is often used for skill development and attitude change.

There are a number of principles for conducting training (Wexley and Yukl, 1984). The first is ensuring trainability. Individuals must have sufficient ability and motivation. Second, an optimum training environment is important. Participants must be able to practice the new behaviors and skills. The material must be learned well enough in training so that it can be transferred, even under adverse conditions, to the work setting. It is very important to maximize the similarity between the work setting and the training setting to ensure the transfer of training. Third, participants should be given knowledge of the results of training. This makes the material meaningful, allows trainees to proceed at their own pace and takes individual differences into consideration.

One sure way to impact negatively an organizational change is to provide the training needed to make the change but fail to remove other barriers from the work environment. These barriers may include a supervisor who is reluctant to allow the trainee to apply new skills in the work place or the lack of available proper equipment to use.

TEAM BUILDING Team building focuses on any defined work group: "family" groups consisting of a boss and subordinates, a "colleague" group such as the regional sales managers of a company, or a project team with members from different specialized departments (Beckhard, 1969). **Team building** is a difficult and time-consuming process. Its effects may also take a long time to be realized.

team building
A form of planned organization change which focuses on the work team in the organizational setting; typically involves training methods designed to improve the interpersonal and working relationships of team members with the final objective of better organizational performance

Team-building efforts often begin with a self-examination. A consultant asks each group member: What can be done to increase the effectiveness of the operations of this team? What are the obstacles to achieving this? Answers are analyzed and then fed back to the team members. The feedback helps to motivate the group to change since problems that hinder group effectiveness are identified. These problems then can be converted into solutions by the group. Then the group sets goals to carry out these solutions. In the goal-setting approach to team building, participation in the group's decisions enhances commitment to problem solutions (Beer, 1980).

A particular type of team building, called **sensitivity training** or T-Groups, emphasizes improving the interpersonal competence of group members (Beer, 1980). Members are taught to share their feelings with one another, to communicate with others in a non-evaluative way, and to provide social support. This type of training is especially useful for organization family groups such as a project team or a department. The family group is more difficult to work with than, say, a group of strangers, because there is a greater threat to cooperation if the family group members have difficulties in training that might damage their personal relationships.

METHODS OF ORGANIZATIONAL CHANGE

organizational development (OD)
Attempts made to take a proactive rather than just a reactive approach to organizational change

Change efforts that focus on the whole organization fall into the broad category of **organizational development** (**OD**). They usually involve an attempt to change through an organization-wide program in which most workers, managers, and professionals participate. Organizational development is concerned with planned change. In other words, change is to be anticipated, planned, and consciously designed rather than approached in a crisis mode when a problem occurs. Often an attempt is made to produce different organizational structures and cultures to support any new systems or approaches introduced. This is because in organizational development, it is assumed that all organizational functioning involves a number of organizational components working together. To change any part of the system requires sensitivity to adjustments across the entire system as in the McKinsey 7-S model.

Organizational members who collaborate with change agents usually execute the change program. Change agents seek to enhance the capacity and motivation of those in the organization to learn, improve, and change through their own efforts in the future. They emphasize development through human growth and improvement. OD practitioners often have training in the behavioral sciences and so they emphasize diagnosis and the use of specific behavioral technologies in helping individuals, groups, or organizations to reach a more successful mode of functioning (Porras and Robertson, 1992).

action research
Occurs when organization members collaborate with outside experts in devising a new program to solve organizational problems

ORGANIZATIONAL ANALYSIS Organization-wide change programs often begin with some type of **action research** showing where and why a particular system is not working so well. **Survey feedback** is an action research method fairly widely used in organizational development. The survey feedback approach begins when an organization recognizes that it has problems. This provides the initial motivation to change, but organizational members still must have confidence that improvements can be realized from the program. A pilot program can provide such assurance by demonstrating in one part of the organization that a system change can be successfully implemented and can produce improvements.

An organizational needs analysis is usually done with a survey, using interviews or structured questionnaires, to identify what should be changed. The survey may reveal problems with performance, employee morale and absenteeism, or failure to achieve unit or organizational goals. The problems identified may also be perceptual or emotional. Once specific problems are identified,

Focus on Change: Who are the Changemasters?

Often, managers think they can intuitively choose those individuals who may be effective change agents. One recent research study carefully analyzed different agents of change and came up with some interesting conclusions.

1 Change agents were easily identified by their energy and their attitudes. Those attitudes included loyalty and respectful questioning of authority.
2 They were rarely individuals initially considered to be among the organization's superstars. They were generally more independent and reacted quickly to situations. Their changes were often not initially approved by their supervisors.
3 They were self-directed by a view that they should do what would benefit the organization and not just what was required by the job. They were more motivated by making a difference and not by promotion.
4 They acted with a sense of urgency and found ways to avoid the bureaucracy.
5 They worked within the context of the organization and were committed to organizational objectives.
6 They expected that they would be successful.
7 They focused their activities on achieving results and were less likely to emphasize teamwork. While they worked within the "system" and were sensitive to the needs of others, they often acted independently (Frohman, 1997).

different remedies may be initiated to change behaviors, perceptions, attitudes, or other unsatisfactory conditions.

ORGANIZATIONAL CHANGE METHODS Organizational development (OD) efforts may be designed and implemented using any of the change methods discussed in this chapter or in chapter 6. For example, team building, positive reinforcement programs, MBO, and HIO strategies have been implemented and been found to be effective in both public and private organizations. The important aspect of any of these approaches is that they systematically involve organizational members throughout the whole change process and that they are based on action research. For example, table 16.1 shows the steps in an action research change program carried out in a firm by external consultants. The external consultants formed a group made up of managers from the company's executive committee to work with them. This helped to ensure the credibility of the change efforts and the solutions that were developed. Two members of this group were designated as internal advisers to assist the consultants in designing approaches to study the problem and to help to implement the solution. Internal advisers are useful for their knowledge of the organization and its history. They can help to ensure that changes are compatible with the organization's culture, history, personnel, and existing practices. The external consultants then gathered data by interviews and structured questionnaires. These data were evaluated, summarized, and presented to the top management project group. But while the data were being collected, this group was trained with respect to various issues involved in the change. They were shown what existing research, theory, and practice suggested about the forces influencing the change effort. When they received the summarized survey feedback data about current problems, they then began developing solutions with the aid of the consultants.

REINFORCEMENT OF ORGANIZATIONAL CHANGES The final step in planned change is to follow up to ensure that the change has been effective. This follow up could take several years and many modifications may be made before a desirable level of effectiveness is achieved. In the survey research program described in table 16.1, there were four separate assessments over a six-year period and, each time, modifications in the system were made as a result.

Improved organizational results can also be reinforced through feedback showing that revenue costs, quality, and quantities are better than before. In the next section, we discuss specific ways to evaluate the organizational change. Once the feedback from this evaluation has been provided to the organization, change programs are then modified and the change process begins anew as shown in table 16.1.

EVALUATION OF ORGANIZATIONAL CHANGE PROGRAMS To change individuals, groups, or organizations takes time and money. There are also hidden costs, such as political issues that make change and improvement difficult when they are not resolved. For these reasons, it makes sense to try to determine whether the change program was effective.

Change programs can be evaluated in very sophisticated ways. These evaluations involve very complicated measurement techniques, statistics, and research designs. The manager can seek help from professionals when it is needed but can look at other factors as well. Managers consider a number of factors in judging the effectiveness of a change program and whether it was worthwhile (Beer, 1976). What is most critical and most important will depend on the organization's situation at the time. Those threatened with bankruptcy do not have the luxury of evaluating the effectiveness of a change by waiting to look at long-term performance improvements.

There are a number of difficult problems in evaluating change.

1 It is difficult to isolate the effects of the change. Suppose, for example, that team building is used to improve relationships between the research group and the manufacturing units and, while the training is being co ducted, a new manager is assigned to the research group. It may be difficult to separate the effects of the new manager from the effects of the training.
2 There is often a time lag between development and evaluation. Both external and internal forces could affect the measured results that would increase the problem of separating the training effects from the other forces. Timing also complicates other issues. For example, some positive changes

Table 16.1 An approach to organizational change

A. The organization or unit perceives it has problems with an existing system and calls in an external consultant.
B. Consultant forms a top management system task force (those with influence and motivation).
C. A group of internal advisers is formed (those with prestige and competence).
D. An organizational audit is conducted to determine current problems with the management system (e.g., communication, performance levels, motivation, intergroup relations, leadership).
E. Top management group and internal advisers are trained.
   1 Training for top management group focuses on broader aspects of program (e.g., long-range planning, policy implications, need for top management support).
   2 Training for internal advisers focuses on implementation issues (e.g., training, answering questions users pose, superior–subordinate goal setting).
F. Results of audit in D above are provided to both top management group and internal adviser group.
G. Group of internal advisers is aided in developing a program tailored to organizational needs.
H. Internal advisers develop the program and communicate to top management group.
I. Top management task force forwards suggestions for change to internal adviser group.
J. Internal adviser group finalizes program with aid of external consultant and obtains approval of top management group.
K. Pilot testing, revision, orientation, and training program are conducted.
L. Program is put into effect. External consultant monitors top management program sessions and activities. Internal advisers monitor middle- and lower-management program sessions and activities.
M. External consultant conducts organizational audit no longer than one year later and feeds results back to top management group and internal advisers.
N. Modifications in program are made by internal advisers and approved by top management.
O. Above steps are repeated at a later time.

may not occur quickly, but take more time. If the assessment is made before the effects take, an incorrect inference of no impact will be made.

3 It is often difficult to specify what to measure. For instance, while the ultimate goal of much training is improved economic performance, the training itself may focus on attitudes and group relationships with the assumption that improvements in them will increase profitability. In this case, assessing changes in profitability may be the wrong measure since it is not likely to be easy to tease out the effects of the training.
4 In complex OD programs, it is possible that several changes are introduced with several different methods. In this case, it is almost impossible to know which method, or combination of methods, produced effects when they occur.

However, there have been many studies on the effectiveness of change and development methods, and the results of this research has been evaluated with meta-analytic techniques. For example, training programs and goal-setting programs have stronger effects on productivity than most approaches (Guzzo et al., 1985). Large-scale OD interventions that involved redesigning work and implementing autonomous work groups were next most powerful (Guzzo et al., 1985). Another analysis showed that the use of self-directed work groups resulted in 38 percent more productivity than when they were not used (Beekun, 1989). The effects were also very durable. They persisted over several years, though they were much greater in the first two years following the intervention. These large-scale OD interventions were also much more effective in changing satisfaction and attitudes (Guzzo et al., 1985). The effects were also greater outside the USA.

Summary

Organizational change is a pervasive aspect of modern organizational life. There are numerous pressures from both the external and internal environments that lead to organizational change. From the external environment, there are pressures to change because of new regulations, new competition, ownership changes, and simply from organizational growth itself. Often, systems and personnel that were appropriate at one time are no longer appropriate. A major pressure for change also comes from dissatisfaction with present performance. Other change pressures stem from changes in the characteristics of people, changes in technologies or internal systems employed, or the personal objectives of powerful managers.

Change can be viewed as a process of unfreezing the status quo (altering the equilibrium), causing transformation, and then refreezing to make the change permanent. Using this model, we can see that factors within the organizational context need to be used to cause the organism to move from a state of equilibrium to a state of disequilibrium. Change can be implemented by considering the levers and barriers to change that exist within the organizational setting, the organization's structure and strategy, the management structure and their skills, the culture and the group.

There are many individual change methods. Counseling and mentoring are two important approaches. Training is used for both individual and group change. Over the years, a great deal of knowledge has been obtained on how to train effectively. Counseling programs can result in a number of positive outcomes, depending on individual needs in the particular situation.

Group change focuses on entire groups or organization units. In group training, the interdependencies among individuals in a group and the importance of any new behavior being reinforced and supported by other group members are recognized. Thus, the whole group is trained together so that the members can support one another in their efforts to change.

Many organization-wide change approaches focus on changing a particular system used throughout the entire organization, such as a performance appraisal system or an inventory system. One widely used approach is survey research, in which organization members collaborate with outside experts in devising a new program to solve organizational problems.

Change is easier if the organization has a climate or culture that is generally supportive of change. Successful changes require effective communication in which concerns and expectations flow easily up and down the organization. There should be a climate of trust in the organization, especially between workers and management, which will help them to cope with the risk, uncertainty, and fear that often accompanies organizational change.

Guide for Managers: Creating Dissatisfaction as a Change Strategy

At the beginning of this chapter, we discussed Lewin's model for organizational change that required unfreezing by disturbing the status quo prior to organization's attempting to cause a transformation by way of change. Another way to think of this is as a method of creating dissatisfaction among organizational members. If they are happy with the status quo, they are unlikely to be motivated to change. Creating dissatisfaction is an important aspect of managing change and here are some ideas for its creation (Spector, 1989).

SHARE COMPETITIVE INFORMATION

Managers often keep the organization's position relative to its competitors a secret. Employees are often unaware of important changes in the market that may effect the long-term health of the organization. As a result, they may view efforts by management to implement new changes as unimportant.

HIGHLIGHT SHORTCOMING IN INDIVIDUAL ON-THE-JOB BEHAVIORS

There is a tendency in organizations to cover for or not publicly discuss the implications of ineffective behavior. For example, when a supervisor knows that her subordinates are generally dissatisfied, she may avoid any systematic attempt by management to assess employee attitudes. This was the case in the consulting effort of one of the authors of this text. He visited an organization where employee opinion surveys were only reported at the ag-gre-gate level. These results were difficult to interpret because there was wide variance in the response but it was obvious that overall employee morale and satisfaction were low despite numerous interventions. The consultant convinced the organization's senior leaders to assess employee attitudes systematically and report them by department level. These results were also made available to everyone in the organization. This helped the organization to identify specific departments with lower morale. It also forced supervisors in those departments to specifically address the underlying issues.

OFFER MODELS THAT SUGGEST WHERE THE COMPANY IS HEADED AND HOW FAR IT IS FROM THAT GOAL

These models can include other successful organizations or perhaps even other successful units within the same organization. The goal is to provide a clear model of success and to demonstrate that the status quo of the organization falls short of "where they should be."

MANDATE DISSATISFACTION

One method of causing change is to inspire change from within the individual, which is the outcome of the previous three points. Quite different is to mandate that organization members must be dissatisfied with the status quo. Remember that the equilibrium state was only achieved over an extended period of time and so significant external force may be required to initiate the transformation process. Bert Spector who authored the article that outlines this checklist provides an excellent example.

> When Don Singer, the newly named chairman of Scranton steel, announced at an executive meeting what changes he considered necessary, one member of his management team objected. "You're talking about participative management – about collaborating with the union, information sharing, cooperative problem solving. But it won't be easy. There's a lot of history to overcome." Singer listened while the executive finished his cautionary speech. He then pointed his finger directly at the executive and said, "Things are going change around here. This is a way of life. And if things don't change", he added, "I won't be the first to go."

Key Concepts

STUDY QUESTIONS

1. What recent changes in the environment of the university have affected its operations?
   What responses are required from the modern university to react to these changes?
   Are all universities the same in terms of having to respond to such change pressures?
   What types of universities would be different?
2. We have indicated that an organization must change in response to its members just as members must change to adapt to the organization.
   What does this mean?
   Give some examples of how organizations must adapt to their members.
3. Everyone has been subject to training, both informal and formal, throughout life.
   List the types of training you have been subject to.
   Then indicate which of these types of training have been most effective in changing you.
   Why have these types of training been most effective?
4. Think of a time in the past when your efficacy for performing a particular task or activity was quite low as you perceived it at the time.
   Did this self-perceived efficacy change?
   In what direction?
   What happened to make it change?
5. For training to be effective, it should be reinforced.
   How is the training received in many college courses reinforced?
   What could colleges and universities do to reinforce more effectively any training they might carry out?
6. Change efforts directed at individuals, groups, or organizations may be effective in the short run but may not be in the long run.
   List some examples of change programs at the level of the individual, group, or organization that might be effective in the short run but not in the long run.
   List some examples of change programs that could be effective in the long run but not in the short run.
7. List two pieces of legislation passed by the US Congress that involved attempts to make changes in the functioning of our society.
   Indicate if you think these were fairly successful or fairly unsuccessful.
   What were some of the factors that had an impact on the success of these programs?
8. What societal problems that presently exist should be the subject of a change program?
   What type of program might work to correct this problem, given what we know about successful change?

Case

A Case of Resistance

Bob Thompson thought that the consultant's approach to managerial performance improvements made a lot of sense. Each manager would be ranked from best to worst on each of several key managerial abilities. These rankings were then to be given to the subordinate and his or her superior. Managers below the median or average would be asked to develop an action plan for themselves to improve on that particular ability. The consultant's program allowed for subordinate participation in change efforts as well as for a change program that was tailored to each individual manager.

The program was presented to higher management by the consultant and Bob Thompson, and they accepted it. It was then implemented throughout the organization. The managers themselves thought that the program made a lot of sense.

Trouble began shortly after the managers had all been ranked on key managerial abilities, and the results fed back to them. Managers receiving rankings that were lower than average reacted very negatively. They claimed that the rankings were in error and did not reflect their true abilities. Given this they saw no need to spend time in developing an action plan to improve these abilities. Bob Thompson wondered what went wrong with this program.

- What went wrong that accounts for the negative reaction by the managers?
- What are some strengths of the approach used by Thompson and the consultant?
- How would you improve on the objectives and methods to deal with this situation?

References

Bandura, A. 1982: Self-efficacy mechanism in human agency. *American Psychologist*, 37, 122–47.

Beckhard, R. B. 1969: *Organizational Development: Strategies and Models*. Reading, MA: Addison-Wesley.

Beekun, R. I. 1989: Assessing the effectiveness of sociotechnical interventions: Antidote or fad? *Human Relations*, 42(10), 877–97.

Beer, M. 1976: The technology of organization development. In M. D. Dunnette (ed.) *Handbook of Industrial and Organizational Psychology*, Chicago: Rand McNally, 937–93.

Beer, M. 1980: *Organization Change and Development: A Systems View*. Santa Monica, CA: Goodyear Publishing.

Carroll, S. J., Olian, J. D. and Giannantonio, C. 1988: Mentor reactions to protégés: An experiment with managers. *Best Papers Proceedings of the Academy of Management, annual meetings*, Anaheim, CA, 273–76.

Fitzgerald-Turner, B. 1997: Myths of expatriate life. *HR Magazine*, 42(b), June, 65–71.

Frohman, A. L. 1997: Igniting organizational change from below: The power of personal initiative. *Organizational Dynamics*, 25(3), Winter, 39–54.

Guzzo, R. A., Jenne, R. D. and Katzell, R. A. 1985: The effects of psychologically based intervention programs on worker productivity: A meta-analysis. *Personnel Psychology*, 38, 275–91.

Hunt, R. G. 1974: *Interpersonal Strategies for System Management: Applications of Counseling and Participative Principles*. Monterey, CA: Brooks. Cole.

Isabella, L. A. 1990: Evolving interpretations as a change unfolds: How managers construe key organizational events. *Academy of Management Journal*, 22(1), 7–41.

Isabella, L. A. 1993: Managing the challenges of trigger events: The mindsets governing adaptation to change. In T. D. Jick (ed.) *Managing Change*, Burr Ridge, IL: Irwin, 18–29.

Kilmann, R. H. 1984: *Beyond the Quick Fix*. San Francisco: Jossey-Bass.

Kilmann, R. H. 1989: A completely integrated program for creating and maintaining organizational success. *Organizational Dynamics*, Summer, 5–19.

Kilmann, R. H., Colman, T. J. and Associates 1988: *Corporate Transformation*. San Francisco: Jossey-Bass.

Kram, K. E. 1985: *Mentoring at Work: Developmental Relationships in Organizational Life*. Glenview, IL: Scott, Foresman.

Lewin, K. 1951: *Field Theory in Social Science*. New York: Harper & Row.

Mendleson, J. L. and Mendelson, C. D. 1996: Workplace diversity: An action plan for difficult communication. *HR Magazine*, 41(10), October, 118–24.

O'Brien, T. L. 1998: 2,250 layoffs set at Chase, or 3% of staff. *The New York Times*, March 18.

O'Connell, S. E. 1998: The virtual workplace moves at warp speed. *HR Magazine*, March.

O'Neill, H. M. and Lenn, D. J. 1995: Voices of survivors: Words that downsizing CEOs should hear. *Academy of Management Executive*, 9(4), 23–34.

Pascale, R. T. and Athos, G. 1981: *The Art of Japanese Management*. Boston: Little, Brown.

Peters, T. J. and Waterman, R. H. 1982: *In Search of Excellence*. New York: Harper & Row.

Petzinger, T. 1997: The Front Lines. *The Wall Street Journal*. October 17. New York: Dow Jones & Company.

Porras, J. I. and Robertson, P. J. 1992: Organizational development: Theory, practice, and research. In M. D. Dunnette and L. M. Hough (eds) *Handbook of Industrial and Organizational Psychology*. Palo Alto: Consulting Psychologists Press Inc., 823–95.

Readdy, A. R. and Mero, N. P. 1998: *Dealing with angst in the ranks: Managerial perspectives on downsizing within the federal government*. Unpublished working paper.

Schellhardt, T. D. 1996: Company memo to stressed out employees: "Deal with it". *The Wall Street Journal*, October 2, B1.

Shoop, T. 1994: True believer. *Government Executive*, September, 16–23.

Skidmore, R. A., Balsam, D. and Jones, O. F. 1974: Social work practices in industry. *Social Work*, 3, 280–6.

Spector, B. A. 1989: From bogged down to fired up: Inspiring organizational change. *Sloan Management Review*, Summer.

Stewart, T. A. 1992: Brace for Japan's hot new strategy. *Fortune*, 126(6), 63–74.

Wagner, J. A. III and Hollenbeck, J. R. 1992: *Management of Organizational Behavior*. Englewood Cliffs, NJ: Prentice Hall.

Wall Street Journal 1998: Unemployment remains at low level. *The Wall Street Journal*, January 12.

Weissman, A. 1975: A social service strategy in industry. *Social Work*, 5, 401–403.

Wexley, K. N. and Yukl, G. A. 1984: *Organizational Behavior and Personnel Psychology*. Homewood, IL: Richard D. Irwin.

Glossary

ability The capacity to carry out a set of interrelated behavioral, or mental, sequences to produce a result

accommodating Giving in to the wishes of another person

achievement motive An internal drive state of the individual that reflects the extent to which success is important and valued

achievement-oriented leadership A style in which leaders set challenging work goals for their work groups

achievement–power theory A motivational model, also used for leadership theory, that is based upon the relative importance of achievement needs, needs for power, and affiliation needs to the individual

action research Occurs when organization members collaborate with outside experts in devising a new program to solve organizational problems

administrative decision-making model A model which attempts to provide a more accurate picture of how managers deal with routine and nonroutine problems

administrative theory An approach to management that is primarily concerned with understanding the basic task of management and of developing guidelines, or principles, on how to manage effectively

affective commitment A strong identity or connection with the organization because it stands for what the person stands for

affective component The positive or negative emotional tone toward the object of the attitude

agreeableness A characteristic in which a person tends to be more tolerant, trusting, generous, warm, kind, good-natured, and is less likely to be aggressive, rude and thoughtless

alarm reaction A reaction from a person experiencing a stressor that causes physiological changes that warn the body that it is under pressure

alienation A type of personal involvement with another or with an organization in which one party wants to escape from the relationship

amended mindset The changing interpretation of change events that unfold over a period of time or stages

antecedent conditions of conflict The conditions that cause or precede a conflict episode

arbitration A third-party approach to conflict resolution, where arbitrators usually make decisions that bind both parties; *see also* mediation

attitude cluster A set, or group, of attitudes consistent with each other, as well as with the specific beliefs, values, and cognitions for each specific attitude in the cluster

attitude object The dimension of an attitude that is the identifiable object to which it is directed

attitude surveys Data collection techniques conducted to assess attitudes and serve as a source of management feedback

attitudes Predispositions or tendencies to react favorably or unfavorably to the world around us, reflecting a person's likes and dislikes, his or her affinities and aversions toward any identifiable aspect of their environment

attraction-selection-attrition cycle People are attracted to and select organizational situations they prefer to enter; upon entry into an organization, they make the situation what it is; as similar people become attracted, and as dissimilar people leave, the organization becomes more homogeneous

attribution theory An approach to understanding how and why people attribute causes to their own and other people's behavior

authoritarian personality A personality type in which the person believes in obedience and respect for authority and that the strong should lead the weak; an excessive concern for power based on prejudices about people

authority The right of decision and control a person has to perform tasks and to meet assigned responsibilities

autocratic leadership The leader makes all decisions and allows the subordinates no influence in the decision-making process

automatic information processing The recognition of some key information, or stimuli, that causes recall of schemas or categories into which that particular information fits, leading our judgment to be biased toward general characteristics of that category

autonomy The level of freedom an individual or team has to do their job

avoidance learning In learning, when an aversive event that follows a behavior is terminated, which increases the frequency of that behavior

avoidant culture A culture in which top management seeks to avoid change; they are passive and purposeless; change is resisted because it may threaten the current organizational values and power structure; the desire of the management to retain control results in little activity, low self-confidence, high anxiety, and an extremely conseruative culture

avoiding Withdrawing from a conflict situation or behaving in a way that ignores or denies the situation

bargaining When one person seeks to influence another through the exchange of benefits or favors

basic organizational types A classification of organizations that reflects different things about the nature of power and control, how authority is distributed, and the degree of flexibility required to accommodate the environment

behavior shaping Involves reinforcing small increments or changes in behavior that are in the direction of desired behavior until a final desired result is achieved

behavioral approaches to leadership Theories and models of leadership that are based on the idea that leader behaviors are related to effectiveness

beliefs Thoughts and ideas about objects or events, not necessarily favorable or unfavorable

belonging needs A desire for love, affection, and belonging; the need to interact with others and have some social acceptance and approval

bounded discretion Self imposed moral and ethical limits we put on our decisions

bounded rationality A theory which proposes that decision makers are limited in their ability to be rational because of limits of human abilities, information, money, and time

brainstorming A technique of idea generation in decision making that requires we let our minds run free and avoid evaluating what we say or think

bureaucracy A form of organization that uses rules and procedures to govern the job behavior of organizational members

bureaucratic culture An organizational culture in which there is more concern with form over substance, that is with the rules of working together than with effective performance

calculative involvement A dependence relationship where both parties make an assessment of the costs and benefits of maintaining the relationship

capacity An individual's ability to solve problems, make judgments, and generally work harder

career The individually perceived sequence of attitudes and behaviors associated with work-related experiences and activities over a person's life

career adaptability The individual's willingness and capacity to make changes in the occupation and/or the work setting so as to maintain his or her own standards of career progress

career attitudes Attitudes about the work itself, where one works, the level of achievement, and the relationship between work and other parts of a person's life

career establishment stage A period, typically from the early thirties to the mid-forties, during which a person becomes established in a career

career exploration stage The period, typically before the twenties in which an individual acquires work values

career identity That particular facet of a person's identity related to occupational activities

career novice stage An early phase of work socialization during which the employee begins to develop some specific competence, experiences some degree of occupational socialization, and makes choices about their first place of work

centralization The degree to which authority and power are concentrated at the higher organizational levels; *see also* decentralization

ceremonials A system of several related rites connected with a specific occasion or event *charismatic culture* An organizational culture in which the emphasis on individualism is exaggerated, particularly at the top level

charismatic power Power that occurs when individuals are susceptible to influence because they identify with another person

classical conditioning Model of learning in which a stimulus that causes a reflexive response is paired with another stimulus presented close in time; eventually the second stimulus triggers the reflexive response

closure, principle of The need for a relatively complete conception, or idea, about things

coaching A superior provides advice and guidance on issues related to subordinates

coalition formation When two or more parties merge their interests

coercive power Power based on the use, or potential use, of punishment to extract compliance

cognitive appraisal The way a person assesses the significance of the various aspects of the environment

cognitive complexity The ability to make sense out of complicated and ambiguous situations

cognitive dimension of attitude The dimension of an attitude that reflects the positive or negative perceptions that are associated with the object

cognitive dissonance A condition that exists when a person experiences a discrepancy among behavior, attitudes, beliefs, or thoughts

Dissonance motivates behavior to reduce the condition. Cognitive dissonance theory is based on the idea that people need to experience consistency, or consonance, between their behavior and attitudes, beliefs or thoughts (cognitions)

cognitive resource theory A leadership theory that integrates a set of trait-like dimensions, called cognitive resources, into Fiedler's contingency model

cognitive restructuring The identification of positive and negative self thoughts and statements, and substitution of positive ones for the negative ones

cohesion The degree to which members of a group are attracted to one another and to group membership

collaborating A willingness to accept the other party's needs, while asserting your own

collection Any group or aggregate of people that do not interact or influence one another

commitment A strong, positive involvement in a dependence relationship

compartmentalization A psychological condition in which one holds contradictory attitudes and beliefs but is able to place them in separate compartments and not connect them

competing Pursuing your own wishes at the expense of the other party

competition Team members showing more concern with their own welfare, sometimes at the expense of others

complex environment A relevant environment that contains many different sectors

complexity, organizational The number of different activities, functions, jobs, and number of levels in the organization

compromising Give-and-take based on the belief that people cannot always have their way, and trying to find a middle ground they can live with

compulsive managers Managers who have high needs for control, view things in terms of domination and submission, and focus on specific, often trivial details

conflict A disagreement, the presence of tension, or some other difficulty between two or more parties

conflict management Strategies in which managers or others take an active role and intervene in the conflict episode

conflict reduction rites Rites intended to reduce or avoid conflict in an organization

conformity The tendency to pattern one's beliefs or behavior after others'; involves direct influence and requires that the person would not act similarly when alone

confrontation techniques Techniques in conflict management that call for the parties in conflict to face each other on the issues, but to do so constructively and peacefully so as to find mutually acceptable and longer lasting solutions

conscientiousness A characteristic or trait in which people are responsible, dependable, persistent, punctual, hard working, and oriented toward work

consideration The extent to which a leader is likely to have job relationships characterized by mutual trust, respect for subordinates' ideas, and concern for their feelings

consistency, principle of The principle that a person's attitudes and perceptions will be congruent with other attitudes, perceptions, and beliefs

content theories of motivation Theories of motivation that emphasize the reasons for individual behavior

contextual performance dimension The dimension of performance that is what one is contributing to the effectiveness of the organization or others in it, in ways other than just your designated work tasks

contingency theories of leadership Theories of leadership that systematically account for how situational factors might result in different relationships between what leaders do and their effectiveness

contingency theory of organization A theory of organization based on the concept that the organization structure and the management approach must be tailored to the situation

continuance commitment An organizational commitment to stay with an organization because one cannot afford to leave

continuous reinforcement schedule Reinforcement, every time a behavior occurs

contrast effect Cues that stand out against their background being more likely to be perceived

controlled information processing Pausing and reflecting on the situation to try to identify both the situational forces and personal causes of behavior before making a judgment about cause/effect relationships

controlling The management function that ensures that activities, when carried out, conform to plans so that objectives are achieved

cooperation Giving support to others, and contributing time and effort in situations where people jointly work together toward some end

cooptation The process of bringing representatives of other groups into the power structure

coping strategies The way a person responds to stress

core job dimensions The core job dimensions in the Job Characteristics approach: skill variety, task identity, task significance, autonomy and feedback

counseling A problem-focused interaction process; its object is learning, growth, and changed behavior

country clusters Groups of countries that share somewhat similar modal personalities, language, geography, and religion

critical psychological states In the job characteristics approach, mental states necessary for the work motivation: meaningfulness of work; experience and responsibility for outcomes; and knowledge of results

cross training Training workers to learn the various skills necessary to perform a wide range of jobs, usually in their unit

cultural metaphors Situations, events, or circumstances that occur in a culture and that capture and clarify its essential elements

culture Patterned ways of thinking, feeling, and reacting acquired and transmitted mainly through socialization and by symbols that constitute the distinct achievements of human groups

decentralization The degree to which power and authority are distributed vertically in an organization; *see also* centralization

decision control The amount of influence you have in the decision-making process

decisional dissonance Cognitive dissonance that is experienced before a decision is made and possibly reduced as a way to justify the decision

degradation rites Rites that surround the removal of someone from a position or an organization

department A distinct area over which a manager has authority for the performance of specific activities

dependence Occurs when one party or both have a need that can be satisfied by the other

dependent variables Those factors in management or research that are treated as outcomes of other factors or events, and are not directly manipulable; *see also* independent variables

depressive personality A person with strong needs for affection and support from others who feels unable to act on and change the course of events

detached personality Managers who have a strong sense of disengagement from others and of not being connected to the environment

directive leadership The style in which the leader gives guidance and direction to subordinates about job requirements

disconfirmed expectations Cognitive dissonance that arises from perceptions of reality not meeting the person's expectations

distress Stress responses that weaken a person's physical and psychological capacity to cope with environmental stressors

distributive justice The degree to which persons believe that they are treated fairly and equitably with respect to work outcomes, or how much they put into work and how much they gain from it

division of labor The way that work in organizations is subdivided and assigned to individuals as a job

dominant coalition The group in an organization that wields the most control and power and whose values are reflected in the organizational culture

dramatic managers Managers with feelings of grandiosity, a strong need for attention from others, and who try to draw attention to themselves, often seeking stimulation and excitement, but lacking self-discipline

dual careers A situation where both husband and wife pursue work careers

dyads Groups of two people

effort–performance expectancy From expectancy theory of motivation, the person's belief about the level of effort put forth and the resulting performance that it will lead to

emotional stability High emotional stability people tend to be less neurotic, less emotional, less tense, less insecure, have low anxiety levels, are less easily upset, less suspicious and are high in self-confidence

employee-centered leadership A style in which the leader is concerned about subordinates' feelings and attempts to create an atmosphere of mutual trust and respect

empowerment The idea that workers should be able to make more decisions about the work that they do, extending these decisions from the task itself to other areas such as selection and discipline of co-workers

enhancement rites Rites that increase the status or position of a person after they are in an organization

equity theory A motivation theory based on the idea that people are motivated to maintain fair relationships with others and to rectify unfair relationships by making them fair

ERG theory A modification to needs theory; three basic needs: existence needs, relatedness needs, and growth needs

escalation of commitment Occurs when managers stick with a decision they made even when it appears to be a bad decision

esteem needs A human need to be respected by others and to have a positive self-image

ethical performance dimension The dimension of performance that focuses on what is the right thing to do

eustress A positive, healthy, and developmental stress response that may lead to better performance and a more adjusted personality

evaluation distortion A condition that occurs when cohesive groups tend to overevaluate their own behavior and accomplishments and to underevaluate outside groups

exhaustion stage The last stage in a person's reaction to stress, in which the person simply wears out

existence needs Needs that encompass psychological and security needs for material things

expectancy A concept in expectancy theory of motivation that a person may do something because he or she believes that the effort made will yield results that the person desires; an individual's estimate, or judgment, of the likelihood that some outcome (or event) will occur

expectancy theory A motivation theory in which the basic idea is that individuals will put forth effort to do those things that will lead to the results (outcomes) they desire; a rational approach to motivation

experienced responsibility for outcome The belief that the person is personally accountable for the results of his or her work

expert career path A career path built on personal competencies or the development of a profession in which the person invests heavily in acquiring a particular skill and then spends most of his or her working time practicing that skill

expert power Power based on a person having valued skill or knowledge in a particular area

expressive meanings The psychological and sociological meaning to members of the various manifestations of culture, e.g. socialization strategies, ideologies, myths, and symbols

external locus of control A belief by persons that they have little influence over the environment and that what happens to them is a matter of luck, fate or due to the actions of others

extinction The cessation of a previously established reinforcer that is maintaining a behavior; the likelihood of behavior decreasing as a result of a lack of reinforcement of the behavior

extrinsic rewards Rewards, such as pay, advancement, and fringe benefits that are administered by someone else to a person

extroversion A trait characterized by a tendency to be sociable, liking to be with others, and being energetic and forceful

feedback The information that a person receives about the results of his or her effort or performance; how their performance compares with some previously developed standard

first impressions Impressions of others, formed early in a relationship; usually lasting impressions

fixed-interval reinforcement schedule A partial reinforcement schedule in which a response is reinforced after a fixed amount of time has elapsed

fixed-ratio reinforcement schedule A partial reinforcement schedule in which a certain number of responses are necessary to produce a consequence

flat organizations An organization with a large span of control with more horizontal dispersion of authority; *see also* lean organization

flexibility The characterisitic of being relatively adaptive to change, somewhat open and responsive toward others

formal groups Groups, such as project teams, that are designed into and make up the formal organization structure

formal organization A configuration of major subunits usually called divisions or departments

formalization The existence of written and institutionalized rules, policies, and procedures in organizations

forming An initial stage of group development in which the group becomes organized; members seek to define the purposes of the group and begin to establish its activities and priorities

functional groups Groups comprised of individuals who accomplish a similar task within the organizational structure

functional organization Activities assigned to major departments are similar; the production activities will be in one unit, marketing in another, and so on

fundamental attribution error A tendency to attribute causes of behavior to the internal characteristics or motives of another rather than to the situation

gainsharing Compensation approach in which employees receive bonuses or other forms of additional pay based on cost savings or profitability increases which occur as a result of the employees' contribution of ideas or more productive work effort

garbage can model Decision-making model for complex organizations; based on the flow of people, problems, solutions, and opportunities

goal emphasis Leader behavior that stimulates enthusiasm for meeting the group's goals or achieving excellent performance

goal-setting theory A motivation theory in which performance is predicted to be caused by a person's intention to perform (or goals)

Good Enough Theory of Promotion A theory based on the assumption that a person's attitudes, values, and beliefs enter into advancement decisions, and that if those beliefs are consistent with the individual or group making promotion decisions, that person has a better chance of advancement than if they were not

group Two or more people who interact and are dependent upon each other to achieve some common objective

group effectiveness A measure of group performance

group performance environment The combined effects of industry, organization, and group factors that form the unique context within which the group operates

group processes Within-group activities and communications that also affect group effectiveness

group structure The roles and relationships among the members and to the forces that maintain the group's organization

groupthink Occurs when a group allows the need for consensus and cohesiveness to be more important than making the best possible decision

growth need strength The extent to which a person desires to advance, to be in a challenging position, and to achieve generally

halo effect A judgment tendency in which one or a few characteristics of an individual affects the evaluation of them on other characteristics; can be positive or negative

hardiness A psychological condition of how much a person feels in control, less alienated from themselves, their sense of personal values and goals, confidence of their own ability and orientation toward challenge and adventure

hierarchical subcultures Subcultures that exist at different organizational levels and are visible in the differences in symbols, status, authority, and power between levels

hierarchy of needs Hypothesis that human needs are arranged in a hierarchy from lower order (safety and physiological needs) to higher order needs (belonging, self esteem, and self actualization)

high involvement organizations (HIOs) A very broad motivational strategy that promotes employee motivation in the work place and improves the effectiveness of the organization by changing the adversarial relationship between workers and managers that dominates many firms and replacing it with a cooperative approach

high LPC leader A leader who has favorable views of the person they least like to work with; *see also* low LPC leader

Hofstede model of culture A model of national culture that profiles the modal personality on five different dimensions that are the basis of attitudes and behaviors, organization practices, and social practices

horizontal distribution of authority The span of control that occurs through decisions that are made in the departmentalization process

horizontal job loading Increasing the job requirements of a person by adding tasks or other activities from the same organizational level; *see also* vertical loading

human relations perspective An early historical perspective on organizational behavior that emphasized the personal and social aspects of employee satisfaction and productivity

hygiene factors Factors in two-factor theory of motivation that create dissatisfaction if they are not present; if added to a job setting, dissatisfaction is reduced

hypotheses Conditional predictions about the relationship between concepts or variables that state how the concepts in a theory go together; the basis for research efforts to test and refine the theory

ideology A relatively coherent set of beliefs that binds a group and explains its world in cause–effect relations

implicit personality theory A tendency to link personality characteristics of others into a pattern

independent variables Those factors that can be manipulated by managers or researchers in dealing with or studying organizational behavior; *see also* dependent variables

indifferent orientation A personal orientation toward work that reflects the belief that work is not a critical part of life

individualism–collectivism A dimension of culture that is the degree to which those in a society prefer individual action to collective action

industrial psychology A field of research and application that focuses on both human and physical resources in the workplace; traditionally a study of selection, performance appraisal, work methods, and group behavior

influence A process by which the behavior or characteristics of people affect the behavior or characteristics of others; operational in all types of human interaction and interdependence

informal groups Groups in an organization that arise out of individual needs and the attraction of people to one another; membership is usually voluntary and based on common values and interests

initiating structure The extent to which a leader is likely to define and structure his or her role and those of subordinates toward goal achievement

instrumental learning *see* reinforcement theories

instrumental meanings The ways that the values and beliefs of the dominant coalition are reflected in what the organization can do (such as its products and services) and how it does it (such as the nature of work relationships, and work processes)

insufficient justification A condition that fosters cognitive dissonance and blocks its reduction when a person lacks a good reason to act against his or her beliefs or attitudes

integration The process of regrouping and relinking system activities into departments in an organization

integration rites Rites that facilitate and increase the interaction of organization members to make working together easier

intended results The outcomes of influence attempts that are desired by the party that exerted the influence

intensity effect Particularly strong, or extreme, cues being more likely to be perceived than smaller ones

interaction facilitation Behavior that encourages members of the group to develop close, mutually satisfying relationships

interactional justice Your perception about whether the decision that affects you and the decision-making process are fully explained to you and whether you are treated with respect and dignity during the decision process

interdependence A measure of the amount of coordination with or approval from others, the team need to complete their assigned tasks

internal locus of control A belief by persons that they can influence their environment, that what they do and how they do it determines what they attain

internal work motivation The level of motivation from the work itself, or the person's own desire, rather than from external factors such as pay and supervision

intersender role conflict Occurs when two different individuals place incompatible demands on a person

intrasender role conflict The inconsistent expectations that one faces from a single person

intrinsic rewards Feelings of growth and status a person has as a result of doing a good job; self-administered by the person

iron law of power The greater the discrepancies in power between the influencer and the target, the higher probability of assertive behavior

job characteristics approach A theory of motivation based on the concept that it is the properties of the work, the core job dimensions, that affect its motivational capacity

job enrichment approach A work design approach in which the activities of a person in a job are changed so that the person does more different things as opposed to a few routine activities, has some autonomy about how to do them, and has responsibility for quality of performance

job satisfaction The attitude toward work in general, or to specific facets of the work

knowledge of results Information that allows a person to make an assessment about the adequacy or inadequacy of work performance

laissez-faire leadership Style of leadership in which supervisors allow their group to have complete freedom in making decisions

leader motive pattern A configuration of personality dimensions that consists of higher power needs, moderate affiliation needs and high power inhibition

leader–member relations The trust a group has in the leader and how well the leader is liked

leader orientation An orientation that is a function of leader's needs and personality, determined by how you view the person you least like to work with

leadership Interpersonal influence – directed toward achieving organization objectives – that occurs when one person is able to obtain compliance from someone else because of the relationship between the two

leadership substitutes The subordinate, the task, and the organization; they, not the action of the leader, contribute to success or failure

lean organization An organization in which fewer people are required to produce the same or more output due to the use of computers and downsizing

learning A relatively permanent change in behavior, or potential for behavior, that is traceable to a person's experience or to practice

legitimate authority Refers to whether the person who is the subject of influence believes that it is right and proper for another to exert influence or attempt to exert it

linear career path The career structure associated with long-term work in a large, bureaucratic organization with a tall pyramid structure where advancement involves a series of upward moves in the organization until you reach your career limit

locus of control The degree to which individuals feel that they are controlled by themselves or mainly by external forces

long- versus short-term patterns of thought The dimension of culture that reflects whether the dominant view about the future is a long-term or a short-term perspective

low LPC leader A leader who is more oriented toward the task; personal relationships tend to have secondary importance; *see also* high LPC leader

LPC scale Least-preferred co-worker scale, from Fiedler's theory of leadership, measures whether the person the leader least likes to work with is viewed in a positive or negative way and the degree of the sentiment

Machiavellianism A personality type which attempts to take advantage of others, seeks to form alliances with people in power to help serve their own goals, and might lie, deceive, or compromise morality, believing that ends justify the means

management by objectives (MBO) A process in which the superior and subordinate, together, establish objectives for the subordinate

management functions Those activities that all executives perform in whole or part that make up the managerial job, such as planning, organizing, and controlling

managerial motivation strategies Attempts to act on the human factors, technological factors, and organizational structural factors in ways that increase the person's motivation to perform, so that they exert more effort and achieve a higher level of performance

manifest conflict A stage of conflict that occurs when parties that have perceived a conflict behave in a way that makes the conflict observable

manifestations of organizational culture The specific form of organizational elements such as selection and socialization, ideologies and myths, and symbols that reflect the values and beliefs of the dominant organization coalition

market environment The consumers of the output of organizations

market-dominated mixed (MDM) organization An organization that exists in an environment that has a stable technological sector, but a volatile market sector

masculinity–femininity A dimension of culture that reflects the degree to which a culture strongly differentiates between typically "male" roles, which have a strong component of assertiveness, and "female" roles, which are characterized by nurturance

matrix organization An organization in which product or project groups are served by and interact with specialist groups

meaningfulness of work The belief that work counts for something important either to the person or to someone else

mechanistic organization An organization with a very clear definition of responsibility and authority; its management structure is rigid and hierarchical

mediation The use of third-party assistance to help arrive at a solution to conflict; *see also* arbitration

mentoring A change method where an older and more experienced organization member helps a younger and less experienced person in the organization to learn to navigate in the world of work

modal organizational personality A representation of organizational culture – shows the degree of homogeneity and strength of the dominant personality orientations in an organization

modeling A type of learning in which people pattern their behavior after others; *see also* social learning theory

motivation An internal mental state of an individual that causes behavior; also defined as a management activity, or something that a manager does to induce others to act in a way to produce the results required organizationally

motivators Factors in the two-factor theory of motivation that are related to high satisfaction and willingness to work harder. When they are present, these job factors may induce more effort, but if they are absent, it will not produce dissatisfaction

multi-focal view of organizational commitment The view that there are several facets of work and the different levels of identification, or orientation, toward each

Myers–Briggs dimensions A number of personality types, based on Jungian personality theory, which are derived from preferences people have for approaching problems and work

myth A dramatic narrative of imagined events, usually to explain origins or transformations of something; an unquestioned belief about the benefits of techniques and behaviors not supported by fact

nature–nurture argument A continuing debate about the role of heredity or the effects of socialization on personality and behavior

needs When a person senses a discrepancy between a present (or future) condition, and some desired state that leads the person to feel tension and act to reduce it

needs theories Motivation or personality theories focusing on needs, which are the internal state of a person that reflects a deprivation or desire he or she has

negative affectivity The tendency to be sad, to focus on failure and for a person to view themselves in negative ways

negative reinforcement Occurs when an undesirable consequence is removed and the behavior is more likely to occur again

negotiation The process of compromise and bargaining to arrive at a solution to conflict

network organization Groups of firms in the relevant organizational environment with which the focal organization does business in which the relationships are based on complementary strengths, reciprocity, mutual strengths, and trust between the organization; also called virtual organization

neurotic organizations Organizations that are in trouble, but still operating, and headed by executives or groups of executives with neurotic tendencies

neuroticism A personality trait characterized by being highly emotional, tense, insecure, suffering from depression, and easily upset, suspicious and having low self-confidence

normative commitment A sense to stay with an organization because of pressures from others in their life that think they should be there

norming The group development stage where group norms are developed

norms Shared group expectations about behavior and how members ought to behave

norms of involvement The expectations that an organization has about the contextual performance and the acceptable ways for its members to show commitment and loyalty

norms of performance Norms that specify the specific task performance components that are to be done and the minimal acceptable levels of performance

objective career success The evaluation of career success based on measurable factors such as increases in pay and staus at work

objective environment The actual conditions in your world in which you are embedded and that may affect you

occupational competence The job related skills, activites, and attitudes that are necessary to perform work tasks in a particular field or occupation

occupational socialization The cultural learning process by which an individual learns the norms, values, and behaviors required in a particular work area or occupation

occupational/task subcultures Subculture with members who are likely to have a strong identification with others that have similar skills when these skills are important to organizational success and the skills have been developed through extensive training

openness to experience A personality characteristic in which people are imaginative, curious, cultured, broad minded, have broad interests and tend to be self-sufficient

organic organization An organization in which relationships and jobs are more loosely defined to permit an easier process of adapting to the changing environment

organizational behavior The systematic and scientific analysis of individuals, groups, and organizations; its purpose is to understand, predict, and improve the performance of individuals and, ultimately, the organizations in which they work

organizational behavior modification (OB Mod) A motivational model with the basic premise that to improve performance (change behavior) it is necessary to change the stimulus (antecedents) and the consequences (reinforcers, punishments, etc.)

organizational citizenship The extent to which a person is willing to go beyond the norms of performance and involvement for his or her work role

organizational commitment The degree to which a person identifies with or feels connected to the organization

organizational culture The patterned ways of thinking, feeling, and reacting that exist in an organization or its subsectors; the unique "mental programming" of that organization which is reflected in the modal organization personality

organizational culture profile The general criteria in an organization used to judge whether actions, ideas, and attitudes of members are right or wrong

organizational design The process of creating the internal conditions that facilitate strategic accommodation to the environment and the implementation of the organization's strategy by arranging the complete range of work activities into organizational subunits and hierarchies

organizational development Attempts made to take a proactive rather than just a reactive approach to organizational change

organizational politics The use of power in an organization

organizational socialization A learning process through which you learn to adapt to the organization; involves competence that you bring to the organization, the organization's norms of performance, and the norms of involvement

organizational status distinctions Accepted power and status relations between individuals and groups in organizations

organizational structure The relationship between the tasks performed by the members of the organization; can be seen in the forms of division of labor, departments, hierarchy, policies, and rules, and coordination and control mechanisms

organizational subcultures Different ideologies, cultural forms, and other practices that are exhibited by identifiable groups of people in an organization

organizational theory A theory concerned with how organizations are structured and how they can be designed to operate more effectively to achieve objectives in a rational way

organizationalist orientation A strong identification with and commitment to the place of work and the organization itself

organizationally based influence Power beyond the range of legitimate authority, because of the position that a person has in an organization

organizing The management function of acquiring and assembling resources in the proper relation to each other to achieve objectives

outcome justice Sense of equity that occurs when individuals compare themselves to other important referents and believe that the efforts and achievements are judged fairly, relative to them

overpayment inequity A sense of inequity that results from getting more out of the job relevant to your referent; leads to dissatisfaction resulting from feelings of guilt

paranoid culture An organizational culture characterized by a strong sense of distrust and a deep sense of suspicion

participative leadership Leaders consult with subordinates on appropriate matters and allow them some influence in the decision-making process

path–goal theory A contingency approach to leadership that focuses on leader behavior and how the situational factors affect what leader behavior is most effective

perceived conflict The requirement that, for conflict to exist, the conflict must be perceived by one or more parties involved

perception The process of using our five senses to relate to the world; includes creating an internal representation of the external world and interpreting what our senses provide so as to give meaning to experience

perceptual bias Any tendency on the part of a person to distort or otherwise misrepresent or organize perceptions in a personalized way

perceptual organization The tendency for people to group stimuli into patterns so that they become "meaningful wholes" rather than fragmented parts

performance components A relatively discrete subtask for which the requisite ability to perform is different from other abilities

performance–outcome expectancy From expectancy theory of motivation, the expectation about the relationship between a particular level of performance and attaining certain outcomes

performing The final stage of group development in which its members move into dealing with problems concerning the structure of the group

personal specialization Occurs when the individual, not the work, is specialized; specialists such as lawyers and doctors often perform such work

personal-based influence Accrues to an individual because he or she possesses attributes valued by others; these attributes are independent of the organization's control

personality The relatively stable organization of a person's characteristics; the enduring pattern of attributes which define the uniqueness of the individual; implies predisposition to act as well as patterns of overt behavior *personalized power motive* Manifested in an interpersonal way between a person and an adversary; those with a personalized power orientation prefer person-to-person competition in which they can dominate

person–organization fit The degree of congruence between organizational values and your own individual values

person–role conflict When organizational demands are in conflict with one's values

physiological needs Basic human requirements for survival such as food and shelter

planning The management function of making decisions about the most effective course of action to take in achieving organization goals and formulating general policies or guides to help in implementing plans

pluralism A cultural value that promotes mutual respect, acceptance, teamwork, and productivity among people who are diverse in work background, experience, age, education, gender, race, ethnic origin, physical abilities, religious belief, sexual orientation, and other perceived differences

polarization The tendency that the average group member's position on an issue will become more extreme as the result of group discussion

politicized culture An organizational culture in which there is no clear direction; the CEO is not strong but detached from the organization, and there are often power struggles among individuals and groups

pooled task interdependence When several units of an organization can operate in an autonomous manner, meaning that what one unit does is not entirely dependent on the other groups

position power Power that exists when a leader has much legitimate authority

positive affectivity A trait characterized by a strong, positive sense of personal well being, being active and involved and overall, a pleasant person in most situations

positive reinforcement Any consequence that is desirable, pleasant, or needed is a positive reinforcer of behavior; when a positive reinforcer is linked to behavior, it increases the probability that the behavior will recur in the same or similar situations

positive-sum interdependence A conflict negotiation condition where compromises are possible that would allow gains for both sides; *see also* zero-sum interdependence

post-decisional dissonance The anxiety experienced by decision makers that occurs after they have made a decision and that causes them to question the decision and the information upon which it is based

power A force that is the basis of influence; the capacity that can be energized to extract compliance

power distance A dimension of culture that is the preferred degree of inequality of power between individuals

power motive The need to have an impact on others, or to establish, maintain, or restore personal prestige or power

power structure The set of influence relationships between different people or subunits in an organization

preliminary work socialization A period prior to joining an organization or beginning a career during which a person begins to develop more specific orientations related to a certain career or to a particular type of organization

primary cognitive appraisal The cognitive appraisal that determines the intensity and quality of the individual's emotional response to stressors

principled negotiation A collaborative approach to bargaining and conflict resolution; stresses problem solving and other techniques for mutual gain of the parties

principles of management General guides to handling the problems that an executive encounters in work situations

procedural justice The extent to which people believe they are treated fairly in terms of "how" decisions are made about things that affect them in the workplace

process control The extent to which you believe that you are allowed to present your position and justify your case before a decision that will affect you is made

process theories Motivation theories that focus on how, not why, behavior changes

process theories of leadership Leadership theories that focus on the processes by which a relationship develops between leaders and subordinates rather than on the leader's traits or behavior

product organization Departments are created around different products and services; each major unit has its own manufacturing operation, marketing, personnel, R&D, and so on

production-centered leadership A style in which the leader is primarily concerned with high levels of production and generally uses high pressure to achieve it

professional orientation A person who is more job centered than organization centered and tends to view organization demands as pressure or a nuisance

project organization An organization in which employees work in temporary work teams, each with a specific project responsibility and duration for the life of the project

projection A form of defense mechanism by which people protect themselves against undesirable characteristics that they themselves possess by projecting their own characteristics or feelings onto others

psychological contract The mutual expectations between an individual and an organization that cover how much work is to be performed for how much pay as well as the whole pattern of rights, privileges, and obligation between the worker and the organization

psychological environment The way that a person experiences and interprets the objective environment

psychological success A measure of career performance that is achieved when self-esteem increases

public boundary Includes those activities that a person wants others, especially his or her superior, to believe are the elements of the psychological contract

punishment Occurs when an undesirable or painful consequence follows behavior or when a desirable consequence is removed; may decrease the frequency of the behavior but often has unintended side-effects

ratebuster An individual who performs at a level above what the group will tolerate

rational or normative models of decision making Models that attempt to show how people should make a decision and they assume that decision makers apply a carefully applied set of criteria or rationale for their decisions

real boundary The "true" limits of the psychological contract

reason An attempt to persuade someone else by providing them with information

reciprocal task interdependence Mutual dependence between two or more units in which interactions vary in complex ways in response to the task

reciprocity norms Widely held social norms that call for returning favors, based on the idea that helping or fairness behaviors fosters similar responses; a norm that tells us to return the favor to those who help us

reference groups Groups which shape our beliefs, values, and attitudes

refreezing The process of making change permanent and achieving a new equilibrium point

reinforcement schedules Consequences of a behavior occurring in different patterns, which affect how quickly the behavior is learned, and how resistant it is to change or to extinction

reinforcement theories Learning theories that describe situations where behavior is affected by its consequences; also called instrumental learning

relatedness needs Security needs for interpersonal matters, love, and belonging needs, and the needs of an interpersonal nature

relevant environment The groups or institutions beyond an organization's boundaries that provide immediate inputs, exert significant pressure on decisions, or make use of the organization's output

renewal rites Rites that have the goal of strengthening and improving the current social structure

resistance Outright sabotage, development of a counter force, or leaving the organization as a way of modifying a relationship

resistance stage The second stage of reaction to stress in which the body tries to restore its balance

reward power Power based on rewards that a second person desires

risky shift The tendency for groups or teams to make riskier decisions about a course of actions than individuals

rites Relatively elaborate, dramatic, planned sets of activities that consolidate various forms of cultural expressions into one event, which is carried out through social interactions

rites of passage Rites that are intended to bring a person into an organization and to convey norms and values

role ambiguity Occurs when people feel uncertain about what is expected of them or when they are not sure what behaviors will earn them acceptance or rejection

role conflict Results when a person is unable to meet conflicting demands; can arise between values within a role, between competing roles, or from external demands of others

role overload Occurs when the work requirements are excessive and exceed the limit of time and/or ability

role underload A condition in which the work does not make use of a person's abilities

roles Expectations that members hold for each other's behavior

safety needs The desire for protection against loss of shelter, food, and other basic requirements for survival; also includes the desire to live in a stable predictable environment

satisficing The tendency to accept the first alternative solution that satisfies the established minimally acceptable criteria

Scanlon Plan A compensation plan intended to be motivational that includes a system of committees for intergroup cooperation between labor and management in which efforts are made to find ways to reduce costs and a formula for determining and sharing the cost savings with the workers

schemas Patterns of information that we have learned from our past experiences; also called categories

scientific management approach An approach to management that emphasizes the systematic study of methods, using techniques such as time study, selection, and incentives to achieve work efficiency

selective perception The tendency to sense some aspects of our environment while paying less attention to or ignoring other aspects

self-actualization needs The individual's desire to do what he or she has the potential of doing; called the "highest-order" need

self-directed teams Teams which place more responsibility on the individuals who make them up, usually with some management responsibility

self-serving bias A judgment tendency reflecting a bias to perceive oneself favorably; crediting oneself when one succeeds but blaming external factors when one fails

separation rites Rites that help a person make a clean break from the organization

sequential task interdependence Where work activities must be performed in a particular sequence and the activities are assigned to different units in such a way that a product must begin at point A, go to point B, then to C

shotgun managers Managers who use the following tactics with above average frequency: reason, coalition formation, bargaining, assertive behavior, and appeals to higher authority

simple environment A relevant environment that contains just a few homogeneous sectors

situational control The level of situational, or contextual, control leaders have determined by their leader–member relations, task structure, and position power

size effect Larger objects being more likely to be perceived than smaller ones

skill variety The number of different abilities and capacities required in performing a job

skill-based pay A pay approach in which workers are paid for the skills they possess, not the actual work that they do

social facilitation A social influence condition in which the mere presence of others can influence behavior; people need only be there, without active involvement, to have an influence

social groups Groups that exist primarily to provide recreational or relaxation outlets for members

social learning Learning that occurs through the observation of others or from modeling (acting) the ways of others; also called vicarious learning; *see also* modeling

social loafing An individual reaction to larger groups that assumes that someone else will do what is needed and thus relieve the individual of the task

social support The communication of positive feelings of liking, trust, respect, acceptance of one's beliefs, and, sometimes, assistance from others who are important people in one's life

social–emotional ambiguity Role ambiguity about how you are evaluated by another person

socialization The process through which a person learns and acquires the values, attitudes and beliefs, and accepted behaviors of a culture, society, organization or group

socialized power motive A person with a socialized power orientation believes that he or she exercises power for the good of others, tends to be careful about the use of personal power, and knows that someone's win is another person's loss

span of control The number of subordinates who report to a manager

specialization A condition in which a person performs only some specific part of a larger set of tasks

spiral career path A career path in which one makes periodic moves from one occupation to another

stable environment An environment in which the degree of changes are relatively small, occurring in small increments, with a small impact on the structure, processes, and output of the organization

status The relative position or standing of a person in a group that causes respect or deference toward them

status incongruence A condition in a group when there is no consensus among the elements making up a person's position in the status hierarchy

stereotyping Connecting characteristics of people to characteristics of the group into which we place them

storming The conflict stage of group development where group goals, purposes and leadership are debated and tested

strategic center The focal firm in the network that must scan and monitor the environment, make critical choices about product design, distribution, and internal coordination, and facilitate the collaboration and cooperation of the network

strategic contingency theory of organizational power Theory based on the concept that a subunit's power depends on whether and how much it controls strategic contingencies for the organization

stress A psychological state that develops because a person is faced with situations that tax or exceed available resources (internal or external), as appraised by that person

stress manifestations Individual responses to stressors; physiological, psychological, or behavioral actions that are triggered by the cognitive appraisal of the situation

stressors Environmental factors and forces that cause stress

strong situations Situations where constraints such as clear and precise cues, rules and task demands act to limit behavior

structural differentiation The process of unbundling all of the work activities in an organization, separating specific sets of activities from others

structural integration The process of creating a management structure by linking the differentiated subunits back together through authority, responsibility, and accountability relationships

substitutability of activities A condition in the organization in which the activities performed by a particular individual or group can be performed by others

sufficient justification A condition helping to reduce cognitive dissonance, when a person is provided with enough reason to act against their beliefs or attitudes

supportive leadership A style in which the leader is concerned with the needs of those who report to him or her

symbols Objects to which meaning has become attached: titles, parking places, special dining rooms, office size, location and furnishings, and other indicators of position and power

systems view of organizations The thinking of an organization as a system of related activities that import resources from their external environment which are then transformed, or changed, by these activities into products or services

tactician managers Managers that attempt to influence others through the use of reason and logic, and about average use of other tactics

task ambiguity Role ambiguity that refers to uncertainty about the work requirements themselves

task groups Groups that are used to accomplish a specific organizational goal

task identity The extent to which a person is responsible for the whole job, from beginning to end

task interdependence Exists when several different tasks required to complete a project, product, or a subassembly are performed by different people

task performance component An element of the person's job that is required to perform the job itself

task performance dimension The dimension of performance that is the set of activities and their results that one must do to accomplish the work

task significance The effect that the work has on others, either in their jobs or their lives

task specialization Occurs when a job is broken down into smaller components or task elements; these are then grouped into jobs and generally assigned to different people

task structure The extent to which jobs are defined and specified

team building A form of planned organization change which focuses on the work team in the organizational setting; typically involves training methods designed to improve the interpersonal and working relationships of team members with the final objective of better organizational performance

team-based incentives Providing similar pay incentives to the whole team instead of the individual members to reinforce the concept of cooperative work

teams A special form of a group that have highly defined tasks and roles and demonstrate high group commitment

technological environment The techniques and the processes that the organization uses to produce the product or service, and the ideas or knowledge underlying the processing or the distribution of the product or service

technology The tools, machines, facilities, and equipment a person uses in performing a task

technology-dominated mixed (TDM) organizations Organizations with uncertainty in the technology environment and stability in the market environment; has a looser structure for internal technical systems

theory A way of organizing knowledge about something; an abstraction of real life; a way of defining a system into variables and their relationships

theory X Beliefs about human beings that assume humans are lazy, with personal goals which run counter to the organization's and hence, they have to be controlled externally

theory Y Beliefs about human beings that assume they are more mature, self-motivated, and self-controlled

total quality management (TQM) A system of organizational processes and values that are intended to develop loyal customers; a culture that supports teamwork, and focuses on continuous product or service improvement

trait theories of leadership Leadership theories based on the idea that personality differences can explain why some people are effective leaders and other people are not

transactional leadership The leader and subordinate are bargaining agents, negotiating to maximize their own position

transfer of learning A condition that occurs when people learn things in one situation and the learned behavior is transferred or applied in another situation

transformation The process of movement that must occur for the organism to change

transformational leadership theory Explains how leaders develop and enhance the commitment of followers; based on the leader's effects on the followers' values, self-esteem, trust, and their confidence in the leader and motivation to perform above and beyond the call of duty

transitory career path A career path in which people seem to not be able to settle down

triads Groups of three people

trigger events Unanticipated events in an organization's history that lead employees to take stock of their situation and interpret the short- and long-term implications of the changing context

Type A behavior pattern People who are hard-driving, highly competitive, impatient with others, irritated when situations prevent them from achieving their goals

Type B behavior pattern People who are less aggressive, competitive, and more relaxed than Type A people
uncertainty avoidance The extent to which individuals and societies wish to have stability and predictability in their lives
underpayment inequity A sense of inequity that results from getting less out of the job relative to what others contribute that results in dissatisfaction that stems from anger from feeling under rewarded
unfreezing The process of placing significant pressure on the organism to recognize the need to change
uniformity Pressure placed on group members holding a position different than the majority to conform to the majority view
valences From expectancy theory of motivation, these are anticipated satisfactions (or dissatisfactions) that result from outcomes; the individual's estimate of the pleasantness – or unpleasantness – of outcomes
values General reflections of people's sense of what they consider to be right
variable-interval reinforcement schedule A partial reinforcement schedule in which the periods of time between reinforcements to occur is varied
variable-ratio reinforcement schedule A partial reinforcement schedule in which the number of behaviors necessary for reinforcements to occur is varied
vertical dyad linkage (VDL) theory Focuses on the relationship between the leader and subordinate in different leader–member relationships that are classified into in-group and out-group categories
vertical loading Enriching a task by adding responsibilities from higher organization levels as opposed to adding more tasks from the same (horizontal) level; *see also* horizontal job loading
virtual organization *See* network organization
volatile environment An environment that is more turbulent, with more intense changes than in the stable one
Vroom–Yetton model A contingency model of leadership that attempts to show how the degree of subordinate influence in decision making should vary according to the situation
weak situations Situations that are loosely structured and ambiguous and characterized by few cues from the environment; no uniform expectancies for those involved, so personality characteristics become a stronger explanation and cause of behavior than the situation the person is in
work ethic The belief that work is good and that it should be valued
work facilitation Activities that help toward achieving goal attainment by doing things such as scheduling, coordinating, planning, and providing resources
work flow centrality The interconnectedness with many others and the work flow immediacy
work flow immediacy The speed and severity with which work flows of a subunit affect the final outputs of the organization
zero-sum interdependence A conflict negotiation condition where a gain by one side means a loss by the other side; *see also* positive-sum interdependence

Author index

Subject index

This covers a broad area but for the purpose of dis essay
I will be focusing on dis....

3500

Sennet bureaucracy